THE
JOHNS HOPKINS
GUIDE TO
DIGITAL MEDIA

THE
JOHNS HOPKINS
GUIDE TO
DIGITAL MEDIA

Edited by Marie-Laure Ryan, Lori Emerson,
and Benjamin J. Robertson

JOHNS HOPKINS UNIVERSITY PRESS   *Baltimore*

Johns Hopkins University Press
2715 North Charles Street
Baltimore, Maryland 21218-4363
www.press.jhu.edu

Library of Congress Cataloging-in-Publication Data

The Johns Hopkins guide to digital media / edited by Marie-Laure Ryan,
Lori Emerson, and Benjamin J. Robertson.
     pages cm
   Includes bibliographical references and index.
   ISBN 978-1-4214-1223-8 (hardcover : alk. paper)—ISBN 978-1-4214-1224-5
(pbk. : alk. paper)—ISBN 978-1-4214-1225-2 (electronic)—ISBN 1-4214-1223-3
(hardcover : alk. paper)—ISBN 1-4214-1224-1 (pbk. : alk. paper)—
ISBN 1-4214-1225-X (electronic)   1. Digital media.   2. Mass media—
Technological innovations—Social aspects.   I. Ryan, Marie-Laure,
1946– editor of compilation.   II. Emerson, Lori editor of compilation.
III. Robertson, Benjamin J., 1973– editor of compilation.   IV. Title: Guide to
digital media.
   P90.J5575 2013
   302.23'1—dc23   2013018847

A catalog record for this book is available from the British Library.

*Special discounts are available for bulk purchases of this book. For more information,
please contact Special Sales at 410-516-6936 or specialsales@press.jhu.edu.*

CONTENTS

vii

Contents

PREFACE

Thanks to the technological developments of the past thirty years, computers have shed their intimidating image of number crunchers, and they have developed into what Theodore Nelson called as early as 1981 "literary machines." By this term one must understand not only word-processing abilities but a manipulation of symbols of all kinds capable of delivering radically new forms of art, entertainment, communication, and social experiences. The study of what is collectively labeled "digital media" or even "new media," the cultural and artistic practices made possible by digital technology, has become one of the most vibrant areas of scholarly activity. It is rapidly turning into an established academic field, with many universities now offering it as a major. More broadly, the so-called digital humanities—whether we conceive of them as media theory, as the study of digital-born artworks, as the investigation of print literature through computer applications, as the design of such applications, or as the creation of online archives devoted to cultural topics—inject new life into an area of knowledge that has been steadily losing ground in academia to the other cultures of science, business, and less art-friendly technologies.

Yet while a plethora of books have been published on the various cultural applications of digital technology, we still lack a systematic and comprehensive reference work to which teachers and students can quickly turn for reliable information on the key terms and concepts of the field. The *Johns Hopkins Guide to Digital Media* fills this need by presenting an interdisciplinary panorama of the ideas, genres, and theoretical concepts that have allowed digital media to produce some of the most innovative intellectual, artistic, and social practices of our time. We envision this book as an easy-to-consult reference work for digital media scholars or for scholars in other disciplines wishing to familiarize themselves with this fast-developing field.

In the age of *Wikipedia*, one may admittedly wonder if a project like this one duplicates information already available online. Has not digital technology, by making possible a free, easily accessible, constantly updated, and (ideally) always current sum of human knowledge, produced the total Encyclopedia that contains all partial encyclopedias and renders them obsolete? Aren't the products of the collective intelligence which *Wikipedia* puts into practice more reliable, more comprehensive, and less biased than the work of individual authors? While honesty forces us to acknowledge that some of our topics are also found on *Wikipedia*, and that it has been a precious source of information for many of our authors, it is our firm belief that this book has a lot to offer that *Wikipedia* does not: it targets a more scholarly audience; its entries are more narrowly focused on issues relevant to the arts, humanities, and cultural studies; and, what is perhaps most important, its authors bear greater responsibility for the content of their contributions than the anonymous authors of *Wikipedia* entries, a responsibility that should lead to greater reliability. In addition, the fact that our contributors are not merely leaders in their field but often the creators of the field they are writing about imparts a perspective that could not be achieved by anonymously written entries.

The main challenge in undertaking a project like this one lies in deciding what information readers will want to look up. It has been more than twenty-five years since digital media penetrated the humanities, and the luddites have largely died down: while in the 1990s there were still many people in academia or other professions who were afraid of computers, ignored the resources of the Internet, refused to use e-mail, or got writer's block at the mere idea of giving up their beloved pen and paper or typewriter, these people have now either retired or been converted. We all conduct business online, and while not everybody has the time (or inclination) to participate in social media, we all do e-mail and use word processors. But there is still widespread ignorance about the more specific applications of computer technology in the area of art, textuality, entertainment, and the humanities, or about the critical concepts that have been developed to theorize digital culture. Moreover, as applications become more diverse, scholars specialize in some areas and cannot keep track of the entire field. For instance, video game scholars may not be up to date on recent developments in electronic literature, and researchers studying print literature through computer programs may not be familiar with the expressive affordances of digital media. The purpose of this volume is to compensate for this trend toward specialization by outlining a wider horizon.

While this horizon is quickly expanding, it is also constantly changing. Many of the applications or ideas that captured people's imagination some twenty years ago have become obsolete, or have been replaced with faster, sexier, and more powerful versions. For those who were born after the digital revolution, MOOs and MUDs, hypertext fiction, or games with low-resolution graphics are the primitive entertainment of a technologically deprived older generation. Virtual reality? Cyberspace? The Information Superhighway? Gone from the headlines, and therefore gone from active memory. Text-based MOOs and MUDs? Largely replaced by sensorially richer online worlds. Does the rapid evolution of digital culture make the present project outdated even before its birth? We think not: on the contrary, as history starts to accumulate, and as the preservation of digital artifacts becomes a major concern, older practices and technologies attract nostalgic interest. Symptomatic of this trend is the fact that at the date of this writing "media archaeology" is one of the most popular fields of investigation in media studies. This guidebook cannot predict the future, but through entries such as "History of Computers," "Game History," or "Early Digital Art and Writing," as well as entries on the textual forms of the 1980s and 1990s, it builds a bridge between the past and the present. Today's students may not have lived through this past, but learning where our cultural forms come from can only enrich their understanding of the present.

The table of contents combines the top-down selection of the editors with the bottom-up input of the contributors, who proposed overlooked topics, or topics they were particularly interested in writing about. Even with the support of the collective intelligence of a community of scholars, however, some relevant topics will be missed, or new topics may emerge in the next few years that are unthinkable today. Our choices are by necessity limited by our focus on art, textuality, entertainment, and culture. The short entries are fact oriented, while the longer ones are more hospitable to the expression of personal positions, though authors have been instructed to give a reasonably comprehensive overview of the topic. We expect that different types of entries will be read for different reasons: some to get a quick definition, some to get suggestions concerning where to find more information, and some for the pleasure of engaging with ideas. Our goal is not to take our readers on a cruise that grants passengers a fixed time at every port of call and then ships them (pun intended) to the next attraction, but to provide them with a GPS and a map of the territory of digital media, so that they will be able to design their own journey through this vast field of discovery.

Algorithm

Bethany Nowviskie

The term *algorithm*, most commonly associated with computer science, may be used for any effective procedure that reduces the solution of a problem to a predetermined sequence of actions. In software, algorithms are used for performing calculations, conducting automated reasoning, and processing data (including digital texts)—but algorithms may also be implemented in mathematical models, mechanical devices, biological networks, electrical circuitry, and practices resulting in generative or procedural art (see CODE, COMPUTATIONAL LINGUISTICS, PROCEDURAL).

In common usage, *algorithm* typically references a deterministic algorithm, formally defined as a finite and generalizable sequence of instructions, rules, or linear steps designed to guarantee that the agent performing the sequence will reach a particular, predefined goal or establish incontrovertibly that the goal is unreachable. The "guarantee" part of this description is important, as it differentiates algorithms from heuristics, which commonly proceed by "rules of thumb." Like algorithms, heuristic methods can be used iteratively to reach a desired end state and may be responsive to feedback from external sources. However, the heuristic process is fundamentally one of informal trial and error rather than of constrained, formally algorithmic activity according to a set of predefined rules. (Nondeterministic algorithms are a class of algorithm that attempts to solve harder problems by finding the best solution available with a given set of constraints. They do not guarantee to find a single, best solution and may, on repetition, present radically different outcomes.)

Almost any everyday problem can be solved heuristically or algorithmically. We proceed by heuristics when, for example, we've lost our car keys: *I look in my bag. I look in my bag again. I search my jacket pockets. I check the front door, because I left them dangling there last week.* The weak point of the heuristic method becomes evident when its user needs to shift gears. I'm not finding my keys in the usual places. *Should I peer with trepidation into the locked car or check the washing machine? Is it possible someone has taken them? Should I keep looking, or is it time to give up and call a cab?* In formal, graph-based problem solving, heuristics are sometimes used to guide the search for solutions by identifying the most promising branches of a tree for further exploration, or by cutting out unpromising branches altogether (see GRAPH THEORY). The basic "problem with heuristics"—which could lead to the inadvertent elimination of the entire branch of a desired outcome branch from the search tree—"is how to decide half-way what would be an appropriate next action, i.e. how to design heuristic rules that lead to good solutions instead of bad ones" (Lagus 1995). Tellingly, we often attribute decisions in successful heuristic processes to intuition and those that result in undesirable outcomes to confusion and bad luck.

If heuristics fail or prove too unsystematic for comfort, we can shift to algorithmic problem solving (expressed here in pseudocode):

For each room in the house,
and for each item in the room;
   pick up and examine the item.
      If the item appears by objective criteria to be the missing object,
         terminate the search.
      If not, put down the item and continue this loop
         until all items in all rooms have been tested.

2
Algorithm

Eventually, if this so-called brute-force algorithm is executed perfectly, we will either find our keys or determine conclusively that they are not in the house. It requires no ingenuity on the part of the performer, and there's a kind of predestination or special providence embedded in the process. That is to say, we know to expect one of two prescribed outcomes before even undertaking the search. And—as its strict definition requires—this algorithm is almost wholly generalizable. If you suspect you have left your keys at a friend's house, you can run the process there. If the misplaced object is a watch, or a hat, these steps are equally applicable. (Admittedly, it isn't a very efficient algorithm, because it requires us, for example, to pick up and examine heavy furnishings, and to reexamine the housecat every time it saunters into a new room, but more elegant versions could be designed.)

At present, advancements in programming frameworks and computing hardware (specifically, the increasing speed and power of processors) are driving new work in concurrency and parallelization of algorithms. This is an active, and even pressing, research area in computer science, with implications for machine learning, a subfield of artificial intelligence (Bekkerman et al. 2011; see ARTIFICIAL INTELLIGENCE). But the development and theorization of algorithms has a long history. The word itself stems from the name of ninth-century mathematician Abū Ja'far Muhammad ibn Mūsa, al-Ḵwārizmī, and was first applied (as *algorism*) to any arithmetical operation using Arabic numerals, before shifting in meaning to its current sense in the late nineteenth and early twentieth centuries. The works of Llull, Leibnitz, Babbage, Lovelace, and Boole (among others) are infused with procedural and proto-algorithmic notions of language, logic, and calculation and raise many of the same questions about the applicability of algorithm to interpretation which underlie present-day concerns about hermeneutics in digital media and the digital humanities (Nowviskie 2013). Chabert and Barbin (1999) offer in-depth discussion of the many ways "algorithms were in use long before it was necessary to give a clear definition" of the term, and they describe how "problems concerning the foundations of mathematical logic" prompted clarification of the concept. This work crystallized largely outside the realm of literature and linguistics in the 1930s, as thinkers such as Kurt Gödel, Alonzo Church, Stephen Kleene, Alan Turing, and Emil Post responded to formalist mathematical questions posed by David Hilbert's *Entscheidungsproblem* and worked to demonstrate the inability of algorithmic processes to establish a truth-value for certain classes of mathematical statements. Chabert and Barbin (1999) note with some irony that "the intuitive idea of an algorithm played an important heuristic role in all those works" which challenged Hilbert's mathematical formalism (455–458). Donald Knuth's *Art of Computer Programming* (1968) helped to codify five widely accepted properties of algorithms: that they are finite in length, are definite or unambiguous, have zero or more inputs and one or more outputs, and are composed of "effective" steps, sufficiently basic as to be executable. Knuth also asserted, "in some loosely-defined aesthetic sense," the desirability of "good" algorithms, citing criteria of efficiency, "adaptability of the algorithm to computers," simplicity, and elegance (1968, 2–9). All of these refinements to the concept of the algorithm are relevant both to artistic production and to the interpretation of texts and artifacts, two domains generally predicated on ambiguity, subjectivity, and flux (see COMBINATORY AND AUTOMATIC TEXT GENERATION, DIGITAL HUMANITIES).

As currently understood, algorithms are expected to be both perfectly precise and entirely implementable. An old bubblegum wrapper joke helps to make this point: How do you fit four elephants into a Volkswagen? The algorithmic answer is that you put two in the front seat and two in the back. Although those steps are clearly unambiguous, they are impossible to implement. In contrast is an algorithm for writing encyclopedia articles: *Step 1. Write a paragraph. Step 2: Repeat Step 1 until the article is complete.* The procedure is clearly implementable—it was performed more than 150 times in the present volume—but it is far too ambiguous to be a "textbook," or even a useful, algorithm. What constitutes a paragraph? What criteria indicate completion? How does the algorithm know that you're writing an article and not a monograph, a novel, or a comic book? And how might a human agent's interpretation and performance of an algorithmic process alter it? That is to say, with what assumptions do we approach algorithmic or procedural activities, and how might those assumptions both shape and be shaped by action within systems of constraint (see WRITING UNDER CONSTRAINT)? In other words, algorithmic methods are productive not only of new texts, but of new readings. In "Algorithmic Criticism," Stephen Ramsay argues that "critical reading practices already contain elements of the algorithmic" and that algorithms "can be made to conform to the methodological project of *inventio* without transforming the nature of computation or limiting the rhetorical range of critical inquiry" (2008, 489). It is also important to acknowledge that even the most clinically perfect and formally unambiguous algorithms embed their designers' theoretical stances toward problems, conditions, and solutions.

Repositioning closed, mechanical, or computational operations as participatory or playful algorithms requires acknowledgement of a primary definition, derived from the studies of game theorist Martin Shubik (see GAME THEORY). Shubik concludes a survey of "the scope of gaming" with the simple statement that "all games call for an explicit consideration of the role of the rules" (1972). He understands this "consideration" not only as adherence by players to a set of constraints, but also as appreciation of the impact of rules on the whole scope of play. The rule set or constraining algorithm in any ludic or hermeneutic system becomes another participant in the process and, in the course of execution or play, can seem to open itself to interpretation and subjective response—in some cases, to real, iterative, or turn-based modification (Suber 2003). In considering the "role of the rules" we must follow C. S. Peirce and interpret algorithmic specifications "in the sense in which we speak of the 'rules' of algebra; that is, as a permission under strictly defined conditions" (1933, 4.361). The permission granted here is not only to perform but also to reimagine and reconfigure.

■ See also RANDOMNESS, SAMPLING, SEARCH, TURING TEST

References and Further Reading

Bekkerman, Ron, Mikhail Bilenko, and John Langford, eds. 2011. *Scaling Up Machine Learning: Parallel and Distributed Approaches*. Cambridge: Cambridge University Press.

Chabert, Jean-Luc, and Évelyne Barbin. 1999. *A History of Algorithms: From the Pebble to the Microchip*. Berlin: Springer.

Knuth, Donald E. 1968. *The Art of Computer Programming*. Volume 1. Boston: Addison-Wesley Professional.

Lagus, Krista. 1995. "Automated Pagination of the Generalized Newspaper Using Simulated Annealing." Master's thesis, Helsinki University of Technology.

Nowviskie, Bethany. 2013. "Ludic Algorithms." In *PastPlay: History, Technology, and the Return to Playfulness*, edited by Kevin Kee, 148–191. Ann Arbor: University of Michigan Press.

Peirce, C. S. 1933. *Collected Papers*. Cambridge, MA: Harvard University Press.

Ramsay, Stephen. 2008. "Algorithmic Criticism." In *A Companion to Digital Literary Studies*, edited by Susan Schreibman and Ray Siemens, 478–491. Oxford: Blackwell.

Shubik, Martin. 1972. "On the Scope of Gaming." *Management Science* 18 (5): 34.

Suber, Peter. 2003. "Nomic: A Game of Self-Amendment." Earlham College. www.earlham.edu /~peters/nomic.htm.

Alternate Reality Gaming

Nicole Labitzke

Alternate reality gaming is "one of the first true art and entertainment forms developed from and exclusively for the Internet" (Szulborski 2005, 1). Beginning around 2001, alternate reality games (ARGs) have been at the center of what Henry Jenkins calls "convergence culture" (2006) (see PARTICIPATORY CULTURE). Native to digital networks, ARGs make use of the core properties that characterize this medium: massive audiences, ubiquity, participation, and searching for and sharing information (see *Wikipedia* entry on ARGs). Though ARGs are a phenomenon of popular culture, they have so far not hit the radar of mass media visibility. However, they are able to generate a very diverse and dedicated hard-core fan base. As a genre they integrate a "massively-scaled, ludic system" (McGonigal 2006, 263) with gameplay and challenges on the one hand and an encyclopedic textual system that projects a complex transmedial story world on the other (see LUDUS AND PAIDIA).

The term *alternate reality game* refers to a gaming environment that is neither an augmented, that is, technologically enhanced, reality (see AUGMENTED REALITY) nor a virtual, that is, simulated 3D, environment (see VIRTUAL REALITY). The players' experience alternates or oscillates between game world and real world (see McGonigal 2003, 112): life and game exist in parallel, and neither of them can be stopped, saved, or played again. The make-believe dimension of the ARG is promoted by the implicit assertion of its authors that "this is not a game" (TINAG). This constitutive formula is an invitation for players to pretend that the game story is real, a pretense that enhances the experience of immersion (see IMMERSION).

Most ARGs operate according to a set of common design principles. Their core mechanics are based on three components: exposition, interaction, and challenges (see Phillips 2008). The lines between these components are normally indistinct, and their relative importance varies greatly, but they determine whether a phenomenon is recognized as ARG or not.

The exposition of the narrative, such as the backstory and basic information about the characters, is usually conveyed via entries on the blogs of the various characters. Other story fragments are scattered on a large number of fake websites of fictional organizations and institutions that are programmed to be accessed by the participants. Usually, there is one central platform that serves as the major hub of player activity; it is called the "rabbit hole." Players are directed there by billboard ads, movie trailers, postal packages, and even pizza deliveries.

The interaction component constitutes the most distinctive characteristic of ARGs. It aims at deepening the engagement and immersive experience of the player. Interacting with the game world in an ARG usually means communicating with a character in a live chat situation or with a chat bot (see CHATTERBOTS). In addition to online devices, every possible communication device, such as e-mail or telephone, can be used to spread information, hints, and challenges. ARGs may also involve live events, online or offline, which engage players in social interaction and contribute to the synchronization of the game with real life. Examples include online poker tournaments, live group chats, real-life protest rallies, and staged car thefts. These live events demonstrate the close relationship between ARGs and live-action role-playing games (see ROLE-PLAYING GAMES).

The gameplay of ARGs consists of challenges that closely resemble the tasks given to players in video games (see GAMEPLAY). The possible variations in this area are numerous. Common puzzles include deciphering encoded texts, finding passwords, dealing with unknown interfaces, and translating uncommon languages. Challenges can also contain so-called social engineering tasks (Phillips 2008, 37) that enhance interaction with the game world and could therefore also be listed as an interaction component. In this case the challenge for players is to convince characters to do something, that is, to give information or to take a certain action. All these challenges and puzzles play a crucial role in the progress of the game. They determine its pace and help regulate "the flow of content to its audience" (Szulborski 2005, 247).

ARG history dates back to the year 2001, when a game that came to be known as *The Beast* was launched in the United States to advertise Steven Spielberg's movie *A.I. Artificial Intelligence*. Though *The Beast* tells a story that is only loosely connected to the events in the movie, it clearly refers to the same story world. It demonstrated the efficiency of ARGs as viral marketing campaigns for big entertainment franchises. In the wake of its success several promotional ARGs created a buzz in the entertainment mainstream, among them *I Love Bees* (2004) for the game *Halo 2* by Microsoft, *The Art of Heist* (2005) for the new car Audi A3, and *Why So Serious?* (2008) for the movie *The Dark Knight* by Christopher Nolan. The concept of alternate reality gaming quickly became a worldwide phenomenon. Data indicate that there are particularly active communities in Canada, Brazil, Germany, Japan, and Sweden (Dena 2008).

In 2004 the success of the Canadian project *ReGenesis* established ARGs as expansions of television shows (see INTERACTIVE TELEVISION), known as "tie-ins." Tie-ins of high-quality series aimed at bridging the gap between seasons and at further engaging audiences. Examples include *Alias* (ABC, USA; 2002), *ReGenesis* (Movie Network, CDN; 2004/2006), *Jamie Kane* (BBCi, UK; 2004), *The Lost Experience* (ABC, USA; 2006), *Heroes Evolutions* (NBC, USA; 2007), *The Truth about Marika* (SVT, SWE; 2007), *Robin sucht Lena* (RTL, GER; 2007), *TrueBlood Revelations* (HBO, USA; 2008), *Torchwood* (BBC, UK; 2008), *Dollplay* (ABC, USA; 2009), and *Dexter* (Showtime, USA; 2010).

While remaining a mainstay of entertainment promotion, the genre later diversified into new applications. ARGs are being developed in grassroots and independent contexts, as well as, more recently, in educational environments (for a taxonomy see Barlow 2006, 15). Independent ARGs usually emerge from fan cultures, initiated by small groups or even single persons. They often refer directly to a large preexisting story world; for instance, *Metacortechs* (2003) by Dave Szulborski et al. ties in with the universe of the *Matrix* movies. Other successful examples that create story worlds of their own are *Chasing the Wish* (2003), by Dave Szulborski; *Sammeeeees* (2006/2007), by Jan Libby; and *MeiGeist* (2007), by Hazel Grian. Player numbers and budgets in grassroots games are smaller, but they do not differ in player dedication.

Educational ARGs, also known as "serious alternate reality games" (SARGs), have developed into a genre in their own right since *World without Oil* (*WWO*), by Ken Eklund and Jane McGonigal, was launched in 2007. Commissioned by the Independent Television Service and sponsored by the Corporation for Public Broadcasting, *WWO* simulated a global oil crisis and asked participants to suggest suitable measures to deal with it. Many SARGs with different subject matters followed: the European Union launched *The Tower of Babel* (2008/2009) to advance foreign language learning; *Traces of Hope* (2008) by the British Red Cross was meant to raise awareness for Ugandan war victims; and *Evoke* (2010), launched by the World Bank Institute, aimed at developing collaborative solutions for problems of water and food security.

ARGs are not only games; they are also story games. They create an intricate narrative within a transmedially constructed story world. Transmedial storytelling in convergence culture (see Jenkins 2006) calls for participation from the audience(s) and offers interactive options on several layers of the story world (see INTERACTIVE NARRATIVE). The participatory options can range from puzzle solving to co-narration and performance. "Story archaeology" (Phillips 2009) is one of the key interactive devices in ARGs. In many cases the progression of the story depends on the actions of players who basically search, follow, and piece together narrative fragments, thereby assembling "a working model of the story" (Phillips 2009). The overall story emerges from a collaborative process within the player community: "instead of telling a story, we would present the evidence of that story, and let the players tell it to themselves" (Stewart 2006). This process of re-narration helps bring an approximate version of the story into the world.

Participants in alternate reality gaming can play yet another important role. They are, as physically engaged players, part of the story world. When participating in challenges and real-world missions, they are actors in the game's story who follow the pre-written script of a group of authors, adequately called the puppet masters. It is the players' "dramatic performance" (McGonigal 2006, 431) that not only constitutes ARGs in the first place but also seems to be their main appeal. The unique character of ARGs arguably lies in their unusual combination of player agency and control of the story by the puppet masters.

The future of alternate reality gaming as a genre in its own right is not guaranteed. ARGs seem to thrive as an innovative and playful way of engaging in collaborative social or political action in a converging media environment (McGonigal 2011). But unlike video games, they so far have not developed financially profitable business models in the entertainment sector (Barlow 2006; Hon 2007). But even if the phenomenon of ARGs does not successfully establish itself, it has, in the first decade of the twenty-first century, significantly contributed to the development of a media-transcending culture in art and entertainment.

■ See also INTERACTIVE DRAMA, LOCATION-BASED NARRATIVE, PARTICIPATORY CULTURE, TRANSMEDIAL FICTION

References and Further Reading

"Alternate Reality Game." *Wikipedia*. http://en.wikipedia.org/wiki/Alternate_reality_game.

Barlow, Nova. 2006. "Types of ARGs." In *Alternate Reality Games White Paper*, edited by IGDA, 15–20. International Game Developers Association. http://archives.igda.org/arg/resources/IGDA-AlternateRealityGames-Whitepaper-2006.pdf.

Dena, Christy. 2008. "ARG Stats." Compiled by Christy Dena, 2005–2008. www.christydena.com/online-essays/arg-stats/.

———. 2009. "Transmedia Practice: Theorising the Practice of Expressing a Fictional World across Distinct Media and Environments." PhD diss., University of Sydney. www.scribd.com/doc/35951341/Transmedia-Practice.

Hon, Adrian. 2007. "The New Alternate Reality Games." Game Developers Conference GDC. http://mssv.net//gdc2007.pdf.

Jenkins, Henry. 2006. *Convergence Culture: Where Old and New Media Collide*. New York: New York University Press.

McGonigal, Jane. 2003. "This Is Not a Game: Immersive Aesthetics & Collective Play." Digital Arts & Culture Conference Proceedings. http://janemcgonigal.com/learn-me/.

———. 2006. "This Might Be a Game: Ubiquitous Play and Performance at the Turn of the Twenty-First Century." PhD diss., University of California, Berkeley. http://janemcgonigal.com/learn-me/.

———. 2011. *Reality Is Broken: Why Games Make Us Better and How They Can Change the World*. London: Jonathan Cape.

Phillips, Andrea. 2008. "Methods and Mechanics." In *Alternate Reality Games White Paper*, edited by IGDA, 31–42. International Game Developers Association. http://archives.igda.org/arg/resources/IGDA-AlternateRealityGames-Whitepaper-2006.pdf.

———. 2009. "WTF Is an ARG? 2009 Edition." www.deusexmachinatio.com/2009/01/wtf-is-an-arg-2009-edition.html.

Stewart, Sean. 2006. "Alternate Reality Games." www.seanstewart.org/interactive/args/.

Szulborski, Dave. 2005. *This Is Not a Game: A Guide to Alternate Reality Gaming*. Macungie, PA: New Fiction.

Analog versus Digital
Jake Buckley

Between the mid-1940s and the late 1960s, the analog and the digital emerged as key concepts for theorizing the layered complexity of communication in human-made devices and, more significantly, within and between organisms, across fields as diverse as mathematics, anthropology, neuroscience, psychology, and engineering (see CYBERNETICS). In basic terms, the analog concerns all that is continuous, fluctuating, and qualitatively variable within communication, whereas the digital concerns all that is discontinuous, boundary marking, and quantitatively controlling within communication. Key to these theorizations was a distinction between analog and digital *computers*. At the level of human-made devices, an example of an analog computer is an analog clock—a display with hour, minute, and second hands. This clock represents time as a continuum using a scale analogous to this continuum. The continuous movement of the hands—over the numbers and markings that the hands point at—elides the gaps between each division on the clock face, thus approximating an experience of time's continuous movement. For the analog clock/computer to become a digital computer, it must shift from *measuring* time in a spatial sense (employing a device that follows or keeps up with a continuous experience, enabling one to imprecisely [or variably] "see" and "feel" this experience) to *calculating* time (employing a device that intervenes in and breaks down a continuum using several discrete, discontinuous, and finite elements [e.g., a row of numbers], enabling one to predict and mark, by a principle of more and more division, the microvariations within this experience that are normally inaccessible to the human senses).

One of the most famous analog computers is the differential analyzer designed by American engineer Vannevar Bush, which was implemented at MIT in 1942. Bush's analyzer comprised a long table-like structure of interconnected shafts, the continuously variable rotations of which were made to represent and compute, by analogy, the relations between changing variables in a differential equation (see Owens 1986, 72–75). The differential analyzer's ability to simulate was significant not only in terms of the high-order, high-speed computations the machine could carry out: as historian Larry Owens asserts, the analyzer "act[ed] out the mathematical equation" (1986, 75), its liveliness bringing engineers and mathematicians physically closer to complexity and change than more abstract methods of calculation. The analyzer, in other words, made its audience *feel* mathematics in action amid mathematics' arbitrarily conventional, rule-bound (digital) array of symbols, which is one reason why this analog device continues to fascinate long after its replacement by powerful digital computers following World War II.

It is important to realize that the analog and the digital do not originate as properties of technological objects such as the computers discussed above. Moving between the domains of theory, philosophy, and language will demonstrate the ways in which the analog and the digital are processes immanent to relationships within and between bodies and things and are important for debating human conduct and life in societies affected by digital media technologies.

Anthropologist Gregory Bateson and communications theorist Anthony Wilden apply the guiding distinctions discussed above to linguistics. Bateson defines analogic communication as a way of conveying meaning through movement, gesture, and varying physical quantities. Shouting, for example, is meaningful independently of phonetic convention, in that an increase in the loudness of the voice might correspond with (be analogous to) the magnitude of physical space between the participants of a conversation, or the magnitude of seriousness of the topic of conversation. This "simple [spatial] connection" (Bateson 1973, 343) is not present in digital communication, because digital communication employs a system of *discrete* linguistic elements, finite in number, which, as Wilden states, combine "autonomously in relation to 'things'" (1972, 163) to enable analog meaning—a nonverbal, "unnameable" flow or continuum of "common experience" (1972, 163)—to be communicated as accurately as possible from organism to organism.

The significance of reading Bateson and Wilden in a digital age is that they emphasize the importance of thinking the analog and the digital relationally and nonhierarchically, in contrast to a popular rhetoric today surrounding new media, which posits mass digitization as a consequence of switching off analog communication. Bateson and Wilden present analog meaning as the movements, sensations, and intensities that continuously and variably attend every relationship, the complexity or "richness" (Wilden 1972, 163) of which is lost when digital language moves its signs through a mechanical oppositional system to signify these relationships. But for Bateson and Wilden the digital does not take over and nullify the analog because of the digital's greater "semiotic freedom" (Wilden 1972, 189); on the contrary, the analog and the digital overlap continuously. For example, Bateson argues that we are continuously moved by, and continue to interpret, the physical gestures and expressions that accompany speech, regardless of the greater organizational sophistication offered by digital language. Communication, then, involves the continuous movement from analog to digital representation, and if one of the primary purposes of mass digitization in media technologies is to augment communicative paths and means, then it seems nonsensical to conceive a digital age that has left behind the analog. Bateson and Wilden remind us that fully digital communication is lifeless, immobile, and devoid of sensation, change, and spontaneity; it appears crucial, therefore, to understand that the analog continues into the present epoch as we communicate our experiences of going digital, whether in everyday conversation, in art, or for political purposes.

The issue of the changing relationship between the analog and digital in response to new technologies has been discussed more explicitly in philosophical debates about digital media. Philosopher Bernard Stiegler argues that analog qualities of continuous movement and sensation are important to any discussion of visual media, new or old, and how these media affect us. Stiegler's concern, though, is that, historically, visual media technologies have been compelled by an uncritical—or "credulous"—belief in the (predominantly analog) images they have produced. In analog photography, Stiegler demonstrates, light touches the material subject of the photograph *once*, before imprinting this materiality onto photosensitive paper. This materiality is then carried forward from generation to generation as a past movement/moment that once was alive (belonged to day) but is now dead or has since "become night" (Stiegler 2002, 152), thus taking on a ghostly quality as it continuously comes to touch and affect—via the light by which it was once touched—those who successively look at the image.

The continuous analog transmission of light unsettles viewers, but, as Stiegler shows, it is also one-way. In other words, while analog photography's transmission of a past movement/moment affects or changes established beliefs in life and death, we remain convinced that the movement/moment imprinted and carried forward in the image "just was" (see Buckley 2011). All analog images are in fact subject to discrete "framing operations and choices" (Stiegler 2002, 155) by the photographer, Stiegler affirms, and the photosensitive paper on which these images are imprinted is composed of discrete grains of silver halide. The credulity effect of analog transmission, though, withholds the viewer from reaching into this process and engaging with (or touching back) the analog image as a mediated, manipulated, and manipulable past.

However, in digital photography, Stiegler claims, we cannot be certain that light once touched the materiality on display, because the light touching the materiality comes from a "digital night" (2002, 152) in which multiple types and degrees of binary treatment have occurred in the dark, as it were, before the image appears on-screen (see FILM AND DIGITAL MEDIA). When we come to look at the "discrete image" imprinted by these treatments of separation, argues Stiegler, we will be touched in the present by mo(ve)ments that never belonged to the day, nor to a night or past that *followed* day sequentially. Instead, for Stiegler, we are presented with an image in which the digital's mediation of the analog is less concealed. In Stiegler's words, these analogico-digital touches come from a "light in the night . . . still deeper than that of a past, the night of a past that was *never present*" (2002, 154–155; emphasis in original). Stiegler's key point is that the analogico-digital urges us to come into contact with hitherto unintelligible bodily acts and ineligible histories, and to have a critical awareness of the ways in which discrete positions are kept as discreet as possible in a continuum. Doubting analog touch means touching more and to different extents, complicating (while still believing in) the notion that the past continuously affects the present.

Whereas for Stiegler the analog is always already digital, for philosopher Brian Massumi (2002) the digital is always *behind* the analog, not as the constitutive condition of the analog, but as a "ploddingly . . . [m]achinic" (2002, 137) representational mode that cannot keep up with the analog's fluid attunement to bodily movement and sensation in a new media age. Drawing on what he terms the technical definition of the analog—"a continuously variable . . . momentum that can cross from one qualitatively different medium to another" (2002, 135)—Massumi argues that the digital aspects of new media are meaningful only for the transformative "analog effects" (2002, 140) they inadvertently enable. Massumi's primary example is web surfing. When we navigate the digital architecture of the web, asserts Massumi, our senses are overwhelmed by an accumulation of multimedia, which distracts us to the extent that our conscious thoughts are always enmeshed in "a knitting of the brows, a pursing of the lips . . . scratching [and] fidgeting" (2002, 138–139). Massumi calls this the "turning in on itself of the body" (2002, 139), whereby any clear-cut, cognitive objective for going online is taken over by a synthesis of nerve receptors, expanding and contracting muscles, and flickering sounds and images, which turns the body into an analog computer, making the body *feel itself being modified* throughout the surfing process.

Even when we experience boredom online, Massumi shows, this does not mean that we are any less actively "fold[ed]" (2002, 139) into analog computation. Indeed, Massumi cites boredom as the exemplary analog effect of this digital medium. Against commonplace understandings of boredom as an experiential void or feeling divested of qualities, Massumi argues that we "click ourselves into a lull" (2002, 139) as part of an ongoing, unmotivated analog process of moving from hyperlink to hyperlink, which Massumi interprets as a bodily impulse toward becoming undone qualitatively as a unitary identity. Thus, for Massumi, the digital programming of the web cannot determine what a body does, because it is precisely this analog undoing of the body in new media that no quantitative method of breaking down, analyzing, and recombining can capture.

Following Stiegler and Massumi, communicating our experiences of going digital would seem to be a case of endorsing one of two critical approaches: that is, either taking time to break down / differentiate the fast-moving components of (always already) technological life using digital media, in order to decide on the democratizing or politically damaging effects of these media in the latest phase of mass communication; or going with the (analog) flow, embracing the new and unpredictable alliances that proliferate as digital media technologies develop, and celebrating the political and ethical import of these alliances as they displace the human from the center of life making.

■ See also CHARACTERISTICS OF DIGITAL MEDIA, COMPUTATIONAL LINGUISTICS, DATA, HISTORY OF COMPUTERS

References and Further Reading

Bateson, Gregory. 1973. *Steps to an Ecology of Mind: Collected Essays in Anthropology, Psychiatry, Evolution and Epistemology.* St Albans, UK: Paladin.

Buckley, Jake. 2011. "Believing in the (Analogico-)Digital." *Culture Machine* 12. www.culture machine.net/index.php/cm/article/view/432/463.

Crogan, Patrick. 2000. "Things Analog and Digital." *Senses of Cinema* 5. www.sensesofcinema .com/2000/5/digital/.

Grosz, Elizabeth. 2005. *Time Travels: Feminism, Nature, Power*. Durham, NC: Duke University Press.

Gruber, Klemens, and Barbara Wurm. 2009. "Elements of Digital Formalism." *Maske und Kothurn* 55 (3): 11–14.

Massumi, Brian. 2002. *Parables for the Virtual: Movement, Affect, Sensation*. Durham, NC: Duke University Press.

Owens, Larry. 1986. "Vannevar Bush and the Differential Analyzer: The Text and Context of an Early Computer." *Technology and Culture* 27 (1): 63–95.

Poster, Mark. 2001. *What's the Matter with the Internet?* Minneapolis: University of Minnesota Press.

Ruesch, Jurgen, and Gregory Bateson. 1968. *Communication: The Social Matrix of Psychiatry*. New York: W. W. Norton.

Sedgwick, Eve Kosofsky, and Adam Frank. 2003. "Shame in the Cybernetic Fold." In *Touching Feeling: Affect, Pedagogy, Performativity*, edited by Eve Kosofsky Sedgwick, 93–122. Durham, NC: Duke University Press.

Stiegler, Bernard. 2002. "The Discrete Image." In *Echographies of Television*, edited by Jacques Derrida and Bernard Stiegler, translated by Jennifer Bajorek, 145–163. Cambridge: Polity Press.

von Neumann, John. 1958. *The Computer and the Brain*. New Haven, CT: Yale University Press.

Watzlawick, Paul, Janet Helmick Beavan, and Don D. Jackson. 1968. *Pragmatics of Human Communication: A Study of Interactional Patterns, Pathologies, and Paradoxes*. London: Faber and Faber.

Wilden, Anthony. 1972. *System and Structure: Essays in Communication and Exchange*. London: Tavistock.

Wilder, Carol. 1998. "Being Analog." In *The Postmodern Presence: Readings on Postmodernism in American Culture and Society*, edited by Arthur Asa Berger, 239–253. Walnut Creek, CA: AltaMira Press.

· ·

Animated Poetry

Philippe Bootz

Premise

Algorithmic text generation regards the poem as the mere result of linguistic computing (see ALGORITHM, COMBINATORY AND AUTOMATIC TEXT GENERATION). In France, this paradigm was preponderant in digital literature throughout the 1980s (see ELECTRONIC LITERATURE). But gradually, due to the increasing power of computers, authors have introduced temporality to make their texts move: in 1982, in France, at the University of Paris 8, Roger Laufer and Michel Brett created the work *deux mots* (two words) in synthesis animation. The same year, Brazilian poet Eduardo Kac created his animated poem *Não*. In 1984, the Canadian experimental poet bpNichol programmed a set of visual poems in the language Basic under the title *First Screening* and published it on diskettes.

L.A.I.R.E. and *Alire*

In France programmed animated poetry becomes a new form: Tibor Papp, an eminent representative of Hungarian avant-garde poetry, projected his work *Les Très Riches Heures de l'ordinateur* onto ten screens during the 1985 Polyphonix Festival.

By doing so, he became the first to put forward a more expressive conception based on animation. Along with Philippe Bootz, Frédéric Develay, Jean-Marie Dutey, and Claude Maillard, he created in 1988 the group L.A.I.R.E (or Lecture, Art, Innovation, Recherche, Ecriture). These authors all come from the field of concrete and sound poetry.

As opposed to the algorithmic conception of the poetic work, L.A.I.R.E. believes that both the program and its execution partake in the work and that they do not constitute a machine designed to produce generated works. These authors claim that literariness lies not only in language but also in the relationships one has to language. For the first time, they argued that programmed digital poetry was a new and intimate form of literature intended to be read at home, on one's own computer, and not in a public place. In this way, the group anticipated the current way of reading digital literature (see DIGITAL POETRY).

To carry out its aesthetic project, the group created in 1989 the first digital magazine specializing in programmed digital poetry: *Alire* (this name is an anagram of the group's acronym). First published on floppy disks, it has been issued on CD since 1994. As the only magazine in the world dedicated to programmed poetry, the journal gradually welcomed other French authors to the group, then digital poets from foreign countries. *Alire* published works of different genres but mainly animated poetry forms (L.A.I.R.E., Burgaud and Castellin in France, Kac and Kendall in the United States, dos Santos in Brazil, Gyori in Argentina). *Alire* thus constitutes one of the most important, though relatively small, collections of works from the 1980s and early 1990s. Only fourteen issues were published between 1989 and 2010.

Alire significantly contributed to the discovery of the specific properties of programmed literature, including the actual role of the execution process. It also gave rise to a distinctly French aesthetic partly based on the failure of traditional modes of reading: the aesthetics of frustration. By revealing a reader's relationship with their natural language throughout the reading process, this aesthetic considers that each and every one of the reader's reactions is part of the work. Thus, frustration is a consequence of the readers' inability to adopt a way of reading that is appropriate for computers and incompatible with books.

Alire has played an important cultural role. Almost unknown to the public because of its very limited distribution, it has contributed since the mid-1990s to general public computer magazines and to educational material destined for secondary education. It also prepared the way for other French magazines that started publishing programmed poetry works through the digital medium, such as KAOS (Balpe 1991) and the digital part of DOCKS (Castellin and Torregrosa 1994), with which it collaborated. It also widely contributed to the meeting of European and American writers, which paved the way for an international field in digital poetry that would come to the fore in 2001, at the occasion of the E-poetry Festival held in Buffalo on Loss Pequeño Glazier's initiative.

The group would gradually disband in the late 1990s owing to the distance separating its members.

Transitoire Observable

Progressively, as a result of the development of computing author languages for animation and video, most digital poets use animation, sometimes publishing their work in a video format (Wilton Azevedo's work, for instance). Animation is no longer a genre, but it is becoming an aesthetic property of the work. In the early 2000s, Alexander Gherban, in France, considered that the development of a Flash-based aesthetic and author languages resulted in a problematic combination of programmed digital poetry and poetry designed for the screen. According to Gherban, one must reaffirm the specificity of programmed art, its irreducibility to any other form of expression, and think through which aesthetic forms are specific to this art, that is, the programmed forms. (He therefore explicitly carried on from the group L.A.I.R.E.) To meet this objective, the group Transitoire Observable (Observable Transient) was created in 2003. Gherban, Papp, and Bootz signed its founding manifesto. They were soon joined by French authors and digital artists. After Transitoire Observable was presented at the 2003 E-poetry Festival, authors from foreign countries joined the group. The group's website (http://transit oireobs.free.fr/to/) gathers theoretical papers of the group's members.

Transitoire Observable was not so much a place for creation or dissemination as a place for reflection. Its website mainly published theoretical papers focusing on the role and aesthetic nature of programming. The group believes that the computer program is the real material utilized during the writing process and that the result produced on the screen is only a transient and observable state, itself produced by the execution of the program. Therefore, writing that appears on the screen cannot be the holder of literariness; instead, literariness is sought through the program and its relationships with the rest of the *"dispositif"* (apparatus, signs, and actors) throughout the execution process. Transitoire Observable integrated the entire digital *dispositif* into its definition of the "work."

The Transitoire Observable project also falls within the aesthetic forms related to coding and code aesthetics (see CODE AESTHETICS). The issue of programmed forms largely broadens this framework by taking into account all of the digital *dispositif* and not only the computer program viewed as a text or its causal relationship to the results produced during the runtime.

The group disbanded in 2007, considering that the distinction between video and programmed arts was now established.

■ See also GLITCH AESTHETICS, HISTORY OF COMPUTERS

References and Further Reading

Balpe, Jean-Pierre, ed. 1991. *KAOS n°1*, January. Puteaux: Kaos.
Castellin, Philippe, and Jean Torregrosa. 1994. *DOC(K)S collection*. Ajaccio: AKENATON. http://akenaton-docks.fr/DOCKS-datas_f/collect_f/COLLECTION.html.

....

Animation/Kineticism
Brian Kim Stefans

Nothing from the era of antiquity suggests that the art of text in motion was of any interest, despite a long history of shaped text that goes back to the Greek poet Simias of Rhodes (300 BCE), huge public texts such as that on the Pantheon (126 CE), "M·AGRIPPA·L·F·COS·TERTIVM·FECIT," and a long tradition of calligraphic scroll poems in Asian art, flutter as they might in the wind. It is not until 1897 that motion is *implied* by a static text. Paul Valéry describes his first visions of Stéphane Mallarmé's poem "Un Coup de dés," a radical venture involving words splayed across the page in highly orchestrated typefaces and sizes, thus: "Inappreciable instants became clearly visible: the fraction of a second during which an idea flashes into being and dies away; atoms of time that serve as the germs of infinite consequences lasting through psychological centuries—at last these appeared as beings, each surrounded with a palpable emptiness" (1972, 309).

The Italian Futurists engaged in cruder, if more visceral, experiments in typography. F. T. Marinetti advocated a poetics of "parole in libertà," in turn influencing Guillaume Apollinaire's suite of "calligrammes" (1918), one of which mimics the motion of falling rain ("Il pleut"). E. E. Cummings's poem "r-p-o-p-h-e-s-s-a-g-r" (1923) encourages the reader to read the poem spatially and temporally, which is to say, cinematically, to encourage seeing, in the shattering and snapping back of the word, the actual flight of a grasshopper. Marcel Duchamp's film *Anémic Cinéma* (1926) consists largely of puns embedded in slowly spinning wheels he termed "rotoreliefs," while American Bob Brown conceived of the "Readies" (1930), poems to be read one word at a time through a viewfinder as the text winds through (like a film loop).

The acclimatization to an *aesthetic* of moving text might have started as an ironic counter-Copernican retroaction: watching billboards, store signage, and street signs whip by when driving in a car. Robert Venturi et al. observe that signage has rendered the landscape symbolic: "This architecture of styles and signs is antispatial; it is an architecture of communication over space; communication dominates space as an element in the architecture and the landscape" (1977, 8). The artist Jenny Holzer (b. 1950) would take this principle of public text to the limit with her series of provocative projections and Times Square–style LED scroll pieces.

The innovative movie titles of graphic designer Saul Bass (1920–1996) are often cited as the origins of the art form of animated typography. The opening sequence for *The Man with the Golden Arm* (1955), for instance, integrates the credits into a dynamic world characterized by an orchestration of sliding constructivist rectangles, text fades, and what would come to be called a "morph," one of the rectangles transforming into the golden arm itself. Bass's title sequence for *North by Northwest* (1959) depicts words in perspective, as if sliding on the glass side of a building, while the sequence for *It's a Mad Mad Mad Mad World* (1963) depicts words exploding from various spherical objects—actually the same sphere reconfigured as an egg, a beach ball, a mechanical top, and so on. These sequences, which convey elements of wit and menace, suggest vector-based Flash animations with their reduction of the image to lines and flat planes of color (indeed, YouTube is replete with parodies of Bass's graphic style applied to recreate titles for newer movies such as *Star Wars*; see FLASH/DIRECTOR).

The Brazilian Noigandres group—including Haroldo De Campos, Augusto De Campos, and Decio Pignatari—authored their "Pilot Plan for Concrete Poetry" in 1958: "Assuming that the historical cycle of verse (as formal-rhythmical unit) is closed, concrete poetry begins by being aware of graphic space as structural agent. Qualified space: space-time structure instead of mere linear-temporistical development." Along with Eugen Gomringer in Switzerland, these poets formulated a visual poetics that privileged the spatialization of words on a page over linear reading, the "word" being seen as "verbi-voco-visual"—semantic, phonemic, and graphemic. Gomringer's conception of the poem as "constellation" elevated Cummings's playful experiments into a poetics in which the shape of the poem itself becomes a single "sign" that impacts its interpretation (see REMEDIATION).

Early kinetic poetry generally retained the principles of concrete poems with the addition of basic motion, often with little regard to the aesthetics of the motion itself. Texts moved mechanically from one stable point—at which it could be "read"—to another. An early suite of kinetic poetry that took these limitations as virtues is Geoff Huth's "Endemic Battle Collage" (1987) (see DIGITAL POETRY), written in Apple Basic and currently surviving as a Quicktime movie. The French poet Philippe Bootz and his group L.A.I.R.E. started the electronic journal *Alire* in 1989 and pursued a poststructuralist visual poetics harking back to Mallarmé (see COMBINATORY AND AUTOMATIC TEXT GENERATION). The Brazilian singer and poet Arnaldo Antunes, inspired by the Noigrandres group and '80s music videos, created a popular body of digital text movies, released on DVD as *Nome* in 1993. This era of pre-web digital poetry was exhaustively surveyed by poet and editor Christopher Funkhouser in his *Prehistoric Digital Poetry: An Archaeology of Forms, 1959–1995* (see EARLY DIGITAL ART AND WRITING [PRE-1990]).

Flash, Macromedia's (now Adobe's) programming environment for animated graphic design, added considerably to the arsenal of tools of the poet/animator, making it easier to create smoother motion using "easing"—the acceleration and deceleration of objects as if moving through physical space—as well as employ fades, changes in color and size, the entire range of True Type Fonts, and motion along curved vectors. Not only could works of animated poetry be rendered with more subtlety, but they could also be quickly distributed due to the quick download time of vector-based graphics on the Internet prior to the present era of universal wide bandwidth (see FLASH/DIRECTOR). This increase in the animation toolbox led to sophisticated paradigms for a *rhetorics* of animation, best exhibited in Alexandra Saemmer's discussion of Brian Kim Stefans's "The Dreamlife of Letters" in "Digital Literature—A Question of Style," where she describes such "figures of animation" as "emergence," "eclipse," "kineasthetic rhymes," and "transfiguration" (Simanowski et al. 2010, 178).

A small sample of recent works that fully realize the possibilities of animated text include David Clark's "feature-length" works such as "A Is for Apple" and "88 Constellations for Wittgenstein," both of which are encyclopedic tour de forces of graphic design; Noah Wardrip-Fruin et al.'s "Screen," an interactive installation for the 3D Cave environment; Alison Clifford's "That Sweet Old Et Cetera," which animates a selection of Cummings's poetry; the giddily animated abecedarian "Bembo's Zoo" by Roberto de Vicq de Cumptich; the text movies of Young-Hae Chang Heavy Industries, which forgo much of the bells and whistles of Flash for clean, quasi-propagandistic parodies; and the Internet meme "What Does Marcellus Wallace Look Like?," which transposes a classic monologue by Samuel Jackson in *Pulp Fiction* as an intoxicatingly dynamic word film.

■ See also ANIMATED POETRY, BOOK TO E-TEXT, CAVE, DIGITAL POETRY, EARLY DIGITAL ART AND WRITING (PRE-1990), ELECTRONIC LITERATURE, FILM AND DIGITAL MEDIA, HOLOPOETRY, WORD-IMAGE

References and Further Reading

de Vicq de Cumptich, Roberto. n.d. "Bembo's Zoo." www.bemboszoo.com/.

Electronic Literature Organization. n.d. "Directory of Electronic Literature." http://directory.eliterature.org/.

Fiore, Quentin, and Marshall McLuhan. 1967. *The Medium Is the Massage: An Inventory of Effects.* New York: Bantam Books.

Goldsmith, Kenneth, et al., eds. n.d. Ubu.com. www.ubu.com.

Higgins, Dick. 1987. *Pattern Poetry: Guide to an Unknown Literature.* Albany: State University of New York Press.

Manovich, Lev. 2008. *Software Takes Command* (draft). http://lab.softwarestudies.com/2008/11/softbook.html.

Rasula, Jed, and Steve McCaffery. 2001. *Imagining Language: An Anthology.* Cambridge, MA: MIT Press.

Simanowski, Roberto, et al., eds. 2010. *Reading Moving Letters: Digital Literature in Research and Teaching.* Bielefeld: Transcript Verlag.

Solt, Mary Ellen. 1970. *Concrete Poetry: A World View.* Bloomington: Indiana University Press.

Valéry, Paul. 1972. Leonardo, Poe, Mallarmé. Translated by Malcolm Cowley and James Lawler. Princeton, NJ: Princeton University Press.

Venturi, Robert, et al. 1977. *Learning from Las Vegas: The Forgotten Symbolism of Architectural Form.* Cambridge, MA: MIT Press.

Young-Hae Chang Heavy Industries. www.yhchang.com/.

....

Archive

Katherine Harris

Digital, electronic, and hypertextual archives have come to represent online and virtual environments that transcend the traditional repository of material artifacts typically housed in a library or other institution (Price 2008, para. 3). Physical archives claim to amass anything that gives evidence of a time that has passed and "is essential for a civilized community" (*OED*). Traditional institutions define an archive as a rare book library, emphasizing the collecting of codex and manuscript representations of writing, authorship, and history. Most rare book and manuscript divisions also collect, preserve, and archive nontraditional forms of printed material and unconventional literary objects. This type of institutional archive is guided by principles of preserving history and an assumption that a *complete* collection will reveal not only that moment, but also its beginning, ending, and connection to other moments. Voss and Werner articulate the duality of the archive as both physical space and, now, an imaginative site, both of which are governed by ideological imperatives (1999, i).

Since 1996, the *digital* archive has revised the traditional institutional archive to represent both a democratizing endeavor and a scholarly enterprise (Manoff 2004, 9). An archive, if truly liberal in its collecting, represents an attempt to preserve and record multiple metanarratives (Voss and Werner 1999). Curators and special collections directors become editors and architects of digital archives to produce "an amassing of material and a shaping of it" (Price 2008, para. 9). However, the digital archive's instability threatens these metanarratives because of its potential for endless accumulation.

Jon Saklofske (2010), among others, proposes that merely offering the materials in a digital archive without editorial intervention is impossible, though Peter Robinson suggests that an archive "is where an impersonal presentation might warrant readerly freedom . . . archives typically provide the data but no tools" (2004, para. 3).

At first, *digital archive* and *scholarly/critical edition* were used interchangeably, but with the interruption of tools, databases, and multimedia objects, the archive now comes to represent something wholly different than its original definition. Flanders notes that "the digital edition could thus, in some settings, be understood more as an archive of source material with an editorial layer built on top: the one operating as the established and immutable facts of the text, and the other operating as the changing domain of human perspective and interpretation" (2005, 60). The digital archive requires, even demands, a set of computational and analytical tools to remix the data. In opposition to Robinson, even the tools become part of the editorial intervention.

The most current debate surrounding tools and digital archives occurred in the 2007 *PMLA* with Ed Folsom's promiscuous claim that the Whitman Archive is, in fact, a database, thus disavowing the long history that attends scholarly editions and digital archives. The database, for Folsom, represents "malleable and portable information" (2007, 1575–1576). Jerome McGann (2007) counters that a database is a prosthetic used to amplify the original material and returns database to its mechanical instantiation instead of the vast metaphor described by Folsom. With a variant on the argument, Meredith McGill proposes that databases offer a "remediation" of archives, not a transformation or a liberation (2007, 1593, 1595) as was supposed originally about digital archives. Folsom answers many of these salvos by reversing the typical hierarchical relationship and posits that archives are contained within databases, as if archives have a taxonomy beyond the database. These essential debates articulate an authenticity battle between database and archive which perhaps stems from academic desire to control, or editorialize, cultural records of knowledge. Kenneth Price (2009) requests that we flatten this discourse to allow for plasticity and create a supple vocabulary for digital scholarly editions and archives.

Most scholarly editors of critical editions (both print and digital) will claim that a digital archive can contain an edition, but that belies the original nature of "archive" itself—a messy compilation of materials. By revising the definition of "archive" to include the original material, its digital surrogates, its database, and its tools, even its visual representation also becomes part of the archive—but not in so messy a heap. With digital archives, we move beyond the physical repository or final resting place of a particular material object. In the digital archive, an object continues to acquire meaning based on users' organization of the material (beyond editorial control of the primary architect), based on the continued re-mixing, re-using, and re-presentation of the object.

■ See also CRITICAL EDITIONS IN THE DIGITAL AGE, DATABASE, HYPERTEXTUALITY, MATERIALITY, PRESERVATION

References and Further Reading

"Archive." *OED*. 1959. Chambers's Encycl. I. 570/1.

Derrida, Jacques. 1998. *Archive Fever: A Freudian Impression*. Chicago: University of Chicago Press.

Flanders, Julia. 2005. "Detailism, Digital Texts, and the Problem of Pedantry." *TEXT Technology* 2:41–70.

———. 2008. "The Productive Unease of 21st-Century Digital Scholarship." *Digital Humanities Quarterly* 3 (3). http://digitalhumanities.org/dhq/vol/3/3/000055/000055.html.

Folsom, Ed. 2007. "Database as Genre: The Epic Transformation of Archives." *PMLA* 122 (5): 1571–1579.

Manoff, Marlene. 2004. "Theories of the Archive from Across the Disciplines." *portal: Libraries and the Academy* 4 (1): 9–25.

McGann, Jerome. 2007. "Database, Interface, and Archival Fever." *PMLA* 122 (5): 1588–1592.

McGill, Meredith. 2007. "Remediating Whitman." *PMLA* 122 (5): 1592–1596.

Price, Kenneth. 2008. "Electronic Scholarly Editions." In *A Companion to Digital Literary Studies*, edited by Susan Schreibman and Ray Siemens. Oxford: Blackwell. www.digitalhumanities.org /companionDLS/.

———. 2009. "Edition, Project, Database, Archive, Thematic Research Collection: What's in a Name?" *Digital Humanities Quarterly* 3 (3). http://digitalhumanities.org/dhq/vol/3/3/000053 /000053.html.

Robinson, Peter. 2004. *Jahrbuch für Computerphilologie Online*. http://computerphilologie.uni-muen chen.de/ejournal.html. Also available in print: *Jahrbuch für Computerphilologie*, 123–143.

Saklofske, Jon. 2010. "NewRadial: Revisualizing the Blake Archive." *Poetess Archive Journal* 2 (1). http://journals.tdl.org/paj/index.php/paj/article/view/8.

Smith, Martha Nell. 2002. "Computing: What's American Literary Study Got to Do with IT?" *American Literature* 74 (4): 833–857.

———. 2007. "The Human Touch: Software of the Highest Order." *Textual Cultures* 2 (1): 1–15.

Voss, Paul, and Marta Werner. 1999. Introduction. "Towards a Poetics of the Archive." *Studies in the Literary Imagination* 32 (1): i–vii.

Walsh, John A. 2008. "Digital Resources for Nineteenth-Century Literary Studies." In *A Companion to Digital Literary Studies*, edited by Susan Schreibman and Ray Siemens. Oxford: Blackwell. www.digitalhumanities.org/companionDLS/.

Artificial Intelligence

David Elson

Artificial intelligence (AI), the notion that a computer can imitate or emulate the thought processes of a human and demonstrate intelligence through action, has been a long-standing area of research at the intersection of computer science, psychology, mathematics, robotics, and other fields (Russell and Norvig 2009).

There is no generally accepted definition of what AI is or what a computer must be capable of doing before we may deem it to possess intelligence. Alan Turing, a founder of modern computer science, considered the problem in the 1940s and decided that the question of whether computers could *think* was extremely difficult to answer. He replaced it with the question of whether computers could *imitate* human thought convincingly. Under this definition, a computer system is intelligent if it appears to be intelligent in a practical test, regardless of the particular computational approach used in its implementation. Turing's eponymous test asks a jury to converse with an agent they cannot see, exchanging written notes and attempting to determine through inquiry whether the agent is a human or a machine. A machine is deemed intelligent if it can convince a preponderance of the jury of its humanity. The Turing test endures as the Loebner Prize, an annual competition between such "chatterbot" programs and their creators (see CHATTERBOTS, TURING TEST).

Other theorists object to the Turing test as a measure for intelligence. Philosopher John Searle (1980) argues that no program can be called intelligent by manipulating symbols while having no true understanding of their meaning (see SEARLE'S CHINESE ROOM). A chatterbot that has been programmed with snippets of conversation understands those snippets only as strings of letters; it is the human judges that ascribe semantics to its output. This has fueled an ongoing debate regarding the nature of human intelligence (how does an individual know that she deeply understands a concept?) and whether a computer can ever truly think; the matter remains unresolved.

While the theoretical debate continues, practical research in AI is carried out on a task-by-task basis, with dialogue systems—such as the chatterbot, which carries out a conversation with a human over teletype—representing one of many possible tasks (see DIALOGUE SYSTEMS). Generally, the more well defined a task is in terms of the logical rules governing its dynamics, the easier the task is for a machine, but the less credit we give to the task as representing intelligence. (Pioneer John McCarthy once noted that "as soon as it works, no one calls it AI any more.") On one end of the spectrum, computers have long surpassed humans in speed and accuracy on the task of arithmetic, but we do not say that a pocket calculator is intelligent. In a celebrated 1997 milestone, IBM's "Deep Blue" supercomputer defeated world chess champion Garry Kasparov in a six-game re-match, $3\frac{1}{2}$–$2\frac{1}{2}$; while this machine and its successors exhibit intelligence in the chess task, they cannot describe a business strategy or devise a war plan, or even know to go indoors when it rains, because the rules that govern the chess domain are far simpler than those that govern business interaction, warfare, and common sense. Similarly, on the other end of the spectrum, humans continue to vastly outperform machines in tasks that involve ambiguities in semantics (meaning), such as language understanding, and those for which the human brain has been conditioned to excel, such as processing visual input (e.g., recognizing objects and faces), physically moving over uneven terrain, and social interaction.

The term *artificial intelligence* was coined by Joseph McCarthy in 1956 at a two-month workshop at Dartmouth College which gave the field its shape. The workshop brought together figures that would dominate the field for decades. The years of effort following the workshop were concerned with building tools for inference, formalizing the rules of various systems about which machines might reason, and building systems that demonstrate intelligence over very small test scenarios in those systems. For instance, the STUDENT system (Bobrow 1967) could solve word problems of the type given to high school students. Here's one example: "The sum of two numbers is 96, and one of the numbers is 16 larger than the other number. Find the two numbers." Using a set of logical rules that describe the structure of language, STUDENT could transform each clause into a mathematical equation (e.g., "$X + Y = 96$") and then solve the system of equations to arrive at an answer. The SHRDLU system (Winograd 1972) could interact with users via teletype and intelligently respond to instructions in the domain of manipulating physical objects:

Person: PICK UP A BIG RED BLOCK.
Computer: OK (does it).
Person: GRASP THE PYRAMID.
Computer: I DON'T UNDERSTAND WHICH PYRAMID YOU MEAN.
Person: FIND A BLOCK WHICH IS TALLER THAN THE ONE YOU ARE HOLDING
AND PUT IT INTO THE BOX.
Computer: BY "IT," I ASSUME YOU MEAN THE BLOCK WHICH IS TALLER THAN
THE ONE I AM HOLDING.
Computer: OK (does it).
Person: WHAT DOES THE BOX CONTAIN?
Computer: THE BLUE PYRAMID AND THE BLUE BLOCK.

Person: WHAT IS THE PYRAMID SUPPORTED BY?
Computer: THE BOX.
Person: HOW MANY BLOCKS ARE NOT IN THE BOX?
Computer: FOUR OF THEM.

SHRDLU not only had a deep understanding of what objects existed in the world and how they could physically relate to one another; it could parse out meaning from text, handle ambiguous pronouns (assigning "it" to a particular block), convert questions into queries, and carry out simple actions. While the computer in this example appears to show general intelligence, its abilities are confined to exactly the types of tasks demonstrated in this dialogue, just as Deep Blue excels only at chess. Still, results such as these caused a great deal of excitement and optimism that general machine intelligence was well under way to being a reality. Herbert Simon, who codeveloped a program that could devise logical proofs, wrote in 1965 that "machines will be capable, within 20 years, of doing any work a man can do." He cited chess as an example, predicting that a champion algorithm would take only ten years to develop (it would take some forty years for Deep Blue to defeat Kasparov).

The issue with the early approaches was one of coverage—the extent of the rules that may be programmed into the computer to "model" the real world. In other words, machines have no common sense, and it turned out to be extraordinarily difficult to teach common sense one axiom at a time. Consider the task of building up SHRDLU to become a robot butler, capable of taking commands and answering questions. A user may ask such a butler to manipulate thousands of possible objects in hundreds of possible ways using language that can be highly ambiguous in intent. If the user asks, "Can I have some water?" the butler would need to know an effectively bottomless set of facts: that the question is a command, rather than a literal inquiry; that water can be obtained from the faucet by turning a handle; that the best route to the faucet is one that avoids the coffee table and steps over the family dog; that water is typically delivered in a glass or cup; that the correct type of glass lives in the cupboard, or perhaps is in the dishwasher; that two-thirds of a glass is a preferred quantity of water; that glasses are carried with the open end away from the pull of gravity, to keep the contents from spilling, which is dangerous, due to the potential for a slip, which can reduce friction enough for a human to fall and injure himself; and so on. While early programs like SHRDLU could deeply understand a small quantity of facts, it eventually became clear to skeptics and practitioners alike that no system could be given broader common-sense knowledge through a manual enumeration of facts and rules; even if the facts could be encoded, the computational resources required to reason over them were far too great to be practical. No computer at the time was fast enough or possessed enough memory to handle such a "combinatorial explosion," and even today, the so-called Strong AI or Good Old-Fashioned AI technique of reasoning over a set of symbols that represent general-purpose facts is unworkable for a real-world application with a nontrivial set of use cases.

The early optimism that characterized the field reversed into pessimism in the late 1970s, leading to a severe contraction in funding for AI research. This period, known as the "AI winter," was also fatal to many startup companies that had attempted to commercialize the field. However, basic research did continue on new approaches to modeling intelligence, especially with respect to particular domains. In the *planning* architecture, a system emulates intelligence by simulating *agents* that perceive the world and carry out actions in an intentional attempt to bring about a particular "goal" state. A navigation system, for instance, knows where it wants to go, sees the obstacles in its way, and can devise a path to circumvent those obstacles, sometimes developing sub-plans to deal with complicated or unexpected barriers. In the *expert system* approach, a machine could be taught to reason about problems in a particular scientific or technical area, given facts about the domain and general rules for combining those facts. One well-known example was developed in the domain of medical diagnosis: MYCIN (Buchanan and Shortliffe 1984) could take as input a set of symptoms, ask questions about other symptoms, and give a diagnosis as to the type of bacteria most likely to have infected the patient. In this case, the facts were the features of various bacteria and kinds of symptoms they often caused; the reasoning engine allowed it to generate a list of candidate bacteria that could be causing the given set of symptoms and then ask questions about other particular symptoms such that the answers could efficiently narrow down the list through elimination. Although MYCIN could outperform junior physicians at the diagnosis task, it, like the earlier systems, was never deployed in practice.

Toward the late 1980s and through the 1990s, AI as a field was revived as tremendous advances in the speed and memory capacity of computers made new approaches possible. In the most impactful new technique, systems could use statistics to *learn about the world from large quantities of data*. In other words, given an algorithm for learning by example and a sizable set of examples, a system can derive its own rules rather than be taught rules by hand. The field of *machine learning* was born, and with it came a new influx of attention and funding. Machine learning approaches can attempt to mimic the structure of the human brain (neural networks) or use mathematical techniques to classify input into one of a set of predetermined categories, such as distinguishing fact from opinion in news text. "Unsupervised" learning techniques do not even require a predetermined set of categories, instead building their own models of the world; these systems discover patterns that emerge from large quantities of data in a bottom-up fashion, such as discovering the syntax of a language by recognizing that certain words tend to occur in certain sequences (much like a young child recognizes words from phonemes by listening to others speak for months on end). The infusion of machine learning made AI more robust than it had been, although the results were more favorable in some tasks than in others. Researchers in language processing made advancements in speech recognition and language translation, for instance, but were still constrained by the small amounts of training data that could be processed with the limited machine resources available.

Since 2000, the proliferation of the Internet, distributed computing (where many machines can tackle one problem simultaneously), and mobile computing have advanced machine learning and AI faster than at any prior time. For many tasks, "cloud computing" is allowing for services where everyday users worldwide can leverage models that have been trained on billions of input examples in data centers. The fruits of AI research have become available on a widespread basis. Accurate speech recognition, for instance, is now common on mobile phones and in call centers (their models trained by analyzing the speech of millions of prior users). Computer vision has allowed us to scan millions of books into a digital form for the first time. Completely autonomous cars are on the road in several states, using laser range finders and other sensors to detect and avoid pedestrians, cars, and other obstacles. Computers are commonly used to control airplanes and other heavy machinery, autonomously perceiving the world and taking action in order to successfully complete their duties.

The intersection of AI and digital media has followed a journey parallel to AI as a whole. In the early days, *story understanding* was a major goal. In this task, a system might read a news article, make inferences about its content, and answer questions that demonstrate understanding. This was possible only in small domains (Schank and Abelson 1977). Story understanding gave way to the more general field of *natural language processing*, which today commonly uses statistical methods that develop models of language use from training data. For instance, the technique of "language modeling" involves compiling histograms of all the n-word sequences that occur in a text, where n varies from 1 to 2, 3, or more. For the training data "To be or not to be," the 3-grams would be "To be or," "be or not," "or not to," and "not to be." These histograms then become a model of normative language use. This can be useful for tasks in understanding—a 4-gram model would suggest that "out for a dink" is less likely to occur in text than "out for a drink," because the latter occurs much more frequently in a corpus of conversational American English. This can guide a language recognition or translation system into synthesizing more accurate results, even without truly understanding what it means to take one out for a drink (in an example of a "Weak AI" approach). By chaining together frequently used n-grams, we can even construct new sentences that, while never before uttered, fit the language model (see n-GRAM); Jurafsky and Martin give Shakespeare-style sentences from a 4-gram model of the Bard's collected works: "It cannot be but so," and "They say all lovers swear more performance than they are wont to keep obliged faith unforfeited!" (2009).

Several tasks in natural language processing have seen rapid improvement and successful integrations into public services. Machine translation has been intensely studied for decades; today, having been statistically trained on vast training corpora, Google's service translates more text for end users in a day than the totality of human translators do in a year. Computers can also summarize news articles by learning how to identify the "gist" of a topic and extracting key sentences. Question answering reached a milestone in 2011 when IBM demonstrated a "Watson" system that used natural language processing over Internet data to beat expert human players in a *Jeopardy!* tournament (Ferrucci et al. 2010). Rather than simply extract n-grams from its training corpus, Watson extracted facts and relationships, such as the directors of films and the relative sizes of world lakes. An online system then parsed each *Jeopardy!* clue, determined what type of response was called for, handled wordplay and other rhetorical complications, and queried the fact database for the most appropriate answer. Watson only offered an answer when its "confidence score" was higher than a given threshold.

AI has also been applied to digital media in the form of interactive or autonomous systems that exhibit creativity or complement the human creative process. The question of whether computers can be *creative* in an artistic or rhetorical sense (see COMBINATORY AND AUTOMATIC TEXT GENERATION) reaches the crux of AI as a whole. Researchers have demonstrated that machines can generate new media by modeling and recombining corpora of existing media; this is not fundamentally different from the human creative process of observation and reformulation (see REMIX). David Cope (1996) has implemented one such system that can analyze the musical style of a composer and generate new music in that style, in a manner analogous to text generation from n-grams. Other domains that have seen machine contributions include the generation of poetry, humor, analogy and metaphor, and narrative (see STORY GENERATION).

Intelligent machines figure into the public imagination. In many works of fiction, they take the role of Frankenstein's monster (or its predecessors, the Golem and the Pygmalion): an inventor unleashes an inhuman force that ultimately destroys him, sometimes overpowering the human race in the process. AI can also fit the Pinocchio mold, in which a machine strives to become more human. Through such an agent, AI serves as a narrative device that permits existential introspection—by interacting with an entity that is human in some ways, but not in others, we are able to explore the boundaries of what it means to be human. For instance, much has been made of the notion of a machine that looks remarkably human, can speak and interact like a human, but lacks the ability to feel and express emotion (in particular, empathy) or be guided by a moral compass. There is a collective anxiety, misplaced as it may be, that AI will ultimately produce machines that are identical to humans in form and function but lack a "soul." This fear has more of a basis in mythology and philosophy than in the technical reality of intelligent machines.

■ See also COMPUTATIONAL LINGUISTICS, INTERACTIVE DRAMA

References and Further Reading

Bobrow, D.G. 1967. "Natural Language Input for a Computer Problem Solving System." In *Semantic Information Processing*, edited by M. Minsky, 133–215. Cambridge, MA: MIT Press.
Buchanan, Bruce G., and Edward H. Shortliffe. 1984. *Rule Based Expert Systems: The MYCIN Experiments of the Stanford Heuristic Programming Project*. Reading, MA: Addison-Wesley.
Cope, David. 1996. *Experiments in Musical Intelligence*. Madison, WI: A-R Editions.
Ferrucci, David, Eric Brown, Jennifer Chu-Carroll, et al. 2003. "Building Watson: An Overview of the DeepQA Project." *AI Magazine* 31 (3): 59–79.
Jurafsky, Daniel, and James H. Martin. 2009. *Speech and Language Processing: An Introduction to Natural Language Processing, Speech Recognition, and Computational Linguistics*. 2nd ed. Upper Saddle River, NJ: Prentice Hall.
Russel, Stuart, and Peter Norvig. 2009. *Artificial Intelligence: A Modern Approach*. 3rd ed. Upper Saddle River, NJ: Prentice Hall.
Schank, Roger C., and Robert P. Abelson. 1977. *Scripts, Plans, Goals and Understanding: An Inquiry into Human Knowledge Structure*. Hillsdale, NJ: Lawrence Erlbaum Associates.
Searle, John. 1980. "Minds, Brains and Programs." *Behavioral and Brain Sciences* 3 (3): 417–457.
Winograd, Terry. 1972. *Understanding Natural Language*. New York: Academic Press.

Artificial Life
Simon Penny

The term *artificial life* arose in the late 1980s as a descriptor of a range of (mostly) computer-based research practices that sought alternatives to conventional artificial intelligence (henceforth AI) methods as a source of (quasi-)intelligent behavior in technological systems and artifacts (see ARTIFICIAL INTELLIGENCE). These practices included reactive and bottom-up robotics; computational systems that simulated evolutionary and genetic processes as well as animal behavior; and a range of other research programs informed by biology and complexity theory. A general goal was to capture, harness, or simulate the generative and "emergent" qualities of "nature"—of evolution, coevolution, and adaptation. "Emergence" was a keyword in the discourse (see EMERGENCE).

Techniques developed in artificial life (henceforth Alife) research are applied in diverse fields, from electronic circuit design to animated creatures and crowds in movies and computer games. Historically, Alife is a reaction to the failures of the cognitivist program of AI and a return to the biologically informed style of cybernetics (see CYBERNETICS). Alife was also informed by various areas of research in the second half of the twentieth century, as discussed below.

Cybernetics and Self-Organizing Systems

Biological and ecological metaphors were the stock-in-trade of cybernetics, along with concepts of feedback, homeostasis, and the notion of a "system." British neurologist Ross Ashby coined the term "self-organising system" in 1947, an idea grouped in the early cybernetic literature with "adaptive," "purposive," and "teleological" systems. The term *self-organization* refers to processes where global patterns arise from multiple or iterated interactions in lower levels of a system. Canonical examples are the organization of social insects and the emergence of mind from neural processes. As a metadiscipline, cybernetics wielded significant influence in the 1960s, in biology (systems ecology), sociology (Luhmann 1995), business management (Beer 1959), and the arts (Burnham 1968).

Computing and Artificial Life

Alife could not have emerged without the easy availability of computation. This is not simply to proclaim (as Christopher Langton—an early spokesman—did) that Alife was an exploration of life on a non-carbon substrate, but that Alife is "native" to computing in the sense that a large-scale iterative process is crucial to the procedures that generate (most) Alife phenomena. One of the enduring fascinations of Alife is that systems that simulate genetic, evolutionary, and animal behavior solve problems in surprising ways, but often they are structurally perplexing and resistant to reverse engineering.

DNA and Computer Code

In 1953, Watson and Crick announced the structure of DNA, building on work by Linus Pauling, Rosalind Franklin, and others. Analogies from both cryptography and computer programming are everywhere in genetics discourse and seem to have been from the outset. Watson and Crick made explicit analogies between computer code and genetic code, with DNA codons being conceived as words in DNA codescript. They explicitly described DNA in computer terms as the genetic "code," comparing the egg cell to a computer tape. The Human Genome Project began in 1990 and was headed by none other than James Watson. Like any structuring metaphor, computer analogies doubtless had significant influence on the way DNA and genetics are conceived, particularly by laying the fallacious hardware/software binary back onto biological matter—constructing DNA as "information" as opposed to the presumably information-free cellular matter. The conception of the genetic "code" as deployed by Watson and Crick did not specifically dissociate the genetic "information" from its materiality, but by the late 1980s, it was possible for Alife adherents to speak in these terms. A basic premise of Alife, in the words of one of its major proponents, Christopher Langton, is the possibility of separation of the "informational content" of life from its "material substrate."

Neural Networks

The idea of an electronic simulation of (a certain understanding of) the behavior of a network of biological neurons was first proposed by Warren McCulloch and Walter Pitts (1943). Such networks were found capable of learning and could be trained, yet they were resistant to reductive analysis. That is, while a network might display a behavior, half the network would not display half the behavior, and one neuron alone would not display one part of the total behavior. The idea of neural nets was a central theme in cybernetic research and rhetoric, and consistent with cybernetic thought. It was felt that the emulation of biological brain mechanisms could result in simulated intelligence. The distinctive qualities of neural networks, namely, freedom from explicit representation, semiautonomous growth, and adaptation, were sympathetic with and informed the emerging Alife paradigm.

Fractals

The desire to describe "nature" mathematically has a long history, a major landmark being the magnum opus *On Growth and Form*, by D'Arcy Wentworth Thompson (1917). In 1977, Benoit Mandelbrot published his highly acclaimed *Fractal Geometry of Nature*. Fractals deploy computing for extensively iterative procedures that capture some formal aspects of biological processes. The basic mathematics of fractals—of symmetry across scale—was over a hundred years old (Cantor). The notion had been exemplified in the early twentieth century by mathematical oddities such as the Koch snowflake, the Sierpinski triangle, and the Menger sponge, but the visual elaboration of extended iteration only became viable with automated calculation. Fractals became a celebrated form of computer graphics and popular poster art and were quickly applied in computer graphics to generate realistic clouds, mountain ranges, vegetation, and coastlines in 3D images, immersive environments, and games.

Chaos Theory and Nonlinear Dynamics

On the heels of fractal hysteria came a more embracing result of iterative computation: nonlinear dynamics and complexity theory. Again, the mathematics behind "chaos" was a century old (Poincaré). It was a meteorologist, Edward Lorenz, who in 1961 found that rounding his figures to three decimal places gave results that were unpredictably different from using the same numbers to six places. That is, the measurement of, say, wind speed as 17.585347 km/hr could give a radically different result than if it was rounded to 17.585. Such results were counterintuitive, to say the least. This phenomenon came to be known as "sensitive dependence on initial conditions," or more colloquially as "the butterfly effect," the notion being that the flap of a butterfly's wing in the Amazon could instigate a chain of events that could result in a tornado in Louisiana.

Through the 1970s the significance of nonlinear mathematics was recognized in many fields. The work of Robert May, for instance, built lasting influence in biology and ecology. These kinds of studies led to a related set of fields and themes: dynamical systems, nonlinear dynamics, complexity theory, emergent complexity, and self-organizing criticality. A later but influential and widely cited paper, "Chaos" (Crutchfield et al. 1986), contributed to increasing popular understanding of these phenomena. It should be noted that the "chaotic regime," contrary to its spectacular name, does not refer to sheer disorder, but to the ragged edges of determinism, referred to as "deterministic chaos" where behaviors, while not predictable, were susceptible to statistical analysis.

Cellular Automata

A key example of Alife dynamics is an iterative mathematical game called "Life," developed by mathematician John Conway in 1970, without the use of computers. Life is a class of mathematical procedures called cellular automata, originally devised by John von Neumann as part of his discussion of the possibility of self-replicating machines. Played out on a simple square grid, cellular automata like Conway's Life demonstrate the emergence of variety and complex behaviors from a few simple rules. In short, the state of every cell in the next time step is determined by its state and the state of its immediate neighbors in the current time step, using simple rules about numbers of neighbors being "on" or "off." As such, Life and other cellular automata became emblematic of the notion of emergent complexity. By the late 1980s it was clear that highly iterative computational processes held the paradoxical potential to simulate processes that seemed to defy the ordered predictability of Boolean logic.

Genetic Algorithms and Synthetic Evolution

In 1975, John Holland published *Adaptation in Natural and Artificial Systems*, in which he outlined the notion of a genetic algorithm as a method of problem analysis based on Darwinian natural selection. "Computer programs that 'evolve' in ways that resemble natural selection can solve complex problems even their creators do not fully understand" (Holland 1975, 66). In such a system, an initial population with randomly generated characteristics is evaluated by some method (called "fitness criteria") to establish the most successful ones. These are mutated and crossbred to produce a new population that is then tested against the same criteria. The process is repeated numerous times in a way that resembles evolution, and increasingly "fit" products are generated. Genetic algorithms have been deployed in a host of application domains to design or evolve: machine vision systems, diesel engines, stock market prediction systems, and coffee tables, as well as artworks and robots. Karl Sims's Evolved Virtual Creatures were a spectacular use of this technique.

Reactive Robotics

By the late 1980s, a level of frustration had developed within the robotics community as the application of conventional AI techniques to robotics had met with limited success. It was in this context that various researchers, including Rodney Brooks and Luc Steels (Steels and Brooks 1995), pursued approaches to robotics based on the idea that most of the creatures that demonstrably survive and thrive in the world have very small brains, are unlikely to reason, and are very unlikely to build internal representations of their worlds upon which to reason. Brooks, reflecting on the challenge of conventional "internal representation based robotics," famously asserted that "the world is its own best model." On the basis of such ideas, researchers developed a range of small robots with very limited computational abilities that demonstrated remarkable success at various mobile tasks. Such results fed the idea in Alife that biological analogies held promise as technological models. In combination with ideas such as flocking and emergence, conceptions of "multi-agent" and "swarm" robotics were developed which linked robotics with the study of social insects such as bees, ants, and termites.

Hard and Soft Artificial Life

The assertion that Alife *is* life divided the community into so-called hard Alifers and soft Alifers. The debate created an ethico-philosophical firestorm concerning intelligence, creativity, and generativity in evolving and adaptive non-carbon-based life-forms. Hard Alifers maintained that silicon-based "life" was indeed alive by any reasonable definition. They argued that biology must include the study of digital life and must arrive at some universal laws concerning "wet life" and digital life. Soft Alifers held that such phenomena were models or simulations (see SIMULATION).

Artificial Life and Media Art

The 1990s were a computer cultural maelstrom during which artists and theorists grappled with the practical and theoretical implications of computing, qua computing, and as cultural practice. Simultaneously, poststructuralism and feminist critiques of science contributed to the rise of science and technology studies (STS) and famously to the "science wars." Notions axiomatic to "normal science" and paradigms accepted within the scientific and technical communities were under interrogation—among them dualism, reductivism, cognitivism, and AI practices rooted in the "physical symbol system hypothesis."

Some in the community of interdisciplinary and technically literate computer artists were highly attentive to the activities of the Alife community. The methods of Alife suggested the "holy grail" of machine creativity and autonomous agency and promised a kind of autonomously behaving art that could make its own decisions, based on its own interpretations of (its/the) world. The artist would become a metadesigner, imposing constraints upon the environments of his creatures, which would then respond in potentially surprising ways. Notions of emergence, generativity, self-organizing systems, autopoiesis, and autonomy were central. In this short synopsis, I will identify and discuss some of the main genres of Alife media art practices, illustrated with some historically key examples (Penny 2009).

Evolved Images and Animation

In addition to the already-mentioned fractals, which are deployed in computer graphic simulations of plants, forests, coastlines, mountains, and other naturally occurring forms, Alife techniques have been applied in animation and interactive and immersive (see IMMERSION) real-time systems. In 1992, Andrew Witkin and Michael Kass won the Ars Electronica Golden Nica for computer graphics for RD (reaction/diffusion) Texture Buttons, which generate plausibly "natural" patterns and textures. This work is historically interesting not simply because it represented significant progress in computer graphics, nor because it deployed the mathematics of nonlinear dynamics, but because it is a simulation of the canonical example of self-organization in chemistry, the Belousov-Zhabotinsky reaction. In the same period, deploying simulated evolution with aspects of fractal math, William Latham evolved an array of biomorphic forms, mostly existing as virtual sculptural objects. Over the next decade, Karl Sims played a leading role in developing technologies and works (an early example being the animation "Panspermia"). In *Turbulence* (1994/1995) John McCormack took another approach, presenting digital animation of an array of evolved and synthetic life-forms in an installation context. User interaction was restricted to navigation of the database of such clips. In this context, mention must also be made of the weirdly hallucinogenic biomorphic and zoo-morphic animations of Yoichiro Kawaguchi.

Virtual Ecologies

One of the early and celebrated Alife experiments was Tierra by Tom Ray, a biologist. In Tierra code objects evolve to compete in a computational environment. Biological survival strategies emerged, such as host/parasite relations and cycles of aggressive behaviors and defensive behaviors (Ray 1995). As an idea Tierra was exciting, but like much scientifico-technical research, its results were statistical. The challenge to the art community was how to open such phenomena to direct sensory experience. A community of "art-breeders" arose in the mid-1990s—Karl Sims, John McCormack, Scott Draves, Jeffrey Ventrella, Bernd Lintermann, and others—who explored the generation of aesthetic artifacts via various Alife and genetic procedures, developing underlying evolutionary and ecological architectures and interaction schemes based on biological and ecological analogies. Digital creatures and communities of life-forms capable of behaving and often interacting became common. Louis Bec remains a visionary artist-theorist in this field.

TechnoSphere by Jane Prophet and Gordon Selley (1995) involved a web-accessible computer-generated landscape/environment in which users could "release" creatures they had built from components available in the application. Creatures would then interact and compete with each other by fighting, attempted mating, and other actions. Along with the modeling of an artificial ecology, *TechnoSphere* engaged other contemporary challenges in digital media arts, such as the creation of navigable virtual landscapes, strategies for real-time interaction, and utilizing the web as a presentation environment. *Time of Doubles* by Haru Ji and Graham Wakefield (2011) is a recent example of this genre.

Physically Instantiated Alife Systems

Another important aspect of Alife art was physically instantiated Alife systems, including mobile robots, robotic sculpture, and interactive environments. Pioneer works include Grey Walter's *Tortoises* (1948) and Edward Ihantowicz's *Senster* (1969). *Flock* (1992) by Ken Rinaldo and Mark Grossman is an installation of, originally, three robotic sculptures suspended from the ceiling. *Flock* was first exhibited in the Machine Culture exhibition at SIGGRAPH'93. *Flock* is a community of devices that sense and move toward visitors and speak to each other using audible telephone dial tones (Penny 1993). It uses "flocking behavior" (Reynolds) to coordinate the activities of the three "arms." *Petit Mal* (Simon Penny 1992–1995) implemented subsumption-like architecture in a robot with capacity for embodied interaction. *Sympathetic Sentience* (Penny 1996) was a hardware instantiated system that manifested emergent complex behavior. *Propagaciones* (2007) by Leo Nuñez is a more recent example of this trajectory. *Propagaciones* is a kinetic sculptural realization of one of the icons of Alife, the cellular automaton. In *Propagaciones*, separate electromechanical sculptural "cells" stimulate each other into mutual action, creating propagating patterns across the field.

Commercial Applications of Artificial Life Art

Much of the research that was prototyped in interdisciplinary media art communities has been applied in the commercial and corporate media industry, particularly cinema special effects and game design (*Myst* and *Spore*: Will Wright / Maxis), and more recently massively multiuser role-playing games (such as *World of Warcraft*) and online communities (Second Life). *Spore* (2008) is reminiscent of virtual ecology art projects discussed above. Less obvious is the fact that the vast array of techniques for generating synthetic but natural-looking landscapes, weather patterns, vegetation and plants, animals, and synthetic characters and crowds (and their autonomous and group behaviors) which we see in movies, computer games, and virtual environments all have some connection to the Alife research of the 1990s. In the movie industry, the rendering of synthetic characters and synthetic crowds has become an entire subindustry leveraging research in procedural modeling, autonomous agents, genetic algorithms, and related Alife fields, a recently celebrated example being crowd and battle scenes in *Lord of the Rings*.

■ See also ANIMATION/KINETICISM, CHATTERBOTS, DIGITAL AND NET ART, DIGITAL INSTALLATION ART, HOLOPOETRY

References and Further Reading

Ashby, Ross. 1956. *An Introduction to Cybernetics.* New York: Wiley.

Beer, Stafford. 1959. *Cybernetics and Management.* London: English Universities Press.

Brooks, Rodney. 1991. "Intelligence without Representation." *Artificial Intelligence* 47 (1–3): 139–159.

Brooks, Rodney A., and Pattie Maes, eds. 1996. *Artificial Life: Proceedings of the Fourth International Workshop on the Synthesis and Simulation of Living Systems.* Cambridge, MA: MIT Press.

Burnham, Jack. 1968. *Beyond Modern Sculpture: The Effects of Science and Technology on the Sculpture of This Century.* New York: Braziller.

Crutchfield, J. P., J. D. Farmer, N. H. Packard, and R. S. Shaw. 1986. "Chaos." *Scientific American* 255 (December 1986): 46–57.

Holland, John. 1975. *Adaptation in Natural and Artificial Systems.* Ann Arbor: University of Michigan Press.

Koza, John R. 1992. *Genetic Programming: On the Programming of Computers by Means of Natural Selection.* Cambridge, MA: MIT Press.

Langton, Christopher G., ed. 1991. *Artificial Life II: Proceedings of the Second Interdisciplinary Workshop on the Synthesis and Simulation of Living Systems.* Reading, MA: Addison-Wesley.

———. 1993. *Artificial Life III: Proceedings of the Third Interdisciplinary Workshop on the Synthesis and Simulation of Living Systems.* Reading, MA: Addison-Wesley.

———, ed. 1995. *Artificial Life: An Overview.* Cambridge, MA: MIT Press.

Luhmann, Niklas. 1995. *Social Systems.* Stanford: Stanford University Press.

Mandelbrot, Benoît B. 1983. *Fractal Geometry of Nature.* San Francisco: W. H. Freeman.

McCulloch, Warren, and Walter Pitts. 1943. "A Logical Calculus of the Ideas Immanent in Nervous Activity." *Bulletin of Mathematical Biophysics* 5:115–133.

Penny, Simon. 1993. "Machine Culture Catalog and Essay Collection." In *Computer Graphics Visual Proceedings: Annual Conference Series, 1993,* ed. Thomas Linehan, 109–184. New York: ACM SIGGRAPH.

———. 2009. "Artificial Life Art—a Primer." *DAC-09 Proceedings.* http://escholarship.org/uc/item/1z07j77x.

Ray, Thomas. 1995. "An Evolutionary Approach to Synthetic Biology: Zen and the Art of Creating Life." In *Artificial Life, an Overview,* edited by C. G. Langton. Cambridge, MA: MIT Press. Previously published in *Artificial Life* 1 (1/2): 179–209.

Sims, Karl. 1991. "Artificial Evolution for Computer Graphics." *Computer Graphics* 25 (4): 319–328. www.karlsims.com/papers/siggraph91.html.

Steels, Luc, and Rodney Brooks, eds. 1995. *The Artificial Life Route to Artificial Intelligence: Building Embodied, Situated Agents.* Hillsdale, NJ: Lawrence Erlbaum Associates.

Thompson, D'Arcy Wentworth. 1917. *On Growth and Form.* Cambridge: Cambridge University Press.

Whitelaw, Mitchell. 2004. *Metacreation: Art and Artificial Life.* Cambridge, MA: MIT Press.

Augmented Reality

Jay David Bolter

Augmented reality (AR) is the term for a constellation of digital technologies that enable users to display and interact with digital information integrated into their immediate physical environment. AR is the technological counterpart of virtual reality (VR), which until recently was much better known, though not necessarily widely used (see VIRTUAL REALITY). In the late 1960s and early 1970s, the digital graphics pioneer Ivan Sutherland developed the first head-worn computer displays permitting the user to see computer graphics overlaid on their visual field. Although Sutherland's displays constituted the beginning of both AR and VR, interest in VR eclipsed that of AR in the following decades, as display and tracking technologies were being developed. Work on AR was revived in the 1990s by Steve Feiner, together with his graduate students Blair MacIntyre and Doree Seligmann at Columbia University, as well as at other universities and research centers. (The term *augmented reality* itself was possibly coined in 1990 by a researcher at the Boeing Company.)

AR and VR are often classed as examples of mixed reality (MR) on a spectrum described by Paul Milgram in 1994. The spectrum indicates the ratio between the amount of information provided by the computer and the amount coming from the user's visual surround. At one extreme there is no computer input (only the so-called real environment); at the other, the computer is providing all the visual information, and possibly sound as well, to constitute a complete "virtual environment" or "virtual reality." AR lies in between these extremes, but typically far more of the user's view is constituted by the actual visual environment and the computer is adding relatively little information. "Augmented virtuality" is a little-used term to describe the case where some elements of the physical world are integrated into a predominantly virtual environment. The spectrum, however, obscures a fundamental distinction between AR and VR. VR cuts the user off from involvement in the physical and, by implication, the social world. AR acknowledges the physical world rather than eliding it. It is one of a trio of such technologies that came to prominence in the 1990s—the other two were ubiquitous computing and tangible computing. Each of these was in its own way a response to the implicit promise of VR to project the user into a disembodied cyberspace (see CYBERSPACE, VIRTUAL BODIES).

Until about 2005, AR was almost exclusively a laboratory technology, because of the expense and technical limitations of the head-worn displays and especially the tracking technologies. The one exception was the development of techniques to alter the video signal in broadcasts of sporting events: for example, to draw the yellow first-down line in American football or to display virtual advertising, which for viewers at home would appear to be on billboards at the stadium. This practice is sometimes called AR, despite the fact that no tracking technology is involved. The advent of smartphones has once again redefined AR as a medium for commercial use and cultural expression. AR on a phone or tablet does not typically require a headset. Instead, the phone's video camera provides a view of the surrounding environment while the processor overlays augmented information on the screen in the appropriate places. A new class of applications has been developed for the two most popular smartphone systems iPhone and Android: these are the

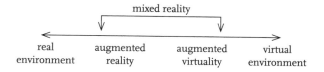

mixed reality

real environment — augmented reality — augmented virtuality — virtual environment

so-called AR browsers, such as Layar and Argon. AR browsers work on analogy with web browsers by accessing a file or "channel" that contains markup for displaying text, images, video, and audio along with geolocational information. As with web browsers, the markup language for AR browsers is relatively easy to learn, so that a broader class of designers and potentially even artists and writers can use them to create AR experiences.

There is a growing interest in the use of AR to enhance the experience of visitors in cultural heritage sites. The idea of using AR technology for tours and educational experiences dates back to the mid-1990s and the "Touring Machine" project at Columbia University. In 2002, Archaeoguide was a project by researchers at the Computer Graphics Center in Darmstadt, Germany, and in Greece, in which a visitor wearing a headset could see, for example, a reconstruction of the temple of Hera appearing on the foundations of the actual site in Olympia in Greece. These experiments and others still required computers, tracking equipment, and bulky headsets. The advent of smartphones makes it possible for the first time to deploy cultural heritage applications for a general population of visitors. Gunnar Liestøl at Oslo University has, for example, created a series of "situated simulations" for the iPhone depicting artifacts and living conditions in the time of the Vikings in Norway. In general, museums and other cultural institutions are beginning to think beyond traditional audioguides and create or commission visual and interactive AR and MR experiences. Another example is the sophisticated cultural heritage application set in the Saint-Etienne Cathedral in Metz, France, created by Maria Engberg from the Blekinge Institute of Technology working with collaborators from the Georgia Institute of Technology. With the Argon browser, the user can visit various locations within the cathedral, hear music as well as historical narrative, examine the stained glass, and see a computer-graphic model of earlier stages in history of the cathedral's architecture.

AR and MR also have potential for locative-based artistic and literary experiences (see DIGITAL INSTALLATION ART). In a sense some installation art from the 1970s could be considered forerunners to the creative use of MR if not AR. Myron Krueger's *Videoplace* was an MR installation that tracked the user's movements, allowing her to interact with the projected images on screens in front of her. Since that time, Krueger's work has been followed by other experimental installations, often exhibited at Ars Electronica, a festival for art and technology founded in 1979. The conceptual artist Jenny Holzer has done important work in large-scale installations with projected text, though not necessarily under computer control. Recent artists working along similar lines include Camille Utterback, Rafael Lozano-Hemmer, and Pablo Valbuena. Since 2006, Paul Notzold has been working on an interactive, text-based MR piece called *TXTual Healing*, in which text messages contributed by passersby are projected in dynamic fonts on the side of a building.

In contrast to MR installation art, instances of "true" AR (in Ron Azuma's sense, with graphics registered in the user's field of view as she looks through a headset or screen) are still rare. In 2010, Sander Veenhof and Mark Skwarek used the Layar browser to stage a "gorilla intervention" at the Museum of Modern Art (MoMA) in New York. Visitors with the browser on their phones could see artwork overlaid in the space of galleries.

These visuals were not approved by MoMA but became part of the exhibits at least for those technologically equipped visitors. Such new art forms become possible precisely because A R allows for the intersection between virtual information spaces and the user's physical location. The potential of locative literature, in which the user would see or hear texts located in space, is also only beginning to be explored.

■ See also LOCATION-BASED NARRATIVE

References and Further Reading

[Contemporary research in augmented reality is presented each year at the flagship conference: International Symposium on Mixed and Augmented Reality (ISMAR)]

Azuma, Ronald T. 1997. "A Survey of Augmented Reality." *Presence: Teleoperators and Virtual Environments* 6 (4): 355–385.

Azuma, Ronald T., Yohan Baillot, Reinhold Behringer, Steve Feiner, Simon Julier, and Blair MacIntyre. 2001. "Recent Advances in Augmented Reality." *IEEE Computer Graphics and Applications* 21 (6): 34–47.

Feiner, Steve, Blair MacIntyre, and Doree Seligmann. 1993. "Knowledge-Based Augmented Reality." *Communications of the ACM* 36 (7): 52–63.

Feiner, Steve, Blair MacIntyre, Tobias Höllerer, and Anthony Webster. 1997. "A Touring Machine: Prototyping 3D Mobile Augmented Reality Systems for Exploring the Urban Environment." *Proc. ISW '97 First* IEEE Int. Symp. on Wearable Computers, October 13–14, Cambridge, MA. http://citeseerx.ist.psu.edu/viewdoc/summary?doi=10.1.1.69.4463.

Milgram, Paul, and Fumio Kishino. 1994. IEICE Transactions on Information Systems, vol. E77-D, no. 12 (December), 1321–1329.

Websites

The Argon Browser: http://argon.gatech.edu
The Layar Browser: www.layar.com/
Paul Notzold, TXTual Healing: www.txtualhealing.com/

....

Authoring Systems
Judy Malloy

The creation of new media literature is a complex process in which the writer works with a combination of words, literary practice, hardware, software, and interface design. Contemporary new media literary forms arise not only from writing practice but also from the exploration and use of computer-mediated authoring systems. A historical precedent is the development of polyphonic music beginning in the Middle Ages when theory composers, such as Guido of Arezzo, Philippe de Vitry, Franco of Cologne, and Marchetto da Padova, explored and developed methods that were at the core of the creation and notation of polyphonic music (Gallo [1977] 1985).

In the field of electronic literature, authoring systems, also called authoring software, may be programming languages, such as Perl, Pascal, or C++, or they may be applications or scripts created with a programming language. Unless the resultant work is print, software is usually inherent to the work itself. Thus, a compiler, application, browser, or "player" is needed to "run" the work and could be considered a component of the authoring system. Additionally, computer operating systems and hardware platforms may also be considered a part of an authoring system, particularly in cases where they are essential to the work: for instance, the historic PDP-1 was central in the creation of *Spacewar!* (Graetz 1981), and the Apple iPad is central in the creation of iPad "apps."

Approaches to the use of authoring systems vary widely from nonprogrammer experimentation with existing applications to the creation of custom-made software to realize a writer's vision, either by the writer or by a programmer working with the writer.

Because the field includes practitioners from very different backgrounds, new media creative projects may or may not follow a traditional software management path from idea to completion. Some writers take the role of project managers. Others begin their work as software engineers. Some begin with an artistic concept and then, either by using a preexisting application or by creating their own authoring software, search for a system to implement their project. Sometimes all of these approaches are combined, or they are alternated in a continual process of exploration.

Additionally, new media writers often choose different authoring systems based on the needs of the work they are creating. For instance, Mark Marino used Juan Gutierrez's Literatronica (Marino 2006) to create *a show of hands*, but to create *Marginalia in the Library of Babel*, he used Diigo social annotation software.

Authoring systems, Storyspace, for example, can be created for the new media writing community by a team of writers and programmers, or they can be created by software companies (see STORYSPACE). Adobe Flash is an example of the latter option. There is also a vibrant tradition of authoring software created by writers and artists for writers and artists. For instance, in the mid-1980s John Cage's "First meeting of the Satie Society" was created using software written by poet Jim Rosenberg and composer Andrew Culver (Couey 1991, 128). Contemporary examples of writer/programmer-written authoring systems are Nick Montfort's interactive fiction system, Curveship, CAVE writing, and the Snapdragon AR authoring environment created in Caitlin Fisher's lab at York University in Toronto (see CAVE).

Although historic programming languages used as authoring systems, such as BASIC, supported the creation of work in many genres, contemporary authoring systems are often genre specific, including poetry generators, interactive social networking platforms, dedicated applications for the creation of interactive fiction or hypertext literature, and applications for the creation of web-based literature, which encompasses digital poetry, among other possibilities.

BASIC, originally designed in the 1960s by John Kemeny and Thomas Kurtz at Dartmouth, was particularly important in the early stages of development of new media writing. Readily available to users of early Apple and IBM PC systems, BASIC encouraged text-friendly authoring that incorporated commented code. BASIC was used by Gregory Yob to create *Hunt the Wumpus* (Wardrip-Fruin and Montfort 2003) and by Scott Adams to create the "adventure virtual machine" for a series of early "Adventure Games." Canadian poet bpNichol's concrete poetry *First Screening* was created using BASIC, and the Apple II and IBM PC versions of Judy Malloy's hypertextual *Uncle Roger*, also programmed online for ACEN Datanet using Unix shell scripts (Malloy 1991, 200–201), were created with BASIC.

Poetry generators were foreseen in *Gulliver's Travels*, in which Jonathan Swift describes a mechanical system where at "every turn, the engine was so contrived, that the words shifted into new places, as the square bits of wood moved upside down." Contemporary poetry generators use a variety of computer-mediated composition systems to create algorithmic poetry or narrative (Balpe 2005). They may generate text using a rule-based system and/or remix, recontextualize, or analyze classic or contemporary author-written texts. They may invite users to input text that is systematically recontextualized. In some cases the literature generator software itself is considered a work of art. Although the intent wasn't always literary, computer-mediated text generator systems—for example, Christopher Strachey's 1952 love letter generator for the Ferranti Mark I computer—are among the earliest new media authoring systems (Link 2006).

There is a continuing tradition of poets and programmers collaborating in the creation and use of authoring systems for generative literature. For instance, Colloquy, an interactive poetry generation system, was created by poet Judith Kerman and programmer Robert Chiles. Poet Chris Funkhouser used poet/programmer Eugenio Tisselli's MIDIPoet to create the performative *MIDIPoetry Songs*, and poet Jackson Mac Low's "Barnesbook: Four Poems Derived from Sentences by Djuna Barnes" was created with programmer Charles O. Hartman's DIASTEXT. Among many others, poetry generation systems include Jean Pierre Balpe's "Babel Poésie," Fox Harrell's GRIOT, Fox Harrell and Kenny Chow's Generative Visual Renku project (Harrell and Chow 2008), Nick Montfort's ppg256-1 (Perl Poetry Generator in 256 characters), and RiTa (Howe 2009). Additionally, the open-source authoring system Processing, which enables the creation of images, animations, and interactive content, has been used to create generative literature, including María Mencía and Alexander Szekely's "Generative Poems" and Scott Rettberg's generative fiction *After Parthenope*.

Software-generated social networking environments that allow the creation and display of creative interventions encompass social networking systems, such as conferencing systems, e-mail, MUDs, MOOs, Twitter, and Second Life (see MUDS AND MOOS, ONLINE WORLDS, SOCIAL NETWORK SITES [SNSs]). Begun as a multiuser MUD "adventure" program by Roy Trubshaw and Richard Bartle at the University of Essex in England, MUDs and MOOs are programmable, text-based, social networking systems. In addition to creative social interaction, LambdaMoo, created by Pavel Curtis at Xerox PARC (Curtis 1992), also fostered virtual world building and allowed for a variety of narrative structures (Malloy 1999). Artist/writer Antoinette LaFarge, director of the MOO-based Plaintext Players, and theater director Robert Allen used a MOO in creating their mixed-reality performance series, *The Roman Forum Project* (LaFarge and Allen 2005). Other social networking systems that have been used to create narrative include Second Life (Joseph DeLappe's reenactment of Mahatma Gandhi's *Salt March to Dandi*) and Twitter (Dene Grigar's *24-Hr. Micro-Elit Project*).

Works in the interactive fiction (IF) genre, historically also called "adventure games," create a simulated environment and involve the reader in interactively navigating a fictional experience or game by entering text-based responses and commands (see INTERACTIVE FICTION). Inspired by *Colossal Cave Adventure*, authored in FORTRAN by Will Crowther (Jerz 2007), the IF Zork was originally written in the MIT Design Language (MDL), a dialect of Lisp (Lebling, Blank, and Anderson 1979). To make IF accessible on home computer systems, Infocom utilized MDL to create Zork Interactive Language (ZIL). Among Infocom Games authored in ZIL and the Z-machine interpreter were Brian Moriarty's *Trinity* and Marc Blank's *Deadline*. Games authored in the IF authoring system Better Than Zork (BTZ), created by William Mataga, included poet Robert Pinsky's *Mindwheel* (programmed by Steve Hales and William Mataga).

Contemporary IF authoring systems embrace Graham Nelson's Inform 7 (Nelson 2005–2006). Based on natural language and incorporating contributions from the IF community, Inform 7 was used by Emily Short to create *Bronze*, by Aaron Reed to create *Blue Lacuna*, and by Andrew Plotkin to create *Hoist Sail for the Heliopause and Home*. Andrew Plotkin is also the author of the portable "virtual machine" Glulx, which can be used to compile work written in Inform. Among other IF authoring systems are Curveship, ChoiceScript, TADS, Hugo, Alan, and Undum, an IF/hypertext hybrid.

With extensive literary content—characterized by linking of units of text called *lexias* or *nodes*—computer-mediated hypertext literature, with roots in hypertext theory and computerized library databases, has been enabled by authoring systems since 1986.

Narrabase, Judy Malloy's authoring system, initially used database system–derived linking structures to access multiple lexias and was later adapted for the World Wide Web. Apple Computer's HyperCard, created by Bill Atkinson, was a widely used commercial hypermedia authoring system for the Macintosh that featured database, scripting, graphic, and audio capabilities. Works made with HyperCard included Fortner Anderson and Henry See's *The Odyssey*, Jean-Pierre Balpe's *Hommage à Jean Tardieu*, Brian Thomas's *The White Rose*, Abbe Don's *We Make Memories*, Deena Larson's *Marble Springs*, and *KAOS*, a special edition of the French literary Magazine *Action Poe(/)tique*.

Initially created by Michael Joyce, Jay David Bolter, and John B. Smith, the hyperfiction authoring system Storyspace is one of the first authoring tools to be written specifically for writers of new media literature. Eastgate's Mark Bernstein, who improved and extended Storyspace, cites the desire for "a hypertext system that would truly embrace links," as well as "concrete writing spaces that students could pick up, hold, and move around" (Bernstein 2010). Storyspace and Storyspace design were used to write *afternoon* by Michael Joyce, *Victory Garden* by Stuart Moulthrop, Judy Malloy's *its name was Penelope*, Carolyn Guyer's *Quibbling*, and Shelley Jackson's *Patchwork Girl*, among many other hyperfictions, including recent works by Steve Ersinghaus and Susan M. Gibb.

Hypertext authoring systems created by individual writers and programmers include Jim Rosenberg's spatial hypertext authoring system, "The Frame Stack Project," "which provides a user interface for overlaying word objects on top of one another, while still allowing them to be read legibly" (Rosenberg 2009), Connection Muse (Kendall and Réty 2000), and Juan B. Guiterrez's Literatronica.

In tandem with browser systems, such as Mosaic, Netscape, Explorer, and Firefox, HyperText Markup Language (HTML) created by Tim Berners-Lee at CERN initiated a flowering of hypertext literature that was publicly accessible on the World Wide Web beginning in 1994. There was and is an internationally read and created body of web-accessible literature, including, among many others, Stuart Moulthrop's *Hegirascope*, Russian new media writer Olia Lialina's *My Boyfriend Came Back from the War*, Muntadas's nonfiction *The File Room*, and Australian poet geniwate's *Rice*.

New media writers adapted and continue to adapt their personal authoring systems on the World Wide Web using content creation systems such as HTML, DHTML (Dynamic HTML), CSS (Cascading Style Sheets), Java, Photoshop, and Dreamweaver. For example, J. R. Carpenter's *Entre Ville* was created with HTML, DHTML, JavaScript, and Apple QuickTime, among other authoring tools.

Adobe Flash, a rich Internet application that is used to create interactive content, such as animated text, graphic images, and video, is one of the most frequently used creative tools for the World Wide Web. Used to create both web-based concrete poetry and a wide variety of new media fiction, Flash includes ActionScript, now an object-oriented language, and was used by Stuart Moulthrop to create *Under Language*, by Donna Leishman to create *RedRidingHood*, by Rob Kendall to create *Pieces*, by M. D. Coverley to create *Accounts of the Glass Sky*, and by Stephanie Strickland and Cynthia Lawson Jaramillo to create *slippingglimpse*. To create FILMTEXT 2.0, a work that is designed to investigate new media writing in the context of interactive cinemas, audiovisual performance, and game and remix culture, Mark Amerika used Flash, Dreamweaver, Photoshop, Illustrator, Pro Tools, Live, Audio Gulch, Final Cut Pro, iMovie, and QuickTime.

Among many other important contemporary authoring systems are rich Internet applications such as HTML5, Adobe Edge, and Microsoft Silverlight; visual and video applications such as Premiere, Final Cut, QuickTime, and iMovie; and sound applications such as Audacity, Max/MSP/Jitter, Sound Forge, and Sound Studio. In the realm of hardware platforms, the Apple iPad is a promising vehicle for electronic fiction, with Eastgate developing iPad versions of adaptable titles.

New authoring systems continue to be developed. For instance, at the University of California at Santa Cruz, *Comme il Faut*, a social artificial intelligence system, was developed by writers/researchers including Josh McCoy, Michael Mateas, and Noah Wardrip-Fruin (McCoy et al. 2010). Additionally, in the contemporary digital humanities, there is renewed interest in the workings of code and in the creation of literate code (see CODE). There is a continuing trend to share and explore experience with using authoring systems, and authoring systems created by individuals or collaborative teams are more frequently being made available to the new media writing community.

■ See also ALGORITHM, CODE AESTHETICS, COMBINATORY AND AUTOMATIC TEXT GENERATION, FLASH/DIRECTOR

References and Further Reading

Balpe, Jean-Pierre. 2005. "Principles and Processes of Generative Literature: Questions to Literature." *Dictung Digital.* http://dichtung-digital.mewi.unibas.ch/2005/1/Balpe/index.htm.

Bernstein, Mark. 2010. "Interview with Mark Bernstein." Interviewed by Judy Malloy. *Authoring Software.* www.narrabase.net/bernstein.html.

Couey, Anna. 1991. "Art Works as Organic Communications Systems." In *Connectivity: Art and Interactive Telecommunications,* edited by Roy Ascott and Carl Eugene Loeffler. *Leonardo* 24 (2): 127–130.

Curtis, Pavel. 1992. "Mudding: Social Phenomena in Text-Based Virtual Realities." Xerox PARC CSL-92-4, April.

Gallo, F. Alberto. (1977) 1985. *Music of the Middle Ages II.* Translated by Karen Eales. Cambridge: Cambridge University Press.

Graetz, J. M. 1981. "The Origin of Spacewar." *Creative Computing.* www.wheels.org/spacewar/creative/SpacewarOrigin.html.

Harrell, D. Fox, and Kenny K. N. Chow. 2008. "Generative Visual Renku: Poetic Multimedia Semantics with the GRIOT System." *HYPERRHIZ.06,* Special Issue: *Visionary Landscapes.* www.hyperrhiz.net/hyperrhiz06/19-essays/79-generative-visual-renku.

Howe, Daniel C. 2009. "RiTa: Creativity Support for Computational Literature." *Proceedings of the 7th ACM Conference on Creativity and Cognition* (Berkeley, CA), 205–210.

Jerz, Dennis. 2007. "Somewhere Nearby Is Colossal Cave: Examining Will Crowther's Original 'Adventure' in Code and in Kentucky." *Digital Humanities Quarterly* 1 (2). www.digitalhumanities.org/dhq/vol/001/2/000009/000009.html.

Kendall, Robert, and Jean-Hugues Réty. 2000. "Toward an Organic Hypertext." *Proceedings of the Eleventh ACM Conference on Hypertext and Hypermedia* (San Antonio, TX). www.wordcircuits.com/connect/ht2000.htm.

LaFarge, Antoinette, and Robert Allen. 2005. "Media Commedia: *The Roman Forum Project.*" *Leonardo* 38 (3): 213–218.

Lebling, P. David, Marc S. Blank, and Timothy A. Anderson. 1979. "Zork: A Computerized Fantasy Simulation Game." *IEEE Computer* 12 (4): 51–59. www.csd.uwo.ca/Infocom/Articles/ieee.html.

Link, David. 2006. "There Must Be an Angel: On the Beginnings of the Arithmetics of Rays." In *Variantology 2. On Deep Time Relations of Arts, Sciences and Technologies*, edited by Siegfried Zielinski and David Lin, 15–42. Cologne: König.

Malloy, Judy. 1991. "Uncle Roger, an Online Narrabase." In *Connectivity: Art and Interactive Telecommunications*, edited by Roy Ascott and Carl Eugene Loeffler. *Leonardo* 24 (2): 195–202.

———. 1999. "Narrative Structures in LambdaMOO." In *In Search of Innovation—the Xerox PARC PAIR Experiment*, edited by Craig Harris, 102–117. Cambridge, MA: MIT Press.

Marino, Mark. 2006. "Literatronica: The Next Generation of Hypertext Authoring." *WRT: Writer Response Theory*. http://writerresponsetheory.org/wordpress/2006/05/22/literatronica/.

McCoy, Josh, Mike Treanor, Ben Samuel, Brandon Tearse, Michael Mateas, and Noah Wardrip-Fruin. 2010. "Authoring Game-Based Interactive Narrative Using Social Games and *Comme il Faut*." *Proceedings of the 4th International Conference & Festival of the Electronic Literature Organization* (Providence, RI). http://games.soe.ucsc.edu/sites/default/files/TheProm-ELOAI.pdf.

Montfort, Nick. 2003. *Twisty Little Passages: An Approach to Interactive Fiction*. Cambridge, MA: MIT Press.

Nelson, Graham. 2005–2006. "Natural Language, Semantic Analysis and Interactive Fiction." http://inform7.com/learn/documents/WhitePaper.pdf.

Rosenberg, Jim. 2009. "Hypertext in the Open Air: A Systemless Approach to Spatial Hypertext." *Journal of Digital Information* 10 (3). http://journals.tdl.org/jodi/article/viewArticle/175/487.

Wardrip-Fruin, Noah, and Nick Montfort, eds. 2003. *The New Media Reader* CD, packaged with *The New Media Reader*. Cambridge, MA: MIT Press. www.newmediareader.com/cd_samples/Basic/index.html.

<hr />

Avatars

Bjarke Liboriussen

Avatar is derived from the Sanskrit *avatāra*, "descent," and can roughly be translated as a Hindu deity's voluntary and temporary incarnation as an animal or human on Earth. In 1980s science fiction literature, a user's engagement with cyberspace was described along the same lines: as a descent into another realm (see CYBERSPACE). Unlike Hindu deities, science fiction's cyberspace users had to split themselves in two. The real body would be left behind in the real world, and the user's consciousness would move through cyberspace. This is, for example, how the protagonist of William Gibson's hugely influential novel *Neuromancer* (1984) navigates cyberspace. Neal Stephenson's novel *Snow Crash* (1992) is often credited with popularizing the idea that the user's consciousness does not float freely through cyberspace but is fixed in a virtual body, an *avatar*.

This conceptual development within literature is mirrored by films such as *Tron* (Steven Lisberger, 1982), a fantasy in which a colorful cyberspace inspired by arcade games is fully entered—with no manifestations of the user left behind in the real world—and *The Lawnmower Man* (Brett Leonard, 1992), a more realistically flavored piece of science fiction in which virtual reality equipment and avatars are employed in order to enter cyberspace (see VIRTUAL REALITY). The hugely popular film *Avatar* (James Cameron, 2009) strengthened the cultural trope of the avatar as a virtual body inhabited by a motionless user in order to enter a fantastic realm (in Cameron's movie the jungle world of the moon Pandora). Importantly, the film's protagonist gains through his avatar a body physically far superior to his own (the protagonist is disabled), and he uses the avatar to pretend he is someone he is not (a member of the alien Na'vi race). Even with only textual means, fluid self-representation, sometimes with an element of wish fulfilment, has been possible on the Internet since its start, as explored by Sherry Turkle in her seminal book *Life on the Screen* (Turkle 1995).

In current usage, an avatar is the graphical representation of a user of a digital media product; for a broader understanding of the term, including nongraphical representation, see Coleman (2011). The term *avatar* is now used very broadly. For example, Yahoo uses *avatar* for the customizable figures associated with their instant messaging service, and Sony uses *avatar* for the interchangeable, static image representing a user of the *PlayStation Network* (such an image would simply be called a "profile picture" on Facebook).

A stronger definition of an avatar would be the graphical representation of a user of a digital media product functioning as a focus for the user's agency within a virtual world. Furthermore, current usage dictates that an avatar resembles a human or an animal. Thus, the player-controlled cars of racing games and the airplanes of flight simulators are not considered avatars.

This definition holds on to the original connotations of descent into another realm but necessitates a clarification of what is meant by "virtual world." The most straightforward examples are those where *virtual world* can be used synonymously with the perceived, three-dimensional space to which the avatar belongs. *Habitat* (Lucasfilm, 1986) was probably the first online world in which *avatar* was used explicitly in this way (see ONLINE WORLDS). Contemporary examples include both virtual worlds that are games, such as the hugely popular *World of Warcraft* (Blizzard, 2004), and virtual worlds that are not, such as Second Life (Linden, 2003). These worlds allow the user to experience an immediate relationship between his or her movements in the real world (typically the manipulation of keyboard and mouse) and the avatar's movements *inside* the space of the virtual world, an effect we can label *felt motor-isomorphism*.

In other examples, "world" is not synonymous with space. Take the avatars of rhythm games such as *Rock Band* (Harmonix, 2007). A *Rock Band* player simulates a musical performance by operating toy instruments or by singing, as instructed to by a stream of on-screen symbols supported by a musical soundtrack. The player has a highly customizable avatar on screen, for example, the drummer of the virtual band. The avatar's drumming movements take place in rough synchronization with the song, and the player who manipulates the toy drum set with drumsticks and bass pedal has a sense of the avatar movements matching his or her own, yet there is no actual motor-isomorphism in this example. The sense of the avatar being a focus for the player's agency within the *Rock Band* "world" depends much more on imagination than in the *World of Warcraft* example where the pressing of buttons has an immediate, unquestionable effect on the avatar's movements through space. The *Rock Band* avatar highlights representational aspects of the relationship between user and avatar. The player's potential sense of ownership over the avatar is based not on motor-isomorphic mastery but on customization of the avatar's clothing, hairstyle, makeup, tattoos, and so on (progress in the *Rock Band* game is partly measured in terms of available customizations).

Scholarly attention to avatars can be characterized roughly by emphasis on either agency or representation. Attention to agency is often found in scholarship aimed at explicating the unique features of computer games, or "interactive media" more broadly, to use another term that can be employed strategically to highlight unique features of digi-

tal media products. Agency can be explored theoretically with recourse to phenomenological philosophy; thus, the work of Maurice Merleau-Ponty features quite prominently
in recent game scholarship (e.g., Gregersen and Grodal 2008; Liboriussen 2012). An interest in representation can be driven by an interest in the psychological effects of having
an avatar (see below) or by more universal concerns about the representation of gender,
ethnicity, and so on (e.g., Nakamura 2008), also known from film and cultural studies
(see GENDER REPRESENTATION).

Most observers will probably find both agency and representation to be important
themes in connection with avatars. It is possible, however, to deem representational issues irrelevant. In order to do just that, noted game scholar (or *ludologist*) Espen Aarseth
uses the tall, voluptuous, and scantily clad avatar of the *Tomb Raider* games, Lara Croft,
as an example (first of many *Tomb Raider* games; Core Design, 1996). Aarseth holds that
"the dimensions of Lara Croft's body, already analyzed to death by film theorists, are
irrelevant to me as a player, because a different-looking body would not make me play
differently. When I play, I don't even see her body, but see through it and past it" (2004,
48). The *Tomb Raider* world experienced by Aarseth is one of puzzles, obstacles, and
labyrinths, an "ergodic" world that requires "nontrivial effort" to be traversed (Aarseth
1997, 1). For representation to be a relevant issue, the user's experience has to be more
akin to that reported by Diane Carr: "I enjoy playing with Lara Croft; I appreciate her
agility, her solitary determination and lethal accuracy" (2002, 171). These specific, experiential qualities of the agency provided by Lara Croft lead Carr toward a discussion of
gender and identification, drawing on film theory; Dovey and Kennedy (2006) contextu-
alize Carr's work and give an overview of related literature.

It might be reasonable to assume that some players of single-player games look past
layers of representation; for discussion of the user's attention being split between surface
layers of representation (fiction, style) and underlying structures (rules, mechanics, code),
see, for example, Juul (2005). When avatars are used to interact with others, however, it is
an assumption incompatible with psychological experiments carried out by Nick Yee and
Jeremy Bailenson (2007). When participants in the experiments interact with each other
through avatars, they do not draw on their underlying real self-image. They do not see
"through and past" their avatars, but almost immediately adjust their behavior in accord
with the avatars they have been assigned: they become confident when using tall avatars,
and less confident with short avatars. Yee and Bailenson term this *the Proteus effect*, after the
Greek sea god who could change his shape at will. Invoking a Greek god might seem rather
poetic for an experimentally based study of communication, but the term aptly points to
the richness of fascinating ways avatars can let their users descend into virtual worlds.

■ See also GAMEPLAY, GAMES AS STORIES, IMMERSION, MUDs AND MOOs,
ROLE-PLAYING GAMES, VIRTUAL BODIES

References and Further Reading

Aarseth, Espen. 2004. "Genre Trouble: Narrativism and the Art of Simulation." In *First Person:
New Media as Story, Performance, and Game*, edited by Noah Wardrup-Fruin and Pat Harrigan,
45–55. Cambridge, MA: MIT Press.

Aarseth, Espen J. 1997. *Cybertext: Perspectives on Ergodic Literature*. Baltimore: John Hopkins University Press.

Carr, Diane. 2002. "Playing with Lara." In *ScreenPlay: Cinema/Videogames/Interfaces*, edited by
Geoff King and Tanya Krzywinska, 171–180. London: Wallflower Press.

Coleman, Beth. 2011. *Hello Avatar: Rise of the Networked Generation*. Cambridge, MA: MIT Press.

Dovey, Jon, and Helen W. Kennedy. 2006. *Game Cultures: Computer Games as New Media*. Maidenhead, UK: Open University Press.

Gregersen, Andreas, and Torben Grodal. 2008. "Embodiment and Interface." In *The Video Game Theory Reader 2*, edited by Mark J. P. Wolf and Bernard Perron, 65–84. New York: Routledge.

Juul, Jesper. 2005. *Half-Real: Video Games between Real Rules and Fictional Worlds*. Cambridge, MA: MIT Press.

Klevjer, Rune. 2006. "What Is the Avatar? Fiction and Embodiment in Avatar-Based Singleplayer Computer Games." PhD diss., University of Bergen.

Liboriussen, Bjarke. 2012. "Collective Building Projects in 'Second Life': User Motives and Strategies Explained from an Architectural and Ethnographic Perspective." In *Virtual Worlds and Metaverse Platforms: New Communication and Identity Paradigms*, edited by Nelson Zagalo, Ana Boa-Ventura, and Leonel Morgado, 33–46. Hershey, PA: IGI Global.

Nakamura, Lisa. 2008. *Digitizing Race: Visual Cultures of the Internet*. Minneapolis: University of Minnesota Press.

Turkle, Sherry. 1995. *Life on the Screen: Identity in the Age of the Internet*. New York: Simon and Schuster.

Williams, M. 2007. "Avatar Watching: Participant Observation in Graphical Online Environments." *Qualitative Research* 7 (1): 5–24.

Yee, Nick, and Jeremy Bailenson. 2007. "The Proteus Effect: The Effect of Transformed Self-Representation on Behavior." *Human Communication Research* 33 (3): 271–290.

B

Biopoetry

Eduardo Kac

Biopoetry is a new poetic form invented by Eduardo Kac in 1999 through his artwork "Genesis," in which Kac created an "artist's gene," a synthetic gene that he produced by translating a sentence from the biblical book of Genesis into Morse code and then converting the Morse code into DNA base pairs according to a conversion principle specially developed by the artist for this work. The sentence reads, "Let man have dominion over the fish of the sea, and over the fowl of the air, and over every living thing that moves upon the earth." It was chosen for what it implies about the dubious notion of divinely sanctioned humanity's supremacy over nature. The Genesis gene was incorporated into bacteria, which were shown in the gallery. Participants on the web could turn on an ultraviolet light in the gallery, causing real, biological mutations in the bacteria. This changed the biblical sentence in the bacteria. The ability to change the sentence is a symbolic gesture: it means that we do not accept its meaning in the form we inherited it, and that new meanings emerge as we seek to change it. "Genesis" explores the notion that biological processes are now writerly and programmable, as well as capable of storing and processing data in ways not unlike digital computers. Further investigating this notion, at the end of the show the altered biblical sentence was decoded and read back in plain English. The artist wishes to reveal that the boundaries between carbon-based life and digital data are becoming as fragile as a cell membrane. "Genesis" is in the permanent collection of the Instituto Valenciano de Arte Moderno (IVAM; Valencian Museum of Modern Art), Valencia, Spain.

Kac first published his biopoetry manifesto in the *Cybertext Yearbook 2002–03*. Since 1999 Kac has created several different biopoems, including "Erratum I" (2006) and "Cypher" (2003/2009), and has exhibited this work worldwide in solo and group shows. In "Cypher," the "reading" of the poem is achieved by transforming E. coli with the provided synthetic DNA. The act of reading is procedural. In following the outlined procedure, the participant creates a new kind of life—one that is at once literal and poetic.

In addition to Kac, poet Christian Bök announced in 2008 his desire to create a literary exercise, which he dubbed "The Xenotext Experiment," also based on encoding poetic information into DNA. As of 2012, this project is still in progress.

■ See also DIGITAL POETRY, ELECTRONIC LITERATURE, HOLOPOETRY, WRITING UNDER CONSTRAINT

References and Further Reading

Bök, Christian. 2008. "The Xenotext Experiment." *SCRIPTed* 5 (2): 227.

Kac, Eduardo. 1999. "Genesis." In *Ars Electronica 99—Life Science*, edited by Gerfried Stocker and Christine Schopf, 310–312. Vienna: Springer.

———. 2003. "Biopoetry." In *Cybertext Yearbook 2002–03*, edited by Markku Eskelinen and Raine Koskimaa, pp. 184–185. Finland: University of Jyvaskyla.

———. 2005. *Telepresence and Bio Art—Networking Humans, Rabbits and Robots*. Ann Arbor: University of Michigan Press.

———. 2007a. *Hodibis Potax*. Ivry-sur-Seine: Édition Action Poétique; Kibla: Maribor.

———, ed. 2007b. *Media Poetry: An International Anthology*. Bristol, UK: Intellect.

———, ed. 2007c. *Signs of Life: Bio Art and Beyond*. Cambridge, MA: MIT Press.

Blogs
Ruth Page

Blogs (also known as web logs) are web pages in which dated entries appear in reverse chronological order, so that the reader views the most recently written entries first. Blogs emerged as a web genre in the late 1990s, and as simple and free publishing tools became available at the turn of the twenty-first century, blogging activity has increased exponentially. Since anyone with an Internet connection can publish a blog, the quality of writing on blogs can vary considerably, and blogs may be written about diverse subjects and for many different purposes. Blogs can be differentiated according to their function, as knowledge-management tools, which filter information, or personal blogs, which are used to document and reflect on the blogger's life history. Both types of blog are highly varied and hybrid genres. Personal blogs are influenced by online forms of communication such as e-mail and personal web pages, along with offline genres of life history, particularly diary writing and autobiography. Filter blogs have their antecedents in bulletin boards and Listservs. Blogs can also be categorized according to their topic or relevance to a particular interest group. Examples of the genre include blogs written about travel, health, politics, sex, legal matters, and cookery, alongside blogs written for professional purposes on behalf of corporations or as part of educational practice.

Although early studies of blogging noted that the textuality of blogs relied primarily on verbal communication (written text), blogs are multimodal genres that rely on recognized conventions of layout. The visual conventions place the updated sequence of blog posts within the frame of the blog's home page, which also contains a sidebar showing the blogger's profile, previously archived posts, and a set of links to other recommended blogs (a blog roll). Other, more explicitly multimodal examples of blogs include photo blogs (as exemplified on Flickr), video blogs (as published on YouTube), and audio blogs (which have their roots in ham radio practices).

The connective affordances of a blog mark them as distinct from offline forms of diary writing and information sharing. A blog is important not just as an outlet for an individual's online publications but for its potential to connect with other bloggers and to the wider resources of the Internet. This connectivity is realized through the use of hyperlinks. Hyperlinks appear in blogs as annotations within individual blog posts and positioned on the blog home page. Although links can be made to any other web page, links can emphasize sources of information or can promote another blogger (of course, there are many cases where these functions overlap). The kind of material that is linked to tends to reflect the topical focus of the blog, suggesting what the blog is "good for." Hyperlinks also have a social dimension, establishing the blogger as an expert source of recommendation who selects and promotes web resources on a particular topic.

Blog posts are usually written episodically and are published over time, with fluctuating regularity. As a result, the content of each post tends to be self-contained rather than forming a unified, coherent progression that is interdependent on the content of preceding or following posts. The style of writing on blogs (see LANGUAGE USE IN ONLINE AND MOBILE COMMUNICATION) is often informal (especially on personal blogs), although some writers employ more polished rhetoric. However, unlike other computer-mediated communication where innovative forms of language are used (such as acronyms or blends), often the typographical conventions in blogging are similar to mainstream standards. Although the blogger's profile may disclose where they are from, Myers (2010) found that bloggers do not often state the geographical location for the reported events. However, like other forms of social media, blogging is influenced by presentism, and reported events tend to take place in close proximity to the time of reporting.

Bloggers usually write with a strong sense of their audience, even where that audience is imagined. While some members of the audience will only ever choose to "lurk," others may interact with the blogger by posting comments on a blog. The nature of commenting varies considerably according to the purpose of the blog itself. Research and political blogs may stimulate debate, while comments on health and personal blogs promote empathy or support. More generally, the commenting facility on blogs points to the blurred roles of production and reception that are entailed in blogging, such that Bruns and Jacobs (2006) refer to bloggers and their commenters as "produsers" (a blend of "producers" and "consumers") who collaboratively create knowledge. However, participation in the blogosphere is not a neutral, evenly distributed activity. Although it would appear that blogging allows anyone to say anything, hierarchies in participation persist.

Blogs (and by default their bloggers) may be ranked according to their authority. Within the blogosphere, "authority" does not correspond to the credibility of content, but rather to the number of links that are made to a particular blog (as calculated by the blog search engine Technorati). The greater the number of links made to a blog, the higher its authority. Blogs may also be promoted through the mechanisms of other search engines, such as Google or Digg, where the number of page views or rankings influences the position of a blog within a series of search results. Blogging thus operates within a system where visibility and attention are the prized values.

Studies of bloggers and their audiences suggest that other hierarchies associated with offline communities influence online participation. Susan Herring and her colleagues (2004) reported that although personal blogging authored by women was the fastest-growing sector of the blogosphere, early academic studies of blogs had focused on filter or knowledge logs. As a result, the role of women in shaping blogging practices had been neglected. Other studies have indicated that women tend to comment more frequently on blogs written by other women, while men tend to comment more frequently on blogs written by other men (Page 2012). However, the demographic profile of blogging participants is not stable and has shifted over time. A recent report for the Pew Internet and Life History project suggested that young bloggers have drifted from blogging as a means of online communication with their peers and now use other social media such as micro-blogging and social network sites instead.

The political implications of blogging have provoked considerable interest. For example, presidential candidates made use of blogs as an early social media genre in order to canvass support from their electorate (a use of social media that has now been extended to other sites such as Facebook or Twitter). Conversely, blogs have also been used by lay writers to express public opinion about politics and current affairs more generally. Although not all blogs are journalistic in nature, blogging practices are part of wider trends in citizen journalism. For example, mainstream news broadcasting has been augmented by the personal testimonials posted on blogs by those directly involved in newsworthy events, bloggers have acted as investigative journalists, while others filter and comment on the mainstream news. However, the citizen journalism associated with blogging is distinct from mainstream news reporting in its explicitly subjective nature: authenticity is prized over credibility (Walker Rettberg 2008).

Like all forms of computer-mediated discourse, bloggers may choose to construct their online identity by drawing on aspects of their offline characteristics, or they may choose to remain anonymous (see IDENTITY). The ability to separate online and offline identities is particularly important if a blogger chooses to write about controversial subject matter, where online anonymity appears to support freedom of expression. Anonymous or pseudonymous blogging may prompt suspicion and subsequent attempts to reveal the blogger's offline identity. Notable cases include exposing the offline identity of sex bloggers (like *Girl with a One Track Mind*), or those who blog about legal matters (such as the British police officer who blogged as *Night Jack*). Other blogs assumed to be authentic have been revealed as fictions, such as the video blogger *Lonelygirl15*, or *Gay Girl in Damascus*. Judgments about inauthenticity and blogging range from pejorative assessments of hoaxes to celebrations of fictional creativity (see HOAXES). These reactions suggest that assumptions about authenticity and fictionality in online contexts are being reworked away from ontological criteria toward expressive resonance. At the same time, offline outcomes of blogging continue to remain potent, with serious consequences for the blogger's status and identity.

The offline consequences of blogging may also entail the gain of economic capital for the blog's author. Some blogs have become clearly commercialized endeavors, accruing income through advertising and marketing strategies. Other corporate blogs have been used to personalize established brands and as the means to announce new products or deal with customer feedback promptly. In some cases, blogs that have attracted significant readership online have been published by the mainstream media, such as *The Julie/Julia Project*, written by Julie Powell (2003) and released as *Julie and Julia* in 2009, and *Wife in the North*, written by Judith O'Reilly and published as a novel by Penguin in 2008. Far from a democratic alternative to mainstream media, blogging has been shaped by neoliberal principles of entrepeneurship as practices have developed in the first decade of the twenty-first century.

■ See also LIFE HISTORY, NARRATIVITY, TWITTER, TUMBLR, AND MICROBLOGGING

References and Further Reading

Bruns, Axel, and Joanne Jacobs. 2006. *Uses of Blogs.* New York: Peter Lang.
Herring, Susan C., Inna Kouper, Lois Ann Scheidt, and Elijah L. Wright. 2004. "Women and Children Last: The Discursive Construction of Weblogs." In *Into the Blogosphere: Rhetoric, Community, and*

Culture of Weblogs, edited by Laura J. Gurak, Smiljana Antonijevic, Laurie Johnson, Clancy Ratliff, and Jessica Reyman. http://blog.lib.umn.edu/blogosphere/women_and_children.html.

Linde, Charlotte. 1993. *Life Stories: The Creation of Coherence.* Oxford: Oxford University Press.

Myers, Greg. 2010. *The Discourse of Blogs and Wikis.* London: Continuum.

Page, Ruth. 2012. *Stories and Social Media: Identities and Interaction.* London: Routledge.

Walker Rettberg, Jill. 2008. *Blogging.* Cambridge: Polity Press.

••

Book to E-text

Kirstyn Leuner

In *Understanding Media*, Marshall McLuhan reflects, "The poet Stephane Mallarmé thought 'the world exists to end in a book.' We are now in a position to go beyond that and to transfer the entire show to the memory of a computer" (1964, 59). Nearly fifty years after McLuhan's prediction, the transfer of content from books to computers has fundamentally changed the way readers, writers, publishers, editors, and technologists interact with text. No longer constrained to produce bound printed pages, authors can now write and publish works without leaving the digital environment, and readers can select from a variety of media with which to browse e-texts. However, during this rapid proliferation of texts to be read on-screen, as well as the hardware and software used to render them, books have not been left behind. The market is, instead, flush with copies of texts available in a variety of print and electronic media.

Early forms of textual transmission have informed the development of digital text technologies. In the first century CE, the Roman author Pliny documented the process of turning papyrus into scrolls that were, on average, thirty to forty feet long (Greetham 1994, 59). Two thousand years later, the "scroll bar" is a standard feature of most electronic document interfaces which enables one to "scroll" down a page that is much longer than the height of the screen. Since the third century, most writing (manuscript or type) has been transmitted in a codex, or book format. Books replaced scrolls, in part, because they are smaller textual storage devices and more easily citable (Greetham 1994, 59). And though lengthy electronic texts have no binding, paper, or cover, they are often referred to as "electronic books," or "e-books," and styled to resemble a printed codex.

In the mid-twentieth century, scholars began to explore computing as a way to work with books using semiautomatic or automatic technologies to convert a printed text into an index or concordance. The genesis of humanities computing is commonly associated with the work of the Italian Jesuit priest Father Roberto Busa, who began a landmark project in 1946 to use both machine and human labor to create an *index verborum* of nearly 11 million words in Medieval Latin that appear in works by St. Thomas Aquinas and others. He completed the first part of that project in 1951 using a reproducing punch, a sorter, a collator, and a tabulator to index and create a lemmatized concordance for four hymns by Aquinas. In the early 1960s, Busa started transferring the Corpus Thomisticus to magnetic tape to process the index electronically using an IBM 750 computer, after indexing the Dead Sea Scrolls to test this machine. Due to the extent of the data set that had to be edited and processed, Busa's *Index Thomisticus* was not published until 1974, after 1 million man-hours of work (Burton 1981, 1; Hockey 1996, 1–3).

Though they predate screen-reading practices and technologies, Busa's projects share with electronic textual studies an interest in textual manipulation, reproduction, and content transfer. Susan Hockey dates early attempts at using computers to create an edition of a book to project OCCULT (The Ordered Computer Collation of Unprepared Literary Text) and Vinton Dearing's work on John Dryden in the 1960s (1996, 1). In the 1970s, Penny Gilbert developed computer programs that could collate manuscripts and store variant readings for processing, while Wilhelm Ott produced a set of text analysis tools called TUSTEP (Hockey 1996, 1–2). By the 1980s, editors had an array of programs available for use in compiling print editions.

Currently, there are several ways to transform a print work into a digital object: the text can be keyboarded (typed) from the original into a text file or a HyperText Markup Language (HTML) file; it can be scanned and uploaded as an image file; or an editor can send the image file through an optical character recognition (OCR) program, which converts the bit-mapped image of the text into a machine-encoded text file similar to the keyboarded text file. OCR-rendered text always requires at least some proofreading; it works best with modern printed texts, and its accuracy declines significantly with damaged pages, multilingual texts, handwriting, and early print, such as texts that feature ligatures and the ever-troublesome "long s."

In order to create archival-quality digital texts from book-born works, it is standard editorial practice to encode the electronic files with descriptive markup before publishing them online, rather than merely reproducing an image of the text. To mark up a text in such a way is to indicate its components—from more objective features, like headings, to subjective properties, like scansion—within the body of the text itself using a collection of predefined "elements" and "attributes" that are commonly called "tags." Each structural component of a text must fall within a unique set of tags that are machine-readable. These tags do not designate the final display of the electronic document—the style sheet and transform files determine that. Rather, descriptive markup communicates a document's original formatting and the pieces of its content (such as paragraphs if the piece is in prose, or lines and stanzas if it is poetry), as well as "metadata" about the electronic text's bibliographic source, its file and encoding description, and the editorial history of the encoded files. Well-formed, descriptive markup of a text has the power to create an interoperable database of the work which can be searched, filtered, and exported for a variety of independent output devices and uses.

For example, the Text Encoding Initiative (TEI) is the current international standard markup language for electronic texts, and the TEI Consortium supports Extensible Markup Language (XML) as its metalanguage—the language with which to deploy the TEI markup system. A group of scholars, computer scientists, and librarians constitute the TEI Consortium and manage the TEI Guidelines—loose rules for how to mark up a text using XML. Mindful that encoding markup is always an analytical editorial act, the Consortium continually modifies the Guidelines to reflect the ways in which editors adapt XML tags to their needs.

After encoding, the final step for publishing XML files online is to process them using XSLT (Extensible Style Sheet Language Transformations) to make HTML or XHTML files that display content on the web. Some drawbacks to the multistep practice of encoding and transforming an electronic text include the time, diverse skill sets, and cost of labor that it requires. However, this procedure enables editors to create several digital versions of a work which each deliver unique information and functionality to an end user: (a) a reader-friendly, searchable HTML text that hyperlinks to notes and related websites, (b) the encoded XML file, (c) a plain text file that one can use to process textual data in other programs, and (d) page and book images of the source object.

N. Katherine Hayles explains in *Writing Machines* that transferring content from one medium to another, as from a book to a computer, alters its meaning: "to change the physical form of the artifact is not merely to change the act of reading . . . but profoundly to transform the metaphoric network structuring the relation of word to world" (2002, 23). While a book's form and content are literally stitched together, an e-text's content and form are discrete. The screen is the point at which a work's digital files meet the reader, and variations in display hardware and user interfaces affect the reading experience, just as a book's print quality, format, and binding also do. Bulky cathode ray tube (CRT) computer monitors—the descendants of early television sets—have been largely replaced by flat panel displays, such as plasma displays (PDPs), liquid crystal displays (LCDs), or light-emitting diode displays (LEDs), that are thinner and lighter. Each type of display has a maximum digital image resolution quality, or sharpness, of how words and images project on the screen. As the desire for portable computers and reading devices has grown, so has the desire for very small machines, some of which are the size of miniature books and possess touch-screen technologies.

Is the phrase "electronic book" an oxymoron? The question bespeaks our current place in media history somewhere between "book" and "screen." Hybrid media creative projects facilitate this inquiry. For example, Stephanie Strickland's book of poetry *V: WaveSon.nets/Losing l'Una* (2002) points to a website, http://vniverse.com, that invites a "reader" to create poetic visualizations by interacting with the screen. Amaranth Borsuk and Brad Bouse's *Between Page and Screen* (2012) is a book with illegible geographic designs on its pages which one can read only by holding them up to a webcam, which translates and projects them as legible text on a computer screen. Two millennia of codex use and the continued influence of book technologies on digital media call for further reflection on the evolution of textual production and consumption, as well as how new text media strive, and fail, to fully subsume and replace the old.

■ See also ARCHIVE, CODE, CRITICAL THEORY, DIGITAL HUMANITIES, ELECTRONIC LITERATURE, HISTORY OF COMPUTERS, INTERFACE, MARKUP LANGUAGES, MEDIALITY, OLD MEDIA / NEW MEDIA, RELATIONS BETWEEN MEDIA, REMEDIATION

References and Further Reading

Borsuk, Amaranth, and Brad Bouse. 2012. *Between Page and Screen*. Los Angeles: Siglio.

Burton, D. M. 1981. "Automated Concordances and Word Indexes: The Fifties." *Computers and the Humanities* 15:1–14.

Drucker, Johanna. 2009. *SpecLab: Digital Aesthetics and Projects in Speculative Computing*. Chicago: University of Chicago Press.

Finneran, Richard J., ed. 1996. *The Literary Text in the Digital Age*. Ann Arbor: University of Michigan Press.

Greetham, D. C. 1994. *Textual Scholarship: An Introduction*. New York: Garland.

Hayles, N. Katherine. 1993. "Virtual Bodies and Flickering Signifiers." *October Magazine* 66. www.english.ucla.edu/faculty/hayles/Flick.html.

———. 2002. *Writing Machines*. Cambridge, MA: MIT Press.

Hockey, Susan. 1996. "Creating and Using Electronic Editions." In *The Literary Text in the Digital Age*, edited by Richard J. Finneran. Ann Arbor: University of Michigan Press.

Kirschenbaum, Matthew. 2008. *Mechanisms: New Media and the Forensic Imagination*. Cambridge, MA: MIT Press.

Manovich, Lev. 2001. *The Language of New Media*. Cambridge, MA: MIT Press.

McGann, Jerome. 2001. *Radiant Textuality: Literature after the World Wide Web*. New York: Palgrave.

McLuhan, Marshall. 1964. *Understanding Media: The Extensions of Man*. New York: McGraw-Hill.

Schreibman, Susan, Ray Siemens, and John Unsworth, eds. 2004. *A Companion to Digital Humanities*. www.digitalhumanities.org/companion/.

Shillingsburg, Peter. 2006. *From Gutenberg to Google: Electronic Representations of Literary Texts*. Cambridge: Cambridge University Press.

Strickland, Stephanie. 2002. *V: WaveSon.nets / Losing l'Una*. New York: Penguin.

Text Encoding Initiative. 2010. *P5: Guidelines for Electronic Text Encoding and Interchange*. www.tei-c.org.

C

Cave
John Cayley

When set in full capitals, "CAVE" is a trademarked, strangely self-referential, "recursive" acronym that stands for "CAVE Automatic Virtual Environment." In a slightly more general use, capitalized, the term may be taken to refer to what is basically a complex computer monitor that, as a minimum, consists of projectors and screens, arranged so as to surround, completely or partially, a user's point of view. Thus, a Cave generally consists of a volume of space large enough for at least one person to move freely within it. Taking the example of the now legacy installation at Brown University's Center for Computation and Visualization (www.brown.edu/Departments/CCV/visualization), this might mean moving "within" four projection-surface "walls" (front, left, right, and floor) of an eight-foot cube missing its "ceiling" and also, ironically, its "fourth" wall. The associated computers render the imagery and project the light and shade of a 3D graphic "world" (this is the technical term used in 3D graphics) onto these surfaces, constantly transforming the patterns of light and shade so as to adapt them in real time both for the multiple projection surfaces and for one specific primary point of view. From the outset Caves provided *stereo* 3D graphics, requiring viewers to wear glasses of some kind to correctly filter, typically, active stereo left-eye and slightly displaced right-eye graphics to each of their eyes. The position and orientation of the primary point of view are tracked, and the stereo 3D world is constantly redrawn in real time to give a sense of its visual coherence and of the depth associated with a human perception of spatial extension. Stereo 3D graphics on enclosing projection surfaces, with a tracked point of view, provide, in the visual realm, what we have come to call *immersion*—an *immersive* artificial visual world (see IMMERSION). Such configurations were foundational for the notion of virtual reality (VR), although it is prudent to remember that VR stands for all of those existing and potential peripheral devices that have been and will be added to computational systems in order to simulate human sensory experience (see VIRTUAL REALITY). The addition of responsive spatialized audio greatly enhances the sense of immersion in Cave devices, and many experiments have been made with haptics and even the olfactory.

The Cave may be considered as an actual existing epitome of media, that is, "new" and "digital" media. Despite the proliferation of 3D stereo graphics as applied to film and games, the experience of immersion is still novel and powerful. Potentially and in theory, the Cave simulates human experience in an artificial environment that is so-called virtually real. Moreover, because of its association with computational, programmable devices, anything—any message or media—can be represented within the Cave in the guise of real-seeming things. Caves could and, in fact, have allowed for the exploration of textual—indeed, literary—phenomena in such artificial environments. Caves have been intermittently employed for works of digital art, but uniquely, at Brown University, thanks to the pioneering efforts of postmodern novelist Robert Coover, there has been an extended pedagogical and research project of this institution's Literary Arts Department to investigate, since 2001, the question of what it might mean to write in and for such an environment. Simple front-end software was developed by undergraduates at Brown which allows writers who are not programmers or computing graphics specialists to create textual objects and develop narrative and poetic structures for the Cave's artificial immersive worlds (Baker et al. 2006; Cayley 2006a). So far, the best-known and most discussed digital literary work to emerge from this project is "Screen" by Noah Wardrip-Fruin et al. (2002; see also Carroll et al. 2004), although this project uses technologies prior to the development of Brown's Cave Writing software as such.

In a Cave environment, language manifests in two material forms: as positional audio, typically voices displaced from human actors or simply as a kind of cinematic voice-over; and as projected graphical inscription—calligraphy or typography—rendered with or without an artificial "depth" applied to these fundamentally 2D graphic linguistic forms. In both cases, instantiation in the Cave forces us to confront the singular, elusive, and sometimes paradoxical problems associated with the phrase "materiality of language," one that often enters into critical discussions of aesthetic literary endeavors, and more especially the innovative, experimental, and multimodal poetics that are influential in the field of digital literature as currently practiced (see ELECTRONIC LITERATURE, MATERIALITY). Considering the case of voices in the Cave, we are confronted with thorny issues concerning the relationship of writing with both the theatrical and the cinematic and both in an entirely new context: outside the theater, what genre, what writing practice inscribes a voice or voices in literal immersive space? In the Cave, we seem to have the potential for a theater of the imagination such as one experiences in the powerful, if culturally marginal, art of radio drama. However, viewers enter into the Cave bodily, hearing and reading any voices they find there in a space that is around them and which may also be filled with corresponding, complementary or contrasting imagery. Indeed, the Cave's graphic world might be filled with . . . anything.

Because computational 3D graphics have, historically, determined the development of work in Caves as primarily a matter of visualization that is inherently responsive to all movements of the primary point of view and optionally transactional—typically point-and-click modes of interaction—language in the Cave appears chiefly as graphical inscription, as the images of letters, words, phrases, sentences, and so on. These may be either captured and rendered as images per se or generated from digital fonts in the same way that all modern inscriptional devices, such as word processors, produce our familiar linguistic symbols on now-numberless 2D screens everywhere. However, in the Cave, these forms are, in fact, "textured models" in the 3D graphics sense of these terms. They are visual forms that have been abstracted to vertices and vectors, composing surfaces and volumes in the graphics world. These are "textured" such that visible surfaces respond appropriately to the artificial lighting of the Cave, simulating as many phenomena of light as possible in our world of visual perception: color, sharpness, dimness, shininess, highlighting, fog, distance. It is a long list, and there is, of course, great and growing expertise (Foley et al. 1995). Rendered in a straightforward, common-sense manner, graphic language, or literal glyphs spelling an extended text, is no more than a set of vertices and vectors all on a 2D zero-depth plane float-ing in the artificial space of the Cave. The "text" on this plane will be a textured surface, the complexities of which are determined by a regular relationship with the orthography of the system of inscription to which this instance of language belongs. In a sense, having zero depth, the surface does not fully "exist" as a volume in this artificial space, apart from the fact that the "front" and "back" of the textured 2D surface will respond to the Cave's artifi-cial lighting and allow a viewer to read the text when facing it. Arguably, this nonexistence of linguistic material in 3D space provides an experiential clue to the strangeness of lan-guage's relationship with media generally (Cayley 2010). In Brown's Cave, a maquette adapted from René Magritte's *La trahison des images* illustrates, in part, the problems (Cay-ley and Valla 2010). If we add artificial depth to letters and words, then they do, of course, exist as volumes, as "things," in the graphics world of the Cave, but what is the symbolic significance of this depth? What is the *linguistic* aesthetic of letters and words as objects or architecture? This architectural use of letter forms surfaces in other digital art contexts, for example, Jeffery Shaw's early and well-known "Legible City" (1989), and many examples in digital video (a recently encountered example is Wiegner 2010). But the problem of legibility does not go away in such pieces. It is bracketed or toyed with. Letters as volumes do not be-come legible from all angles; they must be confronted or assembled *on* or *as* a surface in or-der to be read. Moreover, merely by way of their artificial "presence" they evoke a concrete poetics with which linguistic practice may play for a time—for the pleasure of it and for ef-fects that are marginal and/or supplementary in relation to the significance and affect that derives from the more dangerous supplement of reading itself.

These are fascinating and important problems that face us the moment we enter the Cave in the guise of a programmable inscriptional space, or a complex surface on which to write. The challenge of working to better understand the relationship of language and media would be enough to justify an engagement with this recondite, technologically implicated, and rarified media system. As of 2011, stereo 3D graphics are increasingly com-mon and are already available on portable consumer electronics. Techniques for rendering immersive artificial phenomena must surely come, and textual practices in this environ-ment will have their place. That place must be more than functional or servile to com-merce and marketing; it must also be aesthetic, including an aesthetics informed by the deep appreciation of the linguistic materialities that the Cave makes it possible to experi-ence. Here is a simple example, one that is unambiguously a function of reading and writing and yet is formative of visual experience: letters and words in artificial space give extraordinary positional and depth cues. Letter forms are, at one and the same time, complex and privileged within that which we call "legibility." This causes them to generate expectations of, for example, size and orientation—major distance clues (Cayley 2006b). Graphic worlds made of literal material may have great depth, literally and figuratively, a multimodal depth that digital writers must interrogate.

■ See also DIGITAL POETRY, ELECTRONIC LITERATURE, PLATFORM

References and Further Reading

Baker, Damon, et al. 2006. "Cavewriting 2006: A Hypertext Authoring System in Virtual Reality."
    Poster. ACM SIGGRAPH.
Carroll, Joshua J., et al. 2004. "Screen: Bodily Interaction with Text in Immersive VR." Sketch.
    ACM SIGGRAPH.

Cayley, John. 2006a. "An Interview with John Cayley on *Torus* by Rita Raley." *Iowa Review Web* 8 (3). http://iowareview.uiowa.edu/TIRW/TIRW_Archive/september06/cayley/cayley.html.

———. 2006b. "Lens: The Practice and Poetics of Writing in Immersive VR: A Case Study with Maquette." *Leonardo Electronic Almanac* 14 (5–6). http://programmatology.shadoof.net/pdfs /cayleyLens.pdf.

———. 2010. "The Gravity of the Leaf: Phenomenologies of Literary Inscription in Media-Constituted Diegetic Worlds." In *Beyond the Screen: Transformations of Literary Structures, Interfaces and Genres*, edited by Peter Gendolla and Jörgen Schäfer, 199–226. Media Upheavals. Bielefeld: Transcript.

Cayley, John, and Clement Valla. 2010. *This Is (Not) Writing*. Custom software for Cave Writing. http://treachery.writingdigitalmedia.org.

Foley, James D., et al. 1995. *Computer Graphics: Principles and Practice*. Boston: Addison-Wesley.

Shaw, Jeffrey. 1989. "The Legible City." Web-Based Documentation. www.jeffrey-shaw.net/html _main/frameset-works.php.

Wardrip-Fruin, Noah, et al. 2002. "Screen." Web-Based Documentation. www.noahwf.com/screen/.

Wiegner, Susanne. 2010. "Just Midnight." Web-Based Documentation for an Animated Digital Video. www.susannewiegner.de/lax/start8.html.

··

Cell Phone Novel
Larissa Hjorth

Before the ubiquity of iPad, Kindle, and other tablets ushered in a new appreciation of the literary, there was the cell phone novel. Initiated in Japan around 2000, one of the most popular examples of the cell phone novel (*keitai shōsetsu*), *Koizara*, was successfully adapted into a multimillion-dollar film. The success of *keitai shōsetsu* can be attributed to a variety of factors: Japan's cell phone (*keitai*) market, where screens are big; long commutes on public transport; the specific characteristics of the Japanese language; and the long tradition of the "personal, pedestrian and portable" (Ito 2005) as part of everyday life. As a medium, it has been embraced by young women, as both readers and writers, for its ability to provide new avenues and contexts for expression around previously tacit practices (e.g., domesticity; Hjorth 2009b).

The *keitai shōsetsu* phenomenon began with the founding of one of Japan's most pivotal user-created content (UCC) sites for mobile Internet, Maho No Airando (*maho* meaning "magic"), in 1999. Although *keitai shōsetsu* were initially written by professionals, by the mid-2000s everyday users had begun to be inspired to write and disseminate their own *keitai shōsetsu*. Predominantly written *by* women *for* women, this mode of new media highlights the significance of remediation (Bolter and Grusin 1999); many of the successful *keitai shōsetsu* (millions produced yearly) are adapted into older media such as film, *manga*, and *anime* (see REMEDIATION). This practice can be seen as an extension of earlier gendered tropes of Japanese new media that were dubbed in the 1980s the "Anomalous Female Teenage Handwriting" phenomenon (Kinsella 1995). Characterized by *"kawaii"* (cute) transformations of the Japanese alphabet, *hiragana*, an emerging genre of new media writing (which has a history as "women's language"), soon dominated mobile communication from the pager onward; it became known as the "highschool girl pager revolution" whereby female UCCs hijacked (through personalization techniques) the technologies industry conventionally aimed at businessmen ("salarymen") (Fujimoto 2005; Matsuda 2005; Hjorth 2003).

For Kyoung-hwa Yonnie Kim, *keitai shōsetsu* needs to be understood as "refashioning emails rather than literature" (2012, 9). Often young people move between e-mails (see E-MAIL NOVEL) and *keitai shōsetsu* as both genres and modes of address evoke a similar type of intimacy. Here, it is important to recognize that in Japan the phone has long been the dominant mode for accessing the Internet, and thus mobile Internet e-mails are akin to SMS in other cultural contexts. In addition, *keitai shōsetsu* can also be seen as an extension of literary traditions evoked by arguably one of the most famous novels in the world (written in 1000 CE), *The Tale of Genji*. Drawing on *haiku*, letters, and love sonnets, "Murasaki Shikibu's" (not her real name, thought to be Fujiwara Takako) *The Tale of Genji* deployed *hiragana* to tell both the male and female sides of the numerous lovers of a playboy, "Genji" (Hjorth 2009a).

The popularity of cell phone novels has led to adaptations and adoptions elsewhere, with locations such as China, Taiwan, and Africa developing their own versions. In China—where for many working-class migrants the mobile phone is their only portal to the Internet—deploying new media such as mobile phones and blogging for political means has become an important rite of passage (Qiu 2009). In Africa, the democratic possibilities of the mobile phone as a multimedia device were harnessed in 2007 with the youth cult cell phone novel *Kontax* (Lee 2009). In most cases across the world, cell phone novels have been highly successful with young people as a remediated form of the traditional paperback. The compressed, mobile, and intimate nature of the cell phone has provided many with an accessible way to connect different stories and subjectivities in a fleeting moment. Moreover, the nature of cell phone novels as stories that are often shaped in consultation with readers (especially by experienced cell phone authors) makes them a prime example of new reader-writer relationships (see COLLABORATIVE NARRATIVE).

■ See also LOCATION-BASED NARRATIVE, MOBILE GAMES

References and Further Reading

Bolter, Jay David, and Richard Grusin. 1999. *Remediation*. Cambridge, MA: MIT Press.

Fujimoto, Kenichi. 2005. "The Third-Stage Paradigm: Territory Machine from The Girls' Pager Revolution To Mobile Aesthetics." In *Personal, Portable, Pedestrian: Mobile Phones in Japanese Life*, edited by Mizuko Ito, Daisuke Okabe, and Misa Matsuda, 77–102. Cambridge, MA: MIT Press.

Hjorth, Larissa. 2003. "Kawaii@keitai." In *Japanese Cybercultures*, edited by Nanette Gottlieb and Mark McLelland, 77–102. New York: Routledge.

———. 2009a. "Cartographies of the Mobile: The Personal as Political." *Communication, Policy & Culture* 42 (2): 24–44.

———. 2009b. *Mobile Media in The Asia-Pacific: The Art of Being Mobile*. London: Routledge.

Ito, Mizuko. 2005. "Introduction: Personal, Portable, Pedestrian." In *Personal, Portable, Pedestrian: Mobile Phones in Japanese Life*, edited by Mizuko Ito, Daisuke Okabe, and Misa Matsuda, 1–16. Cambridge, MA: MIT Press.

Kim, Kyoung-hwa Yonnie. 2012. "The Landscape of *keitai shōsetsu*: Mobile Phones as a Literary Medium among Japanese Youth." *Continuum: Journal of Media & Cultural Studies* 26 (3): 1–11.

Kinsella, Sharon. 1995. "Cuties in Japan." In *Women, Media and Consumption in Japan*, edited by Lise Skov and Brian Moeran, 220–54. Surrey, UK: Curzon Press.

Lee, Dave. 2009. "Mobile Novels Switch on South Africa." *BBC News*, October 28, 2009. http://news.bbc.co.uk/2/hi/technology/8329537.stm.

Matsuda, Misa. 2005. "Discourses of *keitai* in Japan." In *Personal, Portable, Pedestrian: Mobile Phones In Japanese Life*, ed. Mizuko Ito, Daisuke Okabe, and Misa Matsuda, 19–40. Cambridge, MA: MIT Press.

Qiu, Jack. 2009. *Working Class Network Society*. Cambridge, MA: MIT Press.

Characteristics of Digital Media

David Golumbia

At least two challenges present themselves in the characterization of digital media in general and digital textual media in particular. The first is the very ubiquity of the digital: scarcely any media can be named that has not been partly or wholly transformed by digitization. Second, there is a strong tendency to look toward predigital formations and to point out those features of such forms that have been changed by digitization. Despite its appeal, this approach tends to maximize breaks over continuities, to privilege features that may be inherent only in particular forms of digital processing, and to overlook new forms of digital production and consumption that may not fit neatly into the categories developed over decades or even centuries of predigital practice (see HISTORY OF COMPUTERS).

Here we focus on the characteristics of those forms of digital media with particular prominence in, consequences for, and relevance in the field of digital textuality. This approach is narrow and not wide; the field of digital media can be arguably understood to be so wide as to encompass virtually everything. Our approach will furthermore be limited to only three principle sites of investigation: those generally understood as relevant for the reading of texts, the writing of texts, and the editing of texts. Despite their apparent comprehensiveness, many areas of digital textuality, to say nothing of digital media in general, fall outside these parameters. Our focus is tightly constrained to existing examples of digital text (first and foremost) and digital media (largely as this relates to digital text); we thus avoid the more expansive but also visionary catalog of properties of so-called new media offered by Manovich in *The Language of New Media*, whose five "Principles of New Media"—numerical representation, modularity, automation, variability, and transcoding (2001, 27–48)—offer themselves much more cleanly as normative desiderata for new forms to come, rather than analytical descriptions of digital media as they exist today.

Digital texts have been said in the critical literature to instance the following characteristics in ways that surpass or altogether exceed those of nondigital or analog texts: nonlinearity, multimedia, hypertextuality, collaboration, portability, and preservation.

Nonlinearity

Especially with regard to writing and editing, digital technology makes possible—or more accurately, makes easy and available—the nonlinear movement of objects. "Linear" in this discussion refers primarily to temporal linearity. The thought is that, using pen and paper, using oral composition techniques, and even using mechanical writing and editing technology such as a typewriter, authors are generally constrained to work according to rough temporal orders. What is composed first comes before what is composed second. Writing by hand or typewriter, the author who wished to insert new text between paragraphs A and B usually found herself compelled to prepare a new version of the manuscript by writing paragraph A again, inserting new paragraph A1, and then continuing on to paragraph B. Manuscript collections of all forms of writing tend to feature many whole versions of works, with, for example, typescripts studded with pen and pencil marginal notes being recomposed into new editions.

The advent of word-processing technology, such as analogous production software for video, images, and audio, allowed authors to move in a *nonlinear* fashion among the elements of manuscripts. Most obviously, this means that paragraph A1 can be inserted between paragraphs A and B without a new manuscript being prepared; less dramatically, marginal changes and other forms of authorial editing can be added whenever the author wishes, so that there is a much less pronounced sense of a novel, for example, being written from beginning to end and then edited by producing an entirely new version, again moving from beginning to end.

Nonlinearity is exemplary, though, in that it demonstrates just that computers make easier or instantly available what had always been implicit and at times explicit in the original process of textual production. Few novelists in fact proceeded in a hard-and-fast linear fashion, simply producing entire new drafts of works from start to finish, without abundant tinkering and even moving of elements; many novelists continue to use nonlinear editing tools while proceeding, roughly, from the start of a manuscript to its end. No thorough study has been prepared of authorial practice to determine whether the papers of digital authors differ in quantity, quality, or at all from those of their predigital peers; the practice of an author like Vladimir Nabokov, who famously composed his works on collections of index cards that allowed for just the kind of cut, copy, and paste actions associated with digital tools, shows that computers were by no means necessary for authors who wished to compose by nonlinear means.

Nonlinearity is often touted as an obvious change in the consumption of many media forms, in part due to the availability of consumer tools where none existed before—the clearest example of such technology is the movement from consumer cassette videotape (VHS or Betamax), in which a film or television program can only be consumed in time order (even when using fast forward or reverse), to the digitized DVD format, where skipping ahead and behind to marked chapters or particular time or index counts became widely available. Yet, paradoxically, print itself seems to fulfill many of the criteria of nonlinear digital media: printed books are easily accessed throughout their length and at random, read in part or in whole, and even decompose easily into constituent parts via copying or cutting (see ANALOG VERSUS DIGITAL). Interestingly, these features of print have been among the features hardest to implement in digital texts, and it is only with somewhat sophisticated tools making features such as bookmarking that e-book readers like the Kindle and Nook have found widespread mainstream acceptance among consumers.

Multimedia

For most of its extended history, "text" has been presumed to indicate largely the presentation of written words on the page. Especially with regard to visual media, it has never actually been the case that printed words and other forms of media occur in complete isolation from each other; from the earliest forms of illuminated and illustrated texts, to the often highly decorative forms of hieroglyphic and calligraphic writing practiced around the world, word and image have often coexisted, to greater and lesser degrees.

In the eras of pen and ink and particularly the typewriter and early typesetting, however, it had become straightforward to produce documents made up largely or exclusively of printed words, without any form of visual or other media objects incorporated. As computing tools became more widely available to the public, and as they became more powerful, it has become more and more straightforward to incorporate not just visual media in its traditional sense of still images, but almost all forms of media within what appear to be traditional printed documents. Ordinary word-processing tools such as Microsoft Word allow the insertion of every kind of still image format (both raster and vector images), as well as most commonly used formats of audio, video, and computational objects such as spreadsheets, chart and graph objects, dynamic shapes, and hypertext links. Often, especially in commercial tools like Microsoft Word and professional documentation presentation software such as QuarkXPress and Adobe InDesign, the objects remain editable, or partly editable, within the text environment.

Similarly, tools first designed primarily for uses other than the printing of text—presentation tools like PowerPoint, but also image editing tools like Adobe's Photoshop, Illustrator, and Fireworks and video and animation software like Adobe's Flash, Premiere, and AfterEffects—all make possible the elaborate editing and even presentation of text as part of the media editing suite. While these tools are rarely used as primary sites for text preparation and editing, they are frequently used for secondary or decorative text editing, and their results are often incorporated into primary text documents.

While such tools have had profound impacts on the production of multimedia texts, their impact on the reception and use of written texts is both less straightforward and less obvious. Most printed books remain in appearance much as they have been for the past few hundred years and may have no more visual illustrations than they have had in the Victorian or modernist periods. Literary novels typically do not include illustrations, and printing costs, particularly for the production of color illustrations, remain prohibitive for the widespread distribution of fully multimedia texts. Electronic readers such as the Kindle and Nook and the use of tablet and mobile computer devices for reading of texts appear to make full multimedia texts an imminent possibility; it has yet to be seen whether, especially for textual narrative, such elements do not occur as a result of technical or commercial limitations or owing to reader preference.

Hypertextuality

Perhaps the single most often identified distinguishing characteristic of digital text, "hypertext" refers to the ability physically to link one element in a text to another element. The worldwide standard for text production, HTML, includes this feature in its title—"HyperText Markup Language"—suggesting its centrality to the popular conception of textual operation in the digital environment.

The earliest association of hypertext with what we have come to see as digital media is arguably the one found in Vannevar Bush's lauded essay "As We May Think" (1945), in which he describes a machine called the Memex (itself, admittedly, not a digital computer, although Bush was deeply involved in the development of such machines) which would store and allow access to intellectual matter according to what Bush considers the actual organization of thoughts in the mind. Bush describes the organization of information into what he calls "trails," which have been generally understood as closely analogous to hypertext: "When numerous items have been thus joined together to form a trail, they can be reviewed in turn, rapidly or slowly, by deflecting a lever like that used for turning the pages of a book. It is exactly as though the physical items had been gathered together from widely separated sources and bound together to form a new book. It is more than this, for any item can be joined into numerous trails" (1945).

In the 1960s, computer scientist and visionary Theodore (Ted) Nelson coined the terms "hypertext" and "hypermedia," in which a vision like that of Bush becomes even more elaborate and complex. Like Bush, Nelson asserts that the brain either stores or processes information in a radically nonlinear fashion, and that the largely linear and structured-category reference materials available to that point (for example, in traditional encyclopedias) would give way to dynamically and conceptually associated data collections.

It is easy to recite the commonplace enthusiasms about the hypertext revolution and less easy to point in a rigorous fashion to those features that distinguish hypertext per se from any digital text. Any HTML document is largely composed of text as such, which would not on the surface be easily distinguishable from all other text. Many hypertext links offer not the many-to-many, conceptually varied connections suggested by enthusiasts like Landow (2006), but instead are made up of buttons and menu choices that offer direct and determinate choices. Nelson himself has proclaimed, contrary to the common sense of many observers, that HTML and the World Wide Web are not embodiments of hypertext but of something like its opposite. Speaking of his long-term visionary Hypertext project Xanadu, Nelson writes, "The Xanadu® project did not 'fail to invent HTML.' HTML is precisely what we were trying to PREVENT—ever-breaking links, links going outward only, quotes you can't follow to their origins, no version management, no rights management" (1999). Further, Nelson abhors the use of XML (Extensible Markup Language) as an adumbration of hypertextual aspirations: "Trying to fix HTML is like trying to graft arms and legs onto hamburger. There's got to be something better—but XML is the same thing and worse. EMBEDDED MARKUP IS A CANCER" (Nelson 1999).

Writers and other practitioners have been divided in their support for, endorsement of, and use of hypertext. Some strongly interested parties, particularly collected around the publisher Eastgate Systems, have promoted a notion of electronic literature in which hypertext plays a central role. Eastgate has published notable works of hypertext literature, such as Michael Joyce's *afternoon, a story* (1987) and Shelly Jackson's *Patchwork Girl* (1995) (see DIGITAL FICTION, INTERACTIVE NARRATIVE, STORYSPACE). Yet the proliferation of web- and browser-based media in the decades since Eastgate began has not been accompanied by a complementary proliferation of hypertextual literature, and traditional literature, even when read and consumed on a variety of electronic devices, continues to thrive today without taking explicit advantage of hypertextual mechanisms. The question of the degree to which hypertext can be seen as a definitive characteristic of digital textual media remains an open one (see HYPERTEXTUALITY).

Collaboration

Theorists of intertextuality, particularly Julia Kristeva (1980), and of the social nature of textual editing (e.g., McKenzie 1999) have long insisted on the collaborative nature of most of what we presume to be singly authored works of texts and even media. Many literary works known to us as the work of one author are known in fact to be the product of intense social interaction between one or more writers and editors; most famously, T. S. Eliot's long poem *The Waste Land* (1922) originally included several hundred lines and phrases excised at the suggestion of Eliot's famous associate, Ezra Pound, calling into question the notion that Eliot is the single author of the poem most people know.

Nevertheless, in the digital age such collaboration is said by some to have become far more widespread than ever before. Within commercial spaces, various forms of text and media—and even more so engineering projects, including ones composed of computer code—take advantage of collaborative tools from the outset, so that source documents can often not be said to have single authors. It is no surprise to find such practices in media production companies and not much of a surprise to think of film and television scripts having been authored by one or more individuals, in some cases lacking a central or lead author or having such a function carried out by a production professional or other professional not technically designated a "writer."

More expansively, the widespread advent of social media has allowed interactive commentary on and response to original productions in such detail and with such rapidity as to suggest their own implication in the production process. Such practices extend from the comment functions on websites hosting images (Flickr), text (newspapers and blogs), video (YouTube), and audio (Soundcloud) to the in-kind production of new media objects that respond to and often incorporate elements of earlier productions (see COLLABORATIVE NARRATIVE, SOCIAL NETWORK SITES [SNSs], TWITTER, TUMBLR, AND MICROBLOGGING, VIRAL AESTHETICS). Watching the spread of LOLcatz memes and copycat YouTube productions, or the long comment threads on original text or video or other media productions on Facebook and Twitter, it seems clear that collaborative media has reached a new level of public availability and influence over its former less public faces.

Portability

Like all digital objects, digital text and other forms of digital media distinguish themselves in their inherent perfect reproducibility. Computers require perfect duplication to run accurately; operating systems and other core programmatic functions must be absolutely or near-absolutely identical in order to guarantee that computer systems work properly at all. When we copy or duplicate or even create a new version of a word-processing document, we rely on the computer's ability to produce perfect copies whose contents will be identical to those of the primary document.

Theorists have long noted that in the transition from analog to digital, perfect copying is the exception rather than the rule. All forms of digitization, from desktop document scanning to professional movie industry creation of digitized versions of analog movies, entail loss and compression of data of various sorts. Some methods of amelioration of loss have been developed, which in some limited circumstances can even improve on qualities of the original, although this typically entails a certain loss of fidelity to the original version. This is especially true for optical character recognition (OCR) of printed documents, which is rarely able to produce perfect fidelity to the underlying text (owing to difficult-to-anticipate variables such as variation in language, spelling, typeface, and printing quality).

Yet it is vital to distinguish lossy copies of analog media from the perfect copying of digital objects, including digital versions of analog objects. Computational processes themselves would be impossible without the perfect copy; many everyday textual and media operations, both production and reception, would be either impossible or radically altered if the producer and consumers could not be certain that each version of the object was not the same as all others.

Preservation

Closely related to the question of portability is that of preservation (see ARCHIVE). While it is beyond question that digital files must be subject to perfect copying under any computational system, it is by no means the case that proper software for processing or even reading the digital copies will be available on systems composed of other hardware, running other operating software, or even operating at different times.

Even minor version changes in standard textual and media protocols including versions of HTML can result in radically different presentations of textual substance. Even consistent uses of software and hardware versions can result in different visual and audio presentations on a variety of platforms. Matthew Kirschenbaum (2007) has been a leader in the effort to identify and preserve not just the media objects themselves but a variety of original and emulative systems in order to preserve access to the media objects. The linguists Steven Bird and Gary Simons in a series of works (e.g., Bird and Simons 2003) have diligently worked to prevent the huge amounts of linguistic data currently being created and preserved in the worldwide digital infrastructure from being inadvertently lost to future technological change (see PRESERVATION).

References and Further Reading

Bird, Steven, and Gary Simons. 2003. "Seven Dimensions of Portability for Language Documentation and Description." *Language* 79:557–582.

Bush, Vannevar. 1945. "As We May Think." *Atlantic Monthly*, July. www.theatlantic.com/magazine/archive/1945/07/as-we-may-think/3881/.

Kirschenbaum, Matthew G. 2007. *Mechanisms: New Media and the Forensic Imagination*. Cambridge, MA: MIT Press.

Kristeva, Julia. 1980. *Desire in Language: A Semiotic Approach to Literature and Art*. New York: Columbia University Press.

Landow, George. 2006. *Hypertext 3.0: Critical Theory and New Media in an Era of Globalization*. Baltimore: Johns Hopkins University Press.

Manovich, Lev. 2001. *The Language of New Media*. Cambridge, MA: MIT Press.

McKenzie, D. F. 1999. *Bibliography and the Sociology of Texts*. New York: Cambridge University Press.

Nelson, Ted. 1965. "A File Structure for the Complex, the Changing, and the Indeterminate." In *Proceedings of the* ACM 20th National Conference, 84–100.

———. 1999. "Ted Nelson's Computer Paradigm, Expressed as One-Liners." http://xanadu.com.au/ted/TN/WRITINGS/TCOMPARADIGM/tedCompOneLiners.html.

Chatterbots
Ragnhild Tronstad

Imitating the conversational skills of a human being, chatterbots (aka chatbots, bots) are interactive agents designed to fill a specific purpose or role. For instance, they may function as an automated online help desk or sales assistant for companies that aim to provide their Internet customers with a more personal interface than the customary menus and search systems. Computer games feature chatterbots in a variety of nonplayer character roles, to confront or assist players, or to hand out tasks for the players to solve (see NPC [NONPLAYER CHARACTER]). Owing to the impact of the Turing test, a number of attempts have also been made to design chatterbots that are able to converse convincingly about general subjects (see TURING TEST).

Depending on their purpose, and what we expect of them, chatterbots are equipped with a more or less complex and elaborate artificial intelligence (AI) (see ARTIFICIAL INTELLIGENCE). Automated assistants and computer game characters are usually expected to operate within a limited knowledge area. For these to function satisfactorily, it may be sufficient that they know how to identify and match key words in the question with a predefined answer in their database. However, to fluently converse on a number of nonspecified topics—as is required to pass the Turing test—a more sophisticated AI based in natural language processing may be needed. Some of today's chatterbots are even designed to learn from their previous conversations—in other words, developing their AI as they speak.

Somehow, it seems natural to attribute a personality to a chatterbot with whom one has interacted, or observed in interaction. The fame and popularity attained by the chatterbot celebrity ELIZA testify to this phenomenon. One of the first chatterbot programs in history, ELIZA was developed by MIT professor Joseph Weizenbaum between 1964 and 1966 (Weizenbaum 1966). The principle guiding ELIZA's responses to an interrogator's input is as simple as it is sly: simulating a Rogerian psychotherapist, her primary purpose is to listen. So instead of contributing any content of her own to the conversation, she supportively rephrases what we have just told her and encourages us to continue talking. As long as we are content to play by these rules, ELIZA may come across as rather convincing in her role. However, if we start pushing her limits, trying to make her reveal parts of her view on the world, it soon becomes obvious that she is really nothing more than a mechanical, empty conversational machine, in possession of no external world of her own.

A relative of ELIZA named PARRY demonstrates how the opposite principle may also be employed to create a convincing chatterbot. Written by Stanford psychiatrist Kenneth Colby in 1972, PARRY is a program that simulates a patient suffering from paranoia. When Parry does not know how to answer, he will aggressively spit out a line of conspiracy theory, thereby forcing his world onto ours. While totally out of context, his response is nonetheless plausible.

A similar trick of the trade is used in artist Ken Feingold's robotic AI installation "Head" (1999), modeling a poetically inclined, slightly disturbed and confused elderly man. Engaging in conversation with *Head* requires a significant share of interpretative effort, but it may also be greatly rewarding to those who are willing to invest in it. Another artist-created chatterbot is Stelarc's *Prosthetic Head*, which simulates the artist's own personality. As it is designed to learn from its conversations, however, this chatterbot may gradually become "more autonomous in its responses" until the artist will "no longer be able to take full responsibility for what his head says" (Stelarc 2003).

While most chatterbots are designed to engage in conversation with human partners, artistic experiments have been made in which chatterbots converse with each other. The result may be hilarious, as in director Annie Dorsen's theatrical performance "Hello Hi There" (2010). Here, Dorsen stages two chatterbots self-reflexively discussing the famous 1971 debate between philosophers Michel Foucault and Noam Chomsky, on the concept of human nature.

■ See also COMPUTATIONAL LINGUISTICS, DIALOGUE SYSTEMS

References and Further Reading

Dorsen, Annie. 2010. "Hello Hi There." Theatre Performance. Video presentation available on www.youtube.com/watch?NR=1&v=3PiwEQQNnBk.

Feingold, Ken. 1999. "Head." Robotic Installation. *Ken Feingold Online Catalog*. www.kenfeingold.com/catalog_html/head.html.

Firunts, Mashinka. 2011. "Talking to Annie Dorsen." Interview in *Culturebot*, January 21, 2011. http://culturebot.net/2011/01/9285/talking-to-annie-dorsen/.

Güzeldere, Güven, and Stefano Franchi. 1995. "dialogues with colorful personalities of early ai." *Stanford Humanities Review, SEHR* 4 (2): "Constructions of the Mind." www.stanford.edu/group/SHR/4-2/text/dialogues.html.

Mauldin, Michael L. 1994. "Chatterbots, Tinymuds, and the Turing Test: Entering the Loebner Prize Competition." Paper presented at AAAI-94. http://robot-club.com/lti/pub/aaai94.html.

Stelarc. 2003. *Prosthetic Head.* http://stelarc.org/?catID=20241.

Turkle, Sherry. 1995. *Life on the Screen. Identity in the Age of the Internet.* London: Phoenix.

Weizenbaum, Joseph. 1966. "ELIZA—a Computer Program for the Study of Natural Language Communication between Man and Machine." *Communications of the ACM* 9 (1): 36–45. http://portal.acm.org/citation.cfm?id=365168.

———. (1976) 2003. "From *Computer Power and Human Reason: From Judgment to Calculation.*" In *The New Media Reader,* edited by Nick Montfort and Noah Wardrip-Fruin, 367–375. Cambridge, MA: MIT Press.

Cheats

Julian Kücklich

Cheating, according to J. Barton Bowyer (1982), is a widespread phenomenon in war and magic, games and sports, sex and religion, business and con games, politics and espionage, art and science. It is within the context of computer games, however, that cheating has come to the attention of researchers in the field of digital media. Here, cheating can be considered as a breach of a game's rules, as an aesthetic phenomenon, as a reading strategy, as a marker of cultural identity, as an ethical choice, as a commodity, and as an act of resistance. It thus opens up avenues of inquiry that lead beyond the field of computer games and into the wider realm of digital media culture.

Historically, cheating in computer games is a practice that can be traced back to early microcomputers, such as the ZX Spectrum or the Commodore 64, and video game consoles such as the Nintendo Entertainment System (NES). Early cheat codes for computer games often consisted of a sequence of alphanumerical symbols (such as "6031769" in *Manic Miner* or "writetyper" in *Jet Set Willy*), while on consoles they usually consisted of a button sequence such as "Up, Up, Down, Down, Left, Right, Left, Right, B, A, Start" (the so-called Konami Code, which gave the player character extra powers in a number of games for the NES, including *Contra* and *Gradius*). For some consoles, hardware cheats existed in the form of special cartridges (e.g., Game Genie and GameShark).

Using walkthroughs is also often considered cheating (see WALKTHROUGH). Walkthroughs have been circulating among gamers since the era of text adventures such as *Zork*, and even today they often contain ASCII art reminiscent of early computer game culture. Walkthroughs are published in books and magazines, and for some games there are lavish "strategy guides" printed on glossy paper with full-color illustrations and maps. Video walkthroughs became popular in the 2000s, when screen-capturing software and video-sharing platforms such as YouTube made it easy to create and distribute gameplay videos.

Personal computers gave rise to the practice of directly manipulating hexadecimal values in games' save files by loading these files into a hex editor. In PC games, particularly in first-person shooter (FPS) games such as *Doom* or *Quake*, certain cheats were conventionalized and came to be expected by players. Thus, most FPS games feature a "god mode" cheat, which renders the player character invincible, and a "no-clip" cheat, which allows the player character to pass through walls. However, cheat codes are used not only to activate power-ups but also to change the visuals of games. For example, typing "thereisnospoon" into the cheat console in *Deus Ex* changes the visual style of the game to that of the Matrix from the Wachowski brothers' eponymous film.

In multiplayer gaming, cheating was virtually nonexistent before the advent of client-server-based games such as *Diablo*. The architecture of *Diablo*'s Battle.net servers proved to be susceptible to the use of so-called trainers, which allowed players to increase the stats of their characters and thus gain an unfair advantage. Subsequently, anticheating measures were introduced in most online multiplayer games. Anticheating software such as PunkBuster was also made available for a number of online games. However, this did not entirely solve the problem of multiplayer cheating, and for some players, it became a challenge to create cheats that could not be detected by the software. Hacking techniques, such as forging network traffic or exploiting latency, also provide opportunities for cheating (see HACKER).

In massively multiplayer online games (MMOGs), such as *EverQuest* or *World of Warcraft* (see ONLINE WORLDS), cheating usually involves practices like "dual-boxing" or "multi-boxing," that is, playing several characters at the same time (see Taylor 2006), or different forms of collusion with other players. Due to the complex nature of social interactions in many MMOGs, a wide variety of controversial practices exist, considered as legitimate by some players and as illegitimate by others. These include bullying ("griefing"), sharing of equipment ("twinking"), hoarding of resources ("farming"), and using scripts ("bots") to automate repetitive tasks. "Real money trading" (RMT), that is, buying avatars and equipment for hard currency, is also often regarded as a form of cheating.

From a theoretical point of view, cheating has traditionally been regarded as a breach of a game's rules in order to gain advantage over other players (Huizinga 1938; Caillois 1961). Computer game play challenges this notion insofar as practices considered cheating often take place in single-player games, and the use of cheat codes is evidently sanctioned by the code of the game in which it takes place (see CODE). This means that cheating in computer games frequently does not provide an advantage over other players, and it is often questionable whether it constitutes a breach of a game's rules.

In multiplayer settings, the distinction between orthodox play and cheating is often quite difficult, due to the fact that the codified rules of the game are complemented by implicit rules (Salen and Zimmerman 2004). For example, in many online FPS games, "camping" (i.e., staying in one place and waiting for one's opponents) and "spawn-killing" (i.e., killing opponents' characters just after they are "reborn") are practices frowned upon by the community, although they are not explicitly forbidden by the rules. At the same time, online multiplayer games often give rise to emergent gameplay practices such as "rocket-jumping" in *Quake*. Emergent gameplay (see EMERGENCE) is usually not intended by designers, but in some cases it is condoned by players.

From an aesthetic perspective, cheating can be considered as a manipulation of the gameplay experience, in which players can engage independently of the advantages it may provide. While some cheat codes are specifically intended to change the gameplay experience (e.g., by altering the gravity or weather of a game world, or by modifying the behavior of nonplayer characters), others can be used in such a way as to deconstruct the space of a game, its narrative, or its internal consistency (Kücklich 2008). Some cheats also establish intertextual links, as in the example from *Deus Ex* given above.

In games with a narrative (see GAMES AS STORIES), cheating can also be regarded as a specific reading strategy, which skips certain parts of the digital texts. As Espen Aarseth has pointed out, it can be compared to what Roland Barthes calls "tmesis," that is, "the readers' unconstrained skipping and skimming of passages, a fragmentation of the linear text expression that is totally beyond the author's control" (1997, 78). It can thus be seen as a constriction of narrative space, which condenses game space in such a way that the internal logic of its fictional world may break down entirely.

Within cultural studies, cheats have been studied as a marker of cultural identity and as a means of accumulating symbolic capital. Canonical cheat codes, such as the Konami Code cited above, can be used by gamers to signal their allegiance to the gamer community, or specific subcommunities within it. The Konami Code in particular has reverberated into other areas of popular culture such as pop music (The Ataris' "Up, Up, Down, Down, Left, Right, Left, Right, B, A, Start") and social networking (an Easter egg on Facebook could be activated using the code; see EASTER EGGS). It is also a popular T-shirt motif.

Mia Consalvo's (2007) in-depth study of cheating is mainly concerned with cheating in multiplayer games and focuses specifically on perceptions of cheating among the gamer community. Considering cheating from an ethical perspective allows her to tease out the remarkable variety of attitudes toward cheating. As she points out, there was hardly any consensus about the definition of cheating among her interviewees beyond the notion that it is "an activity that confers unfair advantage to the player" (2007, 103).

According to Consalvo's research, definitions of cheating range from the purist ("Anything other than getting through the game all on your own") to the liberal ("You can't cheat a GameCube, you can only cheat other players"), with a large segment of players taking a midway position, which assumes that "code is law" (see CODE). This variety draws attention to the large number of different play styles that players bring to computer games, and to the different attitudes they exhibit toward the boundaries of the worlds in which these games take place.

Cheating in multiplayer games can also have political significance (see SUBVERSION [CREATIVE DESTRUCTION]). As a form of resistant play it disturbs the order imposed on game space by the providers and thus draws attention to the power differentials that exist between different stakeholders (Grimmelmann 2006). The politics of using cheats also came to the foreground in the debates surrounding the strict anticheating policy enforced on servers running *America's Army*—a game developed by the U.S. military for recruiting purposes (Nieborg 2009).

As Dyer-Witheford and de Peuter point out, the military training game *Full Spectrum Warrior*, which was released in a commercial version for Microsoft Xbox, could also be reverted to its original state using a cheat code: "While the civilian game presents a war of liberation, the military version familiarizes U.S. soldiers with being unpopular" (2009, 113). René Glas considers different forms of cheating in *World of Warcraft* and arrives at the conclusion that cheats can be used to "circumvent the dominant strategies of progress . . . designed by Blizzard," for "dominating other players," and to gain "agency over the game's design" (2010, 149).

■ See also GAMEPLAY

References and Further Reading

Aarseth, Espen. 1997. *Cybertext. Perspectives on Ergodic Literature.* Baltimore: Johns Hopkins University Press.

Bowyer, J. Barton. 1982. *Cheating: Deception in War & Magic, Games & Sports, Sex & Religion, Business & Con Games, Politics & Espionage, Art & Science.* New York: St. Martin's.

Caillois, Roger. 1961. *Man, Play and Games.* New York: Free Press of Glencoe.

Consalvo, Mia. 2007. *Cheating: Gaining Advantage in Videogames.* Cambridge, MA: MIT Press.

Dyer-Witheford, Nick, and Greg de Peuter. 2009. *Games of Empire: Global Capitalism and Video Games.* Minneapolis: University of Minnesota Press.

Glas, René. 2010. "Games of Stake: Control, Agency and Ownership in *World of Warcraft.*" PhD thesis, University of Amsterdam.

Grimmelmann, James. 2006. "Virtual Power Politics." In *The State of Play: Law, Games, and Virtual Worlds*, edited by Jack M. Belkin and Beth Simone Noveck, 146–157. New York: New York University Press.

Huizinga, Johan. 1938. *Homo Ludens: A Study of the Play Element in Culture.* Boston: Beacon Press.

Kücklich, Julian. 2008. "Forbidden Pleasures: Cheating in Computer Games." In *The Pleasures of Computer Gaming: Essays on Cultural History, Theory and Aesthetics*, edited by Melanie Swalwell and Jason Wilson, 52–71. Jefferson, NC: McFarland.

Nieborg, David B. 2009. "Training Recruits and Conditioning Youth: The Soft Power of Military Games." In *Joystick Soldiers: The Politics of Play in Military Video Games*, edited by Nina B. Huntemann and Matthew Thomas Payne, 53–66. New York: Routledge.

Salen, Katie, and Eric Zimmerman. 2004. *Rules of Play: Game Design Fundamentals.* Cambridge, MA: MIT Press.

Taylor, T. L. 2006. *Play between Worlds: Exploring Online Game Culture.* Cambridge, MA: MIT Press.

Code

Mark C. Marino

Though it can also refer to a system of laws or even a book (cf. codex), "code" becomes an important concept to digital textuality when it refers to either a system of encryption or a system of representing information for machine processes, as in computer source code. The histories for both of these systems overlap notably in the life and work of Alan Turing, who not only worked to crack the German military codes used in the Enigma machine but also developed premises for the prototypical computer using an extremely limited character set (Hodges and Hofstadter 2000). Unlike natural languages, both the Enigma code and programming languages lack ambiguity in translation. However, such one-to-one translation suggests a transparency of code, that its meaning is limited to literal effects. On the contrary, the recent movement to "decode" computer software has resituated the act of reading source code as one of interpretation, drawing upon close-reading techniques and heuristics from the humanities. After first describing the philosophical and technical meanings of *code*, this entry will explore some of the ways code is used in art practices and how code has been read and interpreted as a complex sign system that means far more than merely what it does.

What Is Code?

Computer source code is written in a particular language, which consists of syntax and semantics. A language's level is defined by how closely tied it is to the computer's architecture and operation. Some are compiled, others interpreted, and not all languages are lists of instructions or imperatives, for example, functional languages such as Scheme. The "lowest" level languages offer the least abstraction from the machine processes, which typically indicates fewer conceptual groupings of processes. In machine languages, for example, instructions go directly to the microprocessor. A high-level language, such as Java, needs to be compiled, or translated into processor instructions. High-level languages are marked by greater levels of abstraction, and a subset, including BASIC, COBOL, and even SQL, aspire to greater legibility to human readers. Some of the high-level languages, such as Inform 7, which is used to write interactive fiction, a genre of interactive narrative, can accept statements that read like natural language, such as, "The huge green fierce snake is an animal in Mt King" (Crowther and Conley 2011) (see INTERACTIVE NARRATIVE).

The ontological status of code has been the subject of much debate, particularly whether code can be described in Austinian terms as a performative system, as language that makes things happen. For example, N. Katherine Hayles has argued that "code has become . . . as important as natural language because it causes things to happen, which requires that it be executed as command the machine can run" (2005, 49). However, Wendy Hui Kyon Chun (2008) has warned critics not to confuse source code with executed code and not to treat the code as if it is the hidden essence within the object. Meanwhile, Alexander Galloway stresses the importance of "protocols" over code, arguing that "code only 'matters' when it is understood as being the substance of a network" (2006, 57). Such a point complements Friedrich Kittler's (1995) pronouncement that "there is no software," but instead a set of electrical signals coursing through the hardware. In that sense, there is also no code. Nonetheless, though code may not be able to claim the concrete physical status of hardware, code studies has developed around the material trace, the particular instantiation of an algorithm that is code (see ALGORITHM).

Code studies scholars have begun to reconsider code not as a stand-alone system but as an actor-network, functioning in conjunction with human and machine systems, from the hardware to other software (Critical Code Studies Working Group 2012, 1). In this approach, code is read not as the essence hidden beneath the interface or a self-sufficient object of study, but rather as an axis for discussing all that it unites, the machines (code, hardware, interoperating software) and humans in the circulation of the code through cultures (see INTERFACE).

In other meanings, "code" comes to stand in for the milieu of computationally rendered realities, as in the case of Mark B. N. Hansen's "body-in-code," which he defines as "a body whose (still primary) constructive or creative power is expanded through new interactional possibilities offered by the coded programs of 'artificial reality'" (2006, 38). Code, in this sense, is not important in of itself but metonymically for the realm in which natural world content is represented or encoded.

How Code Is Used in Art

Source code has been a means of making art at least since Christopher Strachey's Love Letter Generator in 1952 on the ancestral computer, the Mark I (Wardrip-Fruin 2005). Works that make their deployment of code central to their meaning constitute an expanding genre of software art. Live coders, such as Andrew Sorensen, perform the writing of code for audiences in prodigious displays akin to musical performers (Ramsay 2010). Other artists invite audiences to collaborate in writing the code, for example,

Jodi, whose works have encouraged interactors to "add and change things" in the code (JODI 2003). Other artists, from Shu Lea Cheang to the Electronic Disturbance Theater, engage in hacktivism, a portmanteau of hack and activism, using code as a political tool to disrupt the functioning of powerful networks (see HACKER). In these projects, code, as medium of activation, takes on a primary role in the artistic intervention, and the cultural practice of hacking is transposed as aesthetic and critical sabotage.

In other genres, code itself becomes the subject of exploration. Perl Poetry and Obfuscated Code competitions play directly with the aesthetics and legibility of compilable code. In a genre of electronic literature called codework, authors create poems in functioning programming languages, in pseudocode, and in nonfunctioning creoles such as Mez's *mesangelle*, which combines codelike elements with natural language. Some of these codeworks compile, but that is not a requirement of the genre. Artist Zach Blas has gone so far as to create an antiprogramming language, transCoder, which has been implemented in several codeworks, including works by Julie Levin Russo and Micha Cárdenas (Blas 2007; Russo 2008; Cárdenas 2011). Additional practitioners of this field include John Cayley, Alan Sondheim, Graham Harwood, Johan Meskens, and Pascale Gustin (see CODE AESTHETICS).

Another genre of code art uses character encodings such as ASCII and Unicode as another artistic palette, generally using fixed-width fonts to produce images out of ordinary character sets. Such approaches were especially popular before computer screen resolutions and storage capacity allowed for the easy transfer of images. Nonetheless, like the eight-bit aesthetic of retro-graphics, the genre has continued well into the age of high-resolution graphics.

How Code Is Read

The works of these artists call attention to the pervasive communicative force of code in digital culture. In his Turing Award lecture, one of the founding fathers of programming, Donald Knuth, argued that programming is an art (1987). Nonetheless, it was not until the turn of the millennium that critics trained in philosophy and literary and new media theory turned their attention to code. While computer source code has been the subject of rich critical inquiry within computer science and programming circles, humanities-style readings of code are a much more recent phenomenon. Pioneering critics Adrian Mackenzie (2006), Florian Cramer (2005), and Loss Pequeño Glazier (2006) wrote on the implications of code. Sadie Plant interrogated the gender play in binary with her *Zeroes and Ones* (1998). A 2003 Ars Electronica called code "the language of our time," and its proceedings show how code has become a focal point in discussions of art, law, and society in this digital moment (Bentley et al. 2003).

More recently, critics have begun close reading source code of digital works as cultural texts. This practice was born of calls by Hayles and others to perform "media specific analysis," readings of works attentive to their particular forms (Hayles and Burdick 2002). Software studies and platform studies have emerged in answer to these calls along with critical code studies (CCS) (see SOFTWARE STUDIES). Books within the software studies series, including Matthew Fuller's edited collection *Software Studies: a Lexicon* (2008), offer tools for close reading concepts in programming, such as loops (see SOFTWARE STUDIES).

CCS is the application of hermeneutics to the interpretation of the extrafunctional significance of computer source code. "Extra" indicates that the meaning does not arise outside of the function but instead emerges from it. Rather than a set theory, CCS names an emerging collection of methodologies applied to the close reading of lines of code. This subfield was named in 2006 but has since burgeoned through conferences, online working groups, articles, and books (Marino 2006, 2010).

Interpretations of code tend to begin with a text-based approach, examining the signs for traces of their production and revision, their cultural context, and the paradigms informing their structures. However, CCS does not examine the code as a literary text but as a semiotic text, as formulated in cultural studies. CCS readings interpret natural language elements of code, such as variable and function names, along with semantic components of the programming language, design choices, and other facets. At the same time, CCS readings do not confine themselves to the functioning processes, as they also scrutinize comments within the code, bugs, and even commented-out code. Despite all these semiotic elements, code is fragmentary, one element of a larger system that connects programmers, users, operating systems, hardware, and other code. Hence, CCS readings use the code as a home base for forays into explorations of the material and historical context in which it was created, functions, and circulates.

CCS readings have included examinations of video games, codework, and other pieces of electronic literature and software. In a book-length manuscript, one group of ten scholars has analyzed a one-line program written in BASIC for the Commodore 64 (Montfort et al. 2013). Code readings have investigated the software that has played a role in contemporary political events, from the Climategate scandal to voting machine software, software used in space exploration, and even software used in health care plans to determine risk. Another group has turned their attention to the code of video games such as *Metropolis* and *Grand Theft Auto*. Others discuss games as programming environments, for example, the game *Dwarf Fortress*, in which a player has created a Turing Machine out of rivers and trees, represented in minimalist ASCII characters (Boluk and Lemieux, forthcoming). Dennis Jerz's essay on William Crowther's *Adventure* included photographs, maps, a discussion of gameplay, and, of course, FORTRAN source code, the entirety of which Jerz has posted for collaborative annotation (Jerz 2007). Code plays a crucial role in these interpretations for it provides the material, historical implementation of the software in question.

Interpreting digital objects through code requires knowledge of their functioning; however, CCS scholars have begun to question whether the conventional literacy metaphors applied to natural written languages also apply in the context of programming. By contrast, David M. Berry has proposed "iteracy" and Annette Vee's "proceduracy" as alternative ways of characterizing programming knowledge born of an iterative cycle of development to embody procedures (Berry 2011; Vee 2010).

Code is a layer of digital textuality whose pointers lead in many directions. Nonetheless, as the semiotic trace of a process or even as the artisitic fodder of codework, code offers an entryway into analysis and interpretation of the particular instantiation of a work, its history, and its possible futures.

■ See also MARKUP LANGUAGES, SUBVERSION (CREATIVE DESTRUCTION)

References and Further Reading

Bentley, Peter, Pierre Levy, Howard Rheingold, Giaco Schlesser, Friedrich Kittler, and Christine Schöpf. 2003. *Ars Electronica 2003: Code: The Language of Our Time*. Ostfildern-Ruit, Germany: Hatje Cantz.

Berry, David. M. 2011. "Iteracy: Reading, Writing and Running Code." *Stunlaw: A Critical Review of Politics, Art and Technology*. http://stunlaw.blogspot.com.es/2011/09/iteracy-reading-writing-and -running.html.

Blas, Zach. 2007. *transCoder|Queer Technologies*. Code. http://users.design.ucla.edu/~zblas/artwork /transcoder_archive/. www.queertechnologies.info/products/transcoder/.

Boluk, Stephanie, and Patrick Lemieux. Forthcoming. "Dwarven Epitaphs." In *Comparative Textual Media: Interplays between Making and Critique*, edited by N. Katherine Hayles and Jessica Pressman. Minneapolis: University of Minnesota Press.

Cárdenas, Micha. 2011. *net.walkingtools.Transformer.shift()*. Code. http://crg.berkeley.edu/content /catalyst-mcardenas.

Chun, Wendy Hui Kyong. 2008. "On 'Sourcery,' or Code as Fetish." *Configurations* 16 (3): 299–324. doi:10.1353/con.0.0064.

Cramer, Florian. 2005. *Words Made Flesh: Code, Culture, Imagination*. Rotterdam: Piet Zwart Institute.

Critical Code Studies Working Group. 2012. "Week 1: Ethics—CCS Working Group 2012." http:// wg12.criticalcodestudies.com/discussion/10/week-1-ethics#Item_49.

Crowther, William, and Chris Conley. 2011. *Adventure*. www.ifarchive.org/if-archive/games/source /inform/Advent_Crowther_source.txt.

Fuller, Matthew. 2008. *Software Studies: A Lexicon*. Illustrated ed. Cambridge, MA: MIT Press.

Galloway, Alexander R. 2006. *Protocol: How Control Exists after Decentralization*. Cambridge, MA: MIT Press.

Hansen, Mark B. N. 2006. *Bodies in Code: Interfaces with Digital Media*. 1st ed. New York: Routledge.

Hayles, N. Katherine. 2005. *My Mother Was a Computer: Digital Subjects and Literary Texts*. 1st ed. Chicago: University of Chicago Press.

Hayles, N. Katherine, and Anne Burdick. 2002. *Writing Machines*. Cambridge, MA: MIT Press.

Hodges, Andrew, and Douglas Hofstadter. 2000. *Alan Turing: The Enigma*. 1st ed. New York: Walker.

Jerz, Dennis G. 2007. "Somewhere Nearby Is Colossal Cave: Examining Will Crowther's Original Adventure in Code and in Kentucky." *DHQ: Digital Humanities Quarterly* 1 (2). http://digital humanities.org/dhq/vol/001/2/000009.html#.

JODI. 2003. *10 Programs Written in Basic © 1984*. BASIC. Electrohype—ROM. www.electrohype .org/rom/jodi/backtobasic.html.

Kittler, Friedrich. 1995. "There Is No Software." *CTheory*, October 18. www.ctheory.net/articles .aspx?id=74.

Knuth, Donald E. 1987. "Computer Programming as an Art." In *ACM Turing Award Lectures: The First Twenty Years: 1966–1985*, 667–673. New York: ACM Press/Addison-Wesley. http://doi .acm.org/10.1145/1283920.1283929.

Mackenzie, Adrian. 2006. *Cutting Code: Software and Sociality*. New York: Peter Lang.

Marino, Mark C. 2006. "Critical Code Studies." *Electronic Book Review*, Electropoetics, December 4. www.electronicbookreview.com/thread/electropoetics/codology.

———. 2010. "Critical Code Studies and the Electronic Book Review: An Introduction." *Electronic Book Review*. First Person. www.electronicbookreview.com/thread/firstperson/ningislanded.

Montfort, Nick, Patsy Baudoin, John Bell, et al. 2013. *10 PRINT CHR$(205.5 + RND(1)); : GOTO 10*. Cambridge, MA: MIT Press.

Pequeño Glazier, Loss. 2006. "Code as Language by Loss Pequeño Glazier: Vol 14 No 5–6 September 2006—Leonardo Electronic Almanac." *Leonardo Electronic Almanac* 14 (5) (September 6). www.leoalmanac.org/journal/vol_14/lea_v14_n05-06/lglazier.html.

Plant, Sadie. 1998. *Zeros and Ones*. New York: HarperCollins.

Ramsay, Stephen. 2010. *Algorithms Are Thoughts, Chainsaws Are Tools*. Lincoln, NE. http://vimeo .com/9790850.

Russo, Julie Levin. 2008. "Thearchive2: The Slash Goggles Algorithm." *LiveJournal. Thearchive2*. http://community.livejournal.com/thearchive2/1465.html.

Vee, Annette. 2010. "Proceduracy: Computer Code Writing in the Continuum of Literacy." ProQuest LLC. 789 East Eisenhower Parkway, P.O. Box 1346, Ann Arbor, MI 48106. Tel: 800-521-0600; website: www.proquest.com/en-US/products/dissertations/individuals.shtml. www.eric.ed.gov /ERICWebPortal/detail?accno=ED523386.

Wardrip-Fruin, Noah. 2005. "Christopher Strachey: The First Digital Artist?" *Grand Text Auto*. www.grandtextauto.org/2005/08/01/christopher-strachey-first-digital-artist/.

· ·

Code Aesthetics
David M. Berry

Code aesthetics refers to a number of different notions applied in particular to the creation of and practices related to computer code and software. As its name suggests, code aesthetics is related to a judgment on the perceived "beauty" or "elegance" of computer code and is used in both a more traditionally aesthetic register and a technical one. In this entry we will concentrate on the main issues related to its usage. Indeed, it is useful to consider the nature of code aesthetics in relation to the computational more generally (Berry 2011). Here, though, the focus will be on (1) new media art and the new aesthetic, (2) computer code as an aesthetic moment, and (3) the aesthetic sensibility in the writing of, and practices that relate to, computer code/software. These formulations tend to separate the aesthetic from the political/economic, and for the sake of brevity this section will reflect that analytic formulation. However, linkages between them are clearly important and indeed form part of the critique that new media art introduces into code and new media practices. The history of code aesthetics also, to some extent, reflects differing conceptions of the "online," "digital," "virtual," and "cyberspace," and how *beauty* or an aesthetic *disinterestedness* can be usefully understood in relation to these concepts.

New Media Art / The New Aesthetic

The most obvious example of the use of aesthetics in relation to code is that of new media art, or related practices, which emerged in the early 1990s. New media art has traditionally defined itself in opposition to older forms and practices of visual art and tends to have a highly technical form or set of practices associated with it. Examples include Mark Amerika, Cory Arcangel, Mez Breeze, Heath Bunting, Stelarc, the Critical Art Ensemble, Golan Levin, Judy Malloy, and Young-Hae Chang Heavy Industries, among others. Many of these artists have tended toward a reflexivity or critical orientation toward the technology and technological society from which they have emerged, including a notion of the aesthetic itself. This is particularly apparent with tactical media and hacktivist art. They have also focused on exploring the tensions between notions of online/offline, digital/physical, and the question of space/cyberspace. New media art has been heavily influenced by the notion of appropriation and "cut and paste" as a form of creative expression and exploration; new media artists have worked in a variety of media forms, combining different mediums into multimodal pieces, as well as experimenting with remediation and open-source techniques (see REMEDIATION, REMIX). Owing to the reliance on digital forms, particularly code and software, many of these works are ephemeral and suffer from rapid obsolescence in their component parts. This has added to the difficulty of curating and the preservation of new media arts (see ARCHIVE, PRESERVATION).

The "New Aesthetic," on the other hand, is an aesthetic that revels in seeing the grain of computation, or perhaps better, seeing the limitations or digital artifacts of a kind of digital glitch, sometimes called the "aesthetic of failure" (see GLITCH AESTHET-ICS). The New Aesthetic was initially introduced at a South by Southwest (SXSW) panel organized by James Bridle and was called "The New Aesthetic: Seeing Like Digital Devices." It was primarily concerned with "giv[ing] examples of these effects, products and artworks, and discuss[ing] the ways in which ways of [computer/robot] seeing are increasingly transforming ways of making and doing" (SXSW 2012). Enabling robot/computer algorithms to "see" by imposing computational code and "pixels" on reality is part of this new aesthetic. However, there is also an element of "down-sampled" representation of a kind of digital past, or digital *passing*, in the kinds of digital glitches, modes, and forms that are chosen, and that are all very much located historically. There has been a certain amount of dismissal of the New Aesthetic by practitioners and artists from, ironically, new media art, who have argued that it either should be subsumed within the category of new media art or else should be seen as an outgrowth of the creative industries, or the Wired Silicon Valley system. Here we merely note that the New Aesthetic has produced some controversy that has clearly been productive and contributes to new thinking about technology and aesthetics (see Berry et al. 2012).

Computer Code as an Aesthetic

The accessibility and influence of computer code as a representative mode, that is, where it is used to convey some form of semiotic function for code/software, is a growing phenomenon. This includes the reproduction of code-like textual forms, including certain kinds of ASCII art, but more particularly programming code, usually from third-generation programming languages, such as C++, Java, Ruby, and so forth, although other representative forms also exist and are used. The growing aestheticization of computer code is related to its mediality, particularly moving from cathode ray tube (CRT) based displays that were constructed through heavily textual interfaces, such as the VT-100/200. Indeed, many of the programmers and hackers of a previous generation remain wedded to a simulated command line aesthetic of white on black text. Increasingly, however, computer programming integrated development environments (IDEs) use color, formatting, and other graphical techniques to create an aesthetic of code that gives the text a signification and depth not available in monochrome versions—for example, marking code commentary green. This increased use of graphics capabilities in the presentation of computer code has correspondingly created new visual forms of programming, such as live-coding, a real-time coding environment for music and visual arts in languages such as Fluxus and Zajal, and visual programming systems that integrate user interface and graphic elements into the programming practices, for example, Sublime Text and Light Table (see INTERFACE). Within the context of an aesthetics of computer code, it is clear that the aesthetic is related to the functional structure of the language, and here we can only gesture toward the increasing reliance on obfuscation in programming language design, and therefore the idea of "hidden" or "private" elements of the structure of the code, as opposed to "available" or "public" elements and the related aesthetic practices associated with them (see Dexter 2012).

Aesthetic Sensibility of Writing Computer Code

Increasingly, the writing practices of computer code, combined with reading and understanding, have become deeply inscribed with practices of an aesthetic sensibility. This is sometimes also linked to the hacker ethic of playfulness and exploratory thinking. The notion of "beautiful code" is intertwined with both aesthetic and functional characteristics that need to be carefully unpacked to appreciate how this beauty is understood and recognized within the coding communities around which computer code is developed (see Oram and Wilson 2007). These practices are deeply related to what Donald Knuth wrote in the highly influential *Literate Programming*, published in 1992, which was described as having a "main concern . . . with exposition and excellence of style . . . [the programmer] strives for a program that is comprehensible because its concepts have been introduced . . . [and] nicely reinforce each other" (Knuth, quoted in Black 2002, 131). That is, well-crafted code is reflected in both its form *and* its content as a "complete" aesthetics of code. In some sense then, aesthetically "beautiful" code avoids what is sometimes referred to as "messy code," although clearly the boundary construction around what is beautiful and what is not is also interesting to explore. Indeed, examples given by obfuscated code also serve to demonstrate the aesthetic and visual, rather than the merely textual, dimension of code aesthetics, and they also serve as counterpoints to Knuth's notions of what is defined as aesthetic (see Berry 2011, 87–93; Mateas and Montfort 2005).

This has led to interesting discussions of the relation of code to poetry, and the related aesthetic sensibility shared between them (see Cox, McLean, and Ward 2006). Sharon Hopkins's Perl poem "rush" is a good example of this (see Berry 2011, 49). Indeed, discussions vary over, for example, the use of camel case, or the contraction of names in code into one word, for example, "ThisIsAFunction," versus the use of underscores, such as "This_is_a_function." Additionally, arguments over formatting, indentation, variable names, namespaces, and so on, are all bound up in the definition of well-constructed computer code. Remarkably, these examples continue to remain an important aspect of contestation over the most aesthetically pleasing code, but which have recently been supplemented with arguments over good typographic design and programming environment design with the move to retina (high-resolution) displays and tablet formats, such as found in Pythonista.

While the importance and relevance of code aesthetic are helpful in understanding computer code and its related practices, Marino cautions, "To critique code merely for its functionality or aesthetics is to approach code with only a small portion of our analytic tools" (2006). This is an important rejoinder to efforts to consider code aesthetics outside the practices and context of its production, use and distribution, and also, crucially, its political economy.

■ See also CODE, CYBERSPACE, DIGITAL AND NET ART, DIGITAL INSTALLATION ART, INTERACTIVE NARRATIVE

References and Further Reading

Berry, David M. 2011. *The Philosophy of Software: Code and Mediation in the Digital Age*. London: Palgrave.

Berry, David M., Michel van Dartel, Michael Dieter, et al. 2012. *New Aesthetic, New Anxieties*. Amsterdam: V2.

Black, Maurice J. 2002. "The Art of Code." PhD diss., University of Pennsylvania.

Cox, Geoff, Alex McLean, and Adrian Ward. 2006. "The Aesthetics of Generative Code." http://generative.net/papers/aesthetics/.

Dexter, Scott. 2012. "The Esthetics of Hidden Things." in *Understanding Digital Humanities*, edited by David M. Berry, 127–144. London: Palgrave.

Marino, Mark C. 2006. "Critical Code Studies." *Electronic Book Review*. www.electronicbookreview.com/thread/electropoetics/codology.

Mateas, Michael, and Nick Montfort. 2005. "A Box, Darkly: Obfuscation, Weird Languages, and Code Aesthetics." http://nickm.com/cis/a_box_darkly.pdf.

Oram, Andy, and Greg Wilson, eds. 2007. *Beautiful Code*. London: O'Reilly.

SXSW. 2012. "The New Aesthetic: Seeing Like Digital Devices." *SXSW*. http://schedule.sxsw.com/2012/events/event_IAP11102.

Cognitive Implications of New Media

Anne Mangen and Jean-Luc Velay

Relations between media (i.e., artifacts/tools/technologies) and human cognition are intimate, complex, and profound. Our modes of reading, writing, communication, and creative expression are closely connected with and continuously shaped by the media, tools, and technologies we use and are familiar with. In a sense, the ways in which we read, write, think, communicate, and express ourselves can be said to reflect the media ecology in which we live and the tools and technologies prevalent in this ecology at the time (see MEDIA ECOLOGY). Reciprocal and symbiotic rather than effectual and unidirectional, the affinities between media and human cognition evolve in a continuous and multifaceted manner, reciprocally impacting each other on both small and large scales, with both short- and long-term effects.

From the earliest times in the history of mankind, humans have developed and employed artifacts, tools, and technologies for everyday life purposes. In a fundamental sense, new media and technologies are merely the most recent additions to an increasingly advanced and comprehensive chain of human-technology relations (see OLD MEDIA / NEW MEDIA). Since the dawn of civilization, humans have been relying on artifacts and technologies to supplement and expand our own, limited cognitive capacity, partially offloading cognitive processes and tasks onto devices such as, for instance, the abacus, the calculator, pencils and paper, the papyrus roll, the codex book, the typewriter, and the computer. For millennia, the repertoire of available technologies was very limited. Writing and drawing were performed by some kind of marking or inscription on a material substrate, eventually mechanized with the typewriter and most recently digitized. For more than five hundred years, since Gutenberg's printing press invention in the fifteenth century, the codex technology of the print book was the dominant if not only reading medium (see BOOK TO E-TEXT). Now, digital reading devices such as e-book technologies based on electronic ink (a digital display technology designed to mimic the visual appearance of ordinary ink on paper, by reflecting ambient light rather than emitting light such as the LCD [liquid crystal display] technology) represent the first major challenge to the print book in the history of reading.

Today, we are witnessing a massive dispersion of reading and writing to a plethora of digital media and devices. Digital technologies are pervading our everyday lives, taking care of an increasing number of activities, tasks, and processes, many of which are, in nature, cognitive. Raymond S. Nickerson classifies tools according to whether the abilities they amplify are motor (e.g., levers, shovels, hammer, and wheels amplifying motor power and carrying capacity), sensory (e.g., eyeglasses, microscopes, telescopes, audio amplifiers, radar and heat detection technology), or cognitive: "Tools that amplify cognition include symbol systems for representing entities, quantities, and relationship, as well as devices and procedures for measuring, computing, inferencing, and remembering" (2005, 3). Digital media are quite probably the most powerful manifestations of a cognitive technology yet to be developed. The digital computer appears to be a cognitive technology par excellence in that it "enhance[s] cognitive functioning through directly affording cognitive support rather than as a side effect" (Salomon and Perkins 2005, 75). The environment and affordances of such a technology are bound to have implications for the processes underlying human attention, perception, and cognition.

New or digital media represent a wide array of different material (see MATERIALITY) and technical platforms and devices, each with its own defining features. However, three features can be conceived as generic to digital media, and these can be assumed to be strongly related to the ways in which digital media impact our modes of reading, writing, communication, and creative expression: (1) interactivity, (2) multimediality, and (3) hypertextuality (see HYPERTEXTUALITY, INTERACTIVITY). In different but closely related ways, these three properties shape and define the cognitive implications of new media.

The first defining concept of digital media, *interactivity*, is quite possibly the most widely used (and, eagerly claimed by several theorists, abused) buzzword in the new media discourse. For the present purposes, we will limit interactivity to denote the affordance of digital media to allow for input from and interaction with the user: "Modern HCI is by definition interactive, in that it allows the user to control the computer in real-time by manipulating information displayed on screen" (Manovich 2001, 55). Of particular significance is the fact that user input and interactivity in some way and to some degree bring about (audio)visual changes in the display, in ways that older media such as print media do not. Torben Grodal defines interactivity as the user's ability to "change to visual appearance of a computer screen (and/or sounds from the speakers) by some motor action via an interface" (2003, 142).

The second defining feature of digital media is *multimediality*. The digital infrastructure of new media allows all types of information and audiovisual representations to be implemented in and displayed on the same technological platform (see ANALOG VERSUS DIGITAL). A digital portable device such as a surf pad (e.g., an iPad) is a multimedium that can generate, store, and display all types of audiovisual modalities (i.e., still and moving images, graphics and animation, sound) and can function simultaneously as a TV, radio, book, typewriter, telephone, camera, photo album, personal broadcast channel, video recorder, and synchronous communication device. In contrast, a print book is restricted to storing and displaying static text and graphics. Hence, the user of an iPad can easily and seamlessly switch between tasks that differ greatly in terms of the nature of processing and the amount and kind of attentional and perceptuo-cognitive expenditure they require. Many of the new media allow and invite extensive multitasking, whereas an "old" medium such as a print book does not allow you to do much else than read and make notes, underline in the text, and so on.

The cognitive implications of multitasking are only beginning to be explored and understood, and so far, findings are inconclusive. For instance, Ophir, Nass, and Wagner

(2009) designed an experiment comparing heavy multitaskers (i.e., subjects who prefer to multitask, and who consider themselves to be performing better when they do) and light multitaskers (i.e., subjects who prefer not to multitask, and who consider themselves to be performing less well when multitasking). The researchers measured the performances of the two groups on (a) attentional focus (i.e., ability to filter out irrelevant information), (b) information retention and recall, and (c) attentional task switching. On all three measures, the light multitaskers outperformed the heavy multitaskers. Ophir et al. conclude that heavy multitaskers show decreased attentional control, in particular when attentional switching. However, replicating the measures of the Ophir et al. study, Alzahabi and Becker (2011) found that heavy media multitaskers have a decreased switch cost compared to light media multitaskers. This means that, in contrast to the findings in the Ophir et al. study, heavy multitaskers are able to switch between two tasks more efficiently. These findings suggest that media multitasking does not interfere with attentional control and may even produce a better ability to switch between tasks (Alzahabi and Becker 2011).

The third main defining feature playing a central role in shaping the cognitive implications of digital media is *hypertextuality* (see HYPERTEXTUALITY). Digitally displayed content is (often, but not always) structured in networks consisting of chunks (or nodes) of information which are internally connected by means of hyperlinks (see LINKING STRATEGIES). The cognitive implications of hypertextuality have been studied extensively, in particular with respect to the cognitive load of navigation and link selection during online reading of web-based hypertexts. A print text has an unequivocal beginning and end, is overly linear, supports sequential reading, and provides the reader with visual as well as tactile access to the totality of the text. By comparison, a digital hypertext is a temporary display of linked chunks of digitized information where the reader is restricted to seeing only what appears on the screen at any time. Digitization allows the digital hypertext to be stored (see PRESERVATION), searched (see SEARCH), sampled (see SAMPLING), revised, and distributed in ways that far surpass that of print text. However, the lack of fixity and physical extension of the digital hypertext might make it more difficult for the reader to get an overview of the text in its entirety—what some call "a sense of the text" (Haas 1996). Such a "sense of the text" might be particularly pertinent when reading potentially complex texts of a certain length. Many studies have shown that the challenges inherent to navigation in a hypertext document entail cognitive costs that can cause cognitive overload for the reader (for a metastudy of hypertext reading and cognitive load, see DeStefano and LeFevre 2007).

In general, different media, technological platforms, and interfaces require, favor, and generate different modes of sensorimotor (physical; ergonomic) and cognitive (mental) interaction and engagement (see INTERFACE). Taken together, the features of interactivity, multimediality, and hypertextuality imply new and sometimes unfamiliar ergonomic, perceptual, and cognitive processes and interactions for the user, compared with those of conventional analog media. Hence, it might make an experiential (cognitive; phenomenological) difference whether we read a text on a printed sheet of paper, on a computer screen, or on a Kindle. In digital media, the connection between the content (whatever is displayed on the screen) and the material support (the technological platform of the device; see MATERIALITY) is split up, allowing the technological device to display a multitude of content that can be altered with a click. A book, in contrast, is a physically and functionally unitary object in which the content cannot be distinguished from the material platform or substrate of paper. Such a detachment in new media might plausibly have important and often neglected cognitive and phenomenological implications for the reading experience. It indicates the potential role of the physicality and tangibility of the document and, by corollary, the fixity of the text, during reading. According to Liu (2008), the tangibility of the printed document is one of the main reasons why digital technologies will not be replacing paper documents any time soon: "People are generally comfortable with information only when they can 'feel it' in their hands and can make sure whether the important information is recorded properly. Why are all the important messages and agreements (e.g., diplomas, certificates, and contracts) put on paper? . . . The saying 'put it on paper' conveys the importance of this tangible document medium" (Liu 2008, 144).

Cognitive implications of new media can be traced in some of the most prominent manifestations of human cognition, namely, reading and writing/drawing. These skills have always relied on the use of technologies and media that provide means of materializing mental content into visible symbols and representations. From the use of clay tablets and animal skins via the medieval manuscript and the ancient papyrus roll to the printing press and the current digitization, writers have always had to handle physical devices and then apply these to some substrate or display. New media and technologies complement and eventually replace old ones, as reading is increasingly performed on a screen rather than on a piece of paper, and as we type and click on keyboards, and tap on touch screens, rather than putting a pen to paper. How does the transition from paper to screen impact the act of reading? And how does the increasing marginalization of writing and drawing by hand impact those skills?

Anecdotal evidence suggests that readers disagree as to what differences in cognitive implications there may be between screen reading and print reading. There is ample reason to expect that this will vary according to the kinds of texts in question (e.g., genre, stylistic, and compositional features; length; level of complexity), as well as the purpose of reading and aspects pertaining to the context and situation in which the reading takes place. A case in point is the differences between study reading and leisure/pleasure reading. The increasing popularity of e-book technologies based on electronic ink (such as Kindle and Kobo) is testimony to the fact that many readers find the experience of longhand reading of, say, novels on these kinds of screens to be equally visually appealing and reader-friendly as reading on paper. Extensive text reading on a computer screen, however, is still often reported as tiring—so much so that readers often resort to print, for instance, by printing out the reading materials. Such fatigue is commonly described as Computer Vision Syndrome (Yan et al. 2008).

Digital drawing and design now require using a graphic tablet and a mouse or a stylus coupled with graphic software. Because it is very simple to use, design software offers the possibility of drawing complex designs without being an expert designer. In spite of all its advantages, in the early 1980s, when computer-aided design (CAD) was being introduced in design offices, surveys conducted among draftsmen showed that they were not totally satisfied with computers (Whitefield 1986). Although they appreciated the speed, accuracy, and ease of making modifications, allowing for very fast product development, they were less satisfied when they had to design a highly complex shape. In such cases, they often preferred to go back to freehand drawing with a good old pencil at the rough draft stage, before resuming designing with the computer, as if there were a cognitive benefit in "thinking with a pencil." In other words, these new graphical tools change drawing habits, but do they really make drawing easier?

One could assume that children would be able to express themselves more freely and be able to produce better designs more easily with these new tools than with pen and paper. Consequently, if their designs become better and more sophisticated, their perceptual capacities and their aptitude in building correct and coherent spatial representations might increase. This is the positive point of view. Conversely, according to the negative point of view, using the new technologies reduces manual activities with respect to traditional ones. The great reduction and simplification of the movements when drawing with a computer could reduce both the sensory-motor and the spatial competence of the children. As a matter of fact, taking ready-made geometrical forms in a toolbox, dragging them with a mouse, and resizing them by simply clicking and pulling on a corner makes the activity much more abstract than when one has to draw the forms "ex nihilo" with a pencil. Drawing a rectangle with a pencil requires making a movement that totally and exactly describes and matches the visual form of the rectangle. The relationship between the visual form and the movement is direct and unique: in that sense we can say it is "concrete." This is not the case with CAD, where this relationship is more "abstract."

Would children, whose motor control of fine and precise hand movements is not completely mastered, learn to draw more easily and more efficiently if they were taught with computerized tools? What would the advantages and disadvantages of their use be? Would using a computerized graphics tool influence children's drawing skills? Do these new digital tools enhance or reduce drawing abilities in terms of planning actions and conceptualizing spatial relationships?

Unfortunately, studies devoted to the impact of computers on children learning to draw and write are still very sparse. In a recent experiment, children were compared in the classical "pen and paper" method and in a computerized method for producing the same drawing (Martin and Velay 2012). The results showed that using a CAD tool might help children while they copy a model, but that it does not improve their ability to draw the same figure using their own, internal model.

The same conclusion was reached for the learning of handwriting versus typewriting and their respective impact on the visual recognition of letters (Mangen and Velay 2010; Velay and Longcamp 2012). It has been shown in children (Longcamp et al. 2005) and in adults (Longcamp et al. 2006, 2008) that character recognition was better when the characters had been learned by handwriting than when they had been learned through typewriting. Furthermore, the brain areas involved during the visual presentation of the characters differed according to how they had been learned previously (Longcamp et al. 2008).

When writing, drawing, and communicating with digital technologies, less precise and less discriminating manual movements are required than when handwriting with pen on paper. In many respects, digitization contributes to making the relationship between the embodied, sensorimotor input and the audiovisual output generated by the technology more abstract and detached. In conclusion, then, theoretical and empirical research indicates that ongoing shifts from analog and print-based media to digital media might have cognitive implications, the full extent of which are yet to be pinned down and explained. As education is increasingly digitized, and as digital screen technologies have begun to replace textbooks and pencils in beginning reading and writing instruction, we need to be attentive to such implications in both a short-term and a long-term perspective.

■ See also ANALOG VERSUS DIGITAL, BOOK TO E-TEXT, CHARACTERISTICS OF DIGITAL MEDIA, INTERACTIVITY, INTERFACE, MATERIALITY, MEDIA ECOLOGY, MEDIALITY, OLD MEDIA / NEW MEDIA, READING STRATEGIES, REMEDIATION

References and Further Reading

Alzahabi, Reem, and Mark W. Becker. 2011. "In Defense of Media Multitasking: No Increase in Task-Switch or Dual-Task Costs." *Journal of Vision* 11 (11): 102.

DeStefano, Diana, and Jo-Anne LeFevre. 2007. "Cognitive Load in Hypertext Reading: A Review." *Computers in Human Behavior* 23 (3): 1616–1641.

Grodal, Torben K. 2003. "Stories for Eye, Ear, and Muscles: Video Games, Media, and Embodied Experience." In *The Video Game Theory Reader*, edited by Mark J. P. Wolf and Bernard Perron, 129–155. New York: Routledge.

Haas, Christina. 1996. *Writing Technology: Studies on the Materiality of Literacy*. Mahwah, NJ: Lawrence Erlbaum Associates.

Liu, Ziming. 2008. *Paper to Digital: Documents in the Information Age*. Westport, CT: Libraries Unlimited.

Longcamp, M. Bouchard, J. C. Gilhodes, J. L. Anton, M. Roth, B. Nazarian, and J. L. Velay. 2008. "Learning through Hand- or Typewriting Influences Visual Recognition of New Graphic Shapes: Behavioral and Functional Imaging Evidence." *Journal of Cognitive Neuroscience* 20 (5): 802–815.

Longcamp, M. Bouchard, J. C. Gilhodes, and J. L. Velay. 2006. "Remembering the Orientation of Newly Learned Characters Depends on the Associated Writing Knowledge: A Comparison between Handwriting and Typing." *Human Movement Science* 25 (4–5): 646–656.

Longcamp, M. Bouchard, M. T. Zerbato-Poudon, and J. L. Velay. 2005. "The Influence of Writing Practice on Letter Recognition in Preschool Children: A Comparison between Handwriting and Typing." *Acta Psychologica* 119 (1): 67–79.

Mangen, Anne, and Jean-Luc Velay. 2010. "Digitizing Literacy: Reflections on the Haptics of Writing." In *Advances in Haptics*, edited by Mehrdad Hosseini Zadeh, 385–401. Vienna: IN-TECH web.

Manovich, Lev. 2001. *The Language of New Media*. Cambridge, MA: MIT Press.

Martin, Perrine, and Jean-Luc Velay. 2012. "Do Computers Improve the Drawing of a Geometrical Figure for 10 Year-Old Children?" *International Journal of Technology and Design Education* 22 (1): 13–23.

Nickerson, Raymond S. 2005. "Technology and Cognition Amplification." In *Intelligence and Technology: The Impact of Tools on the Nature and Development of Human Abilities*, edited by Robert J. Sternberg and David D. Preiss, 3–27. Mahwah, NJ: Lawrence Erlbaum Associates.

Ophir, Eyal, Clifford Nass, and Anthony D. Wagner. 2009. "Cognitive Control in Media Multitaskers." *PNAS—Proceedings of the National Academy of Sciences of the United States of America* 106 (37): 15583–15587.

Salomon, Gavriel, and David Perkins. 2005. "Do Technologies Make Us Smarter? Intellectual Amplification *With, Of,* and *Through* Technology." In *Intelligence and Technology: The Impact of Tools on the Nature and Development of Human Abilities*, edited by Robert J. Sternberg and David D. Preiss, 71–86. Mahwah, NJ: Lawrence Erlbaum Associates.

Velay, Jean-Luc, and Marieke Longcamp. 2012. "Handwriting versus Typing: Behavioral and Cerebral Consequences in Letter Recognition." In *Learning to Write Effectively: Current Trends in European Research*, edited by Mark Torrance, Denis Alamargot, Montserrat Castelló, et al., 306–308. Bingley, UK: Emerald.

Whitefield, Andy. 1986. "An Analysis and Comparison of Knowledge Used in Designing with and without CAD." Paper presented at the CAD 86: Seventh International Conference on the Computer as a Design Tool, London.

Yan, Zheng, Liang Hu, Hao Chen, and Fan Lu. 2008. "Computer Vision Syndrome: A Widely Spreading but Largely Unknown Epidemic among Computer Users." *Computers in Human Behavior* 24 (5): 2026–2042.

Collaborative Narrative

Scott Rettberg

Collaboratively written narratives are not specific to new media: a number of works within the Western cultural and literary canon, for example, the epics of Homer, the Judeo-Christian Bible, and *Beowulf*, are believed to have been developed through collaborative storytelling and writing processes. It can, however, be said that collaborative writing practices are more prevalent in contemporary digital media than in print.

Electronic literature authors most often write within software platforms that are themselves "authored"—every time someone opens up Photoshop, or Flash, they are reminded of the long list of developers who actually wrote the software. So even making use of a particular application is a type of collaboration. There is a greater degree of transparency to the collective efforts involved in digital media production than to traditional literary production.

Network communication technologies more easily enable collaborative writing than did Gutenberg-era writing environments. Technologies as simple as e-mail, Skype, Google docs, and various forms of file sharing make it almost as simple to collaborate with someone on a different continent as with someone down the hall.

Rettberg (2011) proposes a typology of participation in network-based narratives which includes (1) conscious participation, when collaborators are fully aware of the constraints and form of a project and the role of their contribution to it; (2) contributory participation, when contributors take conscious steps to make their text or media available to authors or to a system but do not know how it will fit into the overall project; and (3) unwitting participation, where texts are appropriated by the text machine or harvested from the network. If contributory participation is the most common form of collaborative practice in network narratives, there are also many examples that make use of more appropriative methods.

An early hypertext fiction developed through collaborative writing practices is Judy Malloy and Cathy Marshall's *Forward Anywhere* (1995). Initially written as an exchange of e-mails, in hypertext form, Malloy and Marshall describe it as a "blending of two lives" (1996, 62). The piece explores both e-mail and hypertext as conversational media. In the 1990s net.art practitioners Joan Heemskerk and Dirk Paesmans likewise collaborated and presented their hacker-aesthetic browser-based works under the fictional collective identity of *Jodi*. On a different scale, the *Hypertext Hotel* (1993–1996) produced by Robert Coover's early electronic writing workshops at Brown University was a collaboratively produced narrative architecture, constructed incrementally by many writers over an extended period, subverting and expanding each other's plot lines as they checked in and out of the hotel.

The hypertext novel *The Unknown* (1998) by William Gillespie, Frank Marquardt, Scott Rettberg, and Dirk Stratton is a collaborative fiction in web hypertext form, a sprawling comic novel about a book tour gone horribly wrong. The novel was very much the product of social writing, "jam sessions," constrained writing games, site-specific writing practices, appropriation, and other playful practices. As we wrote, we moved our eponymous characters like pawns, daring each other to write ourselves out of increasingly absurd scenarios.

Collaborative hypertexts can be structured in a number of different ways. The end product could be linear, where each author is building upon previous nodes or in some way stretching the context of a single coherent narrative, or could alternatively have a "branching" structure, as was the case in *Choose Your Own Adventure* books. An early web experiment of the branching variety, *Addventure*, was directed by Alan Firstenberg (1994).

There is likewise a rich history of collaborative writing and coding practice in the genre of interactive fiction. After Will Crowther authored the original version of *Colossal Cave Adventure* in 1976 as a game based on his explorations of Mammoth Cave in Kentucky (see Jerz 2007; Crowther and Woods 1977), Don Woods, then a graduate student, ran across the game on a computer at Stanford and contacted Crowther to ask if he could modify the game to introduce fantasy elements such as elves and dwarves. Woods's version of the game became popular and in turn inspired a group of friends at MIT—Tim Anderson, Mark Blank, Bruce Daniels, and Dave Lebling—to create their own game, *Zork*, loosely based on *Adventure* but making use of a much richer storyline and vocabulary (Lebling, Blank, and Anderson 1979). That collaboration in turn led to the formation of the company Infocom and generally to the birth of an entire genre.

Collaboration in digital narrative can scale from intense collaboration between two or three authors to more grandly conceived collective endeavors involving many contributors. *A Million Penguins* (2007), launched by De Montfort University and Penguin Books, was an experiment in collectively writing a novel in wiki, in which any visitor could modify the text, though some ongoing editing took place. In a report project organizers attested that though the project was not necessarily successful as a novel, it could better be understood as a successful "performance."

The most successful recent large-scale collaborative writing projects indeed merge aspects of fiction, performance, and what might be called "architectures of participation." Judd Morrissey and Mark Jeffery et al.'s *The Last Performance* (2007–2010), for example, offers a collectively written text authored by about 150 contributors with a complex database-driven constrained writing environment. Also promising are Mark Marino and Rob Wittig's recent "netprov" experiments such as Marino's *Work Study Seth* ([2009] 2011) and Wittig's *Grace, Wit & Charm* (2011), mixing structured preplanned narrative scenarios with collective improvisational writing performance and other performative writing practices.

■ See also DATABASE, E-MAIL NOVEL, HYPERTEXTUALITY, PERFORMANCE, ROLE-PLAYING GAMES

References and Further Reading

Coover, Robert, et al. 1993–1996. *The Hypertext Hotel.*

Crowther, Will, and Don Woods. 1977. *Colossal Cave Adventure.*

Firstenberg, Alan. 1994. *Addventure.* www.addventure.com/addventure/.

Gillespie, William, Frank Marquardt, Scott Rettberg, and Dirk Stratton. 1998. *The Unknown.* http://unknownhypertext.com.

Heemskerk, Joan, and Dirk Paesmans. n.d. *Jodi.* http://jodi.org/archive/.

Jerz, Dennis. 2007. "Somewhere Nearby Is Colossal Cave: Examining Will Crowther's Original 'Adventure' in Code and in Kentucky." *Digital Humanities Quarterly* 1 (2). www.digitalhumanities.org/dhq/vol/1/2/000009/000009.html.

Lebling, David P., Marc S. Blank, and Timothy A. Anderson. 1979. "Zork: A Computerized Fantasy Simulation Game." *IEEE Computer* 12 (4): 51–59. www.csd.uwo.ca/Infocom/Articles/ieee.html.

Malloy, Judy, and Cathy Marshall. 1995. *Forward Anywhere*. Cambridge, MA: Eastgate Systems.

———. 1996. "Closure Was Never a Goal in This Piece." In *Wired Women: Gender and New Realities in Cyberspace*, edited by Lynn Cherny and Elizabeth Reba Weise, 56–70. Seattle: Seal Press.

Marino, Mark. (2009) 2011. *The Ballad of Workstudy Seth*. *SpringGun Press*, Fall 2011. www.spring gunpress.com/the-ballad-of-workstudy-seth.

Mason, Bruce, and Sue Thomas. 2008. "A Million Penguins Research Report." Leicester, UK: Institute of Creative Technologies, De Montfort University. www.ioct.dmu.ac.uk/documents/amil lionpenguinsreport.pdf.

A Million Penguins. 2007. Leicester, UK: Institute of Creative Technologies, De Montfort University with Penguin Books.

Morrissey, Judd. 2007–2010. *The Last Performance [dot org]*. http://thelastperformance.org/.

Rettberg, Scott. 2010. "Performative Reading: Attending *The Last Performance [dot org]*." *Dichtung Digital* 40. http://dichtung-digital.mewi.unibas.ch/2010/rettberg/rettberg.htm.

———. 2011. "All Together Now: Hypertext, Collective Narratives, and Online Collective Knowledge Communities." In *New Narratives: Stories and Storytelling in the Digital Age*, edited by Ruth Page and Browen Thomas, 187–204. Lincoln: University of Nebraska Press.

Wittig, Rob. 2011. *Grace, Wit & Charm*. http://gracewitandcharm.com/.

Collective Intelligence
John Duda

"Collective intelligence" refers, broadly, to all those situations in which an aggregate of individual actors manifests a capacity for intelligent behavior that exceeds the individual capacity of the actors alone. A more restricted sense follows the original definition offered by French digital utopian scholar Pierre Lévy in 1994, for whom the term names a particular trajectory in human-machine interaction and the politics of knowledge (Lévy [1994] 1997).

The idea that aggregates of individuals might collectively behave in ways that transcend, in an emergent fashion, the intention and intelligence proper to each of their individual actions is, of course, not new. Indeed, such an assumption lies at the heart of the liberal tradition; Adam Smith's "invisible hand," for instance, describes a process by which the pursuit of private advantage in the market by many individuals increases the general welfare (Smith 1977). Friedrich Hayek will later reformulate these notions in terms of information and communication, arguing that the price system provides a decentralized framework for solving coordination problems intractable for the individual participant in the market (Hayek 1945).

Similar kinds of bottom-up processes that generate emergent order have been studied extensively in the life sciences, especially concerning the formation of schools, swarms, flocks, and the like, in which animals associate in complex and adaptive ways without central control; as Evelyn Shaw put it in a summary of her pioneering work on fish schooling, what is at stake here are "truly egalitarian form[s] of organization in which all members of the group are alike in influence" (Shaw 1978, 166). Critical to all accounts of such phenomena is the idea that no individual animal possesses a mental picture of the whole; instead, emergent order at the collective level is guaranteed by processes of bottom-up interaction and cumulative feedback.

Insect "social" behavior provides numerous suggestive examples, from Grassé's (1959) concept of "stigmergy," describing how termites build complex structures by reacting to the work of their neighbors, to the work of Deneubourg et al. from the 1980s onward clarifying the way that ant colonies use simple local rules to establish and follow efficient pheromone-marked paths to food sources (Deneubourg and Goss 1989). An influential formulation in Douglas Hofstadter's book *Gödel, Escher, Bach* (1979) argued that a system of units following simple combinatorial rules, like an idealized ant colony, could conceivably display intelligence in the full human sense of the word, in analogy with the decentralized system of neurons in the brain.

In the work of some thinkers like *Wired* magazine pundit Kevin Kelly (1995), complexity theorist Eric Bonabeau (Bonabeau, Dorigo, and Theraulaz 1999), and RAND corporation military strategists John Arquilla and David Ronfeldt (2001), a theory of collective or "swarm" intelligence applicable to human aggregates and facilitated by new digital technologies became increasingly prominent starting in the 1990s. Meanwhile, in works such as business journalist James Surowiecki's *The Wisdom of Crowds* (2004), arguments building on and expanding the neoliberal appreciation for the ability of human societies to quickly arrive at optimized solutions to shared problems in a decentralized way have further propagated a notion of collective intelligence as the emergent result of the aggregation of more or less unintelligent individual behaviors.

A more specific use of "collective intelligence" arises from Pierre Lévy's book *L'intelligence collective. Pour une anthropologie du cyberspace* (1994; translated into English in 1997 as *Collective Intelligence: Mankind's Emerging Future in Cyberspace*). For Lévy, collective intelligence is "a form of *universally distributed intelligence*, constantly enhanced, coordinated in real time, and resulting in the effective mobilization of skills. . . . The basis and goal of collective intelligence is the mutual recognition and enrichment of individuals rather than the cult of fetishized or hypostatized communities" (1997, 13). At first glance, Lévy's insistence on the decentralized and antibureaucratic character of collective intelligence ("Totalitarianism . . . was incapable of collective intelligence"; 1997, 3) resonates with the valorization of market-driven modes of emergent collective behavior common in thinkers from Hayek to Surowiecki. But Lévy crucially insists that his vision of collective intelligence is incompatible with the idea of swarm intelligence, where the underlying intelligence of the individual agents in the assemblage is absent or irrelevant: "The ant colony is the opposite of collective intelligence in the sense that I am using the expression" (1997, 16). Similarly, although Lévy characterizes collective intelligence as emerging in a world where "no one knows everything, everyone knows something" (1997, 13–14), this intelligence is not to be understood as a passive statistical aggregation, but as the active co-creation of the space of coordination and communication in which it emerges; Lévy thus understands "cyberspace [as] the shifting space of interaction among knowledge and knowers in deterritorialized intelligent communities" (1997, 15) (see CYBERSPACE).

In Lévy's conception—which is arguably less influential than the broader notion discussed above—collective intelligence is, crucially, not simply an isolated mechanism for the coordination of a limited set of activities, but a total ethical, political, and epistemological horizon in the process of becoming shared by human society at this current stage of social and technological development. As such, it also has its share of antecedents: Emile Durkheim's definition of "collective consciousness" as "the totality of beliefs and sentiments common to the average members of a society [which] forms a determinate system with a life of its own" ([1893] 1997, 37–38); Teilhard de Chardin's notion of a "noosphere"; and, indeed, the utopian visions of networked electronic communication from H. G. Wells's "World Brain" through Marshall McLuhan's "global village," J. C. R. Licklider's "intergalactic network," and Tim Berners-Lee's "world wide web." Lévy himself claims that the first articulations of collective intelligence are to be found in medieval neo-Platonism ([1994] 1997, 92–97). Another important precursor is Karl Marx, whose notion of the "general intellect" in the *Grundrisse*'s "Fragment on Machines" underscores the productivity of shared knowledge, embodied and externalized in the increasingly mechanized means of production (Marx [1857] 1993). Rereading Marx's notion of general intellect in terms of communication and immaterial labor, Antonio Negri and other autonomist Marxists have embraced and extended Lévy's notion of collective intelligence.

In practice, collective intelligence as a discipline and field tends to generally focus less on Lévy's idiosyncratic utopianism and more on the first and broader definition discussed above—"groups of individuals doing things collectively that seem intelligent," as Thomas Malone, founder of MIT's Center for Collective Intelligence, put it in his remarks commemorating the opening of the center (Malone 2006).

Numerous practical techniques exist for extracting collective intelligence from the behavior and beliefs of large numbers of individuals, including so-called prediction markets (as in the cancelled DARPA Policy Analysis Market, which would have allowed trading in futures contracts tied to geopolitical events in the Middle East) and "collaborative filtering," which uses statistical analysis of large data sets of previous interactions to predict future behaviors or preferences (as, for instance, in the case of websites like Netflix and Amazon, which rely on user rankings and other usage data to drive recommendations). A particularly salient example of a practical application of collective intelligence is the Page Rank algorithm underlying Google's search engine, which calculates the relative authority of a given site based on the authority of the sites that link to it, in effect extracting what the network knows about a given topic (see GRAPH THEORY). Similar network effects underpin the phenomena of "viral" content on social networking sites such as Facebook and Twitter, where decentralized coordination between large numbers of users produces emergent behaviors at the macro level.

Another practical technique harnessing digital collective intelligence is the facilitation of the production and the collation of so-called user-generated content: in a case like *Wikipedia*, the design of the system more closely approximates Lévy's vision, since users/editors are not just providing information in a decentralized fashion but also consciously co-creating the norms and structures of the online environment in which the collective intelligence finds its expression.

References and Further Reading

Arquilla, John, and David Ronfeldt. 2001. *Networks and Netwars: The Future of Terror, Crime, and Militancy*. Santa Monica, CA: RAND.

Bonabeau, Eric, Marco Dorigo, and Guy Theraulaz. 1999. *Swarm Intelligence: From Natural to Artificial Systems*. Oxford: Oxford University Press.

Deneubourg, Jean-Louis, and S. Goss. (1989). "Collective Patterns and Decision-Making." *Ethology, Ecology & Evolution* 1:295–311.

Durkheim, Émile. (1893) 1997. *The Division of Labor in Society*. New York: Simon and Schuster.

Grassé, Pierre-Paul. 1959. "La Reconstruction du nid et les Coordinations Inter-Individuelles chez *Bellicositermes Natalensis* et Cubitermes *sp*. La Theorie de la Stigmergie: Essai d'interpretation du Comportement des Termites Constructeurs." *Insect. Soc.* 6:41–80.

Hayek, Friedrich A. 1945. "The Use of Knowledge in Society." *American Economic Review* 35 (4): 519–530.

Hofstadter, Douglas. 1979. *Gödel, Escher, Bach: An Eternal Golden Braid*. New York: Basic Books.

Kelly, Kevin. 1995. *Out of Control: The New Biology of Machines, Social Systems, & the Economic World*. New York: Basic Books.

Lévy, Pierre. (1994) 1997. *Collective Intelligence: Mankind's Emerging World in Cyberspace.* Translated by Robert Bononno. New York: Plenum.

Malone, Thomas. 2006. "What Is Collective Intelligence and What Will We Do about It?" http://cci .mit.edu/about/MaloneLaunchRemarks.html.

Marx, Karl. (1857) 1993. *Grundrisse: Foundations of the Critique of Political Economy.* New York: Penguin.

Shaw, Evelyn. 1978. "Schooling Fishes." *American Scientist* 66 (2): 166–175.

Smith, Adam. 1977. *An Inquiry into the Nature and Causes of the Wealth of Nations.* Chicago: University of Chicago Press.

Surowiecki, James. 2004. *The Wisdom of Crowds.* New York: Random House.

Combinatory and Automatic Text Generation

Philippe Bootz and Christopher Funkhouser

"Text generation" in digital literature refers to processes of producing text by manipulating natural language with algorithms. This type of work emerged during a period when writers, critics, and others were newly exploring language as a system with variable properties.

Combinatory Text Generation

Combinatory generation uses linguistic structures from existing sentences to permute alternative utterances, addressing groupings of language by changing and shifting texts according to fixed rules. Combinatoric procedures can only generate short texts, such as proverbs and poems, because algorithms manage only syntax and not a work's verbal meaning; they are often used to produce free verse but are also applied to construct verse forms. Many different approaches to the task may be identified, such as the "phrase à trous" algorithm invented by the Oulipo, which methodically replaces nouns of a sentence with those taken from vocabulary lists in order to create new statements. Combinatorial generation of text dates back to the fifteenth and sixteenth centuries (in works by Jean Meschinot and Julius Scaliger) and was introduced in digital literature in 1959 with Theo Lutz's *Stochastiche Texte*, which was made with words and phrases from Franz Kafka's novel *The Castle*. In fact, until the 1980s most works of digital poetry were combinatorial generators.

Another renowned pioneering approach to combinatory text generation, Nanni Balestrini's 1961 *Tape Mark* poems, fluidly reinscribed phrases from texts by multiple authors (Lao Tzu, Paul Goldwin, and Michihito Hachiya); such reinscription later became a common trait of digital poetry. The ALAMO (Workshop of Littérature Assisted by Mathematics and Computers), a computing-oriented outgrowth of the Oulipo created by Jacques Roubaud and Paul Braffort in 1980, theorized and attempted to propagate a generative conception of literature. The ALAMO approached literature as a strictly combinatorial task, viewing computers as tools that quickly explore solutions that otherwise could not be solved by humans. The group programmed Oulipian and other methods and attempted to build general languages that authors could use. Pedro Barbosa and Abílio Cavalheiro (1996) developed the program *Syntext*, a "generator of texts" that simulates fifteen previously authored combinatory generators (including Balestrini's). *Syntext* is the first generator that used generative rules as data and not as instructions in its program; it established a difference between algorithms that generate textual material and algorithms that express this material at the level of the screen. *Syntext* demonstrated that different kinds of generation exist, and it created a bridge between generation and animation.

Brion Gysin (1995), Alison Knowles and James Tenney (1968), Jackson Mac Low (1986, 1994), and others also experimented with combinatorial writing during the 1960s. Subsequently, digital poets adapted and expanded these preliminary efforts and techniques in a variety of ways. For example, in *42 Merzgedichte* in Memoriam *Kurt Schwitters*, Mac Low employs Charles O. Hartman's programs DIASTEXT and DASTEX4, as well as Hugh Kenner and Joseph O'Rourke's TRAVESTY, to randomly select linguistic units of a poem he composed for Schwitters and then process its fragments into entirely new literary constellations. TRAVESTY requires its users to provide the input text and then permutes this text by replacing each character group in the text with another (of the same size) located elsewhere in its source; it thereby represented both an aesthetic and technical innovation in combinatoric computer poetry.

Digital combinatory text generation also explores variants of a given text. The process invokes important questions, such as who is the author: the human programmer, the person who selects the input, or the machine applying the program?

Automatic Text Generation

Automatic text generation involves building expressive units of output from separate, basal foundations of speech and was a major advancement in digital poetry. It is a rigorous practice that requires its authors and audience to redefine the notion of text and the roles of author and reader. Author-programmers must programmatically fuse disparate parts of language into sensible speech, requiring significant technological aptitude because this approach to composition is a literary proposal based on simulation, not exploration. The language generated is literally assembled to the specifications of the programmer; formal, precise programming commands are written to perform particular tasks.

More specifically, French poet Jean-Pierre Balpe (1986) invented programs for the automatic generation of literary texts in the early 1980s. The programs he has developed since then can generate infinite novels, which can even be written in the style of a given author. The algorithmic results of Balpe's programs can radically differ and are much more ambitious than combinatory generation because they use deep linguistic structures, and mathematical variables are assigned to each term in the dictionary and associated with selection rules depending on the so-called world of his novels. His programs algorithmically manipulate syntax, pragmatics (conditions for input terms), and style of generated text. In recent years, programmers such as Jim Carpenter have also managed to reflect the authorial styles of specific authors in interactive, automatically generated applications on the web.

Hartman has practiced both combinatory and automatic forms. In addition to creating DIASTEXT to automate Mac Low's "diastic" (manual) process of creating poetic work by extracting and replacing words that share the same verbal or letter patterns in a given text, he later masterfully programmed "Prose," a Python-based text generator that utilizes a personally constructed dictionary to create expertly crafted, syntactically perfect sentences. Applications such as John Cayley and Giles Perring's *Imposition*

(2007) and Nick Monfort's *Taroko Gorge* (2009) effectively perform alternative approaches to generating poems using contemporary network programming modalities on the web.

Most web-based applications at present are combinatorial. As time passes, however, distinctions between combinatory and automatic text processes have in some cases begun to dissolve due to technological capacity. The quantity of sentences with which an author can effectively populate a database, in addition to the number of shifting, interactive parameters a user can adjust within a single work, bestows on a given combinatory piece a more free-form, mutable identity akin to the output of automatically generated texts. Combinatory generation and automatic generation are the two extreme points of generated works. While each adheres to a different ideology, it is possible to mix them, and in fact such mixes occur when a work's aesthetics are routinely mechanical and also dependent on more acutely specified linguistic programming.

■ See also ALGORITHM, DIGITAL POETRY, EARLY DIGITAL ART AND WRITING (PRE-1990), ELECTRONIC LITERATURE

References and Further Reading

Balpe, Jean-Pierre. 1986. *Initiation à la génération de textes en langue naturelle.* Paris: Eyrolles.
Barbosa, Pedro, and Abílio Cavalheiro, eds. 1996. *Syntext.* Diskette. Porto: Edições Afrontamento.
Braffort, Paul. 1984. "La littérature assistée par ordinateur." *Action Poétique* 95:12–20.
Cayley, John, and Giles Perring. 2007. *Imposition.* http://programmatology.shadoof.net/index.php?p=works/impose/impepoetry.html.
Gysin, Brion. 1995. *Recordings 1960–81.* Audio CD. Perdition Plastics.
Hartman, Charles O. n.d. *PyProse.* Computer Program. http://oak.conncoll.edu/cohar/Programs.htm.
Knowles, Alison, and James Tenney. 1968. "A Sheet from 'The House,' a Computer Poem." In *Cybernetic Serendipity: The Computer and the Arts*, edited by Jasia Reichardt. London: Studio International (special issue).
Mac Low, Jackson. 1986. "PFR-3 Poems." In *Representative Works: 1938–1985.* New York: Roof Books.
———. 1994. *42 Merzgedichte in Memoriam Kurt Schwitters*, Barrytown, NY: Station Hill Press.
Montfort, Nick. 2009. *Taroko Gorge.* http://nickm.com/poems/taroko_gorge.html.

• •

Computational Linguistics
Inderjeet Mani

In the 1968 movie *2001: A Space Odyssey*, one of the protagonists was an artificially intelligent computer called HAL (for Heuristically programmed ALgorithmic computer). HAL was entirely fluent in English and was a great conversationalist. While computers today still lack the linguistic prowess of HAL (and thankfully also his cunning!), they are nevertheless able to carry out a variety of linguistically sophisticated tasks. Examples include the Google Translate system (http://translate.google.com/) and IBM's DeepQA question-answering system (Ferrucci 2011), which defeated the two human champions on a 2011 *Jeopardy!* quiz show. Such systems come from the field of computational linguistics, where computer algorithms and linguistic knowledge of one or more languages are used to construct systems that can make sense of human utterances as well as generate them. Since the 1970s, many systems have been developed to understand and generate stories (see ARTIFICIAL INTELLIGENCE, STORY GENERATION).

While great strides have been made in computational linguistics, the processing of narrative presents special challenges.

Endowing computers with linguistic capabilities means addressing the sheer variety of phenomena found across human languages. It is well known that languages differ in the way information is conveyed by words and the way they are ordered into sentences. For example, Spanish packs into each verb (by means of *morphological* inflections) a wealth of information about tense, aspect, number, person, mood (indicative, imperative, and subjunctive), and grammatical voice (active or passive). For a computer to understand a sentence of Cervantes pertaining to an attack on windmills, it will have to unpack this sort of morphological information to determine whether the attack is ongoing or has occurred already. Likewise, to generate a sentence in Spanish (or in Tamil or Turkish, which have thousands of verb inflections), it will have to choose an appropriate verb conjugation based on its ability to memorize the relevant rules. Turning to spoken language, a speech recognition system (of the sort people booking hotels routinely use over the telephone) has to extract *phonological* information, in particular identifying the sequence of linguistic sounds, or phonemes, in the speech signal, using a dictionary that lists phoneme-based pronunciations for words in that particular language. And to utter sentences aloud, a speech synthesis system has to take the words in the written utterance and pronounce them, taking into account linguistic rules for pitch, stress, and intonation.

Of course, the order of the words often conveys important aspects of meaning, so that "Margaret deceived Francis" is quite different in meaning from "Francis deceived Margaret." Systems to understand language therefore have to be able to *parse* out the structure (or *syntax*) of the sentence to figure out that in the former case it is the noun phrase Margaret that fills the role of the instigator or "agent" of the deception, while Francis is the victim or "patient" of it. Syntactic parsers are thus key tools for use in computational linguistics. Similarly, a sentence generator, on being provided with information that the agent of the past deception is Margaret and that Francis is the patient, should go ahead and generate one of the sentences "Margaret deceived Francis," "Francis was deceived by Margaret," "He was cuckolded by Margaret," and so on (see COMBINATORY AND AUTOMATIC TEXT GENERATION). Since sentences can get pretty complex, extracting the agent, patient, and so forth, or expressing them in long utterances, can be challenging, as in parsing the question "Which gun did Robert Wilson tell Francis Macomber he would have Margaret use?" (Answer from Hemingway: a Mannlicher.)

A key problem that a computational linguistics system has to deal with is ambiguity. For example, the sentence "I can fish" can refer to a rather boring factory job or to an ability to carry out a "fun" recreational activity, as a result of the ambiguity in meaning (or *semantics*) of the words "can" and "fish," as well as the corresponding syntactic ambiguities. The latter ambiguities include the ambiguity in part of speech of the word "can" as a noun or modal auxiliary, and "fish" as a noun or verb. Ambiguity in part of speech in turn results in ambiguity of syntactic structure, as to whether "can fish" is a verb phrase made up of the auxiliary "can" and the intransitive verb "fish," or instead (in the "factory job" interpretation) a verb phrase made up of the transitive verb "can" and a noun phrase made up of the noun "fish." Disambiguating the part of speech of words (using a part-of-speech tagger) can obviously be very helpful when parsing a sentence.

As the number of rules in the system increases, or when sentences get longer, the computer faces the problem of having to choose between many possible interpretations or (for generation) realizations, at different levels of linguistic structure, including phonology, morphology, syntax, and semantics. In addition, utterances don't occur in isolation, so expressions like pronouns have to be resolved to the things they refer to, and choices of referring expressions (e.g., "your apple" versus "a large red apple") have to be made based on narrative *context* (this is part of *pragmatics*; see DIALOGUE SYSTEMS).

Until the 1980s, the developers of systems used for story understanding and generation vastly underestimated the number of linguistic rules (especially for syntax, semantics, and pragmatics) required in practice, resulting in systems that were brittle, that is, that would frequently fail on new inputs. The many systems of that era could only process simple stories involving relatively short, unambiguous sentences. Then, in the 1990s, computers had become much faster and there were sufficient bodies of online linguistic data (called *corpora*) that could be used to gather statistics. For example, consider parsing. A computer can simply count how often each type of syntactic configuration is found in a corpus of sentences whose syntax has been parsed by the human. Considering our fishing examples, a sentence could be made up of noun-phrase+verb-phrase, where verb-phrase, as we have seen, can be made up of either auxiliary+intransitive-verb, or transitive-verb oun-phrase. The complete syntactic configuration for each sentence is represented in a data structure called a parse tree, and the corpus of such sentences with trees is called a treebank. A syntactic configuration is represented as a rule, which is "weighted" according to how often it appears in the treebank. Faced with two possible parse trees for the possibly new sentence "I can fish," a statistical parser would search for the most likely one, with the heaviest weighted rules.

Today, linguistic knowledge gleaned from statistical analyses of large corpora has dramatically improved the accuracy with which systems carry out various linguistic tasks, getting around the brittleness problems of the earlier era, while also providing good models of context. Systems have been developed that can read medical narratives and extract information about diseases and symptoms from them (Wang et al. 2008), summarize short stories (Kazantseva and Szpakowicz 2010), infer the order of events in a narrative (Mani 2010), and provide succinct descriptions of object configurations during a computer game (Gabsdil, Koller, and Striegnitz 2002).

A key benefit of modern computational linguistics is the ability to create an empirical subdiscipline of literary studies, going beyond the mainly word- and phrase-level analyses carried out in the field of corpus linguistics. For example, the literary scholar Franco Moretti (1999) has argued that novels set in rural communities, which reflect tightly bound social networks, have fewer characters with more conversational interactions between them, whereas urban novels reflect the looser ties of city life, resulting in more characters sharing fewer conversations. Elson, Dames, and McKeown (2010) have tested this claim by automatically extracting and analyzing conversational "social networks" from a corpus of nineteenth-century novels (including Dickens, Austen, and Conan Doyle). Here a conversational social network, similar to the ones in Facebook (www.facebook .com), is a network where the entities being connected are characters and the links between them are weighted based on the length of their conversations. Elson et al. found that not only do urban novels not contain more characters, but no correlation exists between the number of characters and amount of dialogue between them. However, they did discover a strong correlation between third-person narration and characters who were more frequently connected, suggesting that narrative voice is more crucial for conversational networks than setting.

Despite such results, computational methods that use "machine learning" rely on teams of humans marking up linguistic information in the form of treebanks, discourse banks, time banks, and so on, which is an expensive activity to carry out for texts even as long as short stories. As a result, such methods have not yet had a substantial impact on story understanding or generation systems. In addition, computers have no appreciation of literary and artistic culture and cannot infer the subtle connotations of words and other nuances of language which are hard to formalize. Even metaphor, humor, and irony, for which computational accounts have been developed, have resisted general-purpose solutions.

One key area that remains unsolved has to do with inferences about human behavior and motives, which touches on the vast undercurrent of pragmatic knowledge that underlies language use. Given E. M. Forster's famous story-exemplifying sentence "The king died and the queen died of grief," a child has no difficulty figuring out why the queen was so saddened; however, providing the computer with the knowledge to make such plot-savvy inferences is a formidable task. From the classic systems of the 1970s onward (e.g., Schank and Abelson 1977; Mueller 2006), researchers have devoted considerable attention to encoding rules for commonsense knowledge, for example, by rigorously modeling every action in a story in terms of its causes and effects, and threading these actions together into overall plans (by a character or narrator) to achieve a particular goal (Wilensky 1978; Turner 1994). However, no general-purpose repository of character plans or other such commonsense knowledge could be created. In recent years, the corpus-based approach has tried to revisit plot-level inference without constructing overall plans; for example, Goyal, Riloff, and Daumé (2010) were able to train a system to accurately infer affect states associated with events. Thus, given a sentence like "Margaret killed Francis," the computer could infer that the event outcome is bad for Francis but is positive for Margaret, assuming that she wanted to kill him. Obviously, a character's emotions can be in conflict, and this is something the model doesn't currently handle. Overall, these deeper and more interesting aspects of narrative pose enduring challenges.

In the near future, publishers may benefit considerably from some of these computational linguistics tools. Computers are now reasonably successful at essay grading (Valenti, Neri, and Cucchiarelli 2003) and "sentiment analysis" (e.g., Pang, Lee, and Vaithyanathan 2002, who classify movie reviews based on the Internet Movie Database [IMDb] archive). It should be possible to automatically flag stories for literary magazines, recommending in advance which ones to banish to the slush heap. For writers, computers will be helpful in suggesting cleverer stylistic variants for a sentence, along with offering smarter lookup of various thesauri. In the more distant future, when "plot banks" become feasible, there may be specialized literary search engines that go well beyond today's plagiarism detectors to find snippets of text that match narratological criteria for a particular style of dialogue or variety of plot.

For a more detailed introduction to computational linguistics, see Mani (2006).

References and Further Reading

Elson, David K., Nicholas Dames, and Kathleen R. McKeown. 2010. "Extracting Social Networks from Literary Fiction." *Proceedings of the 48th Annual Meeting of the Association for Computational Linguistics* (ACL'2010), 138–147. www.aclweb.org/anthology/P10-1015.

Ferrucci, David. 2011. "How Watson Works." www-03.ibm.com/innovation/us/watson/building-watson/how-watson-works.html.

Gabsdil, Malte, Alexander Koller, and Kristina Striegnitz. 2002. "Natural Language and Inference in a Computer Game." *Proceedings of the 19th International Conference on Computational Linguistics* (COLING'2002), vol. 1, 1–7. http://dx.doi.org/10.3115/1072228.1072341.

Goyal, Amit, Ellen Riloff, and Hal Daumé III. 2010. "Automatically Producing Plot Unit Representations for Narrative Text." *Proceedings of the 2010 Conference on Empirical Methods in Natural Language Processing* (EMNLP'2010), 77–86. www.aclweb.org/anthology-new/D/D10/D10-1008 .pdf.

Kazantseva, Anna, and Stan Szpakowicz. 2010. "Summarizing Short Stories." *Computational Linguistics* 36 (1): 71–109. http://dx.doi.org/10.1162/coli.2010.36.1.36102.

Mani, Inderjeet. 2006. "Computational Linguistics." In *Introduction to Language and Linguistics*, edited by Ralph Fasold and Jeff Connor-Linton, 465–492. Cambridge: Cambridge University Press.

———. 2010. *The Imagined Moment.* Lincoln: University of Nebraska Press.

Moretti, Franco. 1999. *Atlas of the European Novel, 1800–1900.* London: Verso.

Mueller, Erik T. 2006. *Commonsense Reasoning.* San Francisco: Morgan Kaufmann.

Pang, Bo, Lillian Lee, and Shivakumar Vaithyanathan. 2002. "Thumbs Up? Sentiment Classification Using Machine Learning Techniques." *Proceedings of the 2002 Conference on Empirical Methods in Natural Language Processing* (EMNLP'2002), 79–86.

Schank, Roger C., and Robert P. Abelson. 1977. *Scripts, Plans, Goals, and Understanding: An Inquiry into Human Knowledge Structures.* Hillsdale, NJ: Lawrence Erlbaum Associates.

Turner, Scott R. 1994. *The Creative Process: A Computer Model for Storytelling and Creativity.* Hillsdale, NJ: Lawrence Erlbaum Associates.

Valenti, Salvatore, Francesca Neri, and Alessandro Cucchiarelli. 2003. "An Overview of Current Research on Automated Essay Grading." *Journal of Information Technology Education* 2:319–330.

Wang, Xiaoyan, Amy Chused, Noémie Elhadad, Carol Friedman, and Marianthi Markatou. 2008. "Automated Knowledge Acquisition from Clinical Narrative Reports." *AMIA Annual Symposium* (AMIA'2008), 783–787.

Wilensky, Robert W. 1978. *Understanding Goal-Based Stories.* Yale University Computer Science Research Report.

Conceptual Writing

Darren Wershler

Conceptual writing is an umbrella term for a heterogeneous set of early twenty-first-century writing practices that respond to the implications of a networked digital milieu for the creative process, the social function of authorship, and the economy of publishing. Conceptual writing makes frequent (though not exclusive) use of compositional constraints (e.g., alphabetization, organization by syllabic length; see WRITING UNDER CONSTRAINT), which act as a means for organizing their source material—often appropriated at length from discourses that have been neglected by canonical literature (e.g., weather reports, legal transcripts, Usenet posts). Conceptual writing eschews the syntactic opacity that characterized L=A=N=G=U=A=G=E poetry, even though the former draws inspiration from many of the latter's texts.

Conceptual writing is not a formal movement or school. Largely due to the critical writing of Marjorie Perloff, the term is most frequently associated with the work of Kenneth Goldsmith (n.d., 2011) and an international network of collaborators and correspondents, including (but not limited to) derek beaulieu (2010, 2011), Caroline Bergvall (2010; Bergvall et al., forthcoming), Christian Bök (2001), Craig Dworkin (2008; Dworkin and Goldsmith 2011), Rob Fitterman (2010; Fitterman and Place 2009), Simon Morris (2005,

2007), Vanessa Place (2010), Kim Rosenfield, Nick Thurston (2006), and Darren Wershler-Henry (2000; Wershler-Henry and Kennedy 2006).

Before formulating his practice as "conceptual," Goldsmith had experimented with descriptions of his work as "uncreative," "nutritionless," and "boring," linking it to various pop and neo-avant-garde artists (especially John Cage, Jackson Mac Low, Dick Higgins, and Andy Warhol). Conceptual writing bears strong affinities to Flarf and other contemporary compositional practices (see FLARF; see especially Tan Lin's ambient poetry; see also Farrell 1999, 2000; work by Judith Goldman, Brian Kim Stefans, etc.).

■ See also ALGORITHM, DATABASE, ELECTRONIC LITERATURE

References and Further Reading

beaulieu, derek. 2010. *How to Write*. Vancouver: Talonbooks.
———. 2011. *Seen of the Crime: Essays*. Montreal: Snare Books.
Bergvall, Caroline. 2010. *Meddle English: New and Selected Texts*. Beacon: Nightboat Books.
Bergvall, Caroline, Laynie Browne, Teresa Carmody, and Vanessa Place, eds. 2012. *I'll Drown My Book: Conceptual Writing by Women*. Los Angeles: Les Figues Press.
Bök, Christian. 2001. *Eunoia*. Toronto: Coach House Books.
Dworkin, Craig. 2008. *Parse*. Berkeley: Atelos.
Dworkin, Craig, and Kenneth Goldsmith, eds. 2011. *Against Expression: An Anthology of Conceptual Writing*. Evanston, IL: Northwestern University Press.
Emerson, Lori, and Barbara Cole, eds. 2005. "Kenneth Goldsmith and Conceptual Poetics." *Open Letter* 12 (7).
Farrell, Dan. 1999. *Last Instance*. San Francisco: Krupskaya.
———. 2000. *The Inkblot Record*. Toronto: Coach House Books.
Fitterman, Rob. 2010. *Now We Are Friends*. New York: Truck Books.
Fitterman, Rob, and Vanessa Place. 2009. *Notes on Conceptualisms*. Brooklyn: Ugly Duckling Presse.
Goldsmith, Kenneth. n.d. "Kenneth Goldsmith" [links to complete texts of most major works, essays, interviews, etc.]. Electronic Poetry Center, SUNY Buffalo. http://epc.buffalo.edu/authors/goldsmith/.
———. 2011. *Uncreative Writing: Managing Language in the Digital Age*. New York: Columbia University Press.
Morris, Simon. 2005. *Re-Writing Freud*. York, UK: Information as Material.
———. 2007. *Kenneth Goldsmith: Sucking on Words*. DVD. 59 mins. Colour. York: Information as Material. Distr. Cornerhouse Manchester.
Place, Vanessa. 2010. *Tragodia 1: Statement of Facts*. Los Angeles: Blanc Press.
Thurston, Nick. 2006. *Reading the Remove of Literature*. Edited by Craig Dworkin. York, UK: Information as Material.
Wershler-Henry, Darren. 2000. *the tapeworm foundry andor the dangerous prevalence of imagination*. Toronto: Anansi.
Wershler-Henry, Darren, and Bill Kennedy. 2006. *apostrophe*. Toronto: ECW Press.

....

Copyright
Benjamin J. Robertson

Copyright is a legal sanction that grants monopoly rights to individual or corporate content producers with regard to the use of their productions. Copyright may include a producer's right to be identified as the author of her work, her right to control that work's distribution (commercial or otherwise), and her right to restrict the production of works derivative of the original. Generally, any work fixed in a tangible form (e.g., a story that is written down or a song that is recorded) is eligible for copyright protection through the positive action of the producer (who files for copyright) or by default (as in the United States, where copyright protection accrues automatically upon the production of such a work). Copyright is one branch of intellectual property law, which also includes patent, trademark, and trade secrets law.

The scope and consequence of rights granted under copyright vary from country to country. For example, unlike the United States, France recognizes the perpetual, inalienable, and imprescriptible "moral rights" of authors to be recognized as the creators of their works. Copyright law has also evolved over time in response to shifting social norms and, as this entry makes clear, technological invention and innovation. It has come to focus less on the issue of actually making copies of a copyrighted work and more on the protection of that work as a commodity. For sake of simplicity this entry mainly focuses on copyright in the contemporary United States, where copyright (and intellectual property generally) is instilled in the Constitution's Progress Clause, which grants Congress the power "to promote the Progress of Science and useful Arts, by securing for limited Times to Authors and Inventors the exclusive Right to their respective Writings and Discoveries."

The history of copyright is inextricably tied to the history of the invention and innovation of technologies of cultural production and distribution. The widespread use of the printing press by the sixteenth century led to the regulation of presses (in the sense of the actual technology rather than the sense of "publisher") for purposes of political censorship and reducing competition among printers. For example, the long title of a 1662 British law was "An Act for preventing the frequent Abuses in printing seditious treasonable and unlicensed Bookes and Pamphlets and for regulating of Printing and Printing Presses." Even earlier, the 1556 Charter of the Stationers' Company "gave the stationers the power to 'make ordinances, provisions, and statute' for the governance of 'the art or mistery of [s] tationary' as well as the power to search out illegal presses and books and things with the power of 'seizing, taking, or burning the foresaid books or things, or any of them printed or to be printed contrary to the form of any statute, act, or proclamation'" (Patterson 1993, 9). The Statute of Anne would become in 1709 the first true copyright law by granting regulatory powers to government and its courts rather than to private interests.

In the United States, the Copyright Act of 1909 came about as a means to govern the copying of piano rolls, one of the earliest forms of recorded music. This act also doubled the length of initial copyright in the United States, as established in the Copyright Act of 1790, from fourteen to twenty-eight years, thus beginning a trend of copyright extension that continues to this day.

More significantly, the 1984 case *Sony Corp. of America v. Universal City Studios, Inc.* saw the U.S. Supreme Court uphold Sony's right to continue to produce its Betamax Video Cassette Recorder against the objections of the movie industry and Motion Picture Association of America president Jack Valenti, who told a congressional committee that "the VCR is to the American film producer and the American public as the Boston strangler is to the woman home alone" (quoted in McLeod 2005, 276). The court, by a narrow 5–4 decision, held that, although the VCR could be used to infringe upon copyright, its capacity for substantial, noninfringing use made it permissible under federal law. Such use includes "time shifting," which allows an individual to record programming for future viewing.

In at least this case, the content industries' desire for strong copyright enforcement nearly had the consequence of derailing a technological innovation that would ultimately come to benefit them in the form of increased revenue from the sale of videocassettes and subsequently DVDs and Blu-ray discs. Thus, the Betamax case has become a touchstone for legal and cultural critics concerned about the regulation of creativity and innovation by an American government that appears to value the old over the new and established business models over recent ones. This issue came to a head in 2003's *Eldred v. Ashcroft*, in which lead plaintiff Eric Eldred (an Internet publisher) challenged the constitutionality of the 1998 Sonny Bono Copyright Term Extension Act, which greatly extended the copyright terms set by the Copyright Act of 1976. Eldred claimed that by retroactively extending copyright for past works Congress had violated the Progress Clause, which mandates that such monopolies should only be granted for a limited

time. Because this act was passed in part through the lobbying efforts of Disney (whose copyright on Mickey Mouse was set to expire), it became known as the Mickey Mouse Extension Act in "copyleft" circles. Critics in those circles understood it to chill prospects for future creativity by limiting access to older cultural texts. Notably, a great deal of Disney content derives from such older content, including numerous fairy tales no longer protected by copyright. For a full discussion of the Eldred case from the point of view of Eldred's attorney, see Lessig (2004).

The strong connection between copyright law and technological development continues in the digital age, and, in fact, it might be said that the stakes of debates surrounding copyright law have never been higher. As Lawrence Lessig puts it, contemporary battles over copyright constitute a "war about basic American values . . . the values of balance and measure that should limit the government's role in choosing future forms of creativity" (2002, xvi). In fact, much of the history of copyright, as described here, has become increasingly visible thanks to scholars such as Lawrence Lessig (1999, 2002, 2004), Siva Vaidhyanathan (2001), and Jessica Litman (2001), who situate the contemporary "copyright wars" surrounding peer-to-peer filesharing and other related technological inventions and innovations within and against this history.

In a largely analog world, copyright is relatively easy to enforce. Making and distributing analog copies of films, music albums, or books is a cumbersome task for individuals and tends not to lead to widespread infringement. Lessig (1999) distinguishes between physical architecture and the architecture of code, each of which has different affordances. In the present case, the architecture of the "real world" efficiently regulates behavior with regard to copyright. Books are heavy and difficult to copy; paper is expensive, as are photocopy machines. Digital media, which operate according to different architectures with different affordances and involve costs that are often negligible, make it possible for individuals to, for example, "rip" their music collections to their hard drives and share them through peer-to-peer file-sharing networks such as Napster (itself involved in significant copyright litigation in the early twenty-first century).

In response to the challenges that digital media create for strict copyright enforcement, the U.S. Congress passed the Digital Millennium Copyright Act (DMCA) in 1998, which strengthens the U.S. copyright regime by, among other things, making it illegal for potential infringers to circumvent technological barriers meant to prevent illegal copying. In other words, if a content producer "locks" her content through digital rights management or another mechanism, the owner of, for example, a DVD of that content may not bypass that lock. Critics such as Tarleton Gillespie (2007) have noted that, given the complexity of the law and its protection of such restrictions, fair use (which allows for copying such content under certain conditions, such as education) has become difficult if not impossible to practice for many individuals. As a result, a great deal of digital content is increasingly inaccessible for those who would build upon the cultural past.

The trend toward copyright "maximalism" continues to this day. In 2011, the U.S. Congress considered the Stop Online Piracy Act (SOPA), which would give the government the power to demand that Internet service providers and search engines block access to sites that in some way provide access to copyrighted material. Proponents of the bill, including the Recording Industry Association of America and the Motion Picture Association of America, stated that SOPA is necessary to encourage future cultural production and maintain the sector of the economy that relies on this production. Opponents, including websites such as *Wikipedia* and Google, stated that the proposed legislation would lead to censorship. Moreover, they claimed, blocking access to certain sites would cause significant security issues online for individuals and the nation. Debates on SOPA were delayed indefinitely in early 2012 in response to concerns raised by the bill's opponents.

The copyright wars of the digital age have consequences for nondigital works as well. For example, because copyright is the default in the United States and does not require any positive action on the part of a producer, there is no database of copyright holders. Consequently, there are many "orphaned" works—works for which no author can be identified. However, these works are more or less lost to contemporary culture as no one will distribute them for fear of litigation. In the case of volatile film stock, many works are literally decomposing because no one will archive them in more permanent formats because of the litigious culture of copyright enforcement that has sprung up since the late 1980s. In response to these problems, Creative Commons has established alternatives to copyright. Whereas conventional copyright reserves all rights for the author of a work, Creative Commons licenses reserve "some rights" at the discretion of authors. For example, such licenses might indicate that works can be used for any noncommercial purpose so long as they are attributed to the original author.

Although this entry has focused on the United States and its copyright regime, it would be a mistake to understand copyright strictly in terms of national boundaries. In addition to responding to technological change, early copyright restrictions have historically sought to protect the interests of authors in an international context. In 1893, the United International Bureaux for the Protection of Intellectual Property was established. Today, the World Intellectual Property Organization (an agency of the United Nations established in 1967), according to its Convention, "promotes the protection of intellectual property throughout the world through cooperation among States and, where appropriate, in collaboration with any other international organization." The fluid communication and distribution channels made possible by globalization and the various overlapping networks that compose the Internet and the World Wide Web will ensure that copyright will continue to be an international issue for the foreseeable future.

■ See also CRITICAL THEORY, FREE AND OPEN-SOURCE SOFTWARE, MASHUP, NETWORKING, POLITICS AND NEW MEDIA, SAMPLING, SOUND

References and Further Reading

Gillespie, Tarleton. 2007. *Wired Shut: Copyright and the Shape of Digital Culture*. Cambridge, MA: MIT Press.
Lessig, Lawrence. 1999. *Code and Other Laws of Cyberspace*. New York: Basic Books.

———. 2002. *The Future of Ideas: The Fate of the Commons in a Connected World.* New York: Vintage.

———. 2004. *Free Culture: How Big Media Uses Technology and the Law to Lock Down Culture and Control Creativity.* New York: Penguin.

Litman, Jessica. 2001. *Digital Copyright: Protecting Intellectual Property on the Internet.* Amherst, NY: Prometheus Books.

McLeod, Kembrew. 2005. *Freedom of Expression: Overzealous Copyright Bozos and Other Enemies of Creativity.* New York: Doubleday.

Patterson, L. Ray. 1993. "Copyright and 'the Exclusive Right' of Authors." *Journal of Intellectual Property* 1 (1): 1–48.

Vaidhyanathan, Siva. 2001. *Copyrights and Copywrongs: The Rise of Intellectual Property and How It Threatens Creativity.* New York: New York University Press.

··

Critical Editions in the Digital Age
Claire Clivaz and David Hamidović

Western culture has been concerned with the critical transmission and study of texts at least since the third century BCE: a system of critical commentary with obelisks (daggers) was used by Zenodotus, the first superintendent of the library of Alexandria, to annotate the Homeric *Iliad* and *Odyssey*. In the third century CE, this system was adapted by the Christian author Origen, who produced the *Hexapla*, an impressive critical edition comparing six versions of the Old Testament in different languages. This was the beginning of an interest in producing critical editions of print or manuscript texts which has never declined.

Digital critical editions continue this tradition, since "writing systems, print technology, and now digital encoding license a set of markup conventions and procedures (algorithms) that facilitate the self-reflexive operations of human communicative action" (Buzzetti and McGann 2006, 69). While Vannevar Bush imagined vast electronic libraries as early as 1945, literary text encoding is generally considered to date back to 1949, when Father Roberto Busa began using IBM punched-card equipment for the *Index Thomisticus* (Schreibman, Siemens, and Unsworth 2004). A list of "Literary Works in Machine-Readable Form" was published in 1966 (Carlson 1967). In the late sixties and early seventies machine-readable versions of classical works were created, including the Bible and the complete works of Plato. Classics were a particularly fertile field, producing the *Thesaurus Linguae Graecae Online*, an electronic version of virtually every surviving ancient Greek text from 800 BCE to 600 CE, or the *Perseus Digital Library*, which includes texts and archaeological objects and sites, as well as secondary materials such as a lexicon and an encyclopedia (Solomon 1993).

The 1960s, 1970s, and 1980s saw extensive development of document markup systems. One should distinguish between sets of markup tags for objects of content (such as HTML, XHTML, TEI, and DocBook) and metalanguages for defining such markup languages (such as SGML and XML). The consortium Text Encoding Initiative (TEI) was created in 1987 to coordinate the efforts of electronic editions in the humanities (see DIGITAL HUMANITIES): dozens of scholars collaborated in creating common guidelines, which were fully published for the first time in 2002. After HTML, TEI seems to be the most extensively used SGML/XML text encoding system in scholarly applications. Other projects explore alternative ways, such as Project Gutenberg. Based on a volunteer ethos, this project is conducted by people distrusting all encoding schemes and "believing that the lack of encoding will better allow e-texts to survive changes in hardware, operating systems, and application software. . . . Little can be said for the accuracy of the transcriptions, for there is no central editorial control" (Willett 2004, 244). As of 2013, 42,000 free e-books were gathered in this project. Since highly controlled encoding systems remain expensive and elitist, one can expect literary encoding to explore many different options and to keep evolving in the coming years.

Digital markup is a self-reflexive operation, which can be compared to the work of a modern editor annotating a medieval text by adding diacritical marks to it, such as punctuation. But, as Cerquiglini observed as early as 1989, digital critical editions echo the conception of manuscript culture that preceded the age of print: "Electronic writing, in its mobility, produces the variance of medieval artworks. The computer rediscovers a path leading back in time, beyond Modernity, to an ancient literature whose trace had been erased by print" (1989, 116). Modernity established the reign of the printed critical edition, which uses diverse methods, such as stemmatics (the humanistic discipline that attempts to reconstruct the transmission of a text on the basis of relations between the various surviving manuscripts) or eclecticism (a methodology based on the choices of the modern editor and not on a preferred manuscript), and postulates a single authoritative "original" state of the work, carefully created by a single auctorial voice. As electronic textuality was growing up, medievalists developed a new conception of the variability and malleability of texts. In 1972, Paul Zumthor proposed the notion of *mouvance*, and in 1989, Bernard Cerquiglini wrote a book in praise of the variant. As Buzzetti and McGann observe, "Far from stabilizing the text, the markup actually mobilizes it. . . . Markup is essentially ambivalent and sets forth self-reflexive ambiguous aspects of the text, which can produce structural shifts and make it unstable and mobile" (2006, 65). Nowadays medievalists are often at the forefront of the development of digital critical editions, as demonstrated by the online review *Perspectives Médiévales* and by the new models of digital critical editions collected in *Textes en Liberté* (see Hardy 2009, which extends to medieval music). For medieval studies, the most important digital developments are lexical textual databases (see *Le Nouveau Corpus d'Amsterdam*), as well as the possibility of coordinating lexical and editorial work (Kunstmann 2012).

But much more can be said about the potential of the digital critical editions. They can implement the social-text editing approach promoted by McKenzie (1999), whose central idea was that bibliographical objects are basically social objects. Insofar as the digital can encode and transmit any kind of media object, such as music, pictures, and text, through a uniform electronic procedure, it develops ever new possibilities that transform the notion of textuality. The journal *Digital Philology*, which started in 2012, intends to present examples of philology using any kind of document available. Multimedia and hyperlinks create digital spaces through which readers can break their own paths and retrieve contents previously scattered among separate kinds of documents and artifacts.

The vast potentialities of digital systems make one wonder about the future evolution of critical editions of the New Testament, a collection of texts containing more than 5,700 Greek manuscripts and thousands in other ancient languages such as Coptic, Latin, Ethiopian, Georgian, Syriac, and Arabic. A deep transformation of this critical edition in the digital age is on its way, with institutional networks including notably the INTF (Münster, Germany), ITSEE (Birmingham, United Kingdom), and the CSNTM (Plano, Texas). The *Codex Sinaiticus* online, one of the most important projects in this area, demonstrates that the distinction between facsimile/diplomatic edition and critical edition is no longer tenable in digital culture. New Testament scholars such as Parker (2003), Schmid (2012), and Clivaz (2011) have advocated for many years the creation of an open-ended and multilingual New Testament edition, with an interactive critical apparatus. Lively Internet discussion forums in the field suggest the necessity of a collaborative work to produce a new digital edition of such a vast corpus of texts. A digital New Testament would probably require the adoption of a "versioning perspective," that is, the perspective of the history of readings, over an archival conception of critical edition. This is the approach implemented in the *Homer Multitext* project, a database that devotes equal attention to each manuscript. This approach suggests that in the future it could be necessary to quote the *Iliad* by verse number from a specific manuscript. What these examples show is that the notions of *critical edition* and of *textuality* are themselves subject to further evolution.

To this date, Old Testament digital editions consist mainly of software tools and of digitalized old manuscripts. The biblical softwares BibleWorks and Accordance make it possible to display Old Testament versions in ancient and modern languages on the same screen. The complete version of the softwares remains, however, very expensive; this prevents a wider distribution among scholars. Other texts have been added to the complete version, such as *targumim*, sectarian Qumran texts, treatises of Philo of Alexandria, books of Flavius Josephus, different Apocrypha, works of Origen, and Patristic texts. This technology juxtaposes texts normally known only in codices with texts found in modern books, and it is starting to integrate different manuscripts, such as the Leningrad Codex and Aleppo Codex, which are among the oldest biblical codices. The digitization of other Jewish texts, such as the Dead Sea Scrolls, seeks to promote an interactivity around their corpora that goes beyond what is to be expected from a simple electronic edition.

Collaboration between Israel Antiquities Authority and Google Inc. aims to digitalize every one of the 940 Dead Sea Scroll manuscripts and to make them available on a website. The idea is to allow everybody to see (and perhaps to study) them. The project can be understood as an answer to the public's long-standing fascination with these documents. Anybody who knows Hebrew, Aramaic, and Greek, the languages of the scrolls, will be able to check the manuscripts. Another purpose is to improve the reading of the fragmentary scrolls through the latest digital techniques, such as infrared pictures for the darkest fragments. Since the discovered fragments quickly deteriorate, despite the impressive work of the Israel Museum, the most important goal of the project for the scientific community is the preservation of the manuscripts (see PRESERVATION). Another major project of this kind is the Friedberg Genizah Project website, which gives access to another fantastic archaeological discovery: the *genizah* (i.e., depository) of the Old Cairo synagogue, found in the nineteenth century. The entire corpus of manuscripts and related materials is available with pictures and their identifications, together with descriptions, catalogs, transcriptions, translations, and bibliographical references. The website looks like an exhaustive database on the Cairo *genizah*. This digital edition has another purpose than the Digital Dead Sea Scrolls project: here, the goal is not to communicate with a large public, since access to the database is restricted to the scientific community, but to collect the complete scientific information concerning each manuscript.

■ See also ARCHIVE

References and Further Reading

Buzzetti, Dino, and Jerome McGann. 2006. "Electronic Textual Editing: Critical Editing in a Digital Horizon." In *Electronic Textual Editing*, edited by Lou Burnard, Katherine O'Brien O'Keeffe, and John Unsworth, 53–73. New York: Modern Language Association of America. www.tei-c.org/About/Archive_new/ETE/Preview/mcgann.xml.

Carlson, Gary. 1967. "Literary Works in Machine-Readable Form." *Computer and the Humanities* 1 (3): 75–102.

Cerquiglini, Bernard. 1989. *Éloge de la variante*, Paris: Éditions du Seuil.

Clivaz, Claire. 2011. "The New Testament at the Time of the Egyptian Papyri. Reflections Based on P^{12}, P^{75} and P^{126} (P. Amh. 3b, P. Bod. XIV–XV and PSI 1497)." In *Reading New Testament Papyri in Context—Lire les papyrus du Nouveau Testament dans leur contexte (BETL 242)*, edited by Claire Clivaz and Jean Zumstein, with Jenny Read-Heimerdinger and Julie Paik, 15–55. Leuven, Belgium: Peeters.

Hamidović, David. 2012. "In Quest of the Lost Text. From Electronic Edition to Digital Edition of Dead Sea Scrolls." In *Lire demain. Des manuscrits antiques à l'ère digitale*, edited by Claire Clivaz, Jérôme Meizoz, François Vallotton, and Joseph Verheyden, 155–166. Lausanne, Swizterland: PPUR.

Hardy, Ineke. 2009. "Les chansons attribuées au trouvère picard Raoul de Soissons. Edition critique." PhD diss., Ottawa University. www.uottawa.ca/academic/arts/lfa/activites/textes/ineke/index.htm.

Kunstmann, Pierre. 2012. "L'électronique à l'aide de l'éditeur: miracle ou mirage? Bilan de quatorze années de travaux au LFA." *Perspectives Médiévales* 34. http://peme.revues.org/2245. doi: 10.4000/peme.2245.

Lange, Armin. 1993. *Computer-Aided Text-Reconstruction and Transcription*-CATT Manual. Tübingen, Germany: Mohr-Siebeck.

McKenzie, Donald F. 1999. *Bibliography and the Sociology of Texts*. Cambridge: Cambridge University Press.

Parker, David. 2003. "Through a Screen Darkly: Digital Texts and the New Testament." *Journal for the Study of the New Testament* 25 (4): 395–411.

Schmid, Ulrich. 2012. "Transmitting the New Testament Online." In *Text Comparison and Digital Creativity: The Production of Presence and Meaning in Digital Text Scholarship*, edited by Wido van Peursen, Ernst D. Thoutenhoofd, and Adriaan van der Weel, 189–205. Leiden, Netherlands: Brill.

Schreibman, Susan, Ray Siemens, and John Unsworth, eds. 2004. *A Companion to Digital Humanities*. Oxford: Blackwell. www.digitalhumanities.org/companion/.

Solomon, Jon, ed. 1993. *Accessing Antiquity*. Tucson: University of Arizona Press.

Stoltz, Michael. 2003. "New Philology and New Phylogeny: Aspects of a Critical Electronic Edition of Wolfram's *Parzival*." *Literary and Linguistic Computing* 18 (2): 139–150.

Willett, Perry. 2004. "Electronic Texts: Audiences and Purpses." In *A Companion to Digital Humanities*, edited by Susan Schreibman, Ray Siemens, and John Unsworth, 240–253. Oxford: Blackwell.

Websites

Aleppo Codex: www.aleppocodex.org/

Codex Sinaiticus: www.codexsinaiticus.org

CSNTM: www.csntm.org/

Digital Dead Sea Scrolls: http://dss.collections.imj.org.il/; www.deadseascrolls.org.il/

Digital Philology: http://muse.jhu.edu/journals/digital_philology/

Homer Multitext Project: www.homermultitext.org/

INTF: http://egora.uni-muenster.de/intf/index_en.shtml

ITSEE: www.birmingham.ac.uk/research/activity/itsee/index.aspx

Leningrad Codex: www.echoofeden.com/digest/slaveofone/2010/04/28/leningrad-codex-facsimile-online-toc/

Le Nouveau Corpus d'Amsterdam: www.uni-stuttgart.de/lingrom/stein/corpus/#nca
Old Caire genizah: www.genizah.org/
The Perseus Digital Library: www.perseus.tufts.edu/hopper/
Perspectives Médiévales: http://peme.revues.org/
Project Gutenberg: www.gutenberg.org/
Text Encoding Initiative: www.tei-c.org/index.xml
Textes en Liberté: www.lfa.uottawa.ca/tel.html
Thesaurus Linguae Graecae Online: www.tlg.uci.edu/
West Semitic inscriptions: www.inscriptifact.com/

Critical Theory

David Golumbia

Humanistic research and the modern university are grounded in the belief that the academic mission includes exploring all sides of human phenomena, the good with the bad. In its most general sense the phrase *critical theory* names that side of humanities research which sees its role as subjecting various parts of the human world to *critique*: toward seeing how such phenomena fit into negative or problematic parts of contemporary culture, how problems are perpetuated and/or reflected in cultural and media objects, and how media do and do not provide avenues both for the identification of problems and potentially for solutions to them.

The phrase *critical theory* may include this general sense of critique while indicating two more specific foci. The first and broader of the two is any analysis of society and culture that draws on the long history of theoretical work informed by Marxist critique. The second, narrower meaning, a subset of the broader meaning, takes in that part of Marxist theory specifically associated with the so-called Frankfurt School. The Frankfurt School is the colloquial term used today for the Frankfurt Institute for Social Research, established in the early 1920s by Marxist social critics and philosophers, among whom the preeminent members and associates are Theodor Adorno, Max Horkheimer (whose works explicitly use the phrase *critical theory*), Herbert Marcuse, Erich Fromm, and more recently Jürgen Habermas.

The work of critical theory often seen as exemplary is Horkheimer and Adorno's *Dialectic of Enlightenment* ([1944] 1969), whose title derives from Marx's method of dialectical materialism. The work simultaneously derives from Immanuel Kant's notion of critique (as reflected in the titles of his three great philosophical works, the 1781 *Critique of Pure Reason*, the 1788 *Critique of Practical Reason*, and the 1790 *Critique of Judgment*) and of Enlightenment itself (especially his 1784 essay "What Is Enlightenment?"), a variety of Marxist models, and the forms of Freudian psychological theory practiced at the Frankfurt School. The work is sometimes understood as pessimistic, in that Adorno and Horkheimer take Enlightenment to have both negative and positive aspects, so that "Myth turns into Enlightenment, and nature into mere objectivity," and that "Enlightenment behaves toward things as a dictator toward men. He knows them in so far as he can manipulate them. The man of science knows things in so far as he can make them. In this way their potentiality is turned to his own ends" ([1944] 1969, 9).

As such, *Dialectic of Enlightenment* is a work with deep relevance for the age of the digital, in that the development of technology and the relationship of technology and media form central parts of its substance. In its most famous chapter, "The Culture Industry: Enlightenment as Mass Deception," Adorno and Horkheimer argue that "the basis on which technology acquires power over society is the power of those whose economic hold over society is greatest. A technological rationale is the rationale of domination itself. It is the coercive nature of society alienated from itself" ([1944] 1969, 121). At its heart the critique is most clearly directed at the kinds of mass culture that were especially prominent in the mid-twentieth-century United States and Europe, and it offers a trenchant analysis of the film industry, mass production of cultural products, and the then-nascent broadcast media industries. Its relevance for newer forms of digital media, including apparently or nominally individualized media forms such as social media, has been explored less fully, despite the many clear consequences of the work for contemporary forms.

Perhaps because of the focus of critical theory proper on mass culture, writers on digital media have not taken up the work as directly as they have other methods, such as more optimistic forms of cultural studies that focus on individual resistance as an aspect of media consumption. Nevertheless, one can find a persistent strain of writers drawing very generally on the heritage of critical theory and drawing out its implications for and applications to digital media. Among the most direct heirs to the spirit if not the letter of the work of Adorno and Horkheimer are the British social theorists Kevin Robins and Frank Webster, who in their 1999 *Times of the Technoculture* provide a broad survey of digital phenomena which refuses the presumption that things have changed so radically as to make unnecessary the kinds of critique offered by Adorno and Horkheimer. Among the ideas sometimes thought to be outmoded by the digital but embraced by Robins and Webster are those of propaganda, or the distribution of deceptive ideas by the powerful in order to enforce social control over the less powerful; while digital enthusiasts insist that "the (ideal) role of information and communications in democracies is fundamentally and essentially different from their role in totalitarian states," Robins and Webster insist that "in the nation state of late capitalism, information management is inherently at risk of being totalitarian" (1999, 144).

In a related mode, Robins and Webster draw attention to the tight connections between militarization and the proliferation of the digital, noting that the military has demanded "an anonymous and unexaminable, national and world-wide, web of surveillance and transmission of messages" (1999, 162), that the "surveillance machine is not only directed against external enemies . . . [but] on trade unionists, CND [Campaign for Nuclear Disarmament] activists, educationalists and media personnel," and that "security services also have access on request to a vast array of data banks, including the Police National Computer, Inland Revenue records, British Telecom files, and data held by the Department of Health and Human Security"—in sum, "In the name of security, state surveillance has become a pandemic, and even normative, feature of modern society" (1999, 163). Written before the advent of social media, these words can only have become truer with open National Security State access (both with and without judicial warrant) to almost all existing forms of electronic communication.

Robins and Webster further attend to those effects of digitization on education which tend to maximize the influence of already-entrenched forms of power. They note that "more and more governments regard higher education . . . as a site of 'human capital.' . . . Such an approach accords with a great deal of analysis which emphasizes the emergence of a new post-Fordist paradigm" (1999, 202), and that what the network theorist Manuel Castells calls the "self-programmability" of informational labor is closely tied to the view that universities exist not to create a politically aware citizenry but "to develop flexibility amongst students as a means of appearing attractive to potential employers" (1999, 205). Drawing on Michel Foucault's adumbration of Jeremy Bentham's notion of the socially central spectatorial position as Panopticism, they argue that a "generalized Panopticism operates through individual, and ultimately social, interiorization of social control" based in part on "a vulnerable sense of visibility, such that these subjects come to 'watch themselves,' to exercise power over their own selves . . . [that] also entails the introjection of procedures and behaviors—ways of acting, of speaking, of thinking—appropriate to a disciplinary institution" (1999, 180), all of which have potential special import for social media such as Facebook and Twitter (see SOCIAL NETWORK SITES [SNSs], TWITTER, TUMBLR, AND MICROBLOGGING). Robins and Webster see developments in digital and information technology as part of an ongoing series of revisions of broad academic and intellectual expectations toward what they call "informational progressivism," which they consider "a partial, a misguided, and also a complacent vision" (1999, 224). In its stead, they "suggest that the narrative of what is happening in the field of knowledge might be told from an entirely different perspective—from the perspective of the world whose reality we are being invited to abandon" (1999, 224).

Among the works closest in spirit to that of the original critical theorists with direct application to digital media is *Critique of Information* (2002) by the Goldsmiths sociologist and cultural theorist Scott Lash. Lash expands on the notion of ideology critique associated with the Frankfurt School to a notion appropriate for the digital age which he calls *informationcritique*. Lash notes the existence of two modes of critique: first, "the critique of the particular through the universal . . . the sort of critique we have in Habermas, in which the particularism of 'strategic rationality' is criticized from the universalism of communicative rationality" (2002, 6), a critique that Lash suggests "is difficult in the information age because of the very speed and immediacy of sociocultural processes." Second, "the more widespread notion of critique," he writes, "is the critique of the universal-particular couple itself," which "rejects propositional logic as the space of 'the same,' and operates instead from a critical space of 'the other.'" Rejecting such dualisms even further, Lash writes that the " 'out there' and 'in here' no longer make sense in the information age's Nietzschean problematics of immanence"; "in the age of general informationalization, critique itself must become informational. . . . With the disappearance of a constitutive outside, informationcritique must be inside of information. Critique, and the texts of Critical Theory, must be part and parcel of this general informationalization" (2002, 10). Lash's is the most abstract of recent extensions of critical theoretical methods into the world of the digital.

Nick Dyer-Whitford, among the most persistent and thoroughgoing Marxist critics of digital technology (see especially his 1999 *Cyber-Marx*), has produced in collaboration with Greig de Peuter the signal work of critical theory applied to what is arguably the most dominant form of digital media, namely, video and computer games. Their *Games of Empire* defends the thesis that "video games are a paradigmatic media of Empire" (2009, xv), in which the notion of Empire emerges both from its neo-Marxian formulation by Michael Hardt and Antonio Negri (in their 2000 *Empire*) and from more traditional Marxist and postcolonial perspectives on the worldwide extent of global capital. Dyer-Whitford and de Peuter take issue with the existing strain of video game criticism focusing on formal aspects of gameplay, known as *ludology*, to focus instead on cultural and economic aspects of the worlds of virtual gameplay and their intersection with existing circuits of economic and political power (see LUDUS AND PAIDIA).

Dyer-Whitford and de Peuter develop instead the concept of "immaterial labor," forms of knowledge work and digital labor that include traditional work practices but "extending to everyday life activities that are productive but nonetheless unpaid" (2009, 32). "Hardwired into the category of immaterial labor," they argue, "is the premise that resistance actively alters the course of capitalist development." Examining both the production practices at and reception of the works produced by the major game company Electronic Arts, they note that "despite all the talk of creativity and innovation, EA's production facilities tend much more to a neo-Fordist, re-Taylorized disciplining of the cognitariat" (2009, 58). They explore the development of gaming consoles such as the PlayStation and particularly Microsoft's Xbox, which they describe as "a brutally bulky black box with a lurid green light" that "brandished hard-core appeal. . . . Being hard-core is to control the controls with a tacit, tactile knowledge that makes play easy, fast, and smooth" (2009, 81). Noting that the Xbox Live community "rapidly became (in)famous for an online taunt culture of aggressive sexist, racist, and homophobic insults, including ritualized ingame sexualized humiliations such as 'teabagging' falling Halo opponents" (2009, 82), they also point out that "hacker practices that lie at the base of gaming are a modern form of nomadism" (2009, 84) (see GAMES AND COMMUNITY).

Dyer-Whitford and de Peuter are especially attentive to the military origin of most video game technology and its close association with even the most contemporary video games and game systems. "The best directs of remote-controlled armed aerial drones such as the Predator and Reaper now crucial to the US war in Central Asia are apparently not air force pilots but hard-core video gamers, who, installed in Virginia or Nevada, controller in hand and monitoring multiple screens virtually, deliver actual attacks on villages in Afghanistan and Pakistan" (2009, 121). They develop Michel Foucault's now-popular notion of *biopower* to examine perhaps the single most influential video game, Blizzard Entertainment's *World of Warcraft* (*WoW*), showing that managing *WoW* and other massively multiplayer online games (MMOGs) like it "is an exercise in administering 'life itself'—or at least a 'second life.' It requires recruiting player populations, regulating the spawn cycles of NPCs [nonplayer characters], terraforming digital landscapes, and shaping the 'anatomo-politics' of bizarre creatures while keeping all under panoptic surveillance and disallowing, by account suspension, the life of insubordinate subjects" (2009, 126). "Biopower is about the control of populations," they write, "and nothing more clearly reveals MMOGs as case studies in biopower than the prodigious population-measuring exercises they incite" (2009, 128), up to and including the maintenance of two factions, the Alliance and the Horde, who must remain in perpetual war for the property's overall success. Citing Foucault (2003), they note that "war is intrinsic to Foucault's theory of biopower, which, he says, depends on the 'maintenance of war as a primal and basic state of affairs'; sovereign control of populations is facilitated by a 'general process of war'; and in particular by the sustained hostilities between racial groups, 'a war between races,' which functions as a regulative instrument of power" (2009, 129).

Dyer-Whitford and de Peuter look closely at the hugely popular *Grand Theft Auto* (*GTA*) series of games, noting the centrality of the city to Empire and thus drawing attention not to "the game's inspiration to individual instances of criminal mayhem but the relation of its virtualities to the structural violence of Empire, that is, the systemic patterns of inequality and marginalization inherent to global capital, of which violence and crime are often only symptomatic" (2009, 156). Writing of a recent iteration in the game family, *GTA IV*, they argue that "it is, in fact, vital to the ideological consistency of the games' demonic satire that brutalization, racism, and greed be ubiquitous. In GTA IV a prominent theme is that of the poor exploiting the very poor. There may be other options; but *you can't play them*—and that is what makes GTA a game of Empire" (2009, 180) (see INTERACTIVITY).

Dyer-Whitford and de Peuter are sensitive not just to the reach of Empire but to the claims of both theorists and game enthusiasts alike that certain forms of resistance are not just possible but produced by and within gaming environments. "Contra enthusiasts for game 'empowerment,'" though, they argue that "interactivity does not mean virtual play is free from ideology; rather, it intensifies the sense of free will necessary for ideology to work really well. Players, of their own choice, rehearse socially stipulated subjectivities" (2009, 192). Drawing close parallels with the work of Adorno and Horkheimer, they note,

> Whereas the old broadcast media of industrial capital rather obviously (and often not very successfully) exhorted audiences to specific subject positions, interactive media manifest a more flexible order where users of their own initiative adopt the identities required by the system. In this sense, games are indeed exemplary media of an order that demands not just the obedience of assembly-line worker but also the mandatory self-starting participation of immaterial laborers and global migrants. Empire only wins when played by multitude. But this mode of internalized media discipline, while potentially far more powerful than old-fashioned indoctrination, is also risker. Shaping subjectivity is an ongoing process; people are exposed to various machines of socialization and contain multiple aspects, some of which may be surprisingly activated. Moreover, to be truly involving, a game often has to include some "bad" subject positions, renegade options, outlaw possibilities, even if the logic of play often tends to their being unattractive to play or unlikely to win. (2009, 193)

Such thoughtful and incisive analysis shows that critical theory as a general perspective continues to have much to offer study of digital phenomena. A persistent if small group of writers heavily influenced by Marxist and neo-Marxian approaches continue to probe successfully at the world of the digital. Vincent Mosco's *The Digital Sublime* (2005) and David Golumbia's *The Cultural Logic of Computation* (2009) explore a variety of ways in which fictions, theories, and thoughts about the digital and mind-sets unique to it pervade contemporary culture and make ever more available the kinds of instrumental reason to which Adorno and Horkheimer, as well as more recent critical theorists, draw continued attention. In *Internet and Society* (2003) Christian Fuchs offers perhaps the most direct update of Adorno and Horkheimer for the digital age, arguing that much of their approach to the social world in general can be extended without breaking to the realm of digital media. The U.S. critic Mark Poster has applied work from a number of prominent strains of literary and critical theory, including work influenced by the Frankfurt School, as well as poststructuralist theory, to the realm of the digital, especially in his *The Mode of Information* (1990). A persistent strain of critical thought about the Internet concerns the ubiquity of surveillance; one leading critic of surveillance technologies, David Lyon (see his 2007 *Surveillance Studies* among an impressive oeuvre on the topic), draws heavily on Frankfurt School methodologies and theorists in his articulation of the many critical issues raised by society-wide surveillance technologies. Armand Mattelart, a leading, Marxist-influenced critic of communications technologies in general who has also produced several important works critiquing informatic culture, has recently offered a volume specifically devoted to surveillance technologies, *The Globalization of Surveillance* (2010). Also of note is the thoughtful work of Jodi Dean, who draws on both the economic and psychological aspects of critical theory in her interrogation of informational culture *tout court* and its twin emphasis on privacy and openness (*Publicity's Secret*, 2002) and on the culture of blogs and blogging (*Blog Theory*, 2010).

■ See also BLOGS, POLITICS AND NEW MEDIA

References and Further Reading

Dean, Jodi. 2002. *Publicity's Secret: How Technoculture Capitalizes on Democracy*. Ithaca, NY: Cornell University Press.

———. 2010. *Blog Theory: Feedback and Capture in the Circuits of Drive*. London: Polity Press.

Dyer-Whitford, Nick. 1999. *Cyber-Marx: Cycles and Circuits of Struggle in High-Technology Capitalism*. Urbana: University of Illinois Press.

Dyer-Whitford, Nick, and Greig de Peuter. 2009. *Games of Empire: Global Capitalism and Video Games*. Minneapolis: University of Minnesota Press.

Foucault, Michel. 2003. *Society Must Be Defended: Lectures at the College de France, 1975–76*. New York: Picador.

Fuchs, Christian. 2008. *Internet and Society: Social Theory in the Information Age*. London: Routledge.

Golumbia, David. 2009. *The Cultural Logic of Computation*. Cambridge, MA: Harvard University Press.

Hardt, Michael, and Antonio Negri. 2000. *Empire*. Cambridge, MA: Harvard University Press.

Horkheimer, Max, and Theodor Adorno. (1944) 1969. *Dialectic of Enlightenment*. New York: Continuum.

Lash, Scott. 2002. *Critique of Information*. London: SAGE.

Lyon, David. 2007. *Surveillance Studies: An Overview*. London: Polity Press.

Mattelart, Armand. 2010. *The Globalization of Surveillance*. London: Polity Press.

Mosco, Vincent. 2005. *The Digital Sublime: Myth, Power, and Cyberspace*. Cambridge, MA: MIT Press.

Poster, Mark. 1990. *The Mode of Information: Poststructuralism and Social Context*. Chicago: University of Chicago Press.

Robins, Kevin, and Frank Webster. 1999. *Times of the Technoculture: From the Information Society to the Virtual Life*. London: Routledge.

Crowdsourcing
Klaus-Peter Speidel

The term *crowdsourcing* was coined by Jeff Howe (2006) in an article published by *Wired*. While Howe chose the term polemically, associating it with "outsourcing" and the idea of cheap labor, it rapidly became the standard designation for initiatives where large groups of people execute tasks that are traditionally performed by an individual or a small team, often with a high level of expertise. As this definition implies, crowdsourcing is not limited to specific fields, and the openness of the definition may be one reason for the tremendous success of the concept and practice in recent years.

Another reason is the fact that it perfectly connects to the contemporary myth of the guy in a garage, the lonely inventor, the underdog or nerd, who accomplishes great things through genius and hard work alone. As a matter of fact, one of crowdsourcing's major promises is its radical egalitarianism: you and I can take part in a crowdsourcing initiative, and our contributions will be judged without distinction of person, origin, training, and credentials. In crowdsourcing at its purest single transactions of specific solutions replace reputation-based recruitment and partnerships.

Narratives play an important part in the fantasies that surround crowdsourcing. The Goldcorp Challenge, initiated by a Canadian mining company that wanted to find new gold in an old mine but didn't know where to look, is one of the cases that made crowdsourcing famous. In 2000, Goldcorp's CEO Rob McEwen decided to take a very radical step: the company released a large amount of data about the Redlake mine on the Internet and offered to distribute a total reward of $575,000 among those who would point to the right spots to dig for gold. This openness is typical of companies that use crowdsourcing. The methodology opposes traditional models of corporate management, based on secrecy and in-house research. It therefore contributes to the positive image of progressive and open organizations, and many competitions are in fact paid for by corporate marketing. In other words, some companies are more interested in the "buzz" of the event than the actual results, which are then never implemented. This was not Goldcorp's case. The company had taken a risk and was rewarded: drilling in four of the five spots indicated by the winners, Goldcorp was able to find more than $1 billion worth of gold. Its cost per ounce went down from $360 in 1996 to $59 in 2001 (see Tischler 2002). Cases like this, the Netflix Challenge with its award of $1 million, or NASA's Space Glove Challenge, where two engineers solved a problem a large team of NASA researchers had been stuck with for years, explain why crowdsourcing is such a *fascinandum*. Its advantage for those who launch an initiative is clear too: they access various original ideas or potential solutions, many of which approach their question from new perspectives. In the end, they only pay for what they find most useful. Organizing its Centennial Challenges, NASA has been using the approach since 2005, offering about $10 million per year in reward money.

But while the great stories make for great press, the fact is that crowdsourcing now happens on a daily basis, and the micropayments for simple tasks like those performed on Amazon Mechanical Turk probably add up to more than those paid for the big ideas. Goldcorp's CEO McEwen had been directly inspired by the way the Linux open-source operating system had been built by a large community of contributors (see FREE AND OPEN-SOURCE SOFTWARE). In fact, *Wikipedia* (see WIKI WRITING); Threadless, which sells T-shirts that have been designed by its users; istockphoto, where anyone can offer royalty-free photographs for sale; and Quirky, where new products can be designed by anybody, are other famous examples of constant crowdsourcing. It could even be argued that Google's ranking for websites is based on (implicit) crowdsourcing: people's click and link behavior (see LINKING STRATEGIES) shows Google which websites are on target for certain keywords.

One of crowdsourcing's recent applications has been the funding of projects such as movie, album, or website production. Through crowdfunding a start-up can now do without an investment firm, and a band doesn't need a record label any more. With less commercial pressure, this method has been hailed as truly liberating. Anyone can submit a project and find the funds. Crowdfunding democratizes funding where crowdsourcing democratized access to problems.

There are now multiple models and intermediaries that act as agents between solution seekers and problem solvers in a variety of fields. They replace the trust that was needed in traditional partnerships and help to solve the predicament that is linked to selling ideas: as long as you don't precisely know what I have to offer, you can't pay me, because you don't know if it really is a solution. But once I reveal my solution, you don't have any incentive to pay me anymore. Where the traditional model was based on trust and reputation and thus only very few people had access to the most pressing problems of large organizations, a gifted student can now see many of them, submit solutions, and earn tens of thousands of dollars. In innovation studies, crowdsourcing has been recognized as a way to increase serendipity, the chance to find a solution where you wouldn't have looked for it, and lateral thinking, approaching a problem from a new perspective. Open access to challenges frequently leads to very creative solution approaches. In the Netflix Challenge, an unemployed psychologist from London was first able to get to results that most teams from the world's top universities hadn't been able to achieve (Ellenberg 2008).

While copywriting, proofreading, marketing, and R & D are now crowdsourced, not everything is really as golden as the famous success stories make it seem. In many cases, the only reward for a contribution is the pleasure of participating in something valuable. Some companies offer recognition or a visit to the factory. When participants earn money for their winning proposals, fees usually remain much lower than the ones agreed on in traditional contracts. With services like Amazon Mechanical Turk or Crowdcloud, where people, often in low-income countries, get paid in pennies to accomplish small simple tasks, the link to outsourcing is clear again. The fact that high-level crowdsourcing is strongly linked to competition makes it precarious. After all, you never know if you will win. The relatively low rewards common, for example, in design are possible because of the intrinsic motivation of any contestant trying to win a competition, the truly global market achieved through the Internet, and the fact that many experts don't rely on the competitions to earn a living. Fractal Graphics and Taylor Wall & Associates say that winning the Goldcorp Challenge only covered the cost of their submission. The major value was the boost in their reputations. While there are sometimes high monetary rewards for R & D challenges, the winner usually takes it all and other participants have worked for free. When Netflix offered to pay $1 million to anyone who would achieve an increase of over 10 percent in the reliability of Netflix's movie suggestions ("You liked *Avatar*? You should watch *eXistenZ* too"), Netflix got to see the solution approaches of so many high-level researchers that the price paid per PhD who worked on the precious algorithm seemed insignificant (see ALGORITHM).

■ See also COLLECTIVE INTELLIGENCE, EMERGENCE

References and Further Reading

Ellenberg, Jordan. 2008. "This Psychologist Might Outsmart the Math Brains Competing for the Netflix Prize." *Wired* 16.03. www.wired.com/techbiz/media/magazine/16-03/mf_netflix.

Howe, Jeff. 2006. "The Rise of Crowdsourcing." *Wired* 14.06. www.wired.com/wired/archive/14 .06/crowds.html.

————. 2008. *Crowdsourcing: Why the Power of the Crowd Is Driving the Future of Business*. New York: Three Rivers Press.

Sloane, Paul, ed. 2011. *A Guide to Open Innovation and Crowdsourcing: Advice from Leading Experts*. London: Kogan Page.

Tapscott, Don, and Anthony D. Williams. 2006. *Wikinomics: How Mass Collaboration Changes Everything.* New York: Portfolio.

Tischler, Linda. 2002. "He Struck Gold on the Net (Really)." *Fast Company*, May 31. www.fastcompany.com/44917/he-struck-gold-net-really.

··

Cut Scenes
Rune Klevjer

A cut scene is a nonplayable animated or live-action sequence in a video game, usually employed as a storytelling device, and typically following established conventions of cinema. Cut scenes are closely related to (and may blend into) other storytelling sequences that have no or very limited gameplay functionality, such as text dialogues or comic book panels. The main function of cut scenes is to push the plot forward and give narrative context to the gameplay, often by evoking generic characters, settings, and storylines from popular fiction (see GAMEPLAY). Cut scenes are important to the structure and pacing of single-player games, providing rewards to the player and brief respites from the intensity of gameplay. They may also have specific gameplay functions such as giving mission briefings or providing clues to what lies ahead (Hancock 2002; Klevjer 2002; Salen and Zimmerman 2004).

Donkey Kong (1981), which first presented the character later to be known as Mario, was also the first game to use a series of short animated intermissions to advance the story between levels. During the 1990s, following the introduction of CD-ROM media on home computers and game consoles, full motion video cut scenes—of either animated or live-action footage—proliferated. Since the turn of the century, however, animated cut scenes rendered in real time through the game's graphics engine have been the favored option, offering lower cost and stronger visual seamlessness between gameplay and cut scene imagery. The real-time rendered cut scenes in *Grand Theft Auto III* (2001) were particularly praised for their high quality of motion capture, voice talent, and cinematic direction. The new opportunities opened up by computer game graphics engines also sparked a movement of amateur or small-scale real-time animation production, coined *machinima* (see MACHINIMA).

When cut scenes are being rendered on the fly in real-time 3D environments, the "cut" from gameplay action to cinematic "scene" implies a temporary suspension of avatar-based navigable game space. In contrast, *dramatically scripted events*, as utilized to powerful effect in *Half-Life 2* (2004), unfold within navigable game space, so that the player remains in control of the first-person avatar and needs to be restricted and directed by the game designers in various ways. At the other end, there are innovative games like *Metal Gear Solid 4* (2008) in which cinematic sequences do suspend regular game space, but where the player is invited to choose camera angles and/or conversation lines in a way reminiscent of interactive cinema (see INTERACTIVE CINEMA). The more popular variant of the interactive cut scene, however, would be the so-called quick-time event, which challenges the player to quickly respond to button prompts in a Simon Says fashion in order to make the cinematic interlude unfold successfully.

The role of cut scenes has been much discussed among game designers, players, and theorists alike, as a paradigmatic case in the larger debate on the function and value of prewritten narratives. Klevjer (2002), Weise (2003), and Cheng (2007) all investigate cut scenes as a way of looking into the nature of agency and rhetoric in computer games, emphasizing the ways in which cut scenes and gameplay interact to form a distinct language of dramatic expression.

References and Further Reading

Cheng, Paul. 2007. "Waiting for Something to Happen: Narratives, Interactivity and Agency and the Video Game Cut-Scene." *Situated Play: Proceedings of the 2007 Digital Games Research Association Conference.* www.digra.org/digital-library/publications/waiting-for-something-to-happen -narratives-interactivity-and-agency-and-the-video-game-cut-scene/.

Hancock, Hugh. 2002. "Better Game Design through Cutscenes." *Gamasutra.* www.gamasutra .com/view/feature/3001/better_game_design_through.

Klevjer, Rune. 2002. "In Defence of Cutscenes." *Computer Games and Digital Cultures Conference Proceedings.* www.aqui.rtietz.com/game_design/In_Defense_of_Cutscenes.pdf.

Salen, Katie, and Eric Zimmerman. 2004. *Rules of Play: Game Design Fundamentals.* Cambridge, MA: MIT Press.

Weise, Matthew. 2003. "How Videogames Express Ideas." *Level Up Conference Proceedings: Proceedings of the 2003 Digital Games Research Association Conference.* citeseerx.ist.psu.edu/viewdoc /summary?doi=10.1.1.190.2031.

Cyberfeminism
Kate Mondloch

The evolution of the term *cyberfeminism* is not easy to trace and is evocatively nonlinear and variegated in its applications. Examining the terms that make up the compound word offers a logical starting point. The "cyber" part of cyberfeminism is typically taken to denote cyberspace—"feminisms applied to or performed in cyberspace" is *Wikipedia*'s roomy yet convincing definition (see CYBERSPACE). American feminist theorist Donna Haraway's cyborg feminism (see CYBORG AND POSTHUMAN) is another formative source. Haraway's celebrated 1985 essay "A Cyborg Manifesto: Science, Technology, and Socialist-Feminism in the Late Twentieth Century" (reprinted in Haraway 1991) embraced the cyborg metaphor in order to argue for the inclusive transgression of boundaries (gender, race, difference) and the development of deliberately hybrid social identities. Unsettling cultural feminist critiques of technology with a purposefully ironic stance, her article famously concluded, "I'd rather be a *cyborg* than a goddess." The participants in the 1994 London conference "Seduced and Abandoned: The Body in the Virtual World," among others, describe cyberfeminism as the direct heir of Haraway's cyborg feminism, although the theorist's essay predates both the term *cyberfeminism* and the widespread recognition of cyberspace by several years.

If relatively few writers dispute the relevance of the "cyber" in cyberfeminism, the place of feminism, in contrast, has been frequently debated. The all-female artist and activist collective VNS Matrix (Adelaide, Australia; 1991–1997) was likely the first to unite the terms with their poster entitled "A Cyberfeminist Manifesto for the 21st Century" (1991). The humorous and polemical manifesto provocatively imbued new media technologies with feminine characteristics: "we are the virus of the new world disorder / rupturing the symbolic from within / saboteurs of big daddy mainframe / the clitoris is a direct line to the matrix." British philosopher and writer Sadie Plant, among the earliest proponents of cyberfeminism, proposed that the social relations engendered by new digital technologies are intrinsically associated with women and the feminine. Her best-known text, *Zeros + Ones: Digital Women + the New Technoculture* (1997), argued that actions such as nonlinearly distributed processes should be embraced as "positively feminine."

Many self-identified cyberfeminists took issue with the utopian technophilia and biological essentialism embedded in approaches such as those of VNS Matrix and Plant. American artist and activist Faith Wilding's influential essay "Where Is the Feminism in Cyberfeminism?" (1998b) brought the issue to the forefront, critiquing the deliberate or willed ignorance of alternate political feminisms among many cyberfeminists. Wilding and Cornelia Sollfrank popularized a variant application of the term *cyberfeminism* as part of their work with the activist group Old Boys Network (OBN), founded in 1997 in Berlin. For the OBN, cyberspace was understood as entirely consistent with patriarchal society: "Cyberspace does not exist in a vacuum; it is intimately connected to numerous real-world institutions and systems that thrive on gender separation and hierarchy"; cyberfeminism, accordingly, should be a political undertaking committed to creating and maintaining real and virtual places for women in regard to new technologies—such as creating new feminist platforms and resources, including hands-on techno-education for women and working directly with code—while also critically assessing the "impact of new technologies on the lives of women and the insidious gendering of technoculture in everyday life" (Wilding 1998a, 49).

Cyberfeminism, and the OBN in particular, has had particular resonance within the visual arts. OBN appeared in the spotlight in the 1997 international art exhibition *Documenta X* in Kassel, Germany, where the group hosted the First Cyberfeminist International (CI). Seeking to resist rigid definition, the CI published what they called "100 anti-theses" (OBN and the First Cyberfeminist International 1997). Incorporating several different languages, the one hundred anti-theses defined what cyberfeminism, according to the CI, was *not*; for example: "12. Cyberfeminism is not an institution"; "19. Cyberfeminism is not anti-male"; "40. Cyberfeminism is not essentialist." The subRosa collective (founded by former OBN member Faith Wilding in 1998)—an international group of cultural researchers who combine art, activism, and radical politics to explore and critique the intersections of digital information and biotechnologies in women's bodies, lives, and work—continues to be at the forefront of art and cyberfeminism.

No matter how diverse the strategies proposed by self-identified cyberfeminist activists and writers, all share a commitment to critically engaging rather than hastily discounting all things "cyber" (read: new media technologies, as well as their cultural and social contexts). Social and political activism has been an important component of cyberfeminism, and writers have brought the term to bear in a range of disciplinary contexts—including art, sociology, law, political theory, biology, genetics, computer science, cyberpunk, and sci-fi—both inside and outside of cyberspace (in order to reach those who lack Internet access). The specific terms of cyberfeminist engagement have tended to shift alongside the goals of broader feminist ideological positions. If early efforts concentrated on getting women to participate more fully in what was understood to be "masculine" technological realms, subsequent cyberfeminists, informed by postcolonial theory, have focused on ethnic and racial difference, interrogating the various conditions that uphold our techno-dependent society, as well as the digital divide.

The term *cyberfeminism* was coined in 1991, and cyberfeminist activity flourished throughout the 1990s, coincident with the early excitement and anxiety associated with the wide-scale introduction of the World Wide Web and networked computing. Since then, the term *cyberfeminism* has achieved a global reach (albeit with an Anglo bias). Cyberfeminism has been the topic of conferences, edited volumes, articles, and art exhibitions all over the world, and it is impossible to identify any single definition at present. In today's climate of ubiquitous computing and information flows, some have asked if the term *cyberfeminism* may have outlived its usefulness. In the twenty-first century, it seems apparent that all politics, feminist or otherwise, must confront the "cyber." On the other hand, it's important to note that cyberfeminism has suffered the neglect of other feminist projects; many new media historians and critics consistently overlook the role of cyberfeminism in historical and contemporary theories of technology, lending a special political urgency to its historicization.

■ See also GENDER AND MEDIA USE, GENDER REPRESENTATION, VIRTUAL BODIES

References and Further Reading

Braidotti, Rosi. 1996. "Cyberfeminism with a Difference." *New Formations* 29:9–25.
Fernandez, Maria. 1999. "Postcolonial Media Theory." *Third Text* 47:11–17.
Flanagan, Mary, and Mary Booth Austin, eds. 2002. *Reload: Rethinking Women + Cyberculture.* Cambridge, MA: MIT Press.
Haraway, Donna. 1991. *Simians, Cyborgs and Women: The Reinvention of Nature.* New York: Routledge.
Kember, Sarah. 2003. *Cyberfeminism and Artificial Life.* New York: Routledge.
OBN and the First Cyberfeminist International. 1997. "100 Anti-Theses." www.obn.org/cfundef/100antitheses.html.
Plant, Sadie. 1997. *Zeros + Ones: Digital Women + The New Technoculture.* New York: Doubleday.
Reiche, Claudia, and Verena Kuni, eds. 2004. *Cyberfeminism, Next Protocols.* Brooklyn: Autonomedia.
VNS Matrix. 1991. "Cyberfeminist Manifesto for the 21st Century." www.sysx.org/gashgirl/VNS/TEXT/PINKMANI.HTM.
Wilding, Faith. 1998a. "Notes on the Political Condition of Cyberfeminism." *Art Journal* 57 (2): 46–59.
———. 1998b. "Where Is the Feminism in Cyberfeminism?" *n. paradoxa* 2:6–12.
Wright, Michelle, Maria Fernandez, and Faith Wilding, eds. 2002. *Domain Errors! Cyberfeminist Practices.* Brooklyn: Autonomedia.

....

Cybernetics
Bernard Geoghegan and Benjamin Peters

Cybernetics, like many metadisciplines, evades easy definition: there may now be as many definitions of cybernetics as—or perhaps more than—there are self-identified cyberneticians. Since the mid-1940s, its amalgamation of themes of communication and control in computational biological, social, and symbolic systems has inspired and bedeviled researchers across the natural sciences, social sciences, and humanities. Accounts have variously identified cybernetics as a science of communication and control (Wiener 1948), a universal science (Bowker 1993), an umbrella discipline (Kline, n.d.), a Manichean science (Galison 1994, 232), and a scientific farce founded on sloppy analogies between computers and human organisms (Pierce 1961, 208–227).

MIT mathematician Norbert Wiener is often credited with launching the field with his book *Cybernetics: Or Control and Communication in the Animal and the Machine* (1948). Wiener based *Cybernetics* on his World War II research aimed at better integrating the agency of human gunners and analog computers within antiaircraft artillery fire control systems. Wiener, an inveterate polymath, adapted wartime research on the feedback processes among humans and machines into general science of communication and control. He coined the term *cybernetics*, from the Greek word for "steersman" (a predecessor to the English term *governor*), to designate this new science of control and feedback mechanisms. Wiener's masterworks commingled complex mathematical analysis, exposition on the promise and threat associated with automated machinery, and speculations of a social, political, and religious nature (Wiener 1948, 1950, 1964). The prefix "cyber," now widespread in the description of electronic and digital phenomena, finds its origins in Wiener's speculative efforts in cybernetics.

The Macy Conferences on Cybernetics (1946–1953), as they were informally known, staked out a still broader interdisciplinary purview for cybernetic research (Pias 2004). In addition to Wiener, participants included neurophysiologist Warren McCulloch, who directed the conferences, the mathematician and game theorist John von Neumann, leading anthropologists Margaret Mead and Gregory Bateson, engineer Claude Shannon, sociologist-statistician Paul Lazarsfeld, as well as psychiatrists, psychoanalysts, and philosophers. Relying on mathematical and formal definitions of communication, participants rendered permeable the boundaries that distinguished humans, machines, and animals. The language of cybernetic and informatic analysis—encoding, decoding, signal, feedback, entropy, equilibrium, information, communication, control—sustained the analogies between these ontologically distinct classes (Heims 1991). The "invisible college" constituted by the Macy Conferences proved immensely influential: von Neumann pioneered much of the digital architecture for the computer as well as Cold War game theory (Aspray 1990); Bateson facilitated the adaptation of cybernetics in anthropology and the American counterculture (Turner 2006); Shannon founded American information theory; and Lazarsfeld fashioned much of the conceptual architecture of postwar communication studies. Although American cybernetics found its roots in military and industrial research, England, France, Chile, and the Soviet Union served as home to vibrant and distinct schools of cybernetic research, often with a countercultural or socialist orientation (Pickering 2010; Segal 2003; Medina 2011; Gerovitch 2002).

The methodological hallmarks of cybernetics, especially human-machine interaction and feedback, overlapped with the fields of information theory and game theory (Aspray 1985) (see GAME THEORY). Mainstream American information theory, following Bell Labs engineer Shannon's mathematical theory of communication, concentrates on the efficient and reliable measurement and transmission of data (Shannon 1948) (see DATA). Von Neumann's game theory, influential in economics, developed formal models for human behavior based on strategic decision-making processes (Mirowski 2002). All three methods suggested formal systems for describing communicative activities, often with an emphasis on promoting stability or efficiency, and sought formal systems for describing communicative activities. Wiener defended the importance of grouping these three research fields within cybernetics, and von Neumann did not deploy a rigorous distinction among cybernetics, game theory, and information theory (Kline 2004). From the mid-1950s, however, many information theorists and game theorists have objected to the conflation of these fields (Shannon 1956; Pierce 1973).

Literary and cultural studies have derived a variety of inspirations from cybernetics. In the late 1940s and 1950s American mathematician Warren Weaver, who oversaw the work of Wiener and Shannon during the war, argued for applying their research to machine translation and the analysis of visual arts (Weaver 1949). Throughout the 1950s and 1960s structural linguist Roman Jakobson advocated the selective adaptation of cybernetics to promote a more rigorous and scientific definition of language (Jakobson 1990). His friend and colleague, the French anthropologist Claude Lévi-Strauss, contended that structuralism was an "indirect outcome" of cybernetics, information theory, and game theory, and he saw semiology as part of the communication sciences (Geoghegan 2011). French critics, including Roland Barthes and Jean Baudrillard, later adapted elements of cybernetic modeling within their semiotic studies while arguing that the fields' preoccupation with eliminating noise from communications had a technocratic or politically conservative predisposition (Barthes 1974, 1977; Baudrillard 1981). Jean-François Lyotard's essay *The Postmodern Condition*, ostensibly a critique of the imbrication of informatic and economic terms in global capitalism, also deployed and adapted a number of cybernetic tropes (Lyotard 1984; Galison 1994; Geoghegan 2011).

In the 1980s Donna Haraway and German literary critic Friedrich Kittler developed two contemporaneous but distinct schools of neo-cybernetic criticism. Haraway adapted the themes of cybernetic analysis to develop a new and ironic style of feminist critique concerned with the artifactual, technical, and hybrid conditions of identity in an age of technoscience (Haraway 2004). Subsequent interest in cyborg studies wove the intertwined history of cybernetics and science fiction, from Stanley Kubrick's *Dr. Strangelove* to *The Terminator*, into a refreshing critique of contemporary politics, science, gender, and textuality (Gray 1995; Edwards 1996) (see CYBORG AND POSTHUMAN). Even so, recent historians have noted that only a minor wing of medical cybernetics actually took up the literal fusion of the human and machine in cyborg research (Kline 2009). In this sense, the legacy of cybernetic human-machine interaction appears to splinter into rich literary speculation and pragmatic scientific practice.

Roughly contemporaneous with Haraway's 1980s research, German literary critic Friedrich Kittler, through a sometimes blindingly brilliant antihumanist interpretation of cybernetics and information theory, mobilized the analysis of warfare and communications technology as cultural determinants that spearheaded a new school or approach to German media theory (Kittler 1993; Hörl 2005) (see HISTORY OF COMPUTERS). Like Haraway, Kittler sought to undermine the role of the "human" or "spirit" as an epistemic figure orienting humanistic critique or analysis, an approach that coincided with near disdain toward Anglo-American reflections on gender, politics, and identity.

The two subsequent subfields—variously called cyborg theory and media archaeology— laid the foundation for new literary and cultural interrogations of literature, film, media, biology, gender, and other fields displaced and conjoined by shifting technological regimes. Since the 1990s, the proliferation of digital media in personal, professional, literary, and artistic contexts has prompted major efforts to reevaluate and reclaim aspects of cybernetic analysis. N. Katherine Hayles's literary analysis of cybernetics relies on writers such as Bernard Wolfe and Philip K. Dick advancing a cybernetic complicity in the postmodern disembodiment of human subjects (Hayles 1999). Mark Hansen's *New Philosophy for New Media*, by contrast, finds in the work of British information theorist Donald MacKay (a participant in the Macy Conferences) resources for affirming the role of human embodiment in digital communications (Hansen 2004). Writers and technologists alike from Stanislaw Lem to Cory Doctorow to Rodney Brooks have cited cybernetics as an inspiration (Pickering 2010, 60–69)

Any attempt to reconcile these legion cybernetic understandings would likely be as fruitless as it would be misguided: like many other ambitious projects, contradictions, inconsistencies, paradoxes, and programmatic failures have long been hallmarks of cybernetics. Wiener's failed attempts to improve fire control in the 1940s, the Macy Conferences' failed effort to develop a universal science of control and communication in the 1940s and 1950s, and the ambivalent appropriation of cybernetics by theorists ever since speak to the difficulty—and likely impossibility—of reconciling humans, animals, machines, and societies into a consistent, coherent, or unified intellectual program. It is exactly this disunity of definitions, actors, and exegesis that speaks to cybernetics' continuing promise for future critical inquiry.

■ See also ARTIFICIAL LIFE, CRITICAL THEORY, CYBERPUNK, CYBORG
AND POSTHUMAN, NETWORKING.

References and Further Reading

Aspray, William. 1985. "The Scientific Conceptualization of Information." *Annals of the History of Computing* 7 (2): 117–140.

———. 1990. *John von Neumann and the Origins of Modern Computing*. Cambridge, MA: MIT Press.

Barthes, Roland. 1974. *S/Z: An Essay*. Translated by Richard Miller. New York: Farrar, Straus & Giroux.

———. 1977. "The Photographic Message." In *Image, Music, Text*, translated by Stephen Heath, 15–31. New York: Hill and Wang.

Baudrillard, Jean. 1981. "Requiem for the Media [1972]." In *For a Critique of the Political Economy of the Sign*, translated by Charles Levin, 214. St. Louis, MO: Telos Press.

Bowker, Geof. 1993. "How to Be Universal: Some Cybernetic Strategies, 1943–70." *Social Studies of Science* 23:107–127.

Edwards, Paul N. 1996. *The Closed World: Computers and the Politics of Discourse in Cold War America*. Cambridge, MA: MIT Press.

Galison, Peter. 1994. "The Ontology of the Enemy." *Critical Inquiry* 21:228–268.

Geoghegan, Bernard. 2011. "From Information Theory to French Theory: Jakobson, Lévi-Strauss, and the Cybernetic Apparatus." *Critical Inquiry* 38 (1): 96.

Gerovitch, Slava. 2002. *From Newspeak to Cyberspeak: A History of Soviet Cybernetics*. Cambridge, MA: MIT Press.

Gray, Chris Hables, ed. 1995. *The Cyborg Handbook*. London: Routledge.

Hansen, Mark B. N. 2004. *New Philosophy for New Media*. Cambridge, MA: MIT Press.

Haraway, Donna. 2004. "A Manifesto for Cyborgs: Science, Technology, and Socialist Feminism in the 1980s." In *The Haraway Reader*, 7–46. New York: Routledge.

Hayles, N. Katherine. 1999. *How We Became Posthuman: Virtual Bodies in Cybernetics, Literature, and Informatics*. Chicago: University of Chicago Press.

Heims, Steve J. 1991. *The Cybernetics Group*. Cambridge, MA: MIT Press.

Hörl, Erich. 2005. *Die Heiligen Kanäle: Über Die Archaische Illusion Der Kommunikation*. Berlin: Diaphanes.

Jakobson, Roman. 1990. "Linguistics and Communication Theory." In *On Language*, edited by Linda R. Waugh and Monique Monville-Burston, 489–497. Cambridge, MA: Harvard University Press.

Kittler, Friedrich. 1993. "Signal-Rausch-Abstand." In *Draculas Vermächtnis*, 161–181. Leipzig: Reclam.

Kline, Ronald R. 2004. "What Is Information Theory a Theory Of? Boundary Work among Scientists in the United States and Britain during the Cold War." In *The History and Heritage of Scientific and Technical Information Systems: Proceedings of the 2002 Conference*, edited by W. Boyd Rayward and Mary Ellen Bowden, 15–28. Chemical Heritage Foundation. Medford, NJ: Information Today.

———. 2009. "Where Are the Cyborgs in Cybernetics?" *Social Studies of Science* 39 (3): 331–362.

———. n.d. "Cybernetics in Crisis: Reviving and Reinventing a Postwar Interdiscipline in the United States." Unpublished paper.

Lyotard, Jean-Francois. 1984. *The Postmodern Condition: A Report on Knowledge*. Translated by Geoffrey Bennington and Brian Massumi. Minneapolis: University of Minnesota Press.

Medina, Eden. 2011. *Cybernetic Revolutionaries: Technology and Politics in Allende's Chile.* Cambridge, MA: MIT Press.

Mirowski, Philip. 2002. *Machine Dreams: Economics Becomes a Cyborg Science.* Cambridge: Cambridge University Press.

Pias, Claus, ed. 2004. *Cybernetics—Kybernetik 2: The Macy-Conferences 1946–1953.* Berlin: Diaphanes.

Pickering, Andrew. 1995. "Cyborg History and the World War II Regime." *Perspectives on Science* 3 (1): 1–48.

———. 2010. *The Cybernetic Brain: Sketches of Another Future.* Chicago: University of Chicago Press.

Pierce, John Robinson. 1961. *An Introduction to Information Theory: Symbols, Signals and Noise.* New York: Dover.

———. 1973. "The Early Days of Information Theory." *IEEE Transactions on Information Theory* 19 (1): 3–8.

Rosenblueth, Arturo, Norbert Wiener, and Julian Bigelow. 1943. "Behavior, Purpose, Teleology." *Philosophy of Science* 1:18–24.

Segal, Jérôme. 2003. *Le Zéro et le Un: Histoire de la notion scientifique d'information au 20e siècle.* France: Editions Syllepse.

Shannon, Claude E. 1948. "A Mathematical Theory of Communication." *Bell Systems Technical Journal* 27:379–423, 623–656.

———. 1956. "The Bandwagon." *I. R. E. Transactions on Information Theory* 2 (1): 3.

Turner, Fred. 2006. *From Counterculture to Cyberculture: Stewart Brand, the Whole Earth Network, and the Rise of Digital Utopianism.* Chicago: University of Chicago Press.

Weaver, Warren. 1949. "Recent Contributions to the Mathematical Theory of Communication." In *The Mathematical Theory of Communication*, 1–28. Urbana: University of Illinois Press.

Wiener, Norbert. 1948. *Cybernetics: Or Control and Communication in the Animal and the Machine.* Cambridge, MA: MIT Press.

———. 1950. *The Human Use of Human Beings: Cybernetics and Society.* Boston: Houghton Mifflin.

———. 1964. *God and Golem, Inc.: A Comment on Certain Points Where Cybernetics Impinges on Religion.* Cambridge, MA: MIT Press.

· ·

Cyberpunk
Lisa Swanstrom

It is a truth universally acknowledged (at least among geeks) that science fiction in all of its diverse manifestations—soft, hard, corny, pedantic, operatic, cinematic, sublime—enjoys an intimate relationship with technology. Indeed, the histories of science fiction and technological development are not only coextensive; they are—like the tangle of electrodes which crowns the Data Analyzing Robot Youth Lifeform in a certain film from the mid-1980s (think *D.A.R.Y.L.*)—wholly entwined.

But although one can trace the history of technological progress throughout all science fiction, from at least the Golden Age on, there is one specific stripe of sci-fi that is essential for making sense of the cultural and technological evolution of digitization, in particular. This is cyberpunk fiction. In fact, the evolution of digital culture is so tied to the history of cyberpunk that it is no exaggeration to claim that the digital humanities as a discipline would not exist in its current form without this peculiar science fiction subgenre.

Cyberpunk emerged as a literary genre in the early 1980s and peaked in popularity in the mid-1990s. Cyberpunk was edgy; its landscapes were gritty, its characters jaded technophiles. It offered its readers poetic, frenetic engagements with the dark side of global capitalism and, perhaps most crucially in terms of cyberpunk's relation to the evolution of the digital humanities, allowed readers to imagine the emancipatory potential of computational technology. In spite of several overlapping definitions of cyberpunk from such science fiction luminaries as Bruce Sterling, Rudy Rucker, and William Gibson, however, there remains no firm, universal consensus about what constituted it. The *Encyclopedia Britannica* definition comes close: "Cyberpunk: A science-fiction subgenre characterized by countercultural antiheroes trapped in a dehumanized, high-tech future." And the Russian-based website Project Cyberpunk, a fantastic resource for anyone interested in the subgenre's history and legacy, introduces at least six different perspectives, all of which offer insights into cyberpunk's dystopian attributes. Such definitions point out what everybody needs to know in order to recognize cyberpunk. It *is* often dystopian, dark, and nihilistic. This, however, might be said of any number of fictional narratives. So in addition to these important and defining features, it is important to note that cyberpunk fiction does something quite different from its illustrious precursors in terms of its expression of computation.

Before cyberpunk, our cultural narratives about the digital tended to treat computational technology as something dangerous, manipulative, and antihuman (think of the HAL 9000 in Kubrick's *2001*, the Alpha-60 in Godard's *Alphaville*, or the Demon Seed in the Koontz film by the same name). In contrast to these previous works, digital technology in cyberpunk fiction becomes omnipresent, cheap, and readily accessible, a fact of everyday life. It introduces the idea of technologically *incorporated* beings (see CYBORG AND POSTHUMAN). In many works of cyberpunk the body functions as a site of technological recuperation, of human advancement, creation, and imagination (see MATERIALITY).

In other words, although definitions of cyberpunk that focus on its dystopian aspects provide useful and accurate descriptions of the genre in terms of its literary features, they fall short in addressing the way that cyberpunk has functioned not merely as a collection of aesthetic tropes but as a crucial agent in the shaping of techno-social discourse from the 1980s to today. Key nomenclature used with digital humanities discourse, including cyberspace, hacking, artificial intelligence, information liberation, and the aesthetics of code, either emerged from this subgenre or came to public attention as a result of it (see ARTIFICIAL INTELLIGENCE, CODE AESTHETICS, CYBERSPACE, HACKER, VIRTUALITY). Additionally, during its heyday (mid-1980s to early 1990s, roughly), works of cyberpunk fiction introduced a variety of digital technologies and helped usher these then-nascent technologies into being, both in the cultural imagination and within the real-world sphere of technological innovation and economic enterprise (see VIRTUAL REALITY).

The first use of the term *cyberpunk* occurred in 1982, with a short story entitled "Cyberpunk!" by Bruce Bethke, and the genre took off with the publication of William Gibson's novel *Neuromancer* in 1984, a book that swept every major award that science fiction as a genre bestows and permanently altered the sci-fi landscape. The popularity of Gibson's "Sprawl Trilogy" (*Neuromancer, Count Zero, Mona Lisa Overdrive*) helped pave the way for other authors writing at the same time, such as Pat Cadigan, Bruce Sterling, Joan D. Vinge, and Jonathan Littell. Indeed, Sterling's edited collection *Mirrorshades: The Cyberpunk Anthology* brings several of these authors together and marks one of the most important and lasting contributions to the genre, not only because it showcases an impressive spectrum of literary innovation, but in terms of the way the stories in that collection shaped—and continue to shape—discourse about information technology. In it, writers imagine a future in which technology, society, and identity are entwined. Twenty-five years before augmented reality became a viable technology, the lead story in *Mirror-*

shades, Gibson's "Gernsback Continuum," presents a vision of the American Southwest as something like a palimpsest upon which features of science fiction's past are superimposed against an eerily familiar future (see AUGMENTED REALITY). Cyberpunk fiction in general is filled with such moments of technological prescience. Gibson is most famous, perhaps, for helping to usher the concepts of cyberspace and virtual reality into the cultural imagination, but the very concept of computational data as something imbued with power, control, and a strange sort of agency that hinges upon its status as a product of the complex system of signification that is computer code—all key concepts in digital humanities debates—emerges in one of the earliest stories in the genre, Vernor Vinge's "True Names," published in 1981, in which computer "warlocks" must keep their data secret so as to forestall government interference.

Issues that are very current in digital humanities research today become even more fully sketched in works that come a bit later in cyberpunk's temporal arc. Neal Stephenson's *Snow Crash* (1992), for instance, offers a devastating—and devastatingly funny—critique of hacker culture, copyright, and corporate surveillance. Melissa Scott's *Night Sky Mine*, for another example, grapples with the fact that textual data have become a marker of humanity, "a necessary thing, in whatever form it was stored and accessed . . . the best of all badges of belonging" (1996, 1). And the Wachowski siblings' cyber-gothic *Matrix* franchise, with its alignment of soul-crushing corporate control with the evolution of computer intelligence (1998–2002), is instrumental for promoting the work of hacking as a heroic, even religious, endeavor in the cultural imagination.

While not entirely defunct, cyberpunk is no longer anywhere near its peak popularity. Its wane is perhaps due—at least in part—to the fact that much of the technology it imagined in the 1980s has come to pass and become commonplace, if not obsolete. In 1998, Abel Ferrera's *New Rose Hotel*, a film based upon William Gibson's 1984 short story of the same name, demonstrated just how swiftly the gap between cyberpunk's "imaginary" technology and real-world technology was closing. Among other things, Gibson's original story centers around the production of top-secret, highly mobile computational gadgets that can hold vast amounts of data yet are still small and sleek enough to fit in the palm of one's hand. In 1984, that was exciting stuff. Fourteen years later? Not so much. Ferrara's film had the unfortunate timing of being released shortly after the Nokia PDA found its stride in the marketplace. The techno-speculative aspect of the film fell grossly short, and it never saw wide release, in spite of its elegant production values and high-profile cast.

Despite cyberpunk's decline in popularity, however, it still wields a great deal of cultural influence. Gibson and Sterling's *Difference Engine* (1990) is an important inaugural text for the steampunk genre, which has come into its own as both an artistic movement and a technologically informed counterculture. And cyberpunk in general continues to influence contemporary works. Alex Rivera's 2008 film *Sleep Dealer* plays with several cyberpunk motifs, as do, to large extents, James Cameron's *Avatar* (2009), which plays with cyberpunk's tendency to "plug in" to altered states of consciousness, and Ernest Cline's *Ready Player One* (2011), a novel that breathes fresh life into cyberpunk's past. Indeed, while the future of cyberpunk is uncertain, its history remains an important source of artistic inspiration. This same history also remains crucial for understanding the evolution of digital culture today.

We can trace the charged, wired roots of cyberpunk back to the New Wave science fiction of the 1960s and 1970s, most notably to the work of Harlan Ellison and James

Tiptree Jr.; back to the golden age writing of Gernsback and Del Rey in the 1940s and 1950s; all the way back to the *fin de siècle* writing of H. G. Wells; and back even further to the nineteenth century, to that most famous and quintessential work of science fiction that in some ways launches the entire genre, Mary Shelley's *Frankenstein*. Its etymology has an even more extensive history. Cyberpunk is a portmanteau of "cyber" and "punk." *Cyber* comes to us from the Greek word for "steersman" via Norbert Wiener, who coined the term *cybernetics* to describe the way that animals, and human animals in particular, are in constant correspondence with and receive feedback from the world that surrounds them (see CYBERNETICS). In an essay he wrote for a popular audience in *Scientific American* in 1948, he puts the matter succinctly: "The nervous system, in the cybernetic view, is more than an apparatus for receiving and transmitting signals. It is a circuit in which certain impulses enter muscles and re-enter the nervous system through the senses" (Wiener 1948).

Wiener borrowed this term not only from the Greeks in general, but from Plato in particular, who uses the term in the *Phaedrus* to describe the human soul in terms of a "cybernetes," a pilot or a steersman (Plato, n.d., 247C). Socrates's steersman is a charioteer who must work in conjunction with two horses that, metaphorically, power the human soul. One horse is virtuous and noble, the other base and unruly, and it is the charioteer's job to manage them and create equilibrium—a sort of Socratic differential mechanism. While the *cybernetes* is the captain of this vehicle, he is just as much a part of the circuit of horse and chariot as he is the one who presides over it. In other words, Wiener's word choice is strategic; by referring to Plato's charioteer, Wiener suggests that the feedback that occurs between, in his words, "man, animal, and the world about" has always been at the very essence of what it means to be human, even though the term *cybernetics*, per se, doesn't enter the popular lexicon until the 1950s.

The next term, "punk," is much more current, even though it, too, has roots that date back to at least Elizabethan England. A hotbed of musical innovation and social defiance in London and Birmingham, it is the name used to identify the musical and social subcultures that emerged there in the 1960s and 1970s, quickly spread throughout Europe, leaped across the Atlantic and Pacific Oceans, and became one of the most politically subversive forms of popular culture the world has ever seen. In particular, many works of cyberpunk explicitly reference the work of punk bands such as the Sex Pistols and punk antecedents such as the Velvet Underground.

At first glance it seems an odd combination—what might systems of feedback implied by the "cyber" prefix have to do with the musical and political subversion suggested by the "punk" suffix? The answer is, "Everything." Cyberpunk fiction combines Wiener's ideas of the human nervous system as a supple sensorial interface with punk subculture's particular brand of subversive resistance. The result is a literary subgenre that had—and continues to have—enormous ramifications on technological and cultural discourse.

In spite of the potential positive aspects of digital and network technologies outlined above, the critical response to cyberpunk during the 1980s and 1990s was largely suspicious. During this time period, marked by the advent and popularity of the personal computer, critical approaches to digital culture tended to equate the depiction of "cyber spaces" with a disdain for the material world and its natural spaces. For example, Arthur and Marilouise Kroker's book *Hacking the Future: Stories for the Flesh-Eating 90s* explores the way digitally enabled environments encroach upon the physicality of the real world. In a short piece, "Digital Flesh," the Krokers begin with the following provocative statement:

"Digital flesh? That's life in the 90s as a transitional time when we are stuck with 20th century flesh in 21st century hypertext minds . . . the information highway is paved with (our) flesh" (Kroker and Kroker 1996, 32). The Krokers are far from alone in their critical assertion that digital technology disconnects us from lived, embodied experience.

In her influential book *How We Became Posthuman*, N. Katherine Hayles shares the Krokers' skepticism, yet she also is open to the future, cautiously optimistic regarding posthuman potential. She writes, "If my nightmare is a culture inhabited by posthumans who regard their bodies as fashion accessories . . . my dream is a version . . . that embraces the possibilities of information technologies without being seduced by fantasies of unlimited power and disembodied immortality" (Hayles 1999, 5). The anxieties surrounding these two competing visions of the posthuman—the dream and the nightmare—are expressed throughout all of cyberpunk fiction.

Additionally, strong criticism emerged about the portrayal of gender in cyberpunk fiction. The title of Nicola Nixon's 1992 critical essay, her response to the genre, lays out the stakes of this discussion quite clearly: "Cyberpunk: Preparing the Ground for Revolution or Keeping the Boys Satisfied?" This type of criticism was echoed by virtual reality researcher Mark Pesce, who, after engaging with a "real" virtually immersive art installation, urged readers to "trash all of the adolescent fantasies of violence and disembodiment of William Gibson, the hormone-charged visions of Neal Stephenson and the weakling efforts of a hundred cyberpunk imitators" (Pesce 1998).

In spite of these important and legitimate criticisms, cyberpunk's influence remains evident, not just in terms of the problematic place/non-place of cyberspace, nor in terms of its male-dominated readership, nor even in terms of its alleged disdain for the material world. Its most lasting contribution to our understanding of digital technology is tied to the evolution of cybernetics into the more contemporary concept of wetware. Wetware is the human nervous system—its firing neurons, its opening and closing cerebral synapses and branching dendrites, its "sparks and tastes and tangles" (Rucker 1997, 66). Cyberpunk's most enduring intervention is not only to express man as an embodied network of physical systems but to make the imaginative leap of combining the systems of software and hardware into the similar system of human wetware, in order to see how these systems might interact. That seemed like a wildly speculative combo during the 1980s and 1990s, but it is becoming more possible every day. Indeed, as with many of the technologies that cyberpunk explores, we are about to catch up with the potential of the biotechnological integration that cyberpunk was the first to imagine so vividly.

■ See also CYBERSPACE, HACKER, HISTORY OF COMPUTERS, VIRTUAL REALITY

References and Further Reading

Bethke, Bruce. 1983. "Cyberpunk." *AMAZING Science Fiction Stories* 57:4.
"Cyberpunk." n.d. *Encyclopedia Britannica.* www.britannica.com/EBchecked/topic/147816/cyberpunk.
Foster, Thomas. 2005. *The Souls of Cyberfolk: Posthumanism as Vernacular Theory.* Minneapolis: University of Minnesota Press.
Gibson, William. 1984. *Neuromancer.* New York: Ace Books.
———. 1987. "New Rose Hotel." In *Burning Chrome*, 109–123. New York: Ace Books.
Hayles, N. Katherine. 1999. *How We Became Posthuman.* Chicago: University of Chicago Press.
Kroker, Arthur, and Marilouise Kroker. 1996. *Hacking the Future: Stories for the Flesh-Eating 90s.* New York: Palgrave Macmillan.

"Neuromancer by William Gibson." n.d. *Cyberpunk.ru Information Database: Cyberpunk Project.* http://project.cyberpunk.ru/idb/neuromancer.html.

Nixon, Nicola. 1992. "Cyberpunk: Preparing the Ground for Revolution or Keeping the Boys Satisfied?" *Science Fiction Studies* 19 (2): 219–235.

Pesce, Mark. 1998. "3-D Epiphany." www.immersence.com/publications/1998/1998-MPesce.html.

Plato. n.d. *The Phaedrus. The Internet Classics Archive.* Translated by Benjamin Jowett. http://classics.mit.edu/Plato/phaedrus.html.

Rucker, Rudy. 1997. *Wetware.* New York: Avon Books.

Scott, Melissa. 1996. *Night Sky Mine.* New York: Tor Books.

Stephenson, Neal. 1992. *Snow Crash.* New York: Bantam.

Sterling, Bruce, ed. 1988. *Mirrorshades: The Cyberpunk Anthology.* New York: Ace Books.

———. n.d. "Cyberpunk in the Nineties." *Streetteck.com.* www.streettech.com/bcp/BCPtext/Manifestos/CPInThe90s.html.

Wiener, Norbert. 1948. "Cybernetics." *Scientific American* 179:14–19.

··

Cyberspace
Marie-Laure Ryan

The term *cyberspace* names something that does not exist literally and yet plays an important role in our lives: the environment where networked communication (see NETWORKING) takes place. According to John Perry Barlow, cyberspace is "where you are when you are on the telephone" (1994, 180)—and by analogy, where you are when you are online. Since your physical body remains ensconced in the real world when you surf the web, the "space" of cyberspace can only be a fictional place. This explains why cyberspace has come to be associated with both something very real—the Internet—and a virtual, or alternate, reality (see VIRTUAL REALITY).

The term *cyberspace* was originally coined by the cyberpunk author William Gibson in his novel *Neuromancer* (1984). For Gibson, the word did not originally denote anything in particular: as he wrote seven years later, "Assembled the word cyberspace from small and readily available components of language. Neologic spasm: the primal act of pop poetics. Preceded any concept whatsoever. Slick and hollow—awaiting received meaning" (1991, 27). When cyberspace made its literary debut, however, meaning had already begun to fill its two roots. This meaning prefigures the addictive nature of computer technology and the mastery of this technology by youthful hackers: "[Case] operated on an almost permanent adrenaline high, a byproduct of youth and proficiency, jacked into a custom cyberspace deck that projected his disembodied consciousness into the consensual hallucination that was the matrix" (Gibson 1984, 5). And further: "Cyberspace. A consensual hallucination experienced daily by billions of legitimate operators, in every nation, by children being taught mathematical concepts. A graphic representation of data abstracted from the banks of every computer in the human system. Unthinkable complexity. Lines of light ranged in the nonspace of the mind, clusters of constellations and data. Like city lights, receding" (Gibson 1984, 51). This description of cyberspace ties together two themes: the idea of a world-spanning computer network functioning as meeting place for billions of users separated by physical space, and the idea of being immersed in a graphic display projected by computer data. One idea prefigures the Internet, the other virtual reality technology (see VIRTUAL REALITY).

In Gibson's novel cyberspace embodies the dystopic vision of a world made unlivable by technology. This pessimism turns into wild utopianism in the early nineties, when the term is appropriated by the speculative discourse of developers, promoters, and other prophets of the digital revolution. In 1990, the first Conference on Cyberspace was held at the University of Texas at Austin, gathering computer scientists, artists, architects, and educators. The papers, collected in an influential volume titled *Cyberspace: First Steps* (Benedikt 1991), offer an interdisciplinary cocktail of lyrical effusion, technical discourse, philosophical reflection, and oracular pronouncements. The following quote, from Marcos Novak, captures the diversity of phenomena covered by the umbrella term *cyberspace*, as well as the high hopes placed in the new technologies of networking and simulation: "Cyberspace is a completely spatialized visualization of all information in global information processing systems, along pathways provided by present and future communication networks, enabling full copresence and interaction of multiple users, allowing input and output from and to the full human sensorial, permitting simulations or real and virtual realities, remote data collection and control through telepresence, and total integration and intercommunication with a full range of intelligent products and environments in real space" (1991, 225). For most of the participants in the conference, however, cyberspace was much more than an umbrella term for applications of electronic technology. It was foremost a catalyzer of dreams. As Novak himself declares, "Cyberspace is poetry inhabited, and to navigate through it is to become a leaf on the wind of a dream" (1991, 229).

By the mid-1990s, the term *cyberspace* was solidly established in popular media, advertisement, and common parlance, and *cyber* (from the Greek *kybernetes*, meaning "steersman") was on its way to becoming a standard English prefix denoting a digital support (*cyberculture, cybertext*) or presence on the Internet (*cybernaut, cyberchat, cybersex, cyberporn*).

The key to the association of cyberspace with both the Internet and virtual reality (not necessarily virtual reality technology, but rather, an alternate reality) lies in the suffix of *space*. In the old regime of the imagination, telecommunication was conceived on the model of an epistolary exchange: in a telephone conversation the voice traveled over the lines, like a letter travels through mail carriers. The metaphor of the Internet as cyberspace replaces the idea of mobile information with the idea of a mobile user. The experience of using the Internet is not framed as one of receiving data through a channel of communication, but as one of being transported to a site functioning as host of the data. As a cybernaut of the 1990s declared, "I'm staring at a computer screen. But the feeling really is that I'm 'in' something. I'm some 'where'" (quoted in Dery 1996, 7).

This conception of the Internet as space presupposes that it is made of distinct places, such as home pages and chat rooms connected by the Information Superhighway, a metaphor of the 1990s now largely forgotten. But the Internet is not a space in any geographical sense: far from being limited, it expands indefinitely, as new pages are added to it, and people can homestead by building their own website without depriving others of the same opportunity. Rather than containing places and roads separated by territories full of features, it consists exclusively of places (the pages) and roads (the links), so that visitors cannot wander off-road: in cyberspace you are always at a destination, or waiting to get there. In contrast to real-world travel, the trip is a wait that offers nothing to see. In spite of its abstract nature (prefigured by Gibson's use of the term *nonspace*), cyberspace has been the object of an intense cartographic activity (Dodge and Kitchin 2001). Its maps represent phenomena as varied as the relations between websites (usually visualized on the model of a planetary system, with the kernel of the home pages surrounded by satellites), the flow of traffic, the relations between the real world and individual websites (showing where in the real world the hits originate), or the density of population of various areas of the Internet, measured by which possible IP addresses correspond to an active website. (IP addresses are numbers forming a continuum, but not every one of these numbers is used.)

While the Internet as a whole and most of its component sites are only spaces in a topological sense—a network of relations between discrete elements—cyberspace also contains individual sites that offer a simulation of physical space. These sites are the graphically represented fictional worlds of multiplayer online games, such as *World of Warcraft* or Second Life, and before them, the textually described worlds of MUDs and MOOs (see MUDs AND MOOs, ONLINE GAME COMMUNITIES). These worlds generate a strong loyalty among their users—what geographers would call a sense of place. This sense is reinforced by maps that resemble the maps of the real world, showing cities, roads, rivers, mountains, and the general shape of the land in the case of graphic worlds, or buildings made of separate rooms in the case of MOOs and MUDs. We can move through the space of online worlds through a steady progression, even when they allow teleporting as an alternative mode of transportation, but we can only travel through the abstract space of the Internet in jumps, without experiencing a developing landscape, since there is nothing between our point of departure and our destination.

Nowadays the novelty of the metaphor of cyberspace has worn out and it no longer stirs passions. (Note that most of the references are from the 1990s.) Its slipping out of fashion is due not only to fatigue but also to the development of Web 2.0 and of mobile computing. The new technologies of social networking, such as Facebook, Twitter, blogs, and instant messaging, are asynchronous: messages are stored on the web, and there is no need for people to be simultaneously present in a virtual space (see BLOGS, SOCIAL NETWORK SITES [SNSs]). A large proportion of the messages sent through these technologies stress the actual location of the sender: "I am now at [name place] doing [name activity]." In synchronous communication, such as chat and Skype phone calls, built-in cameras send pictures of the communicating parties in their actual surroundings. Thanks to mobile computing, webcams, and the new forms of social networking, people reconnect to real environments, and they no longer need to imagine themselves meeting in the alternate world of cyberspace.

■ See also SPATIALITY OF DIGITAL MEDIA, WORLDS AND MAPS

References and Further Reading

Barlow, John Perry. 1994. "Leaving the Physical World." In *The Virtual Reality Casebook*, edited by Carl Loeffler and Tim Anderson, 178–184. New York: Van Nostrand Rheingold.

Benedikt, Michael, ed. 1991. *Cyberspace: First Steps*. Cambridge, MA: MIT Press.

Dery, Mark. 1996. *Escape Velocity: Cyberculture at the End of the Century*. New York: Grove Press.

Dodge, Martin, and Rob Kitchin. 2001. *Mapping Cyberspace*. London: Routledge.

Gibson, William. 1984. *Neuromancer*. New York: Ace Books.

———. 1991. "Academy Leader." In *Cyberspace: First Steps*, edited by Michael Benedikt, 27–30. Cambridge, MA: MIT Press.

Heim, Michael. 1991. "The Erotic Ontology of Cyberspace." In *Cyberspace: First Steps*, edited by Michael Benedikt, 59–80. Cambridge, MA: MIT Press.

Novak, Marcos. 1991. "Liquid Architecture in Cyberspace." In *Cyberspace: First Steps*, edited by Michael Benedikt, 225–254. Cambridge, MA: MIT Press.

Wertheim, Margaret. 1999. *The Pearly Gates of Cyberspace: A History of Space from Dante to the Internet*. New York: Norton.

Woolley, Benjamin. 1992. *Virtual Worlds: A Journey in Hype and Hyperreality*. Cambridge, MA: Blackwell.

· ·

Cyborg and Posthuman
Raine Koskimaa

The concept of the cyborg was first defined by Manfred E. Clynes and Nathan S. Kline in their 1960 paper "Cyborgs and Space." In the paper *cyborg* was defined as an "exogenously extended organizational complex functioning as an integrated homeostatic system unconsciously" (1960, 27). In particular, Clynes and Kline were concerned about the well-being of astronauts during space travel and suggested that they should be refashioned as cyborgs, with a mechanism to automatically inject chemicals into the astronaut's body to safeguard them from the perils of violent radiation and other threats (1960, 27, 74). The term *cyborg* is an abbreviation of "cybernetic organism," which directly links the notion to the then-rising field of cybernetics. "Cyborg" is a manifestation of the human-machine symbiosis, where information flows between system and environment, maintaining equilibrium, or homeostasis, in terms of cybernetics.

Cyborgs, or androids, as technologically enhanced persons are also often called, enjoy popularity especially in science fiction literature and film. Philip K. Dick created a series of highly influential android figures in his 1960s novels, *Do Androids Dream of Electric Sheep?* (1968) being the best known of these. In popular media, the TV series *The Six Million Dollar Man* (1974–1979) was based on the novel *Cyborg* by Martin Caidin (1972). In the 1980s the interest in cyborgs was renewed in literature through William Gibson's cyberpunk trilogy *Neuromancer* (1984), *Count Zero* (1986), and *Mona Lisa Overdrive* (1988); in film by Ridley Scott's adaptation of *Do Androids Dream of Electric Sheep?* retitled as *Blade Runner* (1982); and later on by the films *Robocop* (Paul Verhoeven, 1987) and *The Terminator* (James Cameron, 1984). In most of these fictions, the cyborg is a human-like android with technologically enhanced physical capabilities, whereas Gibson's trilogy focuses more on artificial intelligence and enhancing the human mental capabilities through symbiosis with machines.

In academic discussions the term *cyborg* has gone through a process of metaphorization. Donna Haraway's use of cyborg as a transgressive figure in feminist theory has been influential especially in poststructuralist thinking. For Haraway, the cyborg promises to overcome distinctions like human/animal, human/machine, and physical/nonphysical (Haraway 1991, 152–154). As hybrids, cyborgs are necessarily monstrous, but with empowering potential. This extended notion of cyborg has been applied to such earlier fictional figures as Mary Shelley's Frankenstein and E. T. A. Hoffman's Sandman. In cultural theory the representations of the cyborg subject stand for a new phase in history, questioning the old notions of organicity and wholeness of the body (Schwab 1989, 194–195, 200–205). The technological enhancement of the human also often raises issues related to Cartesian dualism.

N. Katherine Hayles (1999) has elaborated the idea of posthuman, on the basis of cybernetics, but also as an answer to the transhumanist thinking as presented by Hans Moravec (1988) and others. "Posthuman" is a wider concept than cyborg, in that it refers not only to technologically enhanced human bodies but also to wider systems of collaboration including human and technological parts. "Posthuman" is also a perspective within which even a biologically unaltered Homo sapiens may be understood in posthuman terms: "The defining characteristics involve the construction of subjectivity, not the presence of nonbiological components" (Hayles 1999, 4). The posthuman, in Hayles's account, is a transformation of the human, where transhumanism implies a more radical exceeding of the limits and disposing of the biological human altogether—the "posthuman" may, however, be understood also synonymously with transhumanism, signaling the end of the human (see Agar 2010, 2).

In the posthuman framework, we may see practically all humans as cyborgs. On one hand, many of us wear technological enhancements, from eyeglasses to pacemakers; on the other, we are wholly reliant on the information and communications technologies in which we are immersed. The question now is more about in which sort of posthuman or cyborg constructions we partake. One direction here is to look at the creative processes of authoring literature for and with digital media. That direction could be labeled as an inquiry into *cyborg authorship*.

With regard to digital literature, we can see what *cyborg* entails. Various software tools (such as HyperCard, Storyspace, ToolBook, Director, and Flash) and, especially in the case of online works, the whole of the World Wide Web enable cooperation between human authors and machines. In addition to serving as parts in the authoring process, computer programs also enable the human author to reflect on language from a new perspective (Montfort 2003, 210). That is, cyborg authorship may be used to promote metareflective functions regarding the linguistic and technological conditions of the creative work.

Cyborg authorship may take various forms, and Espen Aarseth has provided a three-part typology of the possible occasions of the authoring process where the cyborg may appear. Aarseth's cyborg author typology consists of the following positions (1997, 134–136):

1. *Pre-processing*—the human programs and/or loads the machine, which then produces the text.
2. *Co-processing*—the human uses the machine during text production.
3. *Post-processing*—the machine produces a text stream, out of which the human selects and/or modifies parts.

These positions may coexist: pre-processing is almost always involved, whereas co- and post-processing often exclude each other (for an application of the typology, see Montfort 2003, 211–216).

Early examples of the cyborg author can be found in various text generators. Christopher Strachey, a collaborator of Alan Turing, already programmed a love letter generator for the Manchester Mark I computer in 1952, but the most successful has been the dialogue generator Eliza/Doctor (Joseph Weizenbaum, 1966). It simulates a psychiatric analyst (of a Rogerian type) in a text-only context. Eliza/Doctor recognizes a limited set of keywords in the user input and selects a reply according to a relatively simple set of rules, based on keywords identified in the input string. Eliza/Doctor can be considered as a success, much owing to the human want to believe in it (see detailed discussion on Eliza/

Doctor in Wardrip-Fruin 2009). Other well-known text generators include Tale-Spin by James Meehan, which produced short stories, and Racter by William Chamber, which produced poems, stories, and dialogue and, assumedly, "wrote" the book *The Policeman's Beard Is Half Constructed* (Chamberlain 1984).

Some have argued that the computer is more suitable for producing new types of works—cybertexts—than simulating traditional forms such as stories, sonnets, or plays (Aarseth 1997, 141). This notion leads to the more complex forms of cyborg author formations. The extreme form here is the approach where the whole World Wide Web is seen as a *cyborg author* (Wall 1994). The web here is seen as a complex tool that plays an integral part in the creative process of authoring digital literature: "The cyborg Web is the group of circumstances that leads to the creation of a text and the mechanism by which a text is assembled from existing conditions" (Wall 1994). This approach has the advantage that, as an open formation, it escapes the limited and predictable nature of the text generators. It may be argued that online information flows serve as the unconscious of the machine and open up the possibility of unpredictable, genuinely creative productions. In these assemblages the technology (both hardware and software) functions as an integral part of creative processes in a way that cannot be dismissed as a mere tool anymore. Instead, we should consider the whole system of human actors, the World Wide Web, and related software together as the cyborg author.

In this direction, *agent technologies* represent a new type of cyborg formation. Software agents are computer programs that monitor the user's actions and learn to know the user's habits. Based on this learning, the agents make selections on behalf of the human user, automating many actions normally requiring the human user's direct attention. Even though software agents are mainly used for practical purposes, they may be employed also for aesthetic and critical aims. *The Impermanence Agent* (Wardrip-Fruin et al. 1999) is an example of a complex cyborg authorship, where author-created materials, algorithms, user actions, and web contents all contribute to the emergence of the work.

In the early hypertext theory (Bush 1945; Engelbart 1962; Nelson 1965), hypertext was seen as a tool to extend human mental capabilities. This is closely connected to Marshall McLuhan's (1962, 1967) idea of media as an extension of the nervous system. Within this framework the cyborg and the cyborg author can be seen as producing a *mental change* in humanity (comparable to physical change brought along by prostheses). One of the functions of digital literature is to reflect on this mental change currently taking place, investigating what the cyborg and the posthuman condition mean, through the means that the cyborg authorship offers. This may be understood as literally following Clynes and Kline's initial aim with the cyborg as an entity that is able to explore new environments. Whereas the cyborg was meant to explore space, the cyborg author is needed to explore the new digital territory (Montfort 2003, 203–204).

123
Cyborg and
Posthuman

■ See also CYBERNETICS, CYBERPUNK, IDENTITY, NETWORKING

References and Further Reading

Aarseth, Espen. 1997. *Cybertext: Perspectives on the Ergodic Literature.* Baltimore: Johns Hopkins University Press.

Agar, Nicholas. 2010. *Humanity's End: Why We Should Reject Radical Enhancement.* Cambridge, MA: MIT Press.

Bush, Vannevar. 1945. "As We May Think." *Atlantic Monthly* 176 (1): 101–108.

Caidin, Martin. 1972. *Cyborg.* Westminster, MD: Arbor House.

Chamberlain, William. 1984. *The Policeman's Beard Is Half Constructed*. New York: Warner Books.

Clynes, Manfred E., and Nathan S. Kline. 1960. "Cyborgs and Space." *Astronautics* (September), 26–27, 74–76.

Dick, Philip K. 1968. *Do Androids Dream of Electric Sheep?* New York: Doubleday.

Engelbart, Douglas. 1962. *Augmenting Human Intellect: A Conceptual Framework*. Summary Report AFOSR-3223 under Contract AF 49(638)-1024, SRI PRoject 3578 for Air Force Office of Scientific Research, Menlo Park, CA: Stanford Research Institute. [Partially republished in *The New Media Reader*, edited by Noah Wardrip-Fruin and Nick Montfort, 95–108. Cambridge, MA: MIT Press.]

Gibson, William. 1984. *Neuromancer*. New York: Ace Science Fiction.

———. 1986. *Count Zero*. London: Victor Gollancz.

———. 1988. *Mona Lisa Overdrive*. London: Victor Gollancz.

Haraway, Donna. 1991. "A Cyborg Manifesto: Science, Technology, and Socialist-Feminism in the Late Twentieth Century." In *Simians, Cyborgs, and Women: The Reinvention of Nature*. New York: Routledge.

Hayles, N. Katherine. 1999. *How We Became Posthuman: Virtual Bodies in Cybernetics, Literature, and Informatics*. Chicago: University of Chicago Press.

McLuhan, Marshall. 1962. *The Gutenberg Galaxy: The Making of Typographic Man*. Toronto: University of Toronto Press.

———. 1967. *The Medium Is the Massage: An Inventory of Effects*. New York: Random House.

Monfort, Nick. 2003. "The Coding and Execution of the Author." In *The Cybertext Yearbook 2002–2003*, edited by John Cayley, Loss Pequeño Glazier, Markku Eskelinen, and Raine Koskimaa. Jyväskylä: University of Jyväskylä. http://cybertext.hum.jyu.fi.

Moravec, Hans. 1988. *Mind Children: The Future of Robot and Human Intelligence*. Cambridge, MA: Harvard University Press.

Nelson, Theodore H. 1965. "A File Structure for the Complex, the Changing, and the Indeterminate." In *ACM Proceedings of the 20th National Conference*, edited by Lewis Winner, 84–100.

Schwab, Gabriele. 1989. "Cyborgs and Cybernetic Intertexts: On Postmodern Phantasms of Body and Mind." In *Intertextuality and Contemporary American Fiction*, edited by Patrick O'Donnell and Robert Con Davis. Baltimore: Johns Hopkins University Press.

Wall, David. 1994. "The World-Wide Web as a Cyborg Author in the Postmodern Mold." Student paper for ENCR 481: Contemporary Literature and Theory, at the University of Virginia. www.iath.virginia.edu/courses/encr481/wall.paper.html.

Wardrip-Fruin, Noah. 2009. *Expressive Processing: Digital Fictions, Computer Games and Software Studies*. Cambridge, MA: MIT Press.

Wardrip-Fruin, Noah, Adam Chapman, Brion Moss, and Duane Whitehurst. 1999. *The Impermanence Agent*. www.impermanenceagent.com.

D

....

Data

Matthew Fuller

The question of data is a recursive one since it asks what we have to begin with, what is given, a quality made explicit in the French name for data, *les données*. What is given must be gotten; data must be derived, sensed, put on and in the table. This given-ness of data is what makes it controversial, in that it cannot be taken for granted, but also what makes it essential to contemporary forms of computing and of culture where data is donated, abstracted, elicited, mined, shared, protected, opened, analyzed, and normalized. In short, we may say that data comes in three kinds: as data that refers to something outside of itself—encoding or representing changes outside of the computer; data as data, that is, what is handled by a computer; and data that works on data, as a program.

Such a synoptic statement itself requires some metadata. To start with this triple in reverse, data is convoluted. It is not simply the content of a website, or that recorded in the tables of a database, but crucially, at a certain scale, also the material of the programs and operating systems and interfaces by which they run and are worked on (see DATA-BASE). This is a legacy of the formulation of the Turing machine that conceptually stored the symbols for instructions on the same abstract tape as that of the symbols they handled, and that of von Neumann (1945), who designed an electronic version of the universal machine that stored programs as data (see TURING TEST). (Indeed, before *computer science* became the dominant term, an early contender for the name of the field was datalogy [Naur 1992], suggesting that human knowing, language, and discrete structures formed its basis.) What constitutes data, the programs that operate on it, and the structures within which it is placed may therefore at times be obscured, as data becomes active in different ways. A parallel way of formulating this mobility of the category of data in knowledge management has been the hierarchy of forms running from data, to information, to knowledge, in which the organization of data increases as one rises through the hierarchy and the pertaining degree of abstraction.

Conversely, however, one can say that data is a dumb form of programming in that it carries, at a certain level, an instruction to a machine (display this symbol, record this value). Data then, as what is worked on, also does work. A significant example of this is that the question of what constitutes meaningful data has, at numerous times, had consequences for the trajectory of computing. As an example, the 1967 Lyons Electronic Office was an early office computer with hardware designed to meet the needs of a large catering company, and thus it had to be able to process large amounts of information about numerous small transactions, occurring over a long period of time at multiple sites and driven by the kind and rate of the data to be analyzed (Caminer et al 1996). The problem to compute was, in this case, not of speed, as found in tracking the path of a plane or missile, but in understanding the requirements for thousands of cups of tea and slices of cake. In this case, the anticipation of certain kinds of data, to be handled in certain ways, acted on hardware. Thus, the convolution of data extends out, into the systems that anticipate it.

Data as data is what is left when all the noise has been taken out. It may be raw, structured, a stream of variables, or of another kind, but this image of data is now its standard idealization. It is something inert that sits stored on hard drives, rather than as a magnetic charge gradually disturbing them (Kirschenbaum 2008). Data is discovered, studied, held, encrypted, sent, and received, all the while remaining stable. That's quite an achievement, and it takes a lot of activity, or structured inactivity, a lot of stabilization, to keep it that way. At the same time, as with the Lyons machine, data is sometimes said to drive programming; as computing expands to interpolate more aspects of life, life answers back with, and as, data. As computing moves out into the world, as a governing framework for the arrangement of things, in social media, logistics, or geographic information systems, much of what it comes into contact with also becomes data, and if it does not, it is elided, passed over (Gehl 2011).

Data therefore may refer to what, at least partially, lies outside the computer. As Lacan might say, beyond the thing is the thing itself. Data is produced in the interface between the convolutions of computing and the other elements of the world that it enfolds. Equally, in order to generate our understanding of a world that lies out there, that requires bringing into the fold, it must manifest as data. Data sets, collections of data, are what research communities gather around and build along with the corpus of texts of a writer, a set of scans of the heavens, a collection of recordings of interviews with a certain type of person, the "map" of proteomics, the results of experiments (Daston and Galison 2010). Here, data is built, in part, as a means to aggregate other entities, ideas, institutions, and research programs, through speculation on what its manifestation and its analysis might yield. What guarantees the fullness of a data set? Good real-time data about its operations may be necessary for a corporation but a nightmare for a humanities scholar who should, propriety suggests, best wait until after an author's death or a generation after the fading of an art movement until moving in on the territory. Thus, data is intermingled with domain-specific practices, replete with lags, innovations, and standards, but data as a key to the world, what lies beyond the screen or the networks of receptive sensors, also demands a way of attending to it. If you want to catch a putative subatomic particle in order to populate your theorems and pose new questions, you had better arrange some matter, and concatenations of data, in a sufficiently careful way to receive what it gives you.

References and Further Reading

Caminer, David, John Aris, Peter Hermon, and Frank Land. 1996. *User-Driven Innovation: The World's First Business Computer.* Maidenhead, UK: McGraw-Hill.

Daston, Loraine, and Peter Galison, 2010. *Objectivity.* New York: Zone Books.

Gehl, Robert. 2011. "The Archive and the Processor: The Internal Logic of Web 2.0." *New Media & Society* 13 (8): 1228–1244.

Kirschenbaum, Matthew. 2008. *Mechanisms, New Media and the Forensic Imagination.* Cambridge, MA. MIT Press.

Naur, Peter. 1992. *Computing: A Human Activity.* Maidenhead, UK: ACM Press / Addison-Wesley.
von Neumann, John. 1945. *First Draft of a Report on the EDVAC.* Moore School of Engineering, University of Pennsylvania.

....

Database
Christiane Paul

A database, now commonly understood as a computerized record-keeping system, is a structured collection of data which stands in the tradition of "data containers" such as the book, library, and archive (see ARCHIVE, DATA). While the term *database* was first introduced in the early 1960s—coinciding with the emergence of direct-access storage, such as disks—it became a defining principle of cultural storage only in the 1990s. The 1990s were a decade of major digitization, when libraries, archives, and museum collections were translated into digital format, allowing for new forms of filtering and relational connections. In the early twenty-first century the logic and structure of the database have transcended the purely digital realm and the traditional archives of libraries, administrations, and museums. The notion of the database as an organizational model has increasingly infiltrated culture and led to the emergence of the database as, in Lev Manovich's words, a new "symbolic form" (Manovich 1998).

According to the *Oxford English Dictionary*, one of the first appearances of the term *database* was in a 1962 technical memo: "i. 5 A 'data base' is a collection of entries containing item information that can vary in its storage media and in the characteristics of its entries and items" (System Development Corp. 1962). What distinguishes digital databases from their analog predecessors is their inherent possibility for the retrieval and filtering of data in multiple ways (see ANALOG VERSUS DIGITAL). A database essentially is a system that comprises (1) the data container, consisting of tables and structures that house discrete data units; (2) the database management system—the software package that allows for housing the data in its respective container and for retrieving, filtering, and changing it; and (3) the users who browse the data and understand it as information.

Databases can be distinguished according to different "data models"—that is, data containers and the ways in which data are stored in and retrieved from them. The most common model is the relational database, which emerged from the research of E. F. Codd at IBM in the late 1960s and relies on the concept of tables (so-called relations) that store all data. Among the most common data models—some of them subsets of others and sometimes used in combination—are the following:

- *Hierarchical databases*, which arrange the data in hierarchies similar to a tree structure with parent-child relationships.
- *Network databases*, which are still close to the hierarchical model but use "sets" to establish a hierarchy that allows children to have more than one parent and thus establishes many-to-many relationships.
- *Relational databases*, which—contrary to hierarchical or network databases—do not require a close understanding of how exactly information within the database is structured since each table can be identified by a unique name that can be called and found by the database.

- *Client/server databases*, which come in various forms and allow multiple "clients" to remotely and simultaneously access and retrieve information from a database server around the clock.
- *Object-oriented databases*, which are designed to work well with object-oriented programming languages (such as Java and C++) and make entries (objects) in the database appear as programming language objects in one or more languages.

Other approaches to classifying databases would be distinguishing them by the type of their content (e.g., multimedia objects, statistical or bibliographical data) or their application area (e.g., banking and accounting, or manufacturing).

There is no digitally born object in the broadest sense which does not consist of a back-end of algorithms and data sets that are structured according to some underlying principle of organization (see ALGORITHM). This back-end mostly remains hidden and produces a visible front-end—taking the form of anything ranging from complex visuals to abstract communication processes—that is experienced by the viewer/user (see INTERFACE). Manovich has argued that any new media object consists of one or more interfaces to a database of multimedia material, even if it does not explicitly point to its roots in a database (Manovich 2001, 227). Manovich's argument is based on a very broad understanding of the term *database*—rather than the narrower definition of a database management system retrieving and filtering the information in a data container—but captures the importance of a structured collection of data to digital media.

Given the fact that database structure in the broadest sense lies at the root of digital media, it is only natural that the database and its associated logic, aesthetics, and politics now play a major role in digital culture and art. In discourse on digital art, the term *database aesthetics* is frequently used to describe the aesthetic principles applied in either imposing the logic of the database on any type of information, filtering data collections, or visualizing data (Vesna 2007). The term is seldom used to refer to the aesthetics of the database container—although it certainly implies that meaning. The common understanding of "database aesthetics" seems to be more focused on the operations on the front-end—the interactions with the visual manifestations of algorithms, and cultural implications—rather than the back-end of the data container and its structure.

If any new media object consists of one or more interfaces to a database of multimedia material, the object almost always is a visualization of data, which can be culled either from a preselected and stored data set or in real time from a constantly changing source (such as weather data). The visualization and dynamic mapping of data, be it real time or preselected, have become a broad area of exploration in digital art and culture. Various projects can visualize a similar data set (such as stock market data) in distinctly different ways. Database aesthetics has become an important cultural narrative of our time, constituting a shift toward a relational, networked approach to gathering and creating knowledge about cultural specifics. It can be considered a conceptual potential and cultural form—a way of revealing (visual) patterns of knowledge, beliefs, and social behavior. Generally speaking, the aesthetics of a database are inherently relational, be it on the level of the potential opened up by the data stored in its container or by the actual relationships established through the software component.

Database aesthetics suggest the possibilities of tracing process (individual, cultural, communicative, etc.) in its various forms. Apart from visualizations of data sets that often do not explicitly reveal the database as an underlying structure, there have been a multitude of projects that trace cultural subtexts by means of arranging information in a database which then become a means of revealing metanarratives about cultural values and conventions. Examples would be Golan Levin's online data visualization *The Secret Life of Numbers* (Levin et al. 2002), which analyzes the popularity of numbers and exposes their "secret life"—patterns of associations that reflect cultural interests—or Jennifer and Kevin McCoy's *How I Learned*, which exposes the cultural conditioning of learned behavior by creating a video database of the Eastern-Western television series *Kung Fu*, classifying it in categories such as "how I learned about exploiting workers" or "how I learned to love the land" (McCoy and McCoy 2002). Databases lend themselves to a categorization of information that can then be filtered to create metanarratives about the construction and cultural specifics of the original material.

The characteristics of the database, as a collection of information that can be structured according to various criteria and result in a metanarrative, in many ways differ from the concept of the traditional narrative as it unfolds in a book, film, or even single visual image. While narratives can be driven by many different strategies and factors—among them character development, cause-and-effect relationships between events, spatial and temporal movement—they generally establish a sequence of events or defined relationships (for example in a story, an event or even "scene" depicted in a photograph). Lev Manovich sees the database and narrative as natural enemies, pointing out that a database can support narrative, but that nothing in the logic of the database itself fosters the generation of narrative (Manovich 2001, 225). In terms of textuality, Manovich analyzes the semiotics of the database by associating narrative with syntagm and database with paradigm. Ferdinand de Saussure defined syntagmatic relations as those referring intratextually to other words copresent within the text and paradigmatic relations as those referring intertextually to words absent from the text (Saussure [1916] 1983, 122; Saussure [1916] 1974, 123). The syntagmatic dimension is typically constructed in a linear sequence, as words strung together, while the paradigmatic dimension consists of sets of elements (e.g., synonyms) related to any given word. As Manovich puts it, narrative (the syntagmatic dimension) is usually explicit, while (the database of) choices from which the narrative is constructed (the paradigmatic dimension) is implicit. The words making up the narrative materially exist on a piece of paper, while the paradigmatic sets to which these words belong exist in writer's and reader's minds. According to Manovich, the database reverses these relationships on various levels: in the database, the paradigm is privileged and given material existence, while the narrative (arising from the algorithmic filtering of the elements in the database) is downplayed, dematerialized, and virtual (Manovich 2001, 230). The logic and structure of the database therefore constitute a significant shift in the production of meaning.

In the age of social media and the increasing online collection and aggregation of data, there is a growing tension between the dynamics on the front-end, where users interact, and the database back-end, to which owners have access (Stalder 2012, 242) (see SOCIAL NETWORK SITES [SNSs]). The front-end of social media might advance what Elizabeth Stark has defined as semiotic democracy, "the ability of users to produce and disseminate new creations and to take part in public cultural discourse" (Stark 2006), while the back-end largely supports corporate structures. In terms of the politics of the database, the front-end and back-end of the social web create a phenomenon that, as Felix Stalder points out, is characterized by two contradictory dynamics. The front-end, as the creation of voluntary communities, is "decentralized, ad hoc, cheap, easy to use, community oriented and transparent," while the back-end, as the provision of new data-base infrastructures, is "centralized, based on long-term planning, very expensive, difficult to run, corporate and opaque" (Stalder 2012, 248). The new frontier for databases is cloud computing, which requires highly scalable high-performance database management systems and poses challenges with regard to security and the functionality of relational databases. An increasing number of applications are launched in environments with massive workloads that have quickly shifting scalability requirements. The logic, politics, and aesthetics of the database are and will continue to be a defining element of digital culture which affects our daily lives on numerous levels (see POLITICS AND NEW MEDIA).

References and Further Reading

Levin, Golan, Martin Wattenberg, Jonathan Feinberg, Shelly Wynecoop, David Elashoff, and David Becker. 2002. *The Secret Life of Numbers*. www.turbulence.org/Works/nums/.

Manovich, Lev. 1998. "The Database as Symbolic Form." http://transcriptions.english.ucsb.edu/archive/courses/warner/english197/Schedule_files/Manovich/Database_as_symbolic_form.htm.

———. 2001. *The Language of New Media*. Cambridge, MA: MIT Press.

McCoy, Jennifer, and Kevin McCoy. 2002. *How I Learned*. www.mccoyspace.com, www.flickr.com/photos/mccoyspace/sets/327764/.

Saussure, Ferdinand de. (1916) 1974. *Course in General Linguistics*. Translated by Wade Baskin. London: Fontana/Collins.

———. (1916) 1983. *Course in General Linguistics*. Translated by Roy Harris. London: Duckworth.

Stalder, Felix. 2012. "Between Democracy and Spectacle: The Front-End and Back-End of the Social Web." In *The Social Media Reader*, edited by Michael Mandiberg. New York: New York University Press.

Stark, Elizabeth. 2006. "Free Culture and the Internet: A New Semiotic Democracy." www.opendemocracy.net/arts-commons/semiotic_3662.jsp.

System Development Corp. 1962. *Technical Memo*, TM-WD-16/007/00.

Vesna, Victoria, ed. 2007. *Database Aesthetics*. Minneapolis: University of Minnesota Press.

Dialogue Systems
Jichen Zhu

A dialogue system (also dialog system, conversation system) is an interactive computational system designed to provide conversation-like exchanges with human users, typically by natural language. A dialogue system may be stand-alone, such as a chatterbot, or a component of a larger system, such as the mechanism for talking with non-player characters (NPCs) in a computer game (see CHATTERBOTS, NPC [NONPLAYER CHARACTER]). The wide spectrum of dialogue systems can be loosely divided into tool-like and anthropomorphic, based on whether the system's interaction model is framed as a generic information provider or a specific character (Edlund et al. 2008). Dialogue systems also vary significantly in terms of their algorithmic complexity: some simpler systems are designed for constrained scenarios with limited variability, whereas others use artificial intelligence (AI) techniques to handle complex situations and increase user agency (see ARTIFICIAL INTELLIGENCE).

One of the earliest and most influential dialogue systems is ELIZA, a natural language conversation program developed by Joseph Weizenbaum in the mid-1960s. At a time when computers were primarily used for scientific and military applications, ELIZA offered many people their first conversations with an interactive computer character (Murray 1997). Despite ELIZA's brittle illusion due to its simple process of pattern-matching key phrases, people quickly developed an emotional connection to the computer psychotherapist and perceived it as something/someone containing deep understanding of their conditions. The success of ELIZA highlights a human susceptibility to "read far more understanding than is warranted into strings of symbols—especially words—strung together by computers" (Hofstadter 1995, 157). This ELIZA effect offers mixed blessings for interactive storytelling designers. It suggests that human behaviors may be represented by computer algorithms that are far less complex by comparison, but at the same time, that these initially inflated views of the computer's capabilities can quickly fall apart (Wardrip-Fruin 2009).

ELIZA is part of the larger AI research effort in the 1960s to teach computers natural language. For instance, Terry Winograd's SHRDLU system allows the player to manipulate objects in a simulated block world through a natural language interface. Compared with ELIZA's capability to respond to a wide range of topics at the surface level, SHRDLU focuses on deep knowledge of a narrow domain and can reason about its own actions reflexively. Although not directly concerned with storytelling, these systems shed light on the nature of human language. More importantly, they raised the essential question that would set the boundaries for later language-based computer applications, including interactive storytelling systems: Can computers understand language?

As Winograd and Flores later reflected, systems such as SHRDLU are based on the fundamental assumption that the core meaning of words, phrases, and sentences is context independent and can be deduced from a set of rules regardless of the listener. From ELIZA to SHRDLU and even IBM's recent Watson system, these systems have grown more complex, and their limitations have become harder to spot, but their *blindness* (Heidegger 1962) to the contextual meaning of words remained. This fundamental limitation, Winograd and Flores argue, will significantly constrain the computer's ability to understand open-ended human natural language conversations.

As a result, a holodeck-styled dialogue system, if possible, may still be far in the future (see INTERACTIVE NARRATIVE). Existing systems inevitably operate around a set of constraints and simplifications. Dialogue systems in interactive storytelling (e.g., computer games and electronic literature), routinely used to represent NPCs, assume a turn-based interaction model and constrain the conversation to a very limited domain. Based on algorithmic complexity and the amount of user agency they afford, these systems can be broadly classified into three types: (1) noninteractive dialogue system, (2) dialogue tree, and (3) parser-based dialogue systems (Ellison 2010).

The simplest type is the noninteractive dialogue system. The player traverses through a fixed sequence of pre-authored dialogue, only controlling *when* the conversation continues. A slight variation is that the system may choose from multiple conversations, but once selected, the dialogue sequence is fixed. Widely used in many genres of computer games as cut scenes, noninteractive dialogue systems are easy to implement and can effectively deliver key story points in an otherwise interactive environment. In early computer games, this type of dialogue system offers a relatively robust way to incorporate dramatic elements into the gameplay mechanism. For example, the death of the beloved character Aries in *Final Fantasy VII*, a renowned narrative moment for many gamers, is delivered in this way.

The second and more complex type is a dialogue tree, commonly used in role-playing games. Branches of dialogue segments are represented as nodes in the treelike data structure, with specific conditions (e.g., actions and player responses) connecting the nodes (in strict computer science terminology, a lot of dialogue trees are in fact *graph* structures, in that they allow "loops" between dialogue nodes; see GRAPH THEORY). Based on these conditions, a dialogue tree provides a systematic way to model divergent conversations with NPCs. Compared with the previous type, dialogue trees afford more user agency by allowing the player to impact the course of the conversation. It is important to remember that in addition to its storytelling functions, dialogue trees are an important means for the player to make gameplay decisions—certain dialogue choices will also alter the course of the game (Wardrip-Fruin 2009).

User interface design of dialogue trees has a significant impact on the player's experience. A classic dialogue tree interface presents a menu of fully written responses (typically three to five), from which the player can choose. Each option represents what the player character (PC) can say and will trigger responses from NPCs and other potential changes in the gameplay (see GAMEPLAY). For instance, in LucasArts's *The Secret of Monkey Island*, the well-loved swordfight scene requires the player to select, among several similar options, the correct response to the enemy's verbal insults. The effectiveness of the player's dialogue response is directly tied to her character's physical advancement in the swordfight. The advantage of this type of interface is its directness: the player can see all the possible responses ahead of time. However, this design choice also imposes several restrictions on the writing style of the dialogues. It requires the dialogues to be concise enough to fit on the same screen and explicit about the consequences they entail. As a result, they fall short in situations where the story requires the player's quick reaction to narrative events or more nuanced dialogues. Recent games explored dialogue tree interfaces that provide the higher-level intentions behind the dialogues, instead of the exact utterances. For instance, in Quantic Dream's *Heavy Rain*, the player selects among activities such as "reason," "calm," or "threat," which then leads to a full-fledged response enacted by the PC. The interface enables the designer to tap into the player's first reaction and successfully convey a sense of urgency. Similarly, Bioware developed the "dialogue wheel" interface to map responses of similar emotional tones (e.g., "friendly," "investigative," "hostile") to the same buttons on the controller throughout the gameplay.

The third type, the parser-based dialogue system, provides more flexibility in user input by allowing the player to type their conversational turns. The system parses the user's (mostly) natural language input and produces correspondingly appropriate reactions. For example, in Emily Short's dialogue-centric interactive fiction piece *Galatea*, the player can talk to the NPC about a number of different topics at any time through an ASK/TELL interface (see INTERACTIVE FICTION). These dialogues influence the NPC's mood and position and affect the course of the subsequent conversation. The pleasure of figuring out what to ask or tell under different circumstances would be lost in the previous two types of dialogue systems. Mateas and Stern's *Façade* system takes a further step and uses natural language processing algorithms to build a semi-open-ended user interface where the player can type anything. However, because of the difficulties of making computers understand natural language, most parser-based dialogue systems are frail. Especially because of the high expectation raised by the open-ended dialogue interface, parser-based systems require the designer to craft the narrative experience carefully around these technical limitations. For instance, the main characters in *Façade* were given self-absorbed personalities in order to alleviate situations where the system fails to understand the user input.

In summary, realistic and situation-appropriate dialogues between the PCs and NPCs are an essential part of interactive storytelling. Although current dialogue systems are still fairly limited, many authors of interactive stories utilize dialogue systems to reinforce the connection between narrative content and gameplay mechanics.

■ See also ELECTRONIC LITERATURE, INTERACTIVE NARRATIVE

References and Further Reading

Edlund, Jens, Joakim Gustafson, Mattias Heldner, and Anna Hjalmarsson. 2008. "Towards Human-Like Spoken Dialogue Systems." *Speech Communication* 50 (8–9): 630–645.

Ellison, Brent. 2010. Defining Dialogue Systems. *Gamasutra: The Art & Business of Making Games.* www.gamasutra.com/view/feature/3719/defining_dialogue_systems.php.

Heidegger, Martin. 1962. *Being and Time.* Translated by J. Macquarrie and E. Robinson. San Francisco: Harper.

Hofstadter, Douglas R. 1995. "The Ineradicable Eliza Effect and Its Dangers." In *Fluid Concepts and Creative Analogies: Computer Models of the Fundamental Mechanisms of Thought.* New York: Basic Books.

Murray, Janet H. 1997. *Hamlet on the Holodeck: The Future of Narrative in Cyberspace.* New York: Simon & Schuster / Free Press.

Wardrip-Fruin, Noah. 2009. *Expressive Processing: Digital Fictions, Computer Games, and Software Studies.* Cambridge, MA: MIT Press.

Games and Electronic Literature Work

Façade. 2005. Interactive drama. Designed by Michael Mateas and Andrew Stern. www.interactivestory.net/download/.

Final Fantasy VII. 1997. Video game. Designed by Square Product.

Galatea. 2000. Interactive fiction. Designed by Emily Short. www.wurb.com/if/game/1326.

Heavy Rain. 2010. Video game. Designed by Quantic Dream.

The Secret of Monkey Island. 1990. Video game. Designed by Lucasfilm Games.

. . . .

Digital and Net Art
Roberto Simanowski

There is no agreement in the art and academic communities on how to name the type of art that makes creative use of computer technology. Within a few years at the beginning of the century several publications have presented almost the same corpus of works with different labels: Stephen Wilson's *Information Art* (2002); Christiane Paul's *Digital Art* (2003); Julian Stallabras's *Internet Art* (2003); Rachel Greene's *Internet Art* (2004); Michael Rush's *New Media in Art* (2005), which includes a chapter on digital art; Mark Tribe and Reena Jana's *New Media Art* (2006); and Bruce Wands's *Art of the Digital Age* (2006). In most cases the distinction between digital technology and the Internet is neglected; this leads to an interchangeable use of the terms *digital* and *(inter)net art*. It is, however, important to distinguish between a stand-alone computer and a network of connected computers, so as to acknowledge the additional resources that this connectedness brings to artistic projects. While interactivity between different participants at different locations (as in collaborative writing projects; see COLLABORATIVE

NARRATIVE) or between a program and information available online (as in the browsing of social data and in Internet-based installations) requires online connection, interactivity between the audience and the computer (as in the case of hyperfiction, offline computer games, and digital installation art) is made possible by features that are intrinsic to the computer and do not justify the term *net* art (see DIGITAL INSTALLATION ART, INTERACTIVITY).

In addition to the terminological confusion, there is also a lack of clarity concerning the role that the technology should play in an artwork regarded as *digital* art. Thus, the entry on digital art in the Routledge reader on key concepts of cyberculture reads as follows: "At its most basic, the term 'digital art' refers to the use of digital technology, such as computers, to produce or exhibit art forms, whether written, visual, aural—or, as is increasingly the case, in multi-medial hybrid forms" (Bell et al. 2004, 59). According to such a definition, every poem typed on a word processor and every image displayed on a website would deserve to be called either digital poetry or digital painting. But if any artwork represented within digital media is called *digital* art, this will deprive the concept of its heuristic power. The indispensable feature of the definition of digital art is dependency on digital technology not only for distribution but also for aesthetic effect: that is, for a specific mode of expression which cannot be realized without digital technology. As for the defining feature of *net.art*, it is the connectedness provided by the Internet. Hence, calling *digital* art (or any art) *net* art due to its presentation on the Internet would change the basis of the definition and would be as meaningful as saying that a story read on the radio is a radio play.

In this entry, I will regard net.art as a subspecies of digital art, and I will concentrate on the broader category, focusing on two kinds of issues: (1) what are the features—or affordances—of digital technology that the new forms of art exploit; and (2) how digital technology configures the relations between artist, artwork, and audience.

Art or Technology?

The development of this kind of art out of the traditional art world results in a "seismic instability along the edge between art and non-art" (Blais and Ippolito 2006, 231). This distinction is also complicated because of the fact that digital art by definition is concerned with digital technology, which often makes it difficult to decide whether an artifact is art or simply applied technology. A case in point is Warren Sack's *Conversation Map* (2001), a Usenet newsgroup browser that analyzes the content of and the relationships between messages and outputs a diagram that shows the social (who is talking to whom) and semantic (what are they talking about) relationships that have emerged over the course of an online discussion (see http://web.media.mit.edu/~lieber/IUI/Sack/Sack.html). Sack, then a computer science student at MIT, first presented his work in artificial intelligence journals and at anthropology conferences and "wasn't really thinking about it as an art project." It was only after people from the art world showed interest in his work that he started to consider it art (Blais and Ippolito 2006, 160). The question of whether such an artifact is to be considered a technology helping us undertake sociological studies and statistic analysis or whether it possesses aesthetic qualities of its own is brought up, though not explicitly addressed, by Christiane Paul, who includes Sack's *Conversation Map* in her survey on digital art. She concludes, "In all likelihood, these types of dynamic maps of communication will increasingly become part of websites and networked environments that rely on online conversation" (Paul 2003, 189).

Literature or Visual Art?

The specific characteristics of the technology being applied also blur the boundaries between different genres of art, an issue raised by N. Katherine Hayles. In her book *Electronic Literature: New Horizons for the Literary* she states that the "demarcation between digital art and electronic literature is shifty at best, often more a matter of the critical traditions from which the works are discussed than anything intrinsic to the works themselves" (Hayles 2008, 12). Since electronic (or digital) literature cannot by definition be limited to the use of words but needs to employ additional features—such as sensory elements, a specific mode of processing or means of interaction—the boundary between (experimental) *literature* and text-based *art*, that is, between *performance* and *installation*, is a fuzzy one. A case in point is *Text Rain* (1999) by Camille Utterback and Romy Achituv. Here, viewers stand or move in front of a large monitor on which they see themselves as black-and-white projections. Letters fall from the top edge, landing on the participants' bodies; responding to the participants' motions, they can be lifted and dropped again. To the extent that *Text Rain* is more about playing with the text than about reading it, it can hardly be called literature. However, since the falling letters are taken from the lines of a poem, the text is not just a visual object stripped of any linguistic meaning but also a signifying system. The reading process remains as important for understanding this work as in traditional concrete poetry; the way text is presented only reveals its deeper meaning after the text itself is understood.

The Double Life of Text

Text Rain exemplifies the case of a text of digital art functioning either as a linguistic artifact or as a toy for playful interaction, depending on the role the audience allows the text to play. There is a trend in (interactive) installations to use text as an element that is not to be read but to be looked at or played with. Such desemanticization evokes a "cannibalistic" relationship between the semiotic systems of text on the one hand and of visual, installation, or performance art on the other. Other examples of the double life of text and of its transformation into a post-alphabetic object through the deprivation of its linguistic value are *Listening Post* (2001) by Mark Hansen and Ben Rubin (see www.youtube.com/watch?v=dD36IajCz6A) and *Bit.Fall* (2006) by Julius Popp (see www.youtube.com/watch?v=ygQHj1WoPPM). In *Listening Post*, which can be regarded as net art, several computers analyze data from thousands of Internet chat rooms, bulletin boards, and other public forums in order to feed text fragments containing certain phrases (such as "I am" or "I like") into 231 miniature text display screens on a suspended curved grid of eleven rows and twenty-one columns. The displayed text is also read aloud by computer-generated voices. When the spectator stands close to the screens, the text snippets can be read and the work can therefore be considered an example of experimental literature, but when she stands farther away and the letters turn illegible, *Listening Post* becomes visual and sonic art. In *Bit.Fall*, which also requires connection to the Internet, a computer scans news web pages, pulls keywords (nouns, verbs, and proper names), and writes them as a "waterfall of letters" by means of magnetic vents at the top of a frame 157 inches high and 393 inches wide, which enables each of the several water jets to evoke the "WOW factor" that Stephen Pevnick, the original inventor of this technology, achieved through his "Graphical Waterfalls." For this reason, the words, rather than being carefully read, are looked at in awe as a sublime event.

Interaction and Interpretation

The invitation to interact with digital artworks foregrounds exploration and action at the expense of interpretation. Interpretation is often limited to the understanding of the "grammar of interaction" (i.e., the modus of interaction the artist made possible within the interactive environment), not in terms of its meaning but in terms of its configuration. To interact with the work, one needs to understand its rules of operation. Hence, the audience reads the work at hand in order to become an "author"—that is, to contribute to the work without necessarily having to ponder its meaning. Finding out how it works becomes more important than finding out what it means. While in traditional art engaging with a work basically means to search for its deeper meaning, digital art allows us to engage with the work without any attempt at interpretation. One could even say that the dialogue with the work as an interactor gets in the way of a dialogue with it as an interpreter because the initial interactive dialogue may give the interactor the impression that she has engaged thoroughly and sufficiently with the work.

Importance of Code

Code is without doubt an indispensable element in every theoretical discussion of digital art because everything that happens on the screen or on the scene is first and foremost subject to the grammar of code (see CODE, CODE AESTHETICS). In many cases and in many different ways, it is important to understand what has been done and what can be done on the level of code to understand and assess the semantics of a digital artifact. However, a preoccupation with code threatens to divert attention from the actual meaning of an artifact. The formalistic focus on technologies behind the interface neglects the actual experience of the audience and impedes access to the artwork's aesthetics. Code only matters to the extent that it produces text, sound, visual object, and process matters in the experience of the work by its audience.

Craftsmanship

If the artist targets matters of coding itself, rather than conceptual thinking concerning symbolic issues, success and recognition are gained on the level of design and technical execution rather than on the level of ideas. This observation supports Clement Greenberg's assumption that the close concern with the nature of the medium, and hence with "technique," becomes an "artisanal" concern (1971, 46). When the focus of a work is the virtuoso handling of code, fame is based on craftsmanship. When Lev Manovich (1999) states that "avant-garde becomes software," one may ask to what extent software becomes avant-garde and avant-garde, in digital media, becomes a default. A particularly telling example of the return of craftsmanship is the interactive installation *Mondrian* (2004) by Zachary Booth Simpson and his collaborators, allowing the audience to generate Mondrian-like images by drawing lines on a screen with their hand and coloring sections with one of their fingers. The opportunity to create their own Mondrian composition in ten seconds, as advertised by the authors of this Mondrian machine, not only mocks Mondrian but also establishes the virtuosity of the programmer at the expense of the painter, who did not, in contrast to the programmer, make an ostentatious display of his craft in his work.

Technology and Meaning

In digital art, the demands of coding or, alternatively, the constraints of technology may give rise to unintended situations and signals with no implications for the work's significance. A specific feature may actually be a bug the artist was not able to fix, or it may be there for other nonaesthetic reasons. An example of such technological determinism is the interactive drama *Façade* (2005) by Michael Mateas and Andrew Stern (see INTERACTIVE DRAMA). In *Façade*, a text generator based on language processing (see CHATTERBOTS, DIALOGUE SYSTEMS), the interactor plays the role of a guest who influences the outcome of the marriage crisis of her longtime "friends" Grace and Trip, who are represented on the screen by two cartoon characters. In order to sustain the illusion of a real dialogue between the software and the interactor, Mateas and Stern made sure that the core of a dialogue turn's meaning is always communicated in its first few seconds, during which any interruption from the interactor is blocked. Grace and Trip are also, by design, such self-absorbed individuals that they can "believably ignore unrecognized or unhandleable player actions" (Mateas and Stern 2007, 207). The behavior of the characters—reacting to the player only after a long delay and making their point right away instead of working toward it—does not necessarily correspond to a deliberate choice of the authors; rather, it is dictated by the need to keep the interaction plausible despite the technological challenge. Features that in a traditional text would reveal something about the personality of the characters point instead in this context to certain characteristics of the underlying technology. A digital hermeneutics has to take into account the possibility of such technological determinism.

Aesthetic Consequences of Technology

Façade also shows that if a work is avant-garde or advanced in terms of productive mechanisms, its output—the manifestation of the code as text—may very well be conservative. In an interactive drama such as *Façade* the challenge to maintain a convincing dialogue between the interactor and the underlying artificial intelligence requires players to keep the dialogue as ordinary and common as possible. Any absurd reaction would not be understood by the interactor as deliberate, as it would in a play by, say, Alfred Jarry, but would rather be regarded as a malfunction of the program. Since absurdity is the default output of text generators, the author or programmer can only prove her craftsmanship by making the generator produce text that is as conventional as possible. Thus, the trademark of the work's sophistication on the level of generation is the conventionality of its behavior, as it appears via the interface.

Analyzing Digital Media

Scholars of art, or of any hermeneutic discipline, have a choice of two main strategies to analyze digital media. One approach, inspired by cultural studies, focuses on the social context and on its consequences for the production and reception of works of digital art. Its concerns will be with issues such as technology, authorship, copyright, distribution, and the digital divide. Alternatively, and more in the spirit of a semiotic reading, one can opt for a more formal analysis driven by internal factors: attention will then focus on the characteristics of digital language and on codes of meaning—as exemplified in individual artifacts—with the goal of learning how to read a digitally produced sign and how to understand a specific performance of a work of digital art (see

PERFORMANCE). According to this strategy, the codes of art and the codes of technology converge toward a highly interesting nexus of relations, providing multiple, layered domains of signification which have rarely been fully explored simultaneously.

■ See also CONCEPTUAL WRITING, ELECTRONIC LITERATURE, GLITCH AESTHETICS

References and Further Reading

Bell, David J., Brian Loader, Nicholas Pleace, and Douglas Schuler. 2004. *Cyberculture: The Key Concepts*. London: Routledge.

Blais, Joline, and Jon Ippolito. 2006. *At the Edge of Art*. London: Thames & Hudson.

Greenberg, Clement. 1971. "Necessity of 'Formalism.'" In *Late Writings*, 45–49. Minneapolis: University of Minnesota Press.

Greene, Rachel. 2004. *Internet Art*. London: Thames & Hudson.

Hayles, N. Katherine. 2008. *Electronic Literature: New Horizons for the Literary*. Notre Dame, IN: University of Notre Dame Press.

Manovich, Lev. 1999. "Avant-Garde as Software." www.manovich.net/docs/avant garde_as_software .doc.

Mateas, Micheal, and Andrew Stern. 2007. "Writing *Façade*: A Case Study in Procedural Authorship." In *Second Person: Role Playing and Story in Games and Playable Media*, edited by Pat Harrigan and Noah Wardrip-Fruin, 183–207. Cambridge, MA: MIT Press.

Paul, Christiane. 2003. *Digital Art*. London: Thames & Hudson.

Rush, Michael. 2005. *New Media in Art*. London: Thames & Hudson.

Simanowski, Roberto. 2010. "Digital Anthropophagy: Refashioning Words as Image, Sound and Action." *Leonardo* 43 (2): 159–163.

———. 2011. *Digital Art and Meaning: Reading Kinetic Poetry, Text Machines, Mapping Art, and Interactive Installations*. Minneapolis: University of Minnesota Press.

———. 2012. "Text as Event: Calm Technology and Invisible Information as Subject of Digital Arts." In *Throughout: Art and Culture Emerging with Ubiquitous Computing*, edited by Ulrik Ekman. Cambridge, MA: MIT Press.

Stallabrass, Julian. 2003. *Internet Art: The Online Clash of Culture and Commerce*. London: Tate Gallery Publishing.

Tribe, Mark, and Reena Jana. 2006. *New Media Art*. Cologne: Taschen.

Wands, Bruce. 2006. *Art of the Digital Age*. London: Thames & Hudson.

Wilson, Stephen. 2002. *Information Arts: Intersections of Art and Technology*. Cambridge, MA: MIT Press.

Digital Fiction
Maria Engberg

Digital fiction is used as an umbrella term under which many different subgenres or specific writing practices using digital media can be sorted: hypertext fiction (see HYPERTEXTUALITY), network fiction (see NONLINEAR WRITING), interactive fiction (see INTERACTIVE FICTION), e-mail novels (see E-MAIL NOVEL), and multimedia novels are among them. The term is not uncontested and is not universally used among scholars and writers who engage with digital writing, in critical work or in practice. *Digital fiction* is therefore not a standard term for literary narratives in digital form, nor does it have a stable definition. Instead, it encompasses and competes with other terms, some of which may have a longer existence (e.g., hypertext fiction) or are more narrowly defined (e.g., interactive fiction). Some critics, such as Alice Bell et al. (2010), seem to equate digital fiction with other related terms such as electronic literature and e-lit, which both potentially include poetry (see DIGITAL POETRY, ELECTRONIC LITERATURE).

The definitions of digital fiction that have been offered, although few, tend to embrace a wide range of practices. Alice Bell and Astrid Ensslin suggest that "digital fiction is fiction, written for and read on a computer screen, that pursues its verbal, discursive, and/or conceptual complexity through the digital medium and would lose something of its aesthetic and semiotic function if it were removed from that medium" (2011, 311). This definition echoes the one suggested for another, correlate term, *electronic literature*: "works with important literary aspects that take advantage of the capabilities and contexts provided by the stand-alone or networked computer" (Electronic Literature Organization, n.d.). The Electronic Literature Organization's definition of electronic literature also makes a clear distinction between digitized works and what are sometimes called born-digital works, stating that "the confrontation with technology at the level of creation is what distinguishes electronic literature" (Electronic Literature Organization, n.d.). David Ciccoricco, using the term *network fiction* instead, defines it as that which "makes use of hypertext technology in order to create emergent and recombinatory narratives" (2007, 7). Roberto Simanowski elaborates on the combination of materiality and narrative intentionality as key to defining digital, as opposed to digitized, literature: "digital literature must go beyond what could be done without digital media. . . . Digital literature must be more than just literature otherwise it is only literature in digital media" (2009, 12).

As a general term, then, digital fiction encompasses any length of work, any form, any thematic subgroup, any software, and any degree of interaction with the work. Unlike Espen Aarseth's definition of what he called "cybertexts" (Aarseth 1997), the level of interaction from the reader is not an important distinctive feature in existing definitions of digital fiction. Instead, the material origin and intention of how the works are created and received are foregrounded. In addition to a more general understanding of what *digital fiction* means, there are also subgenres and related groups of literary practice. These tend to function as individual groups of digital fiction that have their own communities, audiences, and technological frameworks. These include, for instance, interactive fiction (see INTERACTIVE FICTION), e-mail novels of various kinds (see E-MAIL NOVEL), and fan fiction (see FAN FICTION), as well as SMS or cell phone novels (see CELL PHONE NOVEL), interactive narratives in games and similar platforms (see INTERACTIVE NARRATIVE), and emergent forms such as locative media fiction (see LOCATION-BASED NARRATIVE). The cell phone novel (*keitai shōsetsu*) emerged in Japan in the 2000s as a uniquely digital mobile narrative form and quickly grew to be popular in its native country as the novels were published in print (Onishi 2008). These novels, as well as popular republished fan fiction novels, exist, then, on both sides of the print/digital divide, whereas most other genres defined as digital fiction do not.

The "digital" in digital fiction refers to, as mentioned, digital technologies that are used in some form. However, critics and authors often make a distinction between works that are created specifically with digital media, and are intended to be consumed with digital media as well, and digitized writing, which includes various forms of e-books and digital documents that adhere to print conventions. N. Katherine Hayles suggests that electronic literature is " 'born digital,' a first-generation digital object created on a computer and (usually) meant to be read on a computer" (2008, 3). Similar terms have been suggested, such as "native born digital writing" (Grigar 2008) or "born-digital poetry"

(Engberg 2007). "Born-digital" is a defining distinction between digitized material, such as scanned texts that appear in repositories such as Google Books, or e-books and other digital texts, and literary works created specifically with and for digital media. The "digital" in these terms is also a broad term, as it encapsulates, essentially, all media. There is no distinction at this level of particular software types or programming languages.

Fiction, as "literature created from the imagination" (*Encyclopedia Britannica*, "fiction"), comes from the Latin word *fictiō*, meaning the act of making, fashioning, or molding. A standard definition of fiction is that it is any literary narrative, "whether in prose or verse, which is invented instead of being an account of events that actually happened" (Abrams 2009, 116). Fiction in the term *digital fiction* is generally not defined separately; instead, the distinction between digitized and born-digital works is emphasized.

In "A [S]creed for Digital Fiction," Bell et al. (2010) propose a model for analyzing digital fiction based on close analysis of individual works. They argue that "the aesthetic force, reflexive engagement and complexity of a fiction, rather than its place in a process of technological advancement," are what matter for analysis. Their understanding of the importance of the digital medium for digital fiction, apparent in the works' aesthetic and semiotic functions, differs from media nonspecific concepts such as Hayles's technotext and Aarseth's cybertext, both of which encompass both digital and print texts.

Within scholarship on digital writing at large, various trends can be discerned: the hypertext discussions of the 1990s; digital poetry (and its correlate terms, such as electronic poetry and e-poetry) in the 2000s; electronic literature as an umbrella term, closely related to the American Electronic Literature Organization (ELO) started in 1999; and in the 2010s different notions of procedural or computational narratives (Wardrip-Fruin 2012). There are distinct, and at times isolated, communities that discuss their particular genre of digital fiction. Such communities exist for interactive fiction (Montfort 2003), hypertext fiction (Joyce 1996; Yellowlees Douglas 2001; Ciccoricco 2007; Bell 2010), and digital visual poetry (Glazier 2001; Funkhouser 2007). The collections *First Person: New Media as Story, Performance, and Game* (2004), *Second Person: Role-Playing and Story in Games and Playable Media* (2007), and *Third Person: Authoring and Exploring Vast Narratives* (2009) all include essays on various topics related to digital fiction. Interestingly, the term *digital fiction* appears rarely. However, the range of themes in these three essay collections signals the field of digital creative practices in which digital fiction operates, as a writing practice and a field of critical study.

Whether they are designated communities or subgenres, the term *digital fiction* thus encompasses a series of writing practices, including hypertext fiction, interactive fiction, multimedia fiction, distributed narratives, blog fiction, alternate reality games (ARGs), fan fiction, and cell phone fiction. Digital fiction can also be said to include some forms of digital poetry, machinima, and fictional works on social media sites such as Flickr, Facebook, Twitter, and YouTube. In addition to these named subgenres, works are also grouped according to literary, technical, or aesthetic affiliations. In the Electronic Literature Directory, managed by ELO, tags such as fiction, hypertext, and interactive novel are used to group together similar works. The two volumes of the Electronic Literature Collection, also affiliated with ELO, use keywords. In volume 1, "fiction" is defined as "by analogy with print, story-like or narrative elements appear in the work" (Hayles et al. 2006). Sixteen of the sixty works in volume 1 are defined as fiction, many of which are also defined as hypertext. In volume 2 (Borràs et al. 2011), the keyword "fiction" is taken out, although three out of sixty-two are defined as interactive fiction, and eleven works are marked as hypertext (not specified as fiction or poetry).

Following Marie-Laure Ryan's work on narrative across media forms, Noah Wardrip-Fruin has argued that fiction, particularly digital fiction, can be defined by help of possible-worlds theory and modal logic. Works such as Rob Wittig's e-mail novel *Blue Company* (2001–2002), *The Unknown* (Gillespie et al. 1998–2001), and computer game fiction *Star Wars: Knights of the Old Republic* (Falkner, Brockington, and Hudson 2003) are analyzed as exploring the potentiality of unconventional reading strategies, meaning-making processes involving machine and reader alike, and the gamelike features engendering their poetics (Wardrip-Fruin 2012). The idea of digital fiction as a possible world is an attempt to break away from print conventions that consider fiction in more familiar forms, such as novels, short stories, theater, television, and movies (Wardrip-Fruin 2012, 138), and to instead consider newer definitions that configure the narrative as a world in which constituent parts (images, words, but also computational behaviors and interactivity) become part of the fictional discourse (Ryan 1992).

Historical periods and aesthetic schools that are addressed in literary studies in general, such as modernism and postmodernism, are also applicable to digital fiction. Steve Tomasula's *TOC: A New Media Novel* (2009) can be described as contemporary experimental writing, at least in part written in a late postmodernist mode. *TOC* resides in a contemporary continuation of experimental writing, clearly evident in earlier hypertext works such as Michael Joyce's *afternoon: a story* ([1987] 1990), Shelley Jackson's *Patchwork Girl* (1995), and the 2001 Electronic Literature Award winner in the fiction category, Caitlin Fisher's *These Waves of Girls* (2001). Contemporary fictional works such as *Changed* (2011) and *Dim O'Gauble* (2007) by Andy Campbell (UK) and Kate Pullinger and Chris Joseph's (UK) *Inanimate Alice* series (2005), on the other hand, use storytelling and multimodality to create narrative works that break away from modernist or postmodernist genres. The *Inanimate Alice* series is also described as transmedia storytelling (see TRANSMEDIAL FICTION). Critics such as Sarah Sloane (2000), Loss Pequeño Glazier (2001), and Christopher Funkhouser (2007) have suggested that modernist or postmodernist affiliations are strong in digital writing. Further, critics and writers alike have explored the different connections with the historical avant-garde in certain digital writing, particularly in what is called "codework" (Cayley 2002; Sondheim 2001).

In the 2000s, the application of narratology and narrative theory to the study of longer forms of digital writing emerged as an important theoretical framework. Critics such as Marie-Laure Ryan, Alice Bell, Astrid Ensslin, and David Ciccoricco have applied narratological concepts to the study of primarily hypertext fiction and computer games. In their understanding of digital fiction, these critics tend to exclude blogs, e-books, and fan fiction or "communitarian digital fiction" (Bell et al. 2010).

Theoretical frameworks, media contexts, and audiences for the various writing styles that can be gathered under the term *digital media* vary widely. As with the term *fiction*, the wide reach of the term's meaning and the continuous development of fictional narratives in digital media ensure that the kinds of works that are designated as digital fiction will continue to shift in aesthetics, media, and narrative form.

■ See also NARRATIVITY, NONLINEAR WRITING, TRANSMEDIAL FICTION

References and Further Reading

Aarseth, Espen. 1997. *Cybertext: Perspectives on Ergodic Literature*. Baltimore: Johns Hopkins University Press.

Abrams, M. H. 2009. *A Glossary of Literary Terms*. 9th ed. Boston: Wadsworth Cengage Learning.

Bell, Alice. 2010. *The Possible Worlds of Hypertext Fiction*. Basingstoke, UK: Palgrave-Macmillan.

Bell, Alice, and Astrid Ensslin. 2011. "'I know what it was. You know what it was': Second-Person Narration in Hypertext Fiction." *Narrative* 19 (3): 311–329.

Bell, Alice, Astrid Ensslin, Dave Ciccoricco, Hans Rustad, Jess Laccetti, and Jessica Pressman. 2010. "A [S]creed for Digital Fiction." *electronic book review*. www.electronicbookreview.com/thread/electropoetics/DFINative.

Borràs, Laura, Talan Memmott, Rita Raley, and Brian Stefans, eds. 2011. *Electronic Literature Collection*. Volume 2. College Park, MD: Electronic Literature Organization. http://collection.eliterature.org/2/.

Campbell, Andy. 2007. *Dim O'Gauble*. www.dreamingmethods.com.

———. 2011. *Changed*. www.dreamingmethods.com.

Cayley, John. 2002. "The Code Is Not the Text (Unless It Is the Text)." *electronic book review*. www.electronicbookreview.com/thread/electropoetics/literal.

Ciccoricco, David. 2007. *Reading Network Fiction*. Tuscaloosa: University of Alabama Press.

Electronic Literature Organization. n.d. "About the ELO." http://eliterature.org/about/.

Engberg, Maria. 2007. "Born Digital: Writing Poetry in the Age of New Media." PhD diss., Uppsala University, Sweden.

Falkner, David, Mark Brockington, and Casey Hudson. 2003. *Star Wars: Knights of the Old Republic*. LucasArts.

Fisher, Caitlin. 2001. *These Waves of Girls*. www.yorku.ca/caitlin/waves/.

Funkhouser, Christopher. 2007. *Prehistoric Digital Poetry: An Archaeology of Forms, 1959–1995*. Tuscaloosa: University of Alabama Press.

Gillespie, William, Scott Rettberg, Frank Marquardt, and Dirk Stratton. 1998–2001. *The Unknown*. www.unknownhypertext.com.

Glazier, Loss Pequeño. 2001. *Digital Poetics: The Making of E-poetries*. Tuscaloosa: University of Alabama Press.

Grigar, Dene. 2008. "Electronic Literature: *Where Is It?*" *electronic book review*. www.electronicbookreview.com/thread/technocapitalism/invigorating.

Harrigan, Pat, and Noah Wardrip-Fruin. 2004. *First Person: New Media as Story, Performance, and Game*. Cambridge, MA: MIT Press.

———. 2009. *Third Person: Authoring and Exploring Vast Narratives*. Cambridge, MA: MIT Press.

Harrigan, Pat, Noah Wardrip-Fruin, and Michael Crompton. 2007. *Second Person: Role-Playing and Story in Games and Playable Media*. Cambridge, MA: MIT Press.

Hayles, N. Katherine. 2007. "Electronic Literature: What Is It?" http://eliterature.org/pad/elp.html.

———. 2008. *Electronic Literature: New Horizons for the Literary*. Notre Dame, IN: University of Notre Dame Press.

Hayles, N. Katherine, Nick Montfort, Scott Rettberg, and Stephanie Strickland. 2006. *Electronic Literature Collection*. Volume 1. College Park, MD: Electronic Literature Organization. http://collection.eliterature.org/1/.

Jackson, Shelley. 1995. *Patchwork Girl*. Watertown, MA: Eastgate Systems.

Joyce, Michael. (1987) 1990. *afternoon: a story*. Watertown, MA: Eastgate Systems.

———. 1996. *Of Two Minds: Hypertext Pedagogy and Poetics*. Ann Arbor: University of Michigan Press.

Montfort, Nick. 2003. *Twisty Little Passages: An Approach to Interactive Fiction*. Cambridge, MA: MIT Press.

Morris, Adalaide, and Thomas Swiss, eds. 2009. *New Media Poetics: Contexts, Technotexts and Theories*. Cambridge, MA: MIT Press.

Onishi, Norimitsu. 2008. "Thumbs Race as Japan's Best Sellers Go Cellular." *New York Times*, January 20. www.nytimes.com/2008/01/20/world/asia/20japan.html.

Pullinger, Kate, and Chris Joseph. 2005. *Inanimate Alice*. www.inanimatealice.com.

Ricardo, Francisco J. 2009. *Literary Art in Digital Performance: Case Studies in New Media Art and Criticism*. New York: Continuum Books.

Ryan, Marie-Laure. 1992. *Possible Worlds, Artificial Intelligence, and Narrative Theory*. Bloomington: Indiana University Press.

————. 2004. *Narrative across Media: The Languages of Storytelling*. Lincoln: University of Nebraska Press.

————. 2006. *Avatars of Story*. Minneapolis: University of Minnesota Press.

Simanowski, Roberto. 2009. "What Is and Toward What End Do We Read Digital Literature?" In *Literary Art in Digital Performance: Case Studies in New Media Art and Criticism*, edited by Francisco Ricardo, 10–17. New York: Continuum Books.

Sloane, Sarah. 2000. *Digital Fictions: Storytelling in a Material World*. Stamford, CT: Ablex Publishing.

Sondheim, Alan. 2001. "Introduction: Codework." *American Book Review* 22 (6). www.litline.org/ABR/issues/Volume22/Issue6/sondheim.pdf.

Tomasula, Steve. 2009. *TOC: A New Media Novel*. Fiction Collective 2. Tuscaloosa: University of Alabama Press.

Walker Rettberg, Jill. 2012. "Electronic Literature Seen from a Distance: The Beginnings of a Field." *Dichtung Digital*. http://dichtung-digital.mewi.unibas.ch/2012/41/walker-rettberg/walker-rettberg.htm.

Wardrip-Fruin, Noah. 2012. *Expressive Processing: Digital Fictions, Computer Games, and Software Studies*. Cambridge, MA: MIT Press.

Wittig, Rob. 2001–2002. *Blue Company*. www.robwit.net/bluecompany2002/.

Yellowlees Douglas, Jane. 2001. *The End of Books—or Books without End? Reading Interactive Narratives*. Ann Arbor: University of Michigan.

....

Digital Humanities
Matthew K. Gold

Digital humanities (DH) is a term that has been used since the early 2000s to describe an emerging field of humanities scholarship, teaching, and service which is grounded in digital sources, methodologies, tools, and platforms. Incorporating a range of computational and data-driven approaches, DH work can involve methods such as data mining, text mining, geospatial analysis, information visualization, text encoding, digital scholarly editing, digital archives and preservation, digital forensics, and computational linguistics, among others (see COMPUTATIONAL LINGUISTICS, PRESERVATION). An increasingly prominent strain of digital humanities scholarship focuses on scholarly communication in networked environments, examining the ways in which scholars are using networked platforms to share their work publicly in various states of draft as a way of augmenting or circumventing the traditional social economies of journal- and book-based scholarly production and reception. Such work has begun to transform, or at least to raise significant questions about, the traditional academic processes of peer review, tenure and promotion, and the dissemination of scholarship itself.

Any attempt to define DH represents a foray into contested terrain, since there is wide disagreement and confusion about the contours of the field (if, indeed, one even accepts the proposition that DH is a field rather than a loose constellation of associated methodologies). In "The Humanities, Done Digitally," Kathleen Fitzpatrick locates this confusion at a basic linguistic level: should "digital humanities" take a singular or plural verb ("digital humanities is" or "digital humanities are"?)—a neat externalization of the larger questions surrounding the identity of the field (Fitzpatrick 2011a). As Matthew Kirschenbaum has noted, essays that seek to define DH have become so ubiquitous that they are almost "genre pieces" for DH scholars (Kirschenbaum 2010)—and Kirschenbaum has authored two canonical pieces on the subject. While most DHers might agree with John Unsworth's broad definition of DH as "using computational tools to do the work of the humanities" (Unsworth 2011), key disagreements continue to surround DH: Is DH a discrete field of academic inquiry or a metafield that bridges multiple disciplines? Where does "new media studies" leave off and "digital humanities" begin? Is DH, in the words of Mark Marino, merely a "temporary epithet" that will seem redundant when all work in the humanities becomes digital? Does DH challenge traditional academic practices or merely transpose them into new forms?

What is clear at this moment of emergence and transition is that DH has become a locus for larger debates about the future of the academy and the fate of scholarship in a digital age. But the origins of DH are considerably more constrained. Most scholars locate its beginnings with the Italian Jesuit priest Roberto Busa, whose ambitious project to create a concordance for the collected works of St. Thomas Aquinas in the 1950s is generally considered to be the first DH project. In her history of humanities computing— the name by which DH was known before it became DH—Susan Hockey (2004) divides the history of the field into four periods: Beginnings (1949–early 1970s), Consolidation (1970s–mid-1980s), New Developments (mid-1980s–early 1990s), and the Era of the Internet (Early 1990s–present). Work done during the initial period was dominated by Busa's extraordinary efforts to compile the *Index Thomisticus*, the monumental concordance to the work of Aquinas and related authors which contains over 11 million words of Medieval Latin (Hockey 2004, 4). This work involved a key collaboration with Thomas Watson of IBM, who provided assistance that enabled Busa to transfer written data to punched cards and to create a program for processing that concordance data. Also important during this period were new approaches to authorship and style studies using computational analysis. Such work was constrained by processing and storage technologies of the era, which involved punched cards (with each card holding a maximum of eighty characters of text) and magnetic tape (which allowed only serial processing of data), and significant limitations of character-set representation in such formats.

The next phase described by Hockey saw multiple improvements in storage and processing tools and the beginnings of institutionalization of the field in the form of conferences, journals (*Computers and the Humanities*, founded in 1966, and *Literary and Linguistic Computing*, founded in 1986), and professional organizations (the Association for Literary and Linguistic Computing [1973], the Association for Computers and the Humanities [1978]), along with the establishment of humanities computing centers and college courses. Major work during this period continued to focus on linguistic applications that grew out of concordances and related endeavors (Hockey 2004, 4–7).

During the 1980s and 1990s, professional organs such as the *Humanist* Listserv and the *Humanities Computing Yearbook* allowed humanities computing scholars to stay in better touch with one another and to create directories of projects and active scholars. During this period, the focus of the field shifted as the establishment of new encoding methods (Standard Generalized Markup Language [SGML] and the Text Encoding Initiative [TEI]) resulted in increasing efforts to create digitized texts using shared standards (Hockey 2004, 12). The new availability of personal computers meant that scholars no longer had to register at computing centers in order to use computing resources, which resulted in increased experimentation (Hockey 2004, 10).

With the growth of the World Wide Web during the 1990s, humanities computing projects increasingly sought to use the web as a publication space for digital projects. Pioneering initiatives such as the Blake Archive, the Rossetti Archive, the Walt Whitman Archive, In the Valley of the Shadow, and the Women's Writer's Project took shape during this period, sponsored by key early humanities computing centers such as the Institute for Advanced Technology in the Humanities (IATH) at the University of Virginia. This period also saw the continued institutionalization of humanities computing within the university, as humanities computing scholars began to establish degree programs at institutions such as King's College London, McMaster University, and the University of Alberta.

According to Matthew Kirshenbaum's two influential accounts of the origins of digital humanities (Kirschenbaum 2010, 2012), efforts to establish a degree program at the University of Virginia led to the first usage of the term "digital humanities" in connection with work that had previously been known as "humanities computing." A seminar offered through IATH in 2001–2002 under the codirectorship of John Unsworth and Johanna Drucker was titled "Digital Humanities Curriculum Seminar"; it sought to establish a curriculum for the planned DH program at Virginia (Kirschenbaum 2012, 418). A few years later, as Unsworth and his coeditors Susan Schreibman and Ray Siemens were in the midst of preparing the volume that would become the field-defining *Blackwell's Companion to the Digital Humanities* (2004), the term "digital humanities" was chosen for the title of the volume in place of other options such as "humanities computing" and "digitized humanities" (Kirschenbaum 2010, 5). Around the same time, the Association for Computers in the Humanities (ACH) had joined forces with the Association for Literary and Linguistic Computing (ALLC) to form an umbrella organization called the Alliance for Digital Humanities Organizations (ADHO).

After the Blackwell volume was published in 2004, a series of key developments established DH in the form that has become familiar today. In 2006, the National Endowment for the Humanities launched a DH initiative under the leadership of Brett Bobley; in 2008, that initiative morphed into the National Endowment for the Humanities (NEH) Office of Digital Humanities, thus providing a vital funding stream for both nascent and established DH projects through a series of highly influential grant programs, including the Digital Humanities Start-Up Grants and the Institutes for Advanced Topics in the Digital Humanities (Guess 2008). Other signals of the consolidation of an academic field also appeared, including a book series (Topics in the Digital Humanities from the University of Illinois) and an open-access journal (*Digital Humanities Quarterly*). In the late 2000s, the Modern Language Association (MLA) became a key hub for the popularization of DH work as its annual convention became increasingly dominated by sessions related to DH. The MLA has taken two key steps in recent years which have reinforced the importance of DH to the future of the academy: first, it established the Office of Scholarly Communication under the direction of Kathleen Fitzpatrick; and second, it released revised guidelines for the evaluation of digital work, joining other organizations such as the Conference on College Composition and Communication (CCCC) in providing important guidance to scholars and practitioners whose digital work was being evaluated by their institutions.

Although DH began as a field with easily identifiable roots in computational linguistics and textual editing, its scope has broadened significantly in recent years, no doubt due to the purview licensed by a broad appellation such as "digital humanities." Though debates about exactly what constitutes DH work or digital humanists themselves continue to rage on (Ramsay 2011b; Gold 2012), an examination of projects funded by the NEH Office of Digital Humanities shows support for a wide array of disciplinary, interdisciplinary, and extradisciplinary approaches. Projects traditionally associated with DH such as TEI text-encoding projects continue to receive funding, and newer encoding projects such as TEI Boilerplate, which utilizes HTML5 to render TEI content directly in the web browser, seek to make available simpler and more lightweight options for encoding documents. Innovative multiyear projects such as INKE: Implementing New Knowledge Environments and the Institute for the Future of the Book continue to explore new platforms for networked reading and writing experiences. But DH has begun to encompass a range of other approaches that stray far from the field's origins in textual analysis and digital scholarly editions, and the range of these approaches has led to a significant expansion of the field.

In the early 2010s, several new areas of emphasis have become readily apparent within DH work. First, the increasing availability of large humanities data sets and high-performance computing environments able to process them has led to the popularization of work known generally under the rubric of "big data." This kind of work has been supported in part by a multinational, multiagency funding competition known as "Digging into Data," which asks applicants to grapple with questions such as, "How do you read a million books?" Projects sponsored through this competition include "Data Mining with Criminal Intent," which involves the exploration and visualization of data sets related to millions of records from the Old Bailey, and the Software Studies initiative (see SOFTWARE STUDIES) at the University of California, San Diego (UCSD), which seeks to do with visual material the kind of data mining and visualization that has primarily been explored with textual sources.

If "big data" has increased the scale of DH work, so too have a series of crowdsourcing projects altered their dynamics, especially in relation to the larger public (see CROWDSOURCING). At a moment when archival digitization projects can sometimes have difficulty finding funding, projects such as the University College London's "Transcribe Bentham," the New York Public Library's "What's on the Menu," and Dartmouth College's "Metadata Games" engage the power of the crowd to harvest reliable transcriptions of archival materials or to provide valuable metadata for library materials. In each of these cases and in similar projects, digital humanists have attempted to transform sometimes tedious, detail-oriented work into engaging, community-building projects that add excitement and momentum to the institutions that sponsor them.

Digital humanists have long depended on the affordances of digital platforms, but recent work in DH has involved critical examinations of the hardware and software that undergird those platforms themselves. Examples of such work include Matthew Kirschenbaum's *Mechanisms*, which theorizes the materiality of new media platforms; the Platform Studies book series from MIT Press, which "investigates the relationships between the hardware and software design of computing systems and the creative works produced on those systems"; the Software Studies initiative at UCSD, which examines software as a critical interface; and the Critical Code Studies movement, spearheaded by Mark Marino and Jeremy Douglass, which is invested in "explicating the extra-functional significance of source code" and providing readings of source code that are informed by theoretical hermeneutics (see CODE, CODE AESTHETICS). Relatedly, the tools of digital forensics are increasingly being brought to bear upon humanities manuscripts, as evidenced by the David Livingston Spectral Imaging Project, which used spectral imaging and processing techniques to recover pages from Livingston's diary previously thought to be completely inaccessible due to illegible handwriting and fragile paper.

Other major areas of recent research include geospatial humanities (projects such as UCLA's Hypercities are attempting to link complex layers of social and historical information to interactive maps; see WORLDS AND MAPS) and game studies (projects such as "Preserving Virtual Worlds" have begun to address the possibilities of archiving the transient and ill-preserved environments of digital games and interactive fiction; see PRESERVATION). Also apparent in recent years has been a newfound concentration on DH pedagogy, with a variety of individual scholars and organizations such as the National Institute for Technology in Liberal Education (NITLE) examining the ways in which DH is increasingly entering graduate and undergraduate classrooms. This is both the mark of an increasingly institutionalized field and a shift within the discourse of DH itself, where pedagogy has not always received as much attention as research projects.

Though DHers have, in recent years, begun to share their work publicly on Twitter, the social microblogging service (see TWITTER, TUMBLR, AND MICROBLOGGING), the broadened appeal of DH is shown by a series of commons-based projects aimed at helping DHers connect to one another and to newcomers in the field: Humanities, Arts, Science, and Technology Advanced Collaboratory (HASTAC), the DH Commons, the MLA Commons, the Commons in a Box, and Project Bamboo all seek to create responsive networks around DHers and their projects in part as a way of reducing entry barriers for newcomers. Community resources such as ACH's Digital Humanities Questions & Answers discussion board and Project Bamboo's DiRT directory have provided important points of entry for newcomers. Many of these community resource projects are aimed at creating central repositories of DH projects and methods, in part to realize connections between projects and people, and in part to ensure that DHers build on one another's work in more directed ways. The NEH Office of Digital Humanities has encouraged such work by requiring environmental scans in its applications; relatedly, it has also been concerned with the sustainability of DH projects, as shown by its recently incorporated requirement that applications for DH grants include data-management plans.

DH workshops offer important means of outreach to DH newcomers; the NEH's Institutes for Advanced Topics in the Digital Humanities, the University of Victoria's Digital Humanities Summer Institute (DHSI), and the University of Maryland's Digital Humanities Winter Institute (DHWI) have provided key ways for DHers to share DH knowledge and methods. Innovative new formats for conferences such as the influential "unconference" model of THATCamps have provided unstructured opportunities for informal sharing of methodologies and skills.

DH centers themselves are becoming increasingly linked in a global network through CenterNet, an initiative of the Maryland Institute for Technology in the Humanities (MITH). The global reach of DH has been a long-standing feature of the field, but it has in recent years extended beyond the established axis of the United States, Canada, and Western Europe to include new initiatives in Australia and Asia. Increasingly, DH is a field with global reach.

It is perhaps a measure of that newfound reach and of the growth of the field more generally that DH has come under pressure in recent years, both from within and from without, to take an increasingly activist role in advocating for the humanities and in accounting for a more diverse array of critical approaches. Alan Liu, for instance, has argued that "the digital humanities have been oblivious to cultural criticism" (2012, 491) up to now but that DHers must seize the opportunity before them to advocate for the humanities; the organization cofounded by Liu, *4Humanities*, seeks to do exactly that in response to a cultural moment that has seen widespread defunding of educational institutions and the dismantling of humanities departments in response to fiscal exigencies. Then, too, scholars such as Tara McPherson, who asks in an essay titled "Why Are the Digital Humanities So White?," and Liz Losh, who works on DH and hacktivism, along with new groups such as the *TransformDH* collective, have been pushing the field to take more conscious account of race, ethnicity (see RACE AND ETHNICITY), gender (see CYBERFEMINISM, GENDER REPRESENTATION), sexuality, and class in its projects (see CRITICAL THEORY). These calls for a more politically oriented, activist, and culturally diverse vision of DH have refreshed the field but also posed pointed questions about the assumptions behind its most prominent projects.

Increasingly diverse, increasingly public, and increasing visible, the DH community has been focused in recent years on the very nature of scholarly communication itself. And in this area, several initiatives and groups are attempting to rethink the basic contours of academic life, including publication, peer review, and tenure and promotion. DHers have built emerging publication platforms such as *PressForward*, Scalar, Omeka, Zotero, and Anvil Academic which promise new ways of authoring, displaying, and sharing academic work. New journals such as the *Journal of Digital Humanities* are harnessing algorithmic discovery tools (see ALGORITHM) to surface the best new work in the field, while "middle-state publishing" ventures such as *In Media Res*, the *New Everyday*, and the *Journal of Interactive Technology and Pedagogy* are publishing work that lies somewhere between journal articles and blog posts. Many of these efforts are also exploring new systems of "peer-to-peer" review or postpublication review described by Kathleen Fitzpatrick in her influential book *Planned Obsolescence* (2011b). Increasingly, such innovative models of peer review are being used in the publication of printed books such as *Debates in the Digital Humanities* and *Hacking the Academy*.

Such efforts characterize a field that is, according to Lisa Spiro, committed to the core values of openness (see FREE AND OPEN-SOURCE SOFTWARE), collaboration, collegiality and connectedness, diversity, and experimentation (Spiro 2012, 23–30). Whether *digital humanities* is a term that will soon disappear in the face of the arrival of ubiquitous technology in the academy, as some scholars claim, or whether it heralds the arrival of more collaborative, more open, more engaged, more practical, and more experimental versions of humanities work, DH seems engaged at the moment in answering questions both large and small about the future of the academy. Like much work in DH, it's an iterative process.

References and Further Reading

Berry, David, ed. 2012. *Understanding Digital Humanities*. New York: Palgrave Macmillan.

Fitzpatrick, Kathleen, 2011a. "The Humanities, Done Digitally." *Chronicle of Higher Education*, May 8. http://chronicle.com/article/The-Humanities-Done-Digitally/127382/.

———. 2011b. *Planned Obsolescence: Publishing, Technology, and the Future of the Academy*. New York: New York University Press.

Gold, Matthew K., ed. 2012. *Debates in the Digital Humanities*. Minneapolis: University of Minnesota Press.

Guess, Andy. 2008. "Rise of the Digital NEH." *Inside Higher Ed*, April 3. www.insidehighered.com /news/2008/04/03/digital.

Hockey, Susan. 2004. "The History of Humanities Computing." In *A Companion to Digital Humanities*, edited by Susan Schreibman, Ray Siemens, and John Unsworth, 3–19. Malden, MA: Blackwell.

Kirschenbaum, Matthew G. 2007. *Mechanisms: New Media and the Forensic Imagination.* Cambridge, MA: MIT Press.

———. 2010. "What Is Digital Humanities and What's It Doing in English Departments?" *ADE Bulletin* 150:1–7.

———. 2012. "Digital Humanities As/Is a Tactical Term." In *Debates in the Digital Humanities*, edited by Matthew K. Gold, 415–428. Minneapolis: University of Minnesota Press.

Liu, Alan. 2012. "Where Is Cultural Criticism in the Digital Humanities?" In *Debates in the Digital Humanities*, edited by Matthew K. Gold, 490–509. Minneapolis: University of Minnesota Press.

Moretti, Franco. 2005. *Graphs, Maps, Trees: Abstract Models for a Literary History.* New York: Verso.

Nowviskie, Bethany, ed. 2011. *#alt-academy.* New York: MediaCommons. http://mediacommons .futureofthebook.org/alt-ac/.

Ramsay, Stephen. 2011a. *Reading Machines: Toward an Algorithmic Criticism.* Urbana: University of Illinois Press.

———. 2011b. "Who's In and Who's Out." *Stephen Ramsay*, January 8. http://stephenramsay.us/text /2011/01/08/whos-in-and-whos-out/.

Schreibman, Susan, Ray Siemens, and John Unsworth, eds. 2004. *A Companion to Digital Humanities.* Malden, MA: Blackwell.

Spiro, Lisa. 2012. "'This Is Why We Fight': Defining the Values of the Digital Humanities." In *Debates in the Digital Humanities*, edited by Matthew K. Gold, 16–35. Minneapolis: University of Minnesota Press.

Unsworth, John. 2011. "How Do You Define Humanities Computing / Digital Humanities?" In *Day of Digital Humanities.* CenterNet. http://tapor.ualberta.ca/taporwiki/index.php/How_do_you _define_Humanities_Computing_/_Digital_Humanities%3F.

· ·

Digital Installation Art
Kate Mondloch

The term *installation art* has been used since the 1970s to refer to participatory sculptural environments in which the viewer's spatial and temporal experience with a given exhibition space and the various objects within it forms part of the work itself. These works of art are meant to be experienced as activated spaces, rather than as discrete objects: they are designed to "unfold" during the spectator's experience in time, rather than to be known visually all at once. Installation often overlaps with other genres of art since the 1960s, such as Fluxus, land art, minimalism, video art, performance, conceptual art, and process, all of which share an interest in issues such as site specificity, participation, institutional critique, temporality, and ephemerality. The term *digital installation art* is used to denote installation artworks made with digital technologies. Like installation art in general, digital installation art has proliferated since the 1990s and is now a well-developed mode of artistic practice with established institutional support.

Digital installation can be a confusing term for several reasons (not the least of which is that the label "video art," erroneously, often is used interchangeably). Many installation artworks are consolidated into the common denominator of bits at some point in the production, dissemination, and/or reception of the work without being digital installations per se. For example, while an experimental film installation may be transferred to a digital format (DVD) for easier distribution, typically this would not be called digital installation art because of its fundamental engagement with the analog technology of film. Conversely, sculptural installations might engage with issues pertaining to questions about the digital at the level of content without, however, employing digital technologies. For example, a work might employ a handcrafted or DIY aesthetic as a calculated response to the nearly instantaneous platform transfers made possible by digital technologies.

In general, however, the term *digital installation* is used to describe installation artworks that are nontrivially modified by a computing process in their conception and/or presentation. Code, network, and database also are useful concepts in qualifying what distinguishes digital art from other forms (see CODE, DATABASE, NETWORKING). To say that a work is encoded implies that part or all of it is written in computer code. A networked artwork is designed to be viewed on an electronic communication system, whether a Local Area Network or the Internet (see DIGITAL AND NET ART). New media artist and critic Lev Manovich describes digital art's database logic: "Many new media objects do not tell stories; they don't have a beginning or end; in fact, they don't have any development, thematically, formally or otherwise which would organize their elements into a sequence. Instead, they are collections of individual items, where every item has the same significance as any other" (2001, 218). As such, digital installation art can encompass a wide range of artistic practices, including, but not limited to, animation, net art, cyberart, electronic art, telematic art, genetic/biotech/nanotech art, database art, game design, sound art, virtual reality (VR), and augmented reality (AR) (see AUGMENTED REALITY, SOUND, VIRTUAL REALITY).

Digital installations encourage spectators to engage and/or intervene with various material and conceptual elements as part of the work itself. Australian Jeffrey Shaw's (b. 1944) computer graphic installation *The Legible City* (1989; with Dirk Groeneveld) is an early example. Museum visitors are invited to ride a real stationary bicycle through a screen-based simulated representation of a "city" composed largely of words. A small screen in front of the bicycle depicts an accurate ground plan of one of three cities (Manhattan, Amsterdam, or Karlsruhe), with a marker showing the momentary position of the cyclist. As users pedal the bicycle, computer-generated three-dimensional letters form words and sentences in street-like formations on a large projection screen. Using the ground plans of actual cities, the installation replaces material city architecture with digital textual configurations. On the conceptual level, the artwork's viewers are present in several environments concurrently—the museum space, material city space, and representational/textual space.

The widespread introduction of networked computing technologies in the early 1990s had an enormous impact on digital installation art. North American artist Lynn Hershman's (b. 1941) interactive networked installation the *Dollie Clones* (1995–1998) is representative. The project consists of two telerobotic dolls (*Tillie, the Telerobotic Doll* and *CybeRoberta*), clothes, accessories, video cameras, webcams, monitors, an Internet connection, and custom software. The dolls can be exhibited separately or together. Installed in the *Telematic Connections: The Virtual Embrace* exhibition at the Oklahoma City Museum of Art in 2002, *Tillie*'s Internet-enabled telecamera eyes allowed geographically dispersed viewers to engage with the exhibition space through the doll's perspective. Whether physically or remotely present, all viewers can use a computer to rotate Tillie's head and survey the room. The doll's left eye records the exhibition space in real time and feeds the information to a small monitor nearby. Her right eye, instead, is connected to the Internet, enabling remote users to see what the doll "sees" in the exhibition space (including the unsuspecting museum visitors). Installed together, the telerobotic dolls communicate with each other and occasionally disrupt each other's information feeds, further complicating the installation's multilayered interpenetration between the viewers and objects in the material exhibition space, virtual online space, and remote physical locales.

Digital installation artists have been particularly interested in the phenomena of "telepresence" and "teleaction"—the ability to be functionally present and/or to act in real time at a location other than one's physical location. German art and media theorist Oliver Grau explains how telepresence and teleaction enable the user to be present in three places concurrently: "(a) in the spatio-temporal location determined by the user's body; (b) by means of *teleperception* in the simulated, virtual image space; and (c) by means of *teleaction* in the place where, for example, a robot is situated, directed by one's own movements and providing orientation through its sensors" (2003, 285). Artists have also critiqued these new capacities. As intimated in Hershman's *Dollie Clones*, (telepresent) surveillance and (teleactive) control emerge as the flip side of the expansive spatial realms associated with the Internet. The computer screen's "remote control" activity is potentially bidirectional: every networked viewing environment is potentially subject to being observed and/or acted upon and is also subject to the appearance of simulations. Not every encounter with a computer screen will necessarily make changes in a distant material environment, of course, nor will the viewer's space automatically be compromised by actions from afar. These very possibilities, however, definitively change the viewing subject's relationship to digital interfaces (see INTERFACE).

The production and use of new media technologies in everyday life have a defining impact on digital installation art. Electronic telecommunications now enable the instantaneous transmission of images. Handheld and mobile devices have broadened the possibilities for moving digital art outside of traditional gallery spaces, as well as into entirely computer-based realms. Technical innovations such as VR, telepresence, gesture-based interfaces, touch screens, and three-finger zoom are quickly transmuted among commercial, industrial, military, and artistic applications.

The global convergence of wireless technologies with expanding network infrastructures and miniaturized electronics without a doubt has changed how contemporary subjects understand the world. Some digital installations deploy new technologies self-reflexively to interrogate this situation. Simply put, the ways in which users engage digital technologies can be bracketed out, such that the terms of this engagement themselves are put on display in the art gallery, and to critical effect. One recent example is *T_Visionarium II* (2008)—a 360-degree stereoscopic audio-video environment developed by Neil Brown, Dennis Del Favero, Matthew McGinity, Jeffrey Shaw, and Peter Weibel through the iCinema Centre for Interactive Cinema Research. (Indicative of the resource-intensive nature of certain digital art projects, the large-scale work was sponsored by the University of New South Wales and the ZKM | Center for Art and Media, Karlsruhe.) *T_Visionarium* invites viewers to don 3D glasses and enter a large enclosure (four meters high by ten meters in diameter) fashioned out of a cylindrical screen. Twelve digital projectors create a high-resolution stereoscopic 3D image made up of a massive database of narratives taken from a single day of European television footage in 2006. Each clip has been carefully tagged with identifying data ranging from depicted emotions to character relationships, physical movements, and structural elements. Viewers can use a touch-screen menu to search the database. Clicking on a given keyword immediately draws up "related" footage, bathing viewers in an entirely new nonlinear and multitemporal arrangement of decontextualized sounds and 3D images. In this way, the work investigates the database logic that informs how we inhabit the nearly countless televisual and convergent screen spaces that define our everyday digital lives.

Other installations aspire to effect social and political reflection by confronting viewers with interpretive challenges. North American Nancy Burson's (b. 1948) interactive digital installation *Human Race Machine* (1999–present) uses digital face recognition technology to suggest that race is more a matter of social construction than of genetics. *Human Race Machine* draws on facial recognition and facial alteration software, as well as a database of approximately fifty photographs, to indicate to the viewer what their face might look like if they were of a different race (black, white, Asian, Hispanic, Indian). The viewer looks into a gamelike video mirror and aligns their face using an edge-detection map on the screen. The video image of the viewer's face is then digitized and loaded into the software that allows the viewer to see their face morphed into another race at the touch of a button. That the FBI and America's National Center for Missing and Exploited Children eventually acquired Burson's composite-imaging *software* (to help locate kidnap victims) points again to the multidirectional flow of technological innovation between the arts and commercial or governmental interests.

Other artists are more overtly critical about such exchanges. Artist and activist collaboratives such as ®™ark and subRosa have explored the more disturbing social and political implications of morphing identities and bodies with the help of digital and biotechnologies. ®™ark's *Bio Taylorism* (2000), designed by Natalie Bookchin, consists of a satirical Powerpoint presentation on the "benefits" of biotechnology, while subRosa's installation and website *Cell Track* (2004) examines the privatization and patenting of human, animal, and plant genomes within the context of the history of eugenics.

In many ways, digital art falls in the cracks between artistic categories and academic disciplines. Digital installation artworks often exceed the conventional disciplinary frameworks of fields such as cinema and media studies, art history, and performance studies. As a result, entirely new fields such as electronic literature, software studies, screen studies, and technoculture studies have sprung up to assess this and other hybrid forms of cultural production. While digital installation art need not be seen as categorically different from nondigital variants, many artists, critics, and institutions often proceed as if that were the case. Focusing exclusively on artistic production made with digital technologies, however, can obscure the compelling similarities these works share with nondigital media. Many scholars prefer the term *new media* over *digital* to emphasize the continuities that exist across installations made with a range of media technologies, particularly the well-developed artistic genres of film and video. Others favor the term *screen-based* art as a way to appreciate the commonalities shared among various screen-based art forms.

Irrespective of the critical or disciplinary framework used for assessing specific works, three characteristics are frequently put forth as hallmarks of digital installation art: interactivity, immersion, and virtuality (see INTERACTIVITY, IMMERSION, VIRTUALITY). However helpful these descriptors might be in specific contexts, these broad and unwieldy categories complicate any viable definition of the medium. For example, the "interactivity" of a given work of art is a question of degree and not a qualitative difference separating digital installation from other art forms. Interactivity, often coded as "participation," has been embraced by many theorists and practitioners for its allegedly disruptive and progressive qualities. Michael Rush's *New Media in Art* describes how "the artist has now become a facilitator of the art experience with the interactive artwork becoming, in a sense, an extension of education, a hands-on type of creative learning" (2005, 227). At the same time, a significant counterdiscourse has emerged in recent years to challenge such claims. German literature and media studies scholar Roberto Simanowski, for example, identifies a paradox in so-called interactive art: "There is an irony in the way cultural products that aren't considered interactive nonetheless trigger a participatory culture by turning readers into authors who negotiate meaning among each other and with the original authors, while results of interactive art, such as the installations discussed in this book, may only trigger an instantaneous and momentary interaction with no search for meaning, let alone collective negotiation of whatever meanings are discovered" (2011, 212).

Like interactivity, "virtuality" figures heavily in the literature surrounding digital installation, in this case as a way to distinguish between "real" (material) and "virtual" (immaterial) space. Digital art critic and curator Christiane Paul characterizes installations as "concerned with possible relationships between the physical space and the virtual . . . what distinguishes them are the balance between these two realms and the methods employed to translate one space into the other" (2003, 71–72). From a historical standpoint, however, virtual worlds are neither new nor exclusive to digital technologies. Viewers have gazed upon artistically manipulated virtual spaces at least since Alberti's fifteenth-century formulation of the canvas as a window that opens onto a space "beyond the frame." Furthermore, even "virtual" digital realms have a materiality at the level of mathematical constructs.

The concept of digital installation being characterized by "immersion" similarly is problematic from a historical perspective: viewers have long been engrossed in total environments, from painted tomb chambers to panoramas. The pervasive association of digital installation art with immersion is also unfortunate due to the frequent association of immersion with the critically disparaged qualities of disembodiment and lack of critical distance. In an attempt to rethink this conventional critical dualism—(critical) embodiment in one's immediate surroundings on the one hand, and (complicit) disembodiment and immersion in virtual realms on the other—certain theorists have argued that installations made with digital technologies are in a privileged position to engage spectators simultaneously in the "here-and-now" *and* the "there-and-then" (Mondloch 2010).

The intense discursive focus on interactivity, immersion, and virtuality, coupled with the ease of transferring digital information between platforms, has caused many media installation theorists and critics to neglect the important role of the interface—the conceptual and material point at which the observing subject meets the technological object. This is paradoxical on two accounts: first, because installation art by definition is concerned with spectatorship and the material conditions of reception; and second, because digital data *requires* interfaced computers and other material infrastructures to have utility. Machine-readable symbols must be translated into human-perceivable form for them to have cultural efficacy. As described by Lev Manovich in *The Language of New Media* (2001), the digital art object can be defined as one or more interfaces to a database of multimedia material. Interfaces may be natural, technical, or some combination, but the digital work of art is inescapably bound to the material interface that allows the viewer to experience it.

Digital art, like digital media in general, stores information in immaterial, uncollectable, and nonunique numbers and symbols rather than in objects and events. Digital installation, in contrast, is relatively museum friendly since some part of it necessarily exists in analog sculptural form (although the work of art itself may be site specific and/or deliberately ephemeral). Even so, digital installation artworks present significant challenges in terms of institutionalized collection, exhibition, and preservation (see PRESERVATION). Conservative museum boards and acquisition committees are reluctant to purchase "non-unique" works, although enterprising artists and their galleries have done their best to create alternative hierarchies. Merely exhibiting digital installations can be tricky—it is not uncommon to find that a work of art is closed for repairs.

Preservation presents perhaps the biggest challenge for caretakers of digital installation art. Many problems develop as hardware and software platforms change—what is "the" work and how might one create standards to preserve it, particularly if the original interface is key? Several initiatives have been spawned to attend to this dilemma. The most ambitious of these efforts is the Variable Media Network (VMN), a nontraditional, new preservation strategy that began in 1999 with the Guggenheim Museum's efforts to preserve media-based and performative works in its permanent collection, and which now comprises a group of international institutions and consultants, including the University of Maine, the Berkeley Art Museum/Pacific Film Archives, Franklin Furnace, Rhizome, and Performance Art Festival & Archives. The VMN seeks to define acceptable levels of change within any given art object and to document ways in which a sculpture, installation, or conceptual work may be altered (or not) for the sake of preservation without losing the work's "essential meaning."

The infrastructures to support the creation and exhibition of digital art have become increasingly robust in recent years. Digital installation art is now supported by media labs, institutions, galleries, and festivals worldwide. Prominent examples include V2 (Netherlands), Berlin's transmediale festival (Germany), ZKM|Center for Art and Media (Germany), Ars Electronica Center (Linz, Austria), NTT InterCommunication Center (Tokyo, Japan), the Banff New Media Centre (Canada), Foundation Daniel Langlois (Canada), Bitforms Gallery (United States), Postmasters Gallery (United States), and SIG-GRAPH (United States). Several established online resources devoted to the nexus of art and technology support the history, criticism, and practice of digital installation art; among them are Rhizome, Nettime, Media Art Net, the Adobe Museum of Digital Art (AMODA), the Digital Art Museum, and the Database of Virtual Art. The Database of Virtual Art, a collaborative venture between media art experts and other interested individuals sponsored by Danube University Krems, offers a particularly innovative model for documenting digital installation art practices. This web-based open-access database offers a research-minded overview of "immersive, interactive, telematic, and genetic art" installations by compiling technical data about the interface and technologies employed in a given work. This technical data, along with relevant video documentation and literature, is then richly interlinked via keywords to other pertinent exhibiting institutions, events, and bibliographical references.

■ See also ANIMATION/KINETICISM, CHARACTERISTICS OF DIGITAL MEDIA, CYBERSPACE, INTERACTIVE CINEMA, PROCEDURAL, VIRTUAL BODIES

References and Further Reading

Bishop, Claire. 2005. *Installation Art: A Critical History.* New York: Routledge.
Grau, Oliver. 2003. *Virtual Art: From Illusion to Immersion.* Cambridge, MA: MIT Press.

Huhtamo, Erkki, and Jussi Parikka, eds. 2011. *Media Archaeology: Approaches, Applications, and Implications*. Berkeley: University of California Press.

Jones, Amelia. 2006. *Self/Image: Technology, Representation, and the Contemporary Subject*. New York: Routledge.

Klanten, Robert, Sven Ehmann, and Verena Hanschke, eds. 2011. *A Touch of Code: Interactive Installations and Experiences*. Berlin: Die Gestalten Verlag.

Manovich, Lev. 2001. *The Language of New Media*. Cambridge, MA: MIT Press.

Mondloch, Kate. 2010. *Screens: Viewing Media Installation Art*. Minneapolis: University of Minnesota Press.

Paul, Christiane. 2003. *Digital Art*. New York: Thames & Hudson.

——, ed. 2008. *New Media in the White Cube and Beyond: Curatorial Models for Digital Art*. Berkeley: University of California Press.

Rush, Michael. 2005. *New Media in Art*. New York: Thames & Hudson.

Simanowski, Roberto. 2011. *Digital Art and Meaning: Reading Kinetic Poetry, Text Machines, Mapping Art, and Interactive Installations*. Minneapolis: University of Minnesota Press.

Weibel, Peter, and Jeffrey Shaw, eds. 2002. *Future Cinema: The Cinematic Imaginary after Film*. Karlsruhe: ZKM | Center for Art and Media.

● ●

Digital Poetry

Leonardo Flores

Digital poetry is a poetic practice made possible by digital media and technologies. A genre of electronic literature, it is also known as electronic poetry or e-poetry (see ELECTRONIC LITERATURE). The technologies that shape digital media are diverse, are rapidly evolving, and can be used to such different effects that the term has expanded to encompass a large number of practices.

Digital poetry isn't simply poetry written on a computer and published in print or on the web. The most common use of the computer in the creation of poetry is as a word processor, which "remediates" the typewriter in its capabilities. Jay David Bolter and Richard Grusin coined the term *remediation* to explain the process of representing an old medium in a new one (2000, 45) (see REMEDIATION). Using a word processor to write a poem doesn't necessarily make the result a digital poem because this kind of software is designed primarily to produce printed copies. As an inscription technology it still leaves a mark on a poem, partly in the composition process, and partly in how a poem looks, because it provides a diverse palette of formatting elements and language tools. N. Katherine Hayles distinguishes electronic literature from contemporary works designed with computers for a print publication paradigm: "More than being marked by digitality, electronic literature is actively *formed* by it" (2008, 43).

Loss P. Glazier, who focuses on poetry and the creative process in his book *Digital Poetics*, expands on the notion of "active formation": "The poem is not some idealized result of thinking: the poet thinks *through* the poem. Similarly, investigated here is not the idea of the digital poem as an extension of the printed poem, but the idea of the digital poem as the process of thinking through this new medium, thinking through *making*. As the poet works, the work discovers" (2002, 6). Both Glazier and Hayles focus on the role of digital media in the creative process as a defining factor in the formation of digital poetry, while C. T. Funkhouser broadens the impact of digital media on the work: "A poem is a digital poem if computer programming or processes (software) are distinctively used in the composition, generation, or presentation of the text (or combinations of texts)" (2007, 22). Funkhouser's definition is parallel to Peter Shillingsburg's idea of text as a series of script acts: the creative performance (which produces the conceptual work of art), the production performance (which produces the physical document), and the reception performance (carried out by readers as they interact with the physical document) (1997, 76).

If we combine these three definitions with Shillingburg's model of textuality, then we can define the digital poem as one that distinctively uses digital media in the creation, production, or reception performances of the poem.

But what is poetry? Poetry can be seen as an attempt to capture and communicate remarkable language. The *New Princeton Encyclopedia of Poetry and Poetics* defines poetry as follows: "A poem is an instance of verbal art, a text set in verse, bound speech. More generally, a poem conveys heightened forms of perception, experience, meaning, or consciousness in heightened language, i.e. a heightened mode of discourse" (Preminger et al. 1993, 938). This definition encompasses digital poetry only in the most general sense of the term: it is a verbal art that uses heightened language. It also uses a model based on orality bound in writing, finding its materiality in printed verse. After almost twenty years of the most significant communication media revolution since the invention of the printing press, the 4th edition of the *Princeton Encyclopedia of Poetry and Poetics* avoids defining poetry in any single way, presenting instead a genealogy of the term and concluding that "each of the diverse practices of poetry in the early 21st century derives from some moment in the history of the word, and each stakes a claim that excludes some practice of poetry elsewhere" (Owen 2012, 1068).

Digital poetry is based on notions of textuality ("the word") reconceptualized in digital media, as Strehovec asserts that "digital poetry is based on text. Text, however, can be—in the frame of the new media paradigm—understood as an experimental artistic environment for establishing new (spatial and temporal) relations between text components, as well as for a bold experience of unusual meanings" (2010, 69–70).

Language, especially when heightened, cannot escape the constraints of the medium in which it is created, recorded, and transmitted. Different media place different demands on language—the combination of which gives rise to different poetics, definitions, forms, and traditions. Digital media is no exception and leads to artistic genres and practices unique to its capabilities, yet digital poetry finds itself aligned to poetic tradition as well as to the artistic practices that are "native" to digital media. Matthew Kirschenbaum pinpoints a crucially human point of intersection when he rightly claims that "all electronic poets, however, would surely admit to some level of fascination with digital technology and the way in which its formal logics can be superimposed upon that other formal system par excellence, language" (2012, 395). Because it is positioned between new media–driven artistic practices and literary tradition, digital poetry develops genres of its own that are informed by both cultural paradigms. This entry will elaborate on the most salient of the genres of digital poetry and conclude by framing these practices within a historical context.

There have been numerous attempts at defining genres and producing extensive lists of possible genres because digital media has so many different characteristics and possibilities that it is difficult to encompass the totality of practices. Taking into account the genres described as electronic literature, as well as some listed by C. T. Funkhouser, Loss P. Glazier, and N. Katherine Hayles, this entry will focus on six primary practices to produce the following list of digital poetry genres: generative poetry, code poetry, visual and kinetic poetry, multimedia poetry, and interactive poetry (see ELECTRONIC LITERA-TURE). This is not an exhaustive list, and a given work may fall under more than one category. Each genre will be discussed in terms of its characteristics, history, and connections to prior poetic and/or artistic traditions.

The oldest genre in digital poetry is the generative poem, a tradition that is still in active development. Generative works assemble texts using an algorithm and a data set. Espen Aarseth uses the term "texton" to denote the elements to be assembled (the data set) and "scripton" to refer to the texts that can be produced by the algorithm. An important predecessor from print culture is Raymond Queneau's *Cent mille milliards de poèmes* (1961), which consists of ten sonnets printed in a book with each line cut so that each line could be opened to a different page to generate 10^{14} possible sonnets (scriptons) from 140 parts (textons) (Aarseth 1997, 62). The publication of this book led to the creation of the Oulipo (*Ouvroir de littérature potentielle*, roughly translated as "workshop of potential literature"), which sought to create new literary works based on mathematical and other types of constraints. This kind of generative work is also known as combinatorial or permutational poetry.

Early generative poems sought to produce words, lines, sentences, and entire poems employing diverse techniques, such as templates, variables, and randomized selections from the data sets. C. T. Funkhouser attributes the first digital poem to Theo Lutz in 1959, who used a computer to randomly select and connect sixteen subjects and sixteen titles from Franz Kafka's novel *The Castle* (Funkhouser 2007, 37). Computational linguistics sought to generate a model for the creation of natural language, using Noam Chomsky's research into generative grammar and formal languages (see COMPUTATIONAL LINGUISTICS). The problem with generative language experiments is that computers cannot be instructed to select words that operate within the same conceptual frame of reference, producing illogical sentences. An important work in this genre which illustrates the problems with illogical sentences is the 1983 book titled *The Policeman's Beard Is Half Constructed*, featuring text generated by a computer program named Racter.

The tradition of generative poetry continues with increasingly sophisticated templates, algorithms, data sets, variables, and search engines, producing results that that could lead readers to think they are reading poetry written by a human being—a kind of poetic Turing test (see TURING TEST).

Code poetry exists in the intersection of language written to be read by a computer and language to be read by a person. Computer codes are executable commands for computers which can also be read by humans, usually programmers who know the programming language it was written in. The intended audience of code poetry is therefore both human and machine (see CODE).

There are diverse approaches to code poetry. Some poets, such as Nick Montfort, favor efficiency and compression, seeking the greatest emergent complexity from the most minimal programming possible, as exemplified in his "ppg256 Series" of 256-character Perl poems ([2008] 2012). Other approaches break with executable code to produce a hybrid of natural and machine languages, such as the "mezangelle" language produced by Mary Anne Breeze (Mez), Lionel Kearns's binary code–inspired "Birth of God/uniVerse" (1969), and Jim Rosenberg's "Diagram Poems" ([1979] 1985). Others use the documentation commands in the code to insert poems, as is the case in bpNichol's *First Screening* (1984), which contains a poem between lines 3,900 and 4,000 that constructs its meaning by use of the REM (remark) documentation code.

The traditions of visual, concrete, and Lettrist poetry inform visual digital poetry by exploring a computer's capability to produce visual output through its screen or printer. The computer provides elaborate tools for "drawing" or "painting" language, using vector and raster graphic tools, allowing the production of sophisticated language-based visual art (see WORD-IMAGE). Richard W. Bailey's book *Computer Poems* (1973) contains several works of computer-generated concrete poems, such as Leslie Mezei's pictographical arrangement of the word "Babel" (Funkhouser 2007, 99). Digital media extends the visual poetry tradition beyond the page by simulating two-dimensional and three-dimensional environments in which to place language, layering language, and reimagining the notion of "ink," "paint," or surface used to inscribe language.

Kinetic poetry is perhaps the most important extension of the visual in digital environments because it adds a dimension of motion and time to language. If visual poetry blurs the boundary between language and the visual arts, kinetic poetry can be used to produce language-based films or video poems, as is the case of *First Screening* (1984) by bpNichol, "Amour" (1989) by Philippe Bootz, "Dakota" (2001) by Young-Hae Chang Heavy Industries, and others. The distinction between kinetic poetry and the video poem is the degree of engagement with digital media, particularly its affordances and constraints, beyond its capabilities as a tool for video production (see FILM AND DIGITAL MEDIA, VIDEO). Kinetic typography has long been associated with film and television, both of which display moving words in the credits or through tickers at the bottom of the screen, respectively, yet their use is rarely intended to produce an aesthetic response in the reader.

Multimedia poetry can include one or various elements within the poem, such as images, video, or audio. Its poetic antecedent and inspiration is the Fluxus movement, which focused on the creation of multimedia or "intermedia" art and literature. The use of sound in digital poetry has become more prevalent since authoring programs such as Flash and Shockwave became the industry standard in the mid- to late 1990s. These programs allow for seamless integration of sound and visual elements. HTML and other authoring programs do not allow for such careful integration, because sound elements are loaded as needed, causing potential delays in the presentation of the aural element. The integration of sound in digital poetry is often informed by the tradition of sound poetry and audio writing, an experimental poetic practice built around audio recording technologies. Digital media extends these traditions by engaging the materiality of the audio object through computation operations, such as randomization, algorithms, generation, and interactivity.

Interactive poetry contains interfaces and variables for readers to provide input through the computer's peripheral devices. The poet scripts the role of the reader in the work, creating input cues and feedback loops for that interaction to be incorporated into the textual performance. Interactivity is a strategy for the poem's presentation, in order to produce a meaningful aesthetic effect in the reader. An aspect of interactivity is navigation through virtual environments or using links and nodes, as in the case of hypertexts. Another aspect is the manipulation of language or virtual objects on screen. Combined, these aspects allow for the creation of poetry that is structured by video game dynamics, as is the case of Paul Zelevansky's "SWALLOWS" (1986), Jim Andrews's "Arteroids" ([2001] 2004), and Jason Nelson's "Game, Game, Game, and Again Game" (2007).

An important subgenre of interactive poetry is *hypertext poetry*, which uses nodes as structural units and provides links between them for the reader to choose, producing a sequence of textual portions. It could be considered as a type of generative poetry that uses the reader to make selections rather than using randomization. The interface is important in hypertexts because they inform the reader's choices as they explore the poem. Judy Malloy's pioneering hypertext poem, *Uncle Roger*, was serially published "on Art Com Electronic Network, beginning in 1986. Beginning in 1987, it was published online as a working hypernarrative on the seminal *ACEN Datanet*" (Malloy [1986] 2012). Most early hypertext poetry was produced in HyperCard, such as Amendment Hardiker's *Zaum Gadget* (1987) and Jim Rosenberg's "Intergrams" (1988), and in Storyspace, such as Deena Larsen's *Marble Springs* (1993) and Stephanie Strickland's *True North* (1997).

It bears reminding that there are so many diverse practices and emergent genres in digital poetry that it is impossible to comprehensively list or categorize them all. The genres listed above capture general aspects of digital media which have been broadly explored and accumulated a significant body of work, a necessarily historical approach.

The history of digital poetry has been researched and conceptualized by N. Katherine Hayles, who posited two generations of electronic literature, and by Christopher Funkhouse, whose books *Prehistoric Digital Poetry: An Archaeology of Forms, 1959–1995* and *New Directions in Digital Poetry* review and categorize works from the beginnings of digital poetry to the present. Rather than retell such a history, this entry will frame the history into three generations and suggest the emergence of a fourth generation evidenced in present-day practices.

The first generation of digital poetry can be traced from the beginnings of computer poetry in the late 1950s until the rise of the personal computer in the early 1980s. This was a period of mainframe computers in institutional settings, characterized by algorithmic and generative works that were published in print. Poets such as Emmett Williams, Jackson Mac Low, and others used computers to carry out procedural algorithms to efficiently generate works that would take much longer to do by hand. This was a vibrant period in generative poetry as computational linguists and programmers sought to unlock natural languages through text generation.

The second generation began when personal computers reached wide distribution during the early 1980s and lasted until the rise of the World Wide Web in 1995. Text-based interactive fiction and the development of hypertexts in HyperCard and Storyspace developed a market for digital literature unparalleled to this day. Three writers produced some of the earliest kinetic poetry during the mid-1980s using Applesoft BASIC: bpNichol with *First Screening* (1984), Geof Huth with "Endemic Battle Collage" (1986), and Paul Zelevansky with "SWALLOWS" (1986). This is a period in which works circulated in disk and CD-ROM, and while there was an Internet and works circulated via Internet relay chat, Listservs, and other networking technologies, the bulk of the experience was on standalone personal computers.

The third generation came about with the rise of the web and the development of sophisticated graphical and multimedia authoring tools, such as HTML, VRML, DHTML, Javascript, Director, Flash, and others. These works incorporated multimedia elements, interactivity, animation, and more to produce highly visual and aural works. The creation of virtual environments during this period is an important aspect of the development of digital poetry in this period, as seen in the incorporation of video games and poetry and the production of poetic videos. The ability for networks to create online performance spaces for multiple users promotes collaboration, and poems powered by search engines become new directions for generative works (see FLARF). As of the writing of this entry, we are in this third generation.

A fourth generation of electronic literature and poetry is currently emerging from the development and proliferation of new technologies for users to provide input. For example, mobile networks and platforms allow for the production of poems that take advantage of touch-screen surfaces, accelerometers, GPS (or geolocation), cameras, microphones, and more. The incorporation of technologies that can receive input from the human body and other information (such as QR codes) is blurring the boundaries between physical and virtual worlds and making computing ubiquitous, going beyond the personal computer as a space for the reception of digital poetry. And new genres are developing around these technologies, such as augmented reality, mobile and geolocative literature, and netprov.

Whatever new digital media technologies emerge, there will always be poets interested in how they shape language, and the engagement with their materiality will produce digital poetry (see MATERIALITY).

■ See also CODE, COMPUTATIONAL LINGUISTICS, ELECTRONIC LITERATURE, FILM AND DIGITAL MEDIA, FLARF, MATERIALITY, REMEDIATION, TURING TEST

References and Further Reading

Aarseth, Espen J. 1997. *Cybertext: Perspectives on Ergodic Literature*. Baltimore: Johns Hopkins University Press.

Andrews, Jim. (2001) 2004. "Arteroids." *Vispo.com*. www.vispo.com/arteroids/.

Bailey, Richard W., ed. 1973. *Computer Poems*. Drummond Island, MI: Potagannissing Press.

Bolter, Jay David, and Richard Grusin. 2000. *Remediation: Understanding New Media*. Cambridge, MA: MIT Press.

Bootz, Philippe. 1995. "Amour." Translated by Pierre Joris. *Alire 1*. CD-ROM. Villeneuve d'Ascq: MOTS-VOIR.

bpNichol. 1984. *First Screening: Computer Poems*. Toronto: Underwhich Editions. Reprinted in Vispo.com (2007). http://vispo.com/bp/.

Funkhouser, Christopher T. 2007. *Prehistoric Digital Poetry: An Archaeology of Forms, 1959–1995*. Tuscaloosa: University of Alabama Press.

———. 2012. *New Directions in Digital Poetry*. London: Continuum.

Glazier, Loss Pequeño. 2002. *Digital Poetics: The Making of E-Poetries*. Tuscaloosa: University of Alabama Press.

Hardiker, Amendment. 1987. *Zaum Gadget*. Diskette. Madison, WI: Xexoxial Endarchy.

Hayles, N. Katherine. 2007. "Electronic Literature: What Is It?" Electronic Literature Organization. http://eliterature.org/pad/elp.html.

———. 2008. *Electronic Literature: New Horizons for the Literary*. Notre Dame, IN: University of Notre Dame Press.

Huth, Geof. 1986. "Endemic Battle Collage." In *Electronic Literature Collection*, volume 2, edited by Laura Borrás Castanyer, Talan Memmott, Rita Raley, and Brian Kim Stefans. http://collection.eliterature.org/2/index.html.

Kearns, Lionel. 1969. "Birth of God/uniVerse." In *By the Light of the Silvery McLune: Media Parables, Poems, Signs, Gestures, and Other Assaults on the Interface*. Vancouver: Daylight Press.

Kirschenbaum, Matthew G. 2012. "Electronic Poetry." In *The Princeton Encyclopedia of Poetry and Poetics*, edited by Roland Greene, Stephen Cushman, et al. Princeton, NJ: Princeton University Press.

Larsen, Deena. 1993. *Marble Springs*. Watertown, MA: Eastgate Systems. www.eastgate.com/catalog/MarbleSprings.html.

Lutz, Theo. 2005. "Stochastic Texts." Translated by Helen MacCormack. www.stuttgarter-schule.de/lutz_schule_en.htm.

Malloy, Judy. (1986) 2012. *Uncle Roger—World Wide Web Edition*. www.well.com/user/jmalloy/uncleroger/partytop.html.

Montfort, Nick. (2008) 2012. "ppg256 Series." http://nickm.com/poems/ppg256.html.

Nelson, Jason. 2007. "Game, Game, Game and Again Game." In *Electronic Literature Collection*, volume 2, edited by Laura Borrás Castanyer, Talan Memmott, Rita Raley, and Brian Kim Stefans. http://collection.eliterature.org/2/index.html.

Owen, Stephen. 2012. "Poetry." In *The Princeton Encyclopedia of Poetry and Poetics*, edited by Roland Greene, Stephen Cushman, et al. Princeton, NJ: Princeton University Press.

Preminger, Alex, and T. V. F. Brogan, eds. 1993. *The New Princeton Encyclopedia of Poetry and Poetics*. Princeton, NJ: Princeton University Press.

Queneau, Raymond. 1961. *Cent mille milliards de poemes*. Paris: Gallimard.

Racter, William Chamberlain, and Joan Hall. 1984. *The Policeman's Beard Is Half Constructed: Computer Prose and Poetry by Racter—the First Book Ever Written by a Computer*. New York: Warner Books.

Rosenberg, Jim. (1979) 1985. "Diagram Poems." www.well.com/user/jer/diags.html.

———. 1993. "Intergrams." *Eastgate Quarterly Review of Hypertext* 1 (1). www.eastgate.com/catalog/q11.html.

Shillingsburg, Peter L. 1997. *Resisting Texts: Authority and Submission in Constructions of Meaning*. Ann Arbor: University of Michigan Press.

Strehovec, Janez. 2010. "Digital Poetry beyond the Metaphysics of 'Projective Saying.'" In *Regards Croisés: Perspectives on Digital Literature*. Morgantown: West Virginia University Press.

Strickland, Stephanie. 1997. *True North*. Watertown, MA: Eastgate Systems. www.eastgate.com/catalog/TrueNorth.html.

Young-Hae Chang Heavy Industries. 2001. "Dakota." www.yhchang.com/DAKOTA.html.

Zelevansky, Paul. 1986. "SWALLOWS." In Emerson, Lori. 2012. "Recovering Paul Zelevanksy's Literary Game 'SWALLOWS' (Apple //e, 1985–86)." *lorieemerson.net: reading writing digital textuality*, April 24. http://loriemerson.net/2012/04/24/recovering-paul-zelevanksys-literary-game-swallows-apple-e-1985–86/.

E

Early Digital Art and
Writing (Pre-1990)
Christopher Funkhouser

Decades before digital art and writing became widely transmitted
and accessed online, pioneers in these expressive fields relied predominantly on sponsored exhibitions of their work. Prior to the emergence of the World Wide Web (WWW),
computer-based practitioners desiring to share their compositions—and audiences interested in these contemporary developments—depended on a small number of sympathetic
museums and galleries that promoted such innovations. In the 1960s and early 1970s,
these exhibits tended to unite experiments produced by both digital writers and artists.
Gradually, as electronic arts expanded in a way that digital writing would not until the
proliferation of personal computing and global networks in the 1990s, subsequent exhibitions in the 1970s and 1980s predominantly featured graphical rather than language-
oriented works. The arts, historically familiar with formal shifts in media in ways that
literature was not, quickly responded to the calling of computerized machinery; writers
more gradually adapted to digital possibilities.

The first known group installation of computer art, titled *Cybernetic Serendipity*, was
organized by Jasia Reichardt in London in 1968. This event signaled that experiments
in digital music, dance, sculptural installations, robotics, poetry, texts, paintings, films,
architecture, and graphics—produced by James Tenney, John Cage, Nam June Paik, Nanni
Balestrini, Alison Knowles, Marc Adrian, Ken Knowlton, and others exploring newly available digital modalities—had brought considerable artistic results on an international
scale. With the advent of computers, media and automated or programmed systems
of material structuring clearly had begun to alter aesthetic conditions for artists and
writers.

Geometric patterning is the predominant attribute apparent in many of the visual,
animated, and musical works documented in the catalog. Artists effectively use mathematical features enabled by computers to modulate a work's positioning, shape, and speed.
Verbal works included in the exhibition invented various ways to produce literary texts. For
the *Tape Mark* poems Balestrini created 322 punched cards and twelve hundred instructions in order to produce combinatorial poems built with texts appropriated from other
writers, including Lao Tzu; Margaret Masterman and Robin McKinnon Wood developed
a "slot" mechanism to generate orderly haiku; and combinatoric works featuring open

verse structures were devised by Knowles and Tenney, Jean Baudot, and E. Medoza. Adrian's *Computer Texts* simulated on the screen the aesthetics of concrete poetry, randomly assembling output by using a database of eleven hundred alphabetic symbols to place twenty words at a time on the screen, organizing the interface using a grid system. Edwin Morgan foreshadowed "codework" by making simulated computer poems using the tenets of code, formed as vertical blocks with content containing formatting similar to binary code, denoting a pivotal point where the language of a poem begins to shift in both content and style which exposes the binary, character-driven aspects of encoded expression.

A second major exhibition featuring artists and writers involved with digital technology, *SOFTWARE*, curated by Jack Burnham and sponsored by American Motors Corporation, was installed in 1970 at the Jewish Museum in New York and later exhibited at the Smithsonian Institution. In his notes on the project, Burnham acknowledges the influence of cybernetics and *Cybernetic Serendipity* but also expresses an intention to explore how "personal and social sensibilities" are altered as a result of the digital "revolution."

SOFTWARE was also the location of the first public installation of a hypertext system: Theodor H. Nelson and Ned Woodman's *Labyrinth: An Interactive Catalog*, which enabled viewers to browse through a maze of writings on a computer screen. Works presented in the exhibition also explored the meaning of living in a computerized environment through interactive installations such as *Seek*, a mechanism capable of sensing and affecting an environment that incorporated live animals (gerbils) which was created by MIT's Architecture Machine Group, codirected by Nicholas Negroponte and Leon Grossier. Digital thermal technology played a role in installations such as Sonia Sheridan's *Interactive Paper Systems* and John Goodyear's *Level of Heat*, and works by Hans Haake involved use of interactive teletype terminals. Also featured were audio-based compositions, such as Robert Barry's *Ultrasonic Wave Piece*, in which ultrasonic waves were reflected off interior surfaces, filling selected areas with "invisible, changing patterns and forms"; Allen Raxdow and Paul Conly's music synthesizer *Composer*; and Theodosius Victoria's *Solar Audio Window Transmission*, which transmitted low-volume sound through the museum's glass surfaces. A number of visual artworks appeared in the exhibition, including interactive pieces such as Linda Berris's *Tactile Film*, William Vandouris's *Light Pattern Box*, and Carl Fernbach-Flarsheim's *The Boolean Image / Conceptual Typewriter*, as well as Agnes Denes's device used for mapping thought. Notably, the exhibition also included nondigital technological pieces by Vito Acconci, David Antin, John Baldessari, John Giorno, Allan Kaprow, and Les Levine, as well as assorted conceptual works such as Lawrence Weiner's *An Accumulation of Information Taken from Here to There* and Paik's ... *confessions of a "café revolutionary."*

These groundbreaking events associated their aesthetic aspirations with connections to cybernetics and thus served as demonstrations of contemporary ideas, mixing acts and objects on a computer terminal. Other exhibitions of the era which foregrounded artists who explored digital technology include the Museum of Modern Art's 1966 *Experiments in Art and Technology*, *Polyvision* at Expo 67 in Montreal, and *Art and Technology* held at the Los Angeles County Museum of Art in 1971. A 1972 performance and screening held at Stevens Institute of Technology titled *The Computer Is a Medium* featured a combination of digital music, computer voice, film, and writing. Individual artists working in this discipline not represented in any of these exhibits include Alan Sondheim, whose 1970 experiment *4320* used a program that allowed him to explore the effects of 3D graphics on language, and E. M. de Melo e Castro, whose 1968 video poem *Roda Lume* combines computer-animated letters and shapes to propel an abstract narrative.

In contrast to most events—namely, the graphically oriented gatherings that dominated the spectrum until the 1990s—a 1973 "computer in the arts" symposium at the Cranbrook Academy of Art resulted in *Computer Poems*, the first printed anthology focused on digital writing. Specifically emphasizing works by poets programming computers, this publication includes automatically generated works by Marie Borroff, Archie Donald, Leslie Mezei, John Morris, Robin Shirley, and others.

As technological developments proliferated, so did the range of opportunities for artists and writers to display their works on computer screens and in "virtual environments." The founding of the journal *Leonardo* in 1967, which focused on the application of contemporary science and technology to the arts and music, and SIGGRAPH (Special Interest Group on GRAPHics and Interactive Techniques) in 1974 indicated that electronic art was growing, advancing, and gaining visibility in ways that digital writing did not until the WWW era. By the late 1970s and throughout the 1980s, video, graphical computer programming, computer games, robotics, and laser (holography) technologies all established themselves as colorful creative enterprises, broadening the fields of both digital writing and art. As digital technology became a more accessible means to produce kinetic and static two- and three-dimensional visual imagery, electronic artworks reflecting both narrative and abstract qualities became increasingly vivid and topically diverse. Countless exhibitions and installations featuring digital art, such as *Electra*, *Ars & Machina*, *PIXIM*, *Ars Electronica*, and *ARTEC*, sprang up in the 1980s; the central role technology and machinery played in the arts at this time was indicated by the general title of the 1986 Venice Biennale: *Art and Science*. The advent of Macintosh computers in the 1980s, highly celebrated for prowess in engineering graphics, played a large role in qualitative increases in optical, kinetic, and participatory aspects which the field experienced during this era. On occasion, these advancements included use of language, but more often works were not verbally oriented and their creators aligned themselves with visual, and not literary, arts.

One of the most widely known and renowned works of this period is Jeffrey Shaw's late-1980s participatory construct *Legible City*. Shaw constructed a computer-video-graphic installation in which the viewer rides a stationary bicycle (with moving pedals and handlebars) through the architecture of a city built with three-dimensional letters that take shape as words and sentences along the sides of streets. Sections of New York and Amsterdam were plotted out, and texts were devised to fill the coordinates. Predated in a non-digital form by works such as Morton Heilig's *Sensorama*, which employed film loops, sound, smells, and wind to simulate the experience of riding a motorcycle through Brooklyn circa 1962, Shaw's innovatory piece profoundly managed to bridge a perceived divide between digital art and writing in a manner few others would venture to attempt.

Informal groups of digital writers focusing on common interests, at first disconnected from one another, gradually formed. In France, ALAMO, the Workshop of Littérature Assisted by Mathematics and Computers, an offshoot of the Oulipo group focusing on computer generation, was founded in 1980. At that juncture, author-programmers such as Jean-Pierre Balpe began to revolutionize the automatic generation of literary texts by using deep linguistic structures in his programming. Text processors such as Hugh Kenner and Joseph O'Rourke's *TRAVESTY* and Charles O. Hartman's *DIASTEXT* were developed and used by small groups or individuals working concertedly. In the 1980s, on-screen text animations and interactivity became the focal point of practice for a group of researchers in Europe involved with the hypermedia journal *ALIRE*, as well as in works by inventive language-based artists in the Americas, such as Eduardo Kac's holographic poetry, bpNichol's *First Screening* (1984), and mIEKAL aND's *PataLiterator* (1987).

■ See also ALGORITHM, ANIMATED POETRY, CODE, COMBINATORY AND AUTOMATIC TEXT GENERATION, DIGITAL POETRY, ELECTRONIC LITERATURE, GAMES AS ART/LITERATURE, GLITCH AESTHETICS, HOLOPOETRY, HYPERTEXTUALITY, INTERACTIVE NARRATIVE, PARTICIPATORY CULTURE, VIDEO, VIRTUALITY

References and Further Reading

aND, mIEKAL. 1987. *PataLiterator*. Diskette. Madison, WI: Xexoxial Editions.

Bailey, Richard W., ed. 1973. *Computer Poems*. Drummond Island, MI: Potagannissing Press.

Bootz, Philippe, ed. 1995. *Alire: Le salon de lecture électronique*. CD-ROM. Villeneuve d'Ascq: MOTS-VOIR.

bpNichol. 1984. *First Screening: Computer Poems*. Diskette. Toronto: Underwich Editions.

Burnham, Jack, ed. 1970. *SOFTWARE: Information Technology: Its New Meaning for Art*. New York: Jewish Museum.

Funkhouser, C. T. 2007. *Prehistoric Digital Poetry: An Archaeology of Forms, 1959–1995*. Tuscaloosa: University of Alabama Press.

Hartman, Charles O. 1996. *VIRTUAL Muse: Experiments in Computer Poetry*. Hanover, NH: University Press of New England.

Kac, Eduardo, ed. 1996. *New Media Poetry: Poetic Innovation and New Technologies*. Special issue of *Visible Language* (30.2).

Popper, Frank. 1993. *Art in the Electronic Age*. New York: Abrams.

Reichardt, Jasia, ed. 1968. *Cybernetic Serendipity: The Computer and the Arts*. London: Studio International.

··

Easter Eggs
Laine Nooney

Easter eggs are digital objects, messages, or interactions built into computer programs by their designers. They are intended as a surprise to be found by the user, but they are not required in order to use the program. The term references the secular Western cultural tradition of the springtime Easter egg hunt, where hard-boiled eggs or plastic eggs filled with treats are hidden for children to find on a "hunt." While there are precedents for Easter eggs in nongame computer programs, Easter eggs are usually associated with video games. The classic example of a video game Easter egg is also, historically, the first: in the 1978 Atari VCS game *Adventure*, designer Warren Robinett coded a special room with the phrase "Created by Warren Robinett" spelled out in blinking pixels. It was intended as an authorial signature, Robinett's creative resistance toward a company that denied its programmers design credit. Robinett's room could only be uncovered through intensive exploration and sheer trial and error, ensuring that it would go unnoticed during testing. Thus, the first Easter egg revealed not just itself, but also "the secret of the game's own production" (Montfort and Bogost 2009, 61).

The exploratory qualities of gameplay produce an ideal environment for these intentionally "hidden-to-be-found" components, yet there are no rigid definitions governing how Easter eggs relate to gameplay. Some Easter eggs require keyed commands only uncovered through serendipity or scouring code, or reward exploration in hard-to-reach places, such as the "meta-egg" inscribed at the top of *Grand Theft Auto: San Andreas*'s Gant Bridge, which reads, "There are no Easter Eggs up here. Go away" (Conway 2010, 152). However, many games also include simple extradiegetic references or gags, such as the reoccurring "Maltese Falcon" quest in Sierra On-Line's *Quest for Glory* series, which gamers also refer to as an "Easter egg."

Consalvo divides Easter eggs into roughly two categories: ornamental and functional. Useless hidden objects or a programmer's signature are now common forms of "ornamental" Easter eggs, "designed for display rather than being functional to gameplay" (Consalvo 2007, 19). These in-game ornaments can produce paradoxical moments wherein the Easter egg "breaks the fourth wall" even as it requires deep immersion to locate. Conway addresses this dilemma, defining Easter eggs as "comedic contractions of the magic circle" in which the player finds herself cast outside of the magic circle but nonetheless deriving "pleasure from [her] agency within the postmodern text, for example intertextual recognition and bricolage" (Conway 2010, 152). Functional Easter eggs, in contrast, include the many built-in tricks, codes, and button combinations that release extra game lives or enhance abilities. For Consalvo, these "functional" Easter eggs are the first instantiation of the game "secret," the genealogical origin of cheat codes, god modes, and other paratextual devices. Easter eggs, as secret knowledge forms, "cultivated desire to possess 'gaming capital'" (Consalvo 2007, 18) and are best understood in relation to privileged sources of gamer cultural knowledge such as gaming magazines, strategy guides, and player word of mouth.

■ See also CHEATS, CODE, GAMEPLAY, GAMES AND EDUCATION, GLITCH AESTHETICS, IMMERSION

References and Further Reading

Consalvo, Mia. 2007. *Cheating: Gaining Advantage in Videogames*. Cambridge, MA: MIT Press.
Conway, Steven. 2010. "A Circular Wall? Reformulating the Fourth Wall for Videogames." *Journal of Gaming and Virtual Worlds* 2:145–155.
Montfort, Nick, and Ian Bogost. 2009. *Racing the Beam: The Atari Video Computer System*. Cambridge, MA: MIT Press.
Robinett, Warren. 2005. "*Adventure* as a Video Game: *Adventure* for the Atari 2600." In *The Game Design Reader: A Rules of Play Anthology*, edited by Katie Salen and Eric Zimmerman, 690–713. Cambridge, MA: MIT Press.

E-books
Johanna Drucker

The generic term *e-book* refers to any of several devices used to deliver reading material in a digital form. But the term blurs the important distinction between electronic texts and the format in which they are read. The very term, *e-book*, familiarizes on-screen reading by associating it with the traditional book. This raises questions about how, and in what way, we may refer to the devices and platforms that display digital texts as "books" in any sense, or whether these should be reconceptualized in our understanding and their design. The display of text on a flat screen has little connection to the multidimensional physical structure of a bound codex. The term *e-book* tries to forge a connection between screen modes of delivery/access and behaviors that imitate affordances of their historical predecessors. This basic tension—between the emulation of a prior format and the requirements for on-screen display—has informed the design of e-books since they were first envisioned in the 1970s.

A large number of texts are now available in digital format, but the development of this corpus started slowly. The first electronic texts were assembled through careful rekeyboarding and encoding to create digital files. Page images, or facsimiles, were too memory intensive when storage was limited. Even now many devices continue to use text-only display, gaining benefits of searchability and smaller file size. Project Gutenberg was among the earliest pioneers in the field when its founder, Michael Hart, launched his first e-book in 1971. Hart believed that digital texts could be widely disseminated, even though the World Wide Web was still two decades away and basic equipment for reading digital texts on screen was almost nonexistent in the 1970s outside of a few specialized laboratories.

Alongside the growing corpus of migrated texts (those originally published in print media), hypertext and born-digital content made their appearance in the 1980s as personal computers became popular tools for artists and writers eager to experiment (see HYPERTEXTUALITY). Stored on hard drives, floppy disks, and then CD-ROMs, these electronic texts made use of innovative writing and design techniques. The newly implemented graphical user interface (GUI) exploded visual possibilities for display (see INTERFACE). Eastgate Systems, founded in 1982, developed the first viable commercial hypertext authoring system, Storyspace, which was used to create works whose modular structure and links offered a reading experience along multiple pathways (see AUTHORING SYSTEMS, STORYSPACE). Beginning in 1985, the visionary publisher Voyager created support for electronic texts through its experiments publishing works in CD-ROM.

The Online Books Page at Carnegie Mellon, initiated in 1993, was also among the fledgling cohort of academic units creating digital content. By the time the web was launched in the early 1990s, substantial numbers of digital texts (most from classic, out-of-copyright materials that sidestepped intellectual property restrictions) were available from electronic text centers that had been established in major research universities, whose initial online offerings outstripped those of the commercial outlets, such as Amazon (founded in 1995), or major bookstore chains.

While the web increased distribution possibilities for electronic books, these texts were still being read on multipurpose computers. While an early prototype, the Dynabook, was developed at Xerox PARC in the 1970s, the first specialized commercial reading devices appeared around 1996 when a handheld unit named the Palm Pilot appeared. It had a small low-resolution screen and enough memory to store files for reading and display alongside its other functions (calendars, address book, diary, and so on). The size and mobility of the Palm fueled its popularity, even if the screen resolution was crude by later standards. But the development of so-called smartphones and other networked technology that combined mobility with screens for display radically altered the consumer market. The Rocket eBook (NuvoMedia's first dedicated reading device), the EveryBook, the Millennium eBook, Librius, Nook, Franklin eBookMan, and other specialized items that struggled to capture attention met stiff competition from the Amazon Kindle, launched in 2007. In 2010, Apple's iPad, with its swipe interface and higher screen resolution, achieved instant popularity as a platform for reading, games, online content, downloaded film, video, and networked communication. Long-form texts, such as novels, journal articles, textbooks, technical manuals, and newspapers, are regularly accessed on electronic reading platforms alongside live-feed and subscription-based content.

The generic term *e-book* continues to confuse textual content with a physical format (the codex book). In early designs of e-books, some clumsy attempts were made to imitate physical features of the book, such as page drape or page turning, but the first formats were little more than a continuous stream of text navigated with forward and back arrows. More essential features, such as bookmarks, tables of contents, indices, marginalia, footnotes, and bibliographical references, came more slowly. Among the most dramatic transformations of migrating texts from print to digital formats was that typographic and layout features were eliminated, as if these had no relevance to the experience of reading. Governed by the conviction that content is independent of format or material history, and that the experience of reading a text produces the same results no matter how the reading material is received, this repurposing of text for digital delivery sacrificed some of the crucial aesthetic dimensions of codex books.

A basic conceptual tension continues to drive design of e-books along the lines of emulation and imitation, whether to design them to resemble physical books in a virtual screen space, or whether to let the electronic capabilities push their design toward a new form uniquely suited to the digital, networked environment. Increasing emphasis on repurposable intellectual content and works produced across an array of related platforms is also creating imaginative design solutions. In their brief existence, e-books have acquired increasing sophistication, such as the capacity for annotation, underlining, navigation, search, and cross-reference. Electronic document design has taken advantage of the ability to use embedded media for audio and video, as well as special effects created with augmented and virtual reality platforms. As devices have differentiated, competition for market share has intensified the drive to distinguish pads, platforms, and tablets from each other by pitting price point against specific features, and many major companies are focused on the potential for merging entertainment, games, reading, fiction film, and educational activities in new ways.

The great advantage of e-books is mobility and convenience, replacing the bulk and heft of paper-based volumes with a single device that holds a library of materials in a single place for immediate and repeated use, thus producing the consumerist illusion of infinite supply available on demand.

One of the unexpected consequences of the development of e-books has been the intense reflection it has prompted on the character of the codex book as a material form. Even as pads and tablets become more common and the experience of reading focuses on the screen, interest in the material history and design of the physical codex is growing. As new devices and platforms emerge, attention to the relation between specific materialities and the aesthetic expression may increase, with benefits accruing to all media formats as a result.

■ See also BOOK TO E-TEXT, HISTORY OF COMPUTERS, MOBILE GAMES

References and Further Reading

Auletta, Ken. 2010. "Publish or Perish: Can the iPad Topple the Kindle, and Save the Book Business?" *New Yorker*, April 26.

Ballhaus, Werner. 2010. *Turning the Page: The Future of eBooks*. Price, Waterhouse, Coopers, www .pwc.com.

Diaz, M. H. 2011. "Academic E-books and Their Role in the Emerging Scholarly Communications Landscape." *InfoViews*, August 24.

Lebert, Marie. 2009. *A Short History of eBooks*. Toronto: NEF, University of Toronto.

Rae, Tushar. 2011. "E-books' Varied Formats Make Citations a Mess for Scholars." *Chronicle of Higher Education*, February 6.

Snowhill, Lucia. 2001. "E-books and Their Future in Academic Libraries." *D-Lib Magazine*, July/ August, 7 (7).

Warren, John. 2009. "Innovation and the Future of E-books." Rand Corporation, RP 1385. Champaign, IL: Common Ground Publishing.

....

Electronic Literature
Scott Rettberg

Electronic literature is a generalized term used to describe a wide variety of computational literary practices beneath one broad umbrella, defined by the Electronic Literature Organization (ELO) as "works with important literary aspects that take advantage of the capabilities and contexts provided by the stand-alone or networked computer."

The term is somewhat fraught and often challenged as not sufficiently or accurately descriptive to suit the more taxonomically minded of its scholars and practitioners. By way of reduction and assemblage, one might patch together definitions of "electronic" and "literature" in a way that makes some sense: "electronic literature is the result or product of literary activity carried or performed using the computer." But of course, that would leave us with most literary activity that takes place in the contemporary era. What is really meant by "electronic literature" is that the computer (or the network context) is in some way *essential to* the performance or carrying out of the literary activity in question.

Prior to the 1990s, the term *electronic literature* was most often used to refer more generally to texts that appeared or were stored in electronic form. This usage is still not uncommon, particularly in scientific fields. Research published in online journals or databases might be referred to as "the electronic literature" of the given field.

Jill Walker Rettberg (2012) found evidence that Jay David Bolter was using the term to refer specifically to literary works made for the computer as early as 1985 in an article titled "The Idea of Literature in the Electronic Medium." In their 1987 Hypertext Conference paper "Hypertext and Creative Writing," which was the first presentation of the Storyspace hypertext authoring software, Bolter and Joyce use the term once, writing, "All electronic literature takes the form of a game, a contest between author and reader" (see STORYSPACE). Bolter again uses the term in the 1991 edition of *Writing Space*.

By the mid-1990s the term was in wider circulation and referred specifically to born-digital literary artifacts. Walker Rettberg notes that one prominent use of the term was in Robert Kendall's "Writing for the New Millennium: The Birth of Electronic Literature," published in *Poets & Writers*, a popular magazine targeting an audience of American writers.

In the mid-1990s *electronic literature* was one of many terms in circulation to refer to digital writing practices and was by no means the most prominent. *Hypertext fiction* and the more generic *hypertext* were terms generally used to describe the works published by

Eastgate Systems to refer to node-based literary works connected by links (see HYPER-TEXTUALITY). The generic *hypertext* itself was defined by Ted Nelson, first in 1965 as "a body of written or pictorial material interconnected in such a complex way that it could not conveniently be presented or represented on paper," and then in 1970 as "forms of writing which branch or perform on request." Both of Nelson's definitions of *hypertext* are broadly applicable to the majority of types of work that are understood as electronic literature today. Works of e-lit are generally interconnected in ways that are not easily amenable to print publication, and they branch, or importantly *perform* on request. Yet, as Noah Wardrip-Fruin notes, by the late 1990s "in the literary community, the definition of hypertext shifted so that it applied almost exclusively to chunk-style media" (2004, 127). Owing to both the prominence of Eastgate-published hypertexts such as Michael Joyce's *afternoon, a story* and Shelley Jackson's *Patchwork Girl* and even more profoundly the brand of hypertext encoded in HyperText Markup Language (HTML), in the late 1990s hypertext was largely understood to be works of the link-and-node variety (see MARKUP LANGUAGES). If one forgot Nelson's original definitions, hypertext would seem an awkward fit, for instance, with an aleatory or generative work that produced a new narrative each time it was run, or with a digital poem that moved in the space of the screen yet required little interaction from the reader (see DIGITAL POETRY). While both of these can be understood as hypertexts in Nelson's sense that they perform on request, neither can be easily parsed into a link-and-node structure.

Other terms also presented problems. While one might think, for instance, that the term *interactive fiction* could be applicable to any work of fiction in which the user's interaction plays a significant role in determining the structure or outcome of a story (including the order in which nodes are displayed in a hypertext fiction), the term was already colonized by the devotees of the text adventure game-based genre (see INTERACTIVE FICTION). An active "IF Community" had already by the 1990s developed an elaborate self-sustaining infrastructure for the development and distribution of works in this text parser genre, complete with its own platforms, archives, and competitions. So while hypertext fictions were interactive in the sense that their readers would select links or follow paths, they were distinct from the type of "interactive fiction" that requires its readers to type queries and instructions to participate in the narrative.

In the 1990s, there indeed seems to have been a tension between the literary hypertext community and this definition of interactive fiction. Indeed, hypertext author John McDaid reports that members of Rob Swigart's 1988 hypertext fiction workshop felt that the phrase "This is not a game" was so important to early hypertext practitioners that they put it on a t-shirt "in *real* big letters" (Wardrip-Fruin 2005). In the same article, Stuart Moulthrop reports that in retrospect "our allergy to games looks incredibly foolish, both because Infocom's market experience didn't end all that happily, and more important because there was so much good work coming out of [the interactive fiction] community, and still is." There was clearly anxiety among hypertext fiction writers, who considered their work to be part of a literary tradition, to see their work classified as "mere game."

E-poetry and *digital poetry* are terms that were also in circulation in the mid-1990s and are still used today. The circulation of "e-poetry" is largely due to the success of the Electronic Poetry Center at SUNY Buffalo, spearheaded by poet Loss Glazier and the subsequent launch in 2001 of the E-poetry Festival. The E-poetry Festival has seen five further biennial iterations. As in electronic literature, or e-mail, the e- in e-poetry represents "electronic" and as such is equally ambiguous. While e-poetry does not have any implicit connotation of link-and-node, it is exclusive in the sense that fiction, documentary works, or drama would generally be considered outside the frame. Some might argue that "digital poetry" or "digital literature" would be better terms. "Digital poetry" of course excludes fiction in the same way as "e-poetry," but "digital literature" has a slightly more denotative frame, in that at least one of the *Oxford English Dictionary* definitions of digital ("Of a computer or calculator: that operates on data in digital form; [of a storage medium] that stores digital data") both specifies computers and sets itself in direct contrast to "analog" (see ANALOG VERSUS DIGITAL). Yet "digital" is almost as imprecise as "electronic" as a modifier. And while the involvement of the computer is essential to this sort of work, the underlying binary nature of its operations might seem less so.

Cybertext is a term neologized by Espen Aarseth in the eponymous monograph *Cybertext* and caught on during the 1990s. The "cyber" prefix was derived from the Greek *kubernan*, a verb meaning "to steer or guide," and Aarseth's term directs attention to the configurative operations of many ergodic works, which require nontrivial effort from the reader in order to traverse the text. Of course, there is no particular reason why cybertexts need be electronic—the *I Ching* is one of Aarseth's prominent examples—nor that they be particularly literary. Many computers games that make no effort to offer either narrative or poetry easily could fit within Aarseth's typology.

When the first organizers of the ELO were debating the name of the new nonprofit organization back in 1999, they consciously chose to use this term rather than hypertext, digital poetry, interactive fiction, writing for programmable and networked media, or any other more specific term precisely because of its generality. As previously noted, in 2004, the ELO agreed to define electronic literature as "works with important literary aspects that take advantage of the capabilities and contexts provided by the stand-alone or networked computer."

As a number of people have pointed out subsequently, the phrase "important literary aspects" is a bit slippery. In *Electronic Literature: New Horizons for the Literary*, Hayles excuses the tautology of this phrase, explaining that readers "come to digital work with expectations formed by print" and that "electronic literature must build on these expectations even as it modifies and transforms them." Hayles further draws attention to the distinction between "literature" proper, which one might presume is limited to verbal art forms in which words are dominant, and "the literary," which Hayles proposes as "creative artworks that interrogate the histories, contexts, and productions of literature, including as well the verbal art of literature proper." Hayles felt this distinction important largely because of the fact that when she, Nick Montfort, Scott Rettberg, and Stephanie Strickland were editing the *Electronic Literature Collection*, volume 1, in 2006, they encountered in the submissions, and indeed chose to include in the collections, a number of works in which the written word was not the primary focus if indeed it was present at all. Giselle Beiguelman's *Code Movie 1*, for example, is a movie that presents the hexadecimal code of a jpg in an animation with music. The numbers fly past and would signify nothing were it not for the fact that they are the signifiers underlying an object that is never seen within the work itself. There are no words in the piece, yet the editors chose to include it in the *ELC 1* because it deals in an interesting way with the relationship between code and language, transcodification and transcription (see CODE). So while it is not primarily concerned with language per se, it is about writing, and about how meaning is made in digital environments. As Hayles would argue, it is a literary work even if it itself is not literature.

The ELO's simple definition of electronic literature is supplemented by a list of "forms and threads of practice," including

- hypertext fiction and poetry, on and off the web;
- kinetic poetry presented in Flash and using other platforms;
- computer art installations that ask viewers to read them or otherwise have literary aspects;
- conversational characters, also known as "chatterbots";
- interactive fiction;
- novels that take the form of e-mails, SMS messages, or blogs;
- poems and stories that are generated by computers, either interactively or based on parameters given at the beginning;
- collaborative writing projects that allow readers to contribute to the text of a work;
- literary performances online that develop new ways of writing.

This list was intended not to be exclusive or constraining but to serve as a leaping-off point for further extensions, and that has certainly been the case as one surveys the works that have been published by the ELO in two collections and exhibited by the organization at its conferences in the years since. Some of these forms are clearly established as forms of e-lit: in particular, hypertext fiction and poetry, kinetic poetry (or alternatively "media poetry"), interactive fiction, and generated poetry and fiction all have a substantial history at this point. If hypertext fiction's heyday in the 1990s has come and gone, one can certainly point to a substantial body of creative work and critical discourse around it. Kinetic poetry and its cousins today remain the subject of major international festivals and exhibitions. Interactive fiction is the focus of a thriving amateur creative community. Poetry and fiction generators (see COMBINATORY AND AUTOMATIC TEXT GENERATION, STORY GENERATION) have perhaps the longest history of any of the forms concerned, stretching back to Christopher Stratchey's 1952 *M.U.C. Love Letter Generator* and remaining a subject of considerable creative and computational activity today.

Looking at the ELO list of examples of electronic literature, there are also some (possibly instructive) anomalies. Was it necessary to specify one particular brand of software—Flash? And how precisely do computer art installations "ask viewers to read them"? Perhaps both of these questions point to some of the ambiguities of electronic literature. One such ambiguity is the importance of platform: while Flash was much less dominant in digital poetic practices in 2012 than it was in 2004, it is very much the case that a creative community of digital poets and art makers gathered around that specific platform in the late 1990s and early 2000s, just as a community of early hypertext fiction writers had gathered around the particular platform of Storyspace earlier (see STORYSPACE). The platform in electronic literature constrains and affords practices in a material—and some might even say determinative—way. While it might have mattered very little, for instance, which make of typewriter one used to pound out a manuscript, the use of guard fields in a Storyspace hypertext or tweens in a Flash poem has very specific aesthetic effects on the way that a reader interacts with and perceives a work.

In the other phrase referring to computer art installations, we see one of the ways that we are pulled in different directions. If the person experiencing a computer art installation is a "viewer," but she is also asked to read it, is she not also then already a "reader" (see READING STRATEGIES)? Or is she most likely both a viewer *and* a reader? Many electronic literature installations are what Dick Higgins would have described as *intermedia*. Such an installation might be described as an art installation in one context and a literary work in another, or both simultaneously. The idea of pure forms breaks down, as does a strict ontology of the work itself. Just as it is the case that these sorts of installations are both artwork and literary artifact, calling for both spectacular affect and readerly contemplation, it is most often the case that works of electronic literature are both *written* works in the sense that we understand most literature to be and computer programs that we *run* and of which we are *users*. We encounter electronic literature as both a reading experience and an application, an artifact that may also encompass the tool used to produce it.

The inclusion in the list of "novels that take the form of e-mails, SMS messages, or blogs" (see E-MAIL NOVEL) is an indication of the directions we might expect electronic literature to take in the future. The particular communication platform listed (when is the last time you heard someone refer to a text message as an SMS?) is not particularly important. The essential idea here is that our communication technologies effect changes in the form, style, and content of writing, and that just as literary forms have been modified, and literary genres have emerged, from every previous historical shift in textual communication technologies, we might expect that novels will be written in the networked platforms that have been widely adopted as part of the practice of everyday life. Who will write the Great American Facebook novel, or best encapsulate a moment of epiphany in a work of cathartic Twitterature? And will we even, at that point, recognize the relationship between those and the forms that preceded them?

The last two items on the list, "collaborative writing projects that allow readers to contribute to the text of a work" (see COLLABORATIVE NARRATIVE) and "literary performances online that develop new ways of writing" (see PERFORMANCE), are the least descriptive of precise forms of genres, yet they gesture toward a certain direction of literary practice without necessarily guiding us there by hand. Collaborative writing projects might include many different types of practices. While *Wikipedia* would likely not fit anyone's understanding of electronic literature, projects such as Judd Morrissey, Mark Jeffrey, et al.'s narrative database project *The Last Performance*, which involves contributions by more than a hundred contributors responding to a shared set of constraints and together building a kind of literalized architecture, certainly do. While "literary performances online" might involve just about any kind of writing that unfolds over time on the network, performance is an apt way of describing practices that do not seem intent on sitting still long enough to be understood as discrete artifacts. Particularly when the dominant environments of textual exchange online, such as contemporary social networks, are based more on a model of rapidly flowing conversation than they are on anything approaching the fixity of a book, one can anticipate that performance work, such as Alan Sondheim's various textual and extratextual actions on e-mail lists and virtual worlds, Mez's deconstructive interventions, or Rob Wittig and Mark Marino's "netprov" projects, will increasingly become representative of one type of electronic literature more based on the experience of unfolding process, interaction, and response than on movement toward a fixed literary artifact.

The list of examples of different electronic literature practices provided by the ELO could have gone for pages without arriving at a clear stopping point, and that is ultimately *the* point. Electronic literature is experimental literature and is not as yet tied to any specific market logic. It is literary research and development, but of a particular strain that does not necessarily have any specific destination in mind. Writers and artists will always work with the materials available to them in their cultural moment, and the computer and network are now part of that toolkit. From a creative standpoint, layers of constraints have dropped rapidly away from writers. Consider that it was not so long ago that including a song, or a video clip, or information about the reader's location, or an interface that enables the reader to physically enter a three-dimensional environment would have been completely beyond the reach of most writers. There are a plethora of new tools and techniques available to literary practitioners. The skills and knowledge necessary to make use of all of these new affordances range from trivial to profound—it takes very little knowledge to embed a video clip but a rather long time to learn C++. But the majority of the creative constraints on electronic literature are, at this point, those that the authors choose for themselves.

References and Further Reading

Aarseth, Espen. 1997. *Cybertext*. Baltimore: Johns Hopkins University Press.

Bolter, Jay D. 1985. "The Idea of Literature in the Electronic Medium." *Topic: Computers in the Liberal Arts* 39:23–34.

Bolter, Jay David, and Michael Joyce. 1987. "Hypertext and Creative Writing." In *HYPERTEXT '87 Proceedings of the ACM Conference on Hypertext* (New York, NY), 41–50.

Emerson, Lori. 2011. "on 'e-literature' as a field." Blog post, October 12. http://loriemerson.net/2011/10/12/on-e-literature-as-a-field/.

Hayles, N. Katherine. 2008. *Electronic Literature: New Horizons for the Literary*. Notre Dame, IN: University of Notre Dame Press.

Higgins, Dick. 1967. "Statement on Intermedia." *Dé-coll/age* 6 (July).

Kendall, Robert. 1995. "Writing for the New Millennium: The Birth of Electronic Literature." *Poets & Writers* (November/December). *Word Circuits*. www.wordcircuits.com/kendall/essays/pw1.htm.

Leishman, Donna. 2012. "The Flash Community: Implications for Post-Conceptualism." *Dichtung Digital* 41. www.dichtung-digital.org/2012/41/leishman/leishman.htm.

Morrissey, Judd, et al. 2007–2010. *The Last Performance [dot org]*. http://thelastperformance.org/.

Nelson, Ted. 1965. "A File Structure for the Complex, the Changing, and the Indeterminate." *Association for Computing Machinery: Proc. 20th National Conference*, 84–100.

———. 1970. "No More Teachers' Dirty Looks." *Computer Decisions* 9 (8): 16–23.

Rettberg, Scott. 2012. "Developing an Identity for the Field of Electronic Literature: Reflections on the Electronic Literature Organization Archives." *Dichtung Digital* 41. www.dichtung-digital.org/2012/41/rettberg.htm.

Walker Rettberg, Jill. 2012. "Electronic Literature Seen from a Distance: The Beginnings of a Field." *Dichtung Digital* 41. www.dichtung-digital.org/2012/41/walker-rettberg.htm.

Wardrip-Fruin, Noah. 2004. "What Hypertext Is." In *HYPERTEXT '04 Proceedings of the 15th ACM Conference on Hypertext and Hypermedia* (New York, NY), 126–127.

———. 2005. "Playable Media and Textual Instruments." *Dichtung Digital* 34. http://dichtung-digital.mewi.unibas.ch/2005/1/Wardrip-Fruin/index.htm.

Electronic Literature Organization
Marjorie Luesebrink

The Electronic Literature Organization (ELO) was founded in 1999 to foster and promote the reading, writing, teaching, and understanding of literature as it develops and persists in a changing digital environment. A 501(c)(3) nonprofit organization, the ELO includes writers, artists, teachers, scholars, and developers. The organization's focus is new literary forms that are made to be read on digital systems, including smartphones, web browsers, and networked computers. The ELO's definition of e-literature and its history, goals, activities, and projects/publications contribute to this focus.

The ELO and E-literature

The ELO exists in the context of the computer as a literary element. The term *electronic literature* refers to works with important literary aspects that take advantage of the capabilities and affordances provided by the stand-alone or networked computer. Within the broad category of electronic literature are several forms and threads of practice (see ELECTRONIC LITERATURE).

The field of electronic literature is an evolving one. Current literature not only migrates from print to electronic media; increasingly, "born-digital" works are created explicitly for the networked computer (see BOOK TO E-TEXT). The ELO seeks to bring this network and the process-intensive aspects of literature into visibility.

The confrontation with technology at the level of creation is what distinguishes electronic literature from, for example, e-books, digitized versions of print works, and other products of print authors "going digital" (see E-BOOKS).

Electronic literature often intersects with conceptual and sound arts, but reading and writing remain important to the literary arts. These activities, unbound by pages and the printed book, now move freely through galleries, performance spaces, and museums. But electronic literature does not reside in any single medium or institution.

Because information technology is driven increasingly by proprietary concerns, authors working in new media need the support of institutions that can advocate for the preservation, archiving, and free circulation of literary work. The ELO has continually made common cause with organizations such as Creative Commons, Archiving the Avant Garde, ArchiveIT.org, and the United States Library of Congress, to ensure the open circulation, attributed citation, and preservation of works (see FREE AND OPEN-SOURCE SOFTWARE).

The ELO promotes the discovery of talent and common areas of interest among the membership. The ELO is affiliated with organizations that are allied with the extensive network of people who produce works and the audience that reads, discusses, and teaches e-lit.

History

In the mid- to late 1990s, realizing the promise that electronic media offered for literature but noting the lack of a supporting infrastructure, practitioners, readers, and scholars began discussions on the specifics of groups that would meet this need. Conferences such as "Open Technology Platforms for 21st Century Literature" (hosted by Robert Coover at Brown University in April 1999) and "The CyberMountain Conference" (organized by Deena Larsen in Denver, Colorado, in June 1999) outlined plans for the formation of an electronic literature organization.

The ELO was formally established in late 1999 by electronic author Scott Rettberg, novelist Robert Coover, and Internet business leader Jeff Ballowe. They assembled a board of directors that included writers, publishers, Internet industry leaders, and literary non-profit experts to found this not-for-profit organization. The first office, from 2000 to 2001, was in Chicago. Jeff Ballowe was president of the board, and Scott Rettberg was managing director. Original directors included Ballowe, Mark Bernstein, Peter Bernstein, Coover, Marjorie C. Luesebrink (M. D. Coverley), Cathy Marshall, Stuart Moulthrop, Scott Rettberg, Anne Schott, William Wadsworth, and Rob Swigart.

In the fall of 2001, the ELO moved its headquarters from Chicago to the University of California, Los Angeles (UCLA). Here, under the faculty leadership of N. Katherine Hayles, Managing Director Scott Rettberg, and Presidents Jeff Ballowe and Marjorie C. Luesebrink, the ELO launched conferences and performances and began to develop a network of college and university collaborations. The ELO also inaugurated the *Electronic Literature Literary Advisory Board*, which includes many scholars, experts, and practitioners in the fields of electronic and print literature.

After five productive years at UCLA, in the summer of 2006 the ELO moved to the Maryland Institute for Technology in the Humanities (MITH) at the University of Maryland, College Park, where Matthew Kirschenbaum, MITH's associate director, was the ELO's faculty advisor; Joseph Tabbi became president of the board.

In 2011, the ELO moved to MIT. At MIT the organization is associated with the Comparative Media Studies (CMS) program. Nick Montfort is the current ELO board president; Dene Grigar, vice president; Scott Rettberg, vice president; Sandy Baldwin, treasurer; Mark C. Marino, secretary and director of communication. Additional board members include Jo-Anne Green, Carolyn Guertin, D. Fox Harrell, Robert Kendall, Marjorie C. Luesebrink (M. D. Coverley), Talan Memmott, Stuart Moulthrop, Jason Nelson, Rita Raley, Stephanie Strickland, Joseph Tabbi, Helen Thorington, and Noah Wardrip-Fruin.

The ELO's role in the electronic literature community includes event and conference organization and publication. Landmark events in the organization's history have included the launch of a database-driven directory of electronic literature; readings and outreach events in Chicago, New York, Seattle, Boston, Los Angeles; and an Electronic Literature Awards program that recognizes exemplary works of poetry and fiction.

The ELO's current goals are to bring born-digital literature to the attention of authors, scholars, developers, and the current generation of readers for whom the printed book is no longer an exclusive medium of education or aesthetic practice; to build a network of affiliated organizations in academia, the arts, and business; and to coordinate the collection, preservation, description, and discussion of works in accessible forums, according to peer-to-peer review standards and technological best practices.

Ongoing Activities and Publications

1. *The Electronic Literature Directory*. The directory provides an extensive database of listings for electronic works and their authors. Bibliographic information on preweb and other offline work is included, along with links to currently online work. The entries cover poetry, fiction, drama, and nonfiction works of electronic literature, including hypertexts, animated poems, interactive fiction, multimedia pieces, text generators, and works that allow reader collaboration. The directory allows readers and students to easily list all of an author's works and to browse through different genres of work. Directory entries are shared with affiliated European, Canadian, and Australian organizations (http://directory.eliterature.org/).

2. *The Electronic Literature Collection*, volumes 1 and 2. *The Electronic Literature Collection* is a periodical publication of current and older electronic literature in a form suit-

able for individual, public library, and classroom use. The publications are available both online and as a packaged, cross-platform CD-ROM or DVD, in a case appropriate for library processing, marking, and distribution. The contents of the collections are offered under a Creative Commons license. Volume 1 (http://collection.eliterature.org/1/) was published in 2006, and volume 2 (http://collection.eliterature.org/2/) in 2011. They are available on CD-ROM and on the web.

3. Biyearly ELO Conferences. Regular conferences and symposia bring artists, writers, teachers, developers, and scholars into contact with each other to build a larger audience for the digital arts. Conferences have included "The State of the Arts Symposium," UCLA, 2002; "e(X)literature: The Preservation, Archiving and Dissemination of Electronic Literature," UCSB, 2003; "ELO/MITH Symposium," University of Maryland, 2007; "Visionary Landscapes," Washington State University, Vancouver, 2008; "Archive & Innovate," Brown University, 2010. Future conferences: "Electrifying Literature," West Virginia University, 2012; "Paris 8—Electronic Literature in Translation," Paris, 2012.

4. The ELO Website. The site provides news about the organization, the field of electronic literature, announcements, membership information, links to publications, and the showcase. The ELO showcase, to which new works are continually added, provides a few outstanding examples of electronic literature (http://eliterature.org/).

Past Publications

Electronic Literature: New Horizons for the Literary.—This book by N. Katherine Hayles, published by the University of Notre Dame Press, is published in an edition that includes the *Electronic Literature Collection*, volume 1, on CD-ROM.

Electronic Literature: What Is It?—This publication by N. Katherine Hayles surveys the development and current state of electronic literature, from the popularity of hypertext fiction in the 1980s to the present, focusing primarily on hypertext fiction, network fiction, interactive fiction, locative narratives, installation pieces, "codework," generative art, and the Flash poem. A final section discusses the Preservation, Archiving and Dissemination (PAD) initiative of the ELO, including the *Electronic Literature Collection*, volume 1, and the two white papers that are companion pieces to this essay, "Acid Free Bits" and "Born Again Bits." http://eliterature.org/pad/elp.html.

Toward a Semantic Literary Web.—In this essay, Joseph Tabbi argues that electronic literature is not just a "thing" or a "medium" or even a body of "works" in various "genres." It is not poetry, fiction, hypertext, gaming, codework, or some new admixture of all these practices. E-literature is, arguably, an emerging cultural form, as much a collective creation of new terms and keywords as it is the production of new literary objects. http://eliterature.org/pad/slw.html.

Born-Again Bits: A Framework for Migrating Electronic Literature.—This report, by Alan Liu, David Durand, Nick Montfort, Merrilee Proffitt, Liam R. E. Quin, Jean-Hugues Rety, and Noah Wardrip-Fruin, was published in July 2005 and is an outcome of the PAD project. http://eliterature.org/pad/bab.html.

Acid-Free Bits: Recommendations for Long-Lasting Electronic Literature.—This report, by Nick Montfort and Noah Wardrip-Fruin, was published in June 2004 and is an outcome of the PAD project. http://eliterature.org/pad/afb.html.

State of the Arts Proceedings.—Keynote addresses, papers, and electronic literature from the State of the Arts Symposium are collected in this book and CD. *State of the Arts:*

The Proceedings of the 2002 Electronic Literature Organization Symposium was edited by Scott Rettberg and published in March 2003. http://eliterature.org/state/.

■ See also CELL PHONE NOVEL, DIGITAL FICTION, DIGITAL POETRY, ELECTRONIC LITERATURE, E-MAIL NOVEL, STORYSPACE

References and Further Reading

Borràs, Laura, Talan Memmott, Rita Raley, and Brian Kim Stefans, eds. 2011. *The Electronic Literature Collection.* Volume 2. http://collection.eliterature.org/2/.

Electronic Literature Directory. http://directory.eliterature.org/.

Electronic Literature Organization Website. http://eliterature.org/.

Hayles, N. Katherine. 2007. *Electronic Literature: What Is It?* http://eliterature.org/pad/elp.html.

———. 2008. *Electronic Literature: New Horizons for the Literary.* Notre Dame, IN: Notre Dame University Press.

Hayles, N. Katherine, Nick Montfort, Scott Rettberg, and Stephanie Strickland, eds. 2006. *The Electronic Literature Collection.* Volume 1. http://collection.eliterature.org/1/.

Liu, Alan, David Durand, Nick Montfort, et al. 2005. *Born-Again Bits: A Framework for Migrating Electronic Literature.* http://eliterature.org/pad/bab.html.

Rettberg, Scott, ed. 2003. *State of the Arts: The Proceedings of the 2002 Electronic Literature Organization Symposium.* http://eliterature.org/state/.

Tabbi, Joseph. 2007. *Toward a Semantic Literary Web: Setting a Direction for the Electronic Literature Organization's Directory.* http://eliterature.org/pad/slw.html.

E-mail Novel
Jill Walker Rettberg

E-mail novels present a narrative as a collection of e-mails written between characters in the story. Online e-mail novels have been published both as a web archive of e-mails and as live performances where e-mails are sent directly to readers. There are also a number of print novels constructed as collections of e-mails.

Like blogs and traditional epistolary novels, e-mail novels are a serial form of narrative that makes use of the conventions of a familiar genre and expects the reader to piece together the context (see BLOGS). The intimacy of e-mail allows readers a sense of voyeurism that is often heightened by the e-mails being read in a simulation of a private inbox or arriving in the reader's own inbox but addressed to somebody else. The first e-mail novel may be Carl Steadman's "Two Solitudes" (1994), where readers could subscribe to a series of e-mails between two people who fall in love and finally break up. E-mail novels that are performed live make use of the immediacy and speed of e-mail. The timing of e-mails can also be key. For instance, e-mails in Rob Wittig's *Blue Company* (2001) were usually sent out more or less daily for a month, but one day, five e-mails arrived in rapid succession, giving "live" updates of a tournament in which the protagonist was involved.

While the e-mails in *Blue Company* are all from the protagonist to the woman he is in love with, Scott Rettberg's *Kind of Blue* (2002) consists of e-mails between several characters. Here several e-mails are often sent on any given day, and sometimes within a few minutes of each other as the plot develops. Both these works were first performed live to subscribers and can now be read as web archives. Another technique is to publish the novel as a simulation of a fictional character's web mail, as in Mo Fanning's *Place Their Face* (2007) or Richard Powers's "They Come in a Steady Stream Now" (2004), where the reader appears to have somehow gained access to the main character's private inbox. Some e-mail novels attempt to retain the illusion of authenticity by giving an explanation for the reader's access to the e-mails. For instance, the foreword to Joseph Alan Wachs's series of iPhone apps *Treehouse: A Found E-mail Love Affair* (2009) explains that the e-mails presented were found and painstakingly reconstructed when Wachs was restoring a corrupted hard drive.

Most e-mail novels cast the reader as a voyeur looking in. An exception to this was Rob Bevan and Tim Wright's *Online Caroline* (2000), which directly addresses the reader, making the recipient of the e-mails a character in the fiction. *Online Caroline* consisted of a website with the video diary of Caroline, the protagonist, who eagerly befriended the reader. The reader answered questions and gave advice and, in return, received daily, customized e-mails from Caroline. The story unfolded over twenty-one days in which the reader gradually discovered that Caroline was being held captive as a guinea pig in a bizarre experiment, and that the reader, by keeping her company online, had in fact in some way been complicit in her abuse and possibly, finally, her death (Walker 2004).

E-mail novels share many characteristics with SMS narratives, and with certain narratives told in social media such as Facebook or Twitter. Using the Facebook Application Programming Interface (API), narratives such as Moveon.org's CNNBC Reports (2010) have created customized stories using facts about the actual reader and their friends which can create a similar complicity to Online Caroline. More commonly, in both e-mail novels and other social media narratives, the reader is left outside of the fiction, remaining a voyeur.

■ See also BLOGS, BOOK TO E-TEXT, CHATTERBOTS, DIGITAL FICTION, ELECTRONIC LITERATURE, IMMERSION, INTERACTIVE NARRATIVE, NARRATIVITY, PERFORMANCE, PRESERVATION

References and Further Reading

Bevan, Rob, and Tim Wright. 2000. *Online Caroline*. www.onlinecaroline.com.

Fanning, Mo. 2007. *Place Their Face*. http://placetheirface.com.

Moveon.org. 2010. CNNBC Reports. Personalized video. http://cnnbc.moveon.org.

Powers, Richard. 2004. "They Come in a Steady Stream Now." *Ninth Letter*. www.ninthletter.com/featured_artist/artist/5 [No longer available].

Rettberg, Scott. 2002. *Kind of Blue*. http://tracearchive.ntu.ac.uk/frame/index.cfm?article=77.

Steadman, Carl. 1994. "Two Solitudes." *InterText* 5 (1). www.intertext.com/magazine/v5n1/solitudes.html.

Wachs, Joseph Alan. 2009. *Treehouse: A Found E-Mail Love Affair*. iPhone app.

Walker, Jill. 2004. "How I Was Played by Online Caroline." In *First Person: New Media as Story, Performance, and Game*, edited by Noah Wardrip-Fruin and Pat Harrigan, 302–309. Cambridge, MA: MIT Press.

Wittig, Rob. 2001. *Blue Company*. www.robwit.net/bluecompany2002/.

Emergence
Ragnhild Tronstad

Associated with complexity and unpredictability, a general notion of emergence depicts a situation or phenomenon that evolves in a direction that could not have been predicted beforehand by studying the agents and rules involved. In more specialized terminologies, types of emergence are described by a variety of disciplines, such as economy, philosophy, physics, mathematics, biology, urbanism, and computer science. These types may differ in form as well as degree, from intentionally designed, simple forms of emergence (such as the function of a machine or software code) to strong emergent structures that cannot be reduced to, or explained as, an effect of their underlying properties and laws (Fromm 2005). A distinction has been drawn between *weak* and *strong* emergence: Weak emergence can—in principle, at least—be derived as an effect of the interaction between a system's constituent parts through simulation of the system. However, emergence is strong if entirely new properties are produced that cannot be traced back to the system's parts or their interactions. Unable to provide scientific proof for strong emergence, some scholars recommend that we leave the concept out of scientific discourse: "Although strong emergence is logically possible, it is uncomfortably like magic" (Bedau 1997, 377). Some philosophers argue that consciousness is an example of strong emergence, and that "new fundamental laws of nature" may be needed to explain such phenomena (Chalmers 2006, 245). As a concept emergence is contested, and typical uses of the term "may well express cluster concepts with many different elements" (Chalmers 2006, 253).

A popular biological account of emergence describes the complexity of labor division in ant hills as a decentralized, self-organized form of collective behavior (see COLLECTIVE INTELLIGENCE). Despite there being no central intelligence to keep an overview and assign the tasks, the work appears brilliantly organized with every ant knowing what it has to do. The phenomenon is called swarm intelligence and may be observed in natural form in the organization of ant hills, slime molds, flocks of birds, and schools of fish. Artificial simulations of swarm intelligence are a feature common in software art, generative art, robotics, and artificial life (see ARTIFICIAL LIFE). It is also used to simulate crowds and crowd behavior in fiction film.

Among a number of contemporary cultural forms and genres that have employed emergence as a means of expression, digital games stand out in showing a particular disposition toward emergence in its many configurations. Already traditional, nondigital games are known to embody central principles of emergence. Thus, in John Holland's *Emergence: From Chaos to Order* (1998), board games figure prominently among the examples. For instance, the example of chess is used to demonstrate the general emergent principle of "much coming from little": the phenomenon that "a small number of rules or laws can generate systems of surprising complexity. . . . Chess is defined by fewer than two dozen rules, but humankind continues to find new possibilities in the game after hundreds of years of intensive study" (Holland 1998, 1, 3). The reason why board games are the example of choice for Holland is partly because he wants to restrict his study to emergent phenomena whose underlying rules we are able to identify and describe. However, other emergent systems exist that rely on more complex sets of rules that we may not be able to explain as clearly. Depending on game genre, digital games do include a number of additional complexity layers compared to analog games (see GAME GENRES). In digital games, thus, instances of emergence have been identified that cannot as easily be explained by referring to the underlying game mechanics, or to the deliberate design of the game. While some of these are actual instances of emergence, others may just appear to be emergent (e.g., to the inexperienced player who lacks the necessary knowledge and overview to judge the situation more realistically, as explained below).

Emergence has been described as a relatively simple interaction pattern leading to "variety, novelty and surprise" (Campbell in Salen and Zimmermann 2004, 158). Translated to the field of games, these are characteristics that contribute to making a game interesting. However, we are all familiar with the opposite type of game—games that we have lost interest in playing because, at a point, we started to perceive their outcome as predictable. A well-known example is Tic-Tac-Toe: our initial childhood perception of the "variety, novelty and surprise" provided by this game faded as we became more experienced players. This illustrates how factors associated with emergence, such as complexity and unpredictability, may in fact be relative to the players' experience with and mastery of the game. Thus, where true emergence is considered the hallmark of fine game design, for the player, *apparent* emergence may also do the job—for a while, at least. To the player's experience of being in play it is the apparent *effects* of emergence that are crucial.

Similarly, when the game or game characters behave in ways unpredicted by the game designer, this can be the result of emergence, or it can simply be a high level of complexity preventing the designer from being able to foresee all possible future events. Being second-order design, game design requires the input of players to be complete. Game designers must therefore rely on players to test the game during the design process, to assess whether or not the game will play out as intended. Regular players continue to explore and "test" the game after it has been released on the market, and they will sometimes find glitches in the code or discover new ways of combining rules that introduce a new condition in the game, unpredicted by the designers. In a conference keynote from 2001 on the future of game design, game designer Harvey Smith describes this phenomenon in terms of emergence: as "desirable" when it leads to more interesting gameplay, and "undesirable" when it gives the player an unfair advantage, or otherwise instigates unbalance in the system. Game theorist Jesper Juul has argued against the analytical usefulness of Smith's application of the concept, pointing out that, in technical terms, a game's emergent properties will occur independently of whether or not their designer is aware of them: "The designer may very well have failed to predict an emergent property of the games' rules, but that is not what makes that property emergent" (Juul 2002).

In his influential text, Juul applies the concept of emergence to distinguish analytically between two typical computer game structures: "games of emergence" and "games of progression" (Juul 2002). Games of progression have a linear structure in which the player is assigned tasks sequentially. While many game genres combine emergence and progression, traditional adventure games are predominantly progressive (see GAME GENRES). Often they provide only one possible solution to each task, so that when all puzzles are solved, there is little value in playing the game again: "It is characteristic of progression games that there are more ways to fail than to succeed" (Juul 2005, 73). Allowing the designer to distribute detailed information to the players during gameplay, progression is the superior structure for storytelling and the development of characters in games (see GAMES AS STORIES, QUEST NARRATIVE).

In contrast, games of emergence are characterized by the combination of few and simple rules leading to varied and unexpected outcomes. Ideally, such games are "easy to learn, but difficult to master" (Salen and Zimmermann 2004, xiv). Multiplayer action and strategy games are examples of computer game genres dominated by emergence. Most preelectronic games belong in this category too, while progression games are historically new, according to Juul, originating with the adventure game. "In a game of emergence, a large percentage of the rules and objects in the game can potentially influence each other; in a game of progression, most rules and objects are localized" (Juul

2005, 81–82). Where games of progression have walkthroughs to assist stuck players, games of emergence have strategy guides (see WALKTHROUGH).

A different account of emergence in game studies investigates the development of new strategies and play styles among players of massively multiplayer online games (MMOGs) as emergent properties of these game systems (Karlsen 2009; McGonigal 2008). For instance, the practice of raiding—a central feature of MMOGs today—was not part of the original design of one of the early MMOGs, *EverQuest*. Occurring as a practice among the players first, raiding was implemented in the game and supported by the rules only at a later stage (Taylor 2006, 40–41). In adding yet another layer of complexity to the game, such emergent player cultures represent both a resource and a challenge to game design. There is no doubt that they contribute to a more interesting game experience. The challenge thus is to create a design that facilitates emergence by allowing space for these cultures to flourish, while keeping enough control to make sure that the inherent balance of the game is not threatened.

■ See also CHARACTERISTICS OF DIGITAL MEDIA, DIGITAL AND NET ART, INTERACTIVE NARRATIVE, INTERACTIVITY, SIMULATION

References and Further Reading

Bedau, Mark A. 1997. "Weak Emergence." In *Philosophical Perspectives: Mind, Causation, and World*, volume 11, edited by J. Tomberlin, 375–399. Malden, MA: Blackwell. http://people.reed.edu/~mab/publications/papers/weak-emergence.pdf.

Campbell, Jeremy. 1982. *Grammatical Man: Information, Entropy, Language, and Life*. New York: Simon & Schuster.

Chalmers, David J. 2006. "Strong and Weak Emergence." In *The Re-Emergence of Emergence*, edited by P. Clayton and P. Davies, 244–254. Oxford: Oxford University Press. http://consc.net/papers/emergence.pdf.

Corning, Peter A. 2002. "The Re-Emergence of 'Emergence': A Venerable Concept in Search of a Theory." *Complexity* 7 (6): 18–30.

Fromm, Jochen. 2005. "Types and Forms of Emergence." Cornell University Library. http://arxiv.org/abs/nlin/0506028v1.

Hofstadter, Douglas R. 1979. *Gödel, Escher, Bach: An Eternal Golden Braid*. New York: Basic Books.

Holland, John. 1998. *Emergence: From Chaos to Order*. Cambridge, MA: Perseus Books.

Johnson, Steven. 2001. *Emergence: The Connected Lives of Ants, Brains, Cities and Software*. London: Penguin Books.

Jones, Daniel. 2007. "Swarm Aesthetics: A Critical Appraisal of Swarming Structures in Art Practice." MA diss., Middlesex University. www.erase.net/files/pubs/swarm-aesthetics.pdf.

Juul, Jesper. 2002. "The Open and the Closed: Games of Emergence and Games of Progression." In *Computer Games and Digital Cultures Conference Proceedings*, edited by Frans Mäyrä, 323–329. Tampere, Finland: Tampere University Press. www.jesperjuul.net/text/openandtheclosed.html.

———. 2005. *Half-Real. Video Games between Real Rules and Fictional Worlds*. Cambridge, MA: MIT Press.

Karlsen, Faltin. 2009. *Emergent Perspectives on Multiplayer Online Games: A Study of Discworld and World of Warcraft*. Oslo: Unipub.

McGonigal, Jane. 2008. "Why *I Love Bees*: A Case Study in Collective Intelligence Gaming." In *The Ecology of Games: Connecting Youth, Games, and Learning*, edited by Katie Salen, 199–228. Cambridge, MA: MIT Press. www.avantgame.com/McGonigal_WhyILoveBees_Feb2007.pdf.

Salen, Katie, and Eric Zimmerman. 2004. *Rules of Play: Game Design Fundamentals*. Cambridge, MA: MIT Press.

Smith, Harvey. 2001. "The Future of Game Design: Moving beyond Deus Ex and Other Dated Paradigms." Keynote Lecture at Multimedia International Market, Montreal 2001. www.plan etdeusex.com/witchboy/articles/thefuture.shtml.

Taylor, T. L. 2006. *Play between Worlds: Exploring Online Game Culture.* Cambridge, MA: MIT Press.

Ethics in Digital Media
Charles Ess

Several factors complicate the question "what is digital media ethics (DME)"? DME confronts the ethical challenges evoked by digital media: the ongoing growth and transformations of these media thus spawn new ethical concerns and dilemmas. Specifically, the "mobility revolution"—the rapid diffusion of mobile and then Internet- and GPS-enabled smartphones, netbooks, tablet computers, and related technologies—dramatically expands the sheer *range*, *places*, and *contexts* of communicative and creative engagements facilitated by digital devices, including their increasing intrusion into bathrooms and bedrooms as once iconic private spaces (David 2008).

These developments both make the core issues of DME (Ess 2009) more complex and raise new ones. *Privacy* issues, to start, become increasingly multidimensional as Web 2.0 media such as social networking sites (SNSs), blogging and microblogs (e.g., Twitter and SNS status updates; see TWITTER, TUMBLR, AND MICROBLOGGING), and sites for "broadcasting yourself" (YouTube) depend on users voluntarily offering personal, if not private, information in return for the "free" use of these sites (see SOCIAL NETWORK SITES [SNSs]). Once prevailing *individual* and *exclusive* notions of privacy are increasingly replaced (in Western societies) by various forms of "privately public" and "publicly private" (Lange 2007), "participatory surveillance" (Albrechtslund 2008), and/or the McLuhanesque collapse of the private/public distinction altogether (David 2008). Simultaneously, antiterrorism pressures continue to weaken individual privacy protections in Western nations, while corporations that own and sell "our" data expand these data sets by reaching ever further into our (once) private lives. An emerging domain of DME thus focuses on how such commodification of our data and our identities both threatens privacy and erodes our very capacities for autonomous moral agency (Fuchs & Dyer-Witheford, forthcoming; Ess, forthcoming).

These same developments open new challenges in *research ethics*, beginning with the core norms of Human Subjects Protections—privacy, confidentiality, anonymity, and informed consent. For example, researchers can ask subjects to install an "app" on their smartphones that records and uploads all their uses (and their locations), from text messages to phone calls, status updates and web-browsing histories, contacts and contact changes, "you name it" (anonymous researcher 2012, personal communication). As such devices diffuse ever further into our most intimate spaces, unprecedented challenges to privacy protection follow. Simultaneously, most relevant institutional authorities, including local university oversight committees (where they exist), national legislations, and national research committee policies, have yet to articulate responses to these challenges. Moreover, where guidelines do exist, they vary from nation to nation: determining which, if any, apply to digital communications that routinely cross national borders is no easy task. The Association of Internet Researchers' (AoIR) "2.0" guidelines for "Ethical

Decision-Making and Internet Research" are a critical step in the further development of research ethics (Markham and Buchanan 2012).

Similar observations hold for further core issues, beginning with copyright concerns (see COPYRIGHT). The ease of copying and distributing digital information—including digitized music, photography, films, and other cultural and entertainment creations—early on challenged Western notions of copyright as primarily an *individual* and *exclusive* property right (Ess 2009, 76ff.). These issues have only grown more complex. A telling example is the rise of the Pirate Bay from an (in)famous file-sharing website (one still blocked, for example, in Denmark as it is judged to violate copyright laws) to a growing political party in the Nordic countries that aims to dramatically revise current copyright laws in order to make these laws ostensibly better fit the new realities of such digital media sharing (*BBC News* 2011).

Violent content in computer-based games remains hotly contested. Various so-called effects studies—that is, that seek to demonstrate causal linkages between playing such games and real-world violence—continue to appear, only to face a now-familiar list of criticisms (Talmadge 2008). Additional factors only complicate matters further. First, gamers are "growing up" as their demographic extends significantly into the 30–40- and 40–50-year-old age groups, and as more and more women take up games (Sundén and Sveningsson 2011). As well, some of the most widely used games—massively multiplayer online role-playing games (MMORPGs) most famously represented by *World of Warcraft* (see ONLINE WORLDS)—engage a global and thus cross-cultural audience of players, who thereby bring distinctively different ethical sensibilities and traditions into play (and, for some, design; Consalvo 2011). These cultural differences are further reflected in different national understandings—and rejections—of basic behavioral phenomena such as game addiction: South Korea recognizes game addiction as a psychological problem, unlike the American Psychological Association, for example (Hsu, Wen, and Wu 2009). Finally, the kinds and sophistication of computer-based games themselves have also grown rapidly. This is apparent, for example, in the growth of "serious games," including a "crowdsourcing" approach to complex scientific problems. Most notably, the game *Foldit* turned previously unresolved problems of protein folding into challenges for gamers online (see GAMES AND EDUCATION). The problems were collectively solved within a day (Khatib et al. 2011). At the same time, the relevant literatures on game ethics have rapidly developed into an important field of their own, represented by Miguel Sicart's defining volume (2009).

The globally distributed nature of *World of Warcraft* and the ethical complications it evokes is but one example of how *global citizenship* likewise represents an ever more urgent and complex cluster of issues within DME. The publication of the "Mohammed Cartoons" by the Danish newspaper *Jyllands-Posten* in 2006 and the often-violent aftermath epitomize the point that as nearly one-third of the world's population now has access to the Internet, any digital information we produce and distribute may have literally global consequences. In previous generations, only the few who enjoyed the privileges of travel and extensive education (including languages) required a "cosmopolitan ethics"—that is, one stressing the central importance of deep familiarity with and fundamental respect for diverse cultural traditions. Digital media's continued global diffusion means that such a cosmopolitan ethics is increasingly urgent for "the rest of us."

Pornography likewise develops and becomes more ethically complex. Because pornography remains underresearched, limited empirical findings thus hamper our ethical reflections (Paasonen 2011). Moreover, as our engagements online continue to expand, other concerns eclipse once central ones: in particular, children and young adults in the European Union are more troubled by "cyberbullying" than unwanted encounters with sexually explicit materials (SEMs) online (Livingstone et al. 2011, 25). Lastly, technological advances further blur the ethically crucial difference between what is experienced as *real*—including real-world harms to real-world bodies—and *virtual* (see VIRTUALITY), thereby complicating both our ethical challenges and our capacities to resolve them (Stuart 2008). For example, "virtual" child pornography represents "children" who are entirely digitally produced: no real-world children are thereby harmed. Our ethical responses to the production, distribution, and consumption of such materials may require novel responses to relatively novel problems, including an expansion of the ethical frameworks used to resolve such problems: specifically, *virtue ethics* becomes increasingly significant, alongside more familiar utilitarianisms and deontologies (Ess 2013).

Finally, DME now overlaps at least two new domains—namely, *journalism ethics* and *robot ethics*. First, journalism and thereby journalism ethics have been dramatically transformed by the rise of digital media in general and specifically as the diffusion of mobile-locative devices facilitates "citizen" or "amateur" journalism. Bloggers and eyewitness photos and videos as made with and then uploaded from smartphones—frequently of state violence against protestors—have radically reshaped contemporary news reporting as they have also helped spark and accelerate multiple political revolutions around the world, such as the Arab Spring (Howard et al. 2011). The amateur producers of such material, however, thereby enter into the ethical fields of journalists. Whereas journalism ethics was once the concern of a few professionals and their sustaining institutions, journalistic norms and goals, such as objectivity and fostering of democratic discourse, are increasingly ethical issues for such citizen journalists as well. An emerging hybrid journalism ethics—one conjoining the ethical challenges and resolutions of both amateurs and professionals—is hence beginning to emerge as an important component of DME (Ward 2011; Drushel and German 2011).

Secondly, both "bots" (automated dialogue systems, including "Autonomous Agents" such as "Siri" for iPhones) and increasingly sophisticated robots such as "carebots," "warrior bots," and, of course, "sexbots" become ever more commonplace. These entail our using digital media in new ways and places; hence, *robot ethics* will increasingly overlap with DME (see CHATTERBOTS). For example, "telenoid" robots facilitate an embodied form of communication between loved ones and the elderly, utilizing Internet connections to convey voice, gesture, "hugs," and so on: these new uses of digital media as communicative and expressive media thus open up both new versions of familiar issues in DME (starting with privacy) and new ethical issues per se (Seibt and Nørskov, forthcoming; Vallor 2011). More broadly, Sherry Turkle (2011) argues that increasing reliance on technologically mediated relationships weakens our practices of and thus capacities for such traits as patience, perseverance, empathy, and trust—capacities or *virtues* essential for deep friendships, sexual and family relationships, and the institutions of democratic governance (see Vallor 2010; Ess 2010). DME will thus increasingly confront the question, how ought we design and use robots—as incorporating various forms of digital media—in ethically responsible ways?

■ See also CHEATS, GAMES AND EDUCATION, HOAXES, POLITICS AND NEW MEDIA

References and Further Reading

Albrechstlund, Anders. 2008. "Online Social Networking as Participatory Surveillance." *First Monday* 13 (3). www.uic.edu/htbin/cgiwrap/bin/ojs/index.php/fm/article/view/2142/1949.

BBC News. 2011. "Pirate Parties: From Digital Rights to Political Power." *BBC News*, October 17. www.bbc.co.uk/news/technology-15288907.

Consalvo, Mia. 2011. "MOOs to MMOs: The Internet and Virtual Worlds." In *The Handbook of Internet Studies*, edited by M. Consalvo and C. Ess, 326–347. Oxford: Wiley-Blackwell.

David, Gabriela. 2008. "Clarifying the Mysteries of an Exposed Intimacy: Another Intimate Representation Mise-en-scéne." In *Engagement and Exposure: Mobile Communication and the Ethics of Social Networking*, edited by Kristóf Nyíri, 77–86. Vienna: Passagen Verlag.

Drushel, Bruce E., and Kathleen German. 2011. *The Ethics of Emerging Media: Information, Social Norms, and New Media Technology*. New York: Peter Lang.

Ess, Charles. 2009. *Digital Media Ethics*. Oxford: Wiley-Blackwell.

———. 2010. "The Embodied Self in a Digital Age: Possibilities, Risks, and Prospects for a Pluralistic (Democratic/Liberal) Future?" *Nordicom Information* 32 (2): 105–118.

———. 2013. "Ethics at the Boundaries of the Virtual." In *The Oxford Handbook of Virtuality*, edited by M. Grimshaw. Oxford: Oxford University Press.

———. Forthcoming. Introduction to special issue, "Who Am I Online?" *Philosophy and Technology*.

Fuchs, Christian, and Nick Dyer-Witheford. Forthcoming. "Karl Marx @ Internet Studies." *New Media and Society*.

Howard, Phillip N., Aiden Duffy, Deen Freelon, Muzammil Hussain, Will Mari, and Marwa Mazaid. 2011. "Opening Closed Regimes: What Was the Role of Social Media during the Arab Spring?" Project on Information Technology and Political Islam. http://www.scribd.com/doc/66443833/Opening-Closed-Regimes-What-Was-the-Role-of-Social-Media-During-the-Arab-Spring.

Hsu, Shang Hwa, Ming-Hui Wen, and Muh-Cherng Wu. 2009. "Exploring User Experiences as Predictors of MMORPG Addiction." *Computers & Education* 53:990–999.

Khatib, Firas, Frank DiMaio, Foldit Contenders Group, Foldit Void Crushers Group, Seth Cooper, et al. 2011. "Crystal Structure of a Monomeric Retroviral Protease Solved by Protein Folding Game Players." *Nature Structural & Molecular Biology* 18:1175–1177. doi:10.1038/nsmb.2119. www.nature.com/nsmb/journal/v18/n10/full/nsmb.2119.html.

Lange, Patricia. 2007. "Publicly Private and Privately Public: Social Networking on YouTube." *Journal of Computer-Mediated Communication* 13 (1), article 18. http://jcmc.indiana.edu/vol13/issue1/lange.html.

Livingstone, Sonia, Leslie Haddon, Anke Görzig, and Kjartan Ólafsson. 2011. *EU Kids Online Final Report*. www.eukidsonline.net.

Markham, Annette, and Elizabeth Buchanan. 2012. "Ethical Decision-Making and Internet Research (version 2.0): Recommendations from the AoIR Ethics Working Committee." http://aoirethics.ijire.net/.

Paasonen, Susanna. 2011. "Online Pornography: Ubiquitous and Effaced." In *The Handbook of Internet Studies*, edited by M. Consalvo and C. Ess, 424–439. Oxford: Wiley-Blackwell.

Sicart, Miguel. 2009. *The Ethics of Computer Games*. Cambridge, MA: MIT Press.

Seibt, J., & M. Nørskov. Forthcoming. "'Embodying' the Internet: Towards the Moral Self via Communication Robots?" *Philosophy and Technology*.

Stuart, Susan. 2008. "From Agency to Apperception: Through Kinaesthesia to Cognition and Creation." *Ethics and Information Technology* 10 (4): 255–264.

Sundén, Jenny, and Malin Sveningsson. 2011. *Gender and Sexuality in Online Game Cultures: Passionate Play*. New York: Routledge.

Talmadge, Wright. 2008. "Violence and Media: From Media Effects to Moral Panics." In *Battleground: The Media*, volume 2, edited by R. Andersen and J. Gray, 549–557. Westport, CT: Greenwood Press.

Turkle, Sherry. 2011. *Alone Together: Why We Expect More from Technology and Less from Each Other*. Boston: Basic Books.

Vallor, S. 2010. "Social Networking Technology and the Virtues." *Ethics and Information Technology* 12 (2): 157–170.

———. 2011. "Carebots and Caregivers: Sustaining the Ethical Ideal of Care in the 21st Century." *Philosophy & Technology*. doi:10.1007/s13347-011-0015x.

Ward, S. 2011. *Ethics and the Media: An Introduction.* Cambridge: Cambridge University Press.

F

....

Fan Fiction
Karen Hellekson

It is safe to say that the idea behind fan fiction, a literature based on or derived from another text, has been around as long as texts have: no sooner has a text been created than someone riffs on it, be it Chaucer borrowing from Italian poems, Shakespeare rewriting historical stories, Alice Randall paralleling the events of Margaret Mitchell's *Gone with the Wind* (1936) from another point of view in *The Wind Done Gone* (2001), or a teenager crafting fan comics about the *Star Trek* rebooted film to release online. Although plenty of professional writers have published derivative literature, the term *fan fiction* connotes amateur text creation, usually performed within the context of a community formed around a media property, one that need not be narrative. In addition to writing stories and novels, fans may write and perform new fandom-specific lyrics to well-known songs (a practice known as *filking*); they may create web comics, avatars, or manipulated images; they may role-play; they may craft collaborative narratives via blogs or microblogging sites such as Twitter, perhaps writing from the point of view of a character; they may record their stories as podfic; and they may create videos, with montages from a source text set to music, telling a new story (see AVATARS, BLOGS, COLLABORATIVE NARRATIVE, ROLE-PLAYING GAMES, TWITTER, TUMBLR, AND MICROBLOGGING, WEB COMICS). Often these activities occur within the context of a community, creating dense interassociations of text and response. Sometimes these associations are solicited, rather than unfolding organically. Fans may enjoy writing under constraint, where they write to a prompt or a challenge (see WRITING UNDER CONSTRAINT).

Henry Jenkins famously related fan texts to poaching. Following the work of Michel de Certeau, Jenkins "proposes an alternative conception of fans as readers who appropriate popular texts and reread them in a fashion that serves different interests. . . . Fans construct their cultural and social identity through borrowing and inflecting mass culture images, articulating concerns which often go unvoiced within the dominant media" (1992, 23). This places fans in opposition to the producers, whom fans call "The Powers That Be"—the creators of the media texts, particularly television and film, that fan works are written around, in part because fans are usually powerless to alter the trajectory of the media text. Rather than passively consume, however, fans engage with the text in ways that create meaning for them as individuals and as a collective. By creating and disseminating texts, fans generate complex readings of the source text which reflect concerns often not dealt with by the media source.

These fan concerns vary widely. Marginalized characters are one such concern: in fan fiction, Uhura in the classic *Star Trek* can star in her own stories, perhaps exploring her backstory, gender, and race in an active, rather than passive, mode. Minor characters may also be used to provide a different and parallel perspective on canonical events. Fans may want to fill in perceived gaps in the source text, resulting in story fixes and episode tags, where insufficient narratives are completed. Crossover stories may link together two separate fandoms, with the characters of both media sources interacting. Alternate universe stories, or AUs, throw characters into a totally different milieu: they may be tossed into the Wild West or into the world of the X-Men. Crossovers and AUs fundamentally address the nature of the characters. The author transcends the original source's setting by placing a character in an unfamiliar environment and deciding how he or she reacts, thus illuminating some aspect of the character that the author posits as essential. Some genres revolve around the body: genderswaps and bodyswaps are just what the names describe, and in mpreg stories, a man gets pregnant. These stories address the embodied nature of subjectivity, and they often deal with concerns such as sex, pregnancy, motherhood, and constructions of gender identity. The genre of the Mary Sue similarly deals with subjectivity: in this often-derided genre, an impossibly beautiful original character, an avatar of the author herself, inserts herself into the narrative and saves the day. Finally, two genres deal with cause and effect: futurefic pushes the characters forward into the future, and in deathfic a major character dies, leading to repercussions on the part of those left behind.

Fans write much fiction about romantic pairings—indeed, the presence or absence of a romantic pairing is, after the fandom itself, the primary mode of organization of fan fiction. Fic may posit romantic relationships between a man and a woman, known as *het* or *ship* (from "relationship"), or between two people of the same sex, known as *slash* or, if about women, *femslash* or *femmeslash* ("slash" from the symbol used to separate character names in a romantic pairing, as in Kirk/Spock slash). These pairings may be canonical—that is, the media source presents the characters as a romantic couple—or not. Fic may also posit no relationship at all, in which case it is classified as *gen* (from "general"). Many fans read or write almost exclusively in a single pairing, be it Mulder and Scully in *The X-Files* or Steve McGarrett and Danny Williams in the rebooted *Hawaii Five-0*.

Fan fiction's recent history of dissemination illustrates the way that fan communities appropriate technology. Early fan works, including fan art, meta (that is, fan musings about fandom), letters, stories, and poems, were disseminated by apas, a genre borrowed from science fiction literature fandom. An apa (which stands for "amateur press association") is a text created by a central editor who collects contributions from everyone in a circle, collates them, and then mails them out to group members. Fanzines are another mode of dissemination. These texts are often created by consortiums of fans that form a press; the booklets are duplicated (mimeographed or photocopied, then bound) and sold. Fanzines still exist, although they have been joined by subscription e-zines.

The advent of electronic communication led to targeted dissemination via Usenet, Listservs, e-mail lists, and Yahoo! or Google groups. Much fan activity takes place on blog sites friendly to fans, such as LiveJournal.com and Dreamwidth.org (see BLOGS). Fans use these spaces to post stories, comment on them, and link to related content. Many dedicated fic-archiving sites, including multifandom sites FanFiction.net and An Archive of Our Own (archiveofourown.org), provide space for fans to post stories and engage with each other, and a multitude of fandom-specific archives exist as well, some created with open-source software such as eFiction or WordPress (see FREE AND OPEN-SOURCE SOFTWARE). Fans have proved ingenious at adopting technology to display and organize the plethora of content. For e-mail dissemination, densely meaningful subject lines permit fans to immediately size up a story. Fans can subscribe to fic-archive feeds so they are alerted when stories are uploaded. Blogs have been repurposed as fic archives, often with complex use of tags and categories to create indexes (see BLOGS, PRESERVATION).

The fan cultures that have sprung up to share and disseminate fan writings and other texts are so rich and varied that it is impossible to adequately characterize them, particularly because fandom is increasingly being deployed in virtual spaces by individuals or groups who have no idea they are engaging in an established activity, much less one with a long history, and thus make up their own rules. Suffice it to say that fans engage in a participatory culture that revolves around the object of passion: the media source, rock band, celebrity, or text that identifies the fandom (see PARTICIPATORY CULTURE). Several hallmarks of fan culture exist, however. First, fan texts are now generally written under pseudonyms. Early fan fiction, particularly fan fiction that appeared in fanzines, was often written under the authors' real names, but this is now rare, in part because online search has made it possible to find texts, when previously they were inaccessible except to a chosen few. Second, fans are careful about taking and crediting. Fan fic may not be reprinted, reposted, or otherwise duplicated without the author's permission. Fic also usually includes a disclaimer that names the copyright holder of the media property. Finally, and most crucially for fan communities, fans work for free. Fan fiction is not sold. For work in fanzines, for instance, contributors receive a free copy but are not paid; and although fanzines are sold, they are priced at the cost of materials, with any extra usually going to seed a future publication or given to a specified charity.

The ethos of working for free, a cornerstone of fan activity, is at least partially related to perceptions of copyright infringement: fans reason that if they make no money, The Powers That Be will not send them cease-and-desist letters and they can continue their activities (see COPYRIGHT). The community structures that have sprung up rely on virtual economies and gift culture, with fan fiction and other fan-created artworks, particularly avatars, used in exchanges of (often virtual) items that only hold meaning within the community itself and are otherwise valueless (see VIRTUAL ECONOMIES). Indeed, fandom could be described as the creation and deployment of these artifacts for exchange. Fan fiction is merely one mode of this deployment.

References and Further Reading

Bacon-Smith, Camille. 1991. *Enterprising Women: Television Fandom and the Creation of Popular Myth.* Philadelphia: University of Pennsylvania Press.

"Fanlore." *Wiki.* http://fanlore.org/wiki/Main_Page.

Gray, Jonathan, Cornel Sandvoss, and C. Lee Harrington, eds. 2007. *Fandom: Identities and Communities in a Mediated World.* New York: New York University Press.

Hellekson, Karen, and Kristina Busse, eds. 2006. *Fan Fiction and Fan Communities in the Age of the Internet: New Essays.* Jefferson, NC: McFarland.

Hills, Matt. 2002. *Fan Cultures.* London: Routledge.

Jenkins, Henry. 1992. *Textual Poachers: Television Fans and Participatory Culture.* London: Routledge.

Film and Digital Media

Jens Eder

As a medium, "film" or "cinema" is primarily defined by moving images, while "digital" or "new" media are mainly defined by the computer-based representation, storage, transmission, or manipulation of digital data. Consequently, film may be analog or digital, while new media (video games, the web, etc.) may involve moving images but also other features such as interactive simulations, databases, or hypertext. According to Lev Manovich, one of the first scholars to scrutinize the rapidly changing relations between "cinema and new media," they follow two vectors (2001, 286): cinema has been prefiguring new media, and new media in turn have been influencing cinema. Manovich mentions the use of digital effects in postproduction and digital cameras in independent filmmaking, the influence of new media aesthetics on film style, and the invention of "new forms of computer-based cinema" (2001, 286–333). Today, digital technologies may be involved in all kinds of film practices: preproduction, production, postproduction, distribution, exhibition, marketing, storage, criticism, and viewers' activities (see Daly 2010b). More generally, at least three kinds of relations between film and digital media can be distinguished: (1) *technical relations*—films can be produced and distributed by using digital technologies; (2) *systemic relations*—film is related to digital media in a media system; and (3) *aesthetic relations*—digital media influence the kinds, structures, and styles of film, and vice versa.

Technical Relations in Film Production and Distribution

The prototypical concept associating film with analog photography and theatrical distribution is giving way to the realization that most films are digital. Berys Gaut defines "digital cinema" as "the medium of moving images generated by bitmaps" (2009, 76). While his proposal to include even video games under that heading may be controversial, he concisely points out some characteristics of digital moving images: a fixed amount of information, computability, and the possibility of being infinitely manipulated without degradation.

During the pioneering phase from the 1960s to the 1980s, computers played only a minor role in film production. Because of their limited capacities, their use was confined to short experimental films like *Hummingbird* (1967) or small parts of movies like *Westworld* (1973). From the 1990s on, however, several digital technologies became firmly established (McKernan 2005; Daly 2010b). Preproduction practices such as screenwriting, production design, and production planning all changed with the availability of computers, specific software, and Internet communication. This probably has influenced the films made, for instance, by word-processing software leading to different scripts, digital demos to different casting decisions, and digital graphics to different designs.

Since the mid-1990s the shooting of live-action films has been revolutionized by digital cameras and digital video (DV) in high definition. In comparison to analog film, digital cinematography is cheaper (no costs for film processing), faster (no magazine changes), more mobile (smaller cameras), and has greater light sensitivity. Moreover, DV allows for longer takes, higher shooting ratios, more control by watching the images directly on set, and it can be easily transferred to digital postproduction. All of this has opened up the potential for independent films such as those of the Dogme 95 movement (e.g., *Festen*, 1998). High-budget production also went digital, driven by media corporations and influential filmmakers such as George Lucas and James Cameron. Since the mid-2000s, high-resolution (2K or 4K) digital cameras such as the RED or the Arri Alexa are superseding 35mm film.

More obvious changes have taken place in postproduction since the 1990s. Nonlinear digital editing became a standard practice with systems such as Avid or Final Cut. The computer made editing easier, allowing for instant random access and nondestructive, virtual assembly of images and sounds. Digital editing probably contributed to stylistic innovations, e.g., to an increase of cutting rates and graphic effects. At the same time, the development of digital audio workstations allowed for manipulating, sampling, and mixing all kinds of sounds to make film worlds more immersive or to create new, artificial soundscapes. On the visual level, computer-generated imaging (CGI) and digital effects (compositing, morphing, virtual sets, etc.) have been replacing traditional special effects, particularly in genres such as science fiction and fantasy (Keane 2007, 56–75; McClean 2007; Flückiger 2012; Prince 2012). Many digital effects are meant to operate "invisibly" by providing naturalistic backdrops (via blue-/green-screen techniques) or changing details, for instance, removing stunt wires. Other CGI sequences serve as technical spectacles, bringing to life fantastic creatures like the dinosaurs in *Jurassic Park* (1993) and even convincing humanlike characters such as Gollum (*The Lord of the Rings* trilogy, 2001–2003). By the mid-2000s, digital intermediates became a standard: many films are digitized so that the resulting intermediate can be freely manipulated, for example, by color grading, inserting effects, or correcting flaws. An early example for the narrative use of such possibilities is *Pleasantville* (1998) with its black-and-white world turning into color. Digital cameras and intermediates allow for an intricate amalgamation of photorealistic CGI and live-action photography. Blockbusters like *Avatar* (2009) not only combine keyframe animation, facial performance capture, a virtual camera, and other digital techniques but have also been driving a trend toward digital stereoscopy ("3D").

While the border between live action and animation has become permeable, the animation film itself also has been deeply transformed by digital devices. In the 1980s, new companies began to specialize in computer animation (CA). Pixar's *Toy Story* (1995), the first feature film to be completely computer animated, started a boom of CA family films mixing stylistic features of traditional cartoons, puppet animation, and CGI hyperrealism. Today, those films constitute one of the most successful genres, and traditional cel or stop-trick animation has almost been abandoned. Some CA films are supposed to keep to the typical "2D" look of cel animation, but most of them are "3D" in at least one of two senses: they are made on the basis of 3D digital models, and many of them are then rendered for stereoscopic 3D projection.

3D movies presuppose another recent transformation: the digitization of film distribution and exhibition. Digital sound systems such as Dolby Digital have been in use since the 1990s, but now a complete change "from films to files" (Bordwell 2012), to hard disks or digital streaming, is taking place. The basic plan of organizations such as Digital Cinema Initiatives is to create a digital flow all the way through from preproduction to projection and beyond cinema to other media. This promises high profits for distributors but also high costs for theaters in need of digital projection systems. Therefore, digital distribution has been developing quite differently in the United States, Europe, and

Asia. In the United States, some authors stress the opportunities of digital projection (e.g., Daly 2010b), while others claim that it threatens film culture by favoring big companies at the expense of small exhibitors and independent films (Bordwell 2012).

Systemic and Functional Relations

Film is part of a media system and a media culture, fulfilling certain sociocultural functions in relation to other media (see MEDIALITY), competing, cooperating, or converging with them. Digital media and technologies have transformed the whole system and, accordingly, the position of film therein (see Keane 2005; Tryon 2009; Daly 2010b). New kinds of screens and channels have been proliferating: personal computers, the World Wide Web, DVD, Blu-ray discs, digital television, portable media players, smartphones, tablet computers, game consoles, and public screens. Familiar borders between film, television, and "new" media have been dissolving by various forms of "convergence" in terms of technology, economy, institutions, aesthetics, and content (Jenkins 2006) (see TRANSMEDIAL FICTION). As digital content, moving images are circulating beyond cinema and through all possible channels. Theatrical exhibition has taken the role of generating attention for other release windows. DVDs have been the most lucrative product of the film industry for a while, but since the implementation of broadband access, the majority of films are being streamed and downloaded via the Internet. Video on demand feeds directly into home cinema systems, video platforms such as YouTube store billions of films, and piracy makes film companies lose billions of dollars. Completely transforming film culture, the Internet, digital cameras, editing software, and other digital devices have led to a vast expansion of the number of films; to their permanent availability and global distribution; to new possibilities in mainstream, independent, and amateur filmmaking; to new ways of financing (e.g., by crowdfunding or Internet advertising); to collaborative filmmaking; and to the spread of user-generated films, fan forums, mashups, film blogs, virtual festivals, filmmaking courses, and film recommendations in social networks.

This digital revolution has been discussed controversially. Yannis Tzioumakis, following John Belton, claims that digital technology is merely utilized "as the best available vehicle for the domination of the global entertainment market by a small number of giant corporations" (2011, 11). Recent trends in movie production—spectacular effects, CGI hybrids, and 3D—can be seen as strategies not only of cinema competing with new media but also of establishing event movies as "tentpoles" in large transmedia franchises like *Shrek* or *Avatar*, starting processes of "content streaming" across various channels (see Keane 2007; Thompson 2007). Big-budget films are embedded in a network of digital media fulfilling complementary functions: the Internet is used as a tool for marketing, merchandizing, and stimulating fan activities; DVDs provide extras; and video game spin-offs offer interactive experiences of fictional worlds. The film business is converging with the rapidly grown video game industry: profitable movies are regularly turned into games and vice versa, in spite of frequent conflicts between narrative and gameplay (Keane 2007, 97–117; Brookey 2010) (see GAMEPLAY, INTERACTIVE NARRATIVE, NARRATIVITY).

But digital media also have the potential to empower spectators by turning them into active "produsers" or "viewsers" (Daly 2010a). Nearly everybody has access to means of film production and distribution now, to cheap digital cameras, editing software, DVD printers, and the Internet. The web allows filmmakers to reach large audiences on video platforms and to sell DVDs or downloads to niche audiences. This has led to a huge growth of user-generated content and amateur films. Independent filmmakers and debutants have become more able to compete with big productions by making successful genre movies (e.g., *Paranormal Activity*, 2007) or documentaries (*Super Size Me*, 2004). New forms of collaborative filmmaking and crowdsourcing such as the YouTube production *Life in a Day* (2011) emerge. Moreover, digital media and their omnipresent moving images play a central role in establishing a "participatory culture" (see Jenkins 2006), enabling a new media literacy, and advancing film criticism. For instance, films now can be analyzed with the help of DVDs and computers; older films are digitally restored and made more easily available. Even digital piracy may have its good sides in helping films find their audience or subverting censorship in some countries (Daly 2010b). To evaluate the overall effects of digitization on film culture, then, it is important to consider cultural differences (e.g., between Hollywood, Bollywood, and Nollywood), as well as different kinds of films: movies and documentaries, short and long, amateur and professional, live-action and animation, independent and mainstream.

Aesthetic and Structural Relations

Historically, film has served as a model for the design of many new media. Video games, for instance, have adopted many of film's generic settings, character types, standard situations, visual motifs, and stylistic elements. But new media have also developed their own aesthetic forms, now familiar by pervasive cultural experiences. In combination with the digital transformations of film production and film culture, this has influenced the aesthetics of film, modifying its genres, narratives, structures, looks, and sounds (see Manovich 2001; Hanson 2004; Willis 2005; Keane 2007; Daly 2009, 2010a). Digital media may not lead to a complete revolution of film form, as some authors suggest, but they certainly contribute to an enormous growth and diversification of films by making certain narrative and stylistic options more easily available, stimulating certain trends, and challenging innovative filmmakers to explore new possibilities.

Central aesthetic relations between film and digital media can be understood in terms of three kinds of intermediality (see Rajewsky 2005): media combination (digital media can contain films), media transposition (films adapt digital media texts, and vice versa), and intermedial references (films may cite or imitate typical contents or forms of digital media, and vice versa). For instance, video games can be combined with films in transmedia constellations like the *Matrix* franchise; they can contain cinematic cut scenes or devices to create film sequences (machinima; see MACHINIMA); their stories can be adapted in movies like *Tomb Raider* (2001); and their ludic structures can be emulated by films like *eXistenZ* (1999).

Aesthetic relations between film and new media may also be described in terms of mutual influences. More specifically, digital media have been influencing film in the areas of kinds, narratives, and styles. Digital technologies have been crucial for the development of major trends in film production and for the success of certain genres. The most commercially successful films today are computer-animated films and spectacular CGI/live-action hybrids like *Avatar*, mostly in the genres of fantasy, science fiction, or action-adventure, often in 3D. Those films presuppose digital production and are usually part of transmedia franchises. While times are getting harder for midlevel and independent productions, cheap digital devices and the Internet have also boosted short films, documentaries, amateur films, and certain independent films. The cheapness and small size of digital cameras allow for spontaneous, flexible, unobtrusive, and intimate uses

(Daly 2009): for shooting in slums (*City of God*, 2002), using nonactors (*The Class*, 2008), giving cameras to subjects in critical situations, or having a camera being directed automatically by a computer (*The Boss of It All*, 2006).

Digital production has also influenced the style of films, their look and sound. On a basic level, digital and photographical images differ in several ways (see Daly 2009): digital images have a greater clarity, depth of field, and low-light sensitivity; on the other hand, they have a lower dynamic range, lose details in highlights, lack a grain structure, and tend to look "pixelated" and "cold." Consequently, they are more apt for deep-focus compositions, low-light situations, and cool, analytical narratives. Specific digital devices are used to make them look more "warm" and "cinematic," for instance, by artificially narrowing depth of field to focus on protagonists.

Most importantly, digital images can be easily manipulated. This has caused considerable discussion about their allegedly lost referentiality and indexicality, but today, there is a growing consensus that differences from photographical images may not be so fundamental. After all, Méliès already manipulated images, and viewers still believe digital documentaries. This being said, many feature films take advantage of the possibilities of CGI to create spectacular scenes and elaborate title sequences. Computer animation and effects such as compositing, morphing, virtual sets, and motion capture are contributing to the success of fantastic genres. CGI is also getting more affordable and widespread in low-budget and non-Hollywood productions. CGI/live-action hybrids in Asian cinema (e.g., *House of Flying Daggers*, 2004) boast a freely moving virtual camera, an increase in speed that enhances movement through space, and a mobile framing that emulates perspectives in video games. At the same time, CGI often mimics classical camera work, including deliberate imperfections such as lens flares, blurry pictures, or a shaky "hand camera" (see Rombes 2009). The digital image allows for compositing within the frame, sometimes resulting in a "web browser aesthetic" of "multiple simultaneous-action windows combined with text or animation, where the screen is not purely representational but fulfills a number of roles such as remix surface, textual and graphical information table, and map" (Daly 2009). Moreover, compared to classical montage, digital editing opens up a greater range of options: from rapid cutting and an "MTV aesthetic" to the non-cut as in *Russian Ark* (2003) or to combinations of long takes and multiple screens as in *Time Code* (2000) (Daly 2009).

Digital media also have an impact on the stories and narrative structures of film. Many films represent these media as elements of everyday life and use them as central narrative motifs (e.g., *You've Got Mail*, 1998). Attempts to establish a new genre of "interactive films" (see INTERACTIVE CINEMA) offering viewers the possibility of actively choosing between alternative courses of events have not been very successful. Less obviously but more successfully, digital media advance certain narrative trends in film production. Cross-media productions such as *Star Wars* or *The Blair Witch Project* (1999) engage in forms of "synergistic storytelling" and "transmedial worldbuilding," developing their stories and worlds across films, video games, the web, and other media (Jenkins 2006). Sometimes, this seems to involve a tendency toward a new "cinema of attractions" favoring spectacular digital effects over narrative logic and cohesion (e.g., the *Pirates of the Caribbean* franchise; see Daly 2010a) (see GRAPHIC REALISM). At the same time, digital media also have contributed to a trend of complex, nonlinear or unreliable narratives presupposing active viewers (see Daly 2010a), for instance, in "mind-game films" such as *Memento* (2000) or *Source Code* (2011). These complex narratives may have been influenced by cultural experiences with networked and interactive media. Some film narratives have probably been inspired by specific digital media, for instance, by hypertextual or ludic structures of games that open up different possible paths and worlds (e.g., *eXistenZ*, 1999; *Run Lola Run*, 1999).

To summarize, digital media have transformed film culture, and film itself has become a digital medium, related to (other) digital media by mutual influences and relations of intermediality. We cannot predict where those developments will lead to. But in any case, the varieties of films and film practices have increased considerably because of digital media, and the borders between film and other digital media have begun to dissolve.

196
Film and Digital
Media

■ See also ANIMATION/KINETICISM, CHARACTERISTICS OF DIGITAL MEDIA, MASHUP, MEDIA ECOLOGY, OLD MEDIA / NEW MEDIA, PARTICIPATORY CULTURE, REMEDIATION, TRANSMEDIAL FICTION

References and Further Reading

Bordwell, David. 2012. "Pandora's Digital Box: From Films to Files." In *David Bordwell's Website on Cinema / David Bordwell, Kristin Thompson: Observations on Film Art*. www.davidbordwell.net /blog/2012/02/28/pandoras-digital-box-from-films-to-files/.

Brookey, Robert Alan. 2010. *Hollywood Gamers: Digital Convergence in the Film and Video Game Industries*. Bloomington: Indiana University Press.

Daly, Kristen. 2009. "New Mode of Cinema: How Digital and Computer Technologies Are Changing Aesthetics and Style." *Kinephanos* 1 (1). www.kinephanos.ca/2009/imageries-numeriques -culture-et-reception-digital-imageries-culture-and-reception/.

———. 2010a. "Cinema 3.0: The Interactive-Image." *Cinema Journal* 50 (1): 81–98.

———. 2010b. "How Cinema Is Digital." In *Transitioned Media: A Turning Point into the Digital Realm* (The Economics of Information, Communication, and Entertainment), edited by Gali Einav, 135–147. New York: Springer.

Flückiger, Barbara. 2012. *Resources on Visual Effects and Digital Cinema*. www.zauberklang.ch /resources.html.

Gaut, Berys. 2009. "Digital Cinema." In *The Routledge Companion to Philosophy and Film*, edited by Paisley Livingston and Carl Plantinga, 75–85. New York: Routledge.

Hanson, Matt. 2004. *The End of Celluloid: Film Futures in the Digital Age*. Hove: Rotovision.

Jenkins, Henry. 2006. *Convergence Culture: Where Old and New Media Collide*. New York: New York University Press.

Keane, Stephen. 2007. *CineTech: Film, Convergence, and New Media*. Basingstoke, NY: Palgrave MacMillan.

Manovich, Lev. 2001. *The Language of New Media*. Cambridge, MA: MIT Press.

McClean, Shilo T. 2007. *Digital Storytelling: The Narrative Power of Visual Effects in Film*. Cambridge, MA: MIT Press.

McKernan, Brian. 2005. *Digital Cinema: The Revolution in Cinematography, Postproduction, and Distribution*. New York: McGraw-Hill.

Prince, Stephen. 2012. *Digital Visual Effects in Cinema: The Seduction of Reality*. New Brunswick, NJ: Rutgers University Press.

Rajewsky, Irina O. 2005. "Intermediality, Intertextuality, and Remediation: A Literary Perspective on Intermediality." *Intermédialités* 6. http://cri.histart.umontreal.ca/cri/fr/intermedialites/p6 /pdfs/p6_rajewsky_text.pdf.

Rombes, Nicholas. 2009: *Cinema in the Digital Age*. London: Wallflower.

Rosen, Philip. 2001. "Old and New: Image, Indexicality, and Historicity in the Digital Utopia." In *Change Mummified: Cinema, Historicity, Theory*, 301–349. Minneapolis: University of Minnesota Press.

Thompson, Kristin. 2007. *The Frodo Franchise: The Lord of the Rings and Modern Hollywood*. Berkeley: University of California Press.

Tryon, Chuck. 2009. *Reinventing Cinema: Movies in the Age of Digital Convergence.* New Brunswick, NJ: Rutgers University Press.

Tzioumakis, Yannis. 2011. "From the Business of Film to the Business of Entertainment: Hollywood in the Age of Digital Technology." In *American Film in the Digital Age,* edited by Robert C. Sickels, 11–31. Santa Barbara: Praeger.

Willis, Holly. 2005. *New Digital Cinema: Reinventing the Moving Image.* London: Wallflower.

....

Flarf

Darren Wershler

Flarf is an early twenty-first-century neologism coined by poet/cartoonist Gary Sullivan to describe a poetic composition tactic specific to networked digital media, the sensibility that informs it, and, eventually, a poetic movement. Flarf is organized around a collective; has had its own digital forum, the Flarflist, since May 21, 2001; and produces recognizably "Flarfist" books, recordings, and events on an ongoing basis.

Flarf emerges simultaneously with conceptual writing (see CONCEPTUAL WRITING). Among others, Kenneth Goldsmith has described the movements as "two sides of the same coin." Like conceptual writing, Flarf composition typically involves the application of constraint-based appropriation to digital media; in Flarf, this often involves burrowing into Google search results for inappropriate, awkward, obscene, or otherwise nonliterary text.

Unlike conceptual writing, Flarf typically enlists the language it appropriates for use within conventional forms of versification (e.g., sonnets in K. Silem Mohammad's *Sonnagrams*). As Brian Kim Stefans has noted, "the measure of success for Flarf is actually 'good poems,' whereas the measure of success for conceptual writing . . . is the measure of the depth of the concept—how much it offers a contrast with literature 'as we know it'" (2009). Whereas conceptual writing is concerned with the formal qualities of the "information genres" that literature typically ignores (e.g., news broadcasts, legal documents, scientific papers), Flarf's interest is in discovering new subject matter for poetry.

Though Sullivan compares Flarf's aesthetic to camp, he observes that there are important differences as well. Flarf functions by virtue of its "embarrassing" content overflowing conventional form rather than by camp's glorification of artificial form over mundane content.

Prominent Flarf poets include Gary Sullivan (2008, 2009), Nada Gordon (2007), K. Silem Mohammad (2003), Michael McGee, Drew Gardner (2005), Sharon Mesmer (2008), Rodney Koeneke, and Katie Degentesh.

■ See also ALGORITHM, DATABASE, DIGITAL POETRY, ELECTRONIC LITERATURE

References and Further Reading

Beckett, Tom. 2006. "Interview with Gary Sullivan." Blogspot. *E-X-C-H-A-N-G-E-V-A-L-U-E-S: Primarily Interviews about Poetry, Poetics, Poets by Tom Beckett and Guests.* May 14. http://willtoexchange.blogspot.com/2006/05/interview-with-gary-sullivan.html.

Gardner, Drew. 2005. *Petroleum Hat.* New York: Roof.

Goldsmith, Kenneth. 2009. "Introduction to Flarf vs. Conceptual Writing." New York, April 17, 2009. Electronic Poetry Center at SUNY Buffalo. http://epc.buffalo.edu/authors/goldsmith/whitney-intro.html.

Gordon, Nada. 2007. *Folly.* New York: Roof.

Mesmer, Sharon. 2008. *Annoying Diabetic Bitch.* Combo Books.

Mohammad, K. Silem. 2003. *Deer Head Nation.* San Diego: Tougher Disguises Press.

———. 2010a. "Flarf & Conceptual Poetry Panel Intro." Denver, April 10, 2010. *Lime Tree.* http://lime-tree.blogspot.com/2010/04/awp-2010-flarf-conceptual-poetry-panel.html.

———. 2010b. *Sonnagrams 1–20.* Cincinnati: Slack Buddha Press.

Naik, Gautam. 2003. "Sought Poems." *88: A Journal of Contemporary American Poetry* 3.

———. 2010. "Search for a New Poetics Yields This: 'Kitty Goes Postal / Wants Pizza.'" "The A-Hed." *Wall Street Journal,* May 25. http://online.wsj.com/article/SB10001424052748704912004575252223568314054.html.

Sontag, Susan. 1966. "Notes on 'Camp.'" *Against Interpretation and Other Essays.* New York: Farrar.

Stefans, Brian Kim. 2009. "Re: Appropriation Is the Idea That Ate the Art World." Ed. list, Ubuweb. E-mail from Brian Kim Stefans to Ubuweb mailing list ed. Los Angeles.

Sullivan, Gary. 2008. *PPL in a Depot.* New York: Roof.

———. 2009. "Flarf: From Glory Days to Glory Hole." Books. *Brooklyn Rail,* February. www.brooklynrail.org/2009/02/books/flarf-from-glory-days-to-glory-hole.

Flash/Director

Brian Kim Stefans

Flash is a development suite for the creation of interactive, animated graphics applications. When intended for the Internet, Flash applications, distributed as ".swf" files," run through a free browser plug-in. Flash first reached mainstream attention in the late 1990s when it was developed and supported by Macromedia (it was acquired by Adobe in 2005).

With the introduction of the programming language ActionScript in Flash 2, Flash vied with an earlier Macromedia product, Director—which used the language Lingo, developed by John H. Thompson for ease of use by artists—for dominance in interactive content applications. Director remained viable when interactive CDs were considered a possible successor to the book, but with the rise of the Internet—and the necessity for quick delivery of content over 56k modems—Flash proved the better solution than Shockwave (the Internet file format for Director) for its ability to deliver, in addition to standard raster-based formats such as jpgs and gifs, vector-based graphics, which are defined by points, lines, and fills and which are resizable without deterioration of the image. Vector-based graphics require far less data to transfer than raster-based formats, which contain more information and, when viewed on larger screens, often reveal the infelicities of image compression. Vector-based graphics also allow continued manipulation (beyond basic rotation and resizing) of the image—whether text or picture or something in between—after having been transferred to the user.

Writers in the electronic literature community were initially resistant to the use of Flash because it appeared to betray a central principle in early Internet creativity: keeping your code "open-source" (like HTML and JavaScript, which can be read easily by viewing the source of a webpage) so that they could be adapted by other creators for their own projects (see ELECTRONIC LITERATURE). There was also an understandable, if ultimately self-contradictory, resistance to making work in a commercial software environment in the heady, libertarian early days of the Internet, partly due to the extinction rate of once seemingly ubiquitous programming platforms, such as Apple's HyperCard. Nick Montfort and Noah Wardrip-Fruin argue in "Acid-Free Bits: Recommendations for Long-

Lasting Electronic Literature" (2004) that "community-driven systems have a better track record in terms of enabling migration and emulation" (see FREE AND OPEN-SOURCE SOFTWARE).

There was also a resistance to the "slick" look of Flash applications, especially as some works resembled the interactive Flash ad banners that had gained a wider obtrusive presence on the web. Many electronic writers who have used Flash have quietly addressed the latter issue—Flash's relationship to advertising—by either consciously constraining their use of certain features (Young-Hae Chang Heavy Industries is exemplary), running head-on against any of the norms of quality graphic design (Jason Nelson video game mashups; see MASHUP), or, conversely, excelling as graphic, sound, and video designers and creating magisterial works that can, in the end, still not be considered commercial given the playful, experimental proclivities of the texts (the "feature length" works of David Clark).

The Flash programming language, ActionScript, was initially kept simple to encourage graphic designers to program, but with the increased use of Flash in content delivery—Flash is the leading program for the distribution of video on the web—and use in the transfer of sensitive information, not to mention the platform for countless video games, ActionScript has grown to be a robust, object-oriented language.

Probably the greatest alternative to Flash and ActionScript for the creation of works of electronic literature is Processing, a Java-based, open-source programming language developed by Ben Frye and Casey Reas. The Processing website (http://processing.org) contains numerous tutorials, bits of sample code, user-generated libraries, and a gallery of works. Several instructional books in Processing have already been published. Daniel C. Howe developed an entire library for Processing for language manipulation, RiTa, which has proven popular with electronic writers.

Another contender for the Flash crown—and in greater use by designers and programmers if not by electronic writers—is HTML5, famously preferred by Steve Jobs over Flash, for which he had a justified dislike owing to Flash's poor performance on Mac computers. As of this writing, Flash programs still do not run on Apple mobile products.

■ See also ANIMATED POETRY, ANIMATION/KINETICISM, DIGITAL AND NET ART, DIGITAL POETRY, ETHICS IN DIGITAL MEDIA, FILM AND DIGITAL MEDIA

References and Further Reading

Montfort, Nick, and Noah Wardrip-Fruin. 2004. "Acid-Free Bits: Recommendations for Long-Lasting Electronic Literature." http://eliterature.org/pad/afb.html

Free and Open-Source Software
Luis Felipe Rosado Murillo

By definition, any piece of software licensed to provide the following permissions falls under the category of free software: (1) use the program for any purpose; (2) study the program and modify it; (3) distribute modified copies; and (4) redistribute software without restrictions, providing access to source code.

From the original software-sharing communities created in U.S. research institutions in the 1960s and 1970s to the present day, free and open-source software development has experienced an exponential growth that followed the popularization of the personal computer and the Internet. In a manner similar to academic working papers, software circulated in an economy of sharing among highly skilled technicians until the advent of commercial software companies in the 1980s. At that time, software companies established nondisclosure agreements (NDAs) and began to sell copies of their programs with licenses that restricted developers from communicating about their work and sharing their techniques. Increasingly, more programmers and engineers started to sign these agreements, which prevented software from circulating widely, obstructing the former communication channels of early software-sharing communities.

In 1985 Richard Stallman, a computer hacker from the Artificial Intelligence Lab at MIT, wrote and circulated a manifesto inviting his fellow computer programmers to create free software alternatives to commercial software. His core argument was that software should be a public good, not private property, given that every piece of software is built upon previous common knowledge that must be kept available for every programmer. This manifesto—called GNU Manifesto—was a reaction to the rise of the commercial software industry and the regulation of software by intellectual property laws.

To understand the concept of free software, one has to think of "free speech" instead of "zero price." Gratuity of software is not the issue; rather, at issue is the developers' ability to build and share new software based on previous software code. In order to foster "software freedom," Stallman wrote the GNU General Public License in 1992 (nicknamed "copyleft"), which describes the canonical aforementioned "four freedoms" that every piece of software must carry in order to be defined as free software. The *copyleft* license is often considered a "legal hack" (see HACKER), that is, an inversion and subversion of copyright law to allow unrestrained circulation and refactoring of software. Free software licenses work by inverting the restrictive logic of copyright law and fostering communities of computer experts via a shared commitment to the open, collaborative advancement of technology and the freedom to use, modify, and redistribute software.

By the early 2000s a major transformation occurred within the international free software movement with the advent of the Open Source Initiative (OSI). Defending the importance of replacing free software activism and its strong emphasis on "software freedom," OSI advocates publicly declared that their main goal was to divert the focus away from Richard Stallman's profoundly moral, philosophical, and political discourse. By reorienting the discourse on free software, OSI began to promote the terms *openness* and *choice* to educate corporate executives about the benefits of free software (renamed "open-source software"). OSI was organized around the open-source definition, which exposes the terms and conditions for any piece of software to be licensed as open source. The definition contains ten clauses describing similar software freedoms of the General Public License, except for a very important one: the injunction for sharing derivative software using the same free software license of the original source code, which was put into place to guarantee that contributions would be returned to the community and not turned into closed-source software.

This shift in the history and the politics of free software paved the way for the participation of IT corporations in open-source software production worldwide. Currently, FOSS is a common acronym for free and open-source software in the Anglophone world, encompassing projects, discourses, development practices, and licenses of free software and open-source software, whereas in Europe and Latin America, F/LOSS for free/libre and open-source software is often used, marking the polysemy of *free* in English (meaning both freedom and gratuity) with the Spanish substitute word *libre* to signal "software freedom." In the context of IT industry, "open source" is widely used to signal the distinction with the politics of free software.

In his influential book *The Cathedral and the Baazar* (2000), Eric Raymond offered a set of justifications for superiority of the open-source software production model in contrast with the model of big software companies he identified as centralized and hierarchical. Basically, there are two main points in Raymond's native description of the open model of software production: the first is related to the networking sustained primarily by a gift economy among programmers; the second refers to the "hacker ethics." As open-source advocates put it, "What all the introspections in programming have in common is the emphasis on reputation. Programming is a culture of gift. The value of work of a programmer only comes from sharing of information technology with others. This value is enriched when the work is widely shared in the source code form, not only the results in a pre-compiled binary" (DiBona, Ockman, and Stone, 1999, 13). Raymond's approach to the "hackerdom as a culture of gift" became a highly influential manifestation of his native anthropology of open-source software, having an enormous impact in the IT industry and among Internet communities.

Beyond native discourses, the FOSS model represents sociologically an interesting multifaceted object of inquiry: it is an experiment in socialization, given the techniques that are deployed to coordinate the work of highly complex software projects conducted online among programmers dispersed around the globe; it is a political practice due to its centrality for "information freedom" activism; it is also a subversion of the intellectual property regime, mostly done by the experimental work in which several computer hackers engage in order to define the essential "freedoms" in FOSS licenses. Recent academic accounts of free software as a set of political, technical, and cultural practices (Weber 2004; Kelty 2008; Coleman 2012) further investigated the current transformation through the notion of individual property over intangible goods, as well as the political opposition created by the free software movement to the restrictions of the intellectual property regime. The moral and technical order of free software was ethnographically and historically explored by Kelty (2008). The author coined the concept "recursive public" to describe free software as a "public that is constituted by a shared concern for maintaining the means of association, through which they come together as a public. Geeks find affinity with one another because they share an abiding moral imagination of the technical infrastructure, the Internet, that has allowed them to develop and maintain this affinity in the first place" (Kelty 2008, 28). From a sociotechnical point of view, FOSS projects represent boundary objects: they depend on a form of engagement with the computer and the Internet which is difficult to analyze without tensioning the boundaries of our established categories and their taken-for-granted oppositions in social sciences, such as individual/society, private/public, gift/market, persons/objects, work/leisure, code/expression, self-interest/gratuity, and discourse/practice. In this sense, FOSS can be productively approached in its multiplicity of possibilities of transformation, meanings, and functionalities depending on its local, contextual appropriation.

In the past twenty years with the qualitative and quantitative growth of FOSS projects, the logic of *copyleft* has been transposed to different domains of cultural production. Examples of successful Internet-based projects include the Linux operating system, which started with a small community of developers and became a crucial technology running on Internet servers and cell phones worldwide. Other successful projects include Creative Commons, an initiative to adapt to legal systems around the world a set of flexible *copyleft*-inspired licenses for cultural production (other than software, such as music, literature, illustrations, and photography). Yet another relevant and popular project is *Wikipedia*, which combines an active community of volunteers on the Internet, the flexibility of Creative Commons licenses, and free software applications such as Media-Wiki, successfully transposing the *copyleft* logic and the model of FOSS production to the creation of an entire encyclopedia based on donations and voluntary contributions.

The historical development of FOSS production suggests that its impact is broader than is usually assumed. It provides not only key technologies for the Internet in operation today but also the ethical orientation for the creation of collaborative projects on several domains, such as "open data" (in the public sector, electronic government, and public data management), open access (in the academic domain, making use of free software–based educational platforms such as Moodle and the academic publishing management application Open Journal System), open hardware (the transposition of copyleft logic to the domain of hardware design), and open journalism (through the decentralization of journalism via a multitude of blogs running content management systems, such as WordPress, Joomla, and Drupal). Currently, several Internet projects inspired by the model of FOSS are expanding with a commitment to information openness and the defense of its wide, unrestrained accessibility.

■ See also COPYRIGHT, HACKER

References and Further Reading

Benkler, Yochai. 2002. "Coase's Penguin, or, Linux and 'The Nature of the Firm.'" *Yale Law Journal* 112 (3): 369–446.

Coleman, Gabriella. 2005. "The Political Agnosticism of Free and Open Source Software and the Inadvertent Politics of Contrast." *Anthropological Quarterly* 77 (3): 507–519.

———. 2012. *Coding Freedom: The Ethics and Aesthetics of Hacking.* Princeton, NJ: Princeton University Press.

DiBona, Cris, Sam Ockman, and Mark Stone, eds. 1999. *Open Sources: Voices from the Open Source Revolution.* Sebastopol, CA: O'Reilly.

Feller, Joseph, Brian Fitzgerald, Scott A. Hissam, and Karim R. Lakhani, eds. 2005. *Perspectives on Free and Open Source Software.* Cambridge, MA: MIT Press.

Kelty, Christopher. 2008. *Two Bits: The Cultural Significance of Free Software.* Durham, NC: Duke University Press.

Raymond, Eric. 2000. *The Cathedral and the Bazaar: Musings on Linux and Open Source by an Accidental Revolutionary.* Sebastopol, CA: O'Reilly.

Stallman, Richard. 2002. *Free Software, Free Society: Selected Essays of Richard M. Stallman.* Boston: GNU Press.

Weber, Stephen. 2004. *The Success of Open Source.* Cambridge, MA: Harvard University Press.

G

Game Genres
Andreas Rauscher

The concept of genre is very helpful in understanding the historical evolution of video games (see GAME HISTORY), as well as the interplay between games and other media such as cinema. Yet compared to film and literature, genre is still undertheorized in game studies. This situation may be the result of the tendency of game scholars to focus primarily on formal aspects, such as rules, and to ignore the aesthetic and cultural components of video games. There are also major difficulties in establishing a genre theory for games that goes beyond the commercial classifications of the industry and consumer guides and yet does not result in a system so complex that it is only relevant for scholars. A truly productive concept of genre should serve as a means of communication between audience, producers, and scholars.

In regard to commercial categories employed by retailers and customers, as well as game magazines and websites, the use of genre labels seems to be quite transparent but also restricted to current developments. A gamer knows what she can expect from a new shooter or a strategy game, but this pragmatic knowledge does not provide any satisfying answers in regard to questions like how new genres are created or how retro references to classic arcade games in open-world games work. In order to discuss aesthetic and stylistic developments like these, a dynamic understanding of genre theory can be quite helpful.

One way to approach the problem of the classification of games is to borrow criteria from the concepts of genre used in other media, such as movies or novels. These criteria could be themes, plot types, the aesthetics of the simulated world, or a general similarity with certain types of novels or movies. Yet such an approach would ignore some of the unique attributes of the medium, such as the agency of the player, the game mechanics, and the procedural momentum of the simulation. A medium-specific genre taxonomy for video games should focus on the function of the gameplay and on the rules as a starting point for classification (see GAMEPLAY). The difficulties in constructing a comprehensive taxonomy of game genres are made apparent by the forty-two genres examined by Mark J. P. Wolf in his study *The Medium of the Video Game* (2001, 113–134). More manageable are the nine types listed by British game expert Steven Poole in his book *Trigger Happy: The Inner Life of Video Games* (2000, 35–58), which are based on his long-term experience in game journalism: shooter, racing, platform games, beat 'em up, strategy games, sport games and simulations, adventures, role-playing games (RPGs), and puzzle games. To take into account recent development, this typology should be expanded with categories such as massive multiplayer online role-playing games (MMORPGs) / persistent worlds (see ONLINE WORLDS), casual games, serious games, and independent/art games (see INDEPENDENT AND ART GAMES).

A very useful approach to game genres has been developed by Simon Egenfeldt-Nielsen, Jonas Heide Smith, and Susana Pajares Tosca in *Understanding Video Games* (2008). They "propose a genre system based on a game's criteria for success" (2008, 41) and reduce video game genres to four types:

1. Action games, which are considered by many to be "the archetypical video game" (2008, 43), because classical arcade games such as *Pac-Man* or *Space Invaders* are based on this type of gameplay. Nowadays action challenges that demand fast skills and a good perception are often combined with puzzle elements.

2. Adventure games, which are "characterized by requiring deep thinking and great patience" (2008, 43). Of all basic video game types, this genre has the strongest tendency toward storytelling. The plot is advanced by talking to other characters and solving puzzles.

3. Strategy games, which are "occupying a space between action and adventure games" (2008, 43). This game type focuses on tactical thinking and well-considered moves. Narrative elements can be restricted to simple background information, and visuals are often reduced to window dressing. These games offer a high replay value because of the vast variety of tactics leading to victory.

4. Process-oriented games such as *The Sims* (2000) or *Sim City* (1989), which "could fit the definition of a toy rather than actual games. Think of populating and watching an aquarium as opposed to playing chess." (2008, 44).

This model offers a helpful foundation for game genre analysis, but it remains on a rather abstract theoretical level. The ongoing hybridization process that is characteristic for recent video games demands further combinations based on those four basic types. The most obvious example would be the very popular genre of RPGs, which Egenfeldt-Nielsen, Smith, and Tosca (2008) mention as a challenge to their system. While MMORPGs belong to the category of process-oriented games, single-player RPGs are subsumed under strategy games. But on second thought, strategy games are too close to traditional board games to reflect the specifics of RPGs, which can include elements for all four categories. Strategic gameplay segments in RPGs are combined with the exploration of the game world, which in open-world games can also be experienced in a process-oriented way. Games like the sci-fi RPG *Mass Effect* (2007, 2010) integrate the gameplay of an action shooter game. Epic RPGs such as *Planescape: Torment* (1999) and *Dragon Age: Origins* (2009) not only include puzzle-solving tasks and selectable dialogue typical for the adventure genre but also feature elaborate story arcs (see GAMES AS STORIES) that restrict the player's actions in order to create a dramatic effect corresponding to the games' themes of tragedy and loss. This integration of a configurative storytelling element is a crucial difference between RPGs and traditional board games, and it is what defines them as a video game genre.

A useful concept for the description of current hybrid game genres is the notion of setting, described by Geoff King and Tanya Krzywinska as the "milieu" in which the game takes place (2002, 27). The setting, which can employ the semantic and syntax as well as the iconography of thematic genres from other media, has a strong influence on the types of gameplay employed in the game. Game types such as the action-adventure hybrid survival horror adjust their rules to their cinematic genre settings. The popular *Resident Evil* series (since 1996) restricts the player's perspective as well as the availability of ammunition to create an uncanny experience similar to the apocalyptic *Living Dead* film series (since 1968) by George A. Romero. Elements such as the performance of a selected role and the staging of the mise-en-scène, which are completely secondary in many board and arcade games, become important factors in thematic video games and offer guidance through the three-dimensional navigable spaces. For example, the open-world games of the *Grand Theft Auto (GTA)* series (since 1997), *Red Dead Redemption* (2010), and *L.A. Noire* (2011) produced by developer Rockstar Games all feature similar gameplay combining shooting and driving tasks. Nevertheless, the genre setting communicates important differences to the player. While the gangster satire *GTA* allows the use of exaggerated cartoon violence, the 1940s hardboiled setting of *L.A. Noire* tries to persuade the player to act out a police officer who is less caricatural than the *GTA* characters. In *Red Dead Redemption* the setting during the last days of the Wild West provides a framing for the gameplay inspired by the films of Sergio Leone, Clint Eastwood, Sam Peckinpah, and John Hillcoat (see FILM AND DIGITAL MEDIA). In a complete contrast to the traditional goals of video games, the character controlled by the player, a former outlaw named John Marston, will die during the final mission. The event is not presented in a cut scene, but actively played out (see CUT SCENES). This ending could be regarded as an infringement of the genre contract of games, but it is fully congruent with the violent semantic and syntax of disillusioned melancholic Westerns such as *The Wild Bunch* (1968). The death of the avatar is not experienced as breaking with conventional game rules, but as offering a closure perfectly fitted to the general atmosphere of the game (see AVATARS). This effect is not achieved by the presentation of a cut scene, nor by gameplay alone, but rather by an inspired blending of the conventions of the video game with the syntax of the cinematic genre of the Western.

As this case suggests, the methods for researching game culture should be attentive not only to the blurring of the boundaries between game genres but also to the hybridization of game genres with the genres of other media.

■ See also GAMES AS ART/LITERATURE, INTERACTIVE NARRATIVE

References and Further Reading

Aarseth, Espen. 1997. *Cybertext: Perspectives on Ergodic Literature.* Baltimore: Johns Hopkins University Press.

———. 2004. "Genre Trouble: Narrativism and the Art of Simulation." In *First Person: New Media as Story, Performance, and Game,* edited by Noah Wardrip-Fruin and Pat Harrigan, 45–55. Cambridge, MA: MIT Press.

Apperley, Thomas H. 2006. "Genre and Game Studies." *Simulation and Gaming* 37 (1): 6–23.

Bateman, Chris. 2007. *Game Writing: Narrative Skills for Video Games.* Boston: Charles River Media.

Clearwater, David A. 2011. "What Defines Video Game Genre? Thinking about Genre Study after the Great Divide." *Loading . . . The Journal of Canadian Game Studies Association* 5 (8): 29–49. http://loading.gamestudies.ca.

Davidson, Drew, ed. 2009. *Well Played: Video Games, Value and Meaning.* Volumes 1–3. Pittsburgh: ETC Press. www.etc.cmu.edu/etcpress/wellplayed.

Egenfeldt-Nielsen, Simon, Jonas Heide Smith, and Susana Pajares Tosca. 2008. *Understanding Video Games.* New York: Routledge.

Jarvinen, Aki. 2008. *Games without Frontiers: Theories and Methods for Game Studies and Design.* http://acta.uta.fi/pdf/978-951-44-7252-7.pdf.

Juul, Jesper. 2005. *Half-Real: Video Games between Real Rules and Fictional Worlds.* Cambridge, MA: MIT Press.

King, Geoff, and Tanya Krzywinska, eds. 2002: *ScreenPlay: Cinema/Videogames/Interfaces.* London: Wallflower.

Manovich, Lev. 2001. *The Language of New Media.* Cambridge, MA: MIT Press.

Newman, James. 2004. *Routledge Introduction to Media and Communications: Videogames.* New York: Routledge.

Poole, Steven. 2000. *Trigger Happy: The Inner Life of Video Games.* London: Fourth Estate.

Wolf, Mark J. P. 2001. *The Medium of the Video Game.* Austin: University of Texas Press.

Wolf, Mark J. P., and Bernard Perron, eds. 2011. *Landmark Video Games.* Ann Arbor: University of Michigan Press.

Games

Dragon Age: Origins. 2009. Video game. Designed by Bioware Edmonton.

Grand Theft Auto. Since 1997. Video game. Designed by Rockstar North.

L.A. Noire. 2011. Video game. Designed by Rockstar Games.

Mass Effect. 2007, 2010. Video game. Designed by Bioware.

Planescape: Torment. 1999. Video game. Designed by Black Isle.

Red Dead Redemption. 2010. Video game. Designed by Rockstar San Diego, Rockstar North.

Sim City. Since 1989. Designed by Maxis.

The Sims. Since 2000. Designed by EA Games.

••

Game History
Henry Lowood

Playing games on computers is about as old as the electronic digital computer itself. While digital game history thus can be closely identified with the history of computing, a fundamental historical fact about the "computer game" is that it has been delivered on a remarkably diverse set of platforms, from room-sized mainframe machines to handheld devices, and placed in a variety of settings, from universities to arcades to living rooms. For this reason, terms such as *computer game* and *video game* are not satisfactory for describing the medium in its entirety. Instead, *digital game* will be used in this article as a relatively platform-agnostic term that expresses the historical diversity of the technologies that have supported this medium.

The history of digital games might be considered as two tightly interlocked projects. The first project is the construction of an accurate chronology of participants and events. The second project is the development of appropriate historiography—methods, principles, and theories—to guide the development of analytical and thematic writing on the history of games. These projects are both complicated and enriched by the inherently cross-disciplinary nature of game history. A sampling of the disciplines entangled in game history must include business history, history of technology (computing, networking, display devices, etc.), social history, art history, literary studies, media studies, and gender studies, to name only a few. One of the key challenges for game history will be the sorting of a set of convergent methods and approaches from these diverse fields; it remains to be seen whether this history will emerge as a coherent subdiscipline of game studies or as a collection of topics engaged on a case-by-case basis by existing disciplines.

The main concepts of game chronology have been developed thus far primarily in the game industry or by journalists following the game industry. These concepts include notions such as the "Golden Age of video games," "classic games," the "market crash" of the early 1980s, and the succession of game console "generations." The frequent (and sometimes uncritical) use of terms such as these has tended to conflate game history with nostalgic practices such as retrogaming (also known as "old school" or "classic" gaming) and to focus attention on games of the 1980s and 1990s, in particular. At the same time, it has resulted in valuable work on preservation of games as media objects, such as emulation and re-creation of classic games, or the collection and archiving of documentation such as game magazines and marketing materials.

No history of games can dodge the tricky questions that emerge from efforts to provide an accurate chronology of events, such as priority and invention disputes. These questions generally revolve around "firsts" and credit for innovations that shaped game technology, design, or even business practices. MIT's *Spacewar!* (1962) certainly delivered the approximate configuration of display, controller, software, and game mechanics recognizable as a digital game today. By this standard, we can begin the chronological timeline in 1962, meaning that digital games are at least a half century old. However, the conclusion that *Spacewar!* signaled a moment of invention that provided a stable notion for the artifact "digital game" must be qualified in two respects. First, there are numerous examples of earlier proposals, computer programs, and hardware demonstrations involving games that preceded MIT's project. These examples go back at least as far as Claude Shannon's suggestion that computers could be programmed to play chess in order to explore whether a machine could be "capable of thinking" (1950). Following Shannon's essay, researchers through the 1960s (Samuel 1959; Newell, Shaw, and Simon 1958) used computer programs for playing chess and checkers as laboratories for investigating problems in artificial intelligence. This was play with a "serious purpose," as Shannon put it, meaning that the games themselves—generally traditional board games rendered as software programs—were less important than what they revealed about the computer.

Indeed, through the early 1970s the computer game was a by-product of institutional computer science and other research settings that used computers. This context preceded and shaped the MIT project that resulted in *Spacewar!* The Brookhaven National Laboratory, a center of Cold War science and engineering, was an example of this context. It became the site for what was probably the first interactive electronic game when William ("Willy") Higinbotham, head of the lab's Instrumentation Division, created *Tennis for Two* for its open house event in 1958. The components were an analog computer, control boxes, and an oscilloscope display. *Spacewar!* was distinctly a product of MIT, joining hardware such as Whirlwind, the TX-0, and the PDP-1 in the tradition of what Gordon Bell has called "MIT personal computers." Originally created as a demonstration of the PDP-1 and CRT donated to MIT by the Digital Equipment Corporation, *Spacewar!* was certainly a computer game, and it certified games as an optimal demonstration of computer technology. *Spacewar!* moved beyond MIT during the 1960s mostly via paper tape to the network of research laboratories funded by the Advanced Research Projects Agency of the Defense Department (ARPA, later DARPA) and its Information Processing Techniques Office (IPTO). It also circulated around industrial labs. Thus, it can be said without much exaggeration that the first generation of computer science students in the United States literally was introduced to computers by running a computer game.

Graham Nelson has called computer games emerging from research laboratories during the 1970s "university games." This term reminds that early, precommercial games grew out of a technical and institutional matrix that encouraged their creators to be creative with new technologies and share the results openly, at least initially. The most important of the post-*Spacewar!* university games were William Crowther's *ADVENT* (better known as *Adventure*), which was completed in 1975 or 1976 and expanded by Donald Woods at Stanford University in 1976, and the original MUD (Multi-User Dungeon), developed by Bartle and Trubshaw at the University of Essex in late 1978 and early 1979. Crowther exemplified the university game creator. He was part of the team at Bolt, Beranek and Newman (BBN) that built the first packet-switching Interface Message Processor (IMP) in 1969 under a DARPA contract. Crowther was his group's crack programmer, and he contributed fundamental pieces of the ARPANET infrastructure that provided the underpinning for what would eventually morph into the Internet. The ARPANET connected researchers, graduate students, and programmers who then distributed and played *Adventure* and MUD games, which, like *Spacewar!*, became ubiquitous on the growing network of university-based computer laboratories.

The connections among early games and research institutions in the emerging fields of computer science and networking technology reinforced the contextual relationship between exploratory work in computer science and the emergence of digital games. These games rose out of the very institutions that defined the networked computer—such as MIT, BBN, the University of Utah, and Stanford. The networked and graphics-based games of the PLATO (Programmed Logic for Automated Teaching Operations) Project, close ties between Infocom (publishers of the university game *Zork*) and MIT, and programming projects by graduate students and researchers such as Terry Winograd's SHRDLU and Joseph Weizenbaum's ELIZA (see CHATTERBOTS, DIALOGUE SYSTEMS) refined and extended the academic foundation for exploring digital games through the late 1970s.

By the mid-1980s, however, the open, collaborative culture of university computer games was submerged by the business culture of proprietary game development and the closed technology of the game cartridge and home television console. The early history of the commercial game industry brought together several streams of technical and creative work, some connected to university games and others independent from them. While it may be tempting to generalize from *Spacewar!*, *Adventure*, and the other university games that digital games emerged whole out of laboratories and research centers, this conclusion ignores the significant role of consumer product development in the definition and development of dedicated arcade and home game consoles, as well as the design of games for consumption as a location- or home-based entertainment medium. The few commercial game companies of the late 1970s and early 1980s that spun off from university games, such as Infocom, were exceptions. Atari is a prominent example for illustrating the obstacles in the way of taking university games to market. Atari's founder, Nolan Bushnell, was inspired by *Spacewar!* He sought to design a coin-operated version of that game called *Computer Space* that could be operated in arcades. His efforts to exploit a promising union of technologies—the computer from the university lab and the television from the home—proved impractical; only after replacing the computer with dedicated circuits based on TV technology was Bushnell able to design a working arcade machine. With that breakthrough accomplished, *Computer Space* established a design philosophy and general technical configuration for arcade consoles. Bushnell founded Atari soon thereafter. Al Alcorn's design of *Pong* for the new company reduced the computer game to the format that would launch the arcade game scene and set the stage for Atari's contributions to the development of home console systems.

The television-based home game console was a product of industrial product design. Ralph Baer was the inventor. A television engineer at the military electronics firm Sanders Associates, he designed circuitry in 1966 to display and control moving dots on a television screen, leading to a simple chase game called *Fox and Hounds*. Since the 1950s, he had been intrigued by the idea of interactive television as a way of increasing that medium's educational value (see INTERACTIVE TELEVISION). After proving his concept of interactive television by designing several chase and light-gun games, he received permission from Sanders management to continue his TV Game Project and improve the game system. This work led in 1968 to a version called the Brown Box, a solid-state prototype for a video game console. Sanders licensed the technology and patent rights to Magnavox, and by mid-1971, a working prototype of what would be marketed as the Magnavox Odyssey console was available for consumer testing. Sanders was awarded several U.S. patents for the technology developed by the TV Game Project in 1972, the same year in which Magnavox began selling the Odyssey—the first commercial TV game console designed and marketed for the home.

Pong and the Odyssey inspired numerous imitators, both arcade and home systems. Atari led by creating Atari *Pong*, a home version designed by Alcorn, Harold Lee, and Bob Brown. It was released in 1975 and sold by Sears under its Tele-Games brand. The popularity of *Pong* home consoles established an important synergy between arcade and home systems for Atari. Its phenomenal success also led to brutal competition as more companies entered the market and released new home and arcade systems. Some manufacturers followed the Odyssey's model by offering flexibility in the choice of games. Unlike *Pong*, these platforms accommodated playing multiple cartridge-based games. Atari released its cartridge-based system, the VCS (Video Computer System, later called the 2600), in 1977. While Atari's coin-operated arcade business depended on exclusive distribution of hard-wired games playable only on dedicated machines, home consoles such as the market-leading VCS were programmable. Software contained in a game cartridge's read-only memory (ROM) was read after insertion into a special slot and then executed by the system's processing unit. The separation of game development from hardware manufacturing symbolized by the game cartridge stimulated a boom in demand for new games through the early 1980s. Activision, founded in 1979 by former Atari game designers, became the first third-party game publisher, followed by a rush of competitors.

Rudimentary action games dominated the title lists of arcade and home consoles circa 1980. Display technologies, microprocessors, and other components of the time limited designers, but quick, repetitive games also swallowed more quarters or, in the case of home consoles, could be manufactured cheaply and run reliably on underpowered hardware. While the designs of unqualified hits such as *Breakout* (1976) or Taito's *Space Invaders* (1978) were elegantly streamlined, most of the early console games offered little in terms of strategic and narrative depth. By 1983, competition, overreliance on knockoff imitations of proven hits, and a flood of weak game titles depressed the arcade and home console markets. The disastrous Christmas 1982 release of Atari's *ET* for the 2600 was the beginning of the crash and shakeout, which has since become one of the iconic moments of game history. Companies such as Mattel, Coleco, and Magnavox dropped out of the industry; Atari itself began a long decline, never again leading the industry.

The significance of the "Great Crash" lies in the lessons learned by new companies founded thereafter. The great commercial and cultural success story of the game industry prior to the crash was arguably Namco's *Pac-Man* (1980), designed by Toru Iwatani. It became the most popular arcade game in terms of unit sales, with more than one hundred thousand consoles sold in the United States alone, and its impact on popular culture was unprecedented, due largely to Iwatani's innovative and carefully crafted design work. *Pac-Man* represented the digital game as tightly controlled intellectual property and the product of a closed industrial design studio, rather than an open lab. Given the failure of most crashed hardware manufacturers to control the quality of software cartridges playable on their machines, the next generation of companies would carefully guard their technology platforms and intellectual property. By 1985, this new generation was led from Japan. On the heels of the commercial collapse of the Atari generation, Nintendo released its video console, the Famicom (Family Computer), in Japan in 1983, followed by the Nintendo Entertainment System (NES), a U.S. version of this system, in 1985. Its notable features included improved graphics processing supplied by Nintendo's Memory Map Controller (MMC) chip and the provision of battery-powered backup storage in the game cartridge. The NES and its followers, such as the Sega Genesis (1989), equaled or exceeded contemporary home or personal computers as game machines. Nintendo above all had learned how to control its platform and product, deploying technical, legal, and business measures that restrained access by independent software developers to its cartridge-based console. For example, Nintendo vigorously protected its patent on the cartridge device to restrict game software developers from publishing compatible cartridges without its explicit permission. It also insisted on a high level of quality control, for both titles developed in-house, such as Shigeru Miyamoto's *Super Mario Brothers* (1985) and *The Legend of Zelda* (1986; U.S. version, 1987), and third-party titles. *The Legend of Zelda* played a key role in heightening expectations for video games as an entertainment medium. It exemplified new technology, design aspirations, and business culture by exploiting several capabilities of the NES, such as the graphical rendering of a navigable, two-dimensional world and the ability to use backup storage as one progressed through the lengthy game. Miyamoto also paid careful attention to pacing and play mechanics, with the goal of ensuring that players attained requisite abilities before progressing to increasingly difficult challenges. He raised expectations for both the narrative scope and gameplay offered by digital games. *The Legend of Zelda* initiated a new generation of games, and its success encouraged comparisons of digital games to other media such as cinema in terms not just of sales but also of immersive storytelling potential (see FILM AND DIGITAL MEDIA, GAMES AS STORIES).

Nintendo was not the only game studio built on high production qualities, carefully guarded intellectual property, and auteur designers. LucasArts, founded in 1982 as LucasFilm Games by *Star Wars* filmmaker George Lucas, added interactive media such as game software to his multifaceted vision for the future of entertainment technology. Beginning with *Ballblazer* and *Rescue on Factalus!* in 1984, LucasArts established itself as a leading publisher of adventure games with strong stories, memorable characters, and vivid worlds, such as *Maniac Mansion* (1987), *The Secret of Monkey Island* (1987), and *Grim Fandango* (1998), as well as games from the worlds of *Star Wars* and *Indiana Jones*.

Electronic Arts (EA), founded in 1982, was inspired by United Artists Pictures, the Hollywood "company built by the stars." Just as United Artists had promoted independent production, EA initially left game development to established designers and programmers while gaining control over marketing and publishing of its games. The elements of its business success during the 1980s included strong branding, sports licensing, distinctive packaging and marketing, and control of its distribution network. EA became strong enough to challenge the strict licensing requirements of Nintendo and Sega for access to their consoles, most notably by reverse engineering the 16-bit Sega Genesis and facing down Sega management to secure more favorable terms. Like Sega and Nintendo, its formula for success depended on control of its product.

The success of Nintendo and other postcrash game studios and publishers of the 1980s such as LucasArts, EA, and Sega was not just built on innovative technology and game design; it depended at least as much on high production values, carefully guarded intellectual property, strong branding and marketing, and auteur designers. Control of the product was a common element among the success stories. During the 1990s, however, personal computers began to outpace proprietary game consoles as flexible platforms for innovative game design and proved technically superior for the adoption of elements such as improved graphics. Id Software's *DOOM* (1993) and *Quake* (1996) played a particularly important role by defining a new game genre now known as the first-person shooter (FPS). Id utilized graphics engines, fast networking technology, and a modular, open design philosophy to establish competitive multiplayer games as the leading edge on the powerful, network-connected personal computers of the 1990s.

In recent years, digital games have moved into the mainstream of commerce and culture around the world. Games designed for web browsers and handheld devices alike have explored social media as a new platform, incorporated technologies that rework the interactive and immersive aspects of gameplay, and applied proven game mechanics to many other fields of activity. The importance of social communities for online games emerged from the relatively closed worlds of MUDs (see MUDS AND MOOS) and PC-based massively multiplayer online role-playing games (MMORPGs) with the massive global success of online games such as *Runescape* (2001–) and *World of Warcraft* (2004–), both with more than 10 million subscribers (see ONLINE GAME COMMUNITIES, ONLINE WORLDS). These numbers were then quickly exceeded by games produced by companies such as Zynga and Playfish for casual players who typically played them on Facebook and other social networking services (see SOCIAL NETWORK SITES [SNSs]).

The cultural impact of digital games throughout the world in the early twenty-first century is undeniable. It has been extended and augmented by new and emerging trends such as the growth and acceptance of game art, the serious games movement in education and training (see INDEPENDENT AND ART GAMES), and the controversial advocacy of "gamification," a term for the application of game mechanics to virtually any field of endeavor. Digital game history has more to do, however, than provide a Whiggish account of the succession of ever more successful and technically impressive games. The gradual convergence of leading game console series such as the Sony Playstation and Microsoft Xbox home entertainment systems, the web, personal devices, and computers in the early 2000s has both resolved and masked an important historical tension in the development and business cultures of these platform families, one built on the Nintendo/

Hollywood model of corporate control of content and technology, and the other deriving from the more open culture of university games and id's FPSs.

■ See also GAME GENRES, GAMEPLAY, GAMES AND EDUCATION, GAMES AS ART/ LITERATURE, INTERACTIVITY, INTERFACE, LUDUS AND PAIDIA, PLATFORM, WALKTHROUGH

References and Further Reading

DeMaria, Rusel, and Johnny L. Wilson. 2002. *High Score! The Illustrated History of Electronic Games.* Berkeley, CA: McGraw-Hill Osborne.

Graetz, J. M. 1983. "The Origin of *Spacewar!*" *Creative Computing* 1 (1): 78–85.

Herman, Leonard. 2001. *Phoenix: The Fall and Rise of Videogames.* 3rd ed. Springfield, NJ: Rolenta Press.

Kent, Steven L. 2001. *The Ultimate History of Video Games: From Pong to Pokémon and Beyond: The Story behind the Craze That Touched Our Lives and Changed the World.* Roseville, CA: Prima.

Kushner, David. 2003. *Masters of DOOM: How Two Guys Created an Empire and Transformed Pop Culture.* New York: Random House.

Lowood, Henry. 2009. "Video Games in Computer Space: The Complex History of *Pong.*" *IEEE Annals in the History of Computing* 31 (3): 5–19.

Montfort, Nick. 2003. *Twisty Little Passages: An Approach to Interactive Fiction.* Cambridge, MA: MIT Press.

Montfort, Nick, and Ian Bogost. 2009. *Racing the Beam: The Atari Video Computer System.* Cambridge, MA: MIT Press.

Nelson, Graham. 2001. "A Short History of Interactive Fiction." Chap. 46 in *The Inform Designer's Manual*, 4th ed. St. Charles, IL: Interactive Fiction Library. www.inform-fiction.org/manual /html/s46.html.

Newell, Allen, J. C. Shaw, and Herbert A. Simon. 1958. "Chess-Playing Programs and the Problem of Complexity." *IBM Journal of Research and Development* 2:320–335.

Newman, James. 2012. *Best Before: Videogames, Suppression and Obsolescence.* London: Routledge.

Samuel, Arthur L. 1959. "Some Studies in Machine Learning Using the Game of Checkers." *IBM Journal of Research and Development* 3 (3): 210–229.

Shannon, Claude E. 1950. "A Chess-Playing Machine." *Scientific American* 182 (2): 48–51.

Sheff, David.1999. *Game Over: How Nintendo Conquered the World.* 2nd ed. Wilton, CT: Gamepress.

Game Theory
Travis L. Ross

Game theory provides a method for mathematically formalizing strategic interaction and is named for situations where the outcome of one actor's decision depends on the choices of other actors. Although it is natural to think of strategic interaction in reference only to competitive situations, game theory can also be applied to cooperative situations. Games are typically classified by identifying them as zero-sum, or non-zero-sum. Zero-sum games are always competitive. A positive outcome for one player in a zero-sum game creates a symmetrical negative outcome for the other players, which results in a cumulative score of zero. Non-zero-sum games do not result in a symmetrical outcome, and the cumulative result can be positive or negative. Hence, non-zero-sum games can be classified as either competitive or cooperative. In a cooperative non-zero-sum game (e.g., coordination games), players always improve the score of other players by attempting to maximize their own score. However, in a competitive or mixed-motive non-zero-sum game (e.g., social dilemmas), players can increase their own score at some cost to other players or they can behave cooperatively.

The historical roots of game theory lie in strategic thought such as warfare, sport, and negotiations. The basic premise of game theory, "Make a decision by attempting to predict the decisions of others," has been understood for centuries. Yet a formal solution for games did not become possible until 1944, when John von Neumann and Oskar Morgenstern formalized game theory in their seminal book *Theory of Games and Economic Behavior*. Since then, game theory has been extended to provide insight into a wide range of problems and has been adopted by many scientific disciplines, including economics, political science, psychology, social psychology, anthropology, sociology, biology, and communication.

In order to define a game, it is important to understand three core concepts—players, strategies, and payoffs:

- *Players.*—Games are played by any number of players who compete against one another. A single player can play a game and compete against a stochastic element referred to as nature (uncertainty). Players in a game do not need to be human, and a game can be played by agents such as corporations, governments, or species.
- *Strategies.*—Players take actions by choosing strategies, and a game can be defined with any number of strategies available to the players. In some games, the strategy set of a player is constant and represents a single choice, while other games are repeated over a number of rounds. In addition, a game can be played simultaneously or sequentially. In a sequential game, the strategy set of a player may change between each round based on their previous choices and the choices of other players. Chess is an example of a sequential game played over many rounds.
- *Payoffs.*—When a single strategy for a given player is examined in light of the strategies available to other players, it yields a set of payoffs. Each possible combination of strategies results in a single payoff. For example, the game paper (P), rock (R), scissors (S) has nine possible outcomes, which must be represented by a numeric payoff: S/S, S/R, S/P, P/S, P/R, P/P, R/S, R/R, R/P.

In addition to the three core elements, games also generally operate under a core set of assumptions. These assumptions are not strictly necessary, and researchers have explored game theory outside of them, but without them the solution of a game can quickly become computationally intractable.

It is generally assumed that all players in a game have complete information about their own strategies, the strategies available to other players, and all of the payoffs. This assumption assures that each player is always aware of the best choices available for all players involved and will make a choice knowing that their opponent will also make the best choice. It may appear that this makes a game easily solvable, but the solution to this problem can still be quite complex. A player's best strategy may be contingent on the strategy selected by the opponent, while the opponent's best strategy is contingent on the strategy selected by the player.

Another assumption of game theory is that the numeric definitions of the payoffs completely capture the preferences of each player. Game theory is built on a "rational" utility maximization model of behavior. Payoffs are based on a utility function that maps the preferences of each player onto a numeric quantity. A player who is reasoning in game theory will always do so in a manner that maximizes their utility. In doing so, they will always attempt to play the strategy with the highest payout.

Recently, the rational model of behavior has come under some scrutiny. The fields of psychology and behavioral economics have uncovered consistent irrationality in human decision making. Still, game theory remains applicable for predicting and modeling behavior as long as the irrationalities can be represented in the payoff structure of the game. For example, a player who has an intrinsic preference for cooperation would have this preference represented by a higher payout for cooperative outcomes. Even though human behavior presents frequent inconsistencies, other entities such as corporations, cooperative groups, and species under the selective pressure of evolution may be more accurately modeled with the rational model of behavior.

Games can be solved in a variety of ways. The easiest games to solve are those that have a dominant strategy. In these games, players have a single best response regardless of the choices that other players make. In more complex games, there is no dominant strategy. The best strategy for a player depends on the strategies selected by others. In 1950, John Nash introduced the now-popularized concept of Nash Equilibrium as a means for solving games where players don't have a dominant strategy. The Nash Equilibrium of a game is a set of strategies where no player can improve their payoff by switching to another strategy. It is common for games to have more than one Nash Equilibrium point, and in this case, the equilibrium that the players reach is determined by the starting conditions and context of the game. A coordination game where two players have multiple choices and are attempting to coordinate on the same outcome is one type of a game that has multiple Nash Equilibrium points. Examples of coordination games include a lost child and parent trying to find one another, or choosing which side of the road to drive on.

An equilibrium that has lower payouts than another strategy is referred to as dominated. Players may however reach a dominated equilibrium as a result of errors in judgment or other noise. Dominated outcomes can also be thought of as local maxima in an objective function. The game remains at the local maximum because it is not possible for any player to improve their payoff by switching to a different strategy. Some games do not have a pure Nash Equilibrium. In these cases players can always improve their strategy by switching strategy or choosing another one at random. This type of game is called a mixed strategy game. The game rock, paper, scissors is a mixed strategy game because it is best for a player to play randomly rather than settle on one particular strategy.

One of the most important advances in game theory came in 1977 when John Maynard Smith and George Price extended game theory into biology with the formalization of evolutionary game theory and the evolutionary stable strategy. Evolutionary game theory allows a population of organisms to be modeled using simple behavioral rules in combination with game theory and population dynamics. In order to function correctly, evolutionary game theory requires a replicator dynamic, which can be based on sex and genetics, social learning, or other copying. In evolutionary game theory, a group of players compete and reproduce in an environment that is modeled as a game with strategies and payouts. Players are assigned a strategy, and in each round the strategies of successful players, those with a higher payout, are replicated. Just like game theory, the success, or fitness, of strategies is determined by interactions with other strategies. Evolutionary games are played using repeated interactions; each round represents a time step, and each time step the population of strategies changes based on its fitness. Evolutionary games can also be treated as dynamic systems, where the solutions to the game can be found by solving for what is called the evolutionary stable strategy, a concept similar to the Nash Equilibrium. In practice, evolutionary game theory has proven quite useful. It has been applied to such problems as understanding sex ratios, altruism, and the origin and evolution of culture (Skyrms 1996; Boyd and Richerson 2005).

In recent years, game theory and evolutionary game theory have been applied extensively in behavioral studies of humans and animals. The results of these studies indicate that decision making is very sensitive to contextual features. Two games with the same structure can have very different outcomes when framing, culture, communication bandwidth, or norms are altered (Kahneman and Tversky 1979; Ostrom 2005; Chen, Lakshminarayanan, and Santos 2006; Bicchieri 2006). In addition, game theory has provided a framework for the simulation of social situations and artificial life. Stemming from the pioneering work of Schelling (1978) and Axelrod and Hamilton ([1981] 2006), advances in computing have allowed researchers to investigate increasingly complex agent-based simulations with rules structured using game theory.

■ See also ARTIFICIAL LIFE, GRAPH THEORY, SIMULATION

References and Further Reading

Axelrod, Robert, and William D. Hamilton. (1981) 2006. *The Evolution of Cooperation*. New York: Basic Books.

Bicchieri, Christina. 2006. *The Grammar of Society: The Nature and Dynamics of Social Norms*. New York: Cambridge University Press.

Boyd, Robert, and Peter Richerson. 2005. *The Origin and Evolution of Cultures*. New York: Oxford University Press.

Chen, Keith, Venkat Lakshminarayanan, and Laurie Santos. 2006. "How Basic Are Behavioral Biases? Evidence from Capuchin Monkey Trading Behavior." *Journal of Political Economy* 114 (1): 517–537.

Easley, David, and Jon Kleinberg. 2010. *Networks, Crowds, and Markets: Reasoning about a Highly Connected World*. New York: Cambridge University Press.

Ginits, Herbert. 2000. *Game Theory Evolving*. Princeton, NJ: Princeton University Press.

Kahneman, Daniel, and Amos Tversky. 1979. "Prospect Theory: An Analysis of Decision under Risk." *Econometrica* 47 (1): 263–291.

Maynard Smith, John. 1982. *Evolution and the Theory of Games*. Cambridge: Cambridge University Press.

Nash, John. 1951. "Non-cooperative Games." *Annals of Mathematics Journal* 54 (1): 286–295.

Ostrom, Elinor. 2005. *Understanding Institutional Diversity*. Princeton, NJ: Princeton University Press.

Ross, Don. 2011. "Game Theory." In *The Stanford Encyclopedia of Philosophy (Fall 2011 Edition)*, edited by Edward N. Zalta. http://plato.stanford.edu/archives/fall2011/entries/game-theory.

Schelling, Thomas. 1960. *Strategy of Conflict*. Cambridge, MA: Harvard University Press.

———. 1978. *Micromotives and Macrobehavior*. New York: Norton.

Skyrms, Brian. 1996. *Evolution of the Social Contract*. New York: Cambridge University Press.

———. 2004. *The Stag Hunt and the Evolution of Social Structure*. New York: Cambridge University Press.

von Neumann, John, and Oskar Morgenstern. 1944. *The Theory of Games and Economic Behavior*. Princeton, NJ: Princeton University Press.

Gameplay

Jesper Juul

The concept of gameplay is widely used within game studies, game design, and game culture, to describe not how a game looks, but how it *plays*: how the player interacts with its rules and experiences the totality of challenges and choices that the game offers. In a technical sense, gameplay always concerns the player's interaction with the underlying state of a game, and gameplay is typically used to describe the specific experience of interacting with the game, independently of graphics, fiction, and audio, even if the total player experience is influenced by these other design elements.

Gameplay is a definitional component of games and is not found in other art forms such as literature or cinema. While the audience is active in relation to all art forms by way of interpreting the signs that they are exposed to, games are unique in explicitly evaluating the performance of the audience, and in controlling the audience access to further content based on that evaluation. Colloquially, only games can be won or lost, and only games have GAME OVER.

Sid Meier (designer of *Civilization* and other classics) is credited with the statement "A game is a series of interesting choices" (Rollings 2000, 38). From this perspective, a game's quality hinges on its ability to present interesting choices and challenges to the player. Similarly, Raph Koster's book *A Theory of Fun for Game Design* (2004) describes players as general pattern seekers who will find a game uninteresting once all its patterns have been identified. Rollings and Adams define gameplay as "one or more causally linked series of challenges in a simulated environment" (2003, 201). However, this view overlooks the fact that games also contain passages and moments that are only marginally challenging, or not challenging at all, such as performing the final maneuver against an outplayed opponent in chess (Juul 2005, 112). In a broader perspective, gameplay must therefore be seen as a general rhythm created by a variety of challenges, as well as by the occasional absence of challenge.

Game designers create the gameplay of a game by combining two types of elements: emergent properties (see EMERGENCE) that creators design only indirectly, and linear series of explicitly designed challenge progressions (Juul 2002). When it is said that a game *has* a specific type of gameplay, this is understood in relation to a model player who accepts the game goal, understands the conventions of the game, and possesses the set of skills that the game was designed for.

As we can see, gameplay has a concrete formal existence in the programming of a digital game, or in the rules of an analog game, yet gameplay is always understood in relation to a model player who only experiences gameplay *through* audio, visuals, and fictions. Gameplay is often identified with the challenging aspects of a game, yet the total gameplay experience hinges not only on the types of challenge that an ideal player encounters throughout a game but also on the spacing of these challenges, as well as on their occasional absence.

■ See also GAME GENRES, INTERACTIVITY, INTERFACE, LUDUS
AND PAIDIA, SIMULATION, WALKTHROUGH

References and Further Reading

Juul, Jesper. 2002. "The Open and the Closed: Games of Emergence and Games of Progression." In *Computer Game and Digital Cultures Conference Proceedings*, edited by Frans Mäyrä, 323–329. Tampere, Finland: Tampere University Press. www.jesperjuul.net/text/openandtheclosed.html.

———. 2005. *Half-Real: Video Games between Real Rules and Fictional Worlds*. Cambridge, MA: MIT Press.

Koster, Raph. 2004. *A Theory of Fun for Game Design*. Scottsdale, AZ: Paraglyph Press.

Rollings, Andrew. 2000. *Game Architecture and Design*. Scottsdale, AZ: Coriolis.

Rollings, Andrew, and Ernest Adams. 2003. *Andrew Rollings and Ernest Adams on Game Design*. Indianapolis: New Riders.

· ·

Games and Education
Brian Magerko

As digital games—and digital media in general—have become more prevalent in our everyday lives, employing them for non-entertainment-focused domains has become increasingly popular in the twenty-first century. Games, like many other media, have transitioned from a pure entertainment medium to being used in a broad spectrum of communication domains. The interactive nature of games, which no other cultural form can match, has made them a compelling medium and a potentially powerful tool for informal and formal learning environments.

It has been suggested that learning and play are closely related, if not indistinguishable from one another, which leads to the supposition that games are innately appropriate for education. Ralph Koster has posited that to play any game is to engage in a learning process: "Fun is just another word for learning," and "with games, learning is the drug" (2004, 46). He asserts that, in contrast to traditional, static media, the enjoyment of a gameplay experience resides in learning how to overcome obstacles in the game environment (see GAMEPLAY).

Koster's well-popularized viewpoint does help explain why games could be considered a learning medium. If a game player can learn to overcome obstacles related to fictional situations, it may also help this player to learn about real situations and to acquire real-world-relevant knowledge if the game is mapped to other learning domains, such as biology, finance, or law enforcement. This rationale has been the main drive for the educational game movement of the twenty-first century (also called digital game-based learning or DGBL, when referring to computer games specifically), as well as for the use of games as training and learning tools (war games, role-playing in business training, model government exercises for civics lessons in high school, etc.).

Digital games for education have their roots in the early games of the late 1980s and 1990s, such as *Math Blaster* (Davidson & Associates 1987), *Reader Rabbit* (The Learning Company 1986), and various military flight simulators. Though some of these experiences have had long-lasting commercial success, the impact of educational games during these times was muted. Educational games were fighting against both a lack of widespread integration of computer games as a common and popular media form in the United States and a lack of design-oriented practices for integrating quality educational practices in this relatively new media form. The result was a slow adoption and uninformed design choices when making educational games. As the field of digital games both matured and gained broader societal acceptance, so did the educational subgenre of games.

The popularity of games for education, as part of the larger "serious games" movement (i.e., games used for other purposes than pure entertainment), reached a critical point with the introduction of the first Serious Games Summit at the Game Developer's Conference in 2004. This first major public event centered on serious games was led by Ben Sawyer, whose work on *Virtual U*, a training game for university management (Virtual U Project 2001), was held as an early example of employing solid game design skills to educate people about a real-world problem. In his work on the Serious Games Initiative, Sawyer has been a leading voice for the acceptance of games in education, training, health, and public policy (Sawyer 2012).

Digital games for education can take several different forms. A common form is the off-the-shelf (OTS) approach. It consists of applying a preexisting game to a new learning context, a context possibly unintended by the designers. For example, the *Neverwinter Nights* series has been used in many schools to teach creative writing and storytelling (Robertson and Good 2004; Carbonaro et al. 2008). The rationale is that proper contextualization of the experience can provide learning gains while using a media form that is engaging, relevant to a student's life, and commercially designed to be enjoyable. The *SimCity* series, perhaps the most widely recognized OTS game series used for education, has been used for teaching civics in the classroom (Frye and Frager 1996; Adams 1998; Gaber 2007; Ledesma 2009), and the *Civilization* series has been used for teaching concepts in history (Squire 2002, 2005; Squire and Jenkins 2003; Gwinn 2006). A common criticism of OTS educational uses of commercial games is that the underlying model of the game domain (e.g., world history in *Civilization III*) can be grossly different from the models generally endorsed by scholars for the domain of the real world. This is mainly due to the fact that the game was originally made to entertain by offering an appealing abstraction of its domain as opposed to an accurate one.

Another form of educational game consists of games that were originally created for classroom use (or games that involve substantial modifications of existing games). In the past decades, many of these games have been built as academic projects. Successful modern educational game creation has focused on the incorporation of learning sciences theory into core game development practices. Having an education specialist as part of a project team is becoming more and more common, particularly for projects that are federally funded. For example, *Quest Atlantis* is a 3D, multiuser game that involves learners in inquiry-based activities (Barab et al. 2005). This game also embodies Barab et al.'s concept of transformational play, a theory of learning grounded in play-focused activities (Barab et al. 2009). The products of Happy Neuron, a self-described "brain training company," focus on applying findings in cognitive psychology and neuroscience to the design of games that help increase or maintain mental fitness. Other notable education games of the past decade include *Food Force* (United Nations World Food Programme 2005), which educates players about hunger issues around the globe; *Making History: The Calm & The Storm* (Muzzy Lane Software 2007), a game about living in World War II; and *Re-Mission* (HopeLab 2006), a game that educates children about cancer treatments and the importance of adhering to them.

The games-for-education movement reached a major milestone in 2009, when the Manhattan-based school Quest to Learn (Q2L) announced that it would open with a game-based curriculum (using both digital and nondigital games) for sixth graders which fulfills the New York State curriculum standards (Salen et al. 2010). Funding comes primarily from private institutions, such as the Gates Foundation and the MacArthur Foundation, but it will be taken over by the state of New York in 2015. The founding of this school represents a major achievement in game development and policy in terms of the potential for formal learning environments which it represents. Many informal learning opportunities have also been developed in the past decade, with several informational institutions (e.g., National Geographic, Discovery, and PBS) and companies creating online games to inform their users about relevant subjects (and often to advertise their own projects).

The practice of *gamification* (i.e., the co-opting of gameplay into existing systems as a means of providing engagement or incentives to players) has gained serious interest since 2010 as a way to change how we conduct commerce, educate, exercise, and so on. This approach typically involves taking an existing system (such as a classroom) and providing power-ups, short-term goals, a narrative for the experience, and so on (for an example of classroom gamification, see Sheldon 2011). However, gamification has been highly criticized as being a fad, the renaming of existing practices (e.g., frequent flier programs), and an approach that encourages poor, shallow game design (Deterding 2010; Bogost 2011).

The games-for-education movement, while making steady progress, is not without problems. As is common with other educational media, rigorous evaluation of games for education is rare, thus raising the question, "are games worth the price and effort for actual learning gains?" Games are also often designed with implicit gender and/or cultural biases. Furthermore, games may engage only a specific demographic group rather than an entire classroom composed of culturally diverse students (Cassell 2000; Kafai et al. 2008). And finally, a single game cannot address the variety of learning styles found among students. This decreases the efficiency of games within forced learning environments (Magerko 2008).

■ See also GAME GENRES, GAMEPLAY, INDEPENDENT AND ART GAMES, LUDUS AND PAIDIA

References and Further Reading

Adams, Paul C. 1998. "Teaching and Learning with *SimCity 2000*." *Journal of Geography* 97 (2): 47–55.

Barab, Sasha, Michael Thomas, Taylor Dodge, Robert Carteaux, and Hakan Tuzun. 2005. "Making Learning Fun: *Quest Atlantis*, a Game without Guns." *Educational Technology Research and Development* 53 (1): 86–107.

Barab, Sasha A., Brianna Scott, Sinem Siyahhan, et al. 2009. "Transformational Play as a Curricular Scaffold: Using Videogames to Support Science Education." *Journal of Science Education and Technology* 18 (4): 305–320.

Bogost, Ian. 2011. "Gamification Is Bullshit." www.bogost.com/blog/gamification_is_bullshit.shtml.

Carbonaro, Mike, Maria Cutumisu, Harvey Duff, et al. 2008. "Interactive Story Authoring: A Viable Form of Creative Expression for the Classroom." *Computers & Education* 51 (2): 687–707.

Cassell, Justine. 2000. *From Barbie to Mortal Kombat: Gender and Computer Games*. Cambridge, MA: MIT Press.

Davidson & Associates. 1987. *Math Blaster!* Computer game.

Deterding, Sebastian. 2010. "Pawned: Gamification and Its Discontents." Presented at *Playful 2010*, September 24. Conway Hall, London.

Frye, Beth, and Alan M. Frager. 1996. "Civilization, Colonization, SimCity: Simulations for the Social Studies Classroom." *Learning & Leading with Technology* 24 (2): 21–32.

Gaber, John. 2007. "Simulating Planning SimCity as a Pedagogical Tool." *Journal of Planning Education and Research* 27 (2): 113–121.

Gwinn, Eric. 2006. "New School: Teachers Bring 'Civilization' into the Classroom." *Chicago Tribune*, February 7. http://articles.chicagotribune.com/2006-02-07/features/0602070271_1_pc -game-firaxis-games-teachers.

HopeLab. 2006. *Re-Mission*. Computer game.

Kafai, Yasmin B., Carrie Heeter, Jill Denner, and Jennifer Y. Sun. 2008. *Beyond Barbie and Mortal Kombat: New Perspectives on Gender and Gaming*. Cambridge, MA: MIT Press.

Koster, Ralph. 2004. *A Theory of Fun for Game Design*. Scottsdale, AZ: Paraglyph Press.

The Learning Company. 1986. *Reader Rabbit*. Computer game.

Ledesma, Patrick. 2009. "Gaming in Education: Sim City 4." *EdTechBytes*, October 26. http://edtech bytes.com/?p=305.

Magerko, Brian. 2008. "Adaptation in Digital Games." *Computer* 41 (6): 87–89.

Muzzy Lane Software. 2007. *Making History: The Calm & The Storm*. Computer game.

Robertson, Judy, and Judith Good. 2004. "Children's Narrative Development through Computer Game Authoring." In *Proceedings of the 2004 Conference on Interaction Design and Children: Building a Community*, 57–64.

Salen, Katie, Rebecca Rufo-Tepper, Arana Shapiro, Robert Torres, and Loretta Wolozin. 2010. *Quest to Learn: Developing the School for Digital Kids*. Cambridge, MA: MIT Press.

Sawyer, Ben. 2012. "Serious Games Initiative." *Serious Games Initiative*. www.seriousgames.org /index.html.

Sheldon, Lee. 2011. *The Multiplayer Classroom: Designing Coursework as a Game*. Boston: Cengage Learning.

Squire, Kurt. 2002. "Cultural Framing of Computer/Video Games." *Game Studies* 2 (1). www .gamestudies.org/0102/squire/.

———. 2005. "Changing the Game: What Happens When Video Games Enter the Classroom." *Innovate: Journal of Online Education* 1 (6). www.innovateonline.info/pdf/vol1_issue6/Chang ing_the_Game-__What_Happens_When_Video_Games_Enter_the_Classroom_.pdf.

Squire, Kurt, and Henry Jenkins. 2003. "Harnessing the Power of Games in Education." *Insight* 3 (1): 5–33.

United Nations World Food Programme. 2005. *Food Force*. Computer game.

Virtual U Project. 2001. *Virtual U*. Computer game.

···

Games as Art/Literature
David Ciccoricco

It might appear fairly unproblematic and quite commonplace to discuss the artistry of video games—those primarily entertainment-based digital artifacts played on a personal computer or gaming console. Such discussions might center around instances of dazzling graphical design and animation, from the rendering of live-action combat maneuvers to the depiction of solar systems; they might focus on impressive sound design, from a game's diegetic sound effects to its accompanying musical score; they might focus on the intricacies of a game's narrative design, from compelling characters placed in morally ambiguous situations to unexpected developments in a game's plot or across entire game trilogies. Those on the production end might even point to the elegance of a game engine and its underlying code as a work of art. It is indeed clear that we cannot consider the evolution of video games as an art form without at the same time considering the evolution of the technologies that enable them. The most visible advances, of course, can be seen in the movement toward photorealistic graphics and animation. In fact, it would be possible to claim that video games have become artful only or at least primarily as a result of the affordances of digital media. Nevertheless, the practice of identifying isolated elements of video games as art—each of which are essentially already established artistic media with their own artistic traditions—still does not justify video games as an art form in their own right.

Several factors trouble the status of video games as an art form. They are generally a form of popular entertainment, which might not best serve what may be thought of as the higher purposes of art. But an even more intractable problem lies with their status as vehicles for play, and ones that typically (or arguably by definition) involve competition. That is, no matter how artistic a game may be, the purpose of its creation is arguably located in nonaesthetic goals (see Samyn 2011; Frasca 2003). The competitive nature of video games is especially clear with those based on sports. Video games further trouble the artistic criteria of (1) "artifactuality" and (2) being made or performed for an audience, which are generally accepted as fundamental conditions for any work of art.

That they are not artifactual in the sense of something we can easily point to in space, such as a painting or a sculpture, is not in itself problematic as we similarly experience the so-called temporal arts, such as music, narrative fiction, or cinema, in a time frame that is protracted and in some cases defined by the audience. With video games, however, the player is, in a sense, at once performer and audience of the aesthetic event. For video games to be an art form we would have to account for the fact that the material input of the player in effect creates the "game," which can refer to the result of an individual and idiosyncratic session of gameplay as well as the game as artifact (see GAME-PLAY). There is no shortage of experimentalist avant-garde artwork that demands user participation, but simply adding the "art of video games" to this tradition is a misguided gesture, not least because video games are one of the most dominant forms of cultural activity in the twenty-first-century mainstream. (Focusing on art and art games *arising from* hacking, modifying or "modding," remixing, and regendering, Celia Pearce [2006] productively links avant-garde art history, and specifically the Fluxus emphasis on procedurality and structured play, to the production and experience of video games; see HACKER, REMIX.) More importantly, we need to acknowledge the crucial difference between video games and other forms of representational art: video games are simulations. Or, more accurately, they are simulations that typically employ representational elements.

Although the critical discourse on representation and simulation has yet to coalesce by way of accepting these terms as a discrete conceptual pairing (see Frasca 2003; Ryan 2006, 187–189), what most clearly sets simulations apart is their status as rule-based systems that model behavior in some way (see SIMULATION). In all video games the player assumes a sense of agency in order to produce an outcome. In many contemporary titles, moreover, the player assumes a role in a fictional world (see AVATARS, ROLE-PLAYING GAMES). Can simulations be works of art? For those who embrace the notion that the end goal of the arts is to transform the spectator into an active participant, they might be the ultimate art form. But if we do answer in the affirmative, then who exactly is the artist in or of the video game?

In the context of cinematic production, we are reasonably comfortable with both the notion of a singular artist—the director as auteur with whom we tend to locate artistic or authorial "vision" and a sense of holistic intentionality—and a collective creative team that would include anything from the actors to the set designers or makeup crew. Some game designers have indeed garnered recognition as auteurs for popular contemporary games, among them Shigeru Miyamoto of *Mario Bros.* and *The Legend of Zelda* series, Will Wright of the *Sims* series and *Spore*, and Fumito Ueda of *Ico* and *Shadow of the Colossus*. In video games the notion of a creative team would include some analogous roles in the form of producer, creative director, and script writer, or the potentially overlapping roles of (voice) actors or digital animators, but it would extend to less familiar roles such as programmers and level designers. But with regard to the player as artist, we invite questions of a different order. It is possible to claim that skill is demonstrated artfully through gameplay and that gameplay constitutes an artful form of expression, but equating player to artist is insufficient for an understanding of video games as an art form in its own right.

It is possible, however, to consider video games as a nascent art form (the game industry proper is still only four decades old), and one that has yet to be fully recognized and understood as such (see GAME HISTORY). Art philosophy, for one, can help establish the status of video games as a form of art. Notwithstanding the polemic on the difficulty or even the utility of arriving at a definition of art, philosophers of art approach the question by identifying features peculiar to an artistic work and in the quality of experiencing that work. In constructing definitions, furthermore, one traditional method considers conditions that are *necessary* and *sufficient* to qualify a work of art as such. Working from these premises, treatments of video games as art can first define video games and then attempt to fit this definition into a wider conception of art, or they can start with a definition of art and apply it to video games. Given that the qualities we generally consider necessary to be a video game—the dependency on the computer medium and a media artifact designed to be played primarily for entertainment—are clearly not by themselves enough to be a work of art, the first approach falls short.

The second approach, by contrast, is more productive, especially when we appropriate recent "cluster" theories of art. Rather than adopting a singular, universal definition of art, Denis Dutton (2006), for example, advocates defining art based on a set of twelve characteristics or "recognition criteria." He describes these as a formulation of the first questions one asks of a supposed work of art before more technical concerns such as "authenticity," a question asked only after an object has somehow been qualified as a work of art (though unlike some of his contemporaries, Dutton defends this set as a definition in itself). This set includes the experience of direct pleasure; the display of skill or virtuosity; evidence of style; demonstration of novelty and creativity; an associated body of criticism; the use of representation; some kind of "special" focus in terms of framing or presentation; expressive individuality; emotional saturation; intellectual challenge; traditions and institutions; and—most significantly for Dutton—imaginative experience (2006, 368–373). As Grant Tavinor (2008) observes, a majority of the criteria apply to features peculiar to video games and/or the experience of playing them—although it is worth noting that Dutton (2006, 372) mentions video games in passing as an example of "intellectual challenge" when referring to "non-art" lived experience.

Based on this approach, there would appear to be justification for identifying video games as works of art in their own right, but it would still be possible to object that such discussions of video game aesthetics do not grow out of or necessarily reflect a genuine play-centric theory. Ultimately, the question might hinge on what is valued most for any given player: a competitive experience or an imaginative one, which is not to say that the two are mutually exclusive. A play-centric approach might also accommodate the notion that, despite the typical emphasis on representational material in evaluating a game's artistry, the act of *designing* a compelling gameplay experience is an artistic achievement in itself. In any case, it is necessary to acknowledge that it is entirely possible to understand video games as an art form while at the same time reserving judgment with regard to the

222
Games as
Art/Literature

aesthetic worth or success of any particular game title. Some of the same assumptions that operate for corporate film production, after all, apply to video games as well. That is, independent (or "indie") and art games are generally perceived as more artistic than those produced by major publishers (see INDEPENDENT AND ART GAMES).

The same observation brings into sharp relief the fraught practice of evaluating games in relation to other artistic forms—for example, measuring the success of a game's narrative in relation to twentieth-century novels, or its graphics in relation to contemporary cinematic animation. Will Wright describes the comparison of video games to existing media as both "useful and dangerous" (quoted in Freeman 2004, xxxii), and the practice has stirred video game criticism in both academic forums, as in the "First Person" collection of the *electronic book review* (see Bernstein 2004), and popular ones, as in the prolonged debate carried out between film critic Roger Ebert (2010) and game designer Kellee Santiago (2009).

The related notion of video games as literature, or as possessing literary qualities, is by and large predicated on the extent to which the game draws on or projects a narrative (see GAMES AS STORIES). Video games typically include textual material in the form of instructions or extradiegetic menus, but many games also include narrative interludes after achievements or in between levels. Transcriptions of character dialogue, with or without a quasi-synchronous voice-over, are also common in some game genres (see GAME GENRES). Video games are scripted artifacts, and it is indeed possible to evaluate them on the basis of whether or not they are well *written*. Games, then, can be beautiful, and when they are populated with fictional agents in a fictional world, they can also be meaningful—even ideologically persuasive (Bogost 2007). The question of video games as literature is also a taxonomical one: in academic contexts they have been positioned as a subcategory of the broader artistic field of electronic literature because of their integration of literary and ludic characteristics (see Ensslin and Bell 2007) (see ELECTRONIC LITERATURE). Ironically, many forms of electronic literature, such as digital fiction and digital poetry, struggle to get out of academia, whereas video games have struggled to get in (see DIGITAL FICTION, DIGITAL POETRY).

There is, of course, yet another way to approach questions concerning games as art or literature, one that simply explores how the gamer community situates video games in a cultural and artistic field (see ONLINE GAME COMMUNITIES). In line with the growing artistic—and indeed, literary—sophistication and complexity of certain games, it is clear that game designers see themselves as artists in their own right involved in a defining moment of cultural production (Freeman 2004, 16), and many explicitly situate their work in an artistic tradition. For example, video games constitute perhaps their own unique form of intertextuality in the form of game engines and recycled code (see Bogost 2006, 55–64). But some game worlds are also replete with references to earlier art forms. There are varied intertextual references to Spaghetti Westerns in *Red Dead Redemption* (2010), for instance, as well as historically plausible references to *Captain Billy's Whiz Bang*, a popular humor magazine of the day by the minor nonplayer character Jimmy Saint (see NPC [NONPLAYER CHARACTER]). Allusions can be even more subtle, in the form of technique: when the player-character looks up toward the sun in *Halo* (2001), nested circles appear on screen, a visual invocation of documentary-styled cinema (Smuts 2005).

The practice of granting annual awards by independent publications or bodies and by the industry itself, awards that include recognition for artistic prowess in everything from "technical innovation" to "best character," further reflects their aesthetic appreciation and reception (though the same practice could also be viewed as a self-conscious attempt by the industry to impose the artistic value of games on the wider public). Academic institutions worldwide have exhibited the same trends by introducing programs devoted not only to the creative production of games but also to their critical and aesthetic reception. The Art History of Games Symposium held in February 2010 in Atlanta, Georgia, for instance, marked a productive move to better articulate the importance of games as a form of art. In addition, 2012 saw the opening of a major exhibit on the "Art of Video Games" at the Smithsonian Museum in Washington, D.C. Whatever we ultimately decide about the status of video games as art or literature in critical discourse, they are most certainly already treated as such in practice.

References and Further Reading

Bernstein, Mark. 2004. "Mark Bernstein's Response." *electronic book review*, October 1. www.elec tronicbookreview.com/thread/firstperson/possible.
Bogost, Ian. 2006. *Unit Operations: An Approach to Videogame Criticism.* Cambridge, MA: MIT Press.
———. 2007. *Persuasive Games: The Expressive Power of Videogames.* Cambridge, MA: MIT Press.
Dutton, Denis. 2006. "A Naturalist Definition of Art." *Journal of Aesthetics and Art Criticism* 64 (3): 367–377.
Ebert, Roger. 2010. "Video Games Can Never Be Art." *Chicago Sun Times*, April 16. http://blogs .suntimes.com/ebert/2010/04/video_games_can_never_be_art.html.
Ensslin, Astrid, and Alice Bell, eds. 2007. *Dichtung Digital.* Special Edition: *New Perspectives on Digital Literature.* http://dichtung-digital.mewi.unibas.ch/editorial/2007.htm.
Frasca, Gonzalo. 2003. "Simulation versus Narrative." In *The Video Game Theory Reader*, edited by Mark J. P. Wolf and Bernard Perron, 221–236. London: Routledge.
Freeman, David. 2004. *Creating Emotion in Games.* Berkeley: New Riders.
Halo. 2010. Computer game. Designed by Bungie, Inc. Published by Microsoft Game Studios.
Juul, Jesper. 2005. *Half-Real: Video Games between Real Rules and Fictional Worlds.* Cambridge, MA: MIT Press.
Pearce, Celia. 2006. "Games as Art: The Aesthetics of Interactivity." *Visible Language* 40 (1): 66–89.
Red Dead Redemption. 2010. Computer game. Designed by Rockstar San Diego. Published by Rockstar Games.
Ryan, Marie-Laure. 2006. *Avatars of Story.* Minneapolis: University of Minnesota Press.
Samyn, Michael. 2011. "Almost Art." *Escapist*, February 2. www.escapistmagazine.com/articles /view/issues/issue_291/8608-Almost-Art.
Santiago, Kellee. 2009. "Video Games Are Art." *TEDx Talks*, August 17. www.youtube.com/watch ?v=K9y6MYDSAww&feature=player_embedded.
Smuts, Aaron. 2005. "Are Video Games Art?" *Contemporary Aesthetics* 3. www.contempaesthetics .org/newvolume/pages/article.php?articleID=299.
Tavinor, Grant. 2008. "Definition of Videogames." *Contemporary Aesthetics* 6. www.contempaes thetics.org/newvolume/pages/article.php?articleID=492.

Games as Stories
David Ciccoricco

Video games are not narratives, and they do not *tell stories* in any straightforward sense of the phrase. Although it can be said that play often involves storytelling at a fundamental level and the practices of playing games and telling stories are often interrelated, what ultimately makes video games uniquely compelling has little to do with heralding a new form of narrative media. In fact, the experience that video games yield as rule-based systems sets them apart from other artistic media (see GAMES AS ART/ LITERATURE). Some theorists and game designers (Frasca 2003; Bogost 2006) have drawn distinctions between simulation and representation in an attempt to mark a clear difference between games and other representational art forms such as print fiction or cinema (see SIMULATION). If representations portray worlds and their inhabitants, simulations are systems that model their behavior in some way. Video games can be described as simulations in which an agent directing the output of the system is also a player directing the outcome of a game. Other theorists (Aarseth 1997; Eskelinen 2001) have articulated the dominant activity of gameplay in terms of configuration or exploration rather than interpretation, similarly differentiating games from conventional novels and films (see GAMEPLAY).

At the same time, it is difficult to engage with video games and not engage with narratives in some capacity. Many games employ representational elements and cast the player in the role of a character in a fictional world (see AVATARS, ROLE-PLAYING GAMES). These games engage players in a process of producing narrative events or at least dramatically enacting predetermined ones. Therefore, an *intrinsic* justification for video games as stories—one that posits narrative as an essential property—would fail to recognize the peculiar attributes of the form. A *typological* justification, however, is irrefutable: some games place a heavy investment (in both the generic and the expressly financial sense) in creating sophisticated and emotionally compelling narrative experiences. The growing commitment to developing narratives in video games has gone hand in hand with technical developments in computer animation and ever-increasing computational power (Wolf 2001; Newman 2004), leading some to suggest that the advent of computer technology has initiated "a spectacular reconciliation of competitive *ludus* and narrativity" (Ryan 2005, 355) (see LUDUS AND PAIDIA, NARRATIVITY).

Elaborating on a basic continuum that moves from abstract to representational, Jesper Juul (2005) has proposed a useful way in which to consider such games as a discrete grouping. In his typology, "coherent world games" are those that contain fully developed fictional worlds that can be imagined in great detail (2005, 132). In coherent world games, the rules of the game are inseparable from the fiction, and the relationship between story mechanics and game mechanics—or between "theme and structure" (2005, 15)—is arguably an essential one when it comes to understanding how and why we play them. Juul's distinction dovetails with genre distinctions (see GAME GENRES) that have emerged organically in the industry and gamer community. For example, we can to some extent measure a game's narrative investment in terms of genre, such as a comparably higher degree of narrativity in action-adventure titles compared to strategy games. In addition, a third-person perspective game might be more amenable to narrative mechanics than a first-person game given that our player-character is more visible on screen and therefore more open to characterization and portrayals of subjectivity. Thus, some video games allow for not just perspectival distance in how we see a coherent fictional world and our player-character but also a critical distance in how we interpret them (see Ciccoricco 2010, 244–245).

We can establish that many games make use of fundamental narrative patterns of problem solving and conflict resolution in their plots, narrative in these games can motivate and reward players, and some of these games have grown sophisticated enough to invite acts of interpretation. Significant theoretical questions remain unresolved, however, in terms of articulating *how* and *when* game narratives emerge, and *where* we ultimately locate them. In general, the degree of interactivity is inversely proportional to the level of narrativity, and a tension between user freedom and authorial design arises (see INTERACTIVE NARRATIVE). Some see a disjunction so pronounced as to position games and stories as "opposites" (Costikyan 2000).

While the narratives that games produce in the process of gameplay must occupy a primary place in any conception of diegesis, they are variously described as "potential," "emergent," "enacted," or "experiential" (at times with the same terms used in different ways by different scholars); and the fact that this narrative is arguably closer to dramatic enactment (or mimesis) than narration makes it problematic to frame discussions in terms of diegesis in the first place. The same observation recalls the opposition of simulation and representation, in that representations—especially narrative ones—tend to be oriented toward or about the past, while simulations tend to be oriented toward or designed to project possible future scenarios. Scholars and game designers have also focused on the paradoxically open yet circumscribed quality of game worlds in terms of "narrative architecture" (Jenkins 2004) or "possibility space" (Wright 2006; see also Hayles 2005 for use of this term in relation to electronic literature; see ELECTRONIC LITERATURE).

The narrative that players enact, then, can be considered in relation to narrative elements that might be a priori in the sense of either prescripted narrated backstories and epilogues or prerendered textual interludes and audiovisual cut scenes that are introduced during gameplay (see CUT SCENES). Many of the objections to treating games as narratives—such as claims that they are not narrated or that their temporal dynamics contradict basic models of narrative—stem from an uncertainty surrounding description of the performative aspect of games. But there are also crucial differences across and within game genres governing the extent to which the rule-based system orchestrates the relationship of gameplay and narrative mechanics, from games with hierarchical levels and largely linear narrative arcs to what are effectively toolkits for constructing entirely unscripted narrative experiences, with many combinations of the two extremes in between. Pearce's (2004) model of narrative "operators" and Juul's (2005) discussion of "emergent" and "progressive" games productively account for many of these differences.

Vigorous debate on the place of narrative in video games continues, with cinematic cut scenes—the most overtly narrative (and narrated) qualities of games—often serving as a flash point. Some (players, theorists, and game developers) argue that these nonplayable inserts are nothing more than vestigial remnants from earlier media that interfere with not only the gaming experience but also the evolution of the form. The same notion of vestigiality supports another belief that not only are narratives inessential elements of games, but narrative material can be stripped away to reveal some kind of pure or at least essential game, a view that clouds thorough evaluation (and appreciation) of any given game. For example, while the narrative of *Katamari Damacy* "might be removed without detriment to the gameplay" (Tavinor 2008), it would certainly be to the detriment of the idiosyncratic aesthetic artifact that falls under that title.

While even the most polarizing debates can enliven the field, discussions of narrative in video games which begin by casting certain scholars or certain methodologies in either a "narrativist" or "ludologist" camp are unproductive, as few worthwhile critiques can address either representational material or gameplay mechanics in isolation. Furthermore, several disciplines beyond narrative and literary theory, from education and art history to computer science and information design, promise to make valuable contributions to the study of video games. A division between "narrativists" and "ludologists" not only is artificial but also fails to account for notable narrative theorists who do not admit video games into their model of narrative (such as Abbott 2002); in short, not all narrative theorists are "narrativists" when it comes to video games.

Even though a custom-built discipline of game studies has been a vitally successful enterprise in clearing new institutional ground, the more radical tenets of game scholars who would seek to purge narrative from the domain of game studies scholarship and fashion a hermetically self-sustaining discipline (Aarseth 2004; Eskelinen 2001) have not gained widespread credibility or acceptance. Comprehensive codification and dismantling of the radical ludologist polemic can be found in Ryan (2006) and Rovner (2009). One irony is that in order for game studies to sustain itself as a robust interdisciplinary field, it would need to accommodate narratively complex video games in its critical oeuvre arguably more so than any other kind of game precisely because of the cultural mirror that they hold up to the society in which they are produced and the ideological critiques they carry (see Bogost 2007 on the "procedural rhetoric" of persuasive games).

Scholars have identified a possible trend whereby those players interested in narrative tend to be newer or more casual gamers, whereas those who eschew it tend to be more advanced or "hard-core" gamers (Juul 2005; Ryan 2006). That trend further maps on to Richard Bartle's (1996) famous typology of gamers: his "killers" and "achievers" would align with the ludologist, whereas "socializers" or "explorers" would align with the "narratologist." Whatever the case may be, no matter what discipline one comes from, or how many achievement points one has accumulated, everyone is still relatively new to the notion of a formalized disciplinary study of video games. Furthermore, while it is not only possible but immensely productive to apply narrative-theoretical frameworks to certain video games, it is also necessary to avoid losing sight of the specificity of the gaming experience.

■ See also GAME HISTORY, ONLINE GAME COMMUNITIES

References and Further Reading

Aarseth, Espen. 1997. *Cybertext: Perspectives on Ergodic Literature.* Baltimore: Johns Hopkins University Press.

———. 2004. "Quest Games as Post-Narrative Discourse." In *Narrative across Media: The Languages of Storytelling*, edited by Marie-Laure Ryan, 361–376. Lincoln: University of Nebraska Press.

Abbott, Porter. 2002. *The Cambridge Introduction to Narrative.* Cambridge: Cambridge University Press.

Bartle, Richard. 1996. "Hearts, Clubs, Diamonds, Spades: Players Who Suit MUDs." www.mud.co.uk/richard/hcds.htm.

Bogost, Ian. 2006. *Unit Operations: An Approach to Videogame Criticism.* Cambridge, MA: MIT Press.

———. 2007. *Persuasive Games: The Expressive Power of Videogames.* Cambridge, MA: MIT Press.

Ciccoricco, David. 2010. "Games of Interpretation and a Graphophiliac God of War." In *Intermediality and Storytelling*, edited by Marina Grishakova and Marie-Laure Ryan, 232–257. Berlin: Walter de Gruyter.

Costikyan, Greg. 2000. "Where Stories End and Games Begin." *Game Developer*, September.

Eskelinen, Markku. 2001. "The Gaming Situation." *Game Studies* 1 (1). www.gamestudies.org/0101/eskelinen/.

Frasca, Gonzalo. 2003. "Simulation versus Narrative." In *The Video Game Theory Reader*, edited by Mark J. P. Wolf and Bernard Perron, 221–236. London: Routledge.

Hayles, N. Katherine. 2005. "Narrating Bits: Encounters between Humans and Intelligent Machines." *Comparative Critical Studies* 2 (2): 165–190.

Jenkins, Henry. 2004. "Game Design as Narrative Architecture." In *First Person: New Media as Story, Performance, and Game*, edited by Pat Harrigan and Noah Wardrip-Fruin, 118–131. Cambridge, MA: MIT Press.

Juul, Jesper. 2005. *Half-Real: Video Games between Real Rules and Fictional Worlds*. Cambridge, MA: MIT Press.

Katamari Damacy. 2004. Computer game. Designed by Keita Takahashi. Published by Namco.

Murray, Janet. 1997. *Hamlet on the Holodeck: The Future of Narrative in Cyberspace*. New York: Free Press.

Newman, James. 2004. *Videogames*. London: Routledge.

Pearce, Celia. 2004. "Towards a Game Theory of Game." *electronic book review*, July. www.electron icbookreview.com/thread/firstperson/tamagotchi.

Rovner, Adam. 2009. "A Fable: or, How to Recognize a Narrative When You Play One." *Journal of Gaming and Virtual Worlds* 1 (2): 97–115.

Ryan, Marie-Laure. 2005. "Narrative, Games, and Play." In *The Routledge Encyclopedia of Narrative Theory*, edited by David Herman, Manfred Jahn, and Marie-Laure Ryan, 354–356. London: Routledge.

———. 2006. *Avatars of Story*. Minneapolis: University of Minnesota Press.

———. 2009. "From Narrative Games to Playable Stories: Towards a Poetics of Interactive Narrative." *Storyworlds: A Journal of Narrative Studies* 1 (1): 43–60.

Tavinor, Grant. 2008. "Definition of Videogames." *Contemporary Aesthetics* 6. www.contempaes thetics.org/newvolume/pages/article.php?articleID=492.

Wolf, Mark J. P. 2001. *The Medium of the Video Game*. Austin: University of Texas Press.

Wright, Will. 2006. "Dream Machines." *Wired Magazine* 14 (4). www.wired.com/wired/archive/14.04 /wright.html.

··

Gender and Media Use

Ruth Page

As one of the primary axes used to articulate human identity, *gender* remains a core aspect of self-mediation and choice of communicative style used by participants in computer-mediated communication. *Gender* stands at the heart of a nexus of interrelated terms, which include the designation of individuals within and beyond existing categories such as "male" and "female," the social construction and value of gendered attributes (such as "feminine," "masculine," "butch," "sissy," and so on), and an individual's sexual orientation. The analysis of gender and new media covers a range of topics, including identity and representation, the gendered interpretation of genre and textuality, and, more generally, the sexism that continues to shape the processes of production and reception (for example, in relation to the development of software and computer programming). Analysis of gender in computer-mediated contexts has intersected with the concerns of cyberfeminism but has also drawn on work from sociolinguistics, discourse analysis, and critical discourse analysis in order to explore questions of representation and communicative style.

Research in gender studies in relation to digital textuality has been shaped by changes in feminist thinking, particularly the key changes that took place in the last two decades of the twentieth century. Although the central goal of exposing and contesting inequalities based on gender-related differences remains, approaches to the study of gender and discourse (including digitally mediated discourse) have altered significantly in line with the shift from second-wave to third-wave or postmodern feminist thinking. The politics of second-wave feminism rightly contested the academic and social relegation of women's status (including their social role and the value ascribed to their textual production), drawing a binary, apparently universal, opposition between men and women, patriarchy and feminism.

Some early theorists of hypertextuality mapped this binary opposition of patriarchal oppression and feminist resistance onto textual qualities, so that open-ended, multilinear discourse was ascribed with feminist potential, as exemplified in the polemical writings of feminine *écriture* (Landow 1997; Love 2002). In turn, the parallels between feminine *écriture* and hypertextuality were used to interpret examples of digital fiction. Indeed, the artistic output of creators such as Shelley Jackson (*Patchwork Girl*) and Caitlin Fisher (*These Waves of Girls*) exemplifies some of the ways in which the affordances of hypertextual linking can support the feminist, hypertext fiction inspired by the work of landmark authors such as Mary Shelley and Virginia Woolf. But not all hypertext fiction, and certainly not all hypertextuality per se, need be put to feminist ends or be considered a female or feminine form. An abstract and simplistic pairing of gender and textuality is untenable. From a somewhat different perspective, the cyborg theory of Donna Haraway (1991) also used technology as the inspiration to contest gender boundaries. Cyborg theory inspired examples of print and online cyberpunk fiction and also can be used to interpret the creative use of avatars in virtual worlds that resist simplistic human categorization (e.g., blends of animal and human features).

Later research rejected the binary polarization of gendered categories and reconceptualized gender as a dynamic, fluid aspect of participant identity that could be performed and reworked over time and across different contexts. Drawing on the seminal work of Butler (1990) and postmodern approaches to identity as discursively constructed, the text-based forms of computer-mediated discourse typical of early genres (such as Listserv discussions, MOOs and MUDs) were interpreted as ideal environments for identity play. The possibility of anonymous or pseudonymous discourse enabled participants to choose whether or not to explicitly state a category for their gender identity, an identity that need not map onto the attributes they performed in offline contexts. However, the extent to which online performances destabilized gender boundaries and eradicated difference is questionable. Some studies suggested that gender switching in online contexts was far less extensive than had been assumed initially (Roberts and Parks 1999), while others documented the ongoing conventions of authenticity which prevail in life history genres such as blogs, even for queer communities (Rak 2005).

While participants may not always choose explicitly to state a gendered category in their profile information, they may still "give off" clues via their use of discourse styles which index gendered identities that are consonant with the participants' offline identities and are shaped by the prevailing social norms that govern gendered behavior. Analysis of gendered styles in computer-mediated discourse has extended research from sociolinguistics and the social sciences to explore the extent to which differences in language use according to the participants' gender might occur (or not) in online contexts. This research has included scrutiny of microlinguistic features (such as word choice), discourse style (including turn-taking strategies, speech acts, politeness phenomenon, use of pronouns, typography, tone), and multimodal resources (particularly emoticons, visual self-representation, gaze and gestures). A wide range of computer-mediated genres have been examined, including Listserv discussions, Internet relay chat, blogs, social network sites, and SMS messages.

Results of these studies suggest that even while the boundaries between gendered categories may be destabilized in some contexts, and while online communication might afford pseudonymous self-representation, in many cases participants still use language that indexes gendered identities in ways that reflect stereotypes documented in the study of offline communication. Differences according to gender are not necessarily reflected in microlinguistic features: word choice is often found to be similar in studies of both blogs and Internet relay chat produced by women and men. Nor are the differences universal. Herring and Paolillo (2006) noted that when the topic and genre of online talk are controlled, differences in pronoun use disappear, such that attempts to identify the language of a text's author by automated means (as did the algorithm constructed by Argamon et al. [2003] in the system called "Gender Genie") are found to be inconsistent. Differences in discourse style also vary according to the age of the participants (contrasting teen and adult patterns of self-representation), and discourse styles can change over time (for example, Wolf [2000] notes that men adopted the rate of emoticon use set by women, and Page [2012] notes that the expressive punctuation used by young women on Facebook was later adopted by older women too).

Where differences in discourse style occur, these often relate to pragmatic choices, especially relating to managing interpersonal communication and performing sociality. Hence, even as early as the 1990s, Herring (2003) observed the posts of an academic Listserv, documenting the supportive behavior of women and the aggressive discourse style of men. In later work, Herring and her colleagues have argued that gendered differences are rooted in the complementary and co-constructive patterns of self-representation shaped by heterosexual markets, where the imperative to appear attractive to others influences textual style and self-representation. A recurring trend is the increased pressure on women to appear attractive and playful (Stefanone, Lackaff, and Rosen 2011), although more recent studies suggest that this pressure is also beginning to influence young men's choice of profile photograph on mainstream social network sites (Manago et al. 2008).

The study of discourse styles used online often identified women as the trendsetters of innovative forms and genres (such as the use of expressive punctuation in SMS messages [Herring and Zelenkauskaite 2009] or writing on personal blogs [Page 2008]). However, the contribution of women as producers of digital texts has sometimes been neglected in academic studies of new media (see Herring et al. [2004] for a critique of this). A gap continues to persist in the number of women who pursue careers in information technology (Herring and Marken 2008), and sexist attitudes toward women entrepreneurs in the "tech scene" of Silicon Valley (Marwick 2010) are at odds with the increase in women's participation in online activities, which in some genres (such as social network sites) exceeds that of men (Vollman, Abraham, and Mörn 2010). Discrimination against behavior that falls outside heteronormative ideals also constrains the extent to which sexuality can be expressed online. The first decade of the twenty-first century saw the rise of women "sex-bloggers" who controversially published accounts of their sexual activities and desires. Notable examples include "Girl with a One Track Mind" (Zoe Margolis) and "Belle de Jour" (Dr. Brooke Magnanti), both of which gained popularity in the mainstream media as books and a television series, respectively. However, the need for sex-bloggers to write pseudonymously, as well as the media response to outing their identity, suggests that the freedom of expression promised by the early days of the Internet has not been realized fully. Indeed, while much has changed in terms of widening access to self-publication in online contexts, much has also stayed the same in terms of gendered inequalities. Gender will thus remain a central issue of new media and its participants, for while discursive constructions of gendered identity might appear more open-ended and flexible than ever before, gendered politics continue to constrain and shape online patterns of participation.

■ See also BLOGS, CYBERFEMINISM, IDENTITY, LIFE HISTORY

References and Further Reading

Argamon, Shlomo, Moshe Koppel, Jonathan Fine, and Anat Rachel Shimoni. 2003. "Gender, Genre and Writing Style in Formal Written Texts." *Text* 23 (3): 321–346.

Butler, Judith. 1990. *Gender Trouble: Feminism and the Subversion of Identity.* New York: Routledge.

Haraway, Donna. 1991. "A Cyborg Manifesto: Science, Technology, and Socialist-Feminism in the Late Twentieth Century." In *Simians, Cyborgs and Women: The Reinvention of Nature*, 149–181. New York: Routledge.

Herring, Susan C. 2003. "Gender and Power in Online Communication." In *The Handbook of Language and Gender*, edited by Janet Holmes and Miriam Meyerhoff, 202–228. Oxford: Blackwell.

Herring, Susan C., Inna Kouper, Lois Ann Scheidt, and Elijah L. Wright. 2004. "Women and Children Last: The Discursive Construction of Weblogs." In *Into the Blogosphere: Rhetoric, Community, and Culture of Weblogs*, edited by Laura J. Gurak, Smiljana Antonijevic, Laurie Johnson, Clancy Ratliff, and Jessica Reyman. http://blog.lib.umn.edu/blogosphere/women_and_children.html.

Herring, Susan C., and James Marken. 2008. "Implications of Gender Consciousness for Students in Information Technology." *Women's Studies* 37 (3): 229–256.

Herring, Susan C., and John C. Paolillo. 2006. "Gender and Genre Variation in Weblogs." *Journal of Sociolinguistics* 10 (4): 439–459.

Herring, Susan C., and Asta Zelenkauskaite. 2009. "Symbolic Capital in a Virtual Heterosexual Market." *Written Communication* 26 (1): 5–31.

Landow, George. 1997. *Hypertext 2.0.* Baltimore: Johns Hopkins University Press.

Love, Jane. 2002. "Elécriture: A Course in Women's Writing on the Web." *Kairos* 7 (3). kairos.technorhetoric.net/7.3/binder2.html?coverweb/love/index.html.

Manago, Adrianna M., Michael B. Graham, Patricia M. Greenfield, and Goldie Salimkhan. 2008. "Self-Presentation and Gender on MySpace." *Journal of Applied Developmental Psychology* 29:446–458.

Marwick, Alice 2010. "Status Update: Celebrity, Publicity, and Self-Branding in Web 2.0." PhD diss., New York University.

Page, Ruth. 2008. "Gender and Genre Revisited: Narratives of Illness on Personal Blogs." *Genre* 61 (3–4): 149–172.

———. 2012. *Stories and Social Identity: Identities and Interaction.* London: Routledge.

Rak, Julie. 2005. "The Digital Queer: Weblogs and Internet Identity." *Biography* 28 (1): 166–182.

Roberts, Lynne D., and Malcolm Parks. 1999. "The Social Geography of Gender Switching in Virtual Environments on the Internet." *Information, Communication & Society* 2 (4): 521–540.

Stefanone, Michael, Derek Lackaff, and Devan Rosen. 2011. "Contingencies of Self-Worth and Social-Networking-Site Behavior." *Cyberpsychology, Behavior and Social Networking* 14 (1–2): 41–49.

Vollman, Andrea, Linda Abraham, and Marie Pauline Mörn. 2010. "Women on the Web: How Women Are Shaping the Internet." ComScore Inc. www.comscore.com/Press_Events/Presentations_Whitepapers/2010/Women_on_the_Web_How_Women_are_Shaping_the_Internet.

Wolf, Alecia. 2000. "Emotional Expression Online: Gender Differences in Emoticon Use." *CyberPsychology and Behavior* 3 (5): 827–834.

Gender Representation
Kim Knight

Associations between gender and technology date back as far as the publication of Mary Shelley's *Frankenstein* in 1818. The association between gender and technology that began with Shelley's writing of *Frankenstein* continued into the twentieth century, emerging in subtle, often-unexpected places. For instance, as N. Katherine Hayles points out in *How We Became Posthuman*, "gender appear[s] in this primal scene of humans meeting their evolutionary successors" (1999, xii). Hayles draws on Turing's example of a game in which a subject guesses the gender of an anonymous interlocutor to suggest that because there is the possibility of a wrong answer, there is a disjunction between bodies as enacted and bodies as represented (1999, xiii) (see TURING TEST).

Though Donna Haraway's "Manifesto for Cyborgs: Science, Technology, and Socialist Feminism in the 1980s," first published in 1985, is not explicitly addressing web culture, it presents an image of the cyborg as a postgender construction which has been influential on web theorists because it challenges essentialist notions of "naturalized" gender (see CYBORG AND POSTHUMAN). For many early web scholars, the notion of disembodied posthumanism was a means of challenging essentialist gender hierarchies. Nongendered usernames and the creative use of avatars were seen as a way of refusing the question of gender in an online environment. It was not long, however, before theorists were challenging the notion of disembodiment and the liberation of online identity. Theorists such as Hayles, Lisa Nakamura, Anne Balsamo, and Sadie Plant argued that the materiality of offline life cannot be transcended online (see CYBERFEMINISM, MATERIALITY, VIRTUAL BODIES).

The tension between liberatory rhetoric and material use persists through the development of Web 2.0 technologies. Notable among early Web 2.0 representation is the case of *LonelyGirl15*, a serial fiction that debuted on YouTube in 2006 (see FILM AND DIGITAL MEDIA, VIDEO). The issue of gender does not typically enter into critiques of the series; however, the series is notable for featuring a teenaged female protagonist in what was thought to be a complex and thoughtful relationship with other online users. Though *LonelyGirl15* was criticized for toying with fans, the series paved the way for other notable web series featuring female protagonists. Among these is *The Guild*, an online series that is produced by Felicia Day, Jane Selle Morgan, and Kim Evey.

Other early web tendencies that continue into Web 2.0 platforms include the rhetoric about the liberating potential of anonymity. The "virtual world" Second Life, which parallels early MUDs and MOOs, has been celebrated for the interesting possibilities for gender play in building one's avatar (see AVATARS, MUDS AND MOOS, VIRTUALITY). However, the platform has also been criticized for requiring a user to choose between a male or female character, thereby reinforcing typically binary social constraints on what could be much more fluid gender play. Despite this, users are able to code their own clothing, accessories, and so on, allowing them to push against social norms in a 3D visual environment. The same critiques of disembodiment still apply. However, users continue to explore identity and representation through these platforms.

The questions of gender play and anonymity are increasingly surfacing in the realm of social media. In some sense, the real name policies of social media platforms such as Facebook and Google+ do not necessarily inhibit gender play (see SOCIAL NETWORK SITES [SNSs]). Though users can still play with the system by choosing plausible common names that do not match biological gender or that seem gender neutral, common name policies are indicative of a move toward real name policies that have the potential to greatly diminish the gender play potential of online platforms.

An additional digital environment in which gender play is limited is that of video games (see GAMEPLAY). Researchers have determined that when female characters are present, they are often overtly sexualized and more likely to be depicted nude or in clothing that is inappropriate to the task at hand (Downs and Smith 2010, 725). Surprisingly, the highest percentage of characters with unrealistic body images, both male and female, appear in games rated "E" (for everyone). Downs and Smith speculate that the gender representations in video games may have an effect on body image and relationship expectations as young players are cognitively developing (2010, 723).

The rise in participation and remixing in Web 2.0 platforms has resulted in a proliferation of memes, image macros, and so on that are relevant to issues of gender representation (see REMEDIATION, REMIX). One such mainstream meme is that of "the man your man could smell like," otherwise known as "the Old Spice guy." This series of broadcast commercials that promote Old Spice brand body wash took on a life of their own on the Internet in 2010 as the marketing company began using Twitter and personalized video responses to take advantage of the popularity of the commercial's character, played by Isaiah Mustafa. The "man your man could smell like" campaign is directed at women and includes several problematic gender representations. Old Spice guy's speeches always begin with "Hello, Ladies," implying a heteronormative viewer. The character goes on to list several "wishes" or "demands" of women which he is prepared to fulfill. The campaign relies heavily on satirizing women as materialistic and demanding, while simultaneously depicting men as uncaring and manipulative. In addition, Mustafa's bare torso and highly muscled physique perpetuate unrealistic images of men's bodies, participating in a trend toward depictions of male body image that align with unrealistic body images of women in the media. The proliferation of the Old Spice campaign online suggests that the liberatory "nonspace" of cyberspace is inevitably going to replicate the gender representations of the larger culture.

There are, however, some memes and macros that challenge stereotypes of gender representation. One example, also stemming from a corporate producer of hygiene products, is the online "That's Vaginal" campaign by Summer's Eve. In this campaign, Carlton, a tuxedoed cat on a private plane, attempts to reposition "the human vagina" as a natural wonder. This campaign is reminiscent of a host of feminist work that attempts to celebrate female anatomy and empower women's relationships to their bodies, including *The Vagina Monologues*. Bizarre though it is, its home in an online advertising campaign suggests that the Internet does offer some possibilities for gender play and expression that are excluded from broadcast media.

Danielle Henderson's Tumblr blog "Feminist Ryan Gosling" is a noncorporate example of Web 2.0 technologies challenging stereotypical gender representation. The blog's author describes the posts as "feminist flash cards." Each post to the blog includes an image of actor Ryan Gosling with text superimposed, always beginning with "Hey Girl."

The superimposed text generally cites a feminist principle or author and invites the viewer to engage in the fantasy that these ideas would make her desirable to someone like Gosling, an actor who currently has a fair amount of pop cultural cache. The association is all the more powerful given the way that feminist principles are frequently maligned in popular culture. Though framed playfully, the blog participates in the trend of increasing male objectification, similar to the Old Spice campaign. In addition, it reinforces heteronormativity with its "Hey Girl" tagline (Henderson has included at least one "Hey Boy" post, somewhat destabilizing this tendency).

As in the offline world, the realms of art and literature tend to feature more complex gender representations than those in mainstream production (see ELECTRONIC LITERATURE, HYPERTEXTUALITY, STORYSPACE). Shelley Jackson's *Patchwork Girl*, a prominent work of hyptertext literature from 1995, takes a feminist perspective by telling the story of the female monster whom Frankenstein discards in Shelley's 1818 novel. More recent examples of electronic literature dealing with issues germane to gender representation include Stephanie Strickland and Cynthia Lawson Jaramillo's *V:Vniverse* (2002) and Juliet Davis's *Pieces of Herself* (2006), among others.

In contrast to the longer tradition of electronic literature, mobile applications, or "apps," represent a relatively recent form of digital textuality (see MOBILE GAMES). Gender representation in apps seems to align more closely with that of mainstream media than with more progressive digital forms. Using the search terms "girl" and "boy" in the iTunes app store returns results that reinforce gender binaries and essentialist notions of "gendered" interests (most prominently, dress-up apps for "girl" and a game involving "goo" for "boy"). As with avatar creation and video game characters, gender representation in the development of mobile computing applications suggests a rigidity of gender definition that aligns with the representational tendencies of most popular culture and mainstream digital media.

Just as gender is a fluid category of identification, gender representation in digital environments continues to shift. Hacker communities and STEM (Science, Technology, Engineering, and Mathematics) initiatives have recently begun to acknowledge Ada Lovelace (1815–1852) as the first known computer programmer (see HISTORY OF COMPUTERS). Lovelace's collaborations with Charles Babbage on the difference engine have recently been the subject of increased attention and have led to developments such as the honoring of "Ada Lovelace Day," celebrated annually since 2009. This return to the nineteenth century might suggest a full circle return to the nineteenth-century association of Mary Shelley and technology; however, one might expect that as new technologies develop and others obsolesce, they will continue to be appropriated for gender play while corporate or mainstream uses will continue to reinforce those gender representations that are already culturally dominant.

■ See also CYBERFEMINISM, CYBORG AND POSTHUMAN, GENDER AND MEDIA USE, IDENTITY, RACE AND ETHNICITY

References and Further Reading

Beckett, Miles, Mesh Flinder, and Greg Goodfried. n.d. *LonelyGirl15*. http://lg15.com.
Day, Felicia, Jane Selle Morgan, and Kim Evey. n.d. *The Guild*. http://watchtheguild.com.
Downs, Edward, and Stacy L. Smith. 2010. "Keeping Abreast of Hypersexuality: A Video Game Character Content Analysis." *Sex Roles* 62:721–33.
Fleet Laboratories. n.d. "That's Vaginal." http://thatsvaginal.com/.

Haraway, Donna. 1985. "Manifesto for Cyborgs: Science, Technology, and Socialist Feminism in the 1980s." *Socialist Review* 80:65–108.

Hayles, N. Katherine. 1999. *How We Became Posthuman: Virtual Bodies in Cybernetics, Literature, and Informatics.* Chicago: University of Chicago Press.

Henderson, Danielle. n.d. *Feminist Ryan Gosling.* http://feministryangosling.tumblr.com.

Jackson, Shelley. 1995. *Patchwork Girl.* Watertown, MA: Eastgate Systems.

Linden Labs. n.d. Second Life. http://secondlife.com.

Procter and Gamble. n.d. "The Man Your Man Could Smell Like." www.oldspice.com/videos/video/22/the-man-your-man-could-smell-like/.

Glitch Aesthetics
Lori Emerson

Glitch was first used in the early 1960s to describe either a change in voltage in an electrical circuit or any kind of interference in a television picture. By the 1990s, *glitch* broadly described brief bursts of unexpected behavior in electrical circuits, but it also more specifically was used to describe a style of electronic music that was created from already-malfunctioning audio technology (or from causing technology to malfunction) as a way to explore the life of the digital machine and as a reaction against the push in the computing industry to create an ever more clean, noise-free sound. The term has since been appropriated by musicians, gamers, artists, and designers as a name for what Olga Goriunova and Alexei Shulgin call a "genuine software aesthetics" (2008, 111) (see DIGITAL AND NET ART, GAMEPLAY). Glitch aesthetics, then, involves experimentation with the visible results of provoked or unprovoked computer error. (Such glitches could include aestheticizing the visible results of a virus or even provoking the computer to take on a virus in order to explore its underlying workings; see VIRAL AESTHETICS.)

Its relation, then, to an aesthetics of failure and to the embrace of chance means that glitch aesthetics clearly finds its roots in early twentieth-century avant-garde experiments in art, writing, theater, and music. These experiments on the one hand sought to disrupt the status quo that was supposedly maintained by tranquil, harmonious art, and on the other hand they reflected a search for a new realism—one that represented the noise and chaos of a rapidly industrializing world. Luigi Russolo, for example, wrote the futurist manifesto "The Art of Noises" in 1913, in which he declares that "today music, as it becomes continually more complicated, strives to amalgamate the most dissonant, strange and harsh sounds. . . . This musical evolution is paralleled by the multiplication of machines, which collaborate with man on every front. Not only in the roaring atmosphere of major cities, but in the country too, which until yesterday was totally silent, the machine today has created such a variety and rivalry of noises that pure sound . . . no longer arouses any feeling." Russolo believed, then, that noise—random, dissonant, machine-based sounds as opposed to what he called "pure sound"—was fast becoming the only way to experience the world anew.

Glitch aesthetics also finds its roots in early twentieth-century Dada experiments to escape the outdated notion of the romantic, individual genius whose art and writing were seen to be driven by a singular, self-reliant author with a clear intent. Dadaists such as Tristan Tzara attempted to open writing and art to the chaos and unpredictability of everyday life by, for example, advocating in "To Make a Dadaist Poem" that we cut up words from a newspaper article, randomly draw these words from a hat, and copy them "conscientiously in the order in which they left the bag." It was an attempt to redefine the role of the artist/writer by taking away authorial control and seeking to move away from the egotism of the individual romantic genius. Moreover, it was also an attempt to redefine the nature of an aesthetic object. If a poem could consist of randomly chosen words and if, as Marcel Duchamp demonstrated with his ready-mades, a sculpture could consist of a urinal turned upside down or a bicycle wheel affixed to a stool, then a whole range of traditionally unbeautiful, everyday objects and sounds are available as art.

Glitch, then, takes this radical shift in what counts as an aesthetic object or aesthetic experience, as well as what counts as an author, and asserts that its disruptiveness (in that a glitch constitutes a moment of dysfunctionality in the computer system) defamiliarizes the slick surface of the hardware/software of the computer and so ideally transforms us into critically minded observers of the underlying workings of the computer. As Goriunova and Shulgin put it, "A glitch is a mess that is a moment, a possibility to glance at software's inner structure. . . . Although a glitch does not reveal the true functionality of the computer, it shows the ghostly conventionality of the forms by which digital spaces are organized" (2008, 114). Moreover, the computer itself becomes an author, and we are readers or observers of its aesthetic effects.

One of the best-known creators of glitch art and games is the Dutch-Belgian collective Jodi (whose members are Joan Heemskerk and Dirk Paesmans). Since the mid-1990s, Jodi has, as they put it in a 1997 interview, battled "with the computer on a graphical level. The computer presents itself as a desktop, with a trash can on the right and pull down menus and all the system icons. We explore the computer from inside, and mirror this on the net. When a viewer looks at our work, we are inside his computer" (*Chicago Art Magazine* 2011). For example, their 1996 "untitled game" is a modification of the old video game *Quake* such that its architecture no longer functions according to the conventions of gameplay; one way they do this is by exploiting a glitch that is provoked every time the *Quake* software attempts to visualize the cube's black-and-white-checked wallpaper, causing the player to become entrapped in a cube ("untitled game"). In opposition to the computing industry's attempt to naturalize the interface to the point of invisibility, Jodi makes the interface confusing, unfamiliar, uncomfortable, and malfunctioning.

While *glitch* is rarely used to describe electronic literature, the way in which it is commonly used by musicians, gamers, artists, and designers to describe an artistic practice of experimenting with and even aestheticizing the visible results of computer error makes it a relevant framework for understanding a whole range of early and contemporary works of difficult e-literature (see DIGITAL POETRY, ELECTRONIC LITERATURE). One of the earliest works of digital literature glitch is William Gibson's infamous *Agrippa (a book of the dead)*, which was published in 1992 as a collaborative effort between Gibson, book artist Dennis Ashbaugh, and publisher Kevin Begos Jr. *Agrippa* was packaged as a black box that, once opened, reveals both a hologram of a circuit board on the underside of the lid and inside the box a book inside of which is nested a 3.5″ floppy disk that is programmed to encrypt itself after it is used just once; not surprisingly, once exposed to light, the words and images on the pages of the book also fade altogether.

Finally, it is worth emphasizing that glitches may be provoked or unprovoked. In addition to Jodi's provoked glitch described above, glitch artist Jeff Donaldson writes that one might also provoke a glitch by sending "an audio signal through video input" or by "opening image files in word processing applications. JPGS become text, which can then be randomly edited and saved again as images to be displayed through the filter of co-decs." An unprovoked glitch, then, captures a moment in which an error in the computer system is made visible; it therefore exploits randomness and chance as a way to disrupt the digital ideal of a clean, frictionless, error-free environment in which the computer supposedly fades into the background while we, as creators or workers, effortlessly produce without any attention to the ways in which the computer (or software) determines what and how we produce. As Donaldson puts it, "It is chance made manifest and a spontaneous reordering of data, like the wave function collapse of quantum theory. In its pure, wild sense, a glitch is the ghost in the machine, the other side of intention, a form that is hidden until it manifests itself of its own accord."

■ See also HACKER, INTERFACE, PRESERVATION, RANDOMNESS, SOFTWARE STUDIES

References and Further Reading

Amerika, Mark. n.d. "Museum of Glitch Aesthetics." www.glitchmuseum.com.

Chicago Art Magazine. 2011. "Nick Briz Explains the Glitch-Art Methods of JODI." http://chicago artmagazine.com/2011/09/nick-briz-explains-the-glitch-art-methods-of-jodi/.

Donaldson, Jeffrey. n.d. "Glossing over Thoughts on Glitch. A Poetry of Error." *Artpulse Magazine.* http://artpulsemagazine.com/glossing-over-thoughts-on-glitch-a-poetry-of-error.

Gibson, William. 1992. *Agrippa: a book of the dead.* New York: Kevin Begos.

"Glitch." *Wikipedia.* http://en.wikipedia.org/wiki/Glitch.

Goriunova, Olga, and Alexei Shulgin. 2008. "Glitch." In *Software Studies: A Lexicon,* edited by Matthew Fuller, 110–119. Cambridge, MA: MIT Press.

"jodi." okno.be. http://memoir.okno.be/?id=886.

jodi.org. www.jodi.org/.

Krapp, Peter. 2011. *Noise Channels: Glitch and Error in Digital Culture.* Minneapolis: University of Minnesota Press.

Moradi, Iman, Ant Scott, Joe Gilmore, and Christopher Murphy, eds. 2009. *Glitch: Designing Imperfection.* New York: Mark Batty.

Russolo, Luigi. 1913. "The Art of Noises." www.unknown.nu/futurism/noises.html.

Tzara, Tristan. n.d. "To Make a Dadaist Poem." www.writing.upenn.edu/~afilreis/88v/tzara.html.

"Untitled Game." n.d. jodi.org. www.untitled-game.org/.

Graph Theory
Marie-Laure Ryan

A graph is a spatial figure created by connecting points, known as vertices or nodes, through lines known as edges, links, or arcs. Graph theory (a branch of mathematics) is concerned with the formal properties of graphs and with their use to solve topological problems. The eighteenth-century mathematician Leonhard Euler's drawing of a graph to solve the problem of the seven bridges of Koenigsberg (which asks whether it is possible to cross them all just once and to return to one's starting point) is widely considered the first contribution to graph theory (Tucker 1980). The practical application of graphs to model how pairs of elements are related by some property spans multiple disciplines: computer science, linguistics, business, chemistry, physics, biology, cognitive science, sociology, semiotics, and even literature (Moretti 2005), especially narratology (Ryan 2007).

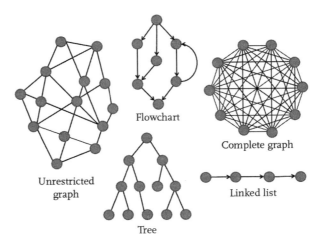

Flowchart

Complete graph

Unrestricted
graph

Linked list

Tree

From a formal point of view graphs can be classified into several categories. Here is a sample of configurations particularly relevant to digital media. Some are formal objects studied by graph theory; others (the linked list and the flowchart) are important special cases of these formal objects.

The *tree* is a hierarchical configuration dominated by a designated node called the root. This root has a number of outgoing links to "children," but no incoming link from a "parent" node. The middle nodes have one parent and any number of children. The terminal nodes, or leaves, have a parent but no children. The distinctive property of the tree is that it allows no circuits: each node can be reached by only one route. If the links are bidirectional, every node can function as a root node: to see this, try hanging the tree by a different node.

The *linked list* (a very thin tree) is a linear configuration with a starting node, an end node, and middle nodes connected to their neighbors by no more than one incoming and one outgoing link.

The *unrestricted graph*, or network, allows nodes to have any number of both incoming and outgoing links. It has consequently no root node, and since it allows circuits, its nodes can be reached through several different paths. In contrast to the linked list and the tree, some links can be removed without breaking up the structure. When all these links have been removed, the remaining graph is a "spanning tree."

The *complete graph* is a network in which every node is connected to every other node.

The *flowchart*, another type of network, is a directed graph whose links can be followed in only one direction. In contrast to unrestricted graphs, it has a specific beginning and end node. In contrast to trees, it allows branches to both split and merge, and it allows circuits, thus making it possible to reach the end state (as well as intermediary states) by different routes. Flowcharts are typically used to represent algorithms consisting of a sequence of steps.

Computer science makes heavy use of data structured as one of these five types of graph. Linked lists are a common type of database, but they present the disadvantage that in order to locate information, it is necessary to inspect every node until a match is found (see DATABASE). In the worst case, it will take n comparisons to find a match for a list of n elements. By contrast, when a database is structured as a binary tree (i.e., a tree with exactly two children per node), it takes no more than $\log_2(n + 1) - 1$ probes to find information in a tree with *n* nodes. It is also by means of tree-shaped diagrams that compilers check the syntax of computer programs, in the same way Chomskyan transformational-generative grammar models the syntactic structures of natural languages. Flowcharts are widely used to represent the steps of algorithms, and graphs with circuits are the preferred organization of computer networks, because when one of the nodes becomes disabled, it remains possible to route the information through a different path (see ALGO-RITHM). Such rerouting would be impossible with a tree or linked list. As a data structure, networks can show a greater variety of relations between their elements than trees, but they are harder to search (see SEARCH).

The contrast between trees and networks lies at the core of Gilles Deleuze and Félix Guattari's influential concept of the rhizome, which they regard as a superior form of culture, social organization, and mode of thinking. What Deleuze and Guattari call rhizome is actually a complete graph, as we can tell by this principle, which, incidentally, is not found in the rhizomes of the plant world, no matter how tangled they appear: "unlike trees or their roots, the rhizome connects any point to any other point" (1987, 21). Yet another of the properties that they attribute to rhizomes is clearly inspired by plant anatomy: "a rhizome may be broken, but it will start up again on one of its old lines, or on new lines." While the rhizome is celebrated by Deleuze and Guattari as a nonhierarchical and nonlinear configuration capable of endless regeneration, fluid transformation, and creative expansion, the tree functions in their vision as the villain of Western thought: as Dan Clinton writes, "the tree comes to symbolize the distinction between subject and object, between signifier and signified, encompassing the whole of dualistic logic through its branching patterns, through its definitions of set pathways between root and branch" (2003). The tree corresponds indeed to the traditional form of thinking and writing that is (or was?) hammered into our heads by high school teachers: when they told us to organize the topic of our essays into subtopics, themselves divided into sub-subtopics whose discussion must be concluded before moving on to the next point, they encouraged us to mold our thinking into a recursive arborescent pattern that prohibits digressions or the classification of ideas under multiple headings, for fear of creating loops forcing the reader to go back. While the tree involves a disciplined organization of thought, the rhizome stands for how the mind operates "naturally," that is, for the free associations of spontaneous thinking. Being less constrained than the tree, the rhizome is believed by its proponents to be more conducive to creativity. Yet the opposition rhizome/tree as "good" versus "bad" mode of thinking and writing remains captive of the dualistic logic that the concept of rhizome is supposed to overcome.

The five types of graph listed above provide useful tools for the description of the basic architecture of interactive texts, whether print or digital (Phelps [1996] 1998; Ryan 2006) (see INTERACTIVE NARRATIVE, INTERACTIVITY).

The linked list corresponds to the zero degree of interactivity. It is represented by those linear texts that must be read in a rigidly prescribed sequential order and offer no choice to the reader.

Tree diagrams have special affinities with stories, because they are particularly efficient at modeling those moments in life when people face decisions that will affect their entire future; the fateful, irreversible character of these decisions corresponds to the fact that once branches split from each other, they never merge again. This property of trees makes them the preferred structure for the branched narratives of the so-called Choose Your Own Adventure stories. Because there is only one path from the root node to any end node, the author can offer choices to the reader while maintaining control over the sequence of events, a control that guarantees narrative coherence. The main drawback of the tree as a model of interactive storytelling is its exponential growth: it would take sixteen different plots, with thirty-one different fragments, to tell a story with four decision points. Another frequent use of trees in digital texts is the structure of a typical website: the home page, or entry point, functions as the root, while the various choices on the menu displayed on the home page correspond to the branches. The tree structure may, however, only appear on the level of the relation between the home page and its immediate children pages: when the original menu remains available after the user has made a choice, this means that the children are interlinked by a network.

The textual implementation of the network is hypertext, a mode of organization found on both the level of the World Wide Web as a whole and the level of individual documents (see HYPERTEXTUALITY). As a model of the user's progression through the text, the network relinquishes the authorial control that makes the tree such an efficient, though limited, model of narrative coherence. The network, as already stated, has no root or leaves, and consequently no beginning or ending; its loops, moreover, allow users to visit the same node many times, and to reach it from different directions. These features are not good for narrative, a type of meaning crucially dependent on a fixed causal and chronological sequence, but they open the door to a new aesthetics, based on a different form of organization (see NONLINEAR WRITING). Roland Barthes's description of the "writerly" is widely regarded as the expression of this network aesthetics: "Let us first posit the image of a triumphant plural, unimpoverished by any constraint of representation (of imitation). In this ideal text, the networks are many and interact, without any one of them being able to surpass the rest; this text is a galaxy of signifiers, not a structure of signifieds; it has no beginning; it is reversible; we gain access to it by several entrances, none of which can be authoritatively declared to be the main one" (1974, 5–6). This shimmering plurality of meaning comes, however, at a price: as Barthes observes, "for the plural text, there cannot be a narrative structure, a grammar or a logic; thus, if one or another of these are sometimes permitted to come forward, it is *in proportion* (giving this expression its full quantitative value) as we are dealing with incompletely plural texts, texts whose plural is more or less parsimonious" (1974, 6). If hypertext remains capable of telling stories, then, it is because it can include stretches of low connectivity, stretches that offer no choices to the reader. It is during these stretches that basic sequences of events—a condition of narrativity—can be established.

Now consider a text modeled on a complete graph. The best-known example of this configuration is Marc Saporta's novel *Composition No. 1* (1961), which was printed on a deck of cards and produced a different sequence of discourse with every reshuffling. Since the text can start with any card, and any card can succeed any other card, the author has no control whatsoever over sequence, and the reader has no reason to choose one path rather than another. The question, of course, is whether the total randomness of the system can really produce anything worth calling meaning (see RANDOMNESS). It certainly cannot create narrative meaning, because narrativity is based on an asymmetric relation between cause and effect (see NARRATIVITY). In a text modeled on a complete graph the effect can precede as well as follow the cause.

The most efficient compromise between breadth of choice and narrative coherence comes from the flowchart. While the directionality of the flowchart models the temporal progression of narrative, the possibility to merge distinct strands protects the system from the combinatory explosion of trees. But the merging of strands also means that the choices taken at the forking points have no definitive consequences, since characters can arrive at the same state through different routes. This type of graph is very efficient at representing the structure of computer games where players can solve problems and reach the next level through different sequences of actions (see GAME GENRES). Every level of a game, typically, will correspond to a different flowchart. But when the actions of the player determine one of many possible endings, in other words, when they have definitive and unique consequences, the flowchart must tail off as a tree.

■ See also LINKING STRATEGIES, PLOT TYPES AND INTERACTIVITY, SPATIALITY OF DIGITAL MEDIA

References and Further Reading

Barthes, Roland. 1974. *S/Z*. Translated by Richard Miller. New York: Farrar, Strauss and Giroux.
Clinton, Dan. 2003. Annotation to "Rhizome." In *A Thousand Plateaus*. http://csmt.uchicago.edu /annotations/deleuzerhizome.htm.
Deleuze, Gilles, and Félix Guattari. 1987. *A Thousand Plateaus: Capitalism and Schizophrenia*. Translated by Brian Massumi. Minneapolis: University of Minnesota Press.
Landow, George. 1997. *Hypertext 2.0*. Baltimore: Johns Hopkins University Press.
Moretti, Franco. 2005. *Graphs, Maps, Trees: Abstract Models for a Literary Theory*. London: Verso.
Phelps, Katherine. (1996) 1998. "Story Shapes for Digital Media." www.glasswings.com.au/mod ern/shapes/.
Ryan, Marie-Laure. 2006. *Avatars of Story*. Minneapolis: University of Minnesota Press.
———. 2007. "Diagramming Narrative." *Semiotica* 165 (1–4): 11–40.
Saporta, Marc. 1961. *Composition No. 1*. Paris: Seuil.
Tucker, Alan. 1980. *Applied Combinatorics*. New York: John Wiley.

Graphic Realism
Rune Klevjer

Graphic realism refers to animated computer-generated imagery that is designed to appear as visually indistinguishable from physical reality as possible. Today, the notion of "realistic graphics" is primarily used with reference to computer games and other real-time navigable 3D environments, as well as to computer-animated film and digital effects. In 3D computer animation, realistic imagery is achieved through geometric modeling of 3D shapes and surfaces; lifelike character animation; simulation of the behaviors of vegetation, water, cloth, and so on; and rendering techniques that capture how light interacts dynamically with surfaces and textures.

Key innovations of 3D computer modeling and animation were developed during the 1970s and 1980s, but it was landmark Hollywood films *Terminator 2: Judgment Day* (1991) and *Jurassic Park* (1993) that introduced the capabilities of realistic 3D graphics to a broad audience. Pixar's *Toy Story* (1995) established a new format of fully computer-animated feature film. Around the same time, personal computers became powerful enough to be able to do real-time rendering of textured 3D graphics, demonstrated by successful computer games such as *Wing Commander* (1990), *Ultima Underworld* (1991), and *DOOM* (1993). *Quake* (1996) was the first game to render a fully polygon-modeled 3D space in real time. The game was also the first to support 3D hardware acceleration, which was followed by a 3D graphics card arms race on the PC market, driven by ever-higher promises and expectations of visual realism.

The standard of graphic realism in PC and console games saw extraordinary rapid development during the years from *DOOM* continuing up to the introduction of the seventh generation of home consoles in 2005–2006 (Xbox 360, Playstation 3, Nintendo Wii), after which point the pace has been slowing down. Today, the quest for more realistic visuals is facing diminishing returns both technologically and in terms of market appeal, corresponding with a general diversification of gaming platforms, formats, and markets. However, graphic realism is still important in the public imagination; it remains at the core of a common teleological understanding of computer game history, and it also informs public debates on games and violence.

In theoretical terms, graphic realism is independent of semantic notions of realism. The characters, events, and settings depicted in, for example, *Monster's Inc.* (2001) are highly improbable and fantastic, yet they look real. Stephen Prince suggests the term *perceptual realism* for this phenomenon. Even if (or precisely because) aliens and monsters "lack reference to any category of being existing outside the fiction" (1996, 32), computer-animated films and special effects specialize in making them appear convincingly real. In their discussion of the concept of "presence" in visual media, Matthew Lombard and Theresa Ditton employ a similar although less specific concept, suggesting that, for example, science fiction may be "low in social realism but high in perceptual realism because although the events portrayed are unlikely, the objects and people in the program look and sound as one would expect if they did in fact exist" (1997, 2). Following Torben Kragh Grodal, we may say that the opposite of "realistic" in this case would not be the fantastic, but the abstract (2009, 252).

As Lev Manovich points out, realistic computer-animated imagery is quintessentially *photorealistic* in nature: "For what is faked is, of course, not reality but photographic reality, reality as seen by the camera lens. In other words, what computer graphics have (almost) achieved is not realism, but rather only photorealism—the ability to fake not our perceptual and bodily experience of reality but only its photographic image" (2001, 200). This simulation of a "reality as seen by the camera lens" is the defining feature of graphical realism. Animated 3D models are being rendered as a 2D image, in a process that simulates the way in which light is being projected through a camera lens. In computer games, this process is taking place in real time, as the player navigates a 3D environment through the virtual camera. In games as well as in computer-animated films, specific camera effects will usually be added in order to heighten cinematographic realism: lens reflections, motion blur, and shallow depth of focus.

Broadly in line with the critique introduced by Jean-Louis Baudry (1986) and other exponents of so-called apparatus theory, Stephen Prince (1996) and David Surman (2003) argue that the classic idea of "realism" in film—famously articulated in Bazin's maxim: "The photographic image is the object itself" (1967, 14)—has been undermined and invalidated by the blatant artifice and nonindexicality of photorealistic 3D graphics. The new digital technology, they argue, demonstrates that realism is a perceptual trick, a *language* of human interpretation, aimed at creating a culturally accepted correspondence between a set of perceptual cues and the viewers' experience of the real world.

There is a sense, however, in which the pseudo-indexicality and apparent transparency of computer-generated 3D imagery have a real basis, in a way that a photorealist painting does not. There *is*, after all, behind the image, as it were, an algorithmically constructed 3D synthetic environment, big or small, which is projected onto a screen, as if filmed by a physical camera. In the live-action variant of 3D computer-animated film, there is also another important indexical relationship, between the performance-captured model and the actors' physical performance.

The notion of photorealism is ambiguous with respect to the simulation of live-action cinematographic images. Live-action realism is achieved through motion-capture or performance-capture animation (facial animation being a particular challenge) and through complex simulations of natural surfaces like skin or fur. The first fully animated film dedicated to live-action realism was *Final Fantasy: Spirits Within* (2001), but the definitive breakthrough of the form in Hollywood was no doubt Andy Serkis's *Gollum* in Peter Jackson's *The Lord of the Rings* trilogy (2001–2003). In contrast, films like *Toy Story*, as well as computer games like the hugely successful *Lego Star Wars* (2005), depict artificial-looking worlds that do not aim to look like live-action imagery. In his thesis on perceptual realism in computer animation, David Surman (2003) refers to the latter type as "*stylised realism*," reserving the term *photorealism* for the live-action variant. This also seems to reflect common usage elsewhere.

However, stylized variants like *Toy Story* nevertheless do depict worlds as perceived through a camera lens—in telling contrast to so-called non-photorealistic rendering, found in video games like *Okami* (2006), which explicitly aims to look like something that is drawn or painted rather than something that is photographed. We could say that toy or Lego worlds are perceptually photorealistic but do not aspire to perceptual *naturalism*. Rather than simulating the look of organic bodies and lifelike human characters in natural environments, non-naturalistic photorealism simulates a world made of wood and plastic, magically come to life in front of a traveling camera.

The idea that there is an inherent conflict between "graphics" and "gameplay" is a long-established trope in computer game discourses. Legendary game designer Chris Crawford is a well-known critic of big-budget graphic realism, arguing that graphics and animation (as well as sound and music) are cosmetic factors, diverting resources away from the design of interesting interactive experiences, which should be the core business of game development (Crawford 2004). His position echoes the widely held view in the games community that the quest for photorealism leads to artistic stagnation and stifles stylistic expression. A related criticism is Salen and Zimmerman's assertion of *the immersive fallacy*: "the idea that the pleasure of a media experience lies in its ability to sensually transport the participant into an illusory, simulated reality." They claim that this ideal "misrepresents the diverse palette of experiences games offer," and that it also contradicts "the many-layered state of mind" that is inherent to the nature of play (2004, 450–455).

Salen and Zimmerman's warning draws attention to the particular immersive quality of digital cinematographic realism; as viewers or players we are invited to look into, or jump into, a seemingly self-contained and autonomous reality. We may indeed see this as a perceptual parallel to the way in which a literary text, according to Marie-Laure Ryan, presents its reader with "a backside to objects, a mind to characters, and time and space extending beyond the display" (2001, 158). In computer games and other real-time 3D environments, however, immersive perceptual realism is not a matter of *looking* as opposed to *acting*, or "visuals" as opposed to interactivity, but is integral to how the player experiences embodied presence within game space, via the navigable "camera-body" (Rehak 2003, 109). In a phenomenological perspective, as offered by, among others, Ryan (2001, 52–66), Wilhelmsson (2006), and Klevjer (2012), this kind of virtual embodiment is constituted through a unity of action and perception, in a way that makes it hard to say where "graphics" ends and "interactivity" begins.

References and Further Reading

Baudry, Jean-Louis. 1986. "Ideological Effects of the Basic Cinematographic Apparatus." In *Narrative, Apparatus, Ideology: A Film Theory Reader*, edited by Philip Rosen, 286–298. New York: Columbia University Press.

Bazin, André. 1967. "The Ontology of the Photographic Image." In *What Is Cinema?*, edited by Hugh Gray, 9–16. Los Angeles: University of California Press.

Crawford, Chris. 2004. "Ga-Ga over Graphics." *Works and Days* 22 (43/44). www.worksanddays.net /2004/File13.Crawford_File13.Crawford.pdf.

Grodal, Torben Kragh. 2009. *Embodied Visions: Evolution, Emotion, Culture, and Film*. Oxford: Oxford University Press.

Klevjer, Rune. 2012. "Enter the Avatar: The Phenomenology of Prosthetic Telepresence in Computer Games." In *The Philosophy of Computer Games*, edited by Hallvard Fossheim, Tarjei Mandt Larsen, and John Richard Sageng. London: Springer.

Lombard, Matthew, and Theresa Ditton. 1997. "At the Heart of It All: The Concept of Presence." *Journal of Computer-Mediated Communication* 3 (2). http://jcmc.indiana.edu/vol3/issue2/lombard.html.

Manovich, Lev. 2001. *The Language of New Media*. Cambridge, MA: MIT Press.

Prince, Stephen. 1996. "True Lies: Perceptual Realism, Digital Images, and Film Theory." *Film Quarterly* 49 (3): 27–38.

Rehak, Bob. 2003. "Playing at Being: Psychoanalysis and the Avatar." In *The Video Game Theory Reader*, edited by Mark J. P. Wolf and Bernard Perron, 103–127. London: Routledge.

Ryan, Marie-Laure. 2001. *Narrative as Virtual Reality: Immersion and Interactivity in Literature and Electronic Media*. Baltimore: Johns Hopkins University Press.

Salen, Katie, and Eric Zimmerman. 2004. *Rules of Play: Game Design Fundamentals*. Cambridge, MA: MIT Press.

Surman, David. 2003. "CGI Animation: Pseudorealism, Perception and Possible Worlds." MA thesis, University of Wales, Newport.

Wilhelmsson, Ulf. 2006. "Computer Games as Playground and Stage." In *Proceedings of the 2006 International Conference on Game Research and Development*. Perth, Australia: Murdoch University.

H

··

Hacker

E. Gabriella Coleman

Hackers—they seem to be everywhere, landing headlines in the news, founding companies in Silicon Valley and hacker spaces around the world, and, at times, facing years in jail. Despite this presence, they are everywhere misunderstood. Generally, a hacker is a technologist with a penchant for computing, and a hack is a clever technical solution arrived at through nonobvious means (Levy 1984; Turkle 2005). It is telling that a hack, as defined by *The Hacker Jargon File*, can mean the complete opposite of an ingenious intervention: a clunky, ugly fix, which nevertheless completes the job at hand. Among hackers, the term is often worn as a badge of honor. In the popular press, however, the connotations of *hacker* are often negative, or at minimum refer to illegal intrusion of computer systems. These differences point to the various meanings and multiple histories associated with the terms *hacker* and *hacking*.

Hackers, especially in the West, tend to uphold a cluster of values: freedom, privacy, and access. They adore computers and networks. They are trained in the specialized—and economically lucrative—technical arts of programming, system/network administration, and security research. Some gain unauthorized access to technologies (though much of hacking is legal). Foremost, hacking, in its distinct incarnations, embodies an aesthetic where craftsmanship and craftiness converge; hackers value playfulness, pranking, and cleverness and will frequently display their wit through source code, humor, or both. But once one confronts hacking historically and sociologically, this shared plane melts into a sea of differences that have, until recently, been overlooked (with a few exceptions) in the literature on hacking (Coleman and Golub 2008; Jordan 2008).

The term *hacker* was first used consistently in the 1960s among technologists at MIT whose lives maniacally revolved around making, using, and improving computer software—a preoccupation that Steven Levy dubbed "a daring symbiosis between man and machine" in his engaging and exhaustive account *Hackers: Heroes of the Computer Revolution* (1984, 39). Levy unbundled the groups' unstated ethical codes from their passionate, everyday collective pursuits and conceptualized them as "the hacker ethic," shorthand for a mix of aesthetic and pragmatic imperatives that included commitment to information freedom, mistrust of authority, heightened dedication to meritocracy, and the firm belief that computers can be the basis for beauty and a better world (1984, 39–46). Levy's book not only represented what had been, at the time, an esoteric community but also inspired others to identify with the moniker "hacker" and its ethical principles.

By the 1980s, many other technologists routinely deployed the term *hacker*, individuals enthralled with tinkering and technical spelunking but whose history and politics were distinct from those chronicled by Levy. Sometimes referred to as the "hacker underground," the story goes that they arose in the 1980s, sullying what had been a pristine and legal tradition. What is often overlooked is their history: their heirs are the phone phreaks who existed at the same time as the first crop of university hackers in the late 1950s and early 1960s. These phreaks, as they were eventually known, tapped into the phone system to make free phone calls, explored "The System," and found each other on phone conferences, also known as party lines (Sterling 1992; Rosenbaum 1971; Thomas 2002; Lapsley 2013).

The end of the analog phone network after the divestiture of "Ma Bell" heralded the end of the golden age of phreaking, which was largely replaced with the exploration of computer networks. The marriage between phreaking and computer hacking was represented in the popular e-zine *Phrack*, first published in 1985 on bulletin board systems, where hackers of all kinds congregated (Scott 2005; Sterling 1992; Thomas 2002). Hackers published prolifically in diverse genres, including manifestos (most famously "The Conscience of a Hacker"), textfiles (written in sparse ASCII text but often filled with ASCII art and audaciously worded content), and zines (such as *Hack-Tic* in the Netherlands and *2600* in the United States). Although many of these underground hackers engaged in technical exploration, often scouting for security vulnerabilities, they also sought forbidden fruit, and their actions included mockery, spectacle, and transgression—a politics and ethics distinct from the university hackers of MIT, Carnegie Mellon, and Stanford (although there was plenty of pranking and irreverence among these hackers as well, and some individuals participated in both domains).

The canonical narrative identifying MIT as hacking's first homeland—a place where the hacker ethic was born—is complicated when we account for other traditions such as phreaking, which existed independently of university-based hacker communities, shaped a subversive tradition that went as far back as the 1960s, and flourished more publicly in the 1980s and 1990s, only to change with the rise of the security industry and new laws criminalizing computer break-ins. Instead of locating a single point of origin for hacking, we should be attentive to multiple origins, distinct lineages, and variable ethics.

By the late 1980s, although various instances of hacking existed, this more subversive tradition became *the* public face of hacking, cemented, and sometimes distorted by, media accounts. Laws, such as the Computer Fraud and Abuse Act, enacted in the United States in 1986, became the weapon of choice to prosecute hackers. Since then, the U.S. government has tended to criminalize hacking under all circumstances, unwilling to differentiate between criminal activities, playful pursuits, and political causes.

Some hackers, concerned by the illicit actions of other hackers and negative, sensationalist media portrayals, started to call those who hacked for illegal or malicious purposes "crackers" (Nissenbaum 2004). The use of "cracker" was a linguistic attempt to reclaim and sanitize "hacker." Unsurprisingly, many hackers also questioned the term. As more automation tools became available, many also started to use the derogatory terms "script kiddies" to designate those who use scripts to circumvent computer security or deface websites, rather than finding a unique compromise. It is a scornful term (no one would elect to self-designate as such) that demarcates boundaries, signals inappropriate behavior, and gives voice to the value placed on ingenuity, inventiveness, and self-sufficiency.

To this day, debate rages among technologists: who deserves the title of "hacker"? What constitutes its parameters? Some readily accept variability, while others starkly demarcate borders. When asked, most can fire off precise definitions. When interviewed, two hackers distinguished between *builders*—often found in free and open-source communities, whose lineage goes back to the university communities explored in Levy—and *breakers* with whom these hackers identify. They define breakers as follows:

DI. I call myself a hacker, what I mean is that I apply creativity and technical knowledge to bypassing defenses.

DA. Yeah I've heard "obtaining lower level understanding of a system to bypass systems" . . . which is a reasonable definition.

As this example demonstrates, to hackers themselves, "to hack" can thus mean distinct activities, from improving the open-source Linux operating system to finding vulnerabilities and "fuzzing" for exploits. Some distinctions are subtle, while others are profound enough to warrant thinking about hacking in terms of genres with distinct aesthetics and histories (Coleman and Golub 2008). Free and open-source hackers—those who have used legal means to guarantee perpetual access to source code—tend to uphold political structures of transparency (Coleman 2012a). In contrast, the hacker underground is more opaque in its social organization (Thomas 2002). These hackers have made secrecy and spectacle into a high art form (Coleman 2012c). For decades in Europe, artistic practice has been marshaled for the sake of hackings (Bazzichelli 2008; Deseriis and Marano 2008). Hardware hacking has also been part of hacking for a long time. Historically, its most notable manifestation was among the Homebrew hackers of the Bay Area who hacked one of the first personal computer kits, the MITS Altair 8800, and helped fuel a nascent personal computer industry. Today, hardware hacking is exploding, buoyed by the spread of hack spaces—physical workshops filled with tools and computers—across North America and Europe but also in Latin America and China. Though in its infancy, biohacking is on the rise, with physical labs being a key locus of activity (Delfanti 2013).

Some hackers run vibrant political collectives whose names, such as Riseup and Mayfirst, unabashedly broadcast their technical crusade to make this world a better one (Juris 2008; Milberry 2012). Other politically minded hackers have gravitated toward Anonymous—an umbrella term for a range of distinct and often-unconnected digital operations—to engage in hacking for the sake of leaking sensitive corporate and government information (Coleman 2012b), extending a longer tradition in hacktivism (Jordan and Taylor 2004). Others—for example, many "infosec" (information security) hackers—are first and foremost committed to security and tend to steer clear of defining their actions in such overtly political terms, even if hacking tends to creep into political territory. Among those in the infosec community there are differences as to whether one should release a security vulnerability (often called full disclosure) or announce its existence without revealing details (referred to as antidisclosure). A smaller, more extreme movement known as anti-sec is vehemently against any disclosure, claiming that it is their "goal that, through mayhem and the destruction of all exploitative and detrimental communities, companies, and individuals, full-disclosure will be abandoned and the security industry will be forced to reform" (Anti-sec_manifesto.png, n.d.).

National and regional differences also make their mark. Southern European hackers have articulated a more leftist, anarchist commitment than their northern European counterparts. Recently, nationalistic hacking—though virtually unexplored by scholars—has spread (Karatzogianni [2006] is an important exception). Pakistani hackers are routinely at war with their Indian neighbors. Chinese hackers are quite nationalistic in their aims and aspirations (Henderson 2007), in contrast to those in North America, Latin America, and Europe, whose antiauthoritarian stance makes many—though certainly not all—wary of joining government endeavors.

It would be a mistake to treat different types of hacking as cultural cocoons. By the 1990s, hackers of all stripes met during annual hacker "cons" (Coleman 2010), and the number of conferences multiplies each year. Technical architectures, the language of codes, and protocols bring together different types of hackers and activities. For instance, as it was developed over the past four decades, the Unix Operating System has worked to bind thousands of hackers together as part of what Chris Kelty calls a "recursive public" (2008). While we can say that hacker action and ethical principles share a common core or general ethos, inquiry demonstrates that we can identify variance and even serious points of contention. Given the multifaceted, rich, and often-controversial political effects engendered by hackers, from the creation of new licensing regimes to exposing the abuses of the surveillance state (Himanen 2001; Söderberg 2008; Wark 2004) and its historical dynamism, it is imperative to keep the variations and full diversity of hacking at the forefront of our inquiries.

■ See also CYBERPUNK, FREE AND OPEN-SOURCE SOFTWARE, GLITCH AESTHETICS, HISTORY OF COMPUTERS, HOAXES, MASHUP, POLITICS AND NEW MEDIA, VIRAL AESTHETICS

References and Further Reading

Anti-sec_manifesto.png. n.d. https://upload.wikimedia.org/wikipedia/commons/b/b7/Anti-sec _manifesto.png.

Bazzichelli, Tatiana. 2008. *Networking: The Net as Artwork*. Aarhus: Digital Aesthetics Research Center. www.networkingart.eu/pdf/networking_bazzichelli.pdf.

Coleman, E. Gabriella. 2010. "The Hacker Conference: A Ritual Condensation and Celebration of a Lifeworld." *Anthropological Quarterly* 83 (1): 47–72.

———. 2012a. *Coding Freedom: The Ethics and Aesthetics of Hacking*. Princeton, NJ: Princeton University Press.

———. 2012b. "Our Weirdness Is Free: The Logic of Anonymous: Online Army, Agent of Chaos, and Seeker of Justice." *Triple Canopy*. http://canopycanopycanopy.com/15/our_weirdness_is _free.

———. 2012c. "Phreaks, Hackers, and Trolls and the Politics of Transgression and Spectacle." In *The Social Media Reader*, edited by Michael Mandiberg. New York: New York University Press.

Coleman, Gabriella, and Alex Golub. 2008. "Hacker Practice: Moral Genres and the Cultural Articulation of Liberalism." *Anthropological Theory* 8 (3): 255–277.

Delfanti, Alesandro. 2013. *Biohackers: The Politics of Open Science*. London: Pluto Press.

Deseriis, Marco, and G. Marano. 2008. *Net.Art: L'arte della Connessione* (Net.Art: The Art of Connecting). Milan: Shake.

Henderson, Scott. 2007. *The Dark Visitor: Inside the World of Chinese Hackers*. n.p.: Lulu.com.

Himanen, Pekka. 2001. *The Hacker Ethic and the Spirit of the Information Age*. New York: Random House.

Jordan, Tim. 2008. *Hacking: Digital Media and Technological Determinism*. Cambridge: Polity Press.

Jordan, Tim, and Paul Taylor. 2004. *Hacktivism and Cyberwars: Rebels with a Cause?* London: Routledge.

Juris, Jeff. 2008. *Networking Futures*. Durham, NC: Duke University Press.

Karatzogianni, Athina. 2006. *The Politics of Cyberconflict*. London: Routledge.

Kelty, Chris M. 2008. *Two Bits: The Cultural Significance of Free Software*. Durham, NC: Duke University Press.

Lapsley, Phil. 2013. *Exploding the Phone: The Untold Story of the Teenagers and Outlaws Who Hacked Ma Bell*. New York: Grove Press.

Levy, Steven. 1984. *Hackers: Heroes of the Computer Revolution*. New York: Delta.

Lindtner, Silvia, and David Li. 2012. "Created in China: The Makings of China's Hackerspace Community." *Interactions* 19 (6): 18–22.

Milberry, Kate. 2012. "Hacking for Social Justice: The Politics of Prefigurative Technology." In *(Re) Inventing the Internet: Critical Case Studies*, edited by Andrew Feenberg and Norm Friesen. Rotterdam: Sense.

Nissenbaum, Helen. 2004. "Hackers and the Contested Ontology of Cyberspace." *New Media and Society* 6 (2): 195–217.

Rosenbaum, Ron. 1971. "Secrets of the Little Blue Box." *Esquire Magazine*. http://www.las.ic.uni camp.br/~gabriel/pub/vigna/~vigna/courses/cs279/HW1/rosenbaum71_bluebox.pdf.

Scott, Jason. 2005. *BBS: The Documentary*. www.bbsdocumentary.com/.

Söderberg, Johan. 2008. *Hacking Capitalism: The Free and Open Source Software Movement*. London: Routledge.

Sterling, Bruce. 1992. *The Hacker Crackdown: Law and Disorder on the Electronic Frontier*. New York: Bantam.

Thomas, Douglas. 2002. *Hacker Culture*. Minneapolis: University of Minnesota Press.

Turkle, Sherry. 2005. *The Second Self: Computers and the Human Spirit*. Cambridge, MA: MIT Press.

Wark, McKenzie. 2004. *A Hacker Manifesto*. Cambridge, MA: Harvard University Press.

....

History of Computers
Jussi Parikka

In a way, there is no history of computers, but multiple histories of computer technologies, components, and practices. Any single historian of the "universal machine" would easily get stuck even with histories and archives of single institutions. A case in point is a glimpse at, for instance, the National Physical Laboratory in the United Kingdom or the 1970s American Xerox Parc research center that produced through its collective work perhaps the most significant technological ideas and software platforms for our graphical user interface culture. One research and development institute can itself reveal a plethora of ideas, clues, blueprints, successful products, but also mistakes, sidetracks, alternatives, and things that never were even realized. In short, there is just too much for a *single* history of the computer. Any history of computing becomes suddenly a metaquestion of how to write a history of such complexity.

Obviously, one can track histories of software and hardware and map some developments specific to the idea that we could think of computing machinery as separate from its instructions. Furthermore, we should complement technology-centered ideas with the wider imaginary and discursive histories and recognize how computers share elements with other media. Computers participate in histories of the typewriter, screen, and storage media, as well as technologies of transmission. In the words of Friedrich Kittler, "Without modern algebra there would be no encoding; without Gutenberg's printing press, no modern cryptology" (2008, 42). What if we can trace pretty much any specific feature of the computer to some other earlier or parallel media historical invention? Paradoxically, if we are *too* persistent, a history of computing becomes a generalized history of almost any media.

This short essay addresses, first, issues of programmability, while progressing to talk through some key themes of computing history. However, a key part of this entry is to introduce a methodology of media archaeology for history of computing research. These ideas are discussed in the last two sections.

Programmability

The complexity of tracking a singular history of the computer follows from the nature of the computer: it is multimedia in the sense of being an assemblage of various technological solutions that are integrated as part of a programmable machine. It would be perhaps easiest, and most intuitive, to focus on the programmability part when defining a computer and outlining its history of development. Yet we should not forget histories of screen technologies, interfaces from keyboards to mouse, audio, or any of the internal parts (such as memory technologies) and the role they play in this programmability. In terms of algorithmic logic of programmability, one possible history leads to spinning looms: in the middle of the eighteenth century, the automata designer Vaucanson was able to automate the process by which looms wove complex patterns. The "programmable" loom used a cylinder, which contained instructions for the interaction of the needles, threads, and cords. It was an automated system with its own implications for the organization of human labor too. Vaucanson's loom thus not only produced beautiful, mechanically produced textile products to be sold on world markets but also consolidated the idea of the program itself, which was far from an abstract principle, but rather a material mechanism for the transportation and implementation of abstractions. What now are thought of as algorithmic programs—step-by-step instructions that tell the machine to do what it needs to do—detached from "hardware," have always been embedded in various materials.

Programmability, or the possibility of breaking down complex tasks into smaller step-by-step parts and encoding those steps into a "program," was embedded in the punch card principle, which persisted for a long time (see ALGORITHM). In addition to pioneers such as Charles Babbage, there were innovators working outside traditional Western histories. For instance, in Russia Semen Korsakov had in the first half of the nineteenth century suggested something similar: punched cards for storage of information, and as a possible program template. From looms to automatic pianos and musical boxes, to computing machines and census data storage (since the late nineteenth century with Hollerith machines used in the U.S. census), punching a card with a hole to indicate a change in value is an early example of a hardware of programming that persists even today; such cards are still used in some voting systems in the United States, for example.

Computers are not just digital, and computer hardware has many other lineages than that of the binary logic of 1 and 0, or the emphasis on silicon and microchips. Indeed, we should not neglect the fact there are such things as analog computers—too often forgotten now in the midst of discourse of digitality—and that all computers are, to an extent, analog (see ANALOG VERSUS DIGITAL). Wendy Hui Kyong Chun emphasizes this point: analog computers are about measuring, digital computers about counting. But even the latter "do so by rendering analog hardware (vacuum tubes, transistors, etc.) signal magnitudes into discrete units" (Chun 2008, 225–226). Hence, referring to Alan Turing and John von Neumann, we can provocatively argue that digital machines do not really exist: as Chun writes, "there are only continuous machines that in Turing's words can be 'profitably thought of as being discrete state machines,' machines in which, 'given the initial state of the machine and the input signals it is always possible to predict all future states'" (2008, 225–226).

Analog computers have a long history and, especially since the 1930s, an important role as simulation machines. Such devices include Vannevar Bush's Differential Analyzer project (started in the late 1920s at MIT Labs) and the curious Moniac machine—at first considered to be named *"financephalograph"* by its inventor Bill Phillips. The machine, still on display at the Science Museum, London, was a simulation of the mechanisms of Keynesian macroeconomics. Unlike the Differential Analyzer, which was built from electromechanical parts, the Moniac works through water flows, giving an added emphasis to the idea of *flow* of money. Indeed, in this machine, "separate water tanks represent households, business, government, exporting and importing sectors of the economy. Coloured water pumped around the system measures income, spending and GDP" (Ng and Wright 2007, 47).

Software Histories

Histories of the computer are useful in reminding us about the nonentertainment media contexts of calculational machines. Indeed, the step from calculation machines to media machines that are controlled through object-oriented programming is important to note (Alt 2011). Similarly, as a problematization of the relation of hardware and software, we need to be aware of the complex histories of software, namely, how it emerged from a concrete wiring of mainframe computers into a self-sustaining product in itself (Chun 2011). Indeed, software history can be seen as a history of how software became a consumer object in a manner similar to how nineteenth-century recording technologies allowed music and images to become discrete marketable consumer products (Crary 1999, 31).

Indeed, the passage from programming to software is important and leads from the wiring of mainframes to the "mathematically oriented functional and declarative [programming] languages that must idealize the machine from which they abstract" of the late 1950s (Hagen 2006, 159). Programming languages are not only ways to govern the hard machine but actually themselves envelopes that produce different ways altogether of grasping what the machine is. Indeed, the later phase—signaled by the gradual mass consumerization of the computer, first through hobbyist kits (1970s), and gradually through consumer products advertised and shipped to consumers as ready working microcomputer packages along with their software packages—suddenly sees us living in a world of computers as media. Indeed, the emphasis of "mediumship" by 1970s pioneers such as Alan Kay extended computers into a matter of subjectivity: personal, dynamic, and reaching to the very foundational development of a person. Here the birth of personal computing became tightly linked with specific software practices. "As with Simula leading to OOP, this encounter finally hit me with what the destiny of personal computing was going to be. Not a personal dynamic vehicle, as in Engelbart's metaphor opposed to the IBM 'railroads,' but something much more profound: a personal dynamic medium. With a vehicle one could wait until high school and give 'drivers ed,' but if it was a medium it had to extend into the world of childhood" (Kay quoted in Alt 2011, 285). Computer history is irrevocably linked to patterns of subjectivity and drilling. Perhaps it is actually a history of training the user to adjust to desires of the computer, so to speak.

Software is both an object of inquiry and a methodological question. For any media archaeology of computing, we need to consider the specific mediatic nature of software and how it affords creative processes, for instance, in electronic literature. Noah Wardrip-Fruin (2011) has challenged us to think about the processuality of software under the umbrella term of digital archaeology. This includes the methodological challenges to expand history of software into a media archaeology of digital arts. By a close reading of Christopher Strachey's text generator program, which produced mock love letters, Wardrip-Fruin elaborates why an investigation into historical software should be an investigation into processuality. This has direct relevance to our histories of, for example, hypertext and introduces an important move. Perhaps even more important than reading foundational documents by key thinkers and engineers of software and other computing systems in the arts, we should be keen to close read algorithmic patterns and codework, in ways that open computer history to critical code studies and more:

> For example, digital media histories generally engage the ideas about hypertext in the writings of early pioneers such as Theodor Holm Nelson, Andries van Dam, and Douglas C. Engelbart, rather than only those of World Wide Web developer Tim Berners-Lee. On the other hand, the ideas expressed by the specific designs of the processes in nondominant systems are very rarely investigated. For example, I am aware of no critical work that investigates the processes in the "Green" and "Gold" Xanadu source code released from Nelson's project or the version of van Dam's still-functioning FRESS project demonstrated by David Durand and Steven J. DeRose. (Wardrip-Fruin 2011, 320)

Similarly, some practitioners have demonstrated how one can do history of computers as a creative enterprise. Besides the larger-scale reconstructions such as Babbage's Difference Engine reconstructed at the Science Museum, London, we have media artists, such as David Link, who investigate media history through a hands-on approach. Link's artistic LoveLetters project constructed a Ferranti Mark I computer emulator to run Strachey's "Loveletters" program. The project won the Tony Sale award for its conservation work in 2012 and demonstrates one way to understand digital practice of computer history, leading us to the discussion of media archaeology.

A Media Archaeological Method

If we approach computer history media-archaeologically, it becomes an interesting methodological challenge: how to reconceptualize the history of computers outside the usual stories of post–World War II research labs and investment which emphasize the linear narrative of "how we got here." This reconceptualization is important and gives a more comprehensive approach to digital culture. It implies that software is always embedded in a wider context of investment and production. A good example is war and the national defense industry, as discussed in media historical inquiries in the style of Friedrich Kittler. In terms of history of computing, World War II focused resources on a functional ad hoc cluster of deciphering machines (human and technological) at Bletchley Park, led by Alan M. Turing, whose Turing machine blueprints can be hailed as one significant prewar investment into thinking the possibilities in abstraction.

In the United States, coordinating much of the effort was the Office of Scientific Research and Development, whose director, Vannevar Bush, was the inventor of the analog computing machine Differential Analyzer (Campbell-Kelly & Aspray 2004, 69). U.S. efforts included R & D investment in specific computing machines instrumental to firing tables (ENIAC) and the building of the first atomic bombs (Manhattan Project at Los

Alamos). Such work mobilized huge numbers of mathematicians, engineers, and other scientists and led to concrete outputs outside of direct military use as well. Such included, for instance, the formulation of the basic infrastructure of computing by John von Neumann: the architecture of separated memory and central processing unit.

After World War II, the commercialization of early computers began to emerge. This was perceived, however, as unnecessary by some pioneers, such as Howard Aiken, developer of the Mark I computer (Ceruzzi 2003, 13). Nonetheless, just a few years after the war, IBM had developed an effective way of reaching a number of early customers. Also, the Cold War provided its own set of priorities and support for technological projects and scientific development, including computing. The heavy investment and research-intensive culture that was risk taking in its R&D, a management specific to the 1970s, contributed to the fact that a lot of our current desktop environment and network technology emerged in the Xerox Palo Alto lab.

All of this points less toward histories of imaginary geniuses—the solitary heroes like Steve Jobs whom the media and digital economy discourse celebrate—than toward the conditions in which ideas are able to develop. This is a more laboratory approach to history of computing, where "laboratory" can be understood quite literally. Firstly, in a way that Bruno Latour and others introduced in science studies, we can observe and learn a lot from the constitutive practices in which epistemologies and facts are born. Latour has called this a shift from matters of fact to matters of concern. By this he means a shift in emphasis from a mere reception of objective facts to a wider concern for the process of production: "A matter of concern is what happens to a matter of fact when you add to it its whole scenography, much like you would do by shifting your attention from the stage to the whole machinery of a theatre" (2008, 39).

Secondly, in a media theoretical way, we are able to track the genealogies of our entertainment devices (mostly digital nowadays) to specific scientific innovations and epistemologies, which they still carry with them. German media theorists such as Wolfgang Ernst and Wolfgang Hagen have, for instance, argued for an approach that looks at the long historical networks of how things ended up as objective parts in our technological machines: histories of vacuum tubes and other radio/computer elements, of technological agencies so gray we have often neglected them as specialist terrain. And yet, such components are historically constituent of what the computerized terrain nowadays itself supports.

In short, we can track a media archaeology of computing, where matters of concern extend back in time too. We should use this idea systematically to claim that a history of computers must be a media archaeology of computing in the sense that we need a thorough account of alternative histories, sidetracks, and failures, as well as of the various minihistories and micronarratives of both human agency and technological components in order to complement otherwise a too linear account of how we got to digital culture. While extending the historical interest into new areas in history of media, we do not need to rely on the idea of being comprehensive; instead, we can be happy to excavate without wanting to write *one* long history. Media archaeology is instead nonlinear.

Tubes, Switches, and Other Transmedia

An alternative look at the history of computers starts from the ground level up. The material basis of computers has for a long time been left as a specialist terrain for engineers, historians of technology, and experts keen to find out, to tinker, and to build. Instead of just specialist histories of engineering and technology, a look at the component basis of computing reveals important aspects hitherto neglected. Following Wolfgang Ernst, we could track a microlevel transmedia history of such technologies, which do not fit into just one particular lineage. Take, for instance, the (vacuum) tube, such a crucial component in the birth of the electronic age as an amplification and switching element, which gradually, since the late nineteenth century, contributed to radio, television, sound, computer industries, and, of course, the spatial medium of artificial light as articulated in the 1884 *A Manifestation of the Edison Lamp*. Indeed, Ernst argues for an alternative to mass media histories. He maps the history of the vacuum, or electron tube, as such an alternative media archaeological history that cannot be reduced to the history of how the broadcasting (or in our case computer) industry emerged, but relates to histories of science and technology and high-frequency oscillation—things not only for human ears or eyes. Methodologically, this can contribute to an extended and therefore richer media archaeology of such gray elements that are only later differentiated into individual media technologies, with seemingly individual histories: "the tube as a basis medium, which transversally unites various media complexes (radio, oscilloscope, television, computer)" (Ernst 2008, 419).

Ernst's work opens up computer history anew by describing vacuum tubes as the essential elements that transported a bit of broadcasting and television history inside the computer—for which tubes were switches, logical parts. They were essential in such early computers as the British Colossus and Colossus mk2, UNIVAC, and ENIAC. The Whirlwind project also used them. Of course, tubes would not be the only transmedia element in such a history. The early German pioneer Konrad Zuse used 35mm film strips as his material for input; the development of screen technologies hovered in various contexts from radar screens and oscillators to emerging computer screens; antennas are not medium-specific, but relate to a transmedia informational history of wireless transmission.

Such an alternative transmedia approach concerns also the transformations in infrastructures. Another case in point is the gradual shift from telephone networks to specifically data networks since the 1970s. With the increasing investment into data networking since the 1960s, ARPANET—and other then-new networks such as the Aloha network in Hawaii, which used a mix of broadcasting and packet switching (Kimbleton and Schneider 1975, 133)—created new demands for transmission. Indeed, for any consideration of computer history, we are nowadays naturally inclined to think of computers as networked. The emergence of networking as a feature of computers and computer-mediated communication relates necessarily to a wider set of technological and infrastructural features. One aspect of this emergence is indeed the sharing of networks for a variety of traffic from human voices to data packets (a history where the role of modems and multiplexing becomes crucial), but it also flags how early on the conflation of such was happening (Davies and Barber 1973). Indeed, even precybernetic networks can be considered complex data networks in the manner that David Mindell outlines concerning the early use of vacuum tubes in telephone networks; besides amplifying the conversation, they allowed the signal itself to become an object that could be standardized and "manipulated on its own terms" (Mindell 2002, 113).

In short, a history of computers cannot neglect material and practices that come from other media contexts; hence, besides opening up a history of the digital to include that of analog computers, we need to be as observant to the gray element in the histories of processing, storage, and transmission.

■ See also CHARACTERISTICS OF DIGITAL MEDIA

References and Further Reading

Alt, Casey. 2011. "Objects of Our Affection: How Object Orientation Made Computers a Medium." In *Media Archaeology: Approaches, Applications and Implications*, edited by Erkki Huhtamo and Jussi Parikka, 278–301. Berkeley: University of California Press.

Campbell-Kelly, Martin, and William Aspray. 2004. *Computer: A History of the Information Machine*. 2nd ed. Boulder, CO: Westview Press.

Ceruzzi, Paul E. 2003. *A History of Modern Computing*. 2nd ed. Cambridge, MA: MIT Press.

Chun, Wendy Hui Kyong. 2008. "Programmability." In *Software Studies: A Lexicon*, edited by Matthew Fuller, 224–229. Cambridge, MA: MIT Press.

———. 2011. *Programmed Visions*. Cambridge, MA: MIT Press.

Crary, Jonathan. 1999. *Suspensions of Perception: Attention, Spectacle, and Modern Culture*. Cambridge, MA: MIT Press.

Davies, Donald W., and Derek L. A. Barber. 1973. *Communication Networks for Computers*. Chichester, UK: John Wiley & Sons.

Ernst, Wolfgang. 2008. "Distory: 100 Years of Electron Tubes, Media-Archaeologically Interpreted vis-á-vis 100 Years of Radio." In *Re-inventing Radio: Aspects of Radio as Art*, edited by Heidi Grundmann et al., 415–430. Frankfurt am Main: Revolver.

Hagen, Wolfgang. 2006. "The Style of Sources: Remarks on the Theory and History of Programming Languages." In *New Media, Old Media: A History and Theory Reader*, edited by Wendy Hui Kyong Chun and Thomas Keenan, 157–175. New York: Routledge.

Kimbleton, Stephen R., and G. Michael Schneider. 1975. "Computer Communication Networks: Approaches, Objectives, and Performance Considerations." *Computing Surveys* 7 (3): 129–173.

Kittler, Friedrich. 2008. "Code." In *Software Studies: A Lexicon*, edited by Matthew Fuller, 40–47. Cambridge, MA: MIT Press.

Latour, Bruno. 2008. *What Is the Style of Matters of Concern?* Spinoza Lecture. Amsterdam: Van Gorcum.

Mindell, David A. 2002. *Between Human and Machine: Feedback, Control, and Computing before Cybernetics*. Baltimore: Johns Hopkins University Press.

Ng, Tim, and Matthew Wright. 2007. "Introducing the MONIAC: An Early and Innovative Economic Model." *Reserve Bank of New Zealand: Bulletin* 70 (4): 46–52.

Wardrip-Fruin, Noah. 2011. "Digital Media Archaeology: Interpreting Computational Processes." In *Media Archaeology: Approaches, Applications and Implications*, edited by Erkki Huhtamo and Jussi Parikka, 302–322. Berkeley: University of California Press.

Hoaxes
Jill Walker Rettberg

We are used to being able to easily tell the difference between truth and fiction, but in the early years of a new medium, these boundaries are sites for negotiation. Hoaxes and scams play with these boundaries and range from aesthetic or satiric to criminal. The following will focus on aesthetic and playful hoaxes on the Internet.

An infamous hoax from the early years of radio was Orson Welles's Halloween 1938 broadcast of *War of the Worlds*, which had thousands of panicked listeners believing that Martians had invaded Earth. Welles had his actors break into a radio concert for supposed "live news" of the attacks. On the Internet, where we are accustomed to using e-mail and websites for information, we can be similarly gullible. E-mail is a well-established channel for both scams and hoaxes, some of which can be seen as contemporary folklore (Kibby 2005). Hoax websites mimic authentic sites to engage or fool readers. Malepregnancy.com uses the interface layout of a typical hospital website and includes links to and facsimiles of fake media coverage of the medical miracle of male pregnancy (see INTERFACE). Bonsaikitten.com, a site that went viral as horrified cat lovers shared it with their friends in 2005, claimed to sell body-modified kittens, shaped by having spent their early weeks in jars, and appropriately used the layout of a typical small online store, including photos of cute kittens, a phone number to call, and explanations of the process and how to order your own modified kitten.

Blogs and video diaries also provide a rich basis for fiction, with or without artistic intent (see BLOGS). An early and renowned blog that turned out to be a hoax featured Kaycee Nicole, a dying teenager who blogged about her battle against cancer, and her mother, Debbie, who started a companion diary about caring for her child with cancer. When Kaycee eventually died in 2002, her online friends were devastated. When they found out that Kaycee and Debbie were fictional, they were furious and felt deceived and used. Unlike Kaycee Nicole, Lonelygirl15 was a project presented in 2006 as the YouTube diaries of a teenage girl, Bree, where the creators turned out to be professional film directors and actors. When fans discovered that Bree was played by an actress, they were as furious as Kaycee Nicole's online friends had been at what they experienced as a betrayal of trust (Rettberg 2008). This shared anger and the accompanying gathering of evidence of how the hoax was conducted can be argued as allowing an audience to construct itself as a community, a medium that both demands and denies the possibility of authentic self-disclosure and stable identity (Nunes 2010). Lonelygirl15 continued as a clearly fictional web series until 2008.

Marketers have used similar strategies to encourage user engagement, and this can also cause severe backlashes when people find out that they have been fooled. An infamous example is the 2009 video featuring a Danish woman looking for her baby's father, a tourist to Copenhagen whose name she has forgotten. After being seen close to a million times, the video was revealed as part of the marketing campaign VisitDenmark. Though heavily criticized, the campaign certainly got media attention.

Many Internet hoaxes are clearly presented as satire, such as the Twitter account @ Queen_UK, which allegedly belongs to the Queen of England and offers mild critique of royalty: "No, Occupy London, one does not 'have room at the Palace for a few tents'" (February 28, 2012). Hoaxes can also be used as tactical media or as propaganda, where false information is presented as reality, as with the white supremacist organization Stormfront's site on Martin Luther King Jr.

■ See also DIGITAL FICTION, NARRATIVITY, NETWORKING, VIRAL AESTHETICS

References and Further Reading

Kibby, Marjorie D. 2005. "Email Forwardables: Folklore in the Age of the Internet." *New Media Society* 7 (6): 770–790.
Nunes, Mark. 2010. "This is Not a Blog Hoax: Narrative 'Provocations' in a Participatory Media Culture." *Explorations in Media Ecology* 9 (2): 71–86.
Rettberg, Jill Walker. 2008. *Blogging*. Cambridge: Polity Press.
Snopes.com. *Urban Legends Reference Pages*. www.snopes.com/.

Holopoetry
Eduardo Kac

A holographic poem, or holopoem, is a poem conceived, made, and displayed holographically. This means, first of all, that such a poem is organized nonlinearly in an immaterial three-dimensional space and that even as the reader or viewer observes it, it changes and gives rise to new meanings. Thus, as the viewer reads the poem in space—that is, moves relative to the hologram—he or she constantly modifies the structure of the text. A holopoem is a spatiotemporal event: it evokes thought processes, and not their result.

A holopoem is not a poem composed in lines of verse and made into a hologram, nor is it a visual poem adapted to holography. The sequential structure of a line of verse corresponds to linear thinking, whereas the simultaneous structure of a visual poem corresponds to ideographic thinking. The perception of a holopoem takes place neither linearly nor simultaneously but rather through fragments seen by the observer according to decisions he or she makes, depending on the observer's position relative to the poem. Perception in space of colors, volumes, degrees of transparency, changes in form, relative positions of letters and words, and the appearance and disappearance of forms is inseparable from the syntactic and semantic perception of the text. The instability of color has poetic function, and the visual mutability of letters extends them beyond the verbal domain. As a result, holopoems are actually quadridimensional because they integrate dynamically the three dimensions of space with the added dimension of time. This is not the subjective time of the reader found in traditional texts, but a perceived time expressed in the holopoem itself.

What defines a holopoem is not the fact that a given text is recorded on holographic film. What matters is the creation of new syntaxes, mobility, nonlinearity, interactivity, fluidity, discontinuity, and dynamic behavior only possible in holographic space-time.

Holopoetry promotes new relationships between the appearance/disappearance of signifiers, which constitutes the experience of reading a holographic text, and our perception of the organizing factors of the text. In this sense, visual perception of parametric behavior of the verbal elements heightens awareness of meanings. As readers move, they continually shift the focus or center or organizing principle of their experience by looking through dispersed viewing zones. The text they experience stands against the fixity of print, and for the instability of holographic space.

In 1983 Eduardo Kac invented this new form, created the terms *holographic poetry* and *holopoetry*, and produced the first holopoem, entitled "Holo/Olho" (now in the permanent collection of the University of Essex, United Kingdom). In 1987 Kac created his digital holopoem "Quando? (When?)." This was the first in a series in which the poet brought digital possibilities to his holographic work. From 1983 to 1993, Kac produced twenty-four holopoems, which have been the object of multiple solo and group shows worldwide.

In addition to Kac, poet Richard Kostelanetz has created what he calls "Literary Holography," language-based holographic works that go from conceptual installations to poems such as "Antitheses" (1985) and a group of poems produced in the late 1980s which include "Ho/Log/Rap/Her" and "Ho/Log/Rap/Hy."

Kac and Kostelanetz collaborated in the holopoem "Lilith" (1987/1989).

■ See also BIOPOETRY, DIGITAL POETRY, ELECTRONIC LITERATURE, INTERFACE

References and Further Reading

Kac, Eduardo. 1986. "Holopoetry and Perceptual Syntax." *Holosphere* 14 (3): 25.
———. 1989. "Holopoetry and Fractal Holopoetry: Digital Holography as an Art Medium." *Leonardo: Special Issue on Holographic Art* 22 (3/4): 397–402.
———, ed. 1995. *Holopoetry: Essays, Manifestoes, Critical and Theoretical Writings*. Lexington, KY: New Media Editions.
———. 2007a. *Hodibis Potax*. Ivry-sur-Seine: Édition Action Poétique.
———. 2007b. *Holopoèmes, Poèmes minitel, poèmes numériques, Biopoèmes*. DVD, Son@art, Paris.
———. 2007c. "Holopoetry." In *Media Poetry: An International Anthology*, 2nd ed., edited by Eduardo Kac. Bristol, UK: Intellect.
Kostelanetz, Richard. 1990. "Literary Holography." *New England Review / Bread Loaf Quarterly* 12 (4): 415–426.

Hypertextuality
Astrid Ensslin

In its broadest technological sense, *hypertext* is an umbrella term denoting a specific principle of electronic document organization. It interlinks digital files of various textual and audiovisual formats into an interactive, associative network. Hypertexts can assume gigantic dimensions: the World Wide Web is widely held to be the largest existing hypertext. Users can freely move through a hypertext by activating hyperlinks through mouse click, gesture, or touch. Owing to their large dimensions, many hypertext documents (such as company websites) offer a site map to facilitate navigation (Shapiro 2006, 518). Hypertext is typically written in HyperText Markup Language (HTML) and its variants.

The term derives from the Greek *hypér* (over, above, beyond) and Latin *texere* (to weave) and refers to the metatextual function of hypertext as a principle of structuring and connecting subordinate electronic texts. It was coined by Theodor Nelson in his 1965 lectures at Vassar College. His frequently quoted definition describes hypertext as "non-sequential writing—text that branches and allows choices to the reader, best read at an interactive screen. As popularly conceived, this is a series of text chunks connected by links which offer the reader different pathways" (Nelson 1984, 0/2) (see LINKING STRATEGIES). The resulting interwoven network enables a dialogue between a variety of texts and contexts, composed in both writing and other different semiotic modes, such as image and sound. Such multimodal hypertextual networks are generally referred to as hypermedia, short for "hypertext multimedia."

Nelson's concept was inspired by Vannevar Bush's revolutionary idea of the memex ("Memory Expander"), an information system designed for the connection and storage of as well as access to all documents and communications in the world, which Bush had first envisaged as early as the 1930s. Intended to emulate the human brain, the memex was designed to operate in terms of indexing, associative connection, and creating paths to help retrieve documents (Bush 1945). Using computational technologies, Nelson aimed to implement Bush's idea, which had never materialized beyond a highly innovative concept. He sought to connect all literary works into a so-called docuverse, an abstract concept anticipating the principles of the World Wide Web, which Nelson wanted to concretize in a project named "Xanadu." This project has so far remained incomplete.

Against a poststructuralist theoretical backdrop, hypertext can be explained metaphorically in terms of the rhizome (Deleuze and Guattari 1987; Moulthrop 1995). Rhizomes are characterized by ramifying, decentralized, horizontally organized root structures, which do not have a clear beginning or end. Therefore, rhizomes conveniently deviate from the arborescent, hierarchical structures associated with logocentrism. Ironically, of course, most functional hypertexts are given a quasi-hierarchical structure all the same, not least in order to provide some guidance for readers. Literary hypertexts such as Storyspace fictions, on the other hand, seek to subvert any sense of hierarchical order or predesigned sequence in order to achieve specific effects in the reader and trigger idiosyncratic receptive and hermeneutic processes.

Among literary hypertext theorists, individual units of a hypertext are widely referred to as "lexias" (nodes, or text chunks), a term borrowed from Barthes (Landow 1992). Typically, each lexia contains a number of links. Therefore, "every reading produces a different text. . . . Whereas the reader of a standard print text constructs personalized interpretations out of an invariant semiotic base, the reader of an interactive text thus participates in the construction of the text as visible display of signs" (Ryan 2001, 5–6) (see INTERACTIVE NARRATIVE). This idea of virtual coauthorship, also referred to as the "(w)reader" (Landow 1992), has been theorized extensively by literary scholars and has gained particular attention since the advent of Web 2.0, its participatory culture, and concomitant forms of social media narrative (e.g., Klaiber 2013) (see PARTICIPATORY CULTURE).

Although the term *hypertext* was coined in the twentieth century, the concepts of multilinear reading, interrelating, annotating, and cross-referencing, as well as the link itself, date back over one thousand years. So-called proto-hypertexts can be traced as far back as the Middle Ages, when glosses (annotations) appeared in the Jewish Talmud, the Bible, and canon law and medical texts. Further on in history, European Enlightenment scholars produced the first printed encyclopedias (e.g., Diderot and d'Alembert, 1751–1780; Johnson, 1755; Black and Black, 1768), thus representing early forms of proto-hypertextual cross-referencing, or "super-scribing" text in order to explain, elaborate, and connect intertextually. In the romantic period, the idea of the "absolute book," inspired by Friedrich Schlegel's utopian idea of a *progressive Universalpoesie*, raised intertextual connectivity to a paradigm of a whole age. (For historical examples of proto-hypertextual, nonlinear fiction, see NONLINEAR WRITING.)

The late 1980s and 1990s saw a growing interest in hypertext as a pedagogic technology. Its capacity for structuring and organizing information in a nonlinear way sparked a number of innovative teaching approaches (e.g., Joyce 1996) and empirical studies within cognitive and educational psychology. Following up Bush's memex idea, psychologists and early representatives of artificial intelligence research adopted the euphoric yet largely hypothetical view that hypertext structures resembled human neurons and could thus be likened to the associative networks of human memory (e.g., Fiderio 1988) (see ARTIFICIAL INTELLIGENCE). Therefore, it was assumed that, if hypertext knowledge bases were to be organized to reflect an expert's or teacher's semantic knowledge structures, learners would adopt these structures over time. This theory came to be known as the cognitive plausibility hypothesis (Jonassen 1986). It was based on the fact that human neurons are made up of intricately interconnected dendrites and axons, which account for human beings' associative capacities. Learning operates in terms of constructing new cognitive structures through generating new nodes and interconnecting them with each other and existing nodes (Norman 1976). Learner knowledge is thus reorganized in such a way as to accommodate new information. Consequently, it was assumed that web structures, with their variously interlinked nodes, are likely to be more easily processed than conventional linear structures and might therefore facilitate learning. Grounding their assumptions in schema theory, psychologists considered those analogies to be highly useful, particularly with respect to mapping expert cognitive structures onto semantic maps, which could then be used as powerful, empowering learning templates (e.g., McKnight, Dillon, and Richardson 1991). Furthermore, it was believed that providing instant, multilinear access to information via associative links rather than logical linearization might further increase learning efficiency. With regard to retaining information via hypertext, however, this hypothesis could not be verified. It was found that learners perform better with linear-format texts than hypertexts, and that considerably less time is spent searching through indexes and contents (McKnight, Dillon, and Richardson 1991).

In literary studies, there have been two major waves of hypertext theory, inspired by a body of fictional, poetic, and dramatic works emerging between the late 1980s and mid-1990s, mostly written in Eastgate's Storyspace and Apple's HyperCard software (see Storyspace). Canonical authors and fictions of the Storyspace School include, for instance, Michael Joyce's *afternoon, a story* (1987), Stuart Moulthrop's *Victory Garden* (1992), and Shelly Jackson's *Patchwork Girl; or, A Modern Monster* (1995). A famous example of HyperCard hypertext is John McDaid's *Uncle Buddy's Phantom Funhouse* (1992). Spearheaded by George P. Landow, Jay David Bolter, and Robert Coover, the first wave of literary hypertext theories outlined major organizing principles of hypertext literature and placed it firmly within the context of poststructuralist theory (see CRITICAL THEORY). In a 1992 essay, Bolter first proclaimed hypertext as a "vindication of postmodern literary theory" (1992, 24). In the same year, Coover published his famous article, "The End of Books," in the *New York Times Book Review*, in which he declared that "hypertext presents a radically divergent technology, interactive and polyvocal, favoring a plurality of discourses over definitive utterance and freeing the reader from the domination of the author" (1992). Landow (1992) systematized these claims in his so-called convergence thesis. He saw in the principle of hypertextuality a convergence between computer technology and poststructuralist theory in the sense that hypertext could be considered a pragmatization of major poststructuralist and deconstructivist theorems (e.g., antilogocentrism, the death of the author, writerly text, nonclosure, decentering). This idea, according to Landow, has considerable liberating, empowering, and democratizing potential because readers become coauthors, thus taking responsibility for the physical *and* mental co-construction of the text. The Storyspace software, authored by Bolter and Michael Joyce, implemented this collaborative potential by allowing readers not only to read in a multilinear fashion but to add notes and comments to the text.

Landow's convergence thesis was met with considerable criticism, which was mostly directed at the theory's inclination toward pragmatic simplification of complex, abstract philosophical concepts, as well as self-righteous, ideologically charged academic spin.

Barthes and Foucault regard the reader as empowered (in the sense of writerly vs. readerly text) in terms of being at liberty to form personal connotations and associations. In a hypertext environment, however, this freedom is considerably restrained given the existence of manifest, technically implemented hyperlinks, which prevent rather than afford creativity. Indeed, hyperlinks have a delimiting rather than empowering function, as they are placed by the author and often lead to confusion, serendipity, and cognitive overhead in the reader. According to Simanowski (2004; see also Ensslin 2007), the only feasible contexts in which the roles of reader and author may legitimately be merged are collaborative writing projects (see COLLABORATIVE NARRATIVE). In such joint ventures, writers coauthor hypertext or other electronic documents, as has been implemented, for example, by Landow in his *Victorian Web* (1994–2011) and in contemporary collaborative writing projects on the web, such as *A Million Penguins* (a 2007 collaboration of Penguin Books and De Montfort University) and Kate Pullinger and Chris Joseph's (2007–2012) *Flight Paths: A Networked Novel* (for further contemporary examples, see Klaiber 2013).

More recently, a second wave of scholars have highlighted the importance of grounding literary, stylistic, and narratological theories of hypertext (and other types of electronic literature) in methodologically rigorous close analyses (see ELECTRONIC LITERATURE). They have embraced the fact that hypertext and other electronic types of writing require a new hermeneutic attitude, which acknowledges and embraces the fact that hypertexts are never read the same way twice but indeed rely on multiple rereadings on the part of the analyst ("aesthetics of revis(itat)ion"; Ensslin 2007). This school of theorists and analysts has been focusing on applying existing, print-born theories and analytical tools to digital *fiction* in particular, and on expanding existing methodological toolkits from stylistics, semiotics, and narratology by introducing new terms and methods of analysis tailored to the affordances of digital media (e.g., Ensslin and Bell 2007; Bell 2010; Bell, Ensslin, and Rustad 2013). Astrid Ensslin (2012), for instance, applies theories of unreliable narration to Michael Joyce's Storyspace fiction *afternoon, a story* and Stefan Maskiewicz's dialogic hypermedia narrative *Quadrego* (2001). Both texts feature unintentional (neurotic and psychopathic) unreliable narrators but make very different uses of hypertextuality and hypermediality to represent the respective characters' perceptions and symptoms. Bell and Ensslin (2011) expand the theoretical discourse and analytical toolset associated with second-person narration by examining the textual *you* in Stuart Moulthrop's *Victory Garden* and Richard Holeton's *Figurski at Findhorn on Acid* (2001). They show how second-person narration in hypertext fiction can not only underscore the interactivity of the medium and the physical participation of the reader but indeed encourage readers to reflect on their role in real-life, extratextual events (see INTERACTIVITY). In a book-length study, Bell (2010) applies select theorems of possible worlds theory to a number of Storyspace hypertext and hypermedia fictions and demonstrates how this approach can be used to analyze the ontological self-consciousness and conflicting first-person perspectives of the narrator, the problematic boundaries between fictional and historical discourses, intertextual references to other fictional characters, appearances of the author figure in the text, and absurdist humor (see DIGITAL FICTION).

Hypertext as a (literary) art form has, since its inception, undergone major creative shifts and transformations. These "generational" shifts (Hayles 2002; Ensslin 2007) have been motivated partly by writers' frustration vis-à-vis hypertext's failure to draw audiences broader than a small number of literary scholars, and partly by the experimental potential afforded by newly evolving digital technologies.

The first generational shift, from hypertext to hypermedia, occurred around the mid-1990s, which marked a watershed in digital technology development. The year 1993 saw the invention of Mosaic, the world's first graphic browser, and, following in its wake, the popularization of the World Wide Web with HTML, its major markup language. The key achievement of HTML as a standardized encoding convention was its propensity to serve a variety of different semiotic systems, which had previously been analog, that is, separated in terms of mediality and materiality. These semiotic systems comprise text, graphics, digitized speech, audio files, animation, and film. Produced, for example, by means of HTML, JavaScript, Flash, and Shockwave technologies, hypermedia is characterized by a variety of pastiche and collage techniques. In these, interactivity emerges through technologically manifested intermediality and, in the case of collaborative, user-generated writing projects, through direct (w)reader interaction and participation via web posts. From an aesthetic point of view, hypermedia readers are confronted not only with interlinked text lexias but a wider semiotic variety, for example, image-text, image-image, and text-image links, as well as dynamic and interactive elements such as film clips and drag-and-drop mechanisms. As opposed to first-generation hypertexts, which use images sparsely and mainly as illustrative or decorative means, hypermedia writings form a coherent intertextual, intermedial, and multimodal whole, which is more than the sum of its constituent parts. Prototypical examples are concrete digital poems such as Judd Morrissey and Lori Talley's (2002) *My Name Is Captain, Captain* and web-based digital fictions such as geniwate and Deena Larsen's *The Princess Murderer* (2003) and Robert Kendall's *Clues* (2002).

A second general shift, from hypermedia to cybertext (Ensslin 2007), can be located in the move toward empowering the software code to take over a considerable degree of control of the reception process without necessarily reducing interactivity (although in some extreme cases reader agency is abandoned completely, such as in the Flash works of Young Hae Chang Heavy Industries). *Cybertext* is a term coined by Espen Aarseth, who sees hypertexts that are programmed in particular ways as autonomous "text/machines," which assume power over the reader by literally "writing themselves" rather than presenting themselves as an existing textual product. The concept of cybertext is based on Aarseth's alternative model of textual communication (1997, 21), which places the text/machine, a mechanical rather than metaphorical concept, at the center of the communicative triangle. The text/machine is symbolically surrounded by the (human) "operator," the "verbal sign," and the material "medium" that disseminates the text. These three elements engage in a complex interplay with the text and each other, which results in a variety of different cybertextual subgenres, depending on which element is emphasized most strongly. What Aarseth aims to communicate is a reversion of some key reader-response principles (e.g., reader-driven hermeneutics; readers "completing" textual meaning through interpretation), which renders the operator a constitutive yet somewhat disempowered element of (cyber)textual performance. Put differently, readers become part of a cybernetic feedback loop, which operates on the basis of mutual stimulus and response between machine and operator. By highlighting this reciprocal contingency, however, Aarseth's model subliminally reconfirms the validity of reader-response theory, as the reader-operator is bound to fill the metatextual gaps opened up by the text by reading cybertextual meanings into it (i.e., meanings that take account of the operator as physical and psychological part of the cybernetic feedback loop, highlighting the importance of code and its effects on interface and interactivity). Inspired by other forms of (ludic) digital narrative, such as video games and massively multiplayer online role-playing games (MMORPGs), the cybertext generation uses the latest achievements in hypermedia technology combined with a variety of plug-ins, which add interactive, playful elements to the text. Early examples include Stuart Moulthrop's (1997) *Hegirascope* and Urs Schreiber's (1998) *Das Epos der Maschine*. *Hegirascope* features tightly timed links, which cause lexias to change at a rapid pace (every eighteen seconds in version 1.0) without giving the reader a chance to take control via mouse click or to close read them. *Das Epos der Maschine* consists of autonomously moving text, which appears, vanishes, expands, diminishes, and wanders across a highly interactive but simultaneously elusive interface.

In 2000, Johannes Auer predicted that, by virtue of such innovations, a more corporeal notion of interactivity, which directly responds to human emotions and physical conditions, may ultimately replace the hyperlink as the central aesthetic and structural feature of hypertext. In fact, as recent "physiocybertextual" (Ensslin 2009) artifacts such as Kate Pullinger, Stefan Schemat, and babel's *The Breathing Wall* (2004) have shown, Auer's vision has to a certain degree become reality. Physiocybertexts integrate the reader's corporeal mechanisms—or select aspects thereof—in the reading process. *The Breathing Wall*, for instance, uses software that measures the reader's breathing rate and intensity and releases or withholds key textual information accordingly.

Based on the aforementioned tripartite system of overlapping generations, Ensslin (2007) suggests a dynamic, multilingual canon of hypertext, hypermedia, and cybertext, which can be modified and expanded to allow it to evolve alongside technological and aesthetic developments. Further attempts at canonizing and/or anthologizing hypertext and related forms of electronic literature include the Electronic Literature Organization's *Electronic Literature Directory* and its two volumes of the *Electronic Literature Collection* (see Electronic Literature Organization).

Despite the technological and concomitant aesthetic developments outlined above, as well as its potentially anti-immersive, alienating, and confusing properties, hypertext as a structuring principle of electronic writing continues to be used by digital writers. That said, more recent creative uses of it reflect a more careful, reader-friendly attitude, which seeks to sustain rather than impede immersion. For instance, as Kate Pullinger and Chris Joseph have shown in episode 4, "Hometown," of their emergent digital fiction *Inanimate Alice* (2005–2012), hypertextual elements can be embedded in a largely linear hypermedia story so as to give readers different options and reading paths without, however, allowing them to get lost in hyperspace. At the beginning of this episode, Alice is dared by her friends to climb a dilapidated staircase. Two-thirds of the way up, the stairs begin to collapse underneath her, at which point the reader is given four hypertextual options to "look at what happened." Each chosen path, however, leads back to the options screen, and all four options, once selected in full, lead to a continuation of the standard linear reading path resulting in Alice's rescue. Another recent attempt to create reader-friendly literary hypertext is Mark C. Marino's (2008) *A Show of Hands*. Using software called the Literatronica storytelling engine, this work seeks to enable readers to situate themselves within the story. It "adapts around the reader's choices, rearranging the content so the reader will always encounter all of the text in an order optimized for narrative coherence" (2008). Thus, hypertext remains a powerful informational and expressive tool for creators and users of both fictional and nonfictional electronic textuality.

■ See also READING STRATEGIES

References and Further Reading

Aarseth, Espen. 1997. *Cybertext: Perspectives on Ergodic Literature*. Baltimore: Johns Hopkins University Press.

Auer, Johannes. 2000. "7 Thesen zur Netzliteratur." www.netzliteratur.net/thesen.htm.

Bell, Alice. 2010. *The Possible Worlds of Hypertext Fiction*. Basingstoke, UK: Palgrave-Macmillan.

Bell, Alice, and Astrid Ensslin. 2011. "'I know what it was. You know what it was': Second Person Narration in Hypertext Fiction." *Narrative* 19 (3): 311–329.

Bell, Alice, Astrid Ensslin, and Hans Kristian Rustad. 2013. *Analyzing Digital Fiction*. New York: Routledge.

Bolter, Jay David. 1992. "Literature in the Electronic Writing Space." In *Literacy Online: The Promise (and Peril) of Reading (and Writing) with Computers*, edited by Myron C. Tuman, 19–42. Pittsburgh: University of Pittsburgh Press.

Bush, Vannevar. 1945. "As We May Think." *Atlantic Monthly*, July, 47–61.

Coover, Robert. 1992. "The End of Books." *New York Times Book Review*, June 21, 23–25. www.nytimes.com/books/98/09/27/specials/coover-end.html.

Deleuze, Gilles, and Félix Guattari. 1987. *A Thousand Plateaus: Capitalism and Schizophrenia*. Minneapolis: University of Minnesota Press.

Ensslin, Astrid. 2007. *Canonizing Hypertext: Explorations and Constructions*. London: Continuum.

———. 2009. "Respiratory Narrative: Multimodality and Cybernetic Corporeality in 'Physio-cybertext.'" In *New Perspectives on Narrative and Multimodality*, edited by Ruth Page, 155–165. New York: Routledge.

———. 2012. "'I Want to Say I May Have Seen My Son Die This Morning': Unintentional Unreliable Narration in Digital Fiction." *Language and Literature* 21:136–149.

Ensslin, Astrid, and Alice Bell. 2007. *New Perspectives on Digital Literature: Criticism and Analysis*. Special issue of *Dichtung Digital* 37. www.dichtung-digital.org/Newsletter/2007.

Fiderio, Janet. 1988. "A Grand Vision." *Byte* 13 (10): 237–243.

geniwate, and Deena Larsen. 2003. *The Princess Murderer*. www.deenalarsen.net/princess/index.html.

Hayles, N. Katherine. 2002. *Writing Machines*. Cambridge, MA: MIT Press.

Holeton, Richard. 2001. *Figurski at Findhorn on Acid*. Watertown, MA: Eastgate Systems.

Jackson, Shelley. 1995. *Patchwork Girl; or, A Modern Monster*. Cambridge, MA: Eastgate Systems.

Jonassen, David H. 1986. "Hypertext Principles for Text and Courseware Design." *Educational Psychologist* 21 (4): 269–292.

Joyce, Michael. 1987. *afternoon, a story*. Cambridge, MA: Eastgate Systems.

———. 1996. *Of Two Minds: Hypertext, Pedagogy, and Poetics*. Ann Arbor: University of Michigan Press.

Kendall, Robert. 2002. *Clues*. www.wordcircuits.com/clues.

Klaiber, Isabell. 2013. "Wreading Together: The Double Plot of Collaborative Digital Fiction." In *Analyzing Digital Fiction*, edited by Alice Bell, Astrid Ensslin, and Hans Kristian Rustad. New York: Routledge.

Landow, George P. 1992. *Hypertext: The Convergence of Contemporary Critical Theory and Technology*. Baltimore: Johns Hopkins University Press.

———. 1994–2011. *The Victorian Web*. www.victorianweb.org.

Marino, Mark C. 2008. *A Show of Hands*. http://collection.eliterature.org/2/works/marino_show_of_hands/hands.htm.

Maskiewicz, Stefan. 2001. *Quadrego*. www.quadrego.de.

McDaid, John. 1992. *Uncle Buddy's Phantom Funhouse*. Watertown, MA: Eastgate Systems.

McKnight, Cliff, Andrew Dillon, and John Richardson. 1991. *Hypertext in Context*. Cambridge: Cambridge University Press.

Morrissey, Judd, and Lori Talley. 2002. *My Name Is Captain, Captain*. Watertown, MA: Eastgate Systems.

Moulthrop, Stuart. 1992. *Victory Garden*. Cambridge, MA: Eastgate Systems.

———. 1995. "Rhizome and Resistance: Hypertext and the Dreams of a New Culture." In *Hyper/Text/Theory*, edited by George P. Landow, 299–320. Baltimore: Johns Hopkins University Press.

———. 1997. *Hegirascope*. http://iat.ubalt.edu/moulthrop/hypertexts/hgs/.

Nelson, Theodor Holm. 1984. *Literary Machines 93.1*. Sausalito, CA: Mindful Press.

Norman, Donald A. 1976. *Studies in Learning and Self-Contained Educational Systems, 1973–1976*. Washington, DC: Office of Naval Research, Advanced Research Projects Agency.

Pullinger, Kate. 2005–2012. *Inanimate Alice*. www.inanimatealice.com/.

Pullinger, Kate, and Chris Joseph. 2007–2012. *Flight Paths: A Networked Novel*. www.flightpaths.net.

Pullinger, Kate, Stefan Schemat, and babel. 2004. *The Breathing Wall*. London: Sayle Literary Agency.

Ryan, Marie-Laure. 2001. *Narrative as Virtual Reality: Immersion and Interactivity in Literature and Digital Media*. Baltimore: Johns Hopkins University Press.

Schreiber, Urs. 1998. *Das Epos der Maschine*. http://kunst.im.internett.de/epos-der-maschine/edm diemaschine.html.

Shapiro, Amy M. 2006. "Site Maps for Hypertext." In *Encyclopedia of Human Computer Interaction*, edited by Claude Ghaoui, 518–522. Hershey, PA: Idea Group Reference.

Simanowski, Roberto. 2004. "Death of the Author? Death of the Reader!" In *poesis: Ästhetik digitaler Poesie—The Aesthetics of Digital Poetry*, edited by Friedrich W. Block, Christiane Heibach, and Karin Wenz, 17–92. Ostfildern-Ruit, Germany: Hatje Cantz.

I

Identity

Steven Edward Doran

Identity has to do with the traits or characteristics possessed by or applied to individuals which allow them to be recognized and situated within the larger social world. Identities point to how people and groups are construed as distinct from one another. Common examples are gender, race, sexual orientation, class, ethnicity, nationality, and so on. Identities provide us with ways of negotiating and understanding social and cultural realms, as well as interior, psychological realms—how we think of ourselves. In this way, identity occurs at the intersection of the public social world and the private interior world of the individual.

Through various discourses, society "interpellates" or hails individuals into certain subject positions. Subject positions are conceptual social spaces occupied by individuals which position them in specific types of relationships with the broader society (Althusser 2006). For example, if a person is arrested for committing a crime, legal discourses interpellate that individual as a criminal, a subject position describing a particular type of relationship between the subject and the rest of society. But identity doesn't end with the ways that society seeks to place us in various subject positions. Identities are "points of temporary attachment" between the subject and the subject position which require "not only that the subject is 'hailed,' but that the subject invests in the position" (Hall 1996a, 5–6). This means that identities are not determined by social and cultural processes alone. For an identity to be fully realized requires that the subject invests in the subject position constructed for them, that they see themselves as fitting into the social category they are being hailed into and that they consent to this. Identity, then, is the point where our sense of self is attached and in agreement with the subject positions created for us by society.

When it is used in everyday speech, identity refers to the sense that a person or group of people is the same over time and social situation, that, regardless of the circumstance, that person or collectivity maintains a constant set of stable characteristics. This is referred to as the essentialist view of identity since it reduces groups and individuals to an essential unchanging identity. Stuart Hall argues that the essentialist view of identity was embodied in the "Enlightenment subject," a way of thinking about the individual based on "the conception of the human person as a fully centered, unified individual, endowed with the capacities of reason, consciousness and action, whose 'centre' consisted of an inner core [identity] which first emerged when the subject was born, and unfolded with it, while remaining essentially the same—continuous or 'identical' with itself—throughout the individual's existence" (Hall 2006b, 597). An essentialist notion of identity holds that identity is fixed, stable, and coherent—a natural and unchanging phenomenon contained within the body.

But when discussed in new media studies and computer-mediated communication (CMC), identity is often thought of in almost completely opposite terms. In contrast to the essentialist view, scholars in these fields often view identity as far less stable or enduring across time. Instead, they have historically adopted the point of view that identities are fractured and fluid, that they are constructed and constantly performed by individuals in different ways at different times and places. So instead of being an innate and unchanging property of the embodied individual, when looking at people's identities from the perspective of CMC, they are thought of as being far more fragmented, malleable, and contingent on other social processes.

As new media technologies became an increasingly prominent feature of day-to-day life in the late 1980s and early 1990s, the ideas of the "posthuman" and the "cyborg" were deployed to describe the changing relationship between human beings and technology (see CYBORG AND POSTHUMAN). These concepts attempted to describe the hybrid human-machine existences people had adopted at both literal and metaphorical levels. As our bodies became integrated with new technologies (e.g., prosthetics, designer drugs), so were our identities becoming hybrids with elements of both physical and virtual realms. By positioning identity in the space between human and machine, both the cyborg and the posthuman reflect a significant break from, and challenge to, earlier understandings of identity that held it to be embodied, stable, and innate to the individual.

This sense of a fractured, decentered, and disembodied identity was met with great enthusiasm by scholars of CMC when the Internet was in its infancy. Unlike the communications technologies that had preceded it, the Internet allowed people to experience anonymity in completely new ways. In the virtual spaces of the pre-web Internet (e.g., MUDs, chat rooms), people existed solely as text, their presence marked only by the descriptions they provided about themselves. This allowed users to manipulate and play with their identities as they interacted with others in these virtual environments; they were able to safely experiment with parts of their selves that they would have typically kept hidden or that would otherwise be impossible to express. In these new virtual spaces, "the self [was] not only decentered but multiplied without limit. There [was] an unparalleled opportunity to play with one's identity and to 'try out' new ones" (Turkle 1996, 356). This act of reimagining, constructing, and performing different selves provided the impetus for much early Internet use; as Bolter and Grusin point out, "MUDs and chatrooms [served] almost no other cultural function than the remediation of the self" (2000, 258). From its earliest days, identity—specifically its construction and performance—played a central role in people's use of the Internet and the World Wide Web.

By presenting themselves through text, early users of the Internet were able to become that which they could not be in the physical world simply through text, leading people to conceive of identity not only as a disembodied, fragmented, and fluid phenomenon, untethered from the constraints of the human body, but also a constructed one, brought into being through people's representation of themselves online. With the emergence of the World Wide Web and widespread public access to the Internet in the mid-1990s, the idea that networked technologies afforded a constructed and disembodied identity for their users persisted. A 1997 TV commercial for MCI—an early Internet service provider—went as far as to claim, "There is no race. There is no gender. There is no age. There are no infirmaries. There are only minds. Utopia? No, the Internet" (Anthem as cited in Nakamura 2000b, 15). In the featureless vacuum of the web, people were whoever they said they were, and many saw this as a great asset.

Since identity on the Internet had no necessary correlation to the embodied identity of the user sitting at the computer, people could elect to take on identities that they did not occupy in the physical world. White people could be black; women could be men; rich people could be poor. By assuming online identities other than their own for the purposes of pleasure or curiosity, people partook in what is referred to as "identity tourism" (Nakamura 2000a). Identity tourism has effects that are potentially positive as well as potentially negative. On the one hand, experiencing, even virtually, the marginalization of an alternate identity can provide users with a greater sense of empathy and understanding of what it is like to be someone with less privilege. On the other hand, the empathy experienced by users can potentially be a false empathy, leading people to diminish or dismiss the marginalization of subordinate groups in society based only on their experience of playing that identity in virtual space. By performing virtual forms of embodied identities such as race, gender, and sexual orientation, identity tourism shows that identity on the Internet can never fully escape the body (see MATERIALITY). This lingering body suggests that online identity is neither as unstable nor as fluid as early new media theorists had thought.

As avatars—visual representations of individuals typically designed or chosen by the user (see AVATARS)—took the place of written descriptions as the predominant mode of self-presentation online, many of the claims made of text-based identity were transferred to discussions of users' avatarial identities in online spaces such as *World of Warcraft* and *Second Life* (see ONLINE GAME COMMUNITIES, ONLINE WORLDS). Through the process of "avatarial introjection" (Van Looy 2010, 177), people would strategically deploy their identities into these virtual spaces, allowing them to experiment and play with identity in ways similar to how they would in earlier text-based environments. As evidence of the prevalence of this type of avatarial identity play, it has become a joke that MMORPG (massively multiplayer online role-playing game) should really stand for "many men online role-playing as girls."

With the emergence of social networking sites (see SOCIAL NETWORK SITES [SNSs]), questions of online identity became less a matter of identity construction and more an issue of identity management. SNS environments like MySpace and Facebook eschew the anonymity of earlier virtual spaces such as chat rooms and MUDs and instead base their platforms on users' "real-life" identities. The shift away from anonymity brings with it a new set of concerns with regard to identity. Whereas text-based and avatarial modes of online presence highlighted the importance of identity construction on the Internet, SNSs draw attention to identity management and performance. Users of SNSs bring their "real-world" identities with them, and thus one of their primary activities on SNSs is the negotiation and deployment of different facets of identity as it straddles both virtual and physical realms.

■ See also AVATARS, CYBORG AND POSTHUMAN, MATERIALITY

References and Further Reading

Althusser, Louis. 2006. "Ideology and Ideological State Apparatuses (Notes towards an Investigation)." In *The Anthropology of the State: A Reader*, edited by Aradhana Sharma and Akhil Gupta, 86–111. Malden, MA: Wiley.

Bolter, Jay David, and Richard Grusin. 2000. *Remediation: Understanding New Media*. Cambridge, MA: MIT Press.

Hall, Stuart. 1996a. "Introduction: Who Needs Identity?" In *Questions of Cultural Identity*, edited by Stuart Hall and Paul Du Gay, 1–17. London: Sage.

———. 1996b. "The Question of Cultural Identity." In *Modernity: An Introduction to Modern Societies*, edited by Stuart Hall, David Held, Don Hubert, and Kenneth Thompson, 595–634. Oxford: Blackwell.

Hayles, N. Katherine. 1999. *How We Became Posthuman: Virtual Bodies in Cybernetics, Literature, and Informatics*. Chicago: University of Chicago Press.

Nakamura, Lisa. 2000a. "Race in/for Cyberspace: Identity Tourism and Racial Passing on the Internet." In *The Cybercultures Reader*, edited by David Bell and Barbara M. Kennedy. New York: Routledge.

———. 2000b. "'Where do you want to go today?' Cybernetic Tourism, the Internet, and Transnationality." In *Race in Cyberspace*, edited by Beth E. Kolko, Lisa Nakamura, and Gilbert B. Rodman. New York: Routledge.

———. 2002. *Cybertypes: Race, Ethnicity, and Identity on the Internet*. New York: Routledge.

Turkle, Sherry. 1995. *Life on the Screen: Identity in the Age of the Internet*. New York: Simon & Schuster.

———. 1996. "Constructions and Reconstructions of the Self in Virtual Reality." In *Electronic Culture: Technology and Visual Representation*, edited by Timothy Druckrey. New York: Aperture.

———. 2011. *Alone Together: Sociable Robots, Digitized Friends, and the Reinvention of Intimacy and Solitude*. New York: Basic Books.

Van Looy, Jan. 2010. *Understanding Computer Game Culture: The Cultural Shaping of a New Medium*. Saarbrücken, Germany: Lambert Academic.

••

Immersion

Jan-Noël Thon

The term *immersion* is now commonly used within game studies to describe the "illusion of immediacy" that, at least for some players, forms an integral part of the experience of playing a computer game. While it has primarily been applied to computer games by scholars such as Murray (1997), Ryan (2001), McMahan (2003), Ermi and Mäyrä (2005), Thon (2008), and Calleja (2011), the term was originally made popular in the context of virtual reality research (see VIRTUAL REALITY) and is also sometimes used to describe certain parts of the experience of appreciating art (e.g., Grau 2003), reading literary texts (e.g., Gerrig 1993), or watching movies (e.g., Schweinitz 2006). Despite its affinity to interactive media, then, immersion may be considered a genuinely transmedial concept in that it can be applied to representational media in general (e.g., Herman 2009, 118–127; Neitzel 2008; Ryan 2001).

Perhaps not surprisingly, however, the concept is rather contested, and the questions of what immersion is and of whether it makes sense at all to speak of immersion with regard to computer games and other digital media have been hotly debated (see Salen and Zimmerman [2004, 450–455] for a critique of the so-called immersive fallacy, or Thon [2008] and Calleja [2011] for a discussion of terminological alternatives). Even among the scholars who do use the term, one cannot necessarily assume a strong consensus regarding its exact meaning. More specifically, one can find a range of opinions as to what aspects of the "immersive experience" should be considered particularly salient.

Murray, for example, describes immersion as the pleasurable "experience of being transported to an elaborately simulated place" which results from the "sensation of being surrounded by a completely other reality, as different as water is from air, that takes over all of our attention, our whole perceptual apparatus" (1997, 98). However, the player of a computer game is not literally transported to another place while playing. Hence, it may seem problematic to rely too strongly on the metaphor of transportation for an appropriate description of the experience of immersion (see also Ermi and Mäyrä 2005; McMahan 2003, 76–77; Ryan 2001, 93–99; the metaphor seems to have been popularized by Gerrig 1993).

Somewhat less metaphorically, Ryan describes immersion as a process of "recentering" by which "consciousness relocates itself to another world" (2001, 103). It is especially noteworthy that her conception of immersion entails not only the shift of attention toward a fictional world but also the construction of a mental representation of that world (Ryan 2001, 110–114). Ryan does not go into too much detail on what role these processes play with regard to computer games, but her discussion of immersion—as well as her distinction between its spatial, temporal, and emotional aspects—remains influential within computer game studies and beyond (see SPATIALITY OF DIGITAL MEDIA, TEMPORALITY OF DIGITAL WORKS).

While both Murray and Ryan conceptualize immersion primarily as a shift of attention to fictional worlds (at least as far as the "metaphor of transportation" can be translated into these terms), McMahan (2003, 68) observes that the player of a computer game can also become immersed in the process of playing itself (see INTERACTIVITY, SIMULATION), and that a consistent experience is more important for evoking a sense of immersion than big screens and impressive surround sound (2003, 68–69). According to McMahan, then, immersion entails more than a shift of attention to the three-dimensional space or the unfolding story of a computer game. Additionally, what is presented becomes more important than how it is presented.

In fact, most scholars within computer game studies seem to agree that it is not necessary for the presentation to "take over . . . our whole perceptual apparatus" (Murray 1997, 98) in order for us to experience immersion. While this kind of "perceptual immersion" may be "accomplished by blocking as many of the senses as possible to the outside world" (McMahan 2003, 77), such a setup does not say too much about the afforded experience or "psychological immersion" (Lombard and Ditton 1997). However, psychological presence research tends to use the term *immersion* primarily to refer to the "perceptual" aspects, describing the "psychological" aspects of the experience as "presence" (e.g., Tamborini and Skalski 2006).

If psychological immersion in computer games and other digital media does not necessarily require perceptual immersion (although it is obviously not independent from perception), the experience of immersion can be more generally described as a shift of attention from the real environment to certain parts of the game, and as the construction of a mental representation of the gameplay, the game spaces, and the game world. Since immersion is often described as a complex, multidimensional experience, however, it also seems worthwhile to examine what elements of computer game structure players shift their attention to and construct situation models of, and how these different kinds of structural properties lead to different kinds of experience.

Both Murray (1997, 109) and Ryan (2001, 120–162) distinguish between immersion in the presented space and immersion in the unfolding story, and it has already been mentioned that McMahan (2003, 68) distinguishes between immersion in the story world and immersion in the game (see NARRATIVITY). Integrating the "perceptual" aspects, Ermi and Mäyrä (2005) distinguish between sensory immersion, challenge-based immersion, and imaginative immersion. The concept of sensory immersion is similar to that of perceptual immersion and entails the assumption that "large screens close to the player's face and powerful sounds easily overpower the sensory information coming from the real world, and the player becomes entirely focused on the game world and its stimuli" (Ermi and Mäyrä 2005, n.p.).

Challenge-based immersion refers to the shift of the player's attention "to sensomotor abilities such as using the controls and reacting fast, and . . . to the cognitive challenges" (Ermi and Mäyrä 2005, n.p.) posed by computer games. The experience of challenge-based immersion is claimed to be strongest when a "satisfying balance of challenges and abilities" (Ermi and Mäyrä 2005, n.p.) is achieved. Imaginative immersion refers to the "dimension of game experience in which one becomes absorbed with the stories and the world, or begins to feel for or identify with a game character" (Ermi and Mäyrä 2005, n.p.). Here, the immersion in the presented space and the immersion in the unfolding story distinguished by both Murray and Ryan are combined.

Expanding the existing models of immersion to account for the experience provided by multiplayer games, Thon (2008) has proposed to distinguish between spatial, ludic, narrative, and social immersion as components of the computer game player's experience. Again, immersion is generally understood as a player's shift of attention to certain game elements and her construction of a situation model related to these elements. Spatial immersion, then, focuses on the game spaces as spaces; ludic immersion focuses on the interaction with the game; narrative immersion focuses on the unfolding of the story and its characters, as well as on the fictional game world as a whole; and social immersion focuses on the other players as social actors and on the relationship between them, as well as on the social space that is constituted through the communication and social interaction between the players.

These different aspects of the computer game player's experience could also be described using different terms. Spatial immersion is very similar to the concept of spatial presence (e.g., Tamborini and Skalski 2006). Ludic immersion could also be described using the concept of flow developed by Csikszentmihalyi (1990). Narrative immersion refers to well-established concepts such as "suspense" and "empathy" (e.g., Ryan 2001, 141–148). Finally, social immersion is very similar to the concept of social presence (e.g., Tamborini and Skalski 2006). It would therefore be possible to reserve the term *immersion* for perceptual immersion and to describe the different dimensions or aspects of psychological immersion—which, depending on the game, may entail not only spatial but also ludic, narrative, and social kinds of experience—using more specialized terminology.

Arguing in a similar vein, Calleja has proposed to describe the experience afforded by computer games in terms of "involvement" and "incorporation" rather than in terms of "immersion," emphasizing that "the problem of viewing the immersive experience as a monolithic phenomenon is addressed by the multidimensional nature of the player involvement model upon which incorporation is built" (2011, 173). However, the six dimensions of player involvement he distinguishes turn out to be rather similar to the dimensions of immersion discussed within computer game studies: kinaesthetic involvement and spatial involvement are entailed in Thon's spatial immersion, shared involvement is roughly equivalent to Thon's social immersion, narrative involvement and affective involvement are entailed in Thon's narrative immersion, and ludic involvement is roughly equivalent to Thon's ludic immersion.

In conclusion, it might be worth stressing that, at least within computer game studies, the term *immersion* is still regularly used in a way that includes some or all of the different dimensions of the gameplay experience discussed above. Against this background, a distinction of different kinds of immersion seems helpful for reasons of terminological clarity alone. Another advantage of the multidimensional models of immersion proposed by Ryan (2001), McMahan (2003), and Ermi and Mäyrä (2005), as well as Thon (2008) and—at least to a certain extent—Calleja (2011), is that they allow us to highlight the similarities and interrelations between different aspects of the computer game player's experience that otherwise would be (and indeed still too often are) discussed separately. Enabling us to look beyond the utopia of a "perfect virtual reality," then, a multidimensional conception of immersion helps to examine similarities and differences in the experiences that computer games and other (digital and nondigital) representational media offer to their users.

References and Further Reading

Calleja, Gordon. 2011. *In-Game: From Immersion to Incorporation*. Cambridge, MA: MIT Press.

Csikszentmihalyi, Mihalyi. 1990. *Flow: The Psychology of Optimal Experience*. New York: Harper & Row.

Ermi, Laura, and Frans Mäyrä. 2005. "Fundamental Components of the Gameplay Experience: Analysing Immersion." In *Digra 2005 Proceedings*. http://people.uta.fi/~tlilma/gameplay_experience.pdf.

Gerrig, Richard J. 1993. *Experiencing Narrative Worlds: On the Psychological Activity of Reading*. New Haven, CT: Yale University Press.

Grau, Oliver. 2003. *Virtual Art: From Illusion to Immersion*. Cambridge, MA: MIT Press.

Herman, David. 2009. *Basic Elements of Narrative*. Malden, MA: Wiley-Blackwell.

Lombard, Matthew, and Theresa Ditton. 1997. "At the Heart of It All: The Concept of Presence." *JCMC* 3 (2). http://jcmc.indiana.edu/vol3/issue2/lombard.html.

McMahan, Alison. 2003. "Immersion, Engagement, and Presence. A Method for Analyzing 3-D Video Games." In *The Video Game Theory Reader*, edited by Mark J. P. Wolf and Bernard Perron, 67–86. New York: Routledge.

Murray, Janet H. 1997. *Hamlet on the Holodeck: The Future of Narrative in Cyberspace*. New York: Free Press.

Neitzel, Britta. 2008. "Facetten räumlicher Immersion in technischen Medien." *montage a/v* 17 (2): 145–158.

Ryan, Marie-Laure. 2001. *Narrative as Virtual Reality: Immersion and Interactivity in Literature and Electronic Media*. Baltimore: Johns Hopkins University Press.

Salen, Katie, and Eric Zimmerman. 2004. *Rules of Play: Game Design Fundamentals*. Cambridge, MA: MIT Press.

Schweinitz, Jörg. 2006. "Totale Immersion, Kino und die Utopien von der virtuellen Realität. Zur Geschichte und Theorie eines Mediengründungsmythos." In *Das Spiel mit dem Medium: Partizipation—Immersion—Interaktion*, edited by Britta Neitzel and Rolf F. Nohr, 136–153. Marburg, Germany: Schüren.

Tamborini, Rob, and Paul Skalski. 2006. "The Role of Presence in the Experience of Electronic Games." In *Playing Video Games: Motives, Responses, and Consequences*, edited by Peter Vorderer and Jennings Bryant, 225–240. Mahwah, NJ: Lawrence Erlbaum Associates.

Thon, Jan-Noël. 2008. "Immersion Revisited: On the Value of a Contested Concept." In *Extending Experiences: Structure, Analysis and Design of Computer Game Player Experience*, edited by Amyris Fernandez, Olli Leino, and Hanna Wirman, 29–43. Rovaniemi, Finland: Lapland University Press.

Independent and Art Games
Celia Pearce

Independent games are those produced outside of the framework of the mainstream video game industry, although they may eventually find more traditional forms of publication. Also called "indie games," they have come into prominence in the past decade as a result of a number of factors, including the expansion of online distribution channels; increased accessibility and declining costs of development tools; lack of innovation among mainstream studios, coupled with the desire for innovation among both developers and players; the perception of games as a medium for creative expression, including games produced under the auspices of "fine art"; the growing role of academic game programs in the video game industry; and the influence of independent game festivals within a flowering indie game community.

History

Independent developers have always been a vital part of the video game ecosystem. Alongside larger companies from the pinball, card game, electronics, and traditional entertainment industries, smaller studios have also contributed to both growth and innovation in the game industry. Many developers that started out indie went on to become or be acquired by major studios. In addition, some indie studios have spun off from larger studies that closed their more creative divisions, such as Double Fine and Telltale, both studios founded by refugees from LucasArts.

In 1995, two years after *Myst*, *DOOM*—two early indies that went on to garner commercial success—and the World Wide Web, the video game industry took a major stride into mainstream entertainment with the launch of E3, a massive expo for video game publishers. With over 1.2 million square feet of theme park–style expo booths aimed at attracting big-box retailers, which were the principal vehicles for success, a compelling argument can be made that E3 marks the moment the video game industry became a victim of its own success. Limited shelf space and a blockbuster mentality resulted in studios that had once been considered innovators falling prey to the new world order of the hit-driven business model, becoming increasingly risk averse.

In spite of its humble beginnings, the success of the video game industry, combined with its hegemonic distribution model, helped to create an industry that, by the 2000s, resembled the film industry of the 1930s. The industry was controlled by a small handful of powerful studios that called the shots on what got made and what got sold. By the 2010s, the industry faced an epidemic of "sequelitis" and licensing mania. Also like the film industry of the 1930s, this studio-based system gave the creative employees of the studios little or no credit and no royalty participation. Just as their predecessors in the film industry had done earlier, creative developers began to rebel in greater numbers, exploring a range of new platforms, genres, and expressive forms for the video game medium.

Platforms and Genres

The rise of indie games has been fueled in part by the growth of casual and browser-based games, combined with increased online distribution and the introduction of new game platforms, such as Facebook and Apple's iOS. Indie developers are particularly well suited for these new platforms since the indie creed is one of experimentation and innovation (see MOBILE GAMES). Especially with new mobile capabilities such as multi-touch and accelerometers, indie developers push the envelope on new features by finding novel ways to "play" with technology. One of the best exemplars of the role of new mobile platforms in advancing indie games is the smash hit *Angry Birds* (2009), which as of this writing had outsold virtually every other app on the iOS platform, as well as many other mainstream video games.

Independent games encompass a wide range of genres, including new twists on traditional video game genres, such as adventure games and platformers, as well as new genres such as serious, documentary (see INTERACTIVE DOCUMENTARY), and activist games; alternate reality and big games; and art games. A new generation of board and card games has also played a growing role in expanding the audience and awareness of indie games.

The burgeoning art games movement has also opened up the field to both new audiences and new creators. Art games are typically targeted to gallery and museum settings, alternative game scene events, festivals, or online distribution, usually for free, and can include both digital and analog forms. These follow some of the traditions of tactical use of games by artists in earlier movements, such as Dada, Fluxus, and Happenings (Pearce 2006; Flanagan 2009). Early exhibitions of art games included Anne Marie Schleiner's online *Cracking the Maze* (1999); *Shift+Ctrl*, at UC Irvine's Beall Center for Art and Technology (2000); and *Trigger*, curated by Rebecca Cannon in Melbourne, Australia (2002). Many early game art works were also made available through the *Select Parks* website (curated by Cannon with Julian Oliver and Chris Dodds), such as Oliver's *Levelhead* and the work of other artists. Other successful game artists have included Mary Flanagan, Eddo Stern, art collective jodi, Cory Archangel, Mark Essen, and Tale of Tales, as well as Brenda Brathwaite, whose *Train*, an art-based board game about the holocaust, has drawn worldwide acclaim.

Art games drew national attention when, in 2011, the U.S. National Endowment for the Arts (NEA) made headlines by rewording its funding solicitations to include new media arts and video games, resulting in a number of headlines in geek and game press proclaiming "U.S. Government Deems Video Games Art" (Hall 2011) (see GAMES AS ART/LITERATURE). This fueled counterarguments to film critic Roger Ebert's famous statements between 2005 and 2010 that "video games would never be an art form" (Ebert 2005, 2010b; Nosowitz 2010). Ebert later tempered his position, conceding to critics that he had failed to provide an adequate definition of "art," as well as having limited experience with video games (2010a). The addition of games to the NEA solicitation opened the door for games like *Walden*, a game based on the classic Henry David Thoreau novel and designed by Tracy Fullerton, who had previously developed the award-winning work *The Night Journey* with video artist Bill Viola.

Availability of Tools

Game development is a time-intensive software development process requiring deep programming skills. Some early attempts at creating easy-to-use tools included HyperCard and Macromedia Director, which eventually evolved into Shockwave and Flash (see FLASH/DIRECTOR). *DOOM* introduced the innovation of licensing game engines, allowing developers to focus on game mechanics while underlying code, such as graphics rendering and physics, could be handled by preexisting software. Initially game engine licenses were available at a high price; however, developers eventually began releasing modifiable versions of their games, allowing players to create their own "mods" using high-end commercial game engines. One of the most notable of these was *Counter-Strike*, produced in 1999 by a distributed team of indie developers. A free mod of Valve's highly successful *Half-Life* first-person shooter game, it became a hit at cybercafes around the world, eventually becoming more popular than *Half-Life* itself. Because playing *Counter-Strike* required the purchase of the original *Half-Life* disk, it therefore drove sales of the original game. Valve subsequently acquired the franchise and published the game and its sequels.

In parallel with the modding movement, a number of new game development tools entered the marketplace at relatively affordable prices. Although the landscape is rapidly changing, as of this writing Adobe Flash had established itself as the principle tool for developing 2D browser-based and casual games. Initially GarageGames's *Torque*, which provided high-quality 3D rendering at a fraction of the price of previous game engines, was the favorite among indie developers, but it has since been supplanted by the Danish *Unity*. The development of open-source tools, as well as code and feature libraries for authoring environments such as Flash and Unity, continue to expand access to indie developers.

New Distribution

The sales of early video games were based principally on the distribution of cartridges and later CDS via large brick-and-mortar retail outlets, such as Best Buy and Walmart. This meant limited shelf space, as well as a rigid genre system that made it easier for marketers and retailers to sell games. Although the United States has been behind the curve on online distribution, in many other countries, most notably Korea, downloading games had become the standard as early as 2000, a decade before it was fully embraced in the United States. The aversion to downloadable games in the United States was due in part to concerns about piracy, as well as to the slow adoption of broadband as compared with regions such as Asia and Northern Europe.

One of the contributing factors to the advancement of indie games and online distribution has been the growth of the casual game market, aided in part by universal adoption of Adobe Flash. In addition to providing a simple tool for authoring interactive content, Flash also allowed for the distribution of browser-based or small downloadable games, further expanding access. A number of games became hits through this mechanism. A notable example is *Diner Dash*, developed at the now-defunct indie studio Game Lab and published by PlayFirst in 2003. A number of game portals, such as Manifesto Games (also now defunct) and Kongregate, allowed developers to publish their own games for general consumption.

Another significant turning point was the introduction of downloadable games for the PC. In 2002, Valve Software, the studio that created *Half-Life*, introduced the first downloadable publishing portal for PC games, *Steam*. Since then a number of online portals have opened, allowing indie developers the opportunity to self-publish. In addition, many indies give away or sell games on their own websites, often gaining traction through word of mouth in the indie game developer and fan communities.

Console developers were slow to follow suit but eventually saw the opportunity to diversify their offerings and, much like the advent of indie film distribution divisions at major movie studios, began to introduce downloadable and indie game portals to their platforms. By 2010, all three major console platforms had introduced downloadable outlets that opened the door for independently produced titles to be published on consoles. In 2012, Jonathan Blow's *Braid* had become one of the most successful indie games released on Xbox Live Arcade.

The Growth of Game Schools

In much the same way that the rise of film schools propelled the explosion of independent films in the 1950s–1970s, video game programs have had a similar effect on the game industry. Following the appearance of early professional schools, such as DigiPen (1988), the first game-focused university programs began to appear in the late 1990s, spearheaded by Georgia Tech's Digital Media graduate program and Carnegie-Mellon's Entertainment Technology Center. These and other programs have taken a leading role in influencing the game industry, especially independent games. These include the MIT Comparative Media Studies Program, UCLA's Design|Media Arts Program, the Interactive Media Program in the University of Southern California's School of Cinematic Arts, and Savannah College of Art and Design's Interactive Design and Game Development, among others. A number of schools also have labs that have produced notable games, such as USC's Game Innovation Lab and MIT's Gambit Lab. A number of international schools have also appeared, including Copenhagen ITU's Center for Computer Games Research, the birthplace of the Copenhagen Game Collective, creators of the award-winning games *B.U.T.T.O.N.* and *Johan Sebastian Joust*.

The growing influence of video game schools and programs is strongly tied to the rise of independent game festivals, which often showcase these games. Two games that epitomize this influence are *Portal* (2007) and *flow* (2008), both successful commercial titles that began as student games. Originally created by students at DigiPen Institute of Technology, *Narbacular Drop* (2005) won the Independent Game Festival's Student Showcase Award in 2006. However, rather than remaining independent, the team accepted an offer by Valve Software to join its staff and develop it as a commercial game. The result was *Portal*, a massive commercial hit, which subsequently won Game of the Year at the Game Developers' Choice Awards (2008), the Academy Award of the video game industry.

flow (2006) began as a master's thesis project at USC's Interactive Media Program, and after being honored as a festival finalist and award winner, it captured the attention of Sony. *flow* was published as a downloadable game on PlayStation 3 (2007) and subsequently won a Game Developers Choice Award for Best Downloadable Game (2008). *flow* was part of a landmark three-game deal between Sony and thatgamecompany that resulted in two other games, *Flower* (2009) and *Journey* (2012), which became the most successful downloadable game on PlayStation Network.

Festivals and the Indie Game "Movement"

The *Portal* and *flow* stories illustrate the growing role of festivals in promoting independent games of all types. The festival movement began with the founding in 1998 of the Independent Game Festival (IGF), a juried exhibition and awards associated with the Game Developers Conference (GDC), the primary annual convening of game creators. While the IGF has remained the most significant influence, it has also been critiqued for its industry-oriented focus, as a subset of a major industry event re-

quiring industry credentials and a high ticket price. A number of festivals that principally cover other media have added games to their purview, including the Slamdance
Guerrilla Game Maker Competition, which ran as part of the Slamdance Film Festival
from 2004 to 2007; South by Southwest (SXSW); the Sundance Film Festival; and the
United Kingdom's BAFTA Awards. The Academia of Interactive Arts & Sciences also
hosts D.I.C.E. and the Interactive Academy Awards. IndieCade, which launched in 2008
and was called the "Sundance of the game industry" by the *Los Angeles Times* (Fritz 2009),
was the first stand-alone independent game festival in the United States to be open to the
public and hosts showcases at E3 (Los Angeles) and Nottingham Game City (United
Kingdom).

These festivals and events support a large and growing independent game scene,
which thrives on blogs, Listservs, and other community vehicles that help to create local,
regional, and international events. The indie community was the centerpiece of the 2012
documentary film *Indie Game: The Movie*, which follows a handful of indie game designers in achieving their vision.

Special thanks to Sam Roberts.

■ See also GAME HISTORY, INTERACTIVE DRAMA, INTERACTIVE FICTION

References and Further Reading

Carroll, Jon. 1994. "Guerillas in the Myst." *Wired* 2 (8).
Cracking the Maze. 1999. Online exhibition curated by Anne Marie Schleiner. http://switch.sjsu
.edu/CrackingtheMaze/.
Ebert, Roger. 2005. "Why Did the Chicken Cross the Genders?" *Chicago Sun-Times*, November, 27.
———. 2010a. "Okay, Kids, Play on My Lawn." Blogpost on the *Chicago Sun-Times* website, July 1.
http://blogs.suntimes.com/ebert/2010/07/okay_kids_play_on_my_lawn.html.
———. 2010b. "Video Games Can Never Be Art." *Chicago Sun-Times*, April 16.
Flanagan, Mary. 2009. *Critical Play: Radical Game Design*. Cambridge, MA: MIT Press.
Fritz, Ben. 2009. "Indiecade, the Video Game Industry's Sundance." *Los Angeles Times*, October 1.
Hall, Brian. 2011. "U.S. Government Declares Roger Ebert Wrong: Video Games Officially Art." *Piki-
Geek*, May 8. http://geek.pikimal.com/2011/05/08/us-government-declares-roger-ebert-wrong
-video-games-officially-art/.
Indie Game: The Movie. 2012. Directed by James Swirsky and Lisanne Pajot. Independently pro-
duced film.
The Indie Game Database. http://db.tigsource.com/.
Nosowitz, Dan. 2010. "Game Designer Kellee Santiago Responds to Roger Ebert's 'Video Games
Are Not Art' Rant." *Fast Company*, April 10. www.fastcompany.com/1621426/game-designer
-kellee-santiago-responds-to-roger-eberts-video-games-are-not-art-rant.
Pearce, Celia. 2006. "Games as Art: The Aesthetics of Play." In *Fluxus and Legacy*, special issue of
Visible Language, edited by Ken Friedman and Owen Smith, 66–89.
Select Parks. www.selectparks.net/.
Sharkey, Mike. 2010. "Robert Ebert Concedes Video Games Can Be Considered Art." *Gamespy*, July
1. www.gamespy.com/articles/110/1103298p1.html.

Interactive Cinema

Glorianna Davenport

Interactive cinema is a genre that combines the language and aesthetics of cinema with a delivery system that enables audience *feedback* and *control.*

Interactive cinema (see INTERACTIVITY) invites its audience to actively engage in the construction, personalization, consumption, and sharing of a movie experience. The "theater" in which it plays out, whether a public venue or a personal space, is enhanced with agencies and devices that empower the audience to "put their hands" onto the story and actively steer its development. In this way, interactive cinema challenges the tradition of cinema in which a story is presented as a fixed, unchangeable linear narrative permanently embedded in a reel of film or videotape. Instead, it "reflects the longing of cinema to become something new, something more complex and personal, as if in conversation with an audience" (Davenport et al. 1993).

Interactive cinema fundamentally alters the relationships between author, audience, and story content. Usually, a machine (often a very complex one) serves as mediator. As all parties collaborate in the co-construction of meaning, new tensions are introduced and new story forms begin to emerge.

As interactive cinema developed and advanced, each project engaged in a heroic struggle to reshape the available technologies of the time into unique, custom-built delivery systems that generally were unsuitable for other content. Further, the costs of creating motion-picture content to support interactivity could be substantial. As a result, most early interactive cinema experiments had limited content and focused on advancing one or two aspects of the genre while neglecting others.

Today, despite many working examples, interactive cinema remains in its infancy as a narrative art. However, twenty-first-century technology is sufficiently advanced that this "holy grail" of narrative may yet become a reality.

Two Faces of Innovations Leading to Interactive Cinema: Art and Technology

Historically, cinema was a mass medium controlled by professional studios, theater owners, and licensed TV broadcasters. Generally, the audience's control was limited to the decision of whether or not to attend. For most movie producers, at least prior to 1967, no other input seemed necessary. However, the role of the artist has always been to challenge the traditional paradigms.

One of the earliest examples of an interactive cinema experience—*KinoAutomat: One Man and His House*—was mounted as a theatrical experience in the Czechoslovakian Pavilion at Expo '67 in Montreal. Raduz Cincera and a crew of Czech "new wave" filmmakers outfitted a 127-seat theater with electronic buttons at each chair. At certain important plot points, a personable human moderator would stop the movie, explain what choices were available, and urge the audience to vote on which direction the story should take by pushing either the red or the blue button. Two 35 mm projectors running in tandem allowed a projectionist to show the film from the reel with the desired scene; after the votes were tallied, the projectionist would put a lens cap over the "losing" projector and play the next part of the story.

Twenty-five years later, Interfilm Inc. attempted to mass-market a theatrical interactive cinema experience using a modernized version of the KinoAutomat. Backed by Sony Entertainment, thirty-five movie theaters were outfitted with red, yellow, and green buttons at each chair for voting. The personable human host of the KinoAutomat was replaced by an on-screen automaton. While 1967 audiences flocked to the Czech Pavilion to witness a new form of entertainment, audiences of the 1980s found the Interfilm productions trivial. In May of 1985, Interfilm folded, and no large-scale theater-based interactive cinema venture has been attempted since.

Mass Media versus My Media: Growing Expectations of Personal Control

As television technology matured, a constant stream of innovative home entertainment devices empowered audiences to increasingly take control over the film experience. This passage to "interactive" engagement can be described as stages of a media revolution that began in 1950 with the mass-marketing of the TV remote control. The handheld controller gave individuals the power to switch channels (and thus select from the matrix of available content) with the push of a button, without having to get up from their chair. A separate, handheld (initially printed) index to content—the *TV Guide*—became a useful (but optional) supplementary tool.

The tyranny of the broadcaster's schedules was shattered in the mid-1970s by the widespread adoption of Betamax and VHS videocassette recorders. Suddenly, people were free to record whatever TV programs they wished and view them whenever they liked. New audience behaviors emerged that changed the nature of viewing, including commercial zapping (fast-forwarding to quickly get past undesired content), time compression (fast-forwarding through desired content), instant replay (reviewing a chunk of video at normal speed or in slow motion), and pausing (stopping the show for bathroom breaks, conversations, and other nonviewing social activities).

VCRs captured the ephemeral TV signal and embedded it within a persistent physical object, the videotape. Cassettes containing TV shows and Hollywood movies became inexpensive commodities that could be copied and swapped with friends, sold in stores, collected in libraries, and otherwise handled in social situations outside of the conventional broadcast channels. In effect, people were free to program their own TV channels.

A compelling early example of audience-driven interactive cinema soon emerged. When the science fiction TV show *Star Trek* was cancelled after three seasons, fans began using their VCRs to reedit footage from the series to make their own episodes and share them with fellow enthusiasts. These "fanvid" remixes (see REMIX) spanned many subcultures, from traditionalists who merely wanted more episodes, to music videos, to "slash fiction" featuring same-sex romances among the major characters (Jenkins 2006, 37–60).

These populist forays required tedious and painstaking editing. Amateur makers had to manually cue playback and record decks, put both decks in "play," and then at the right moment punch in the "record" button, praying that the resulting "edit" would be acceptable. However, this noncomputerized experience foreshadowed a future moment in which an interactive cinema experience would be more like a real-time editing performance, with content seamlessly pieced together "on the fly" from an inventory of premade shots, sounds, text, still images, and other audiovisual elements.

Since the invention of film, there has always been a subculture of personal filmmakers. For many years the 16 mm windup silent camera was the choice of amateur enthusiasts. Silent Super-8 cameras were followed by the introduction of Super-8 sound movie cameras in 1983. Meanwhile the Sony Portapak—a thirty-pound "portable" video camera system first introduced in 1967—had energized hundreds of artists and independent filmmakers. With the appearance of inexpensive, highly portable color camcorders in 1982, the "Do It Yourself" video culture took off. Suddenly, your own personal footage—embedded in a standard videocassette—could be treated interchangeably with Hollywood movies or TV programming.

Another milestone in the media revolution was the mass-marketing of video game consoles and handheld units in the 1970s. Often framed within the context of a story, these games allowed the audience to interact vigorously with audiovisual content. A variety of novel interface devices—joysticks, wands, pressure-sensitive mats, guns, steering wheels, etc.—were closely integrated with the game action. Although these games were very different from movies, a palpable sense that the two were somehow related quickly emerged.

In the late 1970s, as audiovisual appliances for the home became accepted and understood, the first personal computers appeared in the marketplace. People quickly embraced the reality of a powerful, programmable, highly responsive interactive device that combined workaday utilities with tools for artistic creation. By the mid-1990s desktop digital video and audio editors had become common applications. These tools increasingly empowered much of the population to create and share their creative works cheaply and easily.

In 1977, the computer-controllable laser disc player—perhaps the most influential computer accessory up to that time—was first introduced in the United States. The constant angular velocity (CAV) laserdisc held up to 54,000 still frames, or thirty minutes of uncompressed video, two analog audio tracks, and two uncompressed digital audio tracks. The computer-controllable player, equipped with an RS-232 serial port, was capable of addressing audiovisual materials at many levels of granularity, down to the individual frame. In an era of three-hundred-baud network communications and floppy disk storage—when a ten-megabyte hard drive was considered an unaffordable luxury—this relatively huge frame-storing capacity made many pioneering "interactive video" projects possible.

Among the most influential of these early laserdisc-based projects are the following:

- *The Aspen Movie Map* (1978–1980), in which the participant "drives" seamlessly through the streets of the city of Aspen, Colorado, in a manner that predated Google Street View by 25 years (Lippman 1980);
- *Murder, Anyone?* (1982), in which a home audience could engage in solving a murder case (Anderson 1985);
- *New Orleans in Transition, 1983–86* (1986), which served as a video case study in which students could recut and paste video into term papers (Davenport 1987).

The Marriage of Video and Computer

In 1987, Apple Computer released HyperCard, a rapid-prototyping environment that combined a functional database manager with a highly flexible, programmable graphical user interface, an easy-to-learn programming language, and the ability to communicate with other machines via serial and parallel data ports. Most of the early experimenters in interactive cinema had been forced to develop these core functions from scratch; but with HyperCard, a low-cost off-the-shelf solution became widely available, and—when linked to the computer-controlled laserdisc player—the "Golden Age" of interactive multimedia began.

Most interactive cinema experiences move forward as the audience chooses "what to see next" from a menu of possibilities. Where do those menus come from? The earliest projects used *simple branching*, where the story's primary author hard-coded a series of choices at critical plot points. However, tool-building pioneers soon expanded the available options. In his Elastic Tool Kit (first released with the 1989 videodisc *Elastic Charles: A Hypermedia Journal*), H. P. Brondmo added *contextual linking* (where choices appear automatically whenever they are appropriate to the context) and *temporal linking* (where choices only last as long as they are relevant). His tools also featured a method by which participant-viewers could craft their own links using "micons" (movie icons) through a video program. The idea of video-on-video to indicate and actively link segments extended both the concept and language of interactive cinema (Brondmo and Davenport 1989). The Elastic Tool Kit hastened Apple's release of QuickTime and inspired one of the first desktop editing systems, Diva, which was later sold to Avid.

Interactive cinema soon began to plumb artificial intelligence as a basis of cinematic storytelling systems (see ARTIFICIAL INTELLIGENCE). Computational engines crunched metadata descriptions of movie content in order to offer choices of "what to see next." Streams and filters, role-based models, spreading-activation nets, and other computational techniques were matched up with new interface metaphors and eagerly adapted in service of story.

In the mid-1990s, the rise of the World Wide Web provided another opportunity for interactive cinema to make a quantum leap forward. Here minimovies, databases, and graphical user interfaces are easily combined with search facilities, content filters, and interpersonal messaging to serve a widely dispersed but socially connected audience. The web provides a vast infrastructure for individuals and multiplayer teams to actively create, engage with, and share a staggeringly large corpus of video, sound, and text content. So far, the web has inspired some novel interactive works, but web-based cinematic storytelling is still an immature medium. While YouTube and other similar sites provide a venue for publishing and archiving of unique, persistent video artifacts, they have so far fallen short as a nexus for true interactive cinema (see VIDEO).

Conclusion

Today, the tools of interactive cinema have become ubiquitous, and the economics of the channel have moved to a new, less capitally intensive place. However, original examples of interactive cinema are more often developed as unique installation art than as content for home or theatrical consumption (Shaw and Weibel 2003). Despite the theoretical and practical guides to its construction, interactive cinema is not for the faint of heart. Finding the right story with the right granularity, deciding whether to position the participant audience within or outside of the story, building the right interface, designing a seamless system architecture that audiences are familiar with or can quickly learn, keeping to a budget—all of these are critical to bringing this genre into the mainstream.

■ See also FILM AND DIGITAL MEDIA, MACHINIMA

References and Further Reading

Anderson, Frances E. 1985. "Electronic Media, Videodisc Technology, and the Visual Arts." *Studies in Art Education* 26 (4): 224–231.

Bordwell, David, and Kristin Thompson. (1979) 2009. *Film Art: An Introduction*. 9th ed. Reading, MA: Addison-Wesley.

Brondmo, Hans Peter, and Glorianna Davenport. 1989. "Creating and Viewing the Elastic Charles—a Hypermedia Journal." In *Hypertext: State of the ART*, edited by R. McAlesse and C. Green, 43–51. Oxford: Intellect.

Davenport, Glorianna. 1987. "New Orleans in Transition: The Interactive Delivery of a Cinematic Case Study." International Congress for Design Planning and Theory, Park Plaza Hotel, Boston. http://mf.media.mit.edu/pubs/detail.php?id=1415.

Davenport, Glorianna, Barbara Barry, Aisling Kelliher, et al. 1993. "ic_motion.gif." *Interactive Cinema Website*. http://ic.media.mit.edu.

Jenkins, Henry. 2006. *Fans, Bloggers, and Gamers: Exploring Participatory Culture*. New York: New York University Press.

Lippman, Andrew, 1980. "Movie-Maps: An Application of the Optical Videodisc to Computer Graphics." *Proceedings of the 7th Annual Conference on Computer Graphics and Interactive Techniques*, Seattle, Washington, 32–42.

Ryan, Marie-Laure. 2006. *Avatars of Story*. Minneapolis: University of Minnesota Press.

Shaul, Nitzan S. 2008. *Hyper-narrative Interactive Cinema: Problems and Solutions*. Amsterdam: Rodopi.

Shaw, Jeffrey, and Peter Weibel. 2003. *Future Cinema*. Cambridge, MA: MIT Press.

Interactive Documentary

Sandra Gaudenzi

Any project that starts with an intention to document the real and that does so by using digital interactive technology can be considered an interactive documentary (i-doc). This definition does not consider the i-doc as an evolution of linear documentary in the age of digital media but as a new form that uses interactivity to position the viewer within the i-doc itself, demanding her to play an active role in the reconstruction, representation, and negotiation of the facts it wants to convey. "New media doco [documentaries] need not to replay the conventions of traditional, linear documentary storytelling; it offers its own ways of playing with reality" (Whitelaw 2002, 3).

In an i-doc the user must have some level of agency. The act of interpretation of the narrative is not enough. The user needs to be able to physically do something, or else it would not be a digital "interactive" documentary. What type of "doing" this is (whether it is clicking on a link, sending a personal video to a website, recording a statement that can be heard by other people, etc.) is what makes the difference between genres of i-docs. When forms of interactivity inspired by the game world (see GAMES AS STORIES), by interactive narrative (see INTERACTIVE NARRATIVE), by educational software, or by locative media (see LOCATION-BASED NARRATIVE) are applied to factual narrative and use a digital platform, the result is a type of document variously called web-doc, docu-game, collab-docs, edu-doc, art-doc, transmedia, or cross-media doc.

In order to simplify such a fast growing array of names, a few taxonomies have been proposed. The two presented here see interactivity (rather than platform, topic, media, or story genre) as the key differentiator between the types of i-docs:

Galloway, McAlpine, and Harris (2007) see four possible interactive documentary models: the *passive adaptive*, where the documentary (through mechanical observation) displays different content based on how the viewer is reacting to material; the *active adaptive*, where the viewer is in control of the documentary's progression; the *immersive*, where the user is exploring the documentary through a virtual world or augmented reality; and, lastly, the *expansive*, where viewers are actually able to contribute to the documentary itself, making it an organic, ever-growing creation.

Gaudenzi (2013) also describes four modes of i-doc: *Hypertext i-docs* are projects based on the exploration of a closed video archive where the user has an exploratory role, normally enacted by clicking on preexisting options (see any project done using the Korsakov software, *Journey to the End of Coal*, or *Inside the Haiti Earthquake*). *Conversational i-docs*, which simulate a seamless conversation with the computer, position the user in a 3D game world logic (see *Gone Gitmo* or *America's Army*). *Participative i-docs* are based on users' participation: they are therefore growing in content through time (see *6 Billion Others*, *Iranian Stories*, or *18 Days in Egypt*). Finally, *experiential i-docs* place the user interaction outside of the screen and in physical space (see *Rider Spoke* or *Greenwich Emotion Map*).

Whereas MIT's *Aspen Moviemap* (1980) is often cited as the first hypermedia documentary ever produced, it is only in 1989, with the production of *Moss Landing* by the Apple Multimedia Lab, that the term *interactive documentary* comes into use. In the following ten years, Glorianna Davenport's MIT Interactive Cinema group experimented with the form by producing a series of projects—of which *Boston Renewed Vistas* (1995) and *Jerome B. Wiesner 1915–1994: A Random Walk through the Twentieth Century* (1996) are flagged as groundbreaking. But it is only with the emergence of the Web, and especially Web 2.0 after 2004, that i-docs have developed as an independent field. Interactive documentaries look and feel fundamentally different from linear documentaries:

1. i-docs are not necessarily video or screen based (being on a digital platform, they can use any combination of existing media—from sound tagged into physical space to 3D graphics embedded into an augmented reality space).
2. They can be viewed or explored on the move and in physical space (via mobile digital platforms such as mobile phones, portable computers, or tablets).
3. They involve the viewer in an active way: from deciding what to see next to actively producing content for the i-doc itself.
4. Depending on the type of interactivity of the i-doc, the viewer can become a Viewer, User, Participant, Player, or/and an Actor (VUPPA).
5. The VUPPA is not the receiver of an organized narrative coming from the filmmaker, but an actant player in an interactive narrative/experience facilitated by the digital author.

As in any form of interactive narrative, an "interactive paradox" (Louchart and Aylett 2003, 25) is present: which degree of authorial control is necessary to convey a narrative experience? "New media forms pose a fundamental challenge to the principle of narrative coherence, which is at the core of traditional documentary. If we explode and open the structure, how can we be sure that the story is being conveyed?" (Whitelaw 2002, 1). Effectively, by giving agency to the user, the interactive documentary proposes a nonlinear type of narration that is in conflict with the traditional voice of the author, expressed in linear documentaries. This would be a problem if causality and objectivity were still the aims of documentary makers. But Grierson's famous definition of documentary as a "creative treatment of actuality" (Hardy 1946, 11) has been widely challenged since the *cinéma vérité* of the 1960s. The idea of the documentary being a "negotiation" with reality (Bruzzi 2000, 4) has left behind the dream of "objectivity," positioning the filmmaker as a negotiator. Documentary is "a dialectical conjunction of a real space and the filmmaker that invades it" (Bruzzi 2000, 125). But if in a linear documentary the negotiation is taking place among a space, the filmmaker, and its filmed subjects, in an i-doc this negotiation has to involve the user and the medium. It is by clicking, playing, moving, adding, or exploring the medium that the user creates her own i-doc, or re-shapes the i-doc for others to come and modify it again.

Obviously not every user is ready to put such an effort into being an intrinsic part of a digital artifact, and this may explain why i-docs, although growing in number, are not yet a mainstream form of edutainment. But for those willing to engage with digital content and to embrace some level of performance (there are levels of user participation in interactive narratives, as Ryan [2011] and Meadows [2003] have separately described), the i-doc gives the opportunity of being partly responsible for a factual narrative. Interactive documentaries are not just documentaries done with digital technology. They are relational artifacts that allow direct engagement with the reality that they portray.

■ See also DIGITAL FICTION, FILM AND DIGITAL MEDIA, INTERFACE, NONLINEAR WRITING, VIDEO

References and Further Reading

Bruzzi, Stella. 2000. *New Documentary: A Critical Introduction*. London: Routledge.
Galloway, Dayna, Kenneth McAlpine, and Paul Harris. 2007. "From Michael Moore to JFK Reloaded: Towards a Working Model of Interactive Documentary." *Journal of Media Practice* 8 (3): 325–339.
Gaudenzi, Sandra. 2013. "The Living Documentary: From Representing Reality to Co-creating Reality in Digital Interactive Documentary." PhD thesis, Goldsmiths, University of London. http://eprints.gold.ac.uk/7997/.
Hardy, F. 1946. *Grierson on Documentary*. London: Collins.
Louchart, Sandy, and Ruth Aylett. 2003. "Towards A Narrative Theory of Virtual Reality." *Virtual Reality* 7:2–9.
Meadows, M.S. 2003. *The Art of Interactive Narrative*. Indianapolis: New Riders.
Ryan, Marie-Laure. 2011. "Peeling the Interactive Onion: Levels of User Participation in the Narrative Text." In *New Narratives: Theory and Practice*, edited by Ruth Page and Bronwen Thomas, 35–62. Lincoln: University of Nebraska Press.
Whitelaw, Mitchell. 2002. "Playing Games with Reality: *Only Fish Shall Visit* and Interactive Documentary." Catalog essay for *Halfeti: Only Fish Shall Visit*, by Brogan Bunt. Exhibited at Artspace, Sydney, September 19–October 12.
www.interactivedocumentary.net/wp-content/2009/07/sg_panel-yr3_2009_ch1.pdf.

Interactive Drama
Brian Magerko

The term *interactive drama* (sometimes used interchangeably with *interactive narrative*) typically refers to artificial intelligence (AI) based approaches to interactive narrative experiences that involve a user (also called an *interactor*) as a key character in an unfolding story experience (see INTERACTIVE NARRATIVE). The goal of realizing an interactive drama has famously been compared by Janet Murray to creating the fictional technology that supports the holodeck from the *Star Trek: The Next Generation* TV series. In her book *Hamlet on the Holodeck*, Murray describes the concept of user *agency*, which is arguably the chief goal of interactive drama systems, as "the satisfying power to take meaningful action and see the results of our decisions and choice" (1997, 126). In other words, interactive drama seeks to empower a user in a story to have meaningful impacts on its progression and outcome, just like the decisions of a fictional character do in a standard drama.

In contrast to approaches in other interactive narrative domains, AI is employed as a defining feature of interactive drama systems. AI can be responsible for features such as synthetic character (i.e., computer-controlled) behaviors and story management (i.e., deciding what plot elements should happen based on user/character actions in the story world). The prototypical result of applying these technologies is a story-based experience for a single user, typically within a computer game environment, which intelligently adapts itself to the idiosyncratic behaviors of the individual user.

The field, which has its roots in the decades-old field of story generation, was arguably founded in the early 1990s by the research of Joseph Bates and his students on the Oz Project at Carnegie Mellon, which was heavily influenced by the ideas described in Brenda Laurel's book *Computers as Theatre* (1991). These works envisioned a computer-guided experience that, much like the promise of the genre of interactive fiction, puts the user in control of a story as a main character (see INTERACTIVE FICTION). The work in the Oz Project was particularly seminal for its research on drama management (Weyhrauch 1997), synthetic characters (Reilly 1996; Loyall 1997), and sociological study of interactive drama as a potential medium for human enjoyment (Kelso, Weyhrauch, and Bates 1993). The parallel work of researchers such as Hayes-Roth (Hayes-Roth, Brownston, and van Gent 1995), Blumberg (Blumberg and Galyean 1995), and Perlin (Perlin and Goldberg 1996) laid the computational foundation for the spectrum of approaches discussed below.

As stated above, interactive drama is usually associated with a certain degree of user *agency* in a story experience. In other words, the amount of agency in an interactive drama experience is directly related to the degree to which decisions made by the user can affect story content, as well as the narrative experience of the user. The AI-based view of agency is that it can be increased through AI-supported actions such as the real-time rewriting/reorganizing of story content, the simulation of dramatic characters by AI agents, or the dynamic influencing of user behaviors to increase the user's sense of actively contributing to a story as a character/participant. A successful interactive drama experience is, therefore, one where a user feels completely in control of their character, sees coherent dramatic ramifications of their actions, and has a fulfilling story experience.

Mateas and Stern (2002), among others, have described approaches to interactive drama as forming a spectrum of autonomy ranging from *strongly autonomous*, to *semiautonomous*, to *weakly autonomous*. This spectrum, which is explored below, provides a very high level way of categorizing interactive drama systems based on how centralized/decentralized story-relevant decisions are made by the involved AI.

Strong Autonomy

Strongly autonomous approaches rely heavily on AI models of synthetic character behaviors in a story world. These models often include character goals and personal knowledge together with other dramatically relevant capabilities, such as emotion, sociological, psychological, or personality models. The user's role in a strongly autonomous system may consist of impersonating an embodied character or, as shown in Cavazza's work (Cavazza, Charles, and Mead 2002), manipulating the world as a behind-the-scene entity to affect changes in the agents' current intentions.

The story experience in a strongly autonomous interactive drama is said to be an *emergent narrative* (see EMERGENCE). There is no concrete representation of story or authorial intent in a strongly autonomous system (as opposed to weakly autonomous or semiautonomous systems). Story in these systems arises out of the agents' efforts to achieve their goals in the story world, as well as out of the alteration of their intents and goals through the user's interaction with the world. This is a highly distributed model of story with, in its most ideal realization, no background communication or coordination between agents. The model is more closely related to improvisational theater, where story creation involves no behind-the-scenes communication, than to group performances governed by coordination mechanisms (Fuller and Magerko 2011).

Strongly autonomous system research tends to focus on the representation of and interaction with humanlike intelligent virtual agents. While this work shares many of the research challenges of AI as a whole (e.g., natural language interaction, problem solving, decision making, planning), it focuses on the creation of *dramatically believable* agents, rather than of believable agents who coexist with humans in the workplace or daily life, as do more practically oriented AI projects. In other words, the synthetic characters of a strongly autonomous interactive drama system need to portray convincingly the characters of a limited fictional story world, rather than to simulate true-to-life persons (or entities) with a lifetime of experiences in our infinitely more complex real world.

The typical criticism of the strongly autonomous approach is that the stories it creates tend to focus on characters achieving their goals, as opposed to behaving in a way that serves higher narrative (or authorial) goals (Mateas and Stern 2002). This arguably dooms the systems that rely on the strongly autonomous model to creating stories that lack any cohesive global structure, theme, or focus, since characters make decisions that serve their own interests, rather than the long-term interests of a narrative. While this approach has currently fallen out of favor in the AI community, there is a vibrant intelligent virtual agent research group that is tangentially related to the interactive drama community. Recent work by Magerko (Magerko, Fiesler, and Baumer 2010; Magerko, Dohogne, DeLeon 2011) and Zhu (Zhu, Ingraham, and Moshell 2011) has focused on collaboration models that exist within a story experience (e.g., building shared mental models through dialogue interactions) and address the limitations of the canonical strongly autonomous approach.

Weak Autonomy

Alternatively, weakly autonomous approaches can rely on a centralized, behind-the-scenes intelligent agent often referred to as a *drama manager* (also known as a *story manager* or *director agent*) who coordinates the story experience. In this approach, the synthetic characters are little more than "puppets" controlled by the drama manager (see Roberts and Isbell [2008] for a recent overview of the field). Drama managers are typically authored with (1) a *story knowledge* whose logic is typically represented as story graphs (e.g., Yu and Riedl 2012), partial-order planning operators (e.g., Young et al. 2004; Riedl and Young 2010), joint behaviors (e.g., Mateas and Stern 2002), story functions (e.g., Fairclough and Cunningham 2004), or background knowledge about the story domain (e.g., O'Neill et al. 2011); and (2) one or more *processes* that operate on that knowledge and the state of the story world.

The processes employed by a drama manager can be categorized as *external* (e.g., giving commands to synthetic characters or changing physical elements in the story world) or *internal* (e.g., modeling the user's behavior or reconfiguring the structure of the story knowledge with a replanning algorithm). External actions executed by a drama manager are typically called *story mediations* (i.e., attempting to change the environment to support the ongoing story experience). Considerable work has been put into understanding the different reasons to execute story mediation actions, such as to prevent the effects of current or likely future user actions from "breaking" the story in some way (Harris and Young 2005; Magerko 2007). External actions also typically involve the coordination of synthetic character behaviors to serve a story goal, such as the joint behaviors sent to Grace and Trip by the director in *Façade* (Mateas and Stern 2002). Internal actions may involve modeling user behavior as input into the drama manager's decision-making processes. This input may lead to reconfiguring/replanning story content, or simply updating the director's knowledge base about what is true in the story world.

Weakly autonomous systems with drama managers have become the norm for the field in the past several years. As game technologies have become more readily usable, the field has seen an increasing number of working systems with complete visualizations and interaction models which advance the use of drama managers. It is still unclear whether this approach is the optimal technical solution to interactive drama or whether future work will introduce new paradigms that produce more compelling experiences.

Semiautonomy

Semiautonomous systems are mixed models combining the weakly autonomous and strongly autonomous approaches. This approach typically has a centralized agent, similar to a drama manager, who can give commands to synthetic characters at different levels of abstraction. The characters, in turn, are capable of (1) existing on their own and acting to achieve their own goals, (2) enacting very specific commands given to them by another agent, or (3) interpreting an abstract command that allows some flexibility on the part of the character for how that command is carried out. Examples of this approach include the synthetic characters of Blumberg (Blumberg and Galyean 1995) and Magerko's IDA system (Magerko 2007). This approach is not as common as the others because of the inherent difficulty of combining two approaches, as well as the new issues that arise when trying to coordinate a centralized story manager with autonomous agents who remain able to execute actions that conflict with story goals.

■ See also INTERACTIVITY, NARRATIVITY, PLOT TYPES AND INTERACTIVITY

References and Further Reading

Blumberg, Bruce M., and Tinsley A. Galyean. 1995. "Multi-level Direction of Autonomous Creatures for Real-Time Virtual Environments." In *Proceedings of the 22nd Annual Conference on Computer Graphics and Interactive Techniques*, 47–54.

Cavazza, Mark, Fred Charles, and Steven J. Mead. 2002. "Character-Based Interactive Storytelling." *IEEE Intelligent Systems* 17 (4): 17–24.

Fairclough, Chris, and Pádraig Cunningham. 2004. "A Multiplayer OPIATE." *International Journal of Intelligent Games and Simulation* 3 (2): 54–61.

Fuller, Daniel, and Brian Magerko. 2011. "Shared Mental Models in Improvisational Theatre." In *Proceedings of 8th* ACM *Conference on Creativity and Cognition (Atlanta, GA)*, 269–278.

Harris, Justin, and R. Michael Young. 2005. "Proactive Mediation in Plan-Based Narrative Environments." In *Proceedings of the International Conference on Intelligent Virtual Agents*, 292–304.

Hayes-Roth, Barbara, Lee Brownston, and Robert van Gent. 1995. "Multiagent Collaboration in Directed Improvisation." In *Proceedings of the First International Conference on Multi-Agent Systems (ICMAS-95)*, 148–154.

Kelso, Margaret T., Peter Weyhrauch, and Joseph Bates. 1993. "Dramatic Presence." *Presence: The Journal of Teleoperators and Virtual Environments* 2 (1): 1–15.

Laurel, Brenda. 1991. *Computers as Theatre*. Reading, MA: Addison-Wesley.

Loyall, Bryan. 1997. "Believable Agents: Building Interactive Personalities." PhD diss., Computer Science Department, Carnegie Mellon University, Pittsburgh, PA.

Magerko, Brian. 2007. "Evaluating Preemptive Story Direction in the Interactive Drama Architecture." *Journal of Game Development* 2 (3): 25–52.

Magerko, Brian, Peter Dohogne, and Chris DeLeon. 2011. "Employing Fuzzy Concepts for Digital Improvisational Theatre." In *Proceedings of the Seventh Annual International Artificial Intelligence and Interactive Digital Entertainment Conference*, 53–60. Palo Alto, CA: AAAI Press.

Magerko, Brian, Casey Fiesler, and Allan Baumer. 2010. "Fuzzy Micro-Agents for Interactive Narrative." In *Proceedings of the Sixth Annual* AI *and Interactive Digital Entertainment Conference*, 156–161. Palo Alto, CA: AAAI Press.

Mateas, Michael, and Andrew Stern. 2002. "A Behavior Language for Story-Based Believable Agents." *IEEE Intelligent Systems* 17 (4): 39–47.

Murray, Janet. 1997. *Hamlet on the Holodeck: The Future of Narrative in Cyberspace*. Cambridge, MA: MIT Press.

O'Neill, Bryan, Andreya Piplica, Daniel Fuller, and Brian Magerko. 2011. "A Knowledge-Based Framework for the Collaborative Improvisation of Scene Introductions." In *Proceedings of the 4th International Conference on Interactive Digital Storytelling*, 85–96. Vancouver: Springer.

Perlin, Ken, and A. Thomas Goldberg. 1996. "Improv: A System for Scripting Interactive Actors in Virtual Worlds." In *SIGGRAPH 96*, New Orleans, LA.

Reilly, W. Scott Neill. 1996. "Believable Social and Emotional Agents." PhD diss., Computer Science Department, Carnegie Mellon University, Pittsburgh, PA.

Riedl, Mark, and R. Michael Young. 2010. "Narrative Planning: Balancing Plot and Character." *Journal of Artificial Intelligence Research* 39:217–268.

Roberts, David L., and Charles L. Isbell. 2008. "A Survey and Qualitative Analysis of Recent Advances in Drama Management." *International Transactions on Systems Science and Applications, Special Issue on Agent Based Systems for Human Learning* 3 (1): 61–75.

Weyhrauch, Peter W. 1997. "Guiding Interactive Drama." PhD diss., Computer Science Department, Carnegie Mellon University, Pittsburgh, PA.

Young, R. Michael, Mark O. Riedl, Mark Branly, Arnav Jhala, R. J. Martin, and C. J. Saretto. 2004. "An Architecture for Integrating Plan-Based Behavior Generation with Interactive Game Environments." *Journal of Game Development* 1 (1): 51–70.

Yu, Hong, and Mark O. Riedl. 2012. "A Sequential Recommendation Approach for Interactive Personalized Story Generation." In *Proceedings of the 11th International Conference on Autonomous Agents and Multi Agents Systems*, 71–78.

Zhu, Jichen, Kenneth Ingraham, and J. Michael Moshell. 2011. "Back-Leading through Character Status in Interactive Storytelling." In *Proceedings of the 4th International Conference on Interactive Digital Storytelling*, 31–36.

Zhu, Jichen, Kenneth Ingraham, J. Michael Moshell, and Santiago Ontañón. 2011. "Towards a Computational Model of Character Status in Interactive Storytelling." In *Proceedings of the 8th* ACM Conference on Creativity and Cognition, 409–410.

Interactive Fiction
Emily Short

The term *interactive fiction* (see INTERACTIVITY) has several common usages. It may refer to any story that allows reader participation to alter the presentation or outcome of the narrative, especially works such as Quantic Dream's *Heavy Rain* which are marketed to a video game audience but emphasize narrative development over gameplay challenge (see INTERACTIVE NARRATIVE).

Since the mid-1980s, however, *interactive fiction* has been used to refer specifically to works that share the formal characteristics, though not necessarily the genre expectations, of the text adventure, a genre that focused heavily on puzzles and exploration. (See the discussion of *Adventure* below.) The widely used initialism IF will refer hereafter to this interpretation.

IF in this sense refers to a piece of software that makes use of both parsed input and a model world. It takes input in the form of commands written in a subset of natural language, such as

TAKE THE BOX

OPEN THE DOOR

ASK THE QUEEN ABOUT THE TREASURE

The work then responds with a textual reply describing what happens as a result of the player's action. To formulate the reply, it consults a world model represented in code, which may track information such as the player's location within a map of rooms, the objects located in the rooms and those carried by the player, and the qualities or states of objects: open boxes, unlocked doors, angry monsters, and so on.

The emphasis on parsed input distinguishes IF from choice-based narratives or hypertext literature (see HYPERTEXTUALITY); the use of the world model distinguishes it from chatterbot software or interactive poetry (see DIGITAL POETRY).

IF allows for a large but consistent selection of verbs within a given work, such that the player does not always know what all the possible affordances are or even how many there might be. Andrew Plotkin has suggested that the process of choosing a productive action from a large space of possibilities is the truly defining feature of IF. This process requires the player to understand the story in order to recognize and then manipulate the rules of the underlying game. The design of IF is thus intended "not to offer . . . immersion, but to request and require it" (Plotkin 2011, 64).

IF originated with William Crowther and Don Woods's *Adventure* (1977), a simulation of exploring the Mammoth Caves of Kentucky, into which fantasy elements and puzzles had been introduced. The player of *Adventure* encounters dwarfs, threatening creatures, and magic implements; she is challenged to find and collect treasures from the cave and return them safely to the world above ground. This focus on adventures in a fantastic underground realm remained a frequent trope in later IF even as subsequent authors branched out to explore other settings. Early IF was played primarily on mainframes and minicomputers and remained a popular recreation in university or business-computing settings for the next decade.

During the early 1980s, IF became available on home computers, through the efforts of Scott Adams's Adventure International (founded 1979) and Infocom (founded 1979) in the United States, Level 9 (1982) and Magnetic Scrolls (1984) in the United Kingdom, Melbourne House (1982) in Australia, Froggy Software (1983) in France, Dinamic (1984) in Spain, and Enrico Colombini (1982) in Italy. The majority of these works boasted difficult puzzle challenges including mazes, locked doors, logic puzzles, riddles, and segments that had to be solved within a limited number of turns. Hint booklets and magazines containing solutions were a significant secondary revenue channel for several companies.

With improvements in computer graphics and the rise of the graphical adventure, in the late 1980s and early 1990s most commercial IF companies closed their doors. Enthusiasts of IF continued to communicate via bulletin boards and through the Usenet groups rec.arts.int-fiction and rec.games.int-fiction. The IF programming systems Alan (Thomas Nilsson, 1992), TADS (Mike Roberts, 1992), and Inform (Graham Nelson, 1993) significantly improved on the parsing and world modeling available with the existing tools GAGS/AGT and The Quill, allowing for a boom in IF distributed as freeware over the Internet.

Work on IF technology continued in the 2000s, with Inform 7 exploring natural language programming and TADS 3 providing a deep library of simulational processes. Much current work, in the early 2010s, focuses on IF play as part of a web-browsing experience, presenting traditional IF as websites rather than downloadable artifacts.

In contrast to commercial computer games, IF can viably be written by single authors and express a focused authorial vision. Moreover, because most IF is distributed for free, authors have been at leisure to make choices without regard to marketability. Some IF explores particular challenges in interactive narrative, especially the questions of how an interactive story can be narratively satisfying when it incorporates player agency, and how to articulate thematic meaning through the nature of the interaction itself.

One approach is to sharply constrain player agency and to make that constraint an important part of the message of the story. By making a "win" state impossible, Adam Cadre's *Photopia* (1998) reproduces the denial, bargaining, and acceptance of grieving as experienced through the player's attempts to replay the work for a better ending and the inevitable failure of those attempts. *Rameses* (Stephen Bond, 2000) uses a similar conceit of failed player agency in a character study of an unhappy teenager. The protagonist's neuroses prevent him from following through on many of the player's attempts to guide him to a happier social outcome, meeting each suggested action with a resentful or self-serving explanation of why that choice cannot be performed.

Another common method is to center the interactive power of the work on the question of what the player is willing to do or willing to make the protagonist do. Infocom's *Infidel* (Michael Berlyn, 1983) opened this question with a protagonist who is ultimately punished for actions taken during the game, and subsequent IF has delved into the possibilities of an antihero or tragic protagonist. Several authors, notably Victor Gijsbers, have used IF to challenge the player's moral preconceptions, presenting branching narratives in which each decision articulating a particular moral principle leads to an outcome further challenging that stance (see ETHICS IN DIGITAL MEDIA). By confronting the player with a situation in which a morally dubious action is necessary to make narrative progress, such IF encourages the player to consider whether he is willing to be complicit in advancing the story. Aaron Reed's *maybe make some change* (2011) applies this technique to contemporary events, modeling several scenes from the lives of American soldiers in Afghanistan in order to reflect on complicity in military atrocities and the difficulty of finding moral clarity in wartime.

Along with constrained agency and complicity, IF often uses a mechanics of deep exploration, whether of a physical setting or of a narrative possibility space. *Galatea* (Emily Short, 2000) presents a conversational character who develops a relationship with the interactor, with dozens of possible outcomes. *1893: A World's Fair Mystery* (Peter Nepstad, 2003) offers a meticulous re-creation of the 1893 Chicago World's Fair supported by archival photos; though *1893* has a plot and puzzles, it is also designed to be enjoyed as a goalless immersive experience suitable for sightseers and history enthusiasts. In *Aisle* (Sam Barlow, 1999), the reader is only allowed one turn of action before the game ends, but by playing over and over, he is able to construct an understanding of the circumstances that led up to that moment. The narrative structure of exploratory works tends to be loose. The intended process is one of curiosity and resolution, in which the reader is drawn to ask questions and then put these to the test until she feels she has sufficiently understood the story world, forming an aesthetic reaction not to a single playthrough but to the cumulative experience of numerous sessions.

Still other IF invites the player's response to the qualities of the text as a prose object. Infocom's *Nord and Bert Couldn't Make Head or Tail of It* (Jeff O'Neill, 1987) is a comic wordplay puzzler that requires the player to recognize scenarios from popular sayings. More recent wordplay IF has allowed the player to manipulate objects that appear in the text as metaphor (*PataNoir*, Simon Christiansen, 2011), required them to phrase their commands alliteratively (*Ad Verbum*, Nick Montfort, 2000), or even presented a text in which none of the nouns were in English and the game had to be decoded (*The Gostak*, Carl Muckenhoupt, 2001) (see WRITING UNDER CONSTRAINT). Not all such mechanics are playful or surreal in intent, however. *Pale Blue Light* (Dominic Delabruere writing as Kazuki Mishima, 2011) combines traditional parsed IF with passages in which the player types free-form content or responds to interactive poetry; it then incorporates player input into subsequent output, in aid of a meditation on the interaction between writers and readers. *The Warbler's Nest* (Jason McIntosh, 2010) alters outcomes depending on the words the player uses to describe objects in the game, as these are understood to reflect the protagonist's state of mind.

The mode of interaction in a majority of IF, however, is still the challenge to overcome obstacles set before the protagonist, as in *Adventure* and in the majority of IF from the commercial era. Much recent IF design continues to focus on the invention of puzzles, often with an aesthetic preference for those that feel like a fictively plausible part of their surroundings. The noir detective story *Make It Good* (Jon Ingold, 2009) requires the player to manipulate the other characters by displaying, concealing, and even fabricating evidence, a challenge that is both extremely difficult and naturalistic in its rendering. Though puzzle-oriented works are the most gamelike sort of IF, their challenges often serve a significant narrative function by dramatizing the trials the protagonist experiences or requiring the player to come to a deep understanding of some aspect of the fictional world.

■ See also AUTHORING SYSTEMS, DIGITAL FICTION, ELECTRONIC LITERATURE, PLOT TYPES AND INTERACTIVITY

References and Further Reading

Barlow, Sam. 1999. *Aisle.* http://ifdb.tads.org/viewgame?id=j49crlvd62mhwuzu.

Bond, Stephen. 2000. *Rameses.* http://ifdb.tads.org/viewgame?id=ostz0hr7a98bp9mp.

Buckles, Mary Ann. 1985. "Interactive Fiction: The Computer Storygame 'Adventure.'" PhD diss., University of California at San Diego.

Cadre, Adam. 1998. *Photopia.* http://ifdb.tads.org/viewgame?id=ju778uv5xaswnlpl.

Christiansen, Simon. 2011. *PataNoir.* http://ifdb.tads.org/viewgame?id=si9s1jktywxj5vdk.

Cordella, Francesco. 2011. "History of Italian IF." In *IF Theory Reader,* edited by Kevin Jackson-Mead and J. Robinson Wheeler, 379–387. Boston: Transcript On Press.

Delabruere, Dominic, writing as Kazuki Mishima. 2011. *Pale Blue Light.* http://ifdb.tads.org/viewgame?id=xi4s5ne9m6w821xd.

Gijsbers, Victor. 2006. *The Baron.* http://ifdb.tads.org/viewgame?id=weac28l51hiqfzxz.

Ingold, Jon. 2009. *Make It Good.* http://iplayif.com/?story=http://www.archimedes.plus.com/make good.z8.

Jerz, Dennis. 2007. "Somewhere Nearby Is Colossal Cave: Examining Will Crowther's Original 'Adventure' in Code and in Kentucky." *Digital Humanities Quarterly* 1 (2). www.digitalhuman ities.org/dhq/vol/001/2/000009/000009.html.

Labrande, Hugo. 2011. "Racontons une histoire ensemble: History and Characteristics of French IF." In *IF Theory Reader,* edited by Kevin Jackson-Mead and J. Robinson Wheeler, 389–432. Boston: Transcript On Press.

McIntosh, Jason. 2010. *The Warbler's Nest.* http://ifdb.tads.org/viewgame?id=he5spzmz6vr4dgej.

Montfort, Nick. 2000. *Ad Verbum.* http://ifdb.tads.org/viewgame?id=xi4s5ne9m6w821xd.

———. 2003. *Twisty Little Passages.* Cambridge, MA: MIT Press.

———. 2007. "Riddle Machines: The History and Nature of Interactive Fiction." In *A Companion to Digital Literary Studies,* edited by Ray Siemens and Susan Schreibman, 267–282. Oxford: Blackwell.

Montfort, Nick, and Emily Short. 2012. "Interactive Fiction Communities: From Preservation through Promotion and Beyond." *Dichtung Digital* 41. http://dichtung-digital.mewi.unibas.ch /2012/41/montfort-short.htm.

Muckenhoupt, Carl. 2001. *The Gostak.* http://ifdb.tads.org/viewgame?id=w5s3sv43s3p98v45.

Nepstad, Peter. 2003. *1893: A World's Fair Mystery.* http://ifdb.tads.org/viewgame?id=ooeot7swrris5pg6.

Nieto, Ruben. 2005. "The SPAG Interview: International IF Special." Translated by H. Helfgott. *SPAG* 40. www.sparkynet.com/spag/backissues/spag40.html.

Plotkin, Andrew. 2011. "Characterizing, If Not Defining, Interactive Fiction." In *IF Theory Reader,* edited by Kevin Jackson-Mead and J. Robinson Wheeler, 59–66. Boston: Transcript On Press.

Reed, Aaron. 2011. *maybe make some change.* http://ifdb.tads.org/viewgame?id=gugrcz22ghdljosu.

Short, Emily. 2000. *Galatea.* http://ifdb.tads.org/viewgame?id=urxrv27t7qtu52lb.

Interactive Narrative

Marie-Laure Ryan

The combination of narrative, a type of meaning that captivates people in all cultures, with the active user participation afforded by digital media has been called the Holy Grail of digital entertainment. This fascination for interactive narrative rests on the belief that our enjoyment of storytelling will rise to a higher power if instead of listening or watching passively we are able to interact with the story world, play the role of a character (see ROLE-PLAYING GAMES), and determine the development of the plot.

As the metaphor of the Holy Grail suggests, however, interactive narrative is as elusive as it is enticing. Whether or not interactive narrative actually exists depends on what one understands by interactivity: the more prominent the user's role in the story, and the broader the choice of actions—in other words, the more lifelike the user's participation—the more problematic is its integration into a well-formed narrative arc (see INTERACTIVITY). The virtual reality researchers Sandy Louchart and Ruth Aylett call this dilemma "the interactive paradox": "On one hand the author seeks control over the direction of a narrative in order to give it a satisfactory structure. On the other hand a participating user demands the autonomy to act and react without explicit authorial constraint" (2003, 25). If interactive narrative creates a paradox, it is because it must integrate the often-unpredictable, bottom-up input of the user into a global script that presupposes a top-down design, since it must respect the basic conditions of narrativity: a sequence of events linked by some relations of causality, representing believable attempts to solve conflicts, and achieving closure.

Authors such as Andrew Glassner, Carolyn Handler Miller, and Mark Meadows consider the existence of interactive narrative an established fact; in defense of this view, one can point out well-established digital genres, such as hypertext, interactive fiction, and those computer games that are based on the archetypal pattern of the quest of the hero (see GAMES AS STORIES, HYPERTEXTUALITY, INTERACTIVE FICTION). Yet according to Chris Crawford, a respected computer game designer, "not a single interactive story world that commands wide respect has been created" (2003, 259). This divergence of opinion reflects different standards of interactivity and narrativity. Digital narrative is like an onion made of different layers of skin, and interactivity can affect different layers. Those who regard the existence of interactive stories as a fait accompli are satisfied with an interactivity that operates on the outer layers; those who regard interactive stories as something we can dream of but cannot achieve envision an interactivity that penetrates to the core of the story.

In projects of the outer level, which may be called peripheral, narrative is presented through an interactive interface, but the user's actions affect neither the content of the story nor the discourse that presents it (see INTERFACE). The text of the story appears in a fixed order, and the purpose of moving the cursor and clicking on buttons is to take the reader to the next episode. These actions recapture the properties of the book for the digital medium by allowing readers to set their own pace, rather than seeing the text unfold by itself like a film. One may wonder why this formula should be considered interactive, since clicking has the same effect as turning pages, an action generally considered too automatic to be meaningful: where are the choices that, according to Chris Crawford (2004, 191), constitute the hallmark of interactivity? In Kate Pullinger's *Inanimate Alice* (2005–2012), a charming multimedia story of a young girl whose father works at dangerous jobs and moves from country to country, the choice resides in playing games on a handheld electronic device that the girl regards as her most faithful companion. It is occasionally necessary to solve puzzles in order to unlock the next episode (for instance, escaping from a labyrinth in which the heroine is caught), but most of the time the story can be continued with no more effort than clicking on an arrow. On this level of interactivity, the user's input is more a tool to get more data than the result of an interesting choice.

The next layer of interactivity is represented by hypertext narrative (see HYPERTEX-TUALITY). The term *hypertext* refers to a collection of documents interconnected by digital links, so that, when the user selects a link, a new document comes to the screen. Since there are usually several links on a screen, the order of presentation of the units is highly variable. The underlying structure of hypertext can take two forms: the tree and the network (see GRAPH THEORY). In a tree structure there is only one way to reach a certain node. This enables the author to control the path of the reader and to guarantee narrative coherence. A genre that relies on a tree structure is the "Choose Your Own Adventure" stories: the reader follows a branch until it comes to an end, and then starts over at the root node to explore another possible development. In contrast to the tree structure, the network or labyrinth structure presents loops that make it possible to reach the same node through different routes. When a hypertext narrative is based on a network, the author cannot control the user's itinerary through the database. This loss of control has important consequences for the narrative coherence of hypertext. Early theorists such as Landow and Joyce claimed that hypertext is a storytelling machine that generates a different narrative with every run of the program. Since there are an infinite number of different paths through a network, this could be taken to mean that hypertext can produce an infinite number of different stories. But as a series of events connected by temporal and causal relations, narrative is a highly linear type of meaning, and it is unlikely that the unpredictable sequence of data produced by the reader's choices will respect narrative logic. If in order to avoid inconsistencies readers rearrange the information encountered during their traversal of the database in a different order—an order that respects causality—this means that the order of discovery is not constitutive of narrative order, and that different paths can reveal the same story. For instance, the reader who encounters first a lexia describing a character as dead and then a lexia describing this character as alive will not imagine a supernatural resurrection, but rather will construct a narrative sequence that differs from the order of presentation. And if the reader encounters twice the same lexia, she will not imagine a story world in which history repeats itself, but rather will simply assume that the same event is narrated multiple times. Narratologists would say that in hypertext narrative, interactivity operates on the level of discourse, rather than on the level of story. In both this type of interactivity and the previous one, the role of the user can be described as external-exploratory: the user does not play the role of a character in the story but rather manipulates a textual machine, and her actions have no effect on the narrative events.

A deeper level of interactivity can be reached when the user impersonates a character who progresses through a predefined trajectory, a design typical of computer games. This type of participation can be described as internal and ontological. Internal participation means that the user has a body, or avatar, in the fictional world, and that the actions available to him are not merely abstract ways to see more of the story, as was the case with the previous two types, but represent a physical engagement of the avatar with the surrounding world, while ontological participation means that the fate of the avatar and of the story world are at stake in the user's choices (see AVATARS). The dominant narrative structure for this layer of interactivity is the archetypal story of the quest of the hero, as described by Vladimir Propp and Joseph Campbell. In a quest narrative, the hero fulfills his mission by performing a series of tasks of increasing difficulty (see QUEST NARRATIVE). The game determines the theme of the mission and the sequence of the tasks, but the player's performance creates variations on this fixed frame. These variations differ from each other in how the avatar solves problems, in the success or failure of his quest, and in the case of failure, in the time and manner of his death.

It is in games inspired by the epistemic plot of the detective or mystery story that prescripted stories are the most compatible with interactivity. The trademark of the mystery story is the superposition of two plot lines: one constituted by the events that took place in the past, and the other by the investigation that leads to the solving of the puzzle. When the pattern is implemented in a game environment, it combines an authorially defined story—the events being investigated—with a variable story created in real time by the actions of the player, who plays the role of investigator. This structure, which Henry Jenkins calls embedded narrative, is particularly prominent in the textual genre of interactive fiction.

In a computer game, the player's repertory of action consists mainly of physical actions, such as moving, looking around, jumping, building, shooting, killing, collecting objects, and using them or dropping them. But to create an interesting story, the actions of a hero must be motivated by interpersonal relations created through communicative events, such as asking for help, forming alliances, betraying, deceiving, breaking up with, threatening, flattering, seeking revenge, promising and breaking promises, convincing or dissuading. This type of event presupposes verbal communication between characters, a type of interaction still very difficult to achieve in a digital environment (cf. the still-primitive state of dialogue systems; see DIALOGUE SYSTEMS). This explains why the standard way to create reasonably complex stories in this type of design is by means of noninteractive movie clips known as cut scenes (see CUT SCENES). While prescripted cut scenes are used to deliver the back story and the verbal exchanges between the characters, the truly interactive moments are typically limited to those situations when the story progresses through the physical deed of the hero. This is why the most common plot type in computer games is the fundamentally solitary quest of the hero in a world full of danger.

The inner and most radical level of interactivity is an emergent (see EMERGENCE) story generated on the fly out of data that come in part from the system and in part from the user. Every run of the program should result in a different story, and the program should therefore be replayable. In her 1997 classic *Hamlet on the Holodeck*, Janet Murray proposes the holodeck of the TV series *Star Trek* as the model of this level of interactivity. The holodeck is a computer-generated, three-dimensional simulation of a story world (see SIMULATION). The user is invited to step into this world, to impersonate a character, and to interact through language and gestures with synthetic (i.e., computer-created) agents. No matter what the user says or does, the synthetic agents respond coherently and integrate the user's input into a narrative arc that sustains interest. The holodeck, as a whole, may be a castle in the air, but its individual features represent legitimate goals for the designers of interactive narrative. These features are (1) the already-mentioned emergence of the story; (2) natural interface: users should ideally interact with the story world though language and the body, just as they do in the real world; (3) integration of the user's action within the story: these actions should move the plot forward, rather than being merely a means to get more of the story, as in the outer layers discussed above; and (4) frequent interaction: just as in life we interact constantly with the world, in interactive narrative participation should not be limited to decisions separated by long stretches of passive watching. There should be no advancement of the plot through cut scenes on this level.

If we lower our expectations below the lofty standards of the holodeck, there are a few systems in existence that implement a limited degree of emergence. One of them is *Façade*, a project in interactive drama by Michael Mateas and Andrew Stern that was at the time of this writing the only working representative of this genre (see INTERACTIVE DRAMA). The work is designed for a short but intense fifteen-minute experience. The user plays the role of the guest of a dinner party given by Grace and Trip, a couple of successful young professionals who seem to have a perfect marriage. But during the course of the evening, the dialogue between the player and the couple reveals deep cracks in this façade of happiness. At the end of the evening, the visitor is expulsed from the apartment after one of several possible developments. In most of them the marriage is irre-

mediably broken, but in at least one ending the player manages to reconcile the warring spouses. This may sound like a prescripted narrative similar to those of the previous category—especially since all the runs maintain an Aristotelian development of exposition, conflict, and resolution—but the emergence resides in the details of the dialogue. The user, whose participation is internal-ontological, interacts with the characters by typing text, while the characters respond through spoken language. The user hears about 30 percent of the available dialogue during each run, and after five or six runs, the database is exhausted. As the dialogue unfolds, the system ensures that each successive unit increases the tension of the previous unit, until a climax is reached. At this point the system switches to units that decrease tension and lead to the resolution. The natural language interface gives the user an unlimited freedom of expression, in contrast to the menu-driven dialogues of most computer game narratives, but the price to pay for this lifelike freedom is the system's frequent inability to process the contributions of the user and the generation of inconsistent responses. But the frequent incoherence of the dialogue does not lead to a serious loss of credibility, because it can be explained by the self-centered personalities of Grace and Trip and by the general theme of the work. As the initially polite conversation turns into a domestic fight, it is not too surprising that Grace and Trip increasingly ignore the visitor.

Another type of emergent architecture is found in the wildly popular computer game *The Sims*. In contrast to *Façade*, which maintains authorial control by ensuring an Aristotelian development, *The Sims* is a largely bottom-up system. In such a system, stories are generated by creating characters, endowing them with different personalities and possibilities of behaviors, putting them together in a confined space, and letting the user create a story by activating their built-in behaviors. The user plays the role of a puppet master who determines the plot from the position of a (nearly) omnipotent god external to the story world. Imagine that she is currently controlling a character called Nina, and that Nina's sister, Dina, is present on the scene. By moving the cursor over Dina, the player activates a menu of the various actions that Nina can perform with Dina as a patient: actions such as kiss, hug, dance with, play with, talk to, appreciate, or irritate. All these actions have a certain emotional impact on the patient and affect the relation between the two characters. This relation decides how Dina will respond to Nina. Now imagine that instead of just two characters the world includes many, and that the characters can also interact with a variety of objects that affect their mood. The choices offered to the player become too numerous and the interactions of the various objects too complex for the designer to anticipate all the possible developments. This is why this kind of system can be called emergent. But the stories created through bottom-up systems never present the closure of standard literary narratives, and the lack of authorial control makes it virtually impossible to create certain important narrative effects, such as suspense and surprise or an Aristotelian curve of rise and fall in tension. Many developers of interactive narrative (Louchart and Aylett 2003; Szilas, n.d.) advocate the use of a "virtual narrator" or "drama manager" who exercises top-down control over the development of the story, putting it back on the right track when the user's contribution does not fit in a proper trajectory. (In *The Sims*, this top-down element is implemented by having the system generate random events that may interfere with the plans of the characters, such as Death taking a character away, or the house catching fire.)

While the external layers of interactivity require, on the level of code, nothing more complicated than "if then" commands that display the contents of a certain address when a button is activated, the internal layers involve coding and designing tasks of such complexity that they will never be resolved once and for all: tasks such as language understanding and plotting on the fly. Since we don't have to this date a story-generating program sufficiently sophisticated to produce a wide variety of noninteractive stories worth reading for pleasure, we may be raising the stakes to an impossible level by trying to build systems that create stories dynamically on the basis of the unpredictable input of the user (see STORY GENERATION). It is as if Shakespeare had to write Hamlet without having control of all the characters. But it may be wrong to expect of interactive narrative the same kind of gratification that we get from "passives." As Kelso, Weyhrauch, and Bates (1993) have argued, the excitement of role-playing and the satisfaction of being an agent could make up for what will probably be lost on the level of story. Still, the design of interactive narrative faces scores of unanswered questions: what kind of plot (see PLOT TYPES AND INTERACTIVITY) will lend itself to user agency; can this agency be raised to the level of meaningful interpersonal relations, rather than being limited to physical tasks; can interactivity create a genuine aesthetic interest, that is, an interest focused on the story as a whole rather than on the user's success at solving problems; what will be the optimal time frame; and what role should the user play: main protagonist (but will the experience still be pleasurable if the events take a tragic turn?), observer of other people's conflicts (as in *Façade*), or author/puppet master (as in *The Sims*)? For all the fascination inspired by the Holy Grail of emergent narrativity, however, it would be wrong to dismiss the projects of the outer layers as inherently inferior to those of the inner layer simply because they are easier to code: these projects must also solve the aesthetic problem of adapting content to the interface. There are, potentially, good and bad solutions, entertainment and boredom, success and failure in all the layers of interactive narrativity.

■ See also NONLINEAR WRITING, NPC (NONPLAYER CHARACTER), PROCEDURAL, STORYSPACE

References and Further Reading

Campbell, Joseph.1949. *The Hero with a Thousand Faces*. New York: Pantheon.
Crawford, Chris. 2003. "Interactive Storytelling." In *The Videogame Reader*, edited by Mark J. P. Wolf and Bernard Perron, 259–273. London: Routledge.
———. 2004. *Chris Crawford on Interactive Storytelling*. Berkeley: New Riders.
Glassner, Andrew. 2004. *Interactive Storytelling: Techniques for 21st Century Fiction*. Natick, MA: A. K. Peters.
Iurgel, Ido A., Nelson Zagalo, and Paolo Petta, eds. 2009. *Interactive Storytelling: Second Joint International Conference on Interactive Digital Storytelling* (ICIDS). Berlin: Springer.

Jenkins, Henry. 2004. "Game Design as Narrative Architecture." In *First Person: New Media as Story, Performance, and Game*, edited by Noah Wardrip-Fruin and Pat Harrigan, 118–130. Cambridge, MA: MIT Press.

Joyce, Michael. 1995. *Of Two Minds: Hypertext, Pedagogy, and Poetics*. Ann Arbor: University of Michigan Press.

Kelso, Margaret, Peter Weyhrauch, and Joseph Bates. 1993. "Dramatic Presence." *Presence: Teleoperators and Virtual Environments* 2 (1): 1–15.

Landow, George Press. 1997. *Hypertext 2.0: The Convergence of Contemporary Critical Theory and Technology*. Baltimore: Johns Hopkins University Press.

Louchart, Sandy, and Ruth Aylett. 2003. "Towards A Narrative Theory of Virtual Reality." *Virtual Reality* 7:2–9.

Mateas, Michael, and Phoebe Sengers, eds. 2003. *Narrative Intelligence*. Amsterdam: John Benjamins.

Mateas, Michael, and Andrew Stern. n.d. *Façade*. Interactive drama. www.interactivestory.net /download/.

———. 2002. *Façade: An Experiment in Building a Fully-Realized Interactive Drama*. http://www .interactivestory.net/papers/MateasSternGDC03.pdf.

Meadows, Mark Stephen. 2003. *Pause and Effect: The Art of Interactive Narrative*. Indianapolis: New Riders.

Miller, Carolyn Handler. 2004. *Digital Storytelling: A Creator's Guide to Interactive Entertainment*. Amsterdam: Focal Press / Elsevier.

Murray, Janet. 1997. *Hamlet on the Holodeck: The Future of Narrative in Cyberspace*. New York: Free Press.

Propp, Vladimir. (1928) 1968. *Morphology of the Folk Tale*. Translated by L. Scott. Austin: University of Texas Press.

Pullinger, Kate. 2005–2012. *Inanimate Alice*. www.inanimatealice.com/.

Ryan, Marie-Laure. 2008. "Interactive Narrative, Plot Types, and Interpersonal Relations." In *Interactive Storytelling: Second Joint International Conference on Interactive Digital Storytelling*, edited by Nicolas Szilas and Ulrike Spierling. Berlin: Springer.

———. 2009. "From Narrative Games to Playable Stories: Towards a Poetics of Interactive Narrative." *Storyworlds: A Journal of Narrative Studies* 1 (1): 43–60.

———. 2011. "The Interactive Onion: Layers of User Participation in Digital Narrative Texts." In *New Narratives: Stories and Storytelling in the Digital Age*, edited by Ruth Page and Bronwen Thomas, 35–62. Lincoln: University of Nebraska Press.

The Sims 2. 2004. Computer game. Designed by Will Wright. Maxis.

Szilas, Nicolas. n.d. "A New Approach to Interactive Drama: From Intelligent Characters to an Intelligent Virtual Narrator." www.idtension.com.

Szilas, Nicolas, and Ulrike Spierling, eds. 2008. *Interactive Storytelling: Second Joint International Conference on Interactive Digital Storytelling* (ICIDS). Berlin: Springer.

Interactive Television

Jens Jensen

Television is one of the most successful technological consumer products ever produced. It has spread to virtually every household in the global society. TV sets are located in a central part of the main living room in most homes, TV viewing is a dominant part of most people's leisure activities and daily lives, and, for many, TV has become their most important source of information and entertainment. So it is no exaggeration to say that TV has a central place in our global culture, and that TV over the past half century has thoroughly changed our daily lives, leisure, and patterns of consumption (Jensen and Toscan 1999).

TV, however, is not a static medium. Over the past couple of decades, game consoles, VCRs, cable and satellite systems, and so on, have already begun to change the image of what TV is and what it can be as a medium. New features such as interactivity, digitization, convergence, broadband networks, content on demand, two-way cables, and the mixture of TVs and computers and of broadcast and Internet point out some of the aspects involved in this process of change. Briefly, what is at stake here is the delivery of interactive services to the home and to the TV screen: interactive television.

In the broad sense interactive television—also known as ITV or iTV—can be defined as the convergence of conventional television and new interactive information and communication technologies. More specifically, interactive television comprises a number of technologies and program formats that allow viewers to interact with television content as they view it, that is, a new form of television based on actual physical interaction with the media in the form of choices, decisions, and communicative input. In this manner it becomes possible for the viewer to gain control over what to watch, when to watch, and how to watch, or even the potential for active participation in programs or upload of content generated by the user. Understood in this way, interactive television can be considered a fairly broadly defined concept.

There exist a large number of technologies, infrastructures, and delivery systems that can provide homes with new TV-based interactive media content and services. To be truly interactive, the viewer must be able to return information to the broadcaster or program provider, that is, it must be a two-way TV system that enables the viewer to issue commands and give feedback information. However, a return path to the program provider integrated in the TV system is not necessary to have an interactive program experience; the "return path" can also be by another media or channel such as by telephone, text messages from mobile phones, or an Internet connection. Furthermore, interactive television and interactive experiences can also be supported by so-called local interactivity: once an application or program is downloaded, software and interaction can be executed locally at, for example, the set-top box (Jensen and Toscan 1999).

In like manner, there are a number of end-user terminals, devices, and technologies, as well as a multiplicity of services and content types, laying claim to the label of interactive television.

Although the term *interactive television* in this way covers a wide range of content, applications, and services, it is possible to group the variety of interactive television elements into a number of major interactive genres or formats. A brief—and far from exhaustive—list of the most common and popular types of interactive television content and services could look like this (Jensen 2005a, 2005b):

EPGs—electronic program guides or interactive program guides—are new computer-based techniques or advanced interfaces that use various menus and quick scanning of current and upcoming programs to aid navigation through the channels and to identify content that the viewer may want to see.

Enhanced TV refers to different kinds of content (text, graphic, or video) that is overlaid on regularly displayed video content and is accessed interactively.

Content on demand is the reception of content according to individual orders, which enables television viewers to access content whenever they wish. Content on demand covers a wide range of content types or genres: movies on demand, music on demand, news on demand, sports on demand, weather on demand, games on demand, and so on.

Personalized TV—also known as customized TV or individual TV experience—is the personalization of the viewer's television experience based on consumer demands or behavioral patterns and profiling to find out what products and services the individual viewer might find most interesting.

Internet on TV—or television-based Internet access—enables users to carry out many of the activities normally performed on a personal computer connected to the Internet through the television set, for example, to surf the web or search the Internet by keyword or category; to participate in chat groups, discussion groups, or social media; and to read and write e-mails and instant messaging.

Interactive advertising—or iTV advertising, personalized or customized advertising, targeted advertising, one-to-one advertising, or nichecasting—is used to signify the dissemination of marketing and brand messages using the expanded functionality for targeted or personalized communication supported by interactive television.

T-commerce—also known as television commerce, home shopping, iTV-based retail, TRetail, real-time merchandising, or transactional TV—is the e-commerce phenomenon known from the Internet transferred to the medium of television. In other words, T-commerce allows the viewer to purchase products and services that he or she views on the television screen. In this way, viewers become consumers as they transact through television content.

Interactive television games are applications and services that support gaming on the television screen in the form of play-along interactive games, pay-per-play, downloadable games, or multiplayer network games.

Cross-media interaction or two-channel interaction is the use of another medium—for example, telephone, SMS or MMS, e-mail, or web chat—as a "return path" or "feedback channel" from the television viewer to the media sender to produce interactive programs or interactive features. One currently very popular instance of cross-media interaction is the use of SMS services via mobile phones as a return path to live television programming. Popular formats for SMS TV are voting, gaming, and chat.

As can be seen, *interactive television* is a rather ambiguous term. It refers to a variety of different kinds of technologies, different kinds of media content or genres, and different forms and degrees of interactivity.

Concerning the last—different forms and degrees of interactivity—several classifications or typologies for interactivity in interactive television have been introduced (Kiousis 2002). One of the more persistent of these typologies of interactivity is the so-called matrix of interactivity (Jensen 2008b). The distinctive mark of this typology is that it is defined independently of the concrete characteristics such as the technical design of the media, the form of presentation, and the content of information and is instead based on the relatively abstract level of social power relations and power positions, which constitute different "communication patterns" or "information traffic patterns." These patterns are described in relation to who delivers the information and who controls the access to and use of the information, where the latter primarily refers to the choice of the content of information and the time at which it is to be received. By cross-tabulating these two aspects in relation to whether ownership and selection are performed by a centralized information source or by a decentralized information user, we arrive at a four-field matrix of fundamentally distinct media, thus giving four possible combinations: transmission, conversation, consultation, and registration (Bordewijk and Kaam 1986) (see table 1 below).

If (media) interactivity is defined as *a measure of a media's potential ability to let the user exert an influence on the content and/or form of the mediated communication*, then it is possible to develop a typology of interactivity from this matrix. In this way the concept of interactivity is divided into four subconcepts or dimensions (Jensen 1999a, 1999b):

1. *Transmissional interactivity*, defined as a measure of the media's potential ability to let the user choose from a continuous stream of information in a one-way media system without a return channel and therefore without the possibility for making requests. Examples in interactive TV services and formats would be multichannel TV, tele-text, near video on demand, pay-per-view, datacasting, multicasting.

2. *Consultational interactivity*, defined as a measure of the media's potential ability to let the user choose, by request, from an existing selection of preproduced information in a two-way media system with a return channel. Examples in interactive TV services and formats would be (true) video, news, sports, or games on demand; online information services; and so on.

3. *Registrational interactivity*, defined as a measure of a media's potential ability to register information from and thereby also adapt and respond to a given user's needs and actions, or the system's built-in ability to automatically "sense" and adapt. Examples in interaction TV services and formats would be intelligent agents or guides; adaptive or intelligent EPGs; customized, personalized, or adaptive television; and so on.

4. And finally, *conversational interactivity*, defined as a measure of the media's potential ability to let the user produce and input his/her information in a two-way media system that is made available to other users, be it stored or in real time. Examples in interactive TV services and formats would be video conferencing systems, videophone, chat, and various forms of user-generated content (UGC). See table 1.

If you consider the actual and future trends of television's development from the perspective of the matrix, they are best described as a relative movement from the top left position toward the other positions, that is, from the traditional transmission pattern toward the consultation, registration, and conversation patterns. So, another way to conceptualize and describe interactive television is as the television medium's transformation

Table 1. The Matrix of Interactivity with Examples of Interactive Television Services and Content as Prototypical Representatives of the Various Forms of Interactivity

	Information produced by center	Information produced by consumer
Distribution controlled by center	1. Transmissional interactivity (e.g., multichannel TV, tele-text, near video on demand, pay-per-view, datacasting, multicasting)	3. Registrational interactivity (e.g., intelligent agents or guides, adaptive or intelligent EPGs, customized, personalized, or adaptive television)
Distribution controlled by consumer	2. Consultational interactivity (e.g., [true] video on demand, news, sports, or games on demand, online information services)	4. Conversational interactivity (e.g., video conferencing systems, videophone, chat, various forms of UGC)

from a solely transmissional medium to a complex combination of transmissional, consultational, registrational, and even conversational media.

The future of interactive television is unclear. There has been much debate as to how popular and widespread interactive TV will be. Given the significant "interactive turn" in the media landscape over the past decades, it seems likely that some forms of interactive TV will be popular. However, it is also likely that viewing of noninteractive, prescripted, and predefined content will continue to be a dominant part of the TV experience in the future (Jensen 2008b).

■ See also ANALOG VERSUS DIGITAL, CHARACTERISTICS OF DIGITAL MEDIA, GAME GENRES, HISTORY OF COMPUTERS, INTERACTIVITY, OLD MEDIA / NEW MEDIA

References and Further Reading

Bordewijk, Jan L., and Ben Van Kaam. 1986. "Towards a New Classification of Tele-Information Services." *Intermedia* 14 (1): 16–21.

Cesar, Pablo, and Konstantinos Chorianopoulos. 2009. "The Evolution of TV Systems, Content, and Users toward Interactivity." *Foundations and Trends in Human-Computer Interaction* 2 (4): 373–395.

Jensen, Jens F. 1999a. "The Concept of 'Interactivity' in Interactive Television." In *Interactive Television: TV of the Future or the Future of TV?*, edited by Jens F. Jensen and Cathy Toscan, 25–66. Aalborg, Denmark: Aalborg University Press.

———. 1999b. "Interactivity—Tracking a New Concept." In *Computer Media and Communication: A Reader*, edited by Paul A. Mayer, 160–187. Oxford: Oxford University Press.

———. 2005a. "Interactive Content, Applications, and Services." In *Digital Terrestrial Television in Europe*, edited by A. Brown and G. R. Picard, 111–112. Mahwah, NJ: Lawrence Erlbaum Associates.

———. 2005b. "Interactive Television: New Genres, New Format, New Content." In *Proceedings from the Second Australasian Conference on Interactive Entertainment*, Sydney, 89–104.

———. 2008a. "Interactive Television: A Brief Media History." In *Changing Television Environments*, edited by M. Tscheligi, M. Obrist, and A. Lugmayr, 1–19. Berlin: Springer, LICS.

———. 2008b. "The Concept of Interactivity—Revisited: Four New Typologies of a New Media Landscape." In *uxtv08: Designing Interactive User Experience for TV and Video*, edited by Judith Masthoff, Sheri Panabaker, Marc Sullivan, and Artur Lugmayr, 129–132. New York: ACM Press.

Jensen, Jens F., and Cathy Toscan, eds. 1999. *Interactive Television: TV of the Future or the Future of TV?* Aalborg, Denmark: Aalborg University Press.

Kiousis, Spiro. 2002. "Interactivity: A Concept Explication." *New Media & Society* 4 (3): 355–383.

Tscheligi, M., M. Obrist, and A. Lugmayr. 2008. *Changing Television Environments*. Berlin: Springer, LICS.

•••

Interactivity
Peter Mechant and Jan Van Looy

In its most general sense, the term *interactivity* describes an active relationship between at least two entities, which can be people or objects. Often a message is said to be "interactive" when the message is related to a number of previous messages (in contrast to a "reactive" message, which only relates to one previous message). Thus, the "extent to which communication reflects back on itself, feeds on and responds to the past" (Newhagen and Rafaeli 1996, 6), also referred to as "third-order dependency" (Kiousis 2002, 360), is key for assessing the degree of message interactivity. In programming, an application is called "interactive" when it allows for user input while it is running, whereas a batch program does not.

The term *interactivity* was first used by Henry Warren White (1879) to describe atoms mutually affecting one another (Papilloud 2010). Despite its long history, *interactivity* has rarely been defined (McMillan and Downes 2000). Jens F. Jensen (1999) notes that there is no consensus on the characteristics or dimensions of interactivity within the scientific community. Interactivity is a concept that is often used in relation to new media and the (theoretical) discourse on new communication technologies. Scholars working in the discipline of computer-mediated communication (CMC) have been using the concept since the mid-1980s. Early in the study of the Internet and the World Wide Web, interactivity was identified as one of its main features (McMillan 2006). This interest in interactive engagement with media content, as opposed to merely listening or watching passively, led to genres emphasizing the user's role in the story (see INTERACTIVE FICTION, INTERACTIVE NARRATIVE). In the course of the 1990s, *interactivity* became a buzzword, and the term was often indiscriminately employed as a label and selling point for new (communication) technologies such as Interactive Digital TV (IDTV) and Compact Disc Interactive (CD-i) (Quiring 2009).

The academic literature distinguishes between three perspectives on interactivity: (1) as a formal property, (2) as a type of communication, and (3) as a cognitive process (McMillan and Downes 2000). The first perspective positions interactivity as a formal property of a media technology, as "a measure of a media's potential ability to let the user exert an influence on the content and/or form of the mediated communication" (Jensen and Toscan 1999, 59). The second perspective describes interactivity as a communication process. The focus here is not on the analysis of technological characteristics, but on the study of interactivity as a form of information exchange between different actors. These actors can be (groups of) people, but exchanges can also take place between humans and machines. From this perspective interactivity is a "cyclical process in which two actors alternately listen, think and speak" (Crawford 2002, 6). The third perspective describes interactivity as "an information-based process that takes place within the individual" (Newhagen 2004, 397). This viewpoint studies the effects of interactive communication channels and emphasizes the perspective of the user. Interactivity then becomes a "function of both the inclusion of interactive tools as well as of the language used when offering that tool" (Lilleker and Malagon 2010, 27).

Jensen (1999) differentiates between three approaches to defining interactivity: by using a list of prototypical examples, by providing a list of criteria, or by describing a continuum (consisting of one or more dimensions) indicating the degree of interactivity. The disadvantage of the first approach is that it does not demonstrate which properties make a particular medium interactive. Moreover, a definition by examples is closely tied to the cultural and social context of the author and may quickly become outdated. For example, Durlak's (1987, 743) definition of interactive technologies, dating back more than three decades, lists a variety of systems—including the telephone, "two-way television," audio conferencing systems, computers, electronic mail, and so on—but could obviously not anticipate interactivity via more recent technologies. Definitions describing certain criteria that need to be met in order to have interactivity are based on a binary and rigid "all or nothing" approach, making it impossible to differentiate between different levels of interactivity. In contrast, definitions based on continuous scales afford different degrees of interactivity. Some authors (e.g., Rafaeli 1988) use a one-dimensional continuum when defining interactivity as "the capability of new communication systems (usually containing a computer as one component) to 'talk back' to the user" (Rogers 1986, 34). Others define interactivity through multiple criteria. Laurel (1991), for example, uses a three-dimensional conceptual framework based on the dimensions frequency, choice (range), and importance (significance) to define interactivity. Johnson, Bruner, and Kumar (2006, 41) propose a definition of interactivity based on four dimensions: "the extent to which an actor involved in a communication episode perceives the communication to be reciprocal, responsive, speedy, and characterized by the use of nonverbal communication."

Several tendencies in interactivity research can be identified: human-to-human interactivity, human-to-documents interactivity, and human-to-system interactivity (McMillan 2006). In the first tradition, human interaction is placed at the forefront of interactivity research. McMillan notes that the direction of communication and the level of control over the communication environment are key aspects when studying such human-to-human interaction in a computer- or technology-mediated environment. The second tendency, research into human-to-documents interactivity, emphasizes the active role of the audience and focuses on interactive media as opportunities for exchanges between audiences and content creators. The last tendency studies a form of interactivity that is central to new media, that is, the interaction between people and the computer (system) itself. Salen and Zimmerman (2004), for example, differentiate between four overlapping and nonexclusive modes of interactivity between a player (human) and a game (system). The first mode, cognitive interactivity, refers to interpretative participation, for example, the psychological, emotional, and intellectual participation of a player in a digital game. A second level of interactivity is functional interactivity or utilitarian participation. Third, explicit interactivity refers to overt participation "like clicking the non-linear links of a hypertext novel or following the rules of a board game" (2004, 60). The final mode of interactivity is "beyond-the-object-interactivity" (2004, 60) and refers to interaction outside the experience of a single designed system (e.g., fan culture).

A final distinction can be made between open and closed interactivity. "Open" interactivity refers to "productive" or "ontological" interactions with users, not just manipulating but also creating content. "Closed" or "exploratory" interactivity, on the other hand, is restricted to users navigating content and choosing what content to consume (Aarseth 1997; Ryan 2002). This distinction also points to the pseudo- or quasi-interactive services offered by technologies such as interactive TV (see INTERACTIVE TELEVISION), which "retains an asymmetrical structure and limits interactivity to mechanical activities such as on-off requests" (Kim and Sawhney 2002, 229).

■ See also CHARACTERISTICS OF DIGITAL MEDIA, INTERACTIVE CINEMA, INTERACTIVE DOCUMENTARY, INTERACTIVE DRAMA, INTERACTIVE FICTION, INTERACTIVE NARRATIVE, OLD MEDIA / NEW MEDIA

References and Further Reading

Aarseth, Espen. 1997. *Cybertext: Perspectives on Ergodic Literature.* Baltimore: Johns Hopkins University Press.
Crawford, Chris. 2002. *Understanding Interactivity.* San Francisco: No Starch Press.
Durlak, Jerome. 1987. "A Typology for Interactive Media." In *Communication Yearbook 10*, edited by Margaret McLaughlin, 743–757. Newbury Park, CA: Sage.

Jensen, Jens. 1999. "Interactivity: Tracking a New Concept in Media and Communication Studies." In *Computer Media and Communication*, edited by Paul Mayer, 160–187. Oxford: Oxford University Press.

Jensen, Jens, and Cathy Toscan, eds. 1999. *Interactive Television: TV of the Future or Future of the TV?* Aalborg, Denmark: Aalborg University Press.

Johnson, Grace J., Gordon Bruner II, and Anand Kumar. 2006. "Interactivity and Its Facets Revisited: Theory and Empirical Test." *Journal of Advertising* 35 (4): 35–52.

Kim, Pyungho, and Harmeet Sawhney. 2002. "A Machine-like New Medium—Theoretical Examination of Interactive TV." *Media, Culture & Society* 24 (2): 217–233.

Kiousis, Spiro. 2002. "Interactivity: A Concept Explication." *New Media & Society* 4 (3): 355–383.

Laurel, Brenda. 1991. *Computers as Theatre*. Reading, MA: Addison-Wesley.

Lilleker, Darren G., and Casilda Malagon. 2010. "Levels of Interactivity in the 2007 French Presidential Candidates' Websites." *European Journal of Communication* 25 (1): 25–42.

Manovich, Lev. 2001. *The Language of New Media*. Cambridge, MA: MIT Press.

McMillan, Sally. 2006. "Exploring Models of Interactivity from Multiple Research Traditions: Users, Documents and Systems." In *The Handbook of New Media*, edited by Leah Lievrouw and Sonia Livingstone, 205–229. London: Sage.

McMillan, Sally, and Edward Downes. 2000. "Defining Interactivity: A Qualitative Identification of Key Dimensions." *New Media & Society* 2 (2): 157–179.

Newhagen, John. 2004. "Interactivity, Dynamic Symbol Processing, and the Emergence of Content in Human Communication." *Information Society* 20 (5): 397–402.

Newhagen, John, and Sheizag Rafaeli. 1996. "Why Communication Researchers Should Study the Internet: A Dialogue." *Journal of Communication* 46 (1): 4–13.

Papilloud, Christian. 2010. "L'Interactivité." *tic & societé* 4 (1). http://ticetsociete.revues.org/pdf/769.

Quiring, Oliver. 2009. "What Do Users Associate with 'Interactivity'? A Qualitative Study on User Schemata." *New Media & Society* 11 (6): 899–920.

Rafaeli, Sheizaf. 1988. "Interactivity: From New Media to Communication." In *Advancing Communication Science: Merging Mass and Interpersonal Process*, edited by Robert P. Hawkins, John M. Wiemann, and Suzanne Pingree, 110–134. Newbury Park, CA: Sage.

Rogers, Everett. 1986. *Communication Technology: The New Media in Society*. New York: Free Press.

Ryan, Marie-Laure. 2002. "Beyond Myth and Metaphor: Narrative in Digital Media." *Poetics Today* 23 (4): 581–609.

Salen, Katie, and Eric Zimmerman. 2004. *Rules of Play: Game Design Fundamentals*. Cambridge, MA: MIT Press.

Interface

Carl Therrien

The term *interface* refers to the point and/or modalities of communication between two systems. In the study of human-computer interaction, it encompasses the physical means to provide input in a system as well as the feedback produced by the system. A wide variety of input and output devices have been created to communicate with computers, some built with specific work-related tasks in mind (switches, keyboard, mouse), and others dedicated to playing video games. Creators in the field of digital media have also developed custom input methods and have even repurposed cutting-edge technologies in their installations, such as motion sensors, voice recognition, and head-mounted displays. The interface can project the user in specific make-believe scenarios where embodiment is defined precisely: primary actions (P-actions) on the interface are mapped onto actions in a virtual world (Grodal and Gregersen 2009). Depending on the affordances of any given interface, these mappings can be more or less isomorphic in terms of motor activation. At the other end of the spectrum, the interface might be used as a navigation device through a web of documents, or simply as a way to activate an installation without giving the user the same clear sense of agency.

When William Higinbotham created *Tennis for Two* at the Brookhaven National Laboratory in 1958, communication with computers still relied on punch card systems, switches, and knobs. Higinbotham and his team created the first dedicated video game controller: a digital button (a simple on/off variation on the circuit) to hit the ball, and an analog knob (a potentiometer allowing incremental alterations to the electrical current) to affect the angle of the hit. From the controller bundled with the Atari 2600 to the contemporary gamepad, the number of buttons has grown from one to eight or more. A single button press can be made into a great variety of virtual actions depending on the genre. In 1962, *Spacewar!*'s dedicated control box had switches positioned with a directional logic: a vertical switch to move the ship forward or jump to hyperspace, and a horizontal one to rotate the vessel left or right. Electromechanical games had already sought to create symbiotic mappings between P-actions and virtual actions by repurposing directional input devices such as joysticks found in planes and choppers (Sega's *Missile* and Midway's *Whirly Bird*, both from 1969), and video game designers followed suit for flying or racing games early in the history of the medium (*Speed Race*, Taito, 1974; *Gran Trak 10*, Atari, 1974). Digital or analog, the joystick became one of the most common interfaces in the arcade and for home video games. Outside of the vehicular settings, it is typically bound with the legs of a character moving through space. Since the Sony Dual Shock (1997), most game controllers have integrated dual joystick configurations; the second joystick is often dedicated to the manipulation of the point of view in 3D games. Such mappings are not symbiotic, but tangible (Klevjer 2006): the audiovisual depictions are adapted to the user's input in "real time," but the P-actions don't resemble the represented actions. In his installation *Points of View* (1983), media artist Jeffrey Shaw integrated two joysticks: one to steer the projected video content, another to affect the direction of the sound. The joystick has also been used as a steering device in some versions of the Panoscope 360 designed by Luc Courchesne (2000).

When *Spacewar!* was created on the PDP-1, computers were moving away from punch card input systems thanks to the integration of the teletype (a typewriter able to convert the information in electrical form). On the PDP-10's screen, the player of *Colossal Cave Adventure* (Will Crowther, Don Woods, 1976) could navigate and interact with the environment through the use of small sentences, such as "get lamp," and get feedback in written form. Command-line interfaces (CLIS) became preeminent in games at the end of the 1970s: Adventure International's and Infocom's text adventures were best sellers, and the first role-playing games and graphical adventure games used it well into the 1980s. The keyboard interface has also been used to mimic "natural" conversation, for example, with chat bots (ELIZA, Joseph Weizenbaum, 1964–1966) and more recently in the interactive experiment *Façade* (Michael Mateas, Andrew Stern, 2005). Voice recognition interfaces have been explored in video games since the end of the 1990s (*Hey You, Pikachu!*, Nintendo, 1998); with the Nintendo DS or Kinect's microphones, more game companies are starting to integrate voice commands. Lynn Hershman Leeson has explored the potential of this interface to converse with a virtual being in her installation DiNA (2004).

In the early 1980s, personal computer operating systems were moving from CLIS to mouse-driven graphical user interfaces inspired by Doug Englebart's work and the Alto computer. In these work environments, users can execute actions and get feedback more directly: the on-screen pointer mimics the speed and direction of their hand, and objects are selected with a click. The video game *Déjà vu* (Icom Simulations, 1985) was one of the first to use this type of interface. Dragging and dropping items from the main view to the inventory window with the mouse brought a certain degree of motor isomorphism to many adventure games. However, most actions in the game, as in the adventure genre in general, are performed through a rather punctual or even elliptical mapping: selecting action verbs (*Maniac Mansion*, 1987) or icons (*King's Quest V*, 1989) triggers actions that are carried out without further user input (and thus the P-action is restricted to a single "point" of the depicted action), or confirmed through audiovisual/textual cues that sum up the resulting state change, creating a form of ellipse in the depiction. Many artists have created interactive installations using similar point-and-click interfaces, in order to let users navigate through the content in a nonlinear way. Hypertext fiction (*afternoon, a story*, Michael Joyce, 1990; *Patchwork Girl*, Shelley Jackson, 1995) involves navigating a series of interconnected text segments by clicking on words. The advent of larger storage media (CD, DVD) and high-bandwidth Internet connections have set the stage for an explosion of hypermedia art (*Immemory*, Chris Marker, 1997; the database narratives of the Labyrinth Project).

Along with the mouse, the trackballs used in early arcade cabinets are able to capture the hand's movement on two axes. In games like Atari's *Football* (1978) or more recently with the True Swing feature in the *Tiger Woods* PGA Tour (EA) series, the manipulation of the mouse/trackball mimics the action of throwing/hitting a ball to some extent, and the force exerted on the interface is transferred into the virtual world. Many other interfaces seek to create natural manual interaction. For instance, touch screens allow users to interact with their hands on the screen where objects are represented. They have been used in the context of installation art since the 1980s and became part of handheld video games more recently. In Lynn Hershman Leeson's *Deep Contact* (1989), the new physicality afforded by the interface is put forth: users are encouraged to touch a seductive girl's body to initiate their adventure. Chris Hales has explored character interaction via a touch screen in installations such as *Bliss* (1998) and *Len's Stories* (1999). In many Nintendo DS games, the touch screen is used to select items in a menu, but also in more isomorphic scenarios, such as swiping the screen to throw a ball in *Nintendogs* (Nintendo, 2005).

The pursuit of symbiotic interaction has led to the creation of interfaces that involve the body more completely. In the context of the museum, pressure or optical sensors are a simple way for a computer to acknowledge the visitors' movements and adjust audiovisual content in response (such as in *Glowflow*, Myron Krueger, Dan Sandin, Jerry Erdman, and Richard Veneszky, 1969). Toni Dove's *Artificial Changelings* (1998) defines four zones in front of a screen, each associated with a specific situation (inside a character's head, dream state, etc.). The body movements within each zone also affect the images on the screen. The ideal of a natural interface is associated with the development of head-mounted displays (HMDs) and data gloves, devices that seek to capture the movements of the head and the hand in order to create a first-person virtual experience. Since Ivan Sutherland's first attempt in 1968, many technologies have been used with the goal of reducing the latency between the motions and the display. A few HMDs have been introduced in the 1990s to play computer or console video games (VFX-1, Forte, 1994), without any real technological and commercial success. Charlotte Davies has used an HMD in her installation *Osmose* (1995), along with a vest that measures the user's thorax capacity. The body's position and breathing influence a contemplative journey through twelve computer-generated worlds. Manual interfaces such as the Nintendo Wiimote and the Sony Move represent the most recent incarnation of the natural interface ideal. They are able to capture the hand's movements in space through accelerometers and optical sensors and have been mapped to a variety of scenarios, from bowling (*Wii Sports*, Nintendo, 2005) to fantasy sword wielding (*The Legend of Zelda: Skyward Sword*, Nintendo, 2011).

■ See also ANALOG VERSUS DIGITAL, AUGMENTED REALITY, AVATARS, CHATTERBOTS, DIGITAL INSTALLATION ART, GAMEPLAY

References and Further Reading

Bolter, Jay David, and Diane Gromala. 2003. *Windows and Mirrors: Interaction Design, Digital Art, and the Myth of Transparency*. Cambridge, MA: MIT Press.

Burnham, Van. 2003. *Supercade: A Visual History of the Videogame Age 1971–1984*. Cambridge, MA: MIT Press.

Dinkla, Söke. 1994. "The History of the Interface in Interactive Art." Paper presented at ISEA. www.kenfeingold.com/dinkla_history.html.

Grau, Oliver, ed. 2007. *MediaArtHistories*. Cambridge, MA: MIT Press.

Grodal, Torben, and Andreas Gregersen. 2009. "Embodiment and Interface." In *The Video Game Theory Reader 2*, edited by Bernard Perron and Mark J. P. Wolf, 65–83. New York: Routledge.

Huhtamo, Erkki. 2004. "Trouble at the Interface, or the Identity Crisis of Interactive Art." *Framework, The Finnish Art Review*, no. 2.

Klevjer, Rune. 2006. "What Is the Avatar? Fiction and Embodiment in Avatar-Based Singleplayer Computer Games." PhD diss., University of Bergen.

Laurel, Brenda, ed. 1990. *The Art of Human-Computer Interface Design*. Reading, MA: Addison-Wesley.

Shaw, Jeffrey, and Peter Weibel, eds. 2003. *Future Cinema: The Cinematic Imaginary after Film*. Cambridge, MA: MIT Press.

Wolf, Mark J. P., ed. 2008. *The Video Game Explosion: A History from PONG to PlayStation and Beyond*. Westport, CT: Greenwood Press.

L

··

Language Use in Online and Mobile Communication

Naomi S. Baron

The term *electronically mediated communication* (EMC) refers to linguistic messages conveyed via online and mobile media such as computers, mobile phones, and other mobile devices. Originally, the term *computer-mediated communication* (CMC) was used to denote written messages sent on such platforms as Listservs, e-mail, instant messaging (IM), or blogs (see BLOGS). Over time, written messaging has increasingly been done on mobile phones (i.e., text messaging or SMS). Some researchers include CMC under the broader EMC umbrella, while others encompass text messaging as part of CMC. Both online and mobile devices have voice capabilities (e.g., voice over Internet protocols such as Skype on computers; voice calls on mobiles phones). However, discussion of EMC generally focuses on written communication.

EMC began in 1971, with a simple e-mail exchange between two computers in the same room. Other major technological developments included the following:

1971	early computer conferencing
1980	newsgroups
1980s, early 1990s	early IM (e.g., UNIX talk, ytalk, ntalk)
1982	creation of the smiley
1986	Listservs
1988	Internet relay chat (IRC)
1993	text messaging on mobile phones
1996	ICQ ("I Seek You") (modern IM system)
1997	AIM (America Online Instant Messenger)
1997	blogs (weblogs)
2003	Second Life
2003	MySpace
2004	Facebook
2006	Twitter

What are the linguistic characteristics of EMC? The media have commonly depicted such communication as fitting a single mold: badly spelled and punctuated, and rife with grammatical errors (Thurlow 2006). However, EMC corpora offer a different, and more varied, perspective on the linguistic characteristics of EMC messages.

Some sources of variation in EMC are intuitively obvious. For example, full computer keyboards make for easier input than do traditional mobile phone keypads (using the multitap method to input alphabetic characters) or mobile phones with full but tiny QWERTY keypads. Similarly, synchronous messages (e.g., IM) encourage faster transmission of text once it has been composed than asynchronous messages (e.g., e-mail, text messages), which comfortably afford users the opportunity to edit messages before sending them. Third, some platforms allow for messages of any length (e.g., e-mail, blogs), while others restrict the number of characters (e.g., Twitter's 140-character limit). Fourth, individual user personality and style may affect how e-mail messages are written (e.g., whether to proofread before sending; whether to use abbreviations, acronyms, or emoticons). And finally, such variables as gender, age, and culture sometimes shape EMC style.

Empirical studies offer a reality check on assumptions about EMC. We look, in turn, at findings regarding (a) the linguistic character of IM, (b) the use of punctuation in text messaging, and (c) the role of gender in EMC. We then consider (d) whether EMC is a form of speech or of writing, and (e) the future of EMC as a linguistic genre.

The Linguistic Character of IM

Corpora studies indicate that IM texts written by teenagers and young adults—at least during the early 2000s—contained fewer distinctive linguistic characteristics than the popular press (and popular perception) suggested (Baron 2004; Tagliamonte and Denis 2008). For example, Baron's IM corpus of nearly twelve thousand words contained only thirty-one EMC abbreviations (e.g., "k" for "OK" or "bc" for "because"; common written abbreviations such as "hrs" for "hours" were excluded). There were only ninety acronyms, of which "LOL" ("laughing out loud") accounted for seventy-six. Emoticons were also sparse (a total of forty-six, of which thirty-one were a smiley). Moreover, only 171 words were misspelled or lacked necessary apostrophes.

In considering empirical EMC data, it is critical to be mindful of when the data were collected, since usage patterns evolve. In recent years, for example, much of the communication involving teenagers and young adults which earlier took place on IM now occurs through text messaging on mobile phones or through Facebook (see SOCIAL NETWORK SITES [SNSs], TWITTER, TUMBLR, AND MICROBLOGGING). (Users of Twitter tend to be somewhat older.) There is evidence (e.g., Ling and Baron 2007) that text messages contain more abbreviations than IMS sent by young adults. The motivating force may be difficulty of input on mobile devices rather than restrictions on message length (i.e., compared with IM written on computers). While text messages have historically been limited to 160 characters, most users came nowhere near this maximum. Depending on gender, age, and culture, the average is closer to thirty to fifty characters.

Punctuation in Text Messaging

Punctuation in EMC is often characterized as random. Empirical findings offer a different perspective. Baron and Ling (2011) examined punctuation issues in two sets of data: a corpus of text messages sent by undergraduates in 2005, and transcripts of interviews with teenagers regarding text messaging (collected in 2009).

In the first study, the authors found clear patterns regarding where students used punctuation. Overall, subjects were more than twice as likely to use question marks that are "required" by traditional punctuation rules than to use "required" periods or exclamation marks. This strategy makes linguistic sense in that question marks carry more discourse information than periods or exclamation marks. In text messages that contained more than one sentence, users were almost twice as likely to put end marks (periods, question marks, or exclamation marks) at the ends of sentences that were in the middle of the transmission than in sentences appearing at the end (e.g., "I'm correcting this paper. Ill call when im done"). Again, there is a linguistic logic here, since omission of sentence-final punctuation in the middle of a text message is more likely to cause confusion than omission of punctuation at the end of the transmission.

The teenage data revealed interesting perceptions about the role of punctuation in text messaging. While males saw no problem in ending a text with a period (or no punctuation mark), females deemed it important to end with something conveying emotion, such as multiple exclamation marks, a smiley, or an LOL.

It turns out that gender influences on EMC are widespread.

Gender in EMC

There is an extensive literature on the role gender plays in spoken and written language (see GENDER AND MEDIA USE). It has been widely observed that while females frequently use language to facilitate social interaction, men more commonly employ language for conveying information. These findings for spoken and written discourse have been replicated in studies of the content of e-mail (e.g., Boneva, Frolich, and Kraut 2001), IM (e.g., Fox et al. 2007), blogs (e.g., Argamon et al. 2007), and text messages (e.g., Okuyama 2009).

The conversational versus informational dichotomy is also reflected in the linguistic structure of many messages. In IM, for example, Baron (2004) reported that IM conversational closings between female college students took twice as long (in both number of turns and time on the clock) as closings between males. Lee (2003) found that female subjects used explicit openings and closings in IM conversations about 80 percent of the time, compared with 30 percent for males. Females are also more likely than males to use emoticons and exclamation marks in e-mail, IM, and text messages (e.g., Waseleski 2006; Witmer and Katzman 1997).

There are more subtle differences between genders as well. In IM conversations where contractions (e.g., "it's" for "it is") are possible, females use fewer contractions than males (Baron 2004). Moreover, when male and female subjects "chunk" the sentential components of IM messages sent seriatim, for example,

isn't it nice [SEND]
to be in love [SEND]
in the spring [SEND]

(i.e., three messages from the same person, sent one after the other), female "chunking" patterns more closely parallel punctuation in written language, while male patterns are more similar to pauses in speech (Baron 2010).

Is EMC Speech or Writing?

During the 1990s, there was considerable scholarly discussion regarding whether text created on such platforms as Listservs, e-mail, and IM was a form of informal speech "written down" or more akin to traditional writing. On the one hand, the popular press (reflecting user perception) saw these genres as essentially speech. On the other, fine-grained analyses of actual texts revealed a number of traits of more traditional writing (e.g., lexical and grammatical complexity) (Baron 1998; Crystal 2001).

This apparent conundrum results, in part, from the fact that there is so much variation in the kinds of messages sent—and the users sending them. We have already seen that IMS written by young female adults tend to be more "written" in character than those of male counterparts. Similarly, as e-mail and IM have come to replace conventional office communication tools, it is hardly surprising to find a more formal character in communiqués composed in these contexts. Conversely, older users (e.g., parents, grandparents) sometimes adopt teen lingo in their EMC messages as a way of not appearing stodgy.

The Future of EMC as a Linguistic Genre

Scholarly interest in the structure of mediated language began in the 1990s (e.g., Herring 1996) and continues to grow (e.g., Rowe and Wyss 2009; Thurlow and Mroczek 2011). However, it is premature to judge the future of those characteristics that are most commonly said to typify EMC (e.g., abbreviations, acronyms, emotions, and unconventional—though often principled—punctuation patterns). What we can say is that as of the late 2000s, EMC had relatively little effect on conventional speech or writing (Baron 2008, 176–180).

In the year 2000, it would have been difficult to imagine Americans (very few of whom did text messaging, none of whom did Twitter) being interested in pecking out brief messages on small keypads. Ten years later, the use of texting (not to mention Twitter) had exploded, with Americans now sending (and receiving) more text messages on their mobile phones than voice calls (Rosman 2010). Predicting the next new thing in technology—or in language—is a risky undertaking. However, it is fair to predict that the same kinds of linguistic conventions and innovations that have characterized human speech and writing for centuries will continue to be at play.

References and Further Reading

Argamon, Shlomo, Moshe Koppel, James W. Pennebaker, and Jonathan Schler. 2007. "Mining the Blogosphere: Age, Gender, and the Varieties of Self-Expression." *First Monday* 12 (9), September 3.

Baron, Naomi S. 1998. "Letters by Phone or Speech by Other Means: The Linguistics of Email." *Language and Communication* 18 (2): 133–170.

———. 2004. "'See You Online': Gender Issues in College Student Use of Instant Messaging." *Journal of Language and Social Psychology* 23 (4): 397–423.

———. 2008. *Always On: Language in an Online and Mobile World*. New York: Oxford University Press.

———. 2010. "Discourse Structures in Instant Messaging: The Case of Utterance Breaks." *Language@Internet* 7. www.languageatinternet.org/articles/2010/2651.

Baron, Naomi S., and Rich Ling. 2011. "Necessary Smileys and Useless Periods: Redefining Punctuation in Electronically-Mediated Communication." *Visible Language* 45:45–67.

Boneva, Bonka, David Frolich, and Robert Kraut. 2001. "Using E-Mail for Personal Relationships: The Difference Gender Makes." *American Behavioral Scientist* 45 (3): 530–549.

Crystal, David. 2001. *Language and the Internet*. Cambridge: Cambridge University Press.

Eckert, Penelope, and Sally McConnell-Ginet. 2003. *Language and Gender*. New York: Cambridge University Press.

Fox, Annie B., Danuta Bukatko, Mark Hallahan, and Mary Crawford. 2007. "The Medium Makes a Difference: Gender Similarities and Differences in Instant Messaging." *Journal of Language and Social Psychology* 26 (4): 389–397.

Herring, Susan, ed. 1996. *Computer-Mediated Communication: Linguistic, Social, and Cross-Cultural Perspectives.* Amsterdam: John Benjamins.

Lee, Christine. 2003. "How Does Instant Messaging Affect Interaction between the Genders?" The Mercury Project of Instant Messaging Studies, Stanford University. www.stanford.edu/class/pwr3-25/group2/pdfs/IM_Genders.pdf.

Ling, Rich, and Naomi S. Baron. 2007. "Text Messaging and IM: A Linguistic Comparison of American College Data." *Journal of Language and Social Psychology* 26:291–298.

Okuyama, Yoshiko. 2009. "*Keitai Meeru*: Younger People's Mobile Written Communication in Japan." *Electronic Journal of Contemporary Japanese Studies.* www.japanesestudies.org.uk/articles/2009/Okuyama.html.

Rosman, Katie. 2010. "Y U Luv Texts, H8 Calls." *Wall Street Journal,* October 14.

Rowe, Charley, and Eva Wyss, eds. 2009. *Language and New Media: Linguistic, Cultural, and Technological Evolutions.* Cresskill, NJ: Hampton Press.

Tagliamonte, Sali, and Derek Denis. 2008. "Linguistic Ruin? LOL! Instant Messaging and Teen Language." *American Speech* 83 (1): 3–34.

Thurlow, Crispin. 2006, "From Statistical Panic to Moral Panic: The Metadiscursive Construction and Popular Exaggeration of New Media Language in the Print Media." *Journal of Computer-Mediated Communication* 11 (3). http://jcmc.indiana.edu/vol11/issue3/thurlow.html.

Thurlow, Crispin, and Kristine Mroczek, eds. 2011. *Digital Discourse: Language in the New Media.* New York: Oxford University Press.

Waseleski, Carol. 2006. "Gender and the Use of Exclamation Points in Computer-Mediated Communication: An Analysis of Exclamations Posted to Two Electronic Discussion Lists." *Journal of Computer-Mediated Communication* 11 (4). http://jcmc.indiana.edu/vol11/issue4/waseleski.html.

Witmer, Diane, and Sandra Katzman. 1997. "On-Line Smiles: Does Gender Make a Difference in the Use of Graphic Accents?" *Journal of Computer-Mediated Communication* 2 (4). http://jcmc.indiana.edu/vol2/issue4/witmer1.html.

· ·

Life History
Ruth Page

Life history is a qualitative research method used in the social sciences and has currency as a term used to refer to the narrative genre known as the life story. Life histories are distinct from fictional narratives (like digital fiction or e-mail novels) in that the narrator is assumed to be giving an authentic, albeit selective, account of real events so that breaches of authenticity are treated pejoratively as hoaxes, or reconceptualized as artistic endeavours (see HOAXES). In addition, the subject matter of the life history foregrounds the narrator's subjectivity and focuses on their personal experience, where narrative is assumed to be a privileged mode of expression used to construct the narrator's identity (see IDENTITY). Linde's (1993) definition of life story draws attention to the multiple units of discourse which constitute a life (his)story, and which are narrated episodically over the course of the narrator's lifetime. The multiple episodes of a life story are often discontinuous, fluctuating, and contradictory as the narrator tells and retells events from their past, which are deemed to retain reportability over time (often landmark or traumatic events).

In its broadest sense, offline examples of life history are found in conversational narrative genres, in written genres of biography, memoirs, and diary writing, and may be elicited in exchanges such as oral history, pedagogic, and therapeutic interviews. The analysis of life history is thus an interdisciplinary enterprise that spans the social sciences, arts, and humanities, with examples taken from literary, linguistic, heritage, educational, folklore, and medical contexts.

The episodic narration of personal experience found in life stories has adapted readily to online genres, where the evolution of Web 2.0 platforms has enabled individuals with little technical expertise to document their daily experiences with relative ease. As technologies of subjectivity (Ong and Collier 2005), platforms such as blogs, forums, and social network sites enable the narrators to "write themselves into being." Given that many (although not all) social media sites use chronology as an archiving principle (as indicated through the use of time stamps in post templates), and that posts are published episodically over time, the life story that emerges in these contexts is not necessarily a self-contained narrative product, but better regarded as a revisable self-portrait that is aggregated over the unfolding course of the narrator's online interactions, and which might vary according to the narrator's engagement with multiple sites (for example, stories told in Twitter and Facebook have different audiences and so contrast in subject matter and style; see TWITTER, TUMBLR, AND MICROBLOGGING). The styles used in telling a life story also vary over time, not only in relation to shifts in the narrator's subjectivity but also in relation to the dynamic nature of online sites and their communities. For example, some sites fall out of vogue (as did the British social network site Bebo and the North American site MySpace), while other changes occur within particular sites, such as changes to a template design or privacy settings.

The human impulse to tell stories has taken advantage of nearly every form of computer-mediated communication. The conversational examples of life history now exploit the interactive genres available in the forms of e-mail, forums, blogs, social network sites, virtual worlds, instant messaging, and Skype. These day-to-day accounts of lived experience tend to be ephemeral and are embedded in the wider interactions of particular individuals within their online networks. In addition, life stories elicited in interview situations are also found published in online archives. The developments in digital heritage include examples of life history in many localized national projects that focus on particular events (such as World Wars I and II, the Holocaust, and 9/11), social groups (slave narratives, migrants, and lesbian, gay, and bisexual communities), and particular places (local towns, suburbs, or countries). These archives preserve the voices of everyday speakers, particularly from marginalized groups or in the service of providing a memorial for significant national or international events.

Although offline life histories are most often preserved as written transcripts (sometimes with oral recordings), the life stories that are narrated in online contexts take full advantage of the multimodal affordances of the twenty-first-century Internet. Visual examples of life story include the *365 Project* (http://365project.org/) and the photographic storytelling that is disseminated on the photo-sharing site Flickr. Audiovisual examples of life story are best illustrated in the video blogs that populate YouTube, which in turn have antecedents in the amateur use of webcams, popularized particularly by young women (Senft 2008). In keeping with oral history's emphasis on the human voice, many online life histories use sound files (such as MP3 formats) to publish audio recordings of the speakers' voices, as does the StoryCorps Project (http://storycorps.org/), while other life history projects like that promoted by the Center for Digital Storytelling (www.story center.org/) foreground the use of images and music as narrative resources. The increasing ability to access the Internet through Wi-Fi-enabled smartphones has led to the use of life stories in audio tours such as Sound Walk (www.soundwalk.com/), or the international oral history project [*murmur*] (http://murmurtoronto.ca/about.php), which brings everyday storytelling "out onto the street" (see LOCATION-BASED NARRATIVE). These mobile examples of life history draw on the dynamic use of physical spaces and places along with the multisensory, kinaesthetic interactions of the audience to bring to life the narrator's reported personal experiences.

Online examples of life history are varied in the particularities of their subject matter and style, but their narrativity contrasts distinctively with their offline antecedents. While offline life history reports events from the narrator's distant past, examples of life history found in interactive genres (such as e-mail, forums, blogs, and social network sites) are influenced strongly by presentism. Narrators tend to document events assumed to take place in close proximity to the time of narration, and they may elect to use present tense or nonfinite verb forms (in a manner similar to a commentary) or adverbs that reflect the present moment (Page 2012); these events are presented in archives that use reverse chronological ordering (like blogs) and recency of activity (like social network sites) in their dissemination of narrative episodes. The emphasis on presentism is found in many forms of computer-mediated communication but appears to be increasing in the interactive genres that have gained international popularity in the first decade of the twenty-first century.

Offline life history tends to be characterized by the reportability associated with canonical narrativity (that is, reports of landmark events or conflict of some kind). Online examples of life history vary considerably in the subject matter considered appropriate for public dissemination. How far narrators choose to make personal disclosure in their life story may be related to their perceived needs for privacy and their intended audience, both of which are reconfigured by the collapsed contexts of the Internet. Life history may be published on sites that are known to be public, while other sites are semiprivate. Often online audiences bring together members or communities of practice who may be kept separate in offline interactions (as in Facebook friend lists), may have a nonreciprocal relationship with the narrator (such as a Twitter follower and an updater), and may choose only ever to "lurk." Nonetheless, the collaborative contributions of the audience for a life history are made apparent in online contexts, as evidenced through comments on posts or updates, and may shape how the narration unfolds.

Narrative analysts have long recognized that the identities enacted through storytelling are not transparent reflections of reality but are selective, fluid performances. While on one level life history found in online contexts is valued as a means of preserving and making accessible the voices of "everyday" narrators as an antidote to the authorizing discourse of history, it is not understood as a simplistic representation of offline experiences. Instead, life history, like other forms of personal narrative, can vary, often with idealized self-representation that is shaped according to the particular demands of a given context (for example, to project popularity within a peer-to-peer network, or to cultivate professional status or visibility). Although Web 2.0 rhetoric emphasized the apparently democratic nature of social media genres, at the end of the first decade of the twenty-first century, current social media genres have been shaped (at least to some extent) by neoliberal capitalist principles whereby the narrators tell their stories in order to gain social or economic benefit. From this perspective, online examples of life history can be influenced by the practices of microcelebrity, whereby "ordinary" people can self-publish their experiences in an attempt to gain fame, and where an audience of peers becomes reconceptualized as a fan base. Examples of life stories being used for this end include high-profile video bloggers on YouTube, or celebrity practice on the microblogging site Twitter.

Life histories told in online contexts demonstrate the continuing importance of narrative as a mode of self-expression, offering analysts a tractable record of storytelling interactions from a range of "everyday" narrators. These stories have important pragmatic functions, including establishing individual and social identity, and in some cases offering advice or therapeutic support to others (as in illness narratives), and are of interest for their linguistic, thematic, and political features.

■ See also ARCHIVE, DIGITAL FICTION, E-MAIL NOVEL, NARRATIVITY

References and Further Reading

Linde, Charlotte. 1993. *Life Stories: The Creation of Coherence*. Oxford: Oxford University Press.
Ong, Aihwa, and Stephen Collier. 2005. *Global Assemblages: Technology, Politics, and Ethics as Anthropological Problems*. Oxford: Blackwell.
Page, Ruth. 2012. *Stories and Social Media: Identities and Interaction*. London: Routledge.
Senft, Theresa M. 2008. *Camgirls, Community and Celebrity in the Age of Social Networks*. New York: Peter Lang.

Linking Strategies

Susana Pajares Tosca

A linking strategy is the conscious use of hypertextual links (see HYPERTEXTUALITY) in order to attain narrative and lyrical effects. There are two levels of linking strategy: the micro level, which occurs when going from one link to the next and in which the context is more limited, and the macro level, which refers to the more complex structures that all links of a hypertext are organized into. Both levels are dependent on each other but can be distinguished for the analysis.

Tosca deals with the micro level in "The Lyrical Quality of Links" (1999) and "A Pragmatics of Links" (2000). She proposes that hypertext might be more suited to the lyrical than to the narrative form. The intense speculation that precedes choosing a link (a centrifugal movement) and the reconfiguration of meanings which occurs after arriving at the new node (a centripetal movement) are similar to the interpretive movements of reading poetry. Tosca uses relevance theory to conclude that in hyperfiction (as in print fiction) the linking strategy is always to increase the processing effort. The reader's reward "is the exploration of evocative contexts through the search for a wide array of implicatures" (Tosca 2000). Another theorist interested in the link as the carrier of meaning is Licia Calvi (1999).

Tosca also suggests that linking strategies work differently in informational hypertexts versus literary ones (2000). Informational hypertexts want to achieve maximal cognitive effect with minimum processing effort; they provide descriptive links that suggest few strong implicatures, that is, there is no doubt as to the destination of the links. Meanwhile, literary hypertexts want to achieve maximal lyrical effects by increasing the processing effort; links suggest many weaker implicatures that keep readers guessing. In this kind of hypertext, links can sometimes by hidden, playing even more with reader's expectations. Figuring out the structure of the hypertext by piecing together the evocative links (Walker 1999) is an aesthetic strategy in itself.

Several authors have dealt with the configuration of multiple links, that is, linking strategies at a macro level. In "The Structure of Hypertext Activity" (1996), Jim Rosenberg shows how we can understand the movement from individual links to a more holistic understanding of the work. The link's meaning constitutes itself in the next level of the reader's activity (following a link is an acteme, and multiple actemes are combined into an episode, where we can already distinguish meaning).

In "Patterns of Hypertext" (1998), Mark Bernstein defines different "links constructs" or strategies, which he illustrates with abundant examples. Frequently, a single hypertext will contain several of these patterns, or they will even be contained within each other. Discovering the underlying structure of a hypertext is as important as decoding its text. The "cycle" is one of the basic structures of repetition, where readers return to an earlier point and have to embark on a new hypertextual search with new knowledge. Another basic structure is "counterpoint," by which two distinct voices or more coexist in a narration. There is also "mirror world," where two parallel narrative universes run together, meeting at crucial points and letting the reader figure out the connections. Another strategy is "tangle," an apparently chaotic mix of links which intentionally creates confusion. A "sieve" is a classic decision-tree structure. Other examples from patterns/strategies are webrings, contours, montage, neighborhood, split/join, missing link, and navigational feint.

Another important work about linking strategies at the macro level is that of Marie-Laure Ryan (2001). Her focus is narrower than Bernstein's since she is interested in the preservation of narrative coherence in hypertext fiction. She argues that "the narrative potential of the interactive text is a function of the architecture of its system of links" (2001, 246). She identifies the following global structures for narrative, some of which overlap with Bernstein's: the complete graph, the network, the tree, the vector, the maze, the directed network, the hidden story, the braided plot, action-space, epic wandering, and story world (see GRAPH THEORY). Ryan warns us that "the potential of a network to generate well-formed stories for every traversal is inversely proportional to its degree of connectivity" (2001, 256). A linking strategy has the purpose of guiding the path of the reader so that progression makes sense and can produce interesting narrative effects. Ryan believes that a truly narrative experience requires very strong authorial control (see INTERACTIVE NARRATIVE).

■ See also GRAPH THEORY, NETWORKING, NONLINEAR WRITING

References and Further Reading

Bernstein, Mark. 1998. "Patterns of Hypertext." In *Hypertext '98 Proceedings*, Pittsburgh. New York: ACM Press.

Calvi, Licia. 1999. "Lector in rebus: The Role of the Reader and the Characteristics of Hyperreading." In *Hypertext '99 Proceedings*, Darmstadt, Germany. New York: ACM Press.

Rosenberg, Jim. 1996. "The Structure of Hypertext Activity." In *Hypertext '96 Proceedings*, Washington, DC. New York: ACM Press.

Ryan, Marie-Laure. 2001. *Narrative as Virtual Reality: Immersion and Interactivity in Literature and Electronic Media*. Baltimore: Johns Hopkins University Press.

Tosca, Susana. 1999. "The Lyrical Quality of Links." In *Hypertext '99 Proceedings*, Darmstadt, Germany. New York: ACM Press.

———. 2000. "A Pragmatics of Links." In *Hypertext '00 Proceedings*, San Antonio, TX. New York: ACM Press.

Walker, Jill. 1999. "Piecing Together and Tearing Apart: Finding the Story in 'afternoon.'" In *Hypertext '99 Proceedings*, Darmstadt, Germany. New York: ACM Press.

Location-Based Narrative

Scott Ruston

Location-based narrative is an art, entertainment, or education project in which the location of the participant plays an important role in the interaction with story, rendered via mobile media device. This interaction might involve acquisition of narrative components through exploration and puzzle solving, resolving juxtapositions between real and fictional worlds, or simply accessing content cued by location markers. As such, location-based narrative is a form of interactive narrative (see INTERACTIVE NARRATIVE).

Location-based narrative projects may use various techniques and technologies to incorporate location into the narrative experience. *Location-aware* technologies, such as GPS and cell signal triangulation, generally offer passive (to the user) and automated location information updates to the system governing the location-based narrative. This framework is generally considered the least intrusive and most immersive. Other technologies and techniques for location detection include proximity detectors (e.g., Bluetooth, RFID [radio frequency identification]) and user self-reporting. In the former case, the mobile device detects an embedded sensor, which triggers new content delivery, a change in the story world conditions, or some other modification to the narrative structure of the experience. In the latter format, a signpost or other fixed marker provides instructions and a unique code for retrieving narrative content.

By motivating user activity within a space and layering narrative content on top of physical space, location-based narratives can both reveal the layers of human experience that transform an abstract space into a place and contribute new experiences shaping the location into a place. This view, drawn from the theoretical work of human geographers such as Yi-Fu Tuan (1977) and Tim Cresswell (2002), sees "space" as an abstract or as a set of potentials, and "place" as the site of lived experience. An early GPS-powered location-based narrative set in Los Angeles, *34N118W* (2002), triggers fictional audio vignettes as the participants walk downtown streets guided by a one-hundred-year-old map displayed on a tablet device. The vignettes express emotions and activities of fictional residents living in the area over the course of the one-hundred-year span between the map and the contemporary moment, layering the narrative experience with physical exploration and literary imaginings. The effect alters the participant's experience of the downtown locale, enriching the once-abandoned/now-gentrified location with greater nuance and dimension.

While various narrative forms have been portable for a long time (e.g., books), and certain stories have always been inextricably linked to their physical location (consider the June 16 Bloomsday walks in Dublin that take Joyce's *Ulysses* to the streets), a convergence of technology and artistic trends occurred around the turn of the twenty-first century to establish the practice of location-based narrative. First, experimentation with interactive narrative increased, fueled in large part by the advent of hyperlinks and the growth of video games. Second, digital technology such as laptop computers, mobile phones, tablet devices, and other consumer electronics became smaller while incorporating more capability—by the early 2000s, mobile phones included cameras and GPS receivers. The third major technological change leading to location-based narrative was the GPS system. Civilian access to the more precise GPS signal was made available in 2000, increasing both cultural awareness of location specificity and practical uses such as car navigation systems and handheld devices for hikers. Soon developers were making location-based services and entertainments, intersecting digital media content and location. The majority of locative media applications are location-based services (LBSs), such as map and direction-finding applications (e.g., Google Maps) or business-locating applications (e.g., Urban Spoon), or location-specific social networking (e.g., Foursquare). Marketing potential, whether through coupons pushed to a mobile device or location-specific advertisements or other strategies, is a primary driver behind many LBSs.

An early locative hobby or entertainment practice is geocaching. Geocaching involves secreting a container, recording the container's latitude and longitude coordinates, and then publishing the coordinates for others to seek out and find using handheld GPS devices. As a practice, geocachers usually record finding the cache in a notebook at the cache site, as well as online, and may leave tokens behind. In some geocaches, finders are encouraged to add to an ongoing story (see COLLABORATIVE NARRATIVE), so that subsequent geocachers experience a serial narrative.

In the short history of location-based narrative practice, three broad categories have been identified: spatial annotation, games, and mobile narrative experiences (see Ruston 2010). Within each of these categories, individual projects may exhibit a greater or lesser degree of "storiness," and not every spatial annotation project or location-based game incorporates a narrative component (see Ryan [2006] for a scalar definition of narrative suitable for interactive narrative projects).

Spatial annotation projects provide information about a space, in the form of text, audio, image, or video, and accessible by mobile device; frequently they incorporate a participatory component inviting users to upload images, audio, or text that become part of the narrative system for future visitors to encounter. The Canadian project [murmur], now in more than ten installations worldwide, is an excellent example of a spatial annotation that successfully unites a narrative component with the ubiquity and portability of the mobile phone. In establishing a [murmur] installation, the development team collects numerous stories contributed by community members and recorded in the locations about which the stories refer. Project creators curate these stories, resulting in approximately one to four stories per location. Locations are marked with an iconic sign in the shape of a large, green ear indicating a phone number and unique location code. Passersby dial the phone number, enter the code (thus self-reporting location), and hear the stories linked to that location. The [murmur] narrative is a system of stories united by community and the unseen connections produced by the participant's pedestrian navigation through the city.

Location-based games use the real world as a game board and incorporate narrative elements to facilitate play by providing motivation or guidance to players and illustrate the game world / story world for the player to juxtapose with the real world. A game such as *Botfighters* (2001–2005) is similar in many ways to first-person shooter video games, but enacted by real people in the real world. Player and opponent location is tracked via GPS, and battles are controlled by SMS, with game summaries narrated online. With an inhabitable story world available for free play and exploration, coupled with a fixed narrative framework and rule set, games like *Botfighters* exhibit characteristics of both *paidia*-type playable stories and *ludus*-type activities (see LUDUS AND PAIDIA). Art collective

Blast Theory produced a number of search/chase games in the early 2000s which involved collaboration between "street players" (moving through the real world with a handheld mobile device) and "online players" (monitoring street player movements via website and sharing information). Communications scholar Adriana de Souza e Silva (2006) has described this union of cyberspace and real space as a "hybrid reality" (see AUGMENTED REALITY), produced in the collaboration between the two types of players.

In the mobile narrative experience, participants use a mobile media device as the primary interface for accessing a story while moving through space. These location-based narratives capitalize on the ubiquity, portability, and interactivity of mobile media and at the same time incorporate a comprehensive thematic and narrative structure. The interactive component consists of the participant's acquisition of the story elements and engagement with her surroundings in the process. *34N118W*'s vignettes, for example, integrate into different, individualized narrative experiences depending on the sequence in which the participant accesses the vignettes, as well as the triangulations he or she might make between map, city surrounding, and vignette. In the USC Interactive Media Division project *Tracking Agama* (2004–2006), a contained narrative exists, fractured into multiple audio clips, and must be stitched back together by the participant engaged in puzzle-solving activities in multiple Los Angeles locations. In this example, the mobile narrative experience borrows equally from traditional cinematic storytelling practice and newer forms of narrative such as the alternative reality game (see ALTERNATE REALITY GAMING). Seeing a commercially viable market, the travel/tour industry has embraced location-based narrative. Location-based narrative travel guides may feature histories or fictions, as well as game elements, triggered by location-aware technology or user selection (e.g., REXplorer, Storytude, Untravel Media). Artist Jeremy Hight (2003) has called this layering of narrative content "narrative archaeology," positioning the participant in the role of uncovering shards of story and place.

Location-based narrative offers an artistic mode of expression which embraces and engages with the mobile, participatory, and location-aware characteristics of the always-on / always-connected twenty-first-century digital lifestyle. Despite the congruence between narrative mode and cultural valence, however, location-based narrative has yet to see the widespread popularity of location-based services. Contemporary media culture is still highly consumption oriented, and while the popularity of YouTube and other media "prosumption" (see MASHUP) venues indicates a trend toward a participatory culture (Jenkins 2006), experiencing location-based narratives requires a greater level of time and effort than existing mainstream forms of narrative (e.g., books, film, television, and video games). *Botfighters* is among the more commercially successful location-based narratives, having seen forty thousand players subscribed at the peak of its four-year run (Dee 2006). Location-based narrative is uniquely suited to offer immersion in a mixed reality that leverages device portability, an enrichment of place, and the on-demand requirements of contemporary culture, especially as location-aware, multimedia-capable smartphones become more and more widespread with their built-in commercial infrastructure of "apps" and as the trends of immersion, participation, and cross-platform availability continue in digital storytelling and gaming.

■ See also SPATIALITY OF DIGITAL MEDIA

References and Further Reading

34N118W. 2002. Jeremy Hight, Jeffrey Knowlton, Naomi Spellman. Los Angeles.

Blast Theory. 2001–. www.blasttheory.co.uk/.

Botfighters. 2001–2005. It's Alive!

Cresswell, Tim. 2002. "Introduction: Theorizing Place." In *Mobilizing Place, Placing Mobility*, edited by Ginette Verstraete and Tim Cresswell, 11–32. Amsterdam: Rodopi.

de Souza e Silva, Adriana. 2006. "From Cyber to Hybrid: Mobile Technologies as Interfaces of Hybrid Spaces." *Space and Culture* 9 (3): 261–278.

Dee, Johnny. 2006. "G2: Big Kids on the Block." *Guardian*, August 8. Features, 12.

Hight, Jeremy. 2003. "Narrative Archaeology." *Streetnotes*. www.xcp.bfn.org/hight.html.

Jenkins, Henry. 2006. *Convergence Culture*. Cambridge, MA: MIT Press.

[murmur]. http://murmurtoronto.ca/about.php.

Raley, Rita. 2008. "On Locative Narrative." *Genre* 41 (3–4): 123–148.

Ruston, Scott. 2010. "Storyworlds on the Move: Mobile Media and Their Implications for Narrative." *Storyworlds: A Journal of Narrative Studies* 2 (1): 101–119.

Ryan, Marie-Laure. 2006. *Avatars of Story*. Minneapolis: University of Minnesota Press.

———. 2009. "From Narrative Games to Playable Stories: Toward a Poetics of Interactive Narrative." *Storyworlds* 1 (1): 43–59.

Tuan, Yi-Fu. 1977. *Space and Place: The Perspective of Experience*. Minneapolis: University of Minnesota Press.

● ●

Ludus and Paidia

Marie-Laure Ryan

The contrast between ludus and paidia, proposed in 1958 by Roger Caillois as a criterion of classification for play, has been very influential in computer game scholarship. According to Caillois, paidia is a free play characterized by "diversion, turbulence, free improvisation, and careful gaiety," while ludus controls the players' fantasy through arbitrary and imperative conventions that require a great amount of "effort, skills, and ingenuity," even though the conventions are "completely unpractical" (Caillois [1958] 2001, 13).

The best example of paidia games is building imaginary scenarios with toys, using them as "props in a game of make-believe" (Walton 1990, 1:21–24) (see ROLE-PLAYING GAMES). These games do not aim at a specific goal, and they do not lead to losing or winning. The pleasures of paidia reside in the free play of the imagination, in adopting foreign identities, in forming social relations, in building objects, in exploring an environment, and in creating representations. If there are rules, they are spontaneously created by the participants, as when a group of children decides that a certain tree will be the house of the wolf, and they can be renegotiated on the fly. Ludus games, by contrast, are strictly controlled by preexisting rules accepted by the participants as part of a basic game contract; they lead to clearly defined states of winning or losing, and their pleasure resides in the thrill of competition and in the satisfaction of solving problems.

Caillois conceived the contrast ludus/paidia as the two poles of a continuum, and he used it to cross-classify a taxonomy of games which includes four basic categories: *agon* (games of competition, such as chess and football), *alea* (games of chance, such as roulette), *mimicry* (games of simulation, such as building models or playing house), and *ilinx* (games of vertigo, such as extreme sports or riding roller coasters). For Caillois, each one of these four categories includes games that tend toward the ludus pole and games that tend toward the paidia pole. Yet if one regards the presence of rules leading to clearly distinct outcomes as the constitutive feature of ludus, this suggests a much more binary distinction than Caillois had in mind: games are either rule governed or not rule governed, rather than more or less strongly governed by rules. If there is a combination of ludus and paidia, this does not occur in games with weak rules and fuzzy outcomes, but rather in game worlds that allow both ludus and paidia. The ability to combine these two types of experience is one of the most innovative features of computer games. In games such as *Grand Theft Auto* or *World of Warcraft*, players can engage in ludus-type activities, by performing quests that involve competition and lead to advancement in the game, and in paidia-type play, by chatting with other players, building avatars, and exploring the diverse landscapes of the game world. The worlds of such games are both combat zones full of challenges and playgrounds filled with a variety of toys.

■ See also GAME GENRES, GAME HISTORY, GAMEPLAY

References and Further Reading

Caillois, Roger. (1958) 2001. *Man, Play and Games.* Translated by Meyer Burach. Urbana: University of Illinois Press.

Egenfeldt-Nielsen, Simon, Jonas Heide Smith, and Susana Pajares Tosca. 2008. *Understanding Video Games: The Essential Introduction.* London: Routledge.

Juul, Jesper. 2011. *Half-Real: Video Games between Real Rules and Fictional Worlds.* Cambridge, MA: MIT Press.

Salen, Katie, and Eric Zimerman. 2003. *Rules of Play: Game Design Fundamentals.* Cambridge, MA: MIT Press.

Walton, Kendall. 1990. *Mimesis as Make-Believe: On the Foundations of the Representational Arts.* Cambridge, MA: Harvard University Press.

M

Machinima
Michael Nitsche

Machinima is based on the use of virtual environments for the creation of linear cinematic videos. It reflects play as artistic expression and documents an evolving gaming culture through a reframing of games and play. Machinima is not a defined genre but a real-time computer animation practice that combines elements of digital puppetry, filmmaking, and performance to create music videos, full-length feature films, gameplay recordings, and experimental animations, among others.

Machinima evolved from two main origins: One foundation for machinima is found in the early hacker scene. To claim the fame of hacking a particular game first, hackers often added short intro sequences, "crack intros," to the software they distributed once the copy protection was broken. Over time, the artistry of these sequences became more important, spinning off to form its own community: the demoscene (Tasajärvi 2004). Demoscene members aim to code highly compressed yet visually stunning real-time computer-generated imagery (CGI). Their work largely detached itself from games as it evolved into an independent culture of animation and extreme programming.

The second foundation for machinima depends on commercial game engines. Since the early 1980s, developers have used game systems to script animations and to create cut scenes (see CUT SCENES). Eventually, games like *Stunt Island* (1992) made these techniques available to players. Others, such as *DOOM* (1993) and *Quake* (1996), allowed players to record their game sessions in log files, called demos, which could be played back inside the individual game engine. Players recorded virtual performances and distributed these demos to the larger community of fellow video game players, who soon started to experiment with it. Machinima evolved as an example of emergent play (see EMERGENCE) as gamers showed off their skills but also applied basic narrative structures (e.g., *Diary of a Camper* [1996] by The Rangers), created their own demo editing tools (e.g., *Little Movie Processing Center* by Uwe Gierlich [1994]), and formed their own communities (machinima.com [2001–]). Depending on the engine, each demo had its own file structure and reused available game assets. Thus, they could only be played back in the game engine in which they were produced. Machinima remained engine specific but evolved in parallel on different platforms. In this wake, the term itself was assembled by Anthony Bailey and Hugh Hancock as a combination of "cinema" and "machine" to replace the widespread, but increasingly inaccurate, "Quake movies."

With advances in home computer technology, game sessions eventually could be recorded directly from the screen by the late 1990s. Ever since, by far most machinima have been produced and distributed as linear pre-rendered videos. This reduced the once-underlying technical distinction of real-time animation to an optional animation effect, but machinima's transmedia appeal grew as videos could be easily shared. The potential value of machinima "to revolutionize visual-based storytelling as we know it" (Marino 2004, 3) was hailed, and it was tested for commercial productions such as Douglas Gayeton's *Molotov Alva and His Search for the Creator* (2007). But unresolved limitations, particularly the restrictions posed by many games' end-user license agreements, slowed the evolution of a professional machinima community. As a cultural practice, machinima remains in a form of "arrested development" (Salen 2011, 37) that sees many players engaged but no central unifying and evolving core to their art. It largely remains a reflection on and documentation of gaming on the one side and an exercise in guerilla video production and experimental animation on the other.

■ See also DIGITAL AND NET ART, FILM AND DIGITAL MEDIA

References and Further Reading
Hancock, Hugh, and Johnnie Ingram. 2007. *Machinima for Dummies*. Hoboken, NJ: Wiley.
Hanson, Matt. 2004. *The End of Celluloid: Film Futures in the Digital Age*. Mies, Switzerland: Roto-Vision SA.
Kelland, Matt, Dave Morris, and Dave Lloyd. 2005. *Machinima*. Boston: Thomson.
Lowood, Henry, and Michael Nitsche, eds. 2011. *The Machinima Reader*. Cambridge, MA: MIT Press.
Marino, Paul. 2004. *3D Game-Based Filmmaking: The Art of Machinima*. Scottsdale, AZ: Paraglyph Press.
Salen, Katie. 2011. "Arrested Development: Why Machinima Can't (or Shouldn't) Grow Up." In *The Machinima Reader*, edited by Henry Lowood and Michael Nitsche, 37–50. Cambridge, MA: MIT Press.
Tasajärvi, Lassi. 2004. *Demoscene: The Art of Real-Time*. Helsinki: Evenlake Studios.

Markup Languages
Kirstyn Leuner

"In the age of new media, there is no way to avoid markup. . . . Markup is writing" (Dilger and Rice 2010, xi). Markup refers to linguistic expressions or codes within a document that indicate its unique structure and style. These codes are not source or machine codes that execute functions on a computer; rather, markup codes indicate how a person or a machine should understand, organize, and display textual data. Markup elements almost always appear in pairs of tags that enclose the text they describe. For example, at the top of this page, and are "tags" in the "title element" that mark up the title of this entry. If every title in this collection is enclosed in the same set of tags, a computer can retrieve them as data in order to generate, for example, a table of contents. When composing text electronically, especially in a WYSIWYG platform, writing and markup can take place simultaneously—which makes markup less visible but, at the same time, pervasive.

There are two general types of markup language which pertain to electronic texts: procedural and descriptive markup. Procedural markup tells a computer how to process a work and display it to the end user, such as font style and text alignment. Conversely, descriptive markup indicates a document's architecture by identifying its structural components. Descriptive tagging of a poem will identify its stanzas and lines and may even tag its rhyme and meter. The value of descriptive markup is that it organizes content but does not wed it to a certain format. For example, one can publish a marked-up text file of a cookie recipe in two different formats: in a print cookbook and as a web page. The tags that distinguish the ingredients list from the baking instructions enable the data to remain organized properly but also to display differently for each version, as the markup is independent from that which determines styling.

SGML (Standard Generalized Markup Language) is a foundational early electronic markup language. It was invented in the mid-1980s to accommodate the U.S. Department of Defense's need to archive electronic documents with incompatible formats (Bates 2003, 4). Characteristics of SGML include the following: descriptive markup in a hierarchical structure, customizable tag sets, each document contains a Document Type Declaration (DTD) that declares its elements, and elements must be human-readable expressions (DeRose 1997, 195–196). In the 1990s, developers designed HTML (HyperText Markup Language) and XML (Extensible Markup Language) to address SGML's weaknesses (DuCharme 1999, 22). While HTML enables data to display on the web, it lacks XML's flexibility to name and structure elements for various output formats. XML is a meta-markup language that describes a certain grammar of SGML (Bates 2003, 13). When paired with a style sheet and transformed, XML documents can be published online as HTML or XHTML files with a custom format. Many organizations—from businesses to scholarly institutions—that seek a standard for electronic data archiving and publishing adopt an XML "encoding scheme" that they curate specifically for their needs.

■ See also ARCHIVE, CODE, CRITICAL EDITIONS IN THE DIGITAL AGE, DATA

References and Further Reading

Bates, Chris. 2003. *XML in Theory and Practice*. West Sussex, UK: Wiley.

Brown University Women Writers Project. 2007. "What Is Text Encoding?" *Women Writers Project Guide to Scholarly Text Encoding*. http://www.wwp.brown.edu/research/publications/guide/.

Coombs, James H., Allen H. Renear, and Steven J. DeRose. 1987. "Markup Systems and the Future of Scholarly Text Processing." *Communications of the ACM* 30 (1): 933–947.

DeRose, Steven J. 1997. *The SGML FAQ Book: Understanding the Foundation of HTML and XML*. Boston: Kluwer.

Dilger, Bradley, and Jeff Rice, eds. 2010. *From A to <A>: Keywords of Markup*. Minneapolis: University of Minnesota Press.

DuCharme, Bob. 1999. *XML: The Annotated Specification*. Upper Saddle River, NJ: Prentice Hall.

Renear, Alan H. 2004. "Text Encoding." In *A Companion to Digital Humanities*, edited by Susan Schreibman, Ray Siemens, and John Unsworth. Oxford: Blackwell.

Sperberg-McQueen, C. M., and B. Tommie Usdin, eds. 1999–2001. *Markup Languages: Theory and Practice* (Journal). Cambridge, MA: MIT Press.

Text Encoding Initiative. 2013. "A Gentle Introduction to XML." *P5: Guidelines for Electronic Text Encoding and Interchange*. Version 2.3.0. www.tei-c.org/release/doc/tei-p5-doc/en/html/SG.html.

Mashup

Benjamin J. Robertson

A mashup is a cultural production that combines preexisting materials into something new. *Mashup* can also refer to the practices related to such productions and has come to prominence in the wake of personal and networked computing, which has given individuals the means to appropriate, remix, and therefore comment on contemporary culture. *Mashup* most often denotes artistic productions such as videos, songs, and novels which combine extant visual, musical, or textual works, but it can also refer to "a combination of data or functionality from two or more external sources to create a new service" (Sonvilla-Weiss 2010, 8), as when Twitter or similar services allow third parties to develop applications that make use of their functionality.

Mashups apparently share many characteristics with other appropriative practices such as remix and sampling and have antecedents in, among other things, Dada, *musique concrète*, Burroughs and Gysin's cut-ups, the found filmmaking of Bruce Conner, punk DIY, the sonic collage of Negativland, hip-hop's DJ culture, and the plagiarism of Kathy Acker (see REMIX, SAMPLING). Similar to many of these practices, mashups challenge romantic notions of authorship and originality, as well as the business models of the contemporary culture industries. Nonetheless, Stefan Sonvilla-Weiss distinguishes the mashup as a specific form: "mashups follow a logic that is additive or accumulative in that they combine and collect material and immaterial goods and aggregate them into either manifested design objects or open-ended recombinatory and interactive information sources on the Web" (2010, 9). Although Sonvilla-Weiss here refers to the web application sense of "mashup," this definition equally applies to the artistic/musical mashup currently under consideration. In short, mashups tend to be transparent with regard to their sources and rely on this transparency to make their meaning. Whereas artists such as the Beastie Boys might work to mask an audio sample (for fear of litigation or simply for aesthetic reasons), a mashup producer ensures that her listeners will recognize her source material.

Aram Sinnreich (2010) situates the mashup within what he calls "configurable culture." This "newly ascendant paradigm" must be differentiated from the modern paradigm of cultural production because of a contemporary "reciprocal interdependence between communication technology and culture" which has become so symbiotic that "they may no longer be understood in the absence of one another" (2010, 70). Indeed, the rise of the mashup form (and the term itself) follows from the widespread adoption, in the 1990s, of the personal computer, which granted to individuals production tools once reserved for institutions, and of the Internet and World Wide Web, which offered producers easy access to extant cultural materials and inexpensive channels of distribution for their work. Lawrence Lessig (2008) calls cultures that allow for or otherwise encourage cultural productions such as mashups "read/write" (as opposed to "read-only" cultures, which prevent or discourage such production; see also Lessig 2004). Thus, in addition to works that are clearly mashups—such as the Freelance Hellraiser's song "A Stroke of Genius," which combines the Strokes' "Hard To Explain" with Christina Aguilera's "Genie in a Bottle"—we might also identify recent novels such as *Pride and Prejudice and*

Zombies and *Abraham Lincoln: Vampire Hunter* as mashups. These novels mash up pre-existing texts and historical figures with contemporary narrative clichés, but more importantly here, they participate in a general culture of appropriation inspired in part by digital media.

Although contemporary culture seems to broadly accept the mashup and similar forms, established business models and contemporary governments, especially in the United States, often discourage, or "chill," their production. This schism has made of mashups something of an outlaw or pirate form as they, like other forms of appropriation, raise copyright concerns that can have legal ramifications for those who produce, distribute, and consume them (see COPYRIGHT). For example, websites that hosted copies of Danger Mouse's *The Grey Album* and the Kleptones' *A Night at the Hip-Hopera* (which combines music from Queen with vocals from the history of rap) were subject to cease and desist notices from rights holders of those albums' source materials. In the former case, these actions led to online activism as fans of the album and those concerned with the legal and political implications of contemporary cultural production organized "Grey Tuesday" on February 24, 2004 (see POLITICS AND NEW MEDIA). This act of electronic civil disobedience involved approximately 170 websites hosting files of the album in defiance of the cease and desist order (see Howard-Spink 2005). Over one hundred thousand copies of the album were downloaded that day; no one was charged with any crime as a result of these actions.

References and Further Reading

Frere-Jones, Sasha. 2005. "1 + 1 + 1 = 1: The New Math of Mashups." *New Yorker*. www.newyorker.com/archive/2005/01/10/050110crmu_music.

Howard-Spink, Sam. 2005. "Grey Tuesday, Online Cultural Activism, and the Mash-up of Music and Politics." *First Monday* 4. http://firstmonday.org/htbin/cgiwrap/bin/ojs/index.php/fm/article/view/1180/1100.

Lessig, Lawrence. 2004. *Free Culture: How Big Media Uses Technology and the Law to Lock Down Culture and Control Creativity*. New York: Penguin.

———. 2008. *Remix: Making Art and Commerce Thrive in the Hybrid Economy*. New York: Penguin.

Robertson, Benjamin J. 2010. "Mashing-up the Past, Critiquing the Present, Wrecking the Future: The Kleptones' *A Night at the Hip-Hopera*." *Hyperrhiz* 07. www.hyperrhiz.net/hyperrhiz07/27-essays/89-mashing-up-the-past.

Sinnreich, Aram. 2010. *Mashed Up: Music, Technology, and the Rise of Configurable Culture*. Amherst: University of Massachusetts Press.

Sonvilla-Weiss, Stefan. 2010. "Introduction: Mashups, Remix Practices, and the Recombination of Existing Digital Content." In *Mashup Cultures*, edited by Stefan Sonvilla-Weiss, 8–23. New York: Springer.

Materiality

Anna Munster

Much initial scholarship, aesthetic practice, fledgling cyber-ethnographies, and manifestos about digital media proclaimed immateriality to be the medium's inherent quality. During the 1990s, it seemed as though every discipline and practice affected by digital computing—from architecture through to literary studies—was declaring that information technologies would sweep away physical realities, spatial and temporal coordinates, and result in a generalized state of disembodied life. We would,

William Mitchell avowed in 1996, soon come to inhabit a new kind of nonplace, "a city unrooted to any definite spot on the surface of the earth . . . and inhabited by disembodied and fragmented subjects" (1996, 24). Yet simultaneously a number of critiques—often from the perspective of feminism or postcolonialism—of such utopian and dystopian technological visions emerged. These collectively underscored aspects of the materiality of digital media, culture, and its emerging socialities (for example, Nakamura 1995). *Materiality*, then, is a term that enters discussions about the digital from the outside, having already had a long history in various branches of sociology, aesthetics, and political science, for example. More specifically in the context of debates about how digital technologies affect and are affected by the social, cultural, political, and aesthetic spheres, materiality is used in two main ways. It refers both to the physicality of hardware, software, digital objects, artifact, and processes and to the material conditions—including the social relations, political context, and aesthetic experience—of production of all "things" digital.

Katherine Hayles's seminal text, *How We Became Posthuman* (1999), which argued that the broad development and spread of cybernetic theories and practices fundamentally divided information from materiality, in fact set the scene for the return of the material in digital media scholarship. Since the early 2000s, there has been a gathering "material turn" in analyses of digital media, with a growing acknowledgement that the material conditions that give rise to, facilitate interaction with, and embed the digital in distinct social and political practices had previously been overlooked. Materiality should not be now mistaken for a simple quality or property of digital technologies. Instead, it can be discerned as an expanded approach to analyzing neglected questions and areas in computation and culture, such as the laser devices that materially support the writing and reading of electronic print (Kirschenbaum 2008, 3). Importantly, a materialist approach, apparent in areas such as software studies, is a transdisciplinary means of connecting the digital to social relations and historical practices (Mackenzie 2006, 3–5).

The key areas that have emerged as critical to understanding the materiality of the digital are embodiment, hardware-software environments, and the sociocultural situatedness of computation. Although each of these areas has and is being explored as a salve to an earlier digital immaterialism, their aims and approaches and the stakes for materiality differ. There are certainly overlapping concerns; for example, Matthew Fuller's (2005) influential project for tracing the materialist energies at work in informational ecologies carefully draws out the ways in which the software and information embedded in an object mobilize sets of forces and relations that are also social and political. The material (digital or nondigital) media object here is a condensation of relations between hardware-software and broader sociopolitical forces. Fuller inventively releases this knotted material core of digital objects via his analysis: "it is not a question of establishing a static understanding of an apparatus. Understanding the multiple programs and medial drives built into it is also a question of mobilizing it" (2005, 84). But in crossing continuously from the specificity of the apparatus to its situatedness, Fuller also offers a uniquely dynamic materialist approach to technologies. He helps generate a materialist method, or, perhaps more accurately, in his analyses materiality shifts from object of digital media evaluation to becoming a multimodal practice-based theorization of digital cultures. He offers a "hands-on" and tangible mode through the digital, materializing it as it is conceived.

But it is important to also distinguish between the different directions taken in the exploration of digital materiality, for it should not be considered a uniform field or method.

As has already been noted, the so-called disembodiment of cyberspace, of virtual reality and of both screen-based and online mediated communications, had already been contested by feminist and postcolonial digital theorists and by new media artists throughout the 1990s. Yet it was not until Hayles cast the post–World War II history of information theory as one in which information (immaterial and virtual) could be understood as both permeating and separable from materiality (media channels as well as actual bodies and biomass) that an embodied approach to the digital really gathered steam (Hayles 1999, 14). Mark Hansen resituated the aesthetics of new media technologies deployed and developed by artists from around the late 1980s onward as especially concerned with embodiment rather than escaping the body (2006, 20–45).

According to Hansen, new media takes place within an ongoing human-technical ontogenesis, facilitating an expansion of human bodily capacities and engaging the body's latent technicity. Hence, he understands virtual reality, for instance, as a *"technically triggered experience of the organism's power of imaging"* (Hansen 2006, 19; emphasis in the original). Anna Munster provides a different approach to new media's materiality by suggesting that digitality and corporeality should be understood as differential forces, across whose discontinuities and gaps a processual digital embodiment emerges and media materialize (Munster 2006, 142–149). Digital embodiment, then, is a material process of recomposition rather than something that inheres in either media or the body as such. More recently, Frances Dyson has provided a "metadiscursive" analysis of the entwining of embodiment/disembodiment with materiality/immateriality in new media technologies. She argues that much rhetoric around new media's propensities toward virtuality, transcending mediation, and materiality has borrowed from previous configurations of transmitted and reproduced audio, seen as immersive, in flux, and "liquid" (2009, 3). But whereas a critical, historical discourse of sound studies has countered such claims for the aural, this has largely not been the case for digital media. Dyson insists that a broad-ranging materialist reinvestigation of the full range of (historical) conditions—technics, environment, the conditions for phenomenally experiencing any digital media—be taken into account in their theorization.

Rethinking and taking hardware-software relations and situated computing environments into account are closely related concerns for recent materialist approaches to the digital. For example, Matthew Kirschenbaum's exhortations to take better account of the place of fabrication and inscription processes and techniques in computational histories lead him to rethink the importance of hardware, specifically storage as a new media category, and to understand computational hardware's role in situating just this or that practice or behavior in the storing of information (2008, 10–11). Kirschenbaum distinguishes between two forms of materiality with respect to digital objects: forensic and formal. But he sees both as a necessary pair in a fully materialist digital ontology. Forensic materialism takes into account the ways in which, for example, storage capacity is both historically and concurrently always variable: "we find forensic materiality revealed in the amazing variety of surfaces, substrates, sealants, and other materiel that have been used over the years as computational storage media, and in the engineering, ergonomic, and labor practices that attend computation" (2008, 10). Here we can understand the individuated materializations that computational hardware acquires over time—from floppy disks through to the flash memory stick, for example—all of which shape the ongoing culture and technics of digital media. But Kirschenbaum also notes that we need to take into account the techno-social operations carried out by what he calls "multiple computational states" (2008, 14) performed on a digital object (for instance, in a digital image its bitmap information *and* its particular file format). He names this the "formal" level of digital materiality.

Kirschenbaum's nomenclature is deliberately ambiguous, as he clearly wants to engage with and combat previous formalist approaches to the digital. But perhaps what he is really attempting to come to terms with is the *performativity* at the core of digital materiality. Understanding the database, for example, as a *material* digital object, then, means accounting for not simply the way it organizes and stores data but how it *enacts* its mode of organizing multiply, the ways it transduces and interrelates its multiple, proliferating levels of hardware, software, data, and social practices: "Databases are a situation in which

we materially encounter a doing of the multiple" (Mackenzie 2011, 4). Likewise, the explosion of materialist analysis in the burgeoning field of software studies emphasizes the material operations of software as it acts on digital objects; acts in consort with the social and political behaviors of its developers, distributors, and end users; and acts relationally with other computational and noncomputational media.

As digital theorists, writers, media producers, and artists contribute to a growing literature, set of practices, and a debate on materiality, they do more than simply provide a riposte to the seemingly *immaterial* nature of the digital. They are also shifting away from elaborating either typologies or ontologies of digital media as devices, programs, and artifacts. They are instead engaging the digital as a mode or cluster of operations in consort with matter, a way of materially *doing things* in the world. This doing is procedural and constrained by programmability. At the same time the multiple levels of protocol and programs that the digital materially performs make it both error prone and generative. It could be said that to take a digital materiality into account in both theory and practice is to therefore tackle the vibrancy of digital matter(s).

■ See also CYBERSPACE, CYBORG AND POSTHUMAN, VIRTUAL BODIES, VIRTUAL REALITY, VIRTUALITY

References and Further Reading

Dyson, Frances, 2009. *Sounding New Media: Immersion and Embodiment in the Arts and Culture.* Berkeley: University of California Press.

Fuller, Matthew, 2005. *Media Ecologies: Materialist Energies in Art and Technoculture.* Cambridge, MA: MIT Press.

Hansen, Mark B. N. 2006. *Bodies in Code.* London: Routledge.

Hayles, N. Katherine, 1999. *How We Became Posthuman: Virtual Bodies in Cybernetics, Literature, and Informatics.* Chicago: University of Chicago Press.

Kirschenbaum, Matthew G. 2008. *Mechanisms: New Media and the Forensic Imagination.* Cambridge, MA: MIT Press.

Mackenzie, Adrian, 2006. *Cutting Code: Software and Sociality.* New York: Peter Lang.

———. 2011. "More Parts than Elements: How Databases Multiply." *Environment and Planning D: Society and Space* 30 (2): 335–350.

Mitchell, William J., 1996. *City of Bits: Space, Place and the Infobahn.* Cambridge, MA: MIT Press.

Munster, Anna, 2006. *Materializing New Media: Embodiment in Information Aesthetics.* Hanover, NH: Dartmouth College Press.

Nakamura, Lisa. 1995. "Race in/for Cyberspace: Identity Tourism and Racial Passing on the Internet." *Works and Days* 13:181–193.

Media Ecology
Michael Goddard

The concept of media ecology derives from the intuition that rather than merely transmitting messages or delivering content, media generate worlds and therefore need to be understood in complex environmental and/or ecological terms. This environmental approach to media has almost become commonplace in relation to digital media, where talk of "media environments" has become a frequent component of both business and policy discourses. However, this understanding of media environments is frequently an impoverished one that barely goes beyond business practices and official policies, and even a fuller concept of the environment falls short of a truly ecological account of media systems. In order to arrive at this account, it is necessary to first sketch some of the history of the concept of media ecology and its more contemporary vicissitudes that hinge precisely on this distinction between environment and ecology.

Media ecology can claim a direct lineage from the work of Marshall McLuhan, since it was out of conversations with his son Eric McLuhan and Neil Postman in the late 1960s that the term was first explored. As developed by Neil Postman and the Media Ecology Association (MEA), however, media ecology seemed to lose much of McLuhan's technological optimism to become instead a somewhat phobic account of the ways in which media and technology more generally shape and deform human existence, a line that perhaps shows more of an imprint of Jacques Ellul's pessimistic *The Technological Society* (1973) than McLuhan's more celebratory *Understanding Media* (2001). Postman's analysis of the mass media in *Amusing Ourselves to Death* (1987), for example, presents television as an epistemological disaster, while *Technopoly* (1993) extends this analysis to the social dominance of technology in general. As such, these works maintain McLuhan's technological determinism, blended with a humanist technophobia and nostalgia entirely absent in the work of the latter. This is not necessarily the case of the work of the MEA as a whole, which tends to stress more neutral definitions of media ecology, such as "the study of media environments, the idea that technology and techniques, modes of information and codes of communication play a leading role in human affairs" (Lance Strate), or an "emerging meta-discipline . . . broadly defined as the study of complex communication systems as environments. . . . Media ecologists know, generally, what it is they are interested in—the interactions of communications media, technology, technique, and processes with human feeling, thought, value, and behavior" (Christine Nystrom). While more neutrally defined than in the work of Postman, these definitions refer to environments rather than ecological systems and, tellingly, qualify these environments as based around human interactions with technologies and techniques, thereby maintaining an anthropocentric approach to media ecology ultimately derived from McLuhan's prosthetic approach to media as "the extensions of man." In this sense the approaches associated with the MEA can be seen to constitute a human-centered media environmentalism, rather than the full development of an ecological account of media.

However, more recent approaches to plural media ecologies have rejected both the humanism and technological determinism of these earlier accounts in favor of a more dynamic account of media ecologies. Far from eliminating human agency, a less anthropocentric and more materialist account of media ecologies, such as that elaborated in Matthew Fuller's (2005) book of the same name, allows for a more active articulation, emphasizing the way in which circuitries or assemblages of organic life, technological components, and other material and immaterial elements can become powerful and complex systems, often operating in conditions that are far from any stable environmental equilibrium and producing effects beyond both subjective human intentions and predetermined technological capacities (see MATERIALITY). Media ecologies are not just concerned with the effects of reified technical media on a supposedly preexisting and stable human or organic environment, but rather with the codevelopment of humans and technical machines as dynamic systems in which the human and the nonhuman are not clearly dissociable. This is based especially on Félix Guattari's (2000) understanding of ecology as always multiple and including, alongside a physical ecology of material components, a social ecology of relations and a mental ecology of subjectivity and immaterial factors such as thought and affect. This was an account of ecology that was in turn indebted to some of the more advanced expressions of ecological thought such as Arne Naess's (1990) nonanthropocentric account of "Deep Ecology" and especially Gregory Bateson's (2000) cybernetic approach to ecological systems. For example, a phenomenon like the London Pirate Radio, which Fuller analyzes in the first chapter of his book, is not reducible to an inventory of physical components such as micro transmitters, microphones, portable turntables, and mobile phones, nor to the circuitries of sound, electrical impulses, and digital messaging that these devices circulate. Equally important in this media ecology are the social ecology of the East London tower blocks and their Afro-Caribbean inhabitants, social relations that are also connected via parties, clubs, and other events, and specific affects and mental states related not only to the music but also to chemically alterable states of mind and emotion, as well as a specific mode of life in which Pirate Radio plays a crucial role.

Not all contemporary approaches to media ecology, however, engage with such a level of complexity as Fuller's account. In some instances there is a return to what could be described as a "hard" environmentalism as in Richard Maxwell and Toby Miller's article "Ecological Ethics and Media Technology," which focuses on the phenomenon of e-waste, the often hazardous disposal of obsolete media technology from the first world, usually in third-world environments, where it constitutes a seriously toxic threat to the physical environment. This article is written as a deliberate intervention and provocation of the norms of textually based media studies, as is clearly evident from the following quote: "What would happen to game studies if, rather than rehearsing debates about ludological, narratological, and effects approaches, it confronted the fact that . . . cables in Sony's PlayStation 1 consoles were found to contain deadly levels of cadmium, a fiasco that cost Sony US$85 million to fix . . . ?" (Maxwell and Miller 2008, 334). Such an approach, apart from showing no awareness of other media ecological approaches, only touches on important questions of physical and social ecologies, in order to use them as an argument against according any value to the mental ecologies of media systems, and in doing so only reproduces an anthropocentric and moralistic media environmentalism. A fully ecological approach to this important phenomenon of "dead media" would abandon such an either/or approach to physical-social and mental-affective levels of media ecologies and instead attempt to understand this dumping of media waste in dynamic, relational, and political rather than static and moralizing terms. Such an approach characterizes Hertz and Parikka's account of "Zombie Media" (2012), for example, in which such unethical ecological practices are shown as amenable to a pragmatic critique via bricolage and retooling, rendering obsolescent media technology less as dead than as undead. This might not solve the environmental problem of e-waste, but it does have the virtue of connecting up such phenomena with an active account of media ecologies which has a much greater potential to stimulate a creative and activist rather than a moralizing response.

A key reformulation of media ecologies can also be found in the work of Jussi Parikka, both in *Digital Contagions* (2007), his media archaeology of computer viruses, and in his more recent work *Insect Media* (2010), as well as the *Unnatural Ecologies* issue of *Fibreculture* coedited with Michael Goddard (Goddard and Parikka 2011). This is stated especially clearly in the conclusion to *Digital Contagions*, in which his exploration of the anomalous and parasitic life of computer viruses leads to a mutual contagion between new articulations of both media ecology and media archaeology. If a Guattarian inflected media ecology necessarily involves transversal passages between multiple ecologies, then this is highly resonant with the nonlinear and heterogeneous project of media archaeology. What Parikka suggests is that the distinction of media ecology from conventional accounts of media might be one of providing an alternative model of temporality: if the nonhuman durations of technologies and machines have been the frequent focus of media archaeology, then what can be supplemented by media ecology or perhaps more precisely "ecosophy," meaning an ecological, immanent, and ethical mode of knowledge, are evaluations of media ecologies as modes of life that express a political temporality, the capacity to make "cuts in the repetitive nature of Chronos" (2007, 294). In this sense, media ecology, like the practical media archaeological recycling advocated in Hertz and Parikka's "Zombie Media" (2012), can become a form of theoretical circuit bending, in relation to conventional modes of media analysis and history.

References and Further Reading

Bateson, Gregory. 2000. *Steps to an Ecology of Mind: Collected Essays in Anthropology, Psychiatry, Evolution, and Epistemology.* Chicago: University of Chicago Press.

Ellul, Jacques. 1973. *The Technological Society.* New York: Random House.

Fuller, Matthew. 2005. *Media Ecologies: Materialist Energies in Art and Technoculture.* Cambridge, MA: MIT Press.

Goddard, Michael, and Jussi Parikka, eds. 2011. *Unnatural Ecologies: Fibreculture* 17.

Guattari, Félix. 2000. *The Three Ecologies.* Translated by Ian Pindar and Paul Sutton. London: Continuum.

Hertz, Garnet, and Jussi Parikka. 2012. "Zombie Media: Circuit Bending Media Archaeology into an Art Method." *Leonardo* 45 (5): 424–430.

Maxwell, Richard, and Toby Miller. 2008. "Environmental Ethics and Media Technology." *International Journal of Communication* 2:331–353.

McLuhan, Marshall. 2001. *Understanding Media.* 2nd ed. London: Routledge.

Media Ecology Association (MEA). www.media-ecology.org/media_ecology/index.html.

Naess, Arne. 1990. *Ecology, Community and Lifestyle: Outline of an Ecosophy.* Translated by David Rothenberg. Cambridge: Cambridge University Press.

Parikka, Jussi. 2007. *Digital Contagions: A Media Archaeology of Computer Viruses.* New York: Peter Lang.

———. 2010. *Insect Media: An Archaeology of Animals and Technology.* Minneapolis: University of Minnesota Press.

Postman, Neil. 1987. *Amusing Ourselves to Death.* London: Methuen.

———. 1993. *Technopoly: The Surrender of Culture to Technology.* New York: Vintage Books.

Strate, Lance. 2005. "'Taking Issue': Review of *Media Ecologies: Materialist Energies in Art and Technoculture.*" *After-Image* 33 (3): 55–56.

Mediality

Jan-Noël Thon

The term *mediality* refers to the "medial qualities" that can be attributed to various kinds of media. It is primarily used in a medium-specific sense as referring to the set of prototypical properties that can be considered constitutive for a conventionally distinct medium, but it may also refer to more transmedial notions of "medium-ness" (see, e.g., the observations of an increased "mediation" or "mediatization" of contemporary communication in Hepp 2009; Krotz 2009; Livingstone 2009). One way or another, any discussion of mediality necessarily entails an examination of the contested concept of "medium" (for a selection of different approaches to "media" and their mediality see, e.g., Bolter and Grusin 1999; Manovich 2001; McLuhan 1964; Murray 2012; Ryan 2006; Schmidt 2000; as well as the contributions in Münker and Roesler 2008).

As controversial as the question of what a medium is may seem at first glance, one can at least find a certain amount of consensus both within media studies and beyond that the term is best understood as referring to a multidimensional concept. In an attempt to synthesize its various aspects into a coherent model, Schmidt (2000) has proposed to distinguish between four dimensions of media, namely, a semiotic dimension, a technological dimension, an institutional dimension, and a dimension of media products. While the mediality of many newspaper cartoons and web comics, for example, will be rather similar with regard to their semiotic dimension (e.g., both prototypically use combinations of words and images in sequences of panels), there are some striking differences not only with regard to their technological dimension (e.g., one is printed and the other is published online) but also, and perhaps more importantly, with regard to their institutional dimension (e.g., one is published as part of one or several newspapers, while the other is likely published on a dedicated website) (see CHARACTERISTICS OF DIGITAL MEDIA).

In the context of her recent work on transmedial narratology, Ryan (2006, 16–30) similarly discusses media as semiotic phenomena, as technologies with a specific materiality, and as cultural practices, emphasizing the difference that a medium's mediality makes for its narrative affordances and limitations (see NARRATIVITY). If regarded as semiotic phenomena, e-books and paperbacks can usually both be described as "verbal" media; photos on Flickr and photos from a Polaroid can both be described as "visual" media; instrumental music on iTunes and instrumental music in a concert hall can both be described as "aural" media; and movies on a DVD and movies on a videotape can both be described as multichannel media that combine the affordances offered by their respective channel in a specific way (see FILM AND DIGITAL MEDIA, as well as the influential discussion of "multimodality" in Kress 2010; Kress and van Leeuwen 2001; van Leeuwen 2005). However, "the *raw materials* . . . and the *technologies* that support the various semiotic types" (Ryan 2006, 21; emphasis in the original) are radically different in all of these cases, and Ryan also emphasizes that the cultural practices surrounding media are "not entirely predictable from semiotic type and technological support" (2006, 23).

Rather, media such as "newspapers," "books," "comics," "photos," films," or "computer games" are best described as "conventionally distinct means of communication" (Wolf

1999, 40) which can be distinguished not only by way of the technological or material base and/or the semiotic system(s) they use but also by way of the "social fact" that they are conventionally treated as distinct media. However, what we consider to be a "conventionally distinct medium" rests on what we believe to be the social consensus on the matter; hence, it would be more precise to speak of media that are *conventionally perceived as distinct*" (Rajewsky 2010, 61; emphasis in the original). Moreover, the social consensus on what is to be considered as a conventionally distinct medium changes both over time and in different (media) cultures. One cannot therefore treat media as transhistorical and/or transcultural collective constructs, since their construction "necessarily depends on the historical and discursive contexts and the observing subject or system" (Rajewsky 2010, 61; see also the contributions in Huhtamo and Parikka [2011] for a survey of current research on "media archaeology"). Finally, it needs to be acknowledged that even the manifestations of a relatively "well-defined" conventionally distinct medium can be very different, and one should not confuse the individual qualities of media products with their respective medium's mediality. In fact, due to the huge variety of media products that may be realized within the mediality of a conventionally distinct medium, it seems most appropriate to adopt a prototypical understanding of the latter.

Another problem that arises when trying to define a given medium's mediality, however, is the difficulty in distinguishing "medial" from "generic conventions." Privileging technology over semiotic or cultural criteria, Murray, for example, claims that "all things made with electronic bits and computer code belong to a single new medium, the digital medium, with its own unique affordances" (2012, 23). However, different applications of digital technology use different affordances, or different combinations of these affordances: some use networking, some use interactivity, some use multimodality, and so on. If one were to ask a sample of media scholars what, for example, the prototypical features of the mediality of contemporary computer games would entail, the "interactive simulation of gameplay" would probably appear near the top of the list (see GAMEPLAY, SIMULATION). However, there would very likely be diverging opinions regarding the importance of elements such as cut scenes (see CUT SCENES), "photorealistic" representations (see GRAPHIC REALISM), or even the presence of discernible "representations" at all (see GAMES AS STORIES, NARRATIVITY). This is partly because computer games come in a variety of different genres, and the established conventions—and, hence, the prototypical features of a computer game's mediality—may differ significantly depending on the genre in question, as well as on the period of computer game history in which the game is located (see HISTORY OF COMPUTERS).

But even apart from the problematic relation between medial and generic conventions, media can usually be defined through their similarities as well as through their differences. Here, Rajewsky's (2005) proposal to distinguish between "(intra-)medial," "intermedial," and "transmedial" phenomena may prove illuminating. While *intramediality* refers to phenomena that only involve a single medium (e.g., cases of intertextual reference), *intermediality* refers to a variety of phenomena that transcend medial boundaries and involve at least two conventionally distinct media (including both general references to the mediality of other media and specific references to particular texts in these media). Finally, *transmediality* refers to medially unspecified phenomena that are not connected to a specific medium or its mediality and can, hence, be realized using the means of a large number of different media. On the one hand, the concept of mediality is relevant with regard to not only "(intra-)medial" but also "intermedial" and "transmedial" phenomena, since both of the latter are necessarily realized within the mediality of a conventionally distinct medium. On the other hand, digital media with their characteristically hybrid nature may be particularly prone to use what Wolf calls "intermedial transpositions"—to the extent that a number of formerly medium-specific conventions do not anymore have "an easily traceable origin which can be attributed to a certain medium" (Wolf 2002, 19) in digital contexts (see OLD MEDIA / NEW MEDIA, REMEDIATION).

Moreover, while Rajewsky's notion of "transmediality" primarily refers to phenomena that are not connected to a specific medium or its mediality in its semiotic, technological, or institutional/cultural dimension (such as immersion or narrativity, for example), digital media also increasingly allow for another kind of transmediality that manifests itself on the level of what Schmidt (2000) calls "media products." In what has been described as "transmedia storytelling" (Jenkins 2006, 2007, 2011) or "transmedial worlds" (Klastrup and Tosca 2004, forthcoming), the mediality of conventionally distinct media does not dissolve as a result of the hybrid nature of many digital media but is transcended in a coordinated effort to provide complementary entertainment experiences (see TRANSMEDIAL FICTION). While the increasing sociocultural and commercial importance of efforts to disperse "integral elements of a fiction . . . systematically across multiple delivery channels for the purpose of creating a unified and coordinated entertainment experience" (Jenkins 2011) and the increased opportunities of users to contribute to the digital media landscape themselves (see PARTICIPATORY CULTURE) do not obliterate the notion of conventionally distinct media, they may still lead us to conceive of digital media's mediality as more "fluid," more tentative, only valid until the next technological or institutional landslide.

References and Further Reading

Bolter, Jay David, and Richard Grusin. 1999. *Remediation: Understanding New Media*. Cambridge, MA: MIT Press.

Hepp, Andreas. 2009. "Differentiation: Mediatization and Cultural Change." In *Mediatization: Concept, Changes, Consequences*, edited by Knut Lundby, 139–158. New York: Peter Lang.

Huhtamo, Erkki, and Jussi Parikka, eds. 2011. *Media Archaeology: Approaches, Applications, and Implications*. Berkeley: University of California Press.

Jenkins, Henry. 2006. *Convergence Culture: Where Old and New Media Collide*. New York: New York University Press.

———. 2007. "Transmedia Storytelling 101." *Confessions of an Aca/Fan*, March 22. www.henryjen kins.org/2007/03/transmedia_storytelling_101.html.

———. 2011. "Transmedia 202: Further Reflections." *Confessions of an Aca/Fan*, August 1. www .henryjenkins.org/2011/08/defining_transmedia_further_re.html.

Klastrup, Lisbeth, and Susana P. Tosca. 2004. "Transmedial Worlds—Rethinking Cyberworld Design." In *Proceedings of the International Conference on Cyberworlds 2004*, 409–416. Los Alamitos, CA: IEEE Computer Society.

———. Forthcoming. "A Game of Thrones: Transmedial Worlds, Fandom, and Social Gaming." In *Storyworlds across Media: Toward a Media-Conscious Narratology*, edited by Marie-Laure Ryan and Jan-Noël Thon. Lincoln: University of Nebraska Press.

Kress, Gunther. 2010. *Multimodality: A Social Semiotic Approach to Contemporary Communication*. London: Routledge.

Kress, Gunther, and Theo van Leeuwen. 2001. *Multimodal Discourse: The Modes and Media of Contemporary Communication*. London: Arnold.

Krotz, Friedrich. 2009. "Mediatization: A Concept with Which to Grasp Media and Societal Change." In *Mediatization: Concept, Changes, Consequences*, edited by Knut Lundby, 21–40. New York: Peter Lang.

Livingstone, Sonia. 2009. "On the Mediation of Everything." *Journal of Communication* 59 (1): 1–18.

Manovich, Lev. 2001. *The Language of New Media*. Cambridge, MA: MIT Press.

McLuhan, Marshall. 1964. *Understanding Media: The Extensions of Man*. New York: McGraw-Hill.

Münker, Stefan, and Alexander Roesler, eds. 2008. *Was ist ein Medium?* Frankfurt am Main: Suhrkamp.

Murray, Janet H. 2012. *Inventing the Medium: Principles of Interaction Design as a Cultural Practice*. Cambridge, MA: MIT Press.

Rajewsky, Irina O. 2005. "Intermediality, Intertextuality, and Remediation: A Literary Perspective on Intermediality." *Intermédialités/Intermedialities* 6:43–64.

———. 2010. "Border Talks: The Problematic Status of Media Borders in the Current Debate about Intermediality." In *Media Borders, Multimodality and Intermediality*, edited by Lars Elleström, 51–68. Basingstoke, UK: Palgrave-Macmillan.

Ryan, Marie-Laure. 2006. *Avatars of Story*. Minneapolis: University of Minnesota Press.

Schmidt, Siegfried J. S. 2000. *Kalte Faszination: Medien, Kultur, Wissenschaft in der Mediengesellschaft*. Weilerswist: Velbrück Wissenschaft.

van Leeuwen, Theo. 2005. *Introducing Social Semiotics*. London: Routledge.

Wolf, Werner. 1999. *The Musicalization of Fiction: A Study in the Theory and History of Intermediality*. Amsterdam: Rodopi.

———. 2002. "Intermediality Revisited: Reflections on Word and Music Relations in the Context of a General Typology of Intermediality." In *Word and Music Studies: Essays in Honor of Steven Paul Scher and on Cultural Identity and the Musical Stage*, edited by Suzanne M. Lodato, Suzanne Aspden, and Walter Bernhart, 13–34. Amsterdam: Rodopi.

Mobile Games
Anastasia Salter

Mobile entertainment encompasses systems for gaming and media consumption which are portable and thus able to intrude upon and coexist with a range of environments not traditionally seen as spaces for gaming or diversion. To support this freedom, mobile gaming devices are self-contained portable platforms, often designed with the ideal of the "pocket" in mind—they are intended to be continually accessible. As mobile gaming has incorporated more networked technology, it has also adapted to completely transform these environments, with emerging genres such as location-based gaming and augmented reality turning physical locations into virtual game boards. However, looking beyond technological platforms, mobile entertainment is a much older concept, as the traditional book, dice games, card games, and other "mobile" media already have a long history. As Jussi Parikka and Jaakko Suominen have observed, these mobile forms were in part a response to the rise of train travel and other industrial settings that required portable diversions (2006, 20). Our current digital technologies began by simply extending this tradition.

Early digital mobile platforms offered very limited gaming options. The Game and Watch (Nintendo, 1980–1991), arguably the first digital mobile gaming device, doubled as a digital watch and took advantage of cheap LCD screens to create small single-game systems. Nintendo's system emerged during the era of arcade games and, like arcade systems, was hardware based. The games were encoded into the hardware itself, and thus to have any choice a player would need to carry multiple devices. The first game, *Ball* (Nintendo, 1980), was a simple juggling game that launched to "instant success" (Donovan 2010, 155). As Nintendo gained more creative prominence, games featuring their arcade icons, such as *Mario* and *Donkey Kong*, were also released as part of the portable series.

While the Game and Watch systems were produced from 1980 to 1991, the first Nintendo home console (the Family Computer, or "Famicom," which was reinvented as the Nintendo Entertainment System for the U.S. market) wasn't released until 1983 (DeMaria and Wilson 2003, 364) (see GAME HISTORY, GAMEPLAY).

The early history of mobile gaming was defined by its juxtaposition to the arcade gaming industry. While home consoles were associated with family entertainment in Japan, they were first marketed more exclusively to children in the United States. As the industry took off, more portable game consoles emerged, including the Lynx (Atari, 1989), which was the first handheld game system with a color LCD screen. It also featured multiplayer gaming through networked systems and technically advanced hardware, but a lack of games ultimately doomed the system to obscurity. Rival cartridge-based handheld Game Boy (Nintendo) was released the same year. It lacked the power of its competitors, as Nintendo "opted for a monochrome screen and a tiny speaker . . . [but] made up for it with its unrivalled 10-hour battery life and lower retail price" (Donovan 2010, 205). Nintendo bundled the new console with *Tetris*, a deceptively simple game that Henk Rogers suggested would make the device's universal appeal clear: he told the Nintendo president, "If you want little boys to buy your machine then pack in Mario, but if you want everybody to play your game, pack in *Tetris*" (as quoted in Donovan 2010, 205). The combination worked: the bundle of Game Boy and *Tetris* sold more than 40 million copies worldwide (2010, 207).

Tetris marked the start of an entire genre of games that Jesper Juul terms "casual," meaning games that possess "high usability, high interruptibility, and lenient difficulty/ punishment structures" (2010, 54). *Tetris* has not faded from popularity. The game's designer, Alexey Pajitnov, believes the game will last forever because "technology may change but our brains don't" (as quoted in Loguidice and Barton 2009, 301). The genre of casual games includes another enduring example, *Solitaire*, which stands alongside other bundled games that are easy both to install and to play. These aspects of *Solitaire* are in stark contrast to high-investment "hardcore" games that expect "many resources from the player, and require much knowledge of game conventions, much time investment, and a preference for difficulty" (Juul 2010, 54). Thus, while hard-core games are focused activities, intended to consume all of the players' attentions, casual games adapt to the players' circumstances and don't necessarily erase awareness and interaction with the environment. This makes the genre entirely suitable for mobile devices, which themselves are intended to bring playfulness into nontraditional spaces without interrupting the order of those environments.

Other forms of mobile entertainment are more persistent and intrusive, such as Tamagotchi eggs (Bandai, 1996). As one of the most popular examples of smart toys, Tamagotchis were among the first examples of an "artificially intelligent toy . . . programmed to be nurtured by a child" (Allen 2004, 180). A Tamagotchi was a highly portable device, shaped like a plastic egg with a small screen, and its reliance on the child for care made it not only portable but essential. Without the child's continual attention over set intervals, the virtual creature would die. This idea of a virtual pet with demands is precisely the opposite of most mobile entertainment, as Sherry Turkle notes: "as Tamagotchis turn children into caretakers, they teach that digital life can be emotionally roiling, a place of obligations and regrets" (2011, 31). When some schools banned the devices, with their beeping reminders of the Tamagotchis' needs, parents were enlisted to watch them in the children's stead: "the beeping of digital pets became a familiar background noise during business meetings" (Turkle 2011, 32). Other artificial toys would follow, with their own robotic bodies granting them existence outside the screen, but virtual pets would remain part of mobile entertainment. The concept survives on current mobile devices with games such as *Nintendogs + Cats* (Nintendo DS, Nintendo, 2005) and *Edimon* (iPhone, Humble, 2009) offering less demanding virtual pets, sometimes walking the line between game and artificial life simulation (see ARTIFICIAL INTELLIGENCE).

The concept of virtual pets combined with a role-playing game story line and mechanics is at the heart of the *Pokemon* (Game Boy, 1996–) franchise. *Pokemon* combines casual gameplay elements, such as a continually rewarding environment and low consequences for failure, with an extended narrative and progressive goals. The long-lived series has helped cement Nintendo's hold on the market through continual releases interwoven with transmedia storytelling and integrated with other consoles. *Pokemon* brought a new way of using network gaming to the Game Boy consoles. The idea of linking Game Boys for competition (similar to local area network multiplayer on computers) was already established, but *Pokemon* uses the link for cooperation through trading and exchange of resources in the form of captured *Pokemon* creatures and thus has encouraged playing as part of a community, a trend that has continued throughout the evolution of mobile gaming (Donovan 2010, 335) (see ONLINE GAME COMMUNITIES).

The evolution of dedicated gaming platforms has embraced simultaneous multiplayer, color screens, increased battery life, and eventually touch screens as each new entry tried to distinguish itself from previous devices. While the PlayStation Portable (Sony, 2004) markets itself as the "walkman for the 21st century," the Nintendo DS instead relies on the concept of two screens as a way to provide new interactivity (*Wired* Staff 2004, 3). The incorporation of a touch screen brought a new solution to the ongoing interface dilemma: the small scale of portable devices makes it difficult to have a versatile user interface, but a touch screen can continuously adapt. The Nintendo DS was also influenced by the multiple forms of entertainment available on convergent devices: a cartridge filled with literary classics attempts to turn the DS into an e-reader, while the Nintendo DSi (2008) integrates a camera and face recognition capabilities. A further upgrade added the ability to use a digital distribution system and wireless networking capability along with a digital music player. These decisions reflected the new rise in expectations for mobile entertainment due to increased processing power and capabilities of cell phones.

During the period of high profitability for dedicated mobile entertainment platforms, entertainment options on convergent mobile devices were limited. The first iPod (Apple, 2001) revolutionized portable music, moving to immediate digital storage from reliance on external data, but the original iPod's interface (the click wheel) made it a primarily passive mobile entertainment solution. Only one game was bundled with the first system: *Brick* (Wozniak). Eventually, *Parachute*, *Solitaire*, and *Music Quiz*, based on the player's library, were added. There was no rush: in 2001, there was still speculation that the mobile entertainment industry would not be a success outside of Japan; as one anonymous wireless company spokesman observed, "Americans are much more pragmatically focused. Maybe stock quotes or news alerts, but I don't think there's a huge market for cutesy icons or games" (as quoted in Kumar 2001, 17). The market ten years later has proven such predictions wrong.

In 2006, the iTunes store added games to their library, and the number of options began to expand dramatically. With the 2007 release of the iPhone and iPod Touch, Apple added both an improved interface for play and a software development kit (SDK) for third-party development (see INDEPENDENT AND ART GAMES). This system remains at the heart of the ongoing iPod family, including the iPad tablet (Apple, 2010). The iPod Touch and iPhone followed the precedent of the Nintendo DS and introduced the touch screen as a gaming interface alongside the devices' many other functions. While previous generations of dedicated devices had taken their controls from arcade and console systems, and traditional phones had attempted to simulate that interface using the numeric keypad, the touch screen offers the opportunity for direct manipulation of all kinds of data. Unlike the Nintendo DS screen's stylus system, the iPhone and iPod Touch are designed for users to work with their fingers.

Other aspects of the iPhone and competing smartphones, such as cameras and GPS technology, make them the ideal platforms for experiments that dedicated gaming devices did not inherently support. Pseudoportable entertainment, such as Nintendo's failed experiment Virtual Boy, had only gestured toward the emergence of augmented and virtual reality platforms. With the inclusion of video cameras as a standard feature on smartphones and tablets, including the iPhone, the potential for creating a game layer over our physical surroundings is rising. The aforementioned genre of location-based gaming makes use of location awareness to extend mobile games beyond the device through activities such as geocaching, or hunting for "treasure" via GPS, and urban and street gaming. Games and applications that further exploit these technologies can transform a city into a backdrop for battling zombies or participating in multiplayer challenges (see AUGMENTED REALITY).

These powerful convergent devices have ushered in a new generation of casual games, built with the playful touch screen in mind. *Angry Birds* (Rovio Mobile, 2009, multiplatform) has become a defining example of mobile entertainment success. The game's narrative and play are both simple: an army of green pigs has angered the birds, and the player hurls the birds at the pigs' fortresses to ensure their destruction. As of May 2011, sales of the *Angry Birds* app topped 100 million, with Rovio Mobile's marketing executive Peter Vesterbacka quoted as arguing "that most of the innovation in gaming has 'clearly' moved to the mobile platform," as "tablets are killing consoles" (Dredge 2011).

While this remains an overstatement, it is certainly true that the iPad and other tablets offer a larger screen for mobile entertainment with the same touch-based interface, inviting new genres of games, the resurrection of classic games, and a new interaction with spaces through games. As Steven Johnson speculates, "Ten years from now, we will look back at the tablet and see it as an end point, not a beginning. The tablet may turn out to be the final stage of an extraordinary era of textual innovation, powered by 30 years of exponential increases in computation, connection, and portability" (2010). The standard set by tablets is inspiring change in other mobile entertainment devices, such as e-readers, which are now expected to do more than perform their dedicated function well. Even the Kindle (Amazon) now has an emerging market for games. All mobile devices are expected to provide a range of immediate, convergent, playful, and social experiences.

References and Further Reading

Allen, Mark. 2004. "Tangible Interfaces in Smart Toys." In *Toys, Games, and Media*, edited by Jeffrey Goldstein, David Buckingham, and Gilles Brougere, 179–194. Mahwah, NJ: Lawrence Erlbaum Associates.

DeMaria, Rusel, and Johnny L. Wilson. 2003. *High Score! The Illustrated History of Electronic Games.* New York: McGraw-Hill.

Donovan, Tristan. 2010. *Replay: The History of Video Games.* Great Britain: Yellow Ant.

Dredge, Stuart. 2011. "Angry Birds Tops 100m Downloads as Exec Says 'Tablets Are Killing Consoles.'" *Mobile Entertainment*. www.mobile-ent.biz/news/read/angry-birds-tops-100m-down loads-as-exec-says-tablets-are-killing.

Johnson, Steven. 2010. "The End of an Era." *Wired Online*. www.wired.com/magazine/tag/mobile/.

Juul, Jesper. 2010. *A Casual Revolution: Reinventing Video Games and Their Players*. Cambridge, MA: MIT Press.

Kumar, Aparna. 2001. "Games Are Phones' Call for Alms." *Wired Online*. www.wired.com/techbiz /media/news/2001/03/42461.

Ling, Rich. 2004. *The Mobile Connection: The Cell Phone's Impact on Society*. San Francisco: Morgan Kaufmann.

Loguidice, Bill, and Matt Barton. 2009. *Vintage Games: An Insider Look at the History of Grand Theft Auto, Super Mario, and the Most Influential Games of All Time*. Burlington, MA: Focal Press.

Parikka, Jussi, and Jaakko Suominen. 2006. "Victorian Snakes? Towards a Cultural History of Mobile Games and the Experience of Movement." *Game Studies* 6 (1).

Turkle, Sherry. 2011. *Alone Together: Why We Expect More from Technology and Less from Each Other*. New York: Basic Books.

Wired Staff. 2004. "Are Two Screens Better Than One?" *Wired Online*. www.wired.com/gaming /gamingreviews/news/2004/01/62001.

$\bullet\,\bullet$

MUDs and MOOs

Torill Mortensen

The abbreviation *MUD* stands for Multi-User Dungeons/Domains, while *MOO* is a version of this called Multi-User Dungeon, Object Oriented. A MUD is a text-based multiuser area, first developed in 1978 under the name *MUD* by Roy Trubshaw, later expanded and established in cooperation with Richard Bartle (1990). At this time the "D" was for "Dungeon," as it was inspired by a game, unlike later versions where the "D" was reinterpreted as "Dimension" in order to facilitate a wider range of uses for this type of multiuser area. These were early games played utilizing the telnet protocol pretty much as it was available on computers in the shape of written commands in a text window.

MUD was a team effort between Richard Bartle and Roy Trubshaw, and it still runs under the name *British Legends*. On entering the game, a current user will see a strong similarity to another early genre of online multiuser interaction, the Internet relay chat (IRC). Written in 1988 by Jarkko Oikarinen (Oikarinen 2005), it is newer than the original MUD. It did, however, become sufficiently well known that in the early 1990s one way to easily explain what a MUD was would be to say "it's like IRC, but you can play games on it."

The games to be played in MUDs grew out of the adventure genre, where the technology was inspired by the story-game *Adventure*, a simulation of cave exploration by William Crowther turned fantasy game by Donald Woods in 1976 (Aarseth 2004, 51), while the fiction and game elements came from the *Dungeons & Dragons* games first developed by Dave Arneson and Gary Gygax starting in 1970–1971 (Wizards of the Coast 2003).

Several different MUDs developed through the 1980s and 1990s. One of the most distinct advantages of MUDs for creative hackers and eager gamers was the relative simplicity of the code, as well as the easy approach to creating unique environments through text. This led to a wide variety of basic databases: AberMUD, TinyMUD, LPMUD, and

DikuMUD were some of the best-known MUD versions, all variations on a main idea that was strongly game related. As the other major variety of MUDs, the MOO also developed its alternate versions. *LambdaMOO*, developed in 1990, is often seen as the first MOO, but there are at least two other databases available for builders besides Lambda-Core: JHCore and EnCore. EnCore is the base used by Cynthia Haynes and Jan Rune Holmevik to build *LinguaMOO*, designed for teaching purposes (Haynes and Holmevik 1998).

The main difference between MUDs and MOOs can be found in the affordances of the participants or players. MUDs are fairly restricted as to what players can do to the environment. A regular player in a MUD can interact through the objects and orders already written into the program. For instance, besides talking and "emoting" or describing actions to other players, they can pick up already-existing objects, interact with non-player characters (NPCs), attack NPCs as well as other players by using existing abilities, craft a pre-described set of objects from recipes, and move through the descriptions of the game space or the rooms. A MOO affords more freedom to create objects and describe the immediate environment. However, the players' freedom in each room or area of the MOO is restricted by the player who owns or created that room. MUDs and MOOs are most commonly organized geographically, with descriptions of rooms or physical spaces. Navigating them happens in six directions—north, south, east, west, up and down—or by writing out the room name ("go north" or "go ivory tower"). Each order brings you into a new "room," or more precisely to the part of the program where you can access that particular virtual object. In a MOO the room is an object controlled and designed by the player.

This does not mean that a MOO necessarily excludes player attacks, as Julian Dibbell describes in a widely quoted article from 1993. Here Dibbell reports on an episode in *LambdaMOO* where a player uses an object created in the game to make it appear that other players are subjected to humiliating acts, described as a rape.

If we are to make a parallel with graphic digital multiuser games, we can say that the MUD is Blizzard's virtual world and massive game *World of Warcraft* (Mortensen 2006), while the MOO is Linden Labs' virtual world Second Life (see ONLINE WORLDS). The MUDs often had a clearer game structure than MOOs, with rules, affordances, and restrictions. The players' freedom to act depends on the possibilities given them by the administrators, "immortals," or "wizards." MOOs are more dominated by playfulness: the creation of objects is strongly dependent on the players' skill and creativity. These distinctions are, however, just general directions: with the easily available software and the low threshold for setting up a game, players would often create new games, defying norms, and go from being restricted in the creation of one game as regular players to having full access as administrators of another game.

MUDs and MOOs did not originally have a huge impact outside of certain special interest groups, certainly not if we compare them to the immense popularity of multiuser games in 2011. A large MUD would have 200–300 users logged on a good day. By comparison, the online game set in the Star Wars universe, *Star Wars: The Old Republic* (*SWTOR*), launched December 20, 2011, had more than 1 million subscribers registering in one day, most likely the largest single day of user registration in massively multiplayer online role-playing game (MMORPG) history at that time (Muzyka and Zeschuk 2011). They did, however, have a large impact on later game development, as well as game scholarship and the scholarship on online communities, identity formation and experimentation, nonlinear stories, hypertexts, and cybertexts (see NETWORKING, ONLINE GAME COMMUNITIES, SOCIAL NETWORK SITES [SNSs]).

In game development, we can see a pretty clear line leading from MUDs and MOOs to the graphic online world *Ultima Online*, which opened in 1997 (Garriott and Koster 1997), and its successors (see GAME HISTORY). Most of the graphic multiplayer games today contain a chat window. The chat windows contain the same kind of written communication and pretty much the same options as MUDs and MOOs did when they were all text. In *World of Warcraft*, for instance, the chat window will not only carry chat but also give the same type of detailed information on the actions of players and NPCs that would be available to a player in a MUD (Mortensen 2006). The main difference lies in the opportunities created by the visual environment, where it is, for instance, possible to see through a distance or target a player, NPC, or object that would otherwise be several "rooms" away on a MUD grid. This has also eliminated the written descriptions of the rooms and the characters.

Perhaps the first academic approach to analyzing a text-based game was Mary Ann Buckles's thesis from 1985 analyzing the story-game *Adventure*, the game that inspired the MUDs (Erard 2004). But the real academic interest in MUDs and MOOs did not take off until the 1990s. Among the earlier research was Amy Bruckman's work on MOOs and the creation of MOOSE crossing, a MOO for use in teaching (Bruckman 1997), and Sherry Turkle's work on identity formation in computer interaction from the 1990s (Turkle 1995). MUDs also inspired studies of Internet culture and game use (Bruckman 1997; Mortensen 2003), which mingled, expanded, and developed into a strong trend of ethnographic game studies.

MUDs and MOOs did not offer stories as we were used to experiencing them, MOOs even less so than MUDs. MUDs tended to be more fleshed out and built as an arena for games with a basic and somewhat coherent fiction, but MOOs also had a potential for storytelling, as demonstrated in the example of *a midsummer night's dream*, a MOO programmed to give an experience of a Shakespearean text (Walker 1999). By offering an entirely new way to approach and experience a story, MUDs and MOOs challenged the linearity of commonly used texts. This inspired a range of authors to question the structure of texts and the relationship between texts and machines. Espen Aarseth (1997) expanded on the concept of ergodic texts and cybertexts based on his explorations in TinyMUDs, while interactive literature as a genre is reliant on the early text-based games, both single-player and multiplayer (Montfort 2003).

MUDs are still running today. By visiting the Mudconnector at www.mudconnect .com/, it is still possible to find and hence play MUDs. They are mainly nonprofit, community-driven efforts, offering playful interaction for interested players.

■ See also PARTICIPATORY CULTURE

References and Further Reading

Aarseth, Espen. 1997. *Cybertexts: Perspectives on Ergodic Literature.* Baltimore: Johns Hopkins University Press.
———. 2004. "Genre Trouble." In *First Person: New Media as Story, Performance, and Game,* edited by Noah Wardrip-Fruin and Pat Harrigan, 45–55. Cambridge, MA: MIT Press.
Bartle, Richard. 1990. "Early MUD History." www.mud.co.uk/richard/mudhist.htm.

Bruckman, Amy Susan. 1997. "MOOSE Crossing: Construction, Community and Learning in a Networked Virtual World for Kids." PhD diss., Massachusetts Institute of Technology, Program in Media Arts & Sciences.

Dibbell, Julian. 1993. "A Rape in Cyberspace." www.juliandibbell.com/texts/bungle_vv.html.

Erard, Michael. 2004. "2 Decades Later; Let Down by Academia, Game Pioneer Changed Paths." *New York Times*, May 6. www.nytimes.com/2004/05/06/technology/2-decades-later-let-down-by-academia-game-pioneer-changed-paths.html.

Garriott, Richard, and Ralph Koster. 1997. *Ultima Online*. Electronic Arts, Inc.

Haynes, Cynthia, and Jan Rune Holmevik. 1998. *High Wired: On the Design, Use, and Theory of Educational MOOs*. Ann Arbor: University of Michigan Press.

Montfort, Nick. 2003. *Twisty Little Passages: An Approach to Interactive Fiction*. Cambridge, MA: MIT Press.

Mortensen, Torill Elvira. 2003. "Pleasures of the Player: Flow and Control in Online Games." PhD diss., University of Bergen.

———. 2006. "WoW Is the New MUD." *Games and Culture* 1 (4): 397–413.

Muzyka, Ray, and Greg Zeschuk. 2011. "From Ray and Greg: Thank You for Playing." *Star Wars: The Old Republic*, December 23. www.swtor.com/blog/ray-and-greg-thank-you-playing.

Oikarinen, Jarkko. 2005. "IRC History by Jarkko Oikarinen." *Internet Relay Chat*. www.irc.org/history_docs/jarkko.html.

Turkle, Sherry. 1995. *Life on the Screen: Identity in the Age of the Internet*. New York: Simon & Schuster.

Walker, Jill. 1999. *a midsummer night's dream*. Literature on the Web: A Web and MOO Project at Lingo.uib. http://cmc.uib.no/dream/.

Wizards of the Coast. 2003. "Dungeons & Dragons FAQ." *Wizards of the Coast*. www.wizards.com/dnd/DnDArchives_FAQ.asp.

···

Music

Aden Evens

Like so much in this digital age, music can now be comprehended only as a dynamic aggregate of culture, bodies, technologies, and media. But even as music immerses itself so thoroughly in the ascendant (i.e., digital) mode of cultural production, still a purely digital music cannot be, or it would be unhearable. To be heard, to involve ears and the aural, music must become sound, an oscillation of air pressure moving through space. And air pressure waves in variable oscillation defy the single central principle of the digital, that it be discrete rather than continuous (see ANALOG VERSUS DIGITAL). The zeros and ones that constitute the typical code of the digital obtain a perfect individuation, each exactly equivalent to the one or zero that is its definition, whereas the rapid compression and rarefaction of air passes through all intermediate values on its way from a peak to a valley of pressure.

If those last few meters leading up to the listener's ear—with some headphones it might be millimeters—are decidedly analog, then we might yet discover *digital music* somewhere between the breadth of culture at large and the narrow formality of the binary code. Entirely digital music is out of the question, but the intersections of music and the digital are numerous and telling. In fact, though there remain bountiful nondigital forms of music, the musical mainstream has been steeping in the digital, which supports or performs almost every aspect of the experience of music, from recording, generating, analyzing, altering, and storing sound; to disseminating, reproducing, and composing music; to music journalism, instrument design, and sales; and so on.

Digital music means both too much and too little, therefore. Is it music made with digital tools? Recorded using digital devices? Distributed as digital data? Influenced by digital culture?

Origins

For most listeners, the digital announced itself in music through the introduction of the compact disc (starting in Japan in 1982), which for many was also a first significant encounter with any digital medium. Sony boasted that the compact disc offers "perfect sound forever"—history confirms one of these three terms—a brazen idealism that suggests the sort of ideology driving a digital future. Sound aside, the compact disc, in contrast to the vinyl record album, allowed a push-button, random access interface, one of the first mass-cultural digital interfaces (see INTERFACE). (The 1970s technologies of digital watches, calculators, and video games were iconic but not mainstream, associated foremost with a neurasthenic geek subculture.) The buttons on the front of the CD player ("Play," "Pause," "Rewind," etc.) were familiar from older, analog stereo equipment, but the responsiveness and precision of these interfaces, the symbolic exactitude of the numerical indexing of sound, made the experience different. Notably, turntables for playing vinyl record albums could not (usually) be operated with a remote control. This dramatic increase in the immediacy of the experience hinted at the digital difference of the compact disc, its portability, durability, convenience, self-identicalness, and so on—the CD as portent of the coming digital era.

As opposed to the industry-backed introduction of the CD, file sharing and eventually digital music distribution arrived more slowly, not so much a consumer product but an anticonsumer one, responding, some would say, to the digital's invitation to copy.

MP3

The MP3 (Moving Picture Experts Group Audio Layer III) abetted the mass spread of digital-era piracy, grabbing an early lead and holding on to it through a familiar technological phenomenon, format wars. There are alternative ways of making audio files smaller, some of them arguably better sounding or more efficient than the MP3, but the standard that allowed file sharing to blossom in the late 1990s remains the prevalent standard today. The MP3 standard is a *lossy* as opposed to *lossless* data compression format, meaning that the MP3 saves space by discarding information from the original digital representation, information that cannot be recovered. (One can convert an MP3 file back into an uncompressed data format, but the information discarded when the MP3 was created does not return.) As a loose analogy, eliminating the footnotes might save space in a book, and though the book would still probably offer much the same experience as the footnoted version, there would be missing information that could not be deduced from the expurgated text.

Consider the technology underlying the MP3. Extensive studies of human hearing reveal an apparent aural scotoma: when two simultaneous sounds are close together in pitch but different in amplitude (loudness), the louder sound *masks* the softer one. The softer sound is not heard as softer; rather, it is not *heard* at all, according to this experimentally verified theory of perception. Based on this contingency of human hearing, the MP3 technology employs a *perceptual encoding* at the core of its data reduction. Ignoring the *unhearable* sound, the MP3 file only stores the sound that can actually be heard, making for smaller file sizes. (This is a reductive account of a complicated technology: MP3 encoding involves many other methods of reducing data size, and even the psychoacoustic principle of masking is algorithmically delicate to calculate and apply.) It is interesting that this characteristically digital technology relies on such a particular and seemingly contingent aspect of human hearing. Mathematically there is no reason to think that two simultaneous frequencies of different amplitudes would sound the same when the quieter frequency is removed.

When an MP3 is created, calculations must be performed to determine what frequencies are present in the sound at any given moment, so that the unhearable frequencies can be eliminated from the data (and so also from the sound when reproduced from those data during playback). By varying the tolerances that are used to decide which frequencies to eliminate, selecting more data to eliminate by allowing wider frequency differences and smaller amplitude differences to count as masking, the compression algorithm can be directed to throw out more (or less) of the original, uncompressed sound data. The MP3 standard thereby admits different degrees of data compression. To achieve more compression and further reduce the file size, tolerances can be stretched beyond the predicted limits of perceptual masking, and the resultant sound when played back includes perceptible artifacts of the encoding process, such as distortion, a loss of dynamic range, less precise stereo specification, or the attenuation of the highest and lowest frequencies.

Many people claim that they don't hear any difference between lossy/compressed and lossless/uncompressed versions of a song, or that the difference if hearable is insignificant. Mass culture certainly made its decision: more information from the original sound is not as valuable as the convenience of sharing a full-length album over a broadband connection in a couple of minutes. This convenience extends much farther, though, as smaller file sizes allow more music to fit in the same amount of storage, "all your music in one place," as promised by Google Play, the iPod, and plenty of other pretenders to the music-media space.

Accumulation

French political adviser Jacques Attali, writing in the margins of ethnomusicology in the 1970s, diagnoses his century's relationship to music as an age of collecting (Attali 1985). Once music can be stored and automatically recalled in enduring material media such as tape or vinyl, technologies whose origins are roughly coincident with the beginning of the twentieth century, music's acquisition gains a significance of its own, the accumulation of recordings as a way of storing up time, says Attali. He calls for a new age, a new century, where accumulation gives way to production, an age where everyone will participate in the creation of musical sound.

Cast as prognostication, Attali's fantasy both hits and misses. Accumulation has not subsided but has ballooned, buoyed by the ease with which digital files can be exchanged, stored, and accessed. The digital reduces the resistance of material media: since the invention of the computer, computing materials, *hardware*, have become smaller, faster, less demanding of resources, while *software* by definition is mostly abstract, a list of zeros and ones that as such submits without resistance to any arbitrary arithmetic operation, including copying (see HISTORY OF COMPUTERS, SOFTWARE STUDIES). Commercial music distribution prior to digital piracy had relied on the stubborn inertia of material media (records, compact discs, etc.) to contrive a scarcity; to listen to commercial music, you had to have a record. Music could thus behave like a traditional commodity, an item of property to be possessed or coveted. (One can possess the LP record, but it remains ambiguous in what sense one possesses the music thereon.) The music industry seemed unprepared for the rise of digital distribution at the turn of the millennium, and as retailers, distributors, studios, labels, and musicians struggled to find a new sales model, consumers turned to widely available, often free software that made file sharing easy, automatic, and seemingly anonymous. Legislatures and courts introduced regulations intended to preserve the old order while including the new media; witness the Digital Millennium Copyright Act instituted in the United States in 1998 (see COPYRIGHT). In response, software leveraged its eroded materiality in an attempt to perplex the law (see MATERIALITY). One of the key reasons for the success of the file-sharing software Napster was its peer-to-peer sharing principle, which proposed to circumvent existing law by decentralizing the data to be shared, such that downloaders gather a single song (or other file) by retrieving data from many different uploaders; no individual party provides a complete playable version of the song, so no one can be held responsible for distributing stolen property.

The accumulation of stored sound in the digital age may have a different valence from its twentieth-century analog. Where the record collection often symptomatized a bourgeois fetish, the iTunes Library answers to a digital fantasy of immediate availability. It is not so much ownership of the music as *access* to it that measures an individual's relationship to sound media. At least for the moment, in the second decade of the twenty-first century, the industry is moving rapidly toward *the cloud*, the very metonym of dematerialization, wherein one's music collection resides no longer on any particular hard drive but in a distributed aggregation of bits strewn across various servers and tracked using a centralized list of reference numbers and memory locations. Apple, trying to outpace Google, manages personal music collections in part by replacing a user's files with its own copy of the same song, providing higher bitrates (i.e., more of the original, uncompressed file's information) when possible. To own a song no longer establishes a claim over any particular data stored on one's hard drive (if it ever did), but instead retains the right to access *some* data that represent a song declared the same. The music collection has become an abstraction, a set of names, indexes that point to standardized, universal files, while Apple assumes by default the role of arbiter, the keeper of the standard.

In keeping with the premise of the information economy, the music collection derives its value in part from its abstracted existence as information. Music libraries and *playlists* gain a status as cultural artifacts; the playlist represents taste as a list of choices from a large menu, as celebrities offer their curatorial discernment to promote commercial music services. Though hardly a marquee feature of the software, music library sharing (in iTunes, for example) suggests the personalization and self-interpellation of the music library. Subscription music services, which provide large libraries of songs accessible on the Internet from many devices, hint at this same fantasy of universal, ubiquitous, immediate access; whatever information you need or want will be effortlessly available, as easy to summon as your own thoughts.

Playing to the personalization of the playlist and library, commercial music services invent tools to analyze and categorize taste, relying on the precision and ease of digital data collection to provide each user with just what the statistical-analytic algorithm predicts she wants to hear. Depending on the service, tracks are chosen based on broad social factors about the user, or comparisons of listening habits to the habits of other listeners, or analysis of the musical characteristics of the user's preferred music. Industry research aims to develop algorithms that can spontaneously generate new music according to various musical criteria, algorithmic composition tuned to a listener's established listening habits (see ALGORITHM).

Production

If Attali's observation about accumulation has gone unanswered, his proposed positive alternative may find support in the digital. The computer provides the remarkable facility to allow those without access to professional recording studios the possibility of producing high-quality recorded sound, the "home studio revolution." By itself a personal computer performs many of the functions of a professional studio, and partly in response to a growing market, audio recording equipment manufacturers have designed and distributed home-use and semiprofessional gear that makes minimal compromises in sound quality relative to expensive professional equipment, but at prices affordable to nonspecialists.

Even for those without microphones, preamplifiers, mixing boards, and the other ersatz machines that populate *prosumer* recording studios, much software offers access to prerecorded chunks of music, *samples* from individual drum strikes and plucked strings to continuous measures of music played by world-renowned virtuosos specifically for inclusion in a library of sounds out of which to build songs (see SAMPLING). Digital sound synthesis places all the instrumental sounds of the world's orchestras within reach of a garage band, not to mention the unbounded possibilities of creating whole new sounds.

Emulating almost every function of a commercial recording studio and generating instrumental and synthetic sounds in simple software, the computer presents huge numbers of people with an opportunity to exercise their musical expressivity without spending years developing a technical facility with an instrument. Among its many possible representations of sound, software frequently lays out a song visually as a set of simultaneous and successive events placed along a timeline. Individual events can be added or removed but also altered piecemeal and repositioned on the timeline. Whereas traditional instrumental performance requires that music be constantly rescued from the precariousness of its potential dissolution, software-based music production typically invites a more structural approach to sound creation, wherein sounds can be deliberately chosen, placed, repeated, and individually modified to suit their contexts until the composer is satisfied. The *mashup* as a populist art practice incorporates many methods of production but from a top-down perspective, building music mostly by combining existing songs in whole and part (see MASHUP). Digital composition thus bears a closer resemblance to construction or assembly than to improvisation or performance.

Sampling

The primacy of vision in the digital interface produces an overview of the objects on the screen, including representations of sound. Arrayed as blocks of color on the monitor, sounds suggest their own divisibility. Typical of digital media generally, sound can be subdivided in many different ways: a song might be built from separate instrumental tracks—one track for drums, one for rhythm guitar, one for bass, and so on—each of which can be filtered and reorganized separately. (Recording instruments on separate tracks to allow customized editing of each instrument's sound prior to reassembly [*mixing*] of all the sounds together predates the spread of digital recording equipment, but as a method of dividing sound into separate, composable units it is already a digital technique.) Or digital sound can be algorithmically separated by a measurable property of the sound itself, such as frequency (high, mid, low) or amplitude (louder sounds versus softer ones). Software often admits the division of music along the timeline, allowing a sound to be isolated from the sounds that precede and follow it in a recording, so that it can be altered within that recording or copied and inserted elsewhere.

In fact, the isolation and reuse of units of sound define a hallmark of digital music, *sampling*. Sampling, using a small section or sound from one song as an element of a different song, is not unique to the digital domain, but digital tools can easily isolate sounds for alteration and reproduction, which seems tailor-made for the sampling process. As many culture critics have observed, the prevalence of sampling, which sometimes occupies the musical foreground in some genres, guarantees a complex interplay between music and its history, as samples by definition materially incorporate bits of musical history into music of the present.

Sampling names not only a typical technique of digital music but also a technical process at the heart of digital sound representation. To record or construct a sound in a digital medium, it must be converted into a list of numbers, for the digital has no other mode of representation; everything digital amounts to a list of numbers (digits). Because sound is a fluctuation of air pressure over time, the numerical encoding of sound in the digital generally involves a list of numbers that represent successive air pressure levels. To generate such a list, air pressure must be measured very frequently, so that even rapid fluctuations in pressure are included in the resulting list of values. Each measurement produces a single value or *sample*, and the frequency at which measurements are taken is the *sampling frequency*. The compact disc standard specifies a sampling frequency of 44,100 samples per second (44.1 kHz), which was chosen because it is capable of encoding the highest pitches that human hearing registers. Some dogs and sea creatures can hear pitches much higher than a CD can include.

The sampling process may offer a clue as to the thoroughgoing capitulation of music to digital technologies and culture. Because music, as sound, can be reduced to a single dimension, a variation of air pressure over time at a point in space, it offers itself readily to digital capture and reproduction. (A second channel doubles the amount of data but allows stereo sound, which introduces spatial cues into the sound.) Unlike a moving visual image, which has many dimensions (two spatial dimensions, a time dimension, and other data for color and brightness), sound can be compellingly and easily (re)produced in the digital. Moreover, music has rarely relied heavily on representation, instead operating in the realm of affect (inspiring Plato's distrust). Perhaps this alliance with the subrepresentational makes a particularly generative pairing with the powers of digital abstraction. Attali may yet see his fantasy play out.

■ See also REMIX, SOUND

References and Further Reading

Attali, Jacques. 1985. *Noise: The Political Economy of Music*. Translated by Brian Massumi. Minneapolis: University of Minnesota Press.

Evens, Aden. 2005. *Sound Ideas: Music, Machines, and Experience*. Minneapolis: University of Minnesota Press.

Ihde, Don. 2007. *Listening and Voice: Phenomenologies of Sound*. Albany: State University of New York Press.

Kahn, Douglas. 2001. *Noise, Water, Meat: A History of Sound in the Arts*. Cambridge, MA: MIT Press.

Pohlmann, Ken. 2010. *Principles of Digital Audio*. New York: McGraw-Hill.

Sterne, Jonathan. 2003. *The Audible Past: Cultural Origins of Sound Reproduction*. Durham, NC: Duke University Press.

———. 2012. *Mp3: The Meaning of a Format*. Durham, NC: Duke University Press.

N

Narrativity
Jan-Noël Thon

In the past five decades, one of narratology's most stubbornly reoccurring problems has been under which conditions something can be considered to be a narrative and/or to have the quality of narrativity (e.g., Abbott 2009; Ryan 2006, 3–21; Schmid 2010, 1–21; as well as the contributions in Aumüller 2012; Kindt and Müller 2003; Pier and García Landa 2008). As is often the case with concepts central to a discipline, however, the proposed definitions of both *narrative* and *narrativity* vary considerably within classical as well as postclassical narratology. The lack of consensus becomes even more pronounced if one moves beyond the well-entrenched realm of literary criticism into the still-underexplored terrain of digital media in general and interactive digital media such as computer games in particular (see CHARACTERISTICS OF DIGITAL MEDIA, INTERACTIVE FICTION, INTERACTIVITY).

However, let us begin with a brief review of "classical" positions: Schmid (2010, 1–21) distinguishes between (1) broad definitions of narrative that focus exclusively on the "story" side of the canonical "story/discourse" distinction in that they include all media texts that represent a "change of state" and therefore possess at least a minimal degree of "eventfulness" (on "eventfulness" see, e.g., Prince 1982, 4; Hühn 2009; Schmid 2003; on the additional condition of "causality" see also Dannenberg 2008; Kafalenos 2006; Richardson 1997) and (2) narrow definitions of narrative that emphasize, at least to a certain extent, both the verbal nature of storytelling and the presence of a narrator as a necessary condition of narrativity (e.g., Genette 1988; Chatman 1978; Prince 1982; see also the discussion of the "speech-act approach to narrative" in Ryan 2006, 4–6). In the context of a transmedial narratology, however, the broad definition of narrative easily leads one to neglect the striking differences between the "storytelling abilities" of conventionally distinct narrative media, while the narrow definition of narrative appears both unnecessarily restrictive and particularly open to misunderstanding (see MEDIALITY and the discussion of narrators across media in Thon, forthcoming).

Aiming to remedy the caveats of these two kinds of "classical" approaches, then, recent works by scholars such as Fludernik (1996, 12–52), Jannidis (2003), Ryan (2006, 2007), and Wolf (2002, 2004) have developed prototypical definitions of narrative that take the term to refer to a fuzzy set of (media) texts with some of them closer to the prototype than others. Jannidis proposes "to treat the narration in films, the narration in comic strips, and the narration in computer games as different forms of 'narration,' each of which is located at a greater or lesser distance from the prototype, oral narration" (2003, 40). While our understanding of narrative may indeed be determined "by markedly typical exemplars rather than clear boundaries consisting of atomic features" (2003, 40), the notion that one can or should identify oral narration as *the* narrative prototype in human history and/or contemporary society seems rather problematic—the same holds for narration in (interactive) literature, (digital) film, (web) comics, or computer games, though.

Accordingly, a less narrow prototypical understanding of narrative has been proposed by Wolf, who shifts the emphasis from attempting to establish one (and only one) actual prototype of narrative as the primary reference point of a definition to a more explicit awareness of the fact that "a maximum number of traits constitute the ideal prototype as an abstract notion or schema, while concrete phenomena are assessed according to their greater or lesser resemblance with the prototypes" (2004, 86). Even though Wolf still assumes that "verbal, fictional narration yields the prototype of narrative" (2004, 91), focusing on an "ideal" or "abstract" prototype seems preferable to earlier attempts at a more essentialist and sometimes overly reductive typology of different media's narrative potential, which ranked "instrumental music," various kinds of pictures, "films / comic strips," and "drama" on a scale according to their supposed distance from the prototypical narrative form of the "fairy tale" (Wolf 2002).

Despite the various problems inherent in any attempt to define the narrativity of a conventionally distinct medium once and for all, it is necessary to acknowledge that, "when it comes to narrative abilities, media are not equally gifted; some are born storytellers, others suffer from serious handicaps" (Ryan 2006, 4). But particularly because there can be little doubt about "literary narrative's paradigmatic status for the narratological study of narrative representation" (Meister 2009, 343), a definition of narrative should not (or at least not without very good reasons) privilege (or ascribe prototypical status to) any particular narrative medium. This view also seems to be implied in Ryan's proposal to regard "the set of all narratives as fuzzy, and narrativity (or 'storiness') as a scalar property" (2006, 7) that can be defined by eight more or less salient characteristics. By simultaneously describing the latter as "prototypical features" and as optional conditions that "offer a toolkit for do-it-yourself definitions" (2006, 9), Ryan emphasizes that what we choose to consider a narrative is very much a matter of perspective indeed.

A standard understanding of the prototypical properties of a narrative representation would at least include the first three to five of Ryan's conditions, namely, that "narrative must be about a world populated by individuated existents," that "this world must be situated in time and undergo significant transformations," and that these "transformations must be caused by non-habitual physical events" (2006, 8). Moreover, one may choose to demand that "some of the participants in the events must be intelligent agents who have a mental life and react emotionally to the states of the world" and "some of the events must be purposeful actions by these agents," which in turn must be motivated by at least partially "identifiable goals and plans" (Ryan 2006, 8). However, both digital and nondigital media are often "more narrative," that is, possess a higher degree of narrativity, than this definition would require them to have; in other words, they tend to meet the additional conditions that "the sequence of events must form a unified causal chain and lead to closure," that "the occurrence of at least some of the events must be asserted as fact for the storyworld," and that "the story must communicate something meaningful to the audience" (Ryan 2006, 8). Ryan's last three conditions are quite specific, though, and hence can be most readily considered optional rather than mandatory.

The heuristic value of a prototypical definition of narrative and a gradual conception of narrativity becomes particularly apparent in the case of interactive digital media such as computer games. While the somewhat heated controversies of the new millennium, known as the "ludology vs. narratology debate" (e.g., the exchange between Jenkins [2004] and Eskelinen [2004]), have now considerably cooled down, the specific mode of narrativity of computer games remains an interesting problem for both computer game studies and transmedial narratology (e.g., Aarseth 2004; Jenkins 2004; Juul 2005; Neitzel, forthcoming; Ryan 2006, 181–203; Thon, forthcoming). The relevant question here is not so much whether computer games are (or should be) narrative, but rather in what way they are (or can be) narrative and in what way their narrativity differs from the narrativity of other conventionally distinct media. By now, there seems to be a general consensus in computer game studies that many contemporary computer games are set in some kind of fictional world (e.g., Juul 2005; Jenkins 2004; Thon 2007). If one understands "narratives" as representations of a (story) world situated in time and space and populated by individuated existents or characters, most computer games can, indeed, be considered "narratives" (see GAMES AS STORIES). Such a general description of computer games as narratives does remarkably little to explain their medium-specific narrativity, though.

To put it briefly, contemporary computer games often use a variety of "genuinely" narrative techniques such as cut scenes or scripted sequences of events, and the events thus represented are generally highly determined before the game is played (see CUT SCENES). However, the actual gameplay mainly consists of representations of events that are determined while the game is played, so that the mode in which ludic events are represented is more precisely characterized as simulation instead of narration (e.g., Aarseth 2004; Frasca 2003; Thon 2007; see also GAMEPLAY, SIMULATION). However, this distinction between rule-governed simulation and predetermined narration as two fairly different modes of representation does not necessarily imply that only "genuinely" narrative elements are contributing to the representation of a computer game's story world. In fact, the way in which story worlds are represented in contemporary computer games cannot and should not be reduced to either "simulation" or "narration," since it is constituted by the complex interplay between these two modes of representation.

To conclude, then, a prototypical conception of narrative and the resulting gradual notion of narrativity are relevant for both nondigital and digital media. Such a conception makes it possible to examine the specific limitations and affordances of various conventionally distinct media with respect to storytelling, rather than just stating that certain (digital) media "are narrative." What seems particularly interesting here is, on the one hand, what new forms of narrativity arise in digital media and, on the other hand, how these new forms relate to the various kinds of interactivity found in these media. Despite an increasing interest in transgeneric and transmedial problems, contemporary narratology has only just begun to address these questions.

■ See also CELL PHONE NOVEL, DIGITAL FICTION, E-MAIL NOVEL, FILM AND DIGITAL MEDIA, WEB COMICS

References and Further Reading

Aarseth, Espen. 2004. "Genre Trouble: Narrativism and the Art of Simulation." In *FirstPerson: New Media as Story, Performance, and Game*, edited by Noah Wardrip-Fruin and Pat Harrigan, 45–55. Cambridge, MA: MIT Press.

Abbott, H. Porter. 2009. "Narrativity." In *Handbook of Narratology*, edited by Peter Hühn, John Pier, Wolf Schmid, and Jörg Schönert, 309–328. Berlin: De Gruyter.

Aumüller, Matthias, ed. 2012. *Narrativität als Begriff. Analysen und Anwendungsbeispiele zwischen philologischer und anthropologischer Orientierung*. Berlin: De Gruyter.

Chatman, Seymour. 1978. *Story and Discourse: Narrative Structure in Fiction and Film*. Ithaca, NY: Cornell University Press.

Dannenberg, Hillary. 2008. *Coincidence and Counterfactuality: Plotting Time and Space in Narrative Fiction*. Lincoln: University of Nebraska Press.

Eskelinen, Markku. 2004. "Towards Computer Game Studies." In *FirstPerson: New Media as Story, Performance, and Game*, edited by Noah Wardrip-Fruin and Pat Harrigan, 36–44. Cambridge, MA: MIT Press.

Fludernik, Monika. 1996. *Towards a "Natural" Narratology*. London: Routledge.

Frasca, Gonzalo. 2003. "Simulation versus Narrative: Introduction to Ludology." In *The Video Game Theory Reader*, edited by Mark J. P. Wolf and Bernard Perron, 221–235. London: Routledge.

Genette, Gérard. 1988. *Narrative Discourse Revisited*. Translated by Jane E. Lewin. Ithaca, NY: Cornell University Press.

Hühn, Peter. 2009. "Event and Eventfulness." In *Handbook of Narratology*, edited by Peter Hühn, John Pier, Wolf Schmid, and Jörg Schönert, 80–97. Berlin: De Gruyter.

Jannidis, Fotis. 2003. "Narratology and the Narrative." In *What Is Narratology? Questions and Answers regarding the Status of a Theory*, edited by Tom Kindt and Hans-Harald Müller, 35–54. Berlin: De Gruyter.

Jenkins, Henry. 2004. "Game Design as Narrative Architecture." In *FirstPerson: New Media as Story, Performance, and Game*, edited by Noah Wardrip-Fruin and Pat Harrigan, 118–130. Cambridge, MA: MIT Press.

Juul, Jesper. 2005. *Half-Real: Video Games between Real Rules and Fictional Worlds*. Cambridge, MA: MIT Press.

Kafalenos, Irene. 2006. *Narrative Causalities*. Columbus: Ohio State University Press.

Kindt, Tom, and Hans-Harald Müller, eds. 2003. *What Is Narratology? Questions and Answers regarding the Status of a Theory*. Berlin: De Gruyter.

Meister, J. Christoph. 2009. "Narratology." In *Handbook of Narratology*, edited by Peter Hühn, John Pier, Wolf Schmid, and Jörg Schönert, 329–349. Berlin: De Gruyter.

Neitzel, Britta. Forthcoming. "Narrativity in Computer Games." In *the living handbook of narratology*, edited by Peter Hühn, J. Christoph Meister, John Pier, Wolf Schmid, and Jörg Schönert. Hamburg: Hamburg University Press. http://hup.sub.uni-hamburg.de/lhn/.

Pier, John, and José Á. García Landa, eds. 2008. *Theorizing Narrativity*. Berlin: De Gruyter.

Prince, Gerald. 1982. *Narratology: The Form and Functioning of Narrative*. Berlin: Mouton.

Richardson, Brian. 1997. *Unlikely Stories: Causality and the Nature of Modern Narrative*. Newark: University of Delaware Press.

Ryan, Marie-Laure. 2006. *Avatars of Story*. Minneapolis: University of Minnesota Press.

———. 2007. "Toward a Definition of Narrative." In *The Cambridge Companion to Narrative*, edited by David Herman, 22–35. Cambridge: Cambridge University Press.

Schmid, Wolf. 2003. "Narrativity and Eventfulness." In *What Is Narratology? Questions and Answers regarding the Status of a Theory*, edited by Tom Kindt and Hans-Harald Müller, 17–33. Berlin: De Gruyter.

———. 2010. *Narratology: An Introduction*. Berlin: De Gruyter.

Thon, Jan-Noël. 2007. "Unendliche Weiten? Schauplätze, fiktionale Welten und soziale Räume heutiger Computerspiele." In *Computer/Spiel/Räume: Materialien zur Einführung in die Computer Game Studies*, edited by Klaus Bartels and Jan-Noël Thon, 29–60. Hamburg: Department of Media and Communication.

———. Forthcoming. "Toward a Transmedial Narratology: On Narrators in Contemporary Graphic Novels, Feature Films, and Computer Games." In *Beyond Classical Narration: Unnatural and Transmedial Narrative and Narratology*, edited by Jan Alber and Per Krogh Hansen. Berlin: De Gruyter.

Wolf, Werner. 2002. "Das Problem der Narrativität in Literatur, bildender Kunst und Musik: ein Beitrag zu einer intermedialen Erzähltheorie." In *Erzähltheorie transgenerisch, intermedial, interdisziplinär*, edited by Ansgar Nünning and Vera Nünning, 23–104. Trier: W VT.

———. 2004. "'Cross the Border—Close That Gap': Towards an Intermedial Narratology." *European Journal of English Studies* 8 (1): 81–103.

. . . .

Networking
Mark Nunes

Networking describes an interconnection and interrelation of individuals and/or devices within an emergent or preconfigured exchange structure. While dynamic and relational, networking in its most common usages assumes that these exchanges take place between nodes that are spatially dispersed, offering a powerful, contemporary example of what James Carey defines as a "transmission model of communication": "The center of this idea of communication is the transmission of signals or messages over distance for the purpose of control. It is a view of communication that derives from one of the most ancient of human dreams: the desire to increase the speed and effect of messages as they travel in space" (1992a, 15). As such, networking realizes in both concept and material form the arrangement of both technological devices and human practices in a transmission model of communication.

Where to date the start of this "most ancient of human dreams" is a matter of opinion, but as a systematic arrangement of remote exchange, one might consider the rise of modern postal routes as the first examples of networking. Royal posts emerged in Europe and England in the fifteenth century, but it was not until the early 1600s that a significant increase in personal correspondence created a need for a systematic expansion of postal routes beyond the main post roads to include a growing network of interconnected byroads (Robinson 1948, 16–32). From the seventeenth century onward, this networking of roads for the carriage of goods and messages alike becomes increasingly important on a national and international scale.

While telephony, radio, and television follow along this same trajectory of increasingly complex networks of communication-as-transmission, it is the telegraph networks of the nineteenth century that hold a privileged place in the popular imagination as "the mother of all networks," to borrow a phrase from Tom Standage's (1998) history of the telegraph, *The Victorian Internet*. Of critical importance to an evolving concept of networking was the telegraph's ability to supplant a system of material exchange (correspondences) with a system of electronic exchange (signals) (see, for example, Cary 1992b). As Laura Otis (2001) notes, biological and technological metaphors for complex exchange structures converge in the nineteenth century on this image of the network, as researchers exploring the nervous system and proponents of telegraphy struggled to model systems of coordinated communication, and the ability of these systems to facilitate action at a distance. As neuroscience pioneer Emil DuBois-Reymond commented in 1851, "the wonder of our time, electrical telegraphy, was long ago modeled in the animal machine" (quoted in Otis 2001, 11). Key for DuBois-Reymond were parallels in the *system* of communication in both instances, namely, electronic signals conveyed along a complex, interconnecting network of fibers (Otis 2001, 24). Likewise, supporters for expanded telegraph service increasingly described this network as a political, social, and economic nervous system for the nation. In an 1870 U.S. House of Representatives report entitled "Postal Telegraph in the United States," for example, William Orton, president of Western Union, described the telegraph as "the nervous system of the commercial system," capable of reporting business activity at any moment anywhere its network reaches (quoted in Standage 1998, 170; Otis 2001, 131). Networking increasingly serves as a material and conceptual support for economic practices from the late nineteenth century onward. As James Beniger explains in *The Control Revolution*, the increase in productivity that accompanied improvements in manufacturing technology created a "crisis of control," requiring advancements in communication and business practices to manage not only production but also distribution and ultimately consumption (1986, 241–278). Networking as both a set of material practices and a conceptual framework for *doing business* allowed for a coordination of process control functions across an increasingly large and complex economic system. In other words, while telegraphic networking provided an important material underpinning for the coordination of manufacturing and distribution, more broadly speaking, it was the abstraction of labor and production into a system of information-dependent processes that transformed industry and the economy *as a whole* into a system predicated upon networking (Beniger 1986, 1–21).

From the twentieth century onward, networking arises as an increasingly explicit point of interest not only in industry but also in government and military applications. Computers, in their function as computational devices, begin to serve as core processors within "command and control" systems. Under the influence of cybernetics in the 1940s and 1950s, animals and machines alike were described as information *systems* consisting of mechanisms for processing inputs as well as networks for communicating feedback (see, e.g., Wiener 1961). In industry and military alike, advances in computing technology would allow for the development of increasingly powerful and increasingly complex command and control systems (see CYBERNETICS). But with this increase in computing power, networking as both concept and practice would expand considerably as well; in addition to facilitating the transmission of signals across great distances, by the 1960s networking would of necessity become a means for *distributing access* to this computational power, in effect blurring the line between transmission and interaction.

In what has become Internet folklore, popularized in books such as Katie Hafner and Matthew Lyon's (1998) *Where Wizards Stay Up Late*, Bob Taylor and Larry Roberts at the U.S. Department of Defense's Advanced Research Projects Agency (ARPA) undertook the technological challenge of building and sustaining a durable computer network to allow for just this sort of sharing and interaction among researchers. This same popular history of the birth of the Internet emphasizes that the networking of machines was only half of the accomplishment of ARPANET; rather, it was the ability of computer networking to enhance human-to-human collaboration—and interaction—that "revolutionized" research by creating a distributed social space. Much of our contemporary understanding of networking as social and technological practice stems from this notion that distributed collaboration is at the innovative heart of the Internet. Paul Baran's (1964) model for distributed networks provided both a schematic and conceptual framework for rethinking network topology grounded in interaction, rather than merely transmission: once networks could function as centralized (single-hub) or decentralized (multihub) structures, the importance of these networks to economic, military, and governmental functions required a resilient and redundant structure, best described as *distributed* (see COLLECTIVE INTELLIGENCE). With this shift in modeling of networks toward distributed structures, networking increasingly figured as an articulation of emergent, dynamic interactions—defined more by the exchanges themselves than by the preexisting material structures that support these exchanges.

Manuel Castells (1996) provides an in-depth analysis of interactive networking as a relationship between informational processes and the coordinated deployment of labor, goods, and information necessary to sustain its activity. Under informational capitalism, Castells argues, all processes fall under a "networking logic" in which "nodes" (material structures of goods, markets, labor, etc.) transact with and among other nodes in an open-ended structure of informational exchange (1996, 21, 470–471). This networking logic not only privileges a "space of flows" over a "space of places" but also creates "a forever universe, not self-expanding but self-maintaining, not cyclical but random, not recursive but incursive: timeless time" (1996, 433). For Castells, networking supports both the dominant, oppressive power structures of informational capitalism and the potential for marginalized groups (from the left and right alike) to reroute and mobilize this global space of flows toward their own ends. Other contemporary readings of networking have emphasized the enhanced potential for participation among individuals, foregrounding the liberatory possibilities of these structures. In *The Wealth of Networks*, for example, Yochai Benkler argues that networking allows for an "enhanced autonomy" among individuals within a network society by facilitating a greater range of social and economic activities performed "independently of the permission or cooperation of others . . . [and] in loose affiliation with others, rather than requiring stable, long-term relations" (2006, 8–9). In a word, Benkler sees a "radical decentralization of production" in and through technological and cultural networking, resulting in a "shift from an information environment dominated by proprietary, market-oriented action, to a world in which nonproprietary, nonmarket transactional frameworks play a large role alongside market production" (2006, 18).

With the deep penetration of Facebook and other social networking sites into everyday life, the lived practices of networking have become increasingly banal, often with little overt relation to the powerful relational database processes that underlie these informational transactions (see SOCIAL NETWORK SITES [SNSs]). Now, the blending of business and social interactions that we still call "networking" has as much to do with mingling on golf courses and dinner parties as it does with informational exchanges on social networking sites. Social networking as a function of computer interactions allows for a proliferation of contacts in an increasingly complex database structure that, while monetized for social media providers, is experienced by users as a form of what Leisa Reichelt has called *ambient intimacy*: "being able to keep in touch with people with a level of regularity and intimacy that you wouldn't usually have access to, because time and space conspire to make it impossible" (2007). In effect, social networking sites allow users to experience the networking logic of a space of flows on the scale of everyday life.

As contemporary, lived practice, networking facilitates this standing *potential* for interaction across a wide range of social and geographic distances. "The desire to increase the speed and effect of messages as they travel in space" expresses itself in this potential to reach "anywhere, anytime" through one's ability to access this network. Proximity, then, has less to do with individual contacts—the distance between two nodes—than with the "small world" networking structure (what in popular culture has become known as "six degrees of separation") of the system as a whole. In effect, everyday practices of networking—from the link-to-link browsing of hypertext navigation to the "liking" and "friending" of social networking sites—reinforce our experience of the social as an articulation and expression of networking.

■ See also HISTORY OF COMPUTERS

References and Further Reading

Baran, Paul. 1964. *Introduction to Distributed Communications Networks*. RM-3420-PR. Santa Monica, CA: Rand Corporation.

Beniger, James. 1986. *The Control Revolution*. Cambridge, MA: Harvard University Press.

Benkler, Yochai. 2006. *The Wealth of Networks*. New Haven, CT: Yale University Press.

Carey, James. 1992a. "A Cultural Approach to Communication." In *Communication as Culture*, 13–26. New York: Routledge.

———. 1992b. "Technology and Ideology: The Case of the Telegraph." In *Communication as Culture*, 201–230. New York: Routledge.

Castells, Manuel. 1996. *The Rise of the Network Society*. Malden, MA: Blackwell.

Hafner, Katie, and Matthew Lyon. 1998. *Where Wizards Stay Up Late*. New York: Touchstone.

Nunes, Mark. 2006. "Email, the Letter, and the Post." In *Cyberspaces of Everyday Life*, 86–126. Minneapolis: University of Minnesota Press.

Otis, Laura. 2001. *Networking: Communicating with Bodies and Machines in the Nineteenth Century*. Ann Arbor: University of Michigan Press.

Reichelt, Leisa. 2007. "Ambient Intimacy." *Disambiguity* (blog), March 1. www.disambiguity.com /ambient-intimacy/.

Robinson, Howard. 1948. *The British Post Office*. Princeton, NJ: Princeton University Press.

Standage, Tom. 1998. *The Victorian Internet: The Remarkable Story of the Telegraph and the Nineteenth Century's On-Line Pioneers*. New York: Walker.

Watts, Duncan. 1999. *Small Worlds: The Dynamics of Networks between Order and Randomness*. Princeton, NJ: Princeton University Press.

Wiener, Norbert. 1961. *Cybernetics: Or Control and Communication in the Animal and the Machine*. 2nd ed. Cambridge, MA: MIT Press.

N-gram
John Cayley

When applied to linguistic analysis, natural language processing, and text generation, an *n*-gram is, typically, a phrase composed of "*n*" that is "one or more" "grams" that are "tokens" (in the parlance of algorithmic parsing) or "words" (for our purposes). Linguistic *n*-grams are harvested from sequences of words that have, traditionally, been composed by human beings. Clearly, *n*-grams have historically established relative frequencies of occurrence within the corpora where they are found. These frequencies can be used to build a statistical model—most often a Markov model—for a corpus, and the model can be used to generate statistically probable sequences of words. This is the main engine of combinatory and automatic text generation (see COMBINATORY AND AUTOMATIC TEXT GENERATION). Some of the probable sequences generated from a model will, of course, already exist in the corpus, but many of them will not occur, either because these sequences have not yet been composed by human authors or because they would be considered "malformed" for reasons that are beyond the domain of statistical modeling. What, precisely, we can safely deem to be "beyond the domain of statistical modeling" is something of an issue, especially now, although it has been since the early days of the mathematical analysis of language use. Is language choice or chance (Herdan 1966)?

In December 2010, Google made its Ngram Viewer public (http://books.google.com/ngrams/). Intimately allied with this release was the publication of a major multiauthored paper in *Science* (Michel et al. 2011). This was a signal event that allowed us to see that, for some indeterminate amount of time, Google had been taking very seriously the statistical analysis of the corpora it has been harvesting from the Internet and elsewhere. In the case of the Ngram Viewer itself, the corpus is confined to millions of items from the Google Books digitization project. This corpus has also been normalized to a certain extent, as attested in the *Science* article, if not to the degree of thoroughness that is the (always unattainable) ideal of scholarly textual criticism. But there is no question about the "power" of the Ngram Viewer and what it represents for linguistic practice, including aesthetic literary practice. Set out in the *Science* article, there are enough fascinating examples of graphically represented "statements" emerging from the Ngram Viewer as a device of so-called quantitative cultural analysis to establish many major projects of research and, hopefully, language-driven aesthetically motivated data visualization.

Meanwhile, however, there are other service providers, such as Microsoft, also making their *n*-grams available (http://web-ngram.research.microsoft.com/info/), and thus it is becoming clear that this is the tip of a statistical analytic universe that is expanding around us, as language makers, at an explosive rate (Gleick 2011). The *n*-gram model that Google is building—from everything it can crawl from what we inscribe on the digital network—is as close as we may get to a model of "all" inscribed language. Access to this model is now tantalizingly on tap, literally at our finger tips. However, despite all blandishments to the contrary (such as Google's twin mottos "Don't be evil" and "Organize the world's information and make it universally accessible and useful"), access to these vital and potentially productive cultural vectors into and through what should be the inalienable commons of languages is mediated and controlled by the nonreciprocal application of proprietary algorithms; by terms of use or service; by outmoded legal considerations (because whole texts might be reconstituted from 5-gram data sets that include low-frequency *n*-grams, those with less than forty occurrences are not provided within data sets now "freely downloadable"; http://books.google.com/ngrams/datasets); and by the fact that, currently, the provision of these cultural vectors is funded and thus necessarily redirected by the vectors of commerce, via advertising, rather than by the needs and desires of the sciences, humanities, and arts. These data are constructed from language, the very medium of any practice of digital textuality, and so artists and critics of this medium—a commons within which all of us dwell—are increasingly engaging with the *n*-gram.

■ See also COMBINATORY AND AUTOMATIC TEXT GENERATION, COMPUTATIONAL LINGUISTICS, DATA, FLARF, SEARCH

References and Further Reading

Gleick, James. 2011. "How Google Dominates Us." *New York Review of Books* 58 (13). www.nybooks.com/articles/archives/2011/aug/18/how-google-dominates-us/.

Herdan, Gustav. 1966. *The Advanced Theory of Language as Choice and Chance.* Berlin: Springer.

Michel, Jean-Baptiste, Yuan Kui Shen, Aviva Presser Aiden, et al. 2011. "Quantitative Analysis of Culture Using Millions of Digitized Books." *Science* 331:176–182.

Shannon, Claude E., and Warren Weaver. (1949) 1998. *The Mathematical Theory of Communication.* Urbana: University of Illinois Press.

Nonlinear Writing

Astrid Ensslin

Nonlinear writing refers to (a) a writerly activity and (b) a specific type of written document. The first meaning relates to the strategy of composing a text in a nonsequential way by adding, removing, and modifying passages in various places of a manuscript rather than producing it in one piece, from beginning to end. The second meaning refers to documents that are not structured in a sequential way, with a clear beginning, middle, and end. Rather, their macrostructure follows an associative logic, which assembles its composite elements (paragraphs, text chunks, or lexias) into a loosely ordered network. These networks offer readers multiple choices of traversing a document, which can facilitate specific types of reading strategies, such as keyword searches or jumping between main text and footnotes, and complicate others, such as reading for closure or completeness.

The concepts of nonlinear writing, multilinear (or multisequential) reading, interrelating, annotating, and cross-referencing, as well as the abstract and material hyperlink, date back over one thousand years. So-called proto-hypertexts can be traced as far back as the Middle Ages, when glosses (annotations) appeared in the Jewish Talmud, the Bible, canon law, and medical texts. In the baroque period, with its affinity to stylistic conceit in the arts, experimental poets created instances of labyrinth poetry and so-called poetic machines, such as Georg Philipp Harsdörffer's *Wechselsatz* (Permutations) in *Poetischer Trichter* (Poet's Funnel) (1648–1653) and Quirinius Kuhlmann's *Libes-Kuß* (Love Kiss) (1671) (for a history of shaped poems, see George Puttenham's *The Arte of English Poesie* of 1589). Further on in history, European Enlightenment scholars produced the first printed encyclopedias (e.g., Diderot and d'Alembert 1751–1780; Johnson 1755; Black and Black 1768), which represented early forms of proto-hypertextual cross-referencing, or "super-scribing" text in order to explain, elaborate, and connect intertextually. In the romantic period, the idea of the "absolute book," inspired by Friedrich Schlegel's utopian idea of a *progressive Universalpoesie*, raised intertextual connectivity to a paradigm of a whole age.

Nonlinear print fiction first emerged alongside the novel as ultimately nonconformist literary genre. Well-known examples include Lawrence Sterne's antinovel *Tristram Shandy* (1760) and Jean Paul's so-called footnote fiction (e.g., *Siebenkäs*, 1796/1797; *Titan*, 1800–1803). Twentieth-century modernism and postmodernism gave rise to a great variety of nonlinear print fiction. The narrative style of James Joyce's *Finnegans Wake* (1939), for instance, evades linear plot construction and, instead, presents the reader with a discontinuous, ever-changing line of narrative discourse involving rapid changes between focalizers, locations, and plot details. Marc Saporta's *Composition No. 1* (1961) is a "book in a box," whose pages are stored as unnumbered, loose leaves, which readers are expected to shuffle like a deck of cards. A digital edition of *Composition No.1* for iPad was published in 2011, with touch-pad movements replacing the physical shuffling of leaves. Vladimir Nabokov's *Pale Fire* (1962) oscillates between segments of a 999-line poem and an extensive commentary and forces readers to navigate between footnotes in a quasi-hypertextual fashion. Readers of Julio Cortázar's *Rayuela* (Hopscotch, 1963) are offered two different techniques of reading. They can either read up to chapter 56 in a linear fashion, or follow the chapter map provided by the text, which begins with chapter 73 and continues in a seemingly random sequence. Arno Schmidt's German novel *Zettels Traum* (Zettel's Dream, 1970) is organized in three different columns, which display diverse combinations of typewritten text, notes, advertising, and photographs and have to be read in a crisscrossing, associative fashion. Milorad Pavić's Serbian "lexicon novel," *Dictionary of the Khazars* (1984), consists of three cross-referenced encyclopedias and has been published in a "male" and a "female" version, which differ only marginally, however.

Another form of nonlinear print writing is concrete poetry, which first emerged in Switzerland (Eugen Gomringer) and Brazil (Haroldo de Campos, Decio Pignatari, and Augusto de Campos) in the 1950s and subsequently spread around the world. Its earliest precursor is Latin pattern poetry, exemplified by Porphyrius's altar-shaped poem of ca. 400 CE and Venantius Fortunatus's grid poems dated ca. 430–500 CE. Concrete poetry captures a wide range of experimental verbal art forms but is generally defined as short pieces of text intended to be viewed rather than read aloud and as presenting verbal signs as visual artifacts (Bray 2012).

So-called Oulipian writing, which goes back to the 1960s French Oulipo (Ouvroir de littérature potentielle) movement, operates under self-imposed structural and mathematical constraints (see WRITING UNDER CONSTRAINT). This governing principle resulted in various nonlinear works, such as Raymond Queneau's *Cent mille milliards de poèmes* (1961). The collection consists of ten sonnets, each line of which is printed on a separate card and arranged in the physical form of a heads-bodies-and-legs children's book. The individual sonnet lines can be randomly combined, resulting in 10^{14} possible different poems. Oulipian works later inspired numerous digital poets to experiment with similar constraints, implemented through computational processes.

In popular literary and game culture, so-called Choose Your Own Adventure books proliferated from the 1970s to the 1990s. Rather than reading these ludic-fictional artifacts in a sequential fashion, readers choose their own pathways through the book, which results in individualized, diverse experiences and multiple possible outcomes of an adventure. These books became popular at roughly the same time as text and computer game adventures, with which they share early forms of ergodic reader interactivity (see GAME GENRES, GAME HISTORY).

The advent of digital technologies and particularly the World Wide Web in the second half of the twentieth century facilitated electronic applications of and experiments with nonlinear writing. With the invention of hypertext and HTML (HyperText Markup Language), linking documents into online and offline networks became a standard way of representing information and led to the proliferation of nonlinear, electronic writing. To the current day, websites are based on the principle of nonlinear writing, as users navigate their pages in highly individualized ways. Yet the digital medium also inspired artists and writers to experiment with its textual and aesthetic implications and affordances. The late 1980s saw the creation of the first literary hypertexts, which set out to explore the creative and aesthetic potential of digital nonlinear writing. Their success with readers was significantly smaller than that of contemporaneous nonlinear digital nonfiction. Unsurprisingly, digital reference works such as online encyclopedias, glossaries, and dictionaries have by now made their print counterparts virtually obsolete (see HYPERTEXTUALITY).

Other digital forms of nonlinear writing include interactive fiction, which requires readers to interact with the text in a playful, exploratory way by entering commands, as well as various descendents of concrete poetry (see INTERACTIVE FICTION). Kinetic poetry is, quite literally, poetry that moves across the computer screen and has to be read in an interactive, nonsequential fashion, for instance, via drag-and-drop and mouse-over. Generative poetry comprises works that are generated computationally, either with or without previous wreader input. These computational processes trigger poetic sequences that cannot be read in a conventional linear way but rather need to be scanned and watched as pieces of procedural, machine-generated art.

Poststructuralist theories of the 1970s dealt extensively with the idea of nonlinearity in their attempts to challenge the essentialistic, totalizing views of post-Enlightenment philosophical thought. In *Of Grammatology*, for instance, Derrida proposes that linear writing is "rooted in a past of nonlinear writing, . . . a writing that spells its symbols pluri-dimensionally; there the meaning is not subjected to successivity, to the order of a logical time, or to the irreversible temporality of sound" (1976, 85). According to Derrida, linear writing suppressed nonlinear writing until the latter recurred in twentieth-century literature, thus reflecting the impossibility of documenting modern human experience in a linear fashion. Derrida suggests a new way of reading earlier texts as nonlinear artifacts and concludes that "the end of linear writing is indeed the end of the book" (1976, 86; see Bolter 2001, 109). Theories of nonlinearity strongly influenced first-wave hypertext scholarship and criticism in the 1990s.

The receptive counterpart of nonlinear writing is multilinear reading. As reading is a temporal activity, it inadvertently follows a linear trajectory. Whereas in linear writing this trajectory tends to follow a prefabricated path with relatively few diversions, in nonlinear writing it adopts a meandering, crisscrossing fashion. Readers of nonlinear writing might never read the same text twice but will alter their reading paths during and between reading sessions. The result is an array of different mental images, or readings, of the text's content, and multiple rereadings are required to construe a reasonably reliable textual meaning in the reader's mind (Douglas 2000; Ensslin 2007; Ciccoricco 2007). Another result of nonlinearity is a significant degree of intersubjective discrepancy and disagreement between different readers of the same text, which poses both challenges and innovative potential to classroom discourse and critical debate.

■ See also DIGITAL INSTALLATION ART, DIGITAL POETRY

References and Further Reading

Black, Adam, and Charles Black. 1768. *Encyclopaedia Britannica*. Edinburgh: A & C Black.

Bolter, Jay David. 2001. *Writing Space: Computers, Hypertext, and the Remediation of Print*. Mahwah, NJ: Lawrence Erlbaum Associates.

Bray, Joe. 2012. "Concrete Poetry and Prose." In *The Routledge Companion to Experimental Literature*, edited by Joe Bray, Alison Gibbons, and Brian McHale, 298–309. New York: Routledge.

Ciccoricco, David. 2007. *Reading Network Fiction*. Tuscaloosa: University of Alabama Press.

Derrida, Jacques. 1976. *Of Grammatology*. Baltimore: Johns Hopkins University Press.

Diderot, Denis, and Jean le Rond D'Alembert. 1751–1780. *Encyclopédie, ou dictionnaire raisonné des sciences, des arts et des métiers*. Paris: André le Breton, Michel-Antoine David, Laurent Durand, and Antoine-Claude Briasson.

Douglas, Jane Yellowlees. 2000. *The End of Books—or Books without End? Reading Interactive Narratives*. Ann Arbor: University of Michigan Press.

Ensslin, Astrid. 2007. *Canonizing Hypertext: Explorations and Constructions*. London: Continuum.

Johnson, Samuel. 1755. *A Dictionary of the English Language*. London: Consortium.

NPC (Nonplayer Character)

Ragnhild Tronstad

NPC is an abbreviation frequently used within computer gaming and tabletop role-playing games (RPGs) and is commonly translated as an initialism for "nonplayer character," "nonplayable character," or "nonplaying character" (see ROLE-PLAYING GAMES). It refers to the game characters that are not controlled by any player, but rather by the computer or (in tabletop RPGs) by the game master. Characters controlled by players are referred to as player characters (PCs in short) or avatars. Within the context of computer gaming, PCs and NPCs figure in most adventure games, action-adventure games, RPGs, and massively multiplayer online games (MMOGs) (see ONLINE WORLDS, ROLE-PLAYING GAMES). They are also a part of many simulation games.

NPCs fulfill a variety of functions in games. A large number of them represent neutral entities whose main function it is to blend in and populate the game world, for example, shopkeepers, ordinary citizens, and wild or domestic animals that are either friendly or indifferent to the PC's presence.

However, there are also NPCs that play a more prominent role in the game as enemies or allies of the player character. Enemy roles include the aggressive monster physically attacking the PC, as well as the sly antagonist trying to spoil the PC's attempts to accomplish its quest.

Quest giver, informant, and helper are examples of allied NPC roles. Often, an NPC will figure as object of the PC's quest in the role of victim that needs to be saved (see QUEST NARRATIVE). As antagonist or ally in a quest narrative, NPCs are often able to engage in dialogue with the PC. The potential of the dialogue to become more or less elaborate depends on the kind of conversational system with which the NPC is equipped. The simplest and most common solution is a dialogue tree allowing the player to make a choice among a limited number of sentences that are already formulated. In more complex systems based on natural language processing the NPC may function similarly to a chatterbot (see CHATTERBOTS). This is a solution that allows the player more conversational freedom, but it is less functional in terms of securing a desired course of progression in the game (see EMERGENCE).

"Mob," "monster," and "boss" are examples of alternative terms that help us distinguish between different types of NPCs by reflecting their specific purpose in the game. Some of these alternative terms may be ambiguous, though. "Mob," for instance, originated as an abbreviation of "mobile entity" and thus should in principle be a neutral term (Bartle 2003). Today, however, it commonly refers to NPCs whose main purpose it is to be fought, killed, and looted, so that the PC may gain experience points and items to be sold or equipped, which are needed to advance in the game. "Monster" has similar connotations, while "boss" refers to monsters of a higher level that are more difficult and potentially more rewarding for the PC to kill. Quests and game levels often end with a final boss whom the PC must overcome in order to be allowed to proceed to new challenges in the game.

■ See also GAME GENRES

References and Further Reading

Bartle, Richard. 2003. *Designing Virtual Worlds*. Indianapolis: New Riders.

Busey, Andrew. 1995. *Secrets of the* MUD Wizards. Indianapolis: Sams.net.

Ellison, Brent. 2008. "Defining Dialogue Systems." *Gamasutra*. www.gamasutra.com/view/feature /3719/defining_dialogue_systems.php.

Old Media / New Media

Jessica Pressman

The term *new media* announces its relativity. It only has meaning in relation to "old media," and, of course, what is old is always also historically specific. The terms involved are not stable and true but qualitative and changing; and yet, they are often employed rhetorically as if there exists a common definition of *digital, book, print culture,* and so on. This paradox renders it vital that we rigorously and repeatedly examine the ways in which *new* and *old* are used.

In her introductory essay to the collection *New Media, Old Media,* Wendy Chun reminds us of "the importance of interrogating the forces behind any emergence, the importance of shifting from 'what is new' to analyzing what work the new does" (Chun and Keenan 2006, 3). Though many scholarly studies trace the impact of old media on new media, the reverse is rarely pursued. Yet, the work of the new is precisely what inspires us to reconsider the old and to recognize the intersections and convergent histories of old and new. Marshall McLuhan implied as much when he provocatively and metaphorically claimed, "We look at the present through a rear-view mirror. We march backwards into the future" (McLuhan and Fiore 1967, 74–75). More recently, Lisa Gitelman writes, "When media are new, they offer a look into the different ways that their jobs get constructed as such" (2006, 6). In other words, the designation of "newness" indexes an act of mediation and a shift in perspective from a previous cultural norm. It thus invites investigation into how culture operates and operated.

In *The Language of New Media* (2001), Lev Manovich seeks to define "new media"—meaning the new, digital media—by identifying five "principles" that distinguish digital media: numerical representation, modularity, automation, variability, and cultural transcoding. He then sets out to trace the development of new media through the convergence of computing and cinematic technologies. Other scholars pursue similar methodologies of tracing the genealogy of new, digital media through its relation to older media forms. For example, Carolyn Marvin's seminal book about the telegraph, *When Old Technologies Were New,* begins, "*New technologies* is a historically relative term" (1988, 3; emphasis in the original). Tom Standage claims that the telegraph is *The Victorian Internet* (1998), and David Henkin (2006) offers a history of the antebellum American postal service that suggests it as a precursor to our contemporary digital social network. Other scholars use the impetus provided by new media to reexamine older media forms and reconsider them anew. Anne Friedberg examines the window metaphor, such as that used in graphical user interface computing, describing it as "the key measure of epistemic changes in representational systems from painting to photography to moving-image media and computer display" (2006, 5). Such an example shows how new media inspire new ways of thinking about older media.

The impact of new media not only promotes studies of individual old media but also inspires the emergence of new modes of scholarship. The field of book history (or studies in the history of the book) is a ripe example. Over the past few decades, book history has consolidated into a scholarly field around efforts to study the codex as a medium—as a material technology with physical properties and also as an object that mediates cultural process and practices (for more on the history of the book as a field, see Finkelstein and McCleery 2002). This form of old media study now has a scholarly journal (*Book History*, founded in 1998) and a scholarly society (the Society for the History of Authorship, Reading and Publishing, founded in 1991), as well as many titles that fall under the rubric of "book history." In *Too Much to Know*, for example, historian Ann Blair examines the early history of information overload by focusing in early modern England on "one of the longest-running traditions of information managements—the collection and arrangement of textual excerpts designed for consultation," or reference books (2010, 1). So too has a mode of scholarship called "media archaeology" emerged, which seeks to excavate individual technologies and the medial discourses in which they operate in order to challenge a linear historical narrative that describes the shift from old to new media.

Media do not replace one another in a clear, linear succession but instead evolve in a more complex ecology of interrelated feedback loops. "What is new about new media," Jay David Bolter and Richard Grusin write, "comes from the particular ways in which they refashion older media and the ways in which older media refashion themselves to answer the challenges of new media" (1999, 15) (see REMEDIATION). "Remediation" is evidence of how new media impact old media. To take one of Bolter and Grusin's examples, a television news broadcast adopts an interface design akin to a website in an effort to update the older medium. Katherine Hayles (2005) suggests the term "intermediation" instead of "remediation" to showcase the recursive nature of the feedback loop involved in generating the medial ecology between old and new. Bending the line into a circle illuminates the bidirectional impact of old and new media and exposes the ideological interests at work in claiming newness—or, to return to Chun's provocation, questions the work that newness does.

Contemporary literature provides a case study for examining the impact of new media on old media. As the age of print appears to be passing, with more readers turning to screens more often than to books, the threat posed by digital technologies to that old medium of literary culture (the codex) becomes a source of inspiration in contemporary literary arts. The result is a phenomenon that I call "bookishness," wherein the book is figured within literature as an aesthetic object rather than a medium for information transmission, a thing to fetishize rather than to use. Thematically, bookish novels depict books as their main characters or objects of desire. Formally, they expose their mediality with die-cut pages and experiments in collage, color, and design. These books expose themselves to be multimedia objects and archives, and they illuminate the codex to be a medium of endless newness. Bookishness is the result of new media's impact on literature's old media, and it is one example of the complex, poetic, and mutually generative relationship between old and new media.

■ See also CHARACTERISTICS OF DIGITAL MEDIA, HISTORY OF COMPUTERS, MEDIA ECOLOGY, OLD MEDIA / NEW MEDIA, READING STRATEGIES, RELATIONS BETWEEN MEDIA, REMEDIATION

References and Further Reading

Blair, Ann M. 2010. *Too Much to Know: Managing Scholarly Information before the Modern Age.* New Haven, CT: Yale University Press.

Bolter, Jay David, and Richard Grusin. 1999. *Remediation: Understanding New Media.* Cambridge, MA: MIT Press.

Chun, Wendy Hui Kyong, and Thomas Keenan, eds. 2006. *New Media, Old Media: A History and Theory Reader.* New York: Routledge.

Finkelstein, David, and Alistair McCleery, eds. 2002. *The Book History Reader.* New York: Routledge.

Friedberg, Anne. 2006. *The Virtual Window: From Alberti to Microsoft.* Cambridge, MA: MIT Press.

Gitelman, Lisa. 2006. *Always Already New: Media, History, and the Data of Culture.* Cambridge, MA: MIT Press.

Hayles, N. Katherine. 2005. *My Mother Was a Computer: Digital Subjects and Literary Texts.* Chicago: University of Chicago Press.

Henkin, David M. 2006. *The Postal Age: The Emergence of Modern Communications in Nineteenth-Century America.* Chicago: University of Chicago Press.

Manovich, Lev. 2001. *The Language of New Media.* Cambridge, MA: MIT Press.

Marvin, Carolyn. 1988. *When Old Technologies Were New: Thinking about Electric Communication in the Late Nineteenth Century.* New York: Oxford University Press.

McLuhan, Marshall, and Quentin Fiore. 1967. *The Medium Is the Massage: An Inventory of Effects.* New York: Bantam Books.

Standage, Tom. 1998. *The Victorian Internet: The Remarkable Story of the Telegraph and the Nineteenth Century's On-Line Pioneers.* New York: Walker.

Online Game Communities
Celia Pearce

The single-player game is somewhat of an anomaly of the computer era. Prior to the advent of video games, virtually all games, with the exception of a handful of playing card variants, were primarily multiplayer. Indeed, even the very first video games, such as *Tennis for Two*, *OXO*, *Spacewar!*, *Pong*, and the Odyssey platform, were all designed for two or more players (see GAME HISTORY). As early as 1979, the first online game, *MUD1* (for multiuser dungeon or domain), was played over university networks using only text and building off the dice-based conventions of the tabletop role-playing game *Dungeons & Dragons* (see MUDs AND MOOs, ROLE-PLAYING GAMES). This gave rise to an entire hacker community, who modified and built off this genre, which eventually, when combined with graphics, evolved into the massively multiplayer online role-playing game (MMORPG). This pattern of hacking within game communities is a common theme that goes back as far as *Spacewar!*, which went through many iterations as it circulated around college campuses. *MUD1* and its antecedents also precipitated the parallel genre of text-based MOOs (multiuser object oriented), which developed into both games and open-ended social play worlds, such as *LambdaMOO* (1990), the first virtual world whose content was largely player created. This well-documented experiment produced some of the earliest accounts we have of emergent networked communities, of the formation of laws and social conventions, and even of the phenomenon that came to be known as "griefing" (Dibbell 1998), or player harassment.

While there were a few early attempts at graphical user worlds during the 1980s, such as *Lucasfilm Habitat*, it wasn't until the early 1990s with the advent of the World Wide Web and improved PC graphics that distributed play communities began to move toward the mainstream. Three important fictional works were influential on their growth: J. R. R. Tolkien's *The Hobbit* (1937) and its sequels; William Gibson's *Neuromancer* (1984), which introduced the term "cyberspace"; and Neal Stephenson's *Snow Crash* (1992), much of whose action was set in a fictional networked 3D virtual world populated by "avatars," a term originally introduced by the creators of *Lucasfilm Habitat*.

The first major boom in online games and virtual worlds occurred in the mid-1990s and included both open-ended graphical worlds, such as *ActiveWorlds* (1995) and *OnLive* (1995), and a succession of MMORPGs, which borrowed from the conventions originally set forth in *MUD1*, including *Ultima Online* (1996), *EverQuest* (1999), and the Korean *Lineage* (1998) (see ONLINE WORLDS). These games have evolved into their own multiplayer game communities.

From their earliest instantiations, multiplayer games have produced patterns of community and emergent behavior, such as staging "virtual weddings" in online games, doing various forms of hacking and modding, and engaging in griefing, or harassment of other players, as well as acts of civil disobedience. *Ultima Online* and later *EverQuest* players began the practice now colloquially known as "eBaying," selling accounts or virtual loot on auction sites to make money or compensate for time spent in "leveling" characters (Castronova 2001), which has since transformed into the multibillion-dollar gold-farming business (Dibbell 2006) (see VIRTUAL ECONOMIES).

Another boom occurred in the early 2000s with the release of Second Life and There .com (2003), two social virtual worlds that focused on user-created content. The following year saw the launch of *World of Warcraft*, based on Blizzard Entertainment's popular Warcraft franchise, and *MapleStory*, an MMORPG for children and teens. Two games that were poised to be successful because they were based on popular single-player franchises were *The Sims Online*, based on the blockbuster single-player franchise, and the *Myst*-based MMORPG *Uru*. However, both of these games ultimately closed owing to low player participation. First-person shooters (FPSs), which had originated as a single-player genre, also evolved into multiplayer forms during this period. Initially, owing to graphics and speed requirements, these games were played over local area networks (LANs) in cybercafes, or at LAN parties, tournaments, and conventions. Eventually PC graphics processing, network bandwidth, and the integration of networks into game consoles took these games online, with sci-fi combat titles such as *Halo*, as well as more historically themed games such as the *Battlefield* and *Medal of Honor* series. Although these games lack the role-play, persistence, and story focus of fantasy MMORPGs, they have nonetheless precipitated large communities, including professional gamers who play in tournament settings (Taylor 2011; Taylor 2012).

Critiques of conventional MMORPGs have included their narrative and gameplay focus on combat and labor-intensive and often-redundant "grind" mechanics, as well as their "impoverished" approach to gender (Taylor 2006), with a history of oversexualized female representation (see GENDER REPRESENTATION). Extensive research into

MMORPGs has shown that they tend to have a low percentage of female players, ranging from 20 percent to as little as 5 percent for spaceship-based sci-fi games such as *EVE Online* (see GENDER AND MEDIA USE). FPS-style games have a similar disparity in gender, which can often lead to a boys' club ethos and culture of harassment, especially toward female players, although women continue to play these games despite the hostile environment.

Also emerging is a group of outliers that combine the clear rules and mechanics of a game with the user-generated content more commonly associated with virtual worlds. Two of the most successful examples are *Little Big Planet*, a PlayStation 3 game that allows players to build their own levels in a 3D platformer world populated by rag dolls, and *Minecraft*, an independently produced Lego-like game environment where players can mine blocks, craft materials, and build their own massive structures. Significant communities of content creators have grown up around each of these games, resulting in complex emergent behaviors and inventive player-designed environments.

With the introduction of Facebook, as well as new mobile platforms such as the iPad, casual online games have also become a more prevalent feature of the landscape. Some would argue, however, that so-called social network games such as *Farmville*, *Words with Friends*, and *Parking Wars* are minimally social as they typically only support asynchronous interaction and typically involve only two people. However nascent these genres are at this writing, it is likely that they will continue to grow in popularity and become more socially engaging with time.

A growing trend has also been the development of pervasive or alternate reality games (ARGs), games that are played largely in the physical world enabled by networks and mobile devices (see ALTERNATE REALITY GAMING). ARGs have been particularly notable for their emergent behavior. ARG players are ardent puzzle solvers and frequently launch their own wikis and develop other knowledge-sharing mechanisms.

Community Formation and Structure

The popular anxiety that communities that exist inside virtual worlds are somehow less "real" than physical world communities has been refuted by research into online sociality dating back to the 1990s (Curtis 1992; Hine 1998). While virtual worlds have called into question the nature of community itself (Turkle 1997; Boellstorff 2008), research in this area has demonstrated that mediated communities bear more similarities than differences with physical real-world communities. Online researchers have used the metaphor of the "virtual pub" (Kendall 2002) to describe distributed communities, and game scholars have used a variety of similar comparisons, including guilds as mafia families (Taylor and Jakobsson 2003), virtual worlds as "third places" that exist outside of traditional definitions of "public" and "private" as a way to conceptualize virtual worlds, and identifying forms of "fictive ethnicities" that players might adopt as part of their attachment to a specific online game, as well as the notions of "productive play" (Pearce and Artemesia 2009) or "techne" (Boellstorff 2008), which relate to the ways in which play practices can transform into creative activities, and the social roles and status that emerge as a result. Although they have studied a diverse array of communities and practices, virtual world and online game researchers generally agree that game and play communities form genuine bonds between people, which are at the same time distinct from other types of communities in that they engage with fantasy, play, and alternative identities (see IDENTITY).

Typically online game communities are thought of as strictly distributed communities; however, players can also be part of a real-world community of some sort. They may be classmates at a school, coworkers, family members, or members of a real-world gaming community who play together within a cybercafe or LAN club. Cybercafes are particularly popular in Korea and China (Nardi 2010), as well as in Asian communities in the United States.

Online games have also had a tradition of game modding communities, dating back to the earliest games to emerge from university research labs, such as *Spacewar!* and *MUD1*, which continues among players in the commercial sphere. Enterprising hackers create and share plug-ins and add-ons to enhance the player experience of games such as *World of Warcraft*, *Guild Wars*, and *Minecraft*. Modding is also actively practiced in FPS game communities, where new levels and even entirely new games can be built from a preexisting game engine.

In addition to communities within or around a given world, trans-ludic game diasporas can span multiple virtual worlds. This can happen when a new game or virtual world opens, cannibalizing guilds or communities from other worlds, or when a game closes, an increasingly common occurrence. The best-documented instance of this is the *Uru* diaspora, which consists of players from the game *Uru: Myst Online* who dispersed into other games and virtual worlds when the game originally closed in 2004 (Pearce and Artemesia 2009). Owing to player demand, *Uru* was opened and closed several times by different publishers, and as of this writing, it is maintained by the original developer, Cyan Worlds. Throughout this process, *Uru* players have continued to populate other games and virtual worlds, while maintaining a sense of collective identity as "*Uru* refugees," regardless of where they have settled. They do this by cultivating a "fictive ethnicity" within the worlds they inhabit, as well as through the use of extra-virtual community tools, such as forums.

In *Communities of Play* (2009), Pearce presents a number of findings that, though specific to the *Uru* diaspora, can also be applied to other game communities and their emergent behavior and are consistent with previous and subsequent findings by other researchers:

- The type of person attracted to a game, virtual world, or group sets the stage for the types of communities and emergent behaviors that will arise.
- The software affordances of a given virtual world allow for particular types of social interaction and communities to emerge. The values and assumptions embedded in the software have a strong influence on how culture forms.
- Emergent communities are promoted by feedback loops, many of which are instantiated as software features within the game or virtual world itself.
- Play can create powerful bonds that arise out of a shared imagination space, what science fiction author William Gibson, who coined the term "cyberspace," called a "consensual hallucination."
- Play communities often have a sense of communal identity based on shared interests, values, aesthetics, and social conventions.
- Individual identity is socially constructed through play and creative activities, as well as affiliation with the group; players report being surprised by who their avatars become (Bruckman 1992; Taylor 2006; Pearce and Artemesia 2007).
- Creative activities are inherently social, even if the production context is solitary; even solo creators typically have a community in mind for which they are generating content within a play community.

- Communities are labile and organic and can undergo dramatic shifts in a fairly narrow time frame.

- Communities that persist over time or across different worlds tend to have a strong core leadership that keeps the group together.

- The "Magic Circle," previously defined as the ring that surrounds games (Huizinga 1950) and separates them from the world of practical life, is more porous than earlier theories implied. The computer, which creates the magic circle of multiplayer games, is also used for other tasks. When players can use voice, as in There.com and more recently Second Life, this reveals an aspect of their real-world identity.

■ See also AVATARS, INTERACTIVITY, PARTICIPATORY CULTURE, VIRTUALITY

References and Further Reading

Boellstorff, Tom. 2008. *Coming of Age in Second Life: An Anthropologist Explores the Virtually Human.* Princeton, NJ: Princeton University Press.

Bruckman, Amy. 1992. "Identity Workshop: Emergent Social and Psychological Phenomena in Text-Based Virtual Reality." Cambridge, MA: MIT Media Lab.

Castronova, Edward. 2001. "Virtual Worlds: A First-Hand Account of Market and Society on the Cyberian Frontier." Working Paper No. 618, CESifo, Munich. http://papers.ssrn.com/sol3/papers.cfm?abstract_id=294828.

Curtis, Pavel. 1992. "Mudding: Social Phenomena in Text-Based Virtual Realities." In *Proceedings of the 1992 Conference on Directions and Implications of Advanced Computing*, 26–34.

Damer, Bruce. 1997. *Avatars! Exploring and Building Virtual Worlds on the Internet.* Berkeley, CA: Peachpit Press.

Dibbell, Julian. 1998. *My Tiny Life: Crime and Passion in a Virtual World.* New York: Henry Holt.

———. 2006. *Play Money: Or, How I Quit My Day Job and Made Millions Trading Virtual Loot.* New York: Basic Books.

Hine, Christine. 1998. "Virtual Ethnography." Paper from Internet Research and Information for Social Scientists Conference. University of Bristol, UK, March 25–27.

Huizinga, Johan. (1938) 1950. *Homo Ludens: A Study of the Play-Element in Culture.* Translation of the original. New York: Roy.

Kendall, Lori. 2002. *Hanging Out in the Virtual Pub: Masculinities and Relationships Online.* Berkeley: University of California Press.

Nardi, Bonnie. 2010. *My Life as a Night Elf Priest: An Anthropological Account of World of Warcraft.* Ann Arbor: University of Michigan Press.

Pearce, Celia, and Artemesia. 2007. "Communities of Play: The Social Construction of Identity in Persistent Online Game Worlds." In *Second Person: Role-Playing and Story in Games and Playable Media*, edited by N. Wardrip-Fruin and P. Harrigan, 311–318. Cambridge, MA: MIT Press.

———. 2009. *Communities of Play: Emergent Cultures in Multiplayer Games and Virtual Worlds.* Cambridge, MA: MIT Press.

Stephenson, Neal. 1992. *Snow Crash.* New York: Bantam Books.

Taylor, Nick. 2011. "Play Globally, Act Locally: The Standardization of Pro Halo 3 Gaming." *International Journal of Gender, Science and Technology* 3 (1). http://genderandset.open.ac.uk/index.php/genderandset/article/view/130/260.

Taylor, T. L. 2006. *Play between Worlds: Exploring Online Game Culture.* Cambridge, MA: MIT Press.

———. 2012. *Raising the Stakes: E-sports and the Professionalization of Computer Gaming.* Cambridge, MA: MIT Press.

Taylor, T. L., and Mikael Jakobsson. 2003. "*The Sopranos* Meets *EverQuest*: Social Networking in Massively Multiplayer Online Games." Paper read at International Digital Arts and Culture Conference, Melbourne, Australia, May 19–23.

Turkle, Sherry. 1997. "Constructions and Reconstructions of Self in Virtual Reality: Playing in the MUDs." In *Culture of the Internet*, edited by Sara Kiesler, 145–155. Mahwah, NJ: Lawrence Erlbaum Associates.

Online Worlds

Lisbeth Klastrup

Since their mainstream breakthrough in the very late 1990s and early 2000s, graphical online worlds, also known as virtual worlds or multiuser virtual environments (MUVEs), have engaged millions of Internet users as sites of entertainment and play and also as sites of learning and intense social interaction. Today, many types of online worlds exist, ranging from small text-based worlds to large, graphically stunning worlds populated by thousands of users. From a theoretical perspective, being in—and exploring—an online world can be understood as a new form of imaginative experience comparable with, but not entirely similar to, being immersed in the fictional universes of novels, films, and tabletop role-playing games (see ROLE-PLAYING GAMES). Online worlds can therefore, from an analytical perspective, be approached as *cultural entertainment systems*.

Definition

Online worlds are networked, persistent, large, and explorable spatial environments, in which multiple users are represented by an in-world entity, typically a virtual body, referred to as a user's avatar or character (see AVATARS). Whether or not the user consciously performs a role, this mode of participation is often referred to as role-playing (see ROLE-PLAYING GAMES). That online worlds are networked means that it is possible for multiple users to be simultaneously present in the world, and that it is possible for them to talk to or text each other in real time. Characteristic of an online world is also the fact that it seems world-like in its spatial extension, whose size prevents users from exploring all of it in one visit. That they are persistent means that these worlds continuously develop over time, independently of the user's computer, and that changes might be implemented while the user is offline. The system usually keeps track of player data on central servers between active sessions, making it possible for a user to have many characters in one world and for a user's character to develop over time (typically by improving skills and looks), but preventing the user from tampering with the character when offline. In addition to meeting other users in the world, users can also meet and interact with computer-controlled characters known as NPCs (nonplayer characters) (see NPC [NONPLAYER CHARACTER]).

Overall, these characteristics make online worlds different from chat rooms, which are also persistent, but not spatially extended, and in which users are often represented by only a "handle" (nickname) or icon, rather than by a visible body. Online worlds also differ from multiplayer games such as *Counter-Strike* and *Battlefield 1942*, which have some spatial extension but can only hold a limited number of players, and whose characters do not evolve but always reappear ("respawn") exactly the same.

History

Richard Bartle and Ron Trubshaw's purely text-based world MUD (an acronym standing originally for multiuser dungeon, later also for multiuser domain) is generally regarded as the first online world. It was inspired by the *Dungeons & Dragons* role-playing system, as well as by early interactive fiction games such as *ADVENT* and *Zork* (see INTERACTIVE FICTION). Interactive fiction games introduced a text-based command system through which the player could guide her character through a fictional world. All locations and objects were described in text, and these games, like the later MUDs, drew on literary techniques and themes as part of the world creation.

MUDs were the first example of game worlds, a concept that soon became immensely popular. Game worlds are generally characterized by the fact that the world or "game" presents the user with a choice of characters of different races (elf, human, dwarf) and skills (combat skills, dexterity, stealth) to play, and with a set of clear and reachable goals to pursue. The overall goal of the players is to take ("level") their character to the highest possible level of the game by fulfilling a number of "quests" or "missions" presented by the system. These quests earn the players some form of "experience points" and enable them to continuously improve their character's skills. In these early worlds, as well as in today's games, skill improvement typically involved combat and the killing of both computer-controlled characters ("monsters" or "mobs") and characters controlled by other players. To control the gaming experience and to make sure that some players did not get unfair advantages, most often the system does not allow players to alter significantly the design of the game world.

While MUDs inspired by Bartle and Trubshaw's MUD system continued to set up and develop all over the world, some people were growing tired of their so-called hack-and-slash style. This led to the development of MOOs (acronym for MUD, object oriented), a type of world often used as a teaching and learning environment, because it allows players to add content, an activity that requires both verbal and technical skills. Participating in MOOs was therefore an excellent way to teach students both writing and programming (see MUDs AND MOOs).

As a type of social world, MOOs differ from game worlds in that they do not have an explicit leveling system, though some form of status system might exist. Rather than collecting experience points, players add content to the worlds by creating new buildings or entire areas, or by associating objects with programmed behaviors. In some social worlds (Second Life), players improve the status of their characters by dressing them up in progressively fancier clothes and skins.

The first commercial multiuser world with a graphical interface and a social orientation, *Habitat*, was launched as a 2D pilot project as early as 1985 and offered several of the options that we expect today from massive multiplayer worlds. It contained as many as twenty thousand discrete locations and many possibilities for in-world interaction. Owing to the cost of developing and maintaining such a world, *Habitat* remained for a long time the only environment of its kind. It wasn't until the late 1990s that graphical worlds of this scale appeared again. Thus, while different types of online worlds were developed throughout the 1980s, it was not before the late 1990s that online worlds broke through as commercially profitable projects. Several graphically advanced game worlds were launched at that time, run by big production or software companies that could afford to develop, host, and maintain worlds large enough to accommodate several thousands of players on the same server at the same time. These game worlds, known as massively multiplayer online role-playing games (MMORPGs) or massive multiplayer online games (MMOGs), as they are now commonly referred to, generally build upon the early MUD technology.

The first massive multiplayer world to introduce a flat-rate monthly subscription scheme was *Meridian 59*, a fantasy-medieval role-playing game, launched in September 1996. It was soon followed by *Ultima Online* (1997), another fantasy world generally considered to be the first really popular MMOG. It was reportedly the first world to reach a subscription base exceeding one hundred thousand accounts. In 1999, *Ultima Online* got tough competition from *EverQuest*, which was the first online world to attract almost half a million players. Other popular MMOGs at the time were *Asheron's Call* (1999–), yet another fantasy-theme world, and *Anarchy Online* (2001–), the first MMOG set in a science-fictional universe. More worlds of this kind followed in the 2000s, notably the fantasy world *World of Warcraft* (*WoW*), based on the Warcraft stand-alone computer games and launched in 2004. *WoW* quickly attracted several million players, and as of 2012, it remains the most popular MMOG in the Western world, boasting more than 10 million player accounts. Other more recent worlds worthy of notice are *Star War Galaxies* (2003–2011), *Matrix Online* (2005–2009), *Lord of the Rings Online* (2007), and *Star Wars: The Old Republic* (2011). All these worlds are built on already-existing fictional universes (see TRANSMEDIAL FICTION), giving fans the chance to participate actively in their favorite story world. The action of these transmedia games is usually set either before or after the time of the narrative that inspired them. Popular characters from the original narrative typically appear as part of a major quest, while familiar settings are used as attractive "tourist venues." The MMOG *City of Heroes* (2005–) is another game that stands out, in that the player can choose to play either a (super)hero or a villain in a dystopic urban setting located in the future. Another variation on the genre emerged in 2012, when *The Secret World* was launched, one of the first MMOGs set in a modern-day, reasonably realistic world, except that this world is infested by vampires.

It is typical of all these worlds that they are regularly expanded through the addition of new locations, characters, and quests. This continuous expansion is an efficient way to persuade long-time users to keep their subscription to the game world. (See Koster [2002] for a more detailed timeline of early online worlds.) MMOGs are also widespread in Asia, with *Lineage II*, *Final Fantasy XI*, and *MapleStory* being some of the most popular games.

Continuing the MOO tradition and following in the footsteps of a world like *Habitat*, the graphical social worlds of the 1990s focused on elements such as building, decorating, and socializing. In 1995, the graphical universe *ActiveWorlds* (originally *AlphaWorld*) was launched, allowing users to buy a world that they could develop from scratch. In 1998, another relatively popular world named *Cybertown* was created, providing users with a small "home" in 2D and with the possibility to take on "jobs," such as neighborhood watcher (see also Kaneva 2007). *Project Entropia* (now *The Entropia Universe*), released in 2003, introduced a micropayment business model, which Second Life, a descendant of social worlds, also uses. Players can buy in-game currency with real money and sell it back at a variable exchange rate. Money can also be earned by such transactions as selling pieces of land or houses to other players. Two of the most popular commercial social worlds so far have been There.com (2003–2010, 2011–) and Second Life (2003). Both worlds have allowed real-world companies and institutions to advertise their products through such strategies as the creation of virtual versions of these products, or the construction of buildings that mimic real-world buildings. A university may, for instance, advertise itself through the creation of a virtual campus. Though these worlds also contain many unrealistic and fantastic buildings and characters, the presence of such "real-world" objects brings them much closer to everyday life than exotic game worlds set in geographically, ontologically, and temporally remote universes.

Online Worlds as "Texts"

As cultural entertainment systems, online worlds can be regarded as digital "texts" (in the broad sense of the term) that both represent and produce meaning through the activity of users and designers. They differ, however, from the fictional universes of other entertainment systems (books, films) in that users are situated *inside* the world and *inhabit* it through their evolving characters, and in that users themselves help produce the "text" when they move through the world, talk to other characters, and, in some cases, add houses and other objects to the world. These features mean that online worlds differ in nature from the worlds of previous forms of fictions. The border between the fictional or virtual realm and the real world is harder to define in MMOGs than in nonparticipatory fiction because it is continuously transgressed (see Castronova 2005; Taylor 2006; Jakobsson 2006). One form of transgression is due to the fact that the characters we meet and interact with are controlled by real people. As we learn to know the real person behind the avatar, the online world becomes closely interwoven with our social offline world (Taylor 2006). Over time we might start regarding other characters as genuine friends rather than as co-players. Another intrusion of the real into the fictional comes from the fact that online worlds are also technical systems. Players may therefore discuss the online world as a real technological artifact, for instance, by commenting on graphics, lag, or hacks. Another area in which the online world interacts with the offline world is the economy (see VIRTUAL ECONOMIES). As previously noted, in the case of worlds such as *Project Entropia*, *World of Warcraft*, or Second Life, the virtual economies of the online worlds are connected to real-world economies by the fact that actual wealth can be created within online worlds. Thus, even though the setting of the world is fantastic and one's character is imaginary, what one does in the online world is in some cases real work, not merely (social) play (on online worlds and real economy, see Castronova 2005; Dibbell 2006; Nardi 2010).

Another important difference is that online worlds are based on software and therefore function both as a stable representation and as a dynamic real-time *simulation* (see SIMULATION). As already mentioned, the online game version of *Lord of the Rings* both represents and simulates a Tolkien-inspired universe. The user can enter it and meet famous (computer-controlled) characters, such as Aragorn and Gandalf, and visit locations known from the books and films, but she can also *live* the life of a Tolkien-inspired character type by exploring the consequences of making different choices with respect to behavior, skills, or quests. Klastrup and Tosca (n.d.) argue that an analysis of a transmedial world like the *Lord of the Rings* universe should include an evaluation of how the *mythos*, *topos*, and *ethos* of the original world are adapted to its MMOG version and how the possibility to inhabit the world as a character affects the world experience.

The simulation of a fictional reality performed in online worlds is no more complete than the representation that takes place in novels or films. Part of the interpretive process consists therefore of evaluating the technological and ideological choices that have been made concerning which interaction possibilities are available, which aspects of life are included and excluded, and which events are sped up and which are represented in an imitation of real time. Ellipsis, defined in literary theory as nonnarrated passages of time (Genette 1972), plays no less a role in online worlds than in films and novels. Traveling vast distances can, for instance, be done in a much shorter time than in the physical world, and eating may take only a few seconds. Moreover, many forms of action that are part of everyday life are excluded from these worlds, as they are from most types of fictional universes, because they are trivial to perform and boring to watch in real time.

The status of online worlds as texts means that they need to be studied from a variety of perspectives in order to be described and understood in their entirety. Klastrup (2003, 2009) has suggested the concept of "worldness" as a starting point for the systematic study of online worlds as worlds. The study of worldness includes not only the examination of the general properties that define online worlds as a particular new *genre of fictional universes* but also the study of the performative range of the characters (what they can do and say), of the possibilities of interaction, and of the aesthetics and social culture of particular worlds (Klastrup 2003, 2008, 2009). The concept of worldness is applicable on two levels that continuously inform each other: we can speak of worldness on a very abstract level as a number of essential features applicable to all worlds and on a specific level as the defining characteristics of an individual world.

MMOG Research

The history of research into online worlds goes back to studies of the early MUDS. Thus, much research in the area already exists, though up to the mid-2000s it took mostly the form of articles or conference papers. Only a few short overviews of research into online worlds have been written (see Klastrup 2003; Consalvo 2011).

Early research papers often deal with online worlds as "virtual communities." Many researchers with a background in social sciences and social psychology (see, e.g., Taylor 2006; Yee 2006; Williams et al. 2009) or in human-computer interaction and computer-supported cooperative work (CSCW) studies (Duchenaut, Moore, and Nickell 2007; Nardi and Harris 2006) have taken an interest in online game worlds. These worlds have also caught the attention of economists (Castronova 2005), politics and law researchers (Lastowka and Hunter 2003), journalists (Dibbell 1999; Ludlow and Wallace 2007), and of course game researchers (Juul 2005; Aarseth 2008; Williams and Smith 2008). In many of these studies, the worlds are approached primarily as social games, rather than as worlds as such. Game worlds have been further discussed from the point of view of design (e.g., Bartle 2003; Mulligan and Patrovsky 2003; Jakobsson 2006).

Researchers with a background in film, media, and cultural studies have also engaged in game world studies (see Mortensen 2002; Krzywinska 2008; Corneliussen and Walker 2008), discussing aspects such as quests (Tronstad 2001) (see QUEST NARRATIVE), the importance of micronarrative structures (Walker 2008), and mythology (Krzywinska 2006). Tosca and Klastrup (2011) have looked at game worlds as examples of transmedial worlds, described as abstract content systems. Larger recent studies have addressed both social worlds and game worlds, offering anthropological accounts of the virtual life of one researcher or of the experience of participating in a particular community (Boelstorff [2008] on Second Life; Pearce [2009] on the Uru Community in There.com and Second Life; Nardi [2010] and Sundén and Svenningson [2011] on *WoW*). Finally, special issues of journals, anthologies, and monographs have presented diverse perspectives on a specific world (Corneliussen and Walker [2008] on *World of Warcraft*; Hayot and Wesp [2009]; or Krzywinska, MacCallum-Stewart, and Parsler [2011] on *LOTRO*).

Journals such as *Journal of Virtual World Research* (2008–) and *Games and Culture* (2008–) regularly publish research on the social and cultural aspects of online worlds.

■ See also IMMERSION, INTERACTIVE NARRATIVE, INTERACTIVITY, ONLINE GAME COMMUNITIES

References and Further Reading

Aarseth, Espen. 2008. "A Hollow World: *World of Warcraft* as Spatial Practice. " In *Digital Culture, Play and Identity: A World of Warcraft Reader*, edited by Hilde Corneliussen and Jill Walker, 111–122. Cambridge, MA: MIT Press.

Bartle, Richard. 2003. *Designing Virtual Worlds*. Indianapolis: New Riders.

Benedikt, Michael, ed. 1990. *Cyberspace: First Steps*. Cambridge, MA: MIT Press.

Boellstorff, Tom. 2008. *Coming of Age in Second Life: An Anthropologist Explores the Virtually Human*. Princeton, NJ: Princeton University Press.

Boellstorff, Tom, Bonnie Nardi, Celia Pearce, and T. L. Taylor. 2012. *Ethnography and Virtual Worlds: A Handbook of Method*. Princeton, NJ: Princeton University Press.

Castronova, Edward. 2005. *Synthetic Worlds: The Business and Culture of Online Games*. Chicago: University of Chicago Press.

Consalvo, Mia. 2011. "MOOs to MMOs: The Internet and Virtual Worlds." In *The Handbook of Internet Studies*, edited by Mia Consalvo and Charles Ess, 326–347. Oxford: Wiley-Blackwell.

Consalvo, Mia, and Charles Ess, eds. 2011. *The Handbook of Internet Studies*. Oxford: Wiley-Blackwell.

Corneliussen, Hilde, and Jill Walker, eds. 2008. *Digital Culture, Play and Identity: A World of Warcraft Reader*. Cambridge, MA: MIT Press.

Dibbell, Julian. 1999. *My Tiny Life: Crime and Passion in a Virtual World*. New York: Holt.

———. 2006. *Play Money: Or, How I Quit My Day Job and Made Millions Trading Virtual Loot*. New York: Basic Books.

Duchenaut, Nicholas, Robert J. Moore, and Eric Nickell. 2007. "Virtual 'Third Places': A Case Study of Sociability in Massively Multiplayer Games." *Computer Supported Cooperative Work* 16:129–166.

Genette, Gérard. 1972. *Narrative Discourse: An Essay in Method*. Translated by Jane Lewin. Ithaca, NY: Cornell University Press.

Hayot, Eric, and Edward Wesp, eds. 2009. *Special Issue—EQ: 10 Years Later*. http://gamestudies.org /0901/articles/hayot_wesp.

Jakobsson, Michael 2006. "Virtual Worlds & Social Interaction Design." PhD diss., Dept. of Informatics, University of Umeå.

Juul, Jesper. 2005. *Half Real: Video Games between Real Rules and Fictional Worlds*. Cambridge, MA: MIT Press.

Kaneva, Nadezhda. 2007. "Narrative Power in Online Game Worlds." In *The Players' Realm: Studies on the Culture of Video Games and Gaming*, edited by J. Patrick Williams and Jonas Heide Smith, 56–73. Jefferson, NC: McFarland.

Klastrup, Lisbeth. 2003. *Towards a Poetics of Virtual Worlds—Multi-user Textuality and the Emergence of Story*. Copenhagen: IT University of Copenhagen.

———. 2008. "What Makes *World of Warcraft* a World? A Note on Death and Dying." In *Digital Culture, Play and Identity: A World of Warcraft Reader*, edited by Hilde Corneliussen and Jill Walker, 143–166. Cambridge, MA: MIT Press.

———. 2009. "The Worldness of EverQuest—Exploring a 21st Century Fiction." In *Game Studies. Special Issue on EverQuest: EverQuest—10 Years Later*, edited by Eric Hayot and Edward Wesp. http://gamestudies.org/0901.

Klastrup, Lisbeth, and Susana Tosca. n.d. "Transmedial Worlds: Rethinking Cyberworld Design." www.itu.dk/people/klastrup/klastruptosca_transworlds.pdf.

Koster, Raph. 2002. "Online World Timeline." www.raphkoster.com/gaming/mudtimeline.shtml.

Krzywinska, Tanya. 2006. "Blood Scythes, Festivals, Quests and Backstories: World Creation and Rhetorics of Myth in *World of Warcraft*." *Games and Culture* 1 (4): 383–396.

————. 2008. "World-Creation and Lore: *World of Warcraft* as Rich Text." In *Digital Culture, Play and Identity: A World of Warcraft Reader*, edited by Hilde Corneliussen and Jill Walker, 123–142. Cambridge, MA: MIT Press.

Krzywinska, Tanya, Esther MacCallum-Stewart, and Justin Parsler, eds. 2011. *Ringbearers: The Lord of the Rings Online as Intertextual Narrative*. Manchester: Manchester University Press.

Lastowka, Greg, and Dan Hunter. 2003. "The Laws of the Virtual Worlds." Research Paper No. 03–10, Institute for Law and Economics. http://papers.ssrn.com/sol3/papers.cfm?abstract _id=402860.

Ludlow, Peter, and Mark Wallace. 2007. *The Second Life Herald: The Virtual Tabloid That Witnessed the Dawn of the Metaverse*. Cambridge, MA: MIT Press.

Morningstar, Chip, and F. R. Farmer. 1990. "The Lessons of Lucasfilm's *Habitat*." First International Conference on Cyberspace (Austin, TX). In *Cyberspace: First Steps*, edited by Michael Benedikt, 273–302. Cambridge, MA: MIT Press.

Mortensen, Torill. 2002. "Playing with Players: Potential Methodologies for MUDs." *Game Studies* 1 (2). www.gamestudies.org/0102/mortensen/.

Mulligan, Jessica, and Bridgette Patrovsky. 2003. *Developing Online Games: An Insider's Guide*. Indianapolis: New Riders.

Nardi, Bonnie. 2010. *My Life as a Night Elf Priest: An Anthropological Account of World of Warcraft*. Ann Arbor: University of Michigan Press.

Nardi, Bonnie, and Justin Harris. 2006. "Strangers and Friends: Collaborative Play in *World of Warcraft*." Paper presented at CSCW'06, November 2006, Banff, Alberta, Canada.

Pearce, Celia. 2009. *Communities of Play: Emergent Cultures in Multiplayer Games and Virtual Worlds*. Cambridge, MA: MIT Press.

Sundén, Jenny, and Malin Svenningson. 2011. *Gender and Sexuality in Online Game Cultures: Passionate Play*. London: Routledge.

Taylor, T. L. 2006. *Play between Worlds: Exploring Online Game Culture*. Cambridge, MA: MIT Press.

Tosca, Susana, and Lisbeth Klastrup. 2011. "When Fans Become Players: *The Lord of the Rings Online* in a Transmedial World Perspective." In *Ringbearers: The Lord of the Rings Online as Intertextual Narrative*, edited by Tanya Krzywinska, Esther MacCallum-Stewart, and Justin Parsler, 46–69. Manchester: Manchester University Press.

Tronstad, Ragnhild. 2001. "Semiotic and Non-Semiotic MUD Performance." COSIGN, Amsterdam. http://citeseerx.ist.psu.edu/viewdoc/download?doi=10.1.1.16.7155&rep=rep1&type=pdf.

Walker Rettberg, Jill. 2008. "Quests in *World of Warcraft*: Deferral and Repetition." In *Digital Culture, Play and Identity: A World of Warcraft Reader*, edited by Hilde Corneliussen and Jill Walker, 167–183. Cambridge, MA: MIT Press.

Williams, Dmitri, Mia Consalvo, Scott Caplan, and Nick Yee. 2009. "Looking for Gender (LFG): Gender Roles and Behaviors among Online Gamers." *Journal of Communication* 59:700–725.

Williams, J. Patrick, and Jonas Heide Smith, eds. 2007. *The Players' Realm: Studies on the Culture of Video Games and Gaming*. Jefferson, NC: McFarland.

Yee, Nick. 2006. "The Demographics, Motivations and Derived Experiences of Users of Massively Multi-User Online Graphical Environments." *Presence: Teleoperators and Virtual Environments* 15:309–329.

··

Ontology (in Games)

Jose Zagal

An ontology is an organized collection of concepts and relationships used to represent and describe knowledge within a domain. Ontologies are a form of knowledge representation that can allow for organizing information, describing observations, and creating shared vocabularies. In the case of games, this could mean a system of classification and organization which included definitions of games, their properties, and relations to each other. For example, Stewart Culin (1907) classified and illustrated the games played by the indigenous peoples of North America by dividing them into two major classes: chance and dexterity, each with its own subcategories. Culin chose to distinguish games according to what players do and what they are played with, but an ontology of games could be organized differently depending on the goals of its developers. For instance, in the early 1980s, veteran game designer Chris Crawford was interested in providing well-defined terms that game designers could use to communicate with each other while drawing attention to the rich and varied forms in which games have manifested. In Crawford's seminal book *The Art of Computer Game Design*, he describes "five major regions of games: board games, card games, athletic games, children's games, and computer games" (1984). The distinctions Crawford chose to establish, together with the definitions he provided for each of these regions, are perhaps dated since ontological distinctions often shift and change as new games are created or technology advances. Recently, video games have been characterized by their technological platform (e.g., 8-bit video game, computer game, mobile), camera perspective (e.g., first-person, third-person, top-down, side-scrolling), intended audience (e.g., casual, hard-core, children), gameplay (e.g., shooter, puzzle, platformer), and more. Over the years, some categories may achieve greater prominence as more games are created and the terminology used to describe them is adopted more broadly. Similarly, new categorizations often emerge and existing ones may cease to be relevant (see GAME GENRES). These kinds of informal ontologies are commonly developed and used by player communities and gaming media to organize information about games (e.g., release dates, reviews) and provide recommendations.

Many scholars have also tackled questions regarding the fundamental nature of games. This work could be considered as ontological in nature. Roger Caillois (2006), for instance, proposed a conceptual model of play that considered four fundamental categories of games: *agon* (competition), *alea* (chance), *mimicry* (simulation), and *ilinx* (vertigo), in addition to a cross-classification along two extremes of a continuum based on how strongly they are governed by rules (see LUDUS AND PAIDIA). Juul's (2005) analysis of the tensions between the formal (e.g., rules) and representational (e.g., fiction, narrative) aspects of video games led him to propose five main types of games: abstract, iconic, incoherent world, coherent world, and staged. Juul's categories are an attempt to capture the ambiguity and importance that the fictive elements can have in helping players establish meaning in and from the games they play.

Developing an ontology for games is no easy task. Play theorist Roger Caillois despaired when he noted the difficulty of "discovering a principle of classification capable of subsuming [all games] under a small number of well-defined categories" (2006, 129). The issue lies partly in the variety of uses of the word *game*, together with the complex relationship that exists between game and play. Thus, most ontological work in games must either rely on an existing definition or provide one of its own. The latter is often the case since defining what a game is helps establish the framework for an ontology, clarify concepts, and explain their relationships. It should be noted that multiple definitions of games (and thus ontologies) are often inconsistent with each other. For some, a puzzle should not be considered a game, while others may limit themselves to games played by more than one person. Differences in definitions are not a problem since the definition of a game is more often a means to an end, rather than an end in and of itself. In this case what matters is the use and meanings that can be made from a particular game ontology.

There are also other kinds of game ontologies. Rather than classifying and organizing games, these ontologies consist of the structural elements or concepts seen in games. Two notable examples in this area are the Gameplay Design Pattern project (Björk and Holopainen 2005) and the Game Ontology Project (GOP; Zagal et al. 2005).

In 2002 Bernd Kreimeier proposed the use of design patterns for games as a way to collect "reusable solutions to solve recurring problems" in game design (Kreimeier 2002). Björk and Holopainen extended and modified this idea by "replacing the problem-solution pair with a causes/consequences pair describing how [a] pattern can occur in a game design and how it can affect the gameplay and player experiences" (Holopainen, Bjork, and Kuittinen 2007). They argued that this change allowed for "a more detailed relationship structure, having five types of relations in contrast to the original parent and child relations," as well as providing support for people designing games and those seeking to analyze them (Holopainen, Bjork, and Kuittinen 2007). The Gameplay Design Pattern project is thus an attempt to codify knowledge of game design such that it can be shared and applied toward the analysis of games and the design of new ones. Each element of knowledge, called in this case a design pattern, consists of a short description, some examples of games that exhibit this pattern, an explanation of how the patterns can be used, and the effects or consequences that pattern can have in a game's overall design. Additionally, the pattern may be connected to other patterns via one or more relationships. For instance, a pattern may be in conflict with another or might instantiate it. The pattern collection is thus a web of interconnected concepts. The original collection of patterns was published in "Patterns in Game Design" (Björk and Holopainen 2005). It has since been extended and is also available online (Björk 2012).

The GOP also seeks to identify the important structural elements of games and the relationships between them (Zagal et al. 2005). The GOP focuses on things that cause, affect, and relate to gameplay. Representational and narrative details such as issues of setting (e.g., medieval castle, spaceship) or genre (e.g., horror, sci-fi) are not included. Each element of knowledge, called in this case an ontology entry, consists of a description of the element, a number of strong and weak examples of games that embody the element, a parent element, potentially one or more child elements, and potentially one or more part elements (elements related by the part-of relation). The GOP acknowledges that there are "fuzzy boundaries" around certain concepts: strong examples describe how an element is concretely reified in specific games, while weak examples describe border cases of games that partially reify an element. For example, the notion of "Lives" as "a measure of opportunities that a player has to succeed in [a] game" (Game Ontology Wiki 2012) exists in *Pac-Man*: whenever a ghost catches Pac-Man, a life is lost with "the number of lives remaining . . . indicated by the existence of a Pac-Man icon in the corner of the screen." In *Legend of Zelda: A Link to the Past*, however, you can only die once (play continues by reloading from an earlier save point). However, if the player happens to possess a captured fairy when he dies, he is instantly resurrected and can continue playing. "In this sense, the fairy in the bottle is functionally equivalent to Link having an extra 'life' stored away" (Game Ontology Wiki 2012). Using weak and strong examples helps define the center of the ontological entry and illustrate the nuances and interpretations an ontological definition may have. The GOP's hierarchical approach provides a natural way of navigating varying levels of abstraction: more concrete instances are "under" those that are broader or more abstract. The GOP is available online in wiki form, allowing anyone to contribute (Zagal and Mateas 2009). The GOP and Gameplay Design Pattern

Project have also proven useful in game education (Holopainen, Bjork, and Kuittinen 2007; Zagal and Bruckman 2010).

Finally, work has also been done in creating ontologies that are detailed and formal enough that they can be used to support automatic game creation. The idea is that "automatic game generators can serve as highly detailed theories of both game structure and game design expressed operationally as a program" (Nelson and Mateas 2007). Although they are often restricted to specific kinds of games (e.g., chess-like games), they can be useful for generating balanced games (Marks and Hom 2007) or automatically analyzing them (Pell 1992). This work often uses techniques developed in artificial intelligence, and the ontologies created are generally described using mathematical formalisms and logic rather than natural language.

■ See also ARTIFICIAL INTELLIGENCE, GAME GENRES, LUDUS AND PAIDIA, NETWORKING, SEMANTIC WEB

References and Further Reading

Björk, Staffan. 2012. "Game Design Patterns 2.0." http://gdp2.tii.se/.

Björk, Staffan, and Jussi Holopainen. 2005. *Patterns in Game Design*. Hingham, MA: Charles River Media.

Caillois, Roger. 2006. "The Definition of Play and the Classification of Games." In *The Game Design Reader*, edited by K. Salen and E. Zimmerman, 122–155. Cambridge, MA: MIT Press.

Crawford, Chris. 1984. *The Art of Computer Game Design*. Berkeley, CA: Osborne / McGraw-Hill.

Culin, Stewart. 1907. "Games of the North American Indians." In *Twenty Fourth Annual Report of the Bureau of American Ethnology, 1902–1903*, 1–840. Washington, DC: Government Printing Office.

Game Ontology Wiki. 2012. "Lives." http://gameontology.com/index.php/Lives.

Holopainen, Jussi, Staffan Bjork, and J. Kuittinen. 2007. "Teaching Gameplay Design Patterns." In *Organizing and Learning through Gaming and Simulation, Proceedings of* ISAGA 2007, edited by I. Mayer and H. Mastik. Delft: Eburon.

Juul, Jesper. 2005. *Half-Real*. Cambridge, MA: MIT Press.

Kreimeier, Bernd. 2002. "The Case for Game Design Patterns." www.gamasutra.com/features /20020313/kreimeier_01.htm.

Marks, Joe, and Vincent Hom. 2007. "Automatic Design of Balanced Board Games." In *Proceedings of the Artficial Intelligence and Interactive Digital Entertainment International Conference* (AI-IDE), 25–30.

Nelson, Mark J., and Michael Mateas. 2007. "Towards Automated Game Design." In *Proceedings of the 10th Congress of the Italian Association for Artificial Intelligence on AI*IA 2007: Artificial Intelligence and Human-Oriented Computing (AI*IA '07)*, edited by Roberto Basili and Maria Teresa Pazienza, 626–637. Berlin: Springer.

Pell, Barney. 1992. "METAGAME in Symmetric Chess-Like Games." In *Heuristic Programming in Artificial Intelligence 3—The Third Computer Olympiad*, edited by H. J. van den Herik and L. V. A. Allis. Chichester, UK: Ellis Horwood.

Zagal, Jose P., and A. P. Bruckman. 2010. "Designing Online Environments for Expert/Novice Collaboration: Wikis to Support Legitimate Peripheral Participation." *Convergence* 16 (4): 451–470.

Zagal, Jose P., and Michael Mateas. 2009. "Game Ontology Project." www.gameontology.com.

Zagal, Jose P., Michael Mateas, Clara Fernandez-Vara, Brian Hochhalter, and Nolan Lichti. 2005. "Towards an Ontological Language for Game Analysis." In *Changing Views: Worlds in Play, Selected Papers of* DIGRA 2005, edited by S. de Castell and J. Jenson, 3–14. Vancouver, Canada.

P

Participatory Culture
Melissa Brough

Participatory cultures have existed in many historical contexts, but the increasingly decentralized access to producing content in the digital media landscape has facilitated their growth, diversification of forms, and impact. *Participatory culture* is now a widely used term in both the academic and the commercial sectors, most often describing the cultural practices that develop around a network's capacity for producing and sharing content. Yet the term has a much longer history and cultural relevance.

In media studies, Henry Jenkins began applying the term *participatory culture* to the study of fan cultures in the late 1980s. However, Jenkins was more explicit about the characteristics of participatory culture in later work, including *Rethinking Media Change: The Aesthetics of Transition* (with David Thorburn), in which he described media consumers participating in "the archiving, annotation, appropriation, transformation, and recirculation of media content. Participatory culture refers to the new style of consumerism that emerges in this [new media] environment" (2004, 286) (see OLD MEDIA/NEW MEDIA). With his colleagues at the Massachusetts Institute of Technology, Jenkins further developed the concept in relation to learning in the digital media era. "For the moment," they write, "let's define participatory culture as one

- With relatively low barriers to artistic expression and civic engagement;
- With strong support for creating and sharing one's creations with others;
- With some type of informal mentorship whereby what is known by the most experienced is passed along to novices;
- Where members believe that their contributions matter; and
- Where members feel some degree of social connection with one another (at the least they care what other people think about what they have created).

Not every member must contribute, but all must believe they are free to contribute when ready and that what they contribute will be appropriately valued." (Jenkins et al. 2006, 7). This definition is now the most widely cited among scholars and researchers of digital culture.

In media studies more broadly, participatory culture has often been used to describe cultural communities and practices that actively (rather than passively) engage with popular culture, such as fan cultures that remix (see REMIX) or produce their own content in response to, or in dialogue with, mass media content. Jenkins's use of the term stems directly from his early work on fandom. His landmark book *Textual Poachers: Television Fans and Participatory Culture* (1992) analyzed fans' active and participatory media consumption as they reconfigured cultural meanings by "poaching" from mass media content, thus challenging traditional notions of the passive audience (see FAN FICTION). While practiced by fandom for decades, Jenkins argues that participatory culture has spread far beyond fan communities because of the intersection of new media technologies, the proliferation of do-it-yourself (DIY) subcultures, and "economic trends favoring the horizontally integrated media conglomerates [that] encourage the flow of images, ideas, and narratives across multiple media channels and demand more active modes of spectatorship" (2006, 136).

Participatory culture is thus characterized by active participants rather than passive audiences, whose practices often blur the line between production and consumption—prompting the use of terms like "produsage" (Bruns 2008). Similar to alternative media, access and ability to produce one's own content are central to participatory culture. An important distinction, however, is that Jenkins's conceptualization of participatory culture includes how audiences may engage with popular culture and mass media content, whereas alternative media defines itself in opposition to these. For decades, alternative and "citizens" media have employed the concept of participatory media production to highlight their democratic, grassroots, and horizontal approaches to production as distinct from—and outside of—commercial mass media (Downing 2000; Rodriguez 2001). In contrast, Jenkins and others have studied how pop culture content is appropriated and remixed for political meaning making, especially among youth; this phenomenon has led to a growing body of work on the relationship between participatory cultures and civic and political engagement (e.g., Bennett, Freelon, and Wells 2010; Brough and Shresthova 2012).

The concept of participatory culture as one in which media audiences are active and produce their own stories in response to commercial media content has a longer history in the field of media studies—and an even longer historical relevance in Western society. For example, the active theater audiences of Elizabethan England were participatory and even performative in their involvement in the theater, cheering or critically commenting on the actors' performance and using the theater as a space for socializing. As such participation became increasingly associated with the lower classes and seen as "overactive" or unruly, it was subjected to critique and control by elites; more passive reception was encouraged and became the norm for theater etiquette by the nineteenth century (Livingstone 2003). Yet by the mid-twentieth century, avant-garde theorists and practitioners of theater such as Bertolt Brecht (from Germany) and Augusto Boal (from Brazil) had revived and reconfigured the notion of participatory theater to explore its potential for developing political consciousness among audience members.

Paula Petrik (1992) analyzed the participatory culture that developed around the toy printing press in the middle of the nineteenth century and the formation of an amateur press association by young people who printed and circulated their own publications about cultural, political, and everyday life. A related example is the culture of amateur radio operators of the early 1900s, as described by Susan Douglas in *Inventing American Broadcasting, 1899–1922* (1989). Prior to the regulation of the airwaves and the radio boom of the 1920s, American boys "dominated the air" using makeshift wireless radio stations in their bedrooms, attics, or garages. In 1912 there were reportedly several hundred thousand such amateur operators in the United States—surpassing the U.S. Navy in number of radio apparatus—who had organized themselves into a nationwide grass-roots network of 122 "wireless clubs" (De Soto in Douglas 1989, 198, 205). Douglas described this as an "active, committed, and participatory audience" that not only was inspired by the pop culture archetype of the time—the boy inventor-hero—but became pop culture icons themselves (1989, 190).

While the amateur operators were primarily white, middle-class boys and men, other histories of participatory culture can be found in African American storytelling and music traditions such as jazz, influenced by the participatory performance practices of African slaves brought to the Americas and gradually incorporated into various forms of American popular culture (Levine 1978; Ogren 1992).

Mary Celeste Kearney traces the history of cultural production among American girls, another group that has historically been marginalized from the media production process. Kearney describes film fandom by girls and young women in the 1920s and 1930s as highly productive, creating "scrapbooks, letters, diary entries, decorations, and stories . . . openly challenging the stereotype of female youth as passive consumers of culture" (2006, 36). Kearney's book *Girls Make Media* shows how this fandom helped to set the stage "for later generations' more direct engagements with media technologies" (2006, 38). This included girls' participation in the punk and hip-hop cultures of the 1970s and beyond, both of which were active spheres of cultural production that frequently blurred the lines between popular culture consumption and resistant practices. Such DIY ethics and practices were also observable across the countercultures of the 1960s and influenced the development of cyberculture (see CYBERSPACE) in the 1980s and 1990s (Turner 2006).

Other precursors to contemporary participatory cultures can be found across many genres, media forms, and social contexts, from science fiction fandom (see FAN FICTION), to comic book and karaoke cultures, to amateur video and feminist vidding. Yet until the twenty-first century and advances in digital culture, discourses and practices of media participation in the United States remained largely on the periphery of (and sometimes in direct opposition to) pop culture. Indeed, from the Industrial Revolution and the rise of mass media industries until the "digital revolution," the American public was encouraged to see itself primarily as consumers—rather than producers—of media and cultural content. This has shifted somewhat with the rise of Web 2.0 and the commercialization of media participation; but it is also clear that participatory culture predates Web 2.0 by decades.

Noteworthy precursors to contemporary theorizing on participatory culture include Bertolt Brecht's "The Radio as an Apparatus of Communication" (1932), in which he calls for radio to be used as a participatory platform for dialogic communication and for listeners to become producers. Around the same time, Walter Benjamin theorized the political dimension of participation in arguing that a work of art should enable viewers to be involved in the process of production ([1934] 1998). Hans Magnus Enzensberger's article "Constituents of a Theory of the Media" in the *New Left Review* (1970) proposed a participatory media model in contrast to an elite-owned capitalist one. Influenced by Marxist critiques, these thinkers opposed the commercial control of the systems of communication and information dissemination.

In Latin America, Paolo Freire (1970), Augusto Boal (1979), and others theorized participatory pedagogy, communication, and theater as challenges to vertical structures of meaning making and power relations. Their work strongly influenced alternative and community media practices, such as *participatory video*, which aims to include traditionally marginalized groups in decision making and problem solving through grassroots video production (Rodriguez 2001). However, they have been far less influential on participatory culture scholarship that theorizes how active engagement with pop culture may be empowering; this work is less inflected with a critique of the power relations that are structurally embedded within mass media systems.

Reviewing theories of participation in the art world, Claire Bishop observes that "three concerns—activation [of the spectator/consumer]; authorship; community—are the most frequently cited motivations for almost all artistic attempts to encourage participation in art since the 1960s" (2006, 12). For example, Guy Debord and the situationist movement in France addressed all three. They critiqued the "spectacle" of capitalist, mass-produced content for being pacifying, divisive, and nondialogical; the situationists saw participation as a way to do away with the audience problem altogether. On the contrary, political philosopher Jacques Rancière "implies that the politics of participation might best lie, not in anti-spectacular stagings of community or in the claim that mere physical activity would correspond to emancipation, but in putting to work the idea that we are all equally capable of inventing our own translation" (Bishop 2006, 16). Rancière's position is similar to Michel de Certeau's on the creative practices of consumption in *The Practice of Everyday Life* ([1984] 2011), which heavily influenced Henry Jenkins's work on fandom.

Indeed, semiotic analysis and cultural studies have long emphasized the role of the spectator/consumer in the production of meaning, shifting the focus somewhat away from the media system and onto the audience. Roland Barthes's seminal essay "The Death of the Author" (1977) suggested that the interpretation of a text could not be fixed by its author; this was followed by theorizing on the polysemy of texts and the active role of audiences in decoding meanings (Hall 1973).

Despite these diverse histories, theories, and practices, in its contemporary use participatory culture is often conflated with online social networks and user-generated content platforms. This conflation appears technologically deterministic when contrasted with participatory cultures and practices that have long made use of, but not been determined by, a variety of tools and technologies; studies of participatory culture focused solely on digital spaces may obfuscate older practices of participatory media such as those outlined above. Nonetheless, it is clear that contemporary participatory cultures increasingly make use of digital media technologies that facilitate access and enable more horizontal modes of production.

A range of critiques about the concept of participatory culture have been elaborated in scholarly work across several disciplines. The most common of these stem from concern about the ways in which the discourse of participation obscures existing relations of power. Summarized briefly here with key citations for further reading, they include whether scholarly and mainstream discourses of participation obfuscate

- the limited range of active participants in the digital mediascape, who are typically white with middle to upper socioeconomic status (e.g., fans and "early adopters"), and the fact that the vast majority of audiences or users do not produce their own media (Bird 2011);
- the socioeconomic, educational, technological, and other barriers to participation (Seiter 2008; Kelty 2012)—what Jenkins et al. (2006) call the participation gap;

- the implicit, normative value judgment that active participation is inherently better than passive consumption (Bird 2011);
- the kinds of participation happening online, and whether or not these are superficial or meaningful—for example, Nico Carpentier argues that community and alternative media have remained "more successful in organizing more deepened forms of participation in the media" than many of the new media platforms that are frequently described as participatory (2011, 520);
- the "free labor" of participants on user-generated content and social networking platforms (see SOCIAL NETWORK SITES [SNSs]), and the extent to which their production of content and data is exploited by commercial interests (Terranova 2000; Andrejevic 2007; Ouellette and Wilson 2011);
- the increasing concentration of media power; and
- the relations of power embedded in networks, platforms, and practices of participation (Kelty 2012; Fuchs 2011).

Christopher Kelty's recent work on participation and power in online platforms suggests one approach to addressing some of these concerns. Kelty emphasizes questions of ownership and decision making in spaces of participatory culture, and "thinking concretely about the practices, tools, ideologies and technologies that make them up . . . the structures of participation, the processes of governance and inclusion, the infrastructure of software, protocols and networks, as well as the rhetoric and expectations of individuals" (2012, 29).

Participatory cultures have a rich past and quite possibly a prolific future and are thus a crucial area for ongoing research. Not only does participatory culture trouble the problematic active/passive audience binary, but it prompts analysis of the factors that facilitate or limit participation; indeed, it compels us to think about the cultures, practices, discourses, infrastructures, and powers that increasingly structure the contemporary relationship between media and society.

■ See also COLLABORATIVE NARRATIVE, NETWORKING, POLITICS AND NEW MEDIA, SOCIAL NETWORK SITES (SNSs), VIRAL AESTHETICS

References and Further Reading

Andrejevic, Mark. 2007. *iSpy: Surveillance and Power in the Interactive Era*. Lawrence: University Press of Kansas.

Barthes, Roland. 1977. "The Death of the Author." In Roland Barthes, *Image-music-text*, edited and translated by Stephen Heath, 142–148. New York: Hill & Wang.

Benjamin, Walter. (1934) 1998. "The Author as Producer." In *Understanding Brecht*, translated by Anna Bostock. London: Verso.

Bennett, W. Lance, Deen Freelon, and Chris Wells. 2010. "Changing Citizen Identity and the Rise of a Participatory Media Culture." In *Handbook of Research on Civic Engagement in Youth*, edited by Lonnie R. Sherrod, Judith Torney-Purta, and Constance A. Flanagan, 393–424. Hoboken, NJ: John Wiley & Sons.

Bird, S. Elizabeth. 2011. "ARE WE ALL PRODUSERS NOW?" *Cultural Studies* 25:4–5, 502–516.

Bishop, Claire. 2006. *Participation*. Cambridge, MA: MIT Press.

Boal, Augusto. 2000. *Theatre of the Oppressed*. London: Pluto Press.

Brecht, Bertolt. 1964. "The Radio as an Apparatus of Communication." In *Brecht on Theatre: The Development of an Aesthetic*, translated and edited by John Willett, 51–53. New York: Hill & Wang.

Brough, Melissa, and Sangita Shresthova. 2012. "Fandom Meets Activism: Rethinking Civic and Political Participation." *Transformative Works and Cultures* 10.

Bruns, Axel. 2008. *Blogs, Wikipedia, Second Life, and Beyond: From Production to Produsage*. New York: Peter Lang.

Carpentier, Nico. 2011. "CONTEXTUALISING AUTHOR-AUDIENCE CONVERGENCES." *Cultural Studies* 25:4–5, 517–533.

De Certeau, Michel. 2011. *The Practice of Everyday Life*. Berkeley: University of California Press.

Douglas, Susan J. 1989. "Popular Culture and Populist Technology: The Amateur Operators, 1906–1912." In *Inventing American Broadcasting, 1899–1922*. Baltimore: Johns Hopkins University Press.

Downing, John D. H. 2000. *Radical Media: Rebellious Communication and Social Movements*. London: Sage.

Enzensberger, Hans Magnus. 1970. "Constituents of a Theory of the Media." *New Left Review* 64:13–36.

Freire, P. 1970. *Pedagogy of the Oppressed*. Translated by Myra Bergman Ramos. New York: Herder and Herder.

Fuchs, Christian. 2011. *Foundations of Critical Media and Information Studies*. New York: Routledge.

Hall, Stuart. 1973. "Encoding and Decoding in the Television Discourse." Paper for the Council of Europe Colloquy on "Training in the Critical Reading of Televisual Language." Centre for Contemporary Cultural Studies.

Jenkins, Henry. 1992. *Textual Poachers: Television Fans and Participatory Culture*. London: Routledge.

———. 2006. *Fans, Bloggers, and Gamers: Exploring Participatory Culture*. New York: New York University Press.

Jenkins, Henry, Ravi Purushotma, Margaret Weigel, Katie Clinton, and Alice J. Robison. 2006. *Confronting the Challenges of Participatory Culture: Media Education for the 21st Century*. Cambridge, MA: MIT Press.

Kearney, Mary Celeste. 2006. *Girls Make Media*. New York: Routledge.

Kelty, Christopher M. 2012. "From Participation to Power." In *The Participatory Cultures Handbook*, edited by Aaron Delwiche and Jennifer Henderso, 22–31. New York: Routledge.

Levine, L.W. 1978. *Black Culture and Black Consciousness: Afro-American Folk Thought from Slavery to Freedom*. New York: Oxford University Press.

Livingstone, Sonia. 2003. "The Changing Nature of Audiences: From the Mass Audience to the Interactive Media User." In *A Companion to Media Studies*, edited by Angharad N. Valdivia, 337–359. Oxford: Blackwell.

Ogren, Kathy J. 1992. *The Jazz Revolution: Twenties America & the Meaning of Jazz*. New York: Oxford University Press.

Ouellette, Laurie, and Julie Wilson. 2011. "WOMEN'S WORK." *Cultural Studies* 25:4–5, 548–565.

Petrik, Paula. 1992. "The Youngest Fourth Estate: The Novelty Toy Printing Press and Adolescence, 1870–1886." In *Small Worlds: Children and Adolescents in America, 1850–1950*, edited by Elliot West and Paula Petrik. Lawrence: University Press of Kansas.

Rodriguez, Clemencia. 2001. *Fissures in the Mediascape: An International Study of Citizens' Media*. Cresskill, NJ: Hampton Press.

Seiter, Ellen. 2008. "Practicing at Home: Computers, Pianos, and Cultural Capital." In *Digital Youth, Innovation, and the Unexpected*, edited by Tara McPherson, 27–52. Cambridge, MA: MIT Press.

Terranova, Tiziana. 2000. "Producing Culture for the Digital Economy." *Social Text* 63 (18): 33–58.

Thorburn, David, and Henry Jenkins. 2004. *Rethinking Media Change: The Aesthetics of Transition*. Cambridge, MA: MIT Press.

Turner, F. 2006. *From Counterculture to Cyberculture: Stewart Brand, the Whole Earth Network, and the Rise of Digital Utopianism*. Chicago: University of Chicago Press.

Performance
Ragnhild Tronstad

Digital media relate to performance and performativity in a variety of ways: they are used to facilitate performance and to communicate performance. They may instigate a performance, or constitute a performance in themselves. They have been used in order to document and to reenact performance art.

The employment of digital media has become increasingly commonplace within the performative arts in recent decades (Lehmann 2006; Dixon 2007). In the same period we have witnessed the proliferation of a number of digital media genres and phenomena such as video games, interactive fiction, online worlds, and Internet discussion forums that, on the one hand, display characteristics and qualities that are themselves inherently performative and, on the other hand, instigate performance and performativity from their users (see INTERACTIVE FICTION, ONLINE WORLDS). Starting out with examples of how digital media are employed within theater, dance, and performance art, and proceeding to address performative aspects of digital media genres outside of the art sphere, this entry focuses on showing the *variety* of digital phenomena that relate, in different ways, to performance. The multiple ways in which they relate indicate in turn the conceptual and theoretical divergence in the field concerning how performance and the performative may be defined.

Within the performative arts, digital performance is a broad category encompassing the use of digital media to supplement physical actors in theater, dance, and performance art, as well as the staging of theater and performance art productions in cyberspace and online worlds, where the physical actors are replaced by virtual representations (e.g., ATHEMOO, Second Front) (see CYBERSPACE, ONLINE WORLDS). Digital performance may also include interactive installations and performances in which the actors are non-human, for example, robots or chatterbots (see CHATTERBOTS).

In mainstream theater, the use of multimedia and visual projection on stage is well established and a frequent feature, for example, in the productions of the renowned Canadian theater director Robert Lepage. In telematic performance, telecommunication technology is used to include the audiovisual representation of performers situated in a different physical location in a performance situation taking place here and now. This way, the performers are able to interact in real time regardless of the physical distance between them.

Within dance and choreography, experiments with digital media as an expressive tool to supplement or enhance the performative language have been particularly widespread. The use of motion capture and other advanced animation technology has made it possible for dancers to interact in real time with visual representations of themselves or others. While the prospects for technologically enhanced dance and performance are indeed exciting, for the spectator, the end result does not always appear as seamless and convincing as one could have hoped for. Thus, practitioners in the field have often been accused of nurturing technology at the expense of the artistic outcome (see, e.g., Dixon 2007; Salter 2010).

In recent years, location-sensitive smartphones have paved the way for entirely new forms of technologically supported theater and performance. Augmented reality (AR) is a technology that makes it possible to add an extra visual layer to the world as seen through the display of a handheld computer or smartphone (see AUGMENTED REALITY). The surroundings may thus be visually "augmented" to include objects, forms, and colors that are not really there, but which nevertheless appear to be there when the surroundings are viewed through the telephone's display. The technology can be used to visualize history, for instance, by visually reconstructing an old building where there is only a ruin today (Liestøl 2011), but also to inscribe other types of objects in the landscape, such as props or characters in a mixed reality game or interactive drama (see INTERACTIVE DRAMA).

In his doctoral work from 2011, media researcher Anders Sundnes Løvlie launched a version of augmented reality that he called *poetically augmented reality*, in the form of an application for Android phones which makes it possible to download and listen to site-specific poetry and prose as one walks around the city (Løvlie 2011). Standing on the square St. Olavs plass in Oslo, for example, one can listen to a snippet from Hamsun's *Hunger*, where the protagonist is situated in the same geographical location, albeit in a different time and under other circumstances. The idea is that this location-specific, real-time fictional framing will provide the user with an augmented, new sensory experience of the familiar surroundings.

The German reality-oriented theater company Rimini Protokoll has, in a similar manner, "augmented" parts of East Berlin with factual material from the city's recent history. In their production *50 kilometres of files* (*50 Aktenkilometer*) (2011) the audience is equipped with a GPS phone and a map of the area around Alexanderplatz, with a number of locations marked on it. On each location one can listen to file contents, interviews, and other documentation of surveillance conducted in this very place by the Stasi during the Cold War. The cityscape is transformed into an audiovisual map of the oppression of earlier times, where the places marked are given an augmented significance in the awareness of the public, as historical sites.

The British performance group Blast Theory is known to engage the public in experimental outdoor productions that blur the line between the physical and the virtual. Often, they mix elements of gaming and performance as in *Can You See Me Now?* (2001) and *Uncle Roy All around You* (2003). In their more recent performative piece *Ulrike and Eamon Compliant* (2009) the audience is invited to a walk through the city while assuming the role of either of the terrorists Ulrike Meinhof or Eamon Collins. Bringing a mobile phone, participants receive several guiding phone calls along the way, offering stories from Ulrike's or Eamon's life, as well as proposing ethical questions for the participants to reflect upon (Benford and Giannachi 2011).

Online reenactment of historical performance art is a particularly intriguing instance of contemporary digital performance, in that it raises a number of questions concerning what a performance is and the nature of the performative. Video game artist Pippin Barr's *The Artist Is Present* (2010) is a simulation of Marina Abramovic's performance with the same name that took place daily at New York's Museum of Modern Art (MoMA) for several months during the spring of 2010. In the game, as in the original performance, the task for the public is to wait in line for a relatively long period of time in order to finally be allowed to sit down on a chair facing the artist. In the video game version, that is of course a pixelated visual representation of the artist. However beautifully crafted and surprisingly expressive this representation admittedly is, one does not get to face the real artist, which is likely considered by most audience members to be the very point and attraction of the original performance—not the experience of waiting in line, which easily becomes the focus of the game.

In the same vein, represented by two computer-generated characters that resemble their own physical appearances, net artists Eva and Franco Mattes (aka 0100101110101101 .ORG) have staged a series of "synthetic performances" in the virtual world Second Life, some of which were reenactments of famous historical performances such as Chris Burden's "Shoot," Vito Acconci's "Seedbed," and Abramovic/Ulay's "Imponderabilia." Interestingly, none of these original performances are possible to reproduce in a virtual realm where there are no actual bodies involved. The reason is that they all confront the audience with bodily reality as such: in the first example, the risk of the artist's bodily damage or death; in the second, publicly being commented upon as the object of the artist's sexual desire and the (implicit) realization of that desire; and in the last example, having to squeeze in between a naked couple.

According to the net artists, the paradox in choosing just these performances for reenactment in a virtual realm was intentional and based in their declared lack of appreciation of the form itself. Allegedly, they wanted to explore why they found performance art uninteresting (Mattes and Mattes 2007a). Art critic and curator Domenico Quaranta calls their polemical approach "fundamentally Oedipal," while also pointing out the inherent paradox in reenacting any kind of performance art, considering the authenticity claims of the form, its emphasis on the unmediated here and now and on "creating unique, unrepeatable, unpredictable events" (2010).

In fact, within performance studies it is not uncommon to consider the mediation of performance to be a contradiction in terms (e.g., Phelan 1993). This position is influenced by the presence ideology that dominated performance art in the 1970s, according to which the performative was understood to be a direct, unmediated, and nonrepresentational act in contrast to the representational acts of theater. Abramovic, for instance, who began her practice as a performance artist in this period, has claimed that performance only makes sense when it is performed live. Her original performances, typically dealing with risks of pain, bodily damage, and death, were based on the principle "no rehearsal, no repetition, no predicted end" (Abramovic quoted in Cypriano 2009).

The uncompromising focus on presence and the present has since lost some of its impact within the performance field. Philip Auslander and Hans Ulrich Gumbrecht are examples of theorists who have rejected the supposed contradiction between mediation and the experience (Auslander 1999) or production (Gumbrecht 2004) of presence. Recently a common interest in performance and performativity by academics and artists from a number of fields has resulted in the appropriation of concepts of performance across disciplinary borders. This development too is likely to have contributed to a less dogmatic understanding of what performance and performativity are, or may be.

A frequent reference in this discourse today is the philosopher J. L. Austin's theory from 1955, where he introduces the performative as a linguistic function characterized by the fact that it "brings into being that which it names" (Bolt 2008). Austin's theory serves to clarify the relationship between performativity and mediation, in that language primarily has a mediating function but can also function performatively: in its mediational function, language represents an object or a situation, whereas in its performative function, it brings an object or a situation into being. Merely representing performance, the digital reenactments of performances discussed above lack the performative force that characterized the originals and made them art historical landmarks.

The legacy of the 1970s performance art, with its focus on bodily realities, has been continued in bio-art and cyborg-art experiments that started to emerge during the 1990s. In subjecting their bodies to technological intervention, it has often been the expressed aim of these artists to amplify the human body functionally or aesthetically. An example of the latter is Orlan, the French artist who had a number of plastic surgery operations publicly performed on her face and body, in which specific facial features or body parts of female icons from the history of art—such as Botticelli's Venus and da Vinci's Mona Lisa—were copied. Tirelessly working toward the functional amplification of his body, the Australian artist Stelarc has extended it with several artificial limbs and functions, such as a third (mechanical) hand and an extra ear, biologically grown and implanted on his left forearm (Stelarc 1980–2012).

This is not to say that performance and performativity necessarily require the presence of a performer's body, or the co-presence between performer(s) and audience, however. On the contrary, within the context of digital media culture it is just as often the absence of bodies that makes the performative bringing-into-being possible (see, e.g., MacKinnon 1995). A well-known example is the infamous net personality Netochka Nezvanova, who raided mailing lists and Usenet newsgroups during the 1990s with cryptic and often aggressive messages composed of ASCII art, code poetry, and a peculiar grammar and spelling, combined with a total disrespect of netiquette rules. Counted as a genius by some and a terrorist by others, her "real" identity has never been revealed, and the confusion as to who is behind her, one person or many, probably only adds to her status as an almost mythical entity (see, e.g., Mieszkowski 2002).

As with the above-mentioned Internet discussion fora, many digital media genres are implicitly performative in that they instigate role-play and performativity from their users (see ROLE-PLAYING GAMES). Examples include multiuser computer games, online worlds, MUDs, and MOOs (see MUDs AND MOOs, ONLINE WORLDS). The social psychologist Sherry Turkle (1995) has argued that multiuser online environments may fill an important function in the identity development of young adolescents, by providing a "safe" playground for testing out on others aspects of one's personality through role-play. In terms of performance, this kind of identity play may be conceptualized using the concept of performativity developed by the philosopher Judith Butler, in her influential theory on the constitution of gender. According to Butler, gender is not a given part of a person's identity, but constructed through performance. By performing gender differently, bounded gender roles may be subversed (Butler 1990).

Single-user computer games and interactive fiction also possess an inherent performativity that instigates performance from their players, but of a different kind than the ones previously discussed (see INTERACTIVE FICTION). Situated on the textual level of the game, it has the rhetorical function of luring the players into effort and commitment by continuously posing challenges that appear to be closely within reach, yet never instantly accessible (see QUEST NARRATIVE).

A majority of the digital media performances discussed in this entry are characterized by a certain "liveness" as they happen in real time. In this, they provide an experience of emergence that theater scholar Erika Fischer-Lichte (2008) has identified as central to the audience experience of (nondigital) theater and performance art, with regard to the interactive feedback loop between performer(s) and audience in the live performance situation (see EMERGENCE). However, it is not unusual that digital media require significantly more from us in terms of contributing to the feedback loop than does traditional theater—often we are not allowed to remain an audience at all but must become performers ourselves (Eskelinen and Tronstad 2003). Playing with digital media, we see that our moves have consequences, but we are seldom able to predict in advance what these consequences will be. In the words of Steve Dixon, codirector of the Digital Performance Archive, "Interactive works encourage a playful, childlike fascination for the pleasure of cause and effect, where a simple hand movement or facial grimace causes a domino effect, a ripple through time and space that directly affects and transforms something outside of oneself" (2007, 598). This tendency to take effect and to transform is the very essence of performativity and performance, both digital and nondigital.

References and Further Reading

ATHEMOO. 1995–? Professional MOO created by Prof. Juli Burk for the Association for Theater in Higher Education (ATHE), University of Hawaii at Manoa.

Auslander, Philip. 1999. *Liveness: Performance in a Mediatized Culture*. London: Routledge.

Austin, J. L. (1955) 1962. *How to Do Things with Words*. Cambridge, MA: Harvard University Press.

Barr, Pippin. 2010. *The Artist Is Present*. Video game. www.pippinbarr.com/games/theartistispresent /TheArtistIsPresent.html.

Benford, Steve, and Gabriella Giannachi. 2011. *Performing Mixed Reality*. Cambridge, MA: MIT Press.

Blast Theory. 1991–present. Artists' group. www.blasttheory.co.uk/bt/index.php.

Bolt, Barbara. 2008. "A Performative Paradigm for the Creative Arts?" *Working Papers in Art and Design* 5. http://sitem.herts.ac.uk/artdes_research/papers/wpades/vol5/bbfull.html.

Butler, Judith. 1990. *Gender Trouble: Feminism and the Subversion of Identity*. New York: Routledge.

Cypriano, Fabio. 2009. "Performance and Reenactment: Analyzing Marina Abramovic's Seven Easy Pieces." http://idanca.net/lang/en-us/2009/09/02/performance-e-reencenacao-uma -analise-de-seven-eeasy-pieces-de-marina-abramovic/12156.

Digital Performance Archive (DPA). www.ahds.ac.uk/performingarts/collections/dpa.htm.

Dixon, Steve. 2007. *Digital Performance: A History of New Media in Theater, Dance, Performance Art, and Installation*. Cambridge, MA: MIT Press.

Eskelinen, Markku, and Ragnhild Tronstad. 2003. "Video Games and Configurative Performances." In *The Video Game Theory Reader*, edited by Mark J. P. Wolf and Bernard Perron, 195–220. New York: Routledge.

Fischer-Lichte, Erika. 2008. *The Transformative Power of Performance: A New Aesthetics*. London: Routledge.

Gumbrecht, Hans Ulrich. 2004. *Production of Presence: What Meaning Cannot Convey*. Stanford, CA: Stanford University Press.

Lehmann, Hans-Thies. 2006. *Postdramatic Theatre*. London: Routledge.

Liestøl, Gunnar. 2011. "Learning through Situated Simulations: Exploring Mobile Augmented Reality." *Research Bulletin* 1. Boulder, CO: EDUCAUSE Center for Applied Research. www.educause .edu/Resources/LearningthroughSituatedSimulat/221754.

Løvlie, Anders Sundnes. 2011. *Textopia: Experiments with Locative Literature*. PhD diss. Oslo: Unipub.

MacKinnon, Richard C. 1995. "Searching for the Leviathan in Usenet." In *Cybersociety*, edited by Steven G. Jones, 112–137. Thousand Oaks, CA: Sage.

Mattes, Eva, and Franco Mattes (aka 010010111010101.ORG). 2007a. "Nothing Is Real, Everything Is Possible." Excerpts from interviews with Eva and Franco Mattesaka 010010111010101.ORG. http://010010111010101.org/press/2007-07_Nothing_is_real.html.

———. 2007b. *Synthetic Performances*. www.010010111010101.org/home/reenactments/index.html.

Mieszkowski, Katharine. 2002. "The Most Feared Woman on the Internet." *Salon Magazine*, March 1. www.salon.com/2002/03/01/netochka/.

Phelan, Peggy. 1993. *Unmarked: The Politics of Performance*. London: Routledge.

Quaranta, Domenico. 2010. "Eva and Franco Mattes aka 010010111010101.ORG *Reenactment of Marina Abramovic and Ulay's Imponderabilia*." www.reakt.org/imponderabilia/index.html.

Rimini Protokoll. 2011. *50 Kilometers of Files (50 Aktenkilometer)*. Radio drama / audio walk. www
.rimini-protokoll.de/website/en/project_4969.html.

Salter, Chris. 2010. *Entangled: Technology and the Transformation of Performance*. Cambridge, MA:
MIT Press.

Second Front. 2006–2009. Performance art group based in the virtual world Second Life. www
.secondfront.org/.

Stelarc. 1980–2012. *Projects*. Prosthetic installations. http://stelarc.org/?catID=20247.

Turkle, Sherry. 1995. *Life on the Screen: Identity in the Age of the Internet*. New York: Simon &
Schuster.

....

Platform

Nick Montfort and Ian Bogost

The term *platform* is used in digital media and textuality to describe the
material and formal construction of a system that enables developers to write applications and users to run them. Platforms of this sort, known as computational platforms,
can be hardware systems such as the Commodore 64, software environments such as
Adobe Flash, or combinations of the two like Apple iDevices and the iOS operating system. One builds on a computational platform by producing symbolic instructions that
tell the platform how to behave and respond. Marc Andreessen (2007) explains that to
determine whether or not something is truly a platform, one should ask, "Can it be programmed?" A true computational platform may be specialized in certain ways, but will
be capable of general-purpose computation.

There are other uses of the term *platform* which relate to digital media. For example, some speak of the Canon EOS platform in photography, indicating cameras that
use the same lenses and accessories. *Platform* can also refer to a communication system, a social networking service, or a file format and player device for digital media that
is not capable of general computation. The term is regularly used in its central computational sense, however, by software developers of all sorts (Bogost and Montfort 2009),
along with those working in industry (Evans, Hagiu, and Schmalensee 2006) and in
organizations that deal with digital media development. It is the awareness of platform
in this sense that has led to platform studies, a new engagement with computational
systems and with how they relate to creativity (Bogost and Montfort 2007; see also
http://platformstudies.com).

Every creator must create in some particular form. A visual artist must work with
particular materials such as oil, bronze, or marble. Bookmaking can be done in several
different formats, including hand-created poetry, chapbooks, and cheaply produced
mass-market paperbacks. Photographers can also work in different formats, for example,
the 135 film format we most commonly associate with 35 mm film cameras and the 8×10
film plate, which is used with large-view cameras. While many different kinds of work
can be done in each of them, both material conditions and creative traditions help establish standards and conventions for these formats. For example, a mass-market paperback
is made cheaply and at low quality to be able to sell long novels on thin paper to a large
audience at limited cost. Understanding the qualities of different media and formats has
been essential to both the practice and study of the arts. Platform studies extends these
sorts of insights into digital art, literature, and media, by considering the importance of
a work's platform.

The creator of a computational work must take into account the hardware and/or software features of that platform in conceiving, planning, structuring, and executing the creative work. Likewise, the user of a computational work must have access to the platform in question and know how to operate it. The particular features of platform constrain and enable the development of software while also influencing how it is accessed—who is allowed to run it, and how users interact with software in physical space. The appearance that is characteristic of particular game platforms can, for instance, influence the aesthetics of future games, sometimes very directly (Camper 2009) and sometimes obliquely.

Five levels of analysis help to situate the study of platforms in creative computing (Montfort and Bogost 2009). All of these levels are permeated by cultural factors, which should be given serious consideration wherever a study is positioned, rather than being treated as merely icing on top.

Reception/operation is the level that includes the various existing theories of how digital media are understood, along with empirical studies of the behavior of readers, players, and other interactors. While only interactive media can be programmed and operated, all media are meant to be received and understood. This means that on this level, insights from other disciplines can often be usefully adapted to digital media.

Interface studies include the whole discipline of human-computer interface along with studies of user interface done by humanists, including film theorists and art historians. The concept of remediation (Bolter and Grusin 1999) concerns itself with interface, although this particular approach also deals with reception and operation (see RE-MEDIATION). It is not unusual for studies to span several levels, even when they focus on one specific level.

Form/function is the main concern of cybertext studies and of much of the work in game studies and ludology. Narratology, used for decades to understand literature and cinema, deals with form and function and has now been profitably applied to digital media (see GAMES AS STORIES, NARRATIVITY).

Code is a level that has only recently been explored by new media scholars (see CODE). Among the emergent fields of investigation concerned with code are software studies and code aesthetics (see CODE AESTHETICS, SOFTWARE STUDIES). Software engineering is a related field that concerns itself with the code level in an effort to improve productivity and the maintenance of systems.

Platform is that for which code is written. Platform studies is in some ways similar to the study of computing systems and computer architecture. A humanistic perspective on platforms will study the relations between the more or less fixed ideas that are embodied in their design and the many types of creative software development that have been done, often over a long period of time, on those platforms.

Some of the clearest and most prominent examples of platforms are video game consoles, which are packaged and sold to the public and explicitly advertised as platforms. Any console for which games can be developed should be regarded as a computational platform. This definition does not include the original Home Pong by Atari (see GAME HISTORY), because it was a single-purpose device, but it covers the Atari Video Computer System, aka Atari 2600 (Montfort and Bogost 2009), the Fairchild Channel F (Whalen 2012), the Nintendo Entertainment System, the Nintendo Game Boy, the Nintendo Wii (Jones and Thiruvathukal 2012), and consoles of the Xbox and Playstation series.

Game systems are not the only platforms that support creative computing, however. All computer and operating systems are platforms, including early home systems such as the Apple II and Amiga (Maher 2012); later systems running Mac OS X, Windows, and GNU/Linux; and unique early computers such as the Manchester Mark I.

In addition to specialized hardware platforms, there are also software platforms that serve as tools for everyday computer users. Flash and Java are examples of such systems. They run on different platforms and provide a stable, consistent platform of their own upon which a great deal of significant software development has been done. Of particular interest to scholars of digital textuality (see ELECTRONIC LITERATURE) are specialized platforms such as HyperCard and the Infocom Z-Machine, which are capable of general computation but well adapted for literary use: multimedia hypertext for the former, interactive fiction for the latter (see INTERACTIVE FICTION).

■ See also ALGORITHM, CHARACTERISTICS OF DIGITAL MEDIA, HISTORY OF COMPUTERS

References and Further Reading

Andreessen, Marc. 2007. "The Three Kinds of Platforms You Meet on the Internet." Pmarca.Com 7. http://blog.pmarca.com/2007/09/the-three-kinds.html.

Bogost, Ian, and Nick Montfort. 2007. "New Media as Material Constraint: An Introduction to Platform Studies." Paper presented at 1st International HASTAC Conference, Durham, NC.

———. 2009. "Platform Studies: Frequently Questioned Answers." Paper presented at Digital Arts and Culture Conference, Irvine, CA, December 12–15. www.escholarship.org/uc/item /01r0k9br.

Bolter, Jay David, and Richard Grusin. 1999. *Remediation: Understanding New Media*. Cambridge, MA: MIT Press.

Camper, Brett. 2009. "Fake Bit: Imitation and Limitation." Paper presented at Digital Arts and Culture Conference, Irvine, CA, December 12–15. http://escholarship.org/uc/item/3s67474h.

Evans, David S., Andrei Hagiu, and Richard Schmalensee. 2006. *Invisible Engines: How Software Platforms Drive Innovation and Transform Industries*. Cambridge, MA: MIT Press.

Jones, Steven E., and George K. Thiruvathukal. 2012. *Codename Revolution: The Nintendo Wii Platform*. Cambridge, MA: MIT Press.

Maher, Jimmy. 2012. *The Future Was Here: Commodore Amiga*. Cambridge, MA: MIT Press.

Montfort, Nick, and Ian Bogost. 2009. *Racing the Beam: The Atari Video Computer System*. Cambridge, MA: MIT Press.

Whalen, Zach. 2012. "Channel F for Forgotten: The Fairchild Video Entertainment System." In *Before the Crash: Early Video Game History*, edited by Mark J. P. Wolf, 60–80. Detroit: Wayne State University Press.

Plot Types and Interactivity
Marie-Laure Ryan

The design of interactive narratives, more particularly of video games, begins with the choice of a narrative structure that gives the player something to do (see INTERACTIVE NARRATIVE). The plot types available in oral and written literature present various degrees of compatibility with active user involvement.

Epic Plot

The narrative structure typical of epic poetry is the most easily adaptable to the demands of interactivity. The epic plot is focused on the exploits of a solitary hero who shows his valor in battles against human enemies, monsters, or the powers of nature. Since every feat adds to the glory of the hero, the story can be endlessly expanded by adding new feats and new episodes (De Jong 2005). Epic narratives focus on physical actions, and the human relations that motivate the hero to act remain fairly simple. Throughout the plot of the folktales described by Vladimir Propp ([1928] 1968), for instance, the hero is the faithful servant of the dispatcher; he remains opposed to the villain until the end (there is no reconciliation); nobody changes sides during the fight between the two factions; and if the hero is rewarded with the hand of a princess, they live happily ever after (see QUEST NARRATIVE).

All these features make it very easy to adapt epic structures to the demands of games: we find it in shooters, in adventure games, and in the quests of multiplayer online worlds (see ONLINE WORLDS). The most common mode of interaction in computer games is through the keyboard, or through game pads. The range of actions that can be symbolically performed in real time through these controls is limited to the physical kind: players can move the body of their avatar, inspect or pick up objects by clicking on them, and trigger the behaviors encoded in these objects, such as firing weapons (see AVATARS). The archetypal narrative pattern of the quest makes the most out of these limitations. The deeds of the hero are relatively easy to simulate through the game controls; the basic sequence of accomplishment-reward can be repeated endlessly, allowing the player to reach higher and higher levels in the game; and the solitary nature of the hero's quest makes interpersonal relations dispensable. Another reason for the popularity of the epic pattern in video games lies in the graphic capabilities of computers. Epic narratives are basically travel stories that recount the adventures of the hero in a world full of danger. The ability of 3D graphic engines to adapt the display to the position of the player's virtual body makes them very efficient at simulating movement as an embodied experience (see VIRTUAL BODIES), thereby creating spatial immersion (see IMMERSION).

Mystery Plot

Another type of narrative easily implemented in an interactive environment is the epistemic plot—a plot driven by the desire to know. Its standard representative is the mystery story. The trademark of the epistemic plot is the superposition of two stories: one constituted by the events that took place in the past, and the other by the investigation that leads to their discovery. The intellectual appeal of the mystery story lies in challenging the reader to find the solution before it is given out by the narrative; in order to do so, the reader needs to sort out the clues from accidental facts, and to submit these clues to logical operations of deduction and induction.

Interactive implementations of the epistemic plot cast the player in the well-defined role of detective, thereby combining an authorially predefined story—the events being investigated—with a variable story created in real time by the actions of the player. These games take advantage of the visual resources of digital systems by sending the player on a search for clues disseminated throughout the story world. The activity of the detective can be easily simulated through the types of action executable by game controls: moving across the world, picking objects, examining them for clues, finding documents, and interrogating nonplayer characters (NPCs), ideally through a language-understanding system that works in real time but, more efficiently, through a menu of canned questions (see DIALOGUE SYSTEMS). When participation takes the form of spatial exploration (see SPATIALITY OF DIGITAL MEDIA) and leads to unexpected discoveries, its motivation is curiosity, and its reward is surprise. These two effects play a major role in creating temporal immersion.

Dramatic Plot

A much more problematic narrative structure for the designer of interactive narratives is the dramatic plot, which Aristotle, in his *Poetics*, opposes to the epic plot. The focus of the dramatic plot is not the adventures of a solitary hero, but the evolution of a network of human relations. In a dramatic plot, the action is mental rather than physical: most of the events consist of acts of verbal communication between the characters; and when the characters perform physical actions, the significance of these actions resides in what they reveal about the mind of the agent and in how they affect interpersonal relations. Another difference from epic plots is that dramatic narratives present a closed pattern of exposition, complication, crisis, and resolution (corresponding roughly to the three points of the Freytag triangle) which defies expansion. The focus on interpersonal relations of the dramatic plot describes both the tragic and the comic genre.

The interactive implementation of the dramatic plot raises countless problems (see INTERACTIVE DRAMA). What will be the goals of the player, and what kind of algorithm will it take to make these goals interact with the goals of NPCs? In an epic and epistemic plot all the efforts of the player are geared toward the accomplishment of a mission. But in a dramatic plot with evolving interpersonal relations, the goals of characters evolve together with their relations, and they must be constantly redefined. This requires an ability to simulate human reasoning, which makes enormous, if not unrealistic, demands on the artificial intelligence that runs the application.

The principal appeal of the dramatic plot resides in the emotional impact of the characters on the audience. Aristotle defined this impact as *catharsis*, arguing that the effect of tragedy should be purification through terror and pity. Creating characters who inspire emotions, whether positive or negative, is currently a major goal of game designers, because it would diversify the audience of their products. Video games have managed to insert dramatic moments in a globally epic structure by creating ethical dilemmas: for instance, by asking players to kill an NPC who has helped them in the past (Nitsche 2008). But so far the only working specimen of a dramatic structure is *Façade* by Michael Mateas and Andrew Stern, a noncommercial "playable story" (rather than game proper) in which the user plays the role of a guest who unintentionally triggers a fight between Grace and Trip, the couple he or she is visiting, thereby revealing deep cracks in the façade of their seemingly happy marriage. The dramatic character of *Façade* resides not only in its Aristotelian structure of exposition, crisis, and dénouement, but also in the intense feelings of contempt that the player develops toward Grace and Trip.

When the problem of creating emotion-inducing characters is resolved, the question will remain of what kind of role should be given to the player, in order to make the visit to the story world a truly pleasurable experience. Would people enjoy emulating the heroes of tragedy and comedy by turning themselves into objects of pity or laughter? The safest role for the player is that of a marginally involved observer or confidante whose interventions serve mainly as a stimulant that affects the behavior of the NPCs and trigger changes in their relations. Jesper Juul has suggested that time may be ripe for games in which the player's character suffers a truly tragic fate. But a genuine sense of the tragic will not be created by merely giving players disturbing tasks such as committing suicide (Juul 2012), because insofar as it takes problem-solving skills to reach this goal, success in the game will most likely convey a sense of achievement that negates the tragic character of the act.

Soap Opera

As a type of plot, soap operas owe their existence to the unlimited time resources of television. They can run for decades, and like life itself, they have no beginning or end, except for the cancellation of the show due to shrinking audiences. As a serial form, soap operas are written on the fly, a few episodes ahead of the current show, in contrast to most films, novels, and games, which are only presented to the public once they have been fully conceived. Soap operas follow the entangled destinies of a large number of characters, alternating between parallel plot lines that correspond to mostly amorous relations. When the relation ends for good, so does the plot line, but new subplots are continually created as characters find different partners, new characters are brought in, and individual destinies cross each other in ever new pairings.

This pattern has been successfully simulated in the game franchise *The Sims* (see INTERACTIVE NARRATIVE for more details on the functioning of the game). *The Sims* is a god game in which players create and control several characters (typically, a family) from a perspective external to the story world. They may also adopt characters created by the system, together with their backstory. Each character is defined by individual personality traits, aspirations, goals, likes and dislikes, and affective relations to other characters. All characters, however, have the same basic repertory of actions. The game also contains a number of NPCs who drop into the life of the player's characters and interact with them in ways specified by the system. The vast number of characters, the types of action of which they are capable, the possibility for the user to switch control from one character to another, and the fact that the game never ends predispose *The Sims* to generating massively parallel stories driven by love affairs and social relations. Many of these soaps can be found on fan fiction websites (see FAN FICTION). While in many other games the plot remains subordinated to gameplay (this is particularly the case with epic and epistemic games), in *The Sims* the creation of stories becomes the reason to play (see GAMEPLAY). The narrative appeal of *The Sims* lies in the game's ability to offer a compromise between the situation of an author who is in full control of the plot and that of a reader who follows a predefined plot line. In *The Sims* players choose the behaviors of their characters, but they must deal with the constraints of the system and with the unpredictable events that destiny (=the system) throws in the life of their characters. It is this combination of relative freedom of action and exposure to the randomness of fate, as well as to the will of others, which makes *The Sims*' soap operas into a believable simulation of life.

■ See also GAME GENRES, GAMES AS ART/LITERATURE, GAMES AS STORIES, NARRATIVITY

References and Further Reading

Aristotle. 1996. *Poetics*. Translated and introduction by Malcolm Heath. London: Penguin.

De Jong, Irene. 2005. "Epic." In *The Routledge Encyclopedia of Narrative Theory*, edited by David Herman, Marie-Laure Ryan, and Manfred Jahn, 138–140. London: Routledge.

Jenkins, Henry. 2004. "Game Design as Narrative Architecture." In *First Person: New Media as Story, Performance, and Game*, edited by Noah Wardrip-Fruin and Pat Harrigan, 118–130. Cambridge, MA: MIT Press.

Juul, Jesper. 2012. *The Art of Failure: On the Pain of Playing Video Games.* Cambridge, MA: MIT Press.

Mateas, Michael, and Andrew Stern. *Façade.* Interactive drama. www.interactivestory.net/download/.

Nitsche, Michael. 2008. *Video Game Spaces: Image, Play and Structure in 3D Worlds.* Cambridge, MA: MIT Press.

Propp, Vladimir. (1928) 1968. *Morphology of the Folk Tale.* Translated by L. Scott. Austin: University of Texas Press.

Ryan, Marie-Laure. 2009. "From Narrative Games to Playable Stories: Towards a Poetics of Interactive Narrative." *Storyworlds: A Journal of Narrative Studies* 1:56–75.

The Sims 3. 2010. Computer game. Designed by Will Wright. Maxis.

Szilas, Nicolas, and Jean-Hugues Réty, eds. 2006. *Création de récits pour les fictions interactive: simulation et realisation.* Paris: Lavoisier.

●●

Politics and New Media
Joss Hands

The topic of new media and politics ranges over such a potentially large area that it is necessary to talk of distinct, if interlinked, domains. This entry discusses four such domains: actually existing representative political democracy, activist and direct democracy, the politics of new media technologies themselves, and the politics of everyday life.

Likewise any definition of new media and politics must include some specification of the use of the two terms. Firstly, with regards to "new media," the "new" is immediately suspect given that it has deep roots and decays so quickly, but for the purposes of this entry we can understand new media as those devices, systems, and processes of communication and mediation which cluster around the key characteristics of digital computers and distributed digital networks, primarily the Internet (see CHARACTERISTICS OF DIGITAL MEDIA, NETWORKING).

Politics also commands a varied set of classifications, but we can define it pragmatically as the organization, distribution, and expression of power in any particular society or group. Within this definition we can see politics occupying a wide range of subcategories, but a broad distinction can be made between formal politics and governance and the personal or micropolitics of everyday life. The extent to which the "micro" and "macro" are politically distinct is a matter of controversy, but it is historically inscribed nevertheless. The division of politics, as a public life (the life of the polis), from private life in ancient Greece is often seen as the roots of such a division (Arendt 1958) and also a source of top-down, or "constituted," power, formed in the separation of the domain of the "vita activa," instigating an associated conceptual hierarchy between classes, genders, and races which persists to this day.

Network Politics

Political power is increasingly played out in, and expressed through, digital network technologies, in what can be described as a network politics that revolves around struggles over the uses, protocols, and affordances of new media. Consider the central questions of network politics: what affordances are offered by new media that previous media could not provide, and how are they being used? One significant characteristic of new media is the combination of the flexibility of digital microprocessors with networked communications. The Internet's multidirectional, open, and distributed structure offers the capacity to disseminate messages to large numbers of people outside of the control of traditional media outlets (see Chomsky and Herman's [1994] propaganda model), such as newspapers and television stations, and to facilitate multiple person-to-person interactions and coordination (see SOCIAL NETWORK SITES [SNSs]). As such it can be seen to provide the possibility of undermining traditional political institutions, hierarchies, and power relations.

Actually Existing Democracy

With regard to formal (or actually existing) democratic politics, new media's area of impact comes with the emergence of "e-democracy." Here issues of voting, representation, deliberation, and the public sphere are key, as new media have often been offered as a solution to perceived problems in areas such as voter turnout and citizen participation. Al Gore's vision of the "information superhighway" entailed the hope that the scalability of new media would lead to a mass "electronic town hall" to offset voter exclusion and apathy. But, as John Street (1997) has observed, such claims often cover up more fundamental problems with actually existing democracies which limit participation, such as disparities of wealth, access to education, and fundamental problems with voting systems that distort representation and create "elected dictatorships."

Here the issue of new media as providing the means for a new, more inclusive and effective public sphere becomes paramount, given its capacity for expanded interactions between interlocutors, which can readily include matters of public interest. Exploring whether Jürgen Habermas's (1989, 1996) conditions for an active public sphere could be met, Lincoln Dahlberg (2005) argues that while the Internet certainly expands the opportunities for engaging in forms of public reason, Habermas's conditions may be too stringent to be fully realized online. Yochai Benkler (2007) has posited the existence of a "networked public" that is replacing the physical spaces of meeting with newer aggregations of online commons, following on from commentators such as Howard Rheingold (2000) who have championed the notion of the "virtual community" as a real and meaningful form of socialization. Joss Hands (2011) argues that the concept of publicness in network societies may need to be rethought as the idea of a "public" becomes less meaningful in fast and fluid modes of interaction, suggesting the form of the "quasi-autonomous recognition network" as an alternative.

Activism and Direct Democracy

Beyond the confines of actually existing democracy, new media can also be understood as working toward more direct ends. There has been an increasing amount of direct action supported and augmented by new media. The most notable early manifestation of this was the use of the Internet by the Zapatistas, an indigenous insurgent movement in Chiapas, Mexico, in the early 1990s. The impact of this movement has been attributed (Olesen 2005) to a community of supporters who leveraged the affordances of the Internet to publicize the cause of the Zapatistas and to help organize networks of solidarity and support, not least of whom was the academic and activist Harry Cleaver, who set up a website and mailing list to aggregate support networks, and who has also written on the topic (Cleaver 1998).

In that regard the Internet provides a similar advantage as posited in the reformulation of the public sphere, but the difference here is the collective decision to act outside of systems of formal representation and to undertake direct action. In 2009/2010 a number of uprisings took place around the globe, including what has become known as the "Arab Spring" and the global "occupy movement," as well as student rebellions in the United Kingdom and elsewhere. These seemingly disparate movements appeared to have in common that they were augmented by digital networked computing, and in particular the rise of "social media." Social media afforded the key to these movements' rapid growth as they provide easy-to-use platforms, built on the Internet and World Wide Web, that can be readily used for dissent, the organization of protests, and acts of mass resistance that can easily "scale." The extent to which this was true of the Arab Spring was a source of much debate both in the mainstream media and within social media itself. One of the notable examples was a debate between media commentators Clay Shirky and Evgeny Morozov (Shirky 2009).

In some respects the character of these events—lots of horizontal coordination, loose affiliations, on-the-fly communication using distributed network communications via mobile devices—reflects a new social formation that echoes the evolution of the political form of "multitude." "Multitude" is a concept that comes from the Italian tradition of autonomist Marxism, in the work of Paulo Virno and Antonio Negri, among others, and gained prominence with the publication of the series of books *Empire* (2000), *Multitude* (2004), and *Commonwealth* (2009), in which Negri and cowriter Michael Hardt attempt to build a framework for understanding political sovereignty and democracy in a post-Fordist economy and "post-political" era. They argue for a democracy of the multitude that moves beyond collectives and individuals toward a coming together of networked "singularities" in intensive cooperation, in a quest for a new form of commons suitable to the digital age.

Despite the enthusiasm of "net optimists," there is a strain of thought that suggests that the capacity of new media to act as a catalyst for liberation is more limited. Jodi Dean (2009) argues that the Internet is not, nor could it be, a public sphere, or anything like it, in the context of what she refers to as "communicative capitalism." In this form of capitalism, characterized by the circulations of data through global networks, messages are never "received" but merely endlessly circulate, never influencing or impacting on formal democratic power. In this way politicians are able to pay lip service to democracy and free speech, while never actually allowing the circulating discourses to take root. She uses the example of the huge anti–Iraq War protests on February 15, 2003, as just such an instance.

The Politics of New Media Technology

This moves us into the realm of the politics of new media itself. Theorists such as Alex Galloway, Eugene Thacker, and Greg Elmer have all argued in various ways that digital media are as much oriented to forms of control as liberation. Drawing from Gilles Deleuze's influential essay "Postscript on Control Societies" (1995), Galloway (2004) argues that the protocols of the Internet and the World Wide Web actually create forms of algorithmic control, directing and containing the use of the web in its very fabric, and as such proscribing or instilling action. This debate also extends into issues of intrusion and surveillance, spying on e-mails, Google searches, and other forms of data mining. Greg Elmer (2004) has argued that we have moved into an era of "profiling machines," in which the use of mass compiled data can allow for preemptive action to curtail political resistance and opposition before it has even happened.

Yet here we can also argue for the potential of tactical media use in political resistance, often involving the use of new media in ways unintended by its designers and producers. Such politically motivated hacking or "hacktivism" was pioneered by Critical Art Ensemble (CAE) in their support of the Zapatistas with their creation of "floodnet," which was used to overload and slow down or crash particular websites (Jordan 2002, 121) (see HACKER). The rise of hacktivism, according to Tim Jordan, reconfigured hacking "within a broader political landscape" (2002, 121). CAE talks about a "nomadic resistance" as its orientation against "nomadic power" (1996, 3). One aligned political strategy, which is thought possible by Galloway and Thacker (2007), is one of action as a practice of "non-existence." This has been described as a way to escape the control mechanisms entailed in the categorization and organization in databases and associated techniques of micromanagement (see DATABASE). Seb Franklin argues that this is a way of becoming "nonexistent culturally, impossible to classify in terms of the user-programmer distinction that is definitive of identity in the digital age" (2009). This kind of "tactical" media use shifts the aim of politics away from traditional revolutionary aims into a "micropolitics of disruption, intervention, and education" (Raley 2009, 1).

New Media and the Politics of Everyday Life

Thus, new media have also long become a contested site in areas that can be referred to as identity politics, micropolitics, or the politics of everyday life (see IDENTITY). Early notions that the abstract geometry of cyberspace would allow an escape from binary structures and the concrete constraints of power (Haraway 1991) have been challenged by a recognition of the integration of cyberspace and everyday life. This is instanced in the development of a cluster of "new materialist" theory (Coole and Frost 2010) and in the work of network theorists such as Manuel Castells (2009). Such a perspective is also visible in art practice and activism, for example, with groups such as the "subRosa" collective—"a reproducible cyberfeminist cell of cultural researchers committed to combining art, activism, and gender politics to explore and critique the effects of the intersections of the new information and biotechnologies on women's bodies, lives, and work" (cyberfeminism.net) (see CYBERFEMINISM). In this practice we can see the employment of a form of cultural politics as a tactic of micropolitical activism. Other such projects include "Angry Women" by Annie Abrahams, which explores digital video calling as networked performance art, integrating concrete and virtual spaces with expressions of rage, empathy, affect, and solidarity. Such engaged cultural politics in the field of new media art has been the focus of the Furtherfield Collective since its foundation in 1997.

We can also question the extent to which the shift to a purely "nomadic resistance" remains in the wake of the Arab Spring. The fundamental importance of space in political power has again become clear in the occupations of Tahrir Square and the subsequent occupation movement around the world. The foregoing examples display a process in which the struggle over the "production of space" (Lefebvre 1991) is again central to political struggle.

So it is that as devices have become cheaper and we have moved into an era of mobile computing and networking, the ubiquity of new media has meant political struggle now crossing the borderline between traditional notions of private and public, the virtual and the concrete, and perhaps also working to erase the hierarchies traditionally found therein.

References and Further Reading

Arendt, Hannah. 1958. *The Human Condition*. Chicago: University of Chicago Press.

Benkler, Yochai. 2007. *The Wealth of Networks*. New Haven, CT: Yale University Press.

Castells, Manuel. 2009. *Communication Power*. Oxford: Oxford University Press.

Chomsky, Noam, and Edward S. Herman. 1994. *Manufacturing Consent: The Political Economy of the Mass Media*. London: Vintage.

Cleaver, Harry. 1998. "The Zapatista Effect: The Internet and the Rise of an Alternative Political Fabric." *Journal of International Affairs* 51 (2): 621–640.

Coole, Diana, and Samantha Frost. 2010. *New Materialisms: Ontology, Agency, and Politics*. Durham, NC: Duke University Press.

Critical Art Ensemble. 1996. *Electronic Civil Disobedience*. New York: Autonomedia.

Dahlberg, Lincoln. 2005. "The Habermasian Public Sphere: Taking Difference Seriously." *Theory and Society* 34 (2): 111–136.

Dean, Jodi. 2009. *Democracy and Other Neoliberal Fantasies*. Durham, NC: Duke University Press.

Deleuze, Gilles. 1995. *Negotiations*. Translated by Martin Joughin. New York: Columbia University Press.

Elmer, Greg. 2004. *Profiling Machines*. Cambridge, MA: MIT Press.

Franklin, Seb. 2009. "On Game Art, Circuit Bending and Speedrunning as Counter-Practice: 'Hard' and 'Soft' Nonexistence." *CTheory*. www.ctheory.net/articles.aspx?id=609.

Galloway, Alex. 2004. *Protocol*. Cambridge, MA: MIT Press.

Galloway, Alex, and Thacker, Eugene. 2007. *The Exploit: A Theory of Networks*. Minneapolis: Minnesota University Press.

Habermas, Jürgen. 1989. *The Structural Transformation of the Public Sphere*. Translated by Thomas Burger and Frederick Lawrence. Cambridge: Polity Press.

———. 1996. *Between Facts and Norms*. Translated by William Rehg. Cambridge: Polity Press.

Hands, Joss. 2011. *@ Is for Activism: Dissent, Residence and Rebellion in a Digital Culture*. London: Pluto Press.

Haraway, Donna. 1991. "A Cyborg Manifesto: Science, Technology, and Socialist Feminism in the Late Twentieth Century." In *Simians, Cyborgs and Women: The Reinvention of Nature*, 149–181. New York: Routledge.

Hardt, Michael, and Antonio Negri. 2000. *Empire*. Cambridge, MA: Harvard University Press.

———. 2004. *Multitude: War and Democracy in the Age of Empire*. New York: Penguin.

———. 2009. *Commonwealth*. Cambridge, MA: Harvard University Press.

Jordan, Tim. 2002. *Activism! Direct Action, Hacktivism and the Future of Society*. London: Reaktion Books.

Lefebvre, Henri. 1991. *The Production of Space*. Oxford: Blackwell.

Olesen, Thomas. 2005. *International Zapatismo*. London: Zed Books.

Raley, Rita. 2009. *Tactical Media*. Minneapolis: Minnesota University Press.

Rheingold, Howard. 2000. *The Virtual Community: Homesteading on the Electronic Frontier*. Cambridge, MA: MIT Press.

Shirky, Clay. 2009. "The Net Advantage." *Prospect Magazine*, December 11, 2009. www.prospectmagazine.co.uk/2009/12/the-net-advantage/.

Street, John. 1997. "Remote Control? Politics, Technology and Electronic Democracy." *European Journal of Communication* 12 (1): 27–42.

···

Preservation

Matthew Kirschenbaum

Strictly speaking, digital preservation encompasses the narrowest of three interrelated sets of activities which are often discussed interchangeably: preservation, archiving (see ARCHIVE), and curation. While preservation ensures the integrity and longevity of a given sequence of bits, digital archiving embeds the bitstream within a workflow that includes such traditional archival functions as identification, appraisal, arrangement and description, management, and retrieval. Digital curation, meanwhile, embraces the entire life cycle of a digital object, from creation to use (and reuse) through preservation and archiving. Though the preceding terminology thus has specific usages in the professional literature, here we will take "preservation" to include access and archival functions, as well as the mere ongoing maintenance of the bitstream.

Given the amount of digital information in the world (by some estimates, upward of three hundred exabytes created per annum), it is not surprising that professionals in industry, government, and cultural heritage are increasingly preoccupied with the survival of so-called *born-digital* material, ranging from data files to executable software to content in distributed networked environments such as the web or even virtual worlds. It is difficult to imagine understanding contemporary politics or world affairs without future access to a wide array of digital media, for example. Moreover, individuals are increasingly aware of the irreplaceability of their own digital mementos, with digital photographs, video, and e-mail augmenting traditional heirlooms and keepsakes.

Many commentators have weighed in with dire predictions of an approaching "digital dark ages," whereby a wealth of knowledge and achievement will be effaced from the collective human record. Analogies are frequently drawn to the history of early cinema, where some half of the films made before 1950 have been lost through neglect and decay. One key difference, however, is the large-scale collective awareness of the importance of digital preservation, and the amount of research and investigation proactively being channeled toward its challenges—for example, through the Library of Congress's National Digital Information Infrastructure and Preservation Program (NDIIPP) program. Likewise, small groups of activists are sometimes taking matters into their own hands, like Jason Scott's Archive Team, which leaps into action to scrape and torrent imperiled web content.

At the heart of the preservation challenge is a paradox about the nature of digital information: it is simultaneously uniquely vulnerable and uniquely stable and persistent. This duality is itself an artifact of the fundamentally symbolic dimension of digital data representation: the ubiquitous ones and zeros of binary code are themselves merely abstractions, or symbolic representations, of physical phenomena such as voltage differentials and magnetic flux reversals (see ANALOG VERSUS DIGITAL). Thus, as Friedrich Kittler has memorably proclaimed, "there is no software" (1995). Abby Smith puts it this way: "A digital art-exhibition catalog, digital comic books, or digital pornography all present themselves as the same, all are literally indistinguishable one from another during storage, unlike, say, a book on a shelf" (1998). Yet, this same symbolic regimen also means that bits are easy to reproduce. Error detection and algorithmic hashing ensure that whatever the vagaries of their interactions with physical media, a given sequence of bits can nearly always be reconstituted with perfect fidelity since the value of any individual bit is effortlessly disambiguated and differentiated. "A computer," as Cory Doctorow often says, "is a machine for copying bits." In digital preservation, this principle is instantiated as the catchphrase "lots of copies keep stuff safe," and the LOCKSS system is a series of redundant repositories allowing participating institutions to share responsibility for the long-term maintenance of the data committed to their distributed servers.

But lots of copies, while necessary, are not sufficient for meaningful digital preservation. Digital preservation is all but inseparable from access, and access depends on the reliable transmission of *context*. There is no way to know whether a given eight-bit string represents an ASCII character, a binary number, a decimal number, a musical tone, a piece of bitmap, or a machine instruction (see DATA). Digital data thus always depend on more data—additional layers of context and representation information—to reconstitute themselves in the form intended by their originator. This requirement for context—which can be logically instantiated through a file header or software application, or (less reliably) inferred through documentation and forensic analysis—means that if any link in the representational chain is broken, the data revert to an opaque binary sequence. The Open Archival Information System places so-called representation information at the center of its reference model, meaning that an archive or repository must assume responsibility for not only the bits themselves but also the preservation of contextual material. For example, in order to preserve a simple ASCII text file, the repository would also maintain (or reference) a copy of the ASCII character standard.

Traditionally the digital preservation community has relied on three strategies or approaches for preserving bits and their contexts: migration, emulation, and re-creation. Migration, as the name implies, entails moving bits from one physical medium to another, as well as (sometimes) updating their format and logical (symbolic) context. Finding creative ways to move bits off of obsolescent and deteriorating storage media that may no longer be supported by appropriate hardware devices in the consumer marketplace is one of the most immediate and formidable obstacles to digital preservation. In addition, a file saved as, say, a Microsoft Word document might be formatted instead as a PDF. Such migrations of format and logical context almost always introduce changes to the appearance and behavior of digital objects, necessitating trade-offs in terms of fidelity to its original manifestation as a digital artifact. Nonetheless, migrating bits from older to newer media and updating their format is the most common method of digital preservation.

Emulation (and the associated concepts of virtual machines and interpretation) essentially entails the literal, formal reproduction of the logic instantiated in the hardware or software of some now-vanished platform. The gaming community is the largest constituency for emulation, and many emulators have been written to allow play of classic arcade, computer, and console games (see GAME HISTORY). Importantly, an emulator is actually executing the original machine instructions in the reproduced logical context of the absent platform. Nonetheless, emulation is not perfect, and the experience of the original game or program can be altered by such environmental variables as screen quality, processor speeds, sound cards, controllers or peripherals, and so forth. Note too that migration and emulation are not mutually exclusive: bits must first be migrated from their original media in the form of a disk image or ROM image, and the distribution of these can entail trafficking in legally gray areas (see COPYRIGHT). Moreover, since an emulator is ultimately a piece of software, as time passes the emulator itself will need to be migrated or emulated. Effort is increasingly being focused on universal cloud-based emulators, by which users will (in theory) be able to reconstitute any given operating environment on demand.

Re-creation (sometimes also called reimplementation) covers a variety of practices that depend on documentation (usually some combination of source code, screenshots and still images, video, design notes, artist's statements, fan products, reviews, and published scholarship) to remake the original digital artifact with contemporary tools, techniques, and materials. Re-creation is typically labor intensive and may result in, at best, an approximation of the original experience; however, particularly in artistic settings, some artists will embrace this form of renewal and preservation through change as an ongoing aspect of the trajectory of their work, rather than simply viewing it as a compromise of their vision. The interactive fiction game *Mystery House* offers a useful example: though the game was released into the public domain by Sierra On-Line in 1987, its source code had been lost. In 2004, a team of developers re-created the game in the programming language Inform 6, even recapitulating some of its original bugs; they subsequently made their code available for others to modify and released a set of online derivative interpretations of the original game, dubbed *Mystery House Taken Over.*

A fourth method, suitable for use on small, specialized scales, consists in working installations of vintage hardware, typically maintained through hobbyist know-how and spare parts purchased online. Defamiliarizing basic tenets of human-computer interaction—for example, booting a computer from a floppy disk instead of a hard drive—can offer today's users a valuable historical perspective (see HISTORY OF COMPUTERS). The Deena Larsen Collection at the University of Maryland and the Media Archaeology Lab at the University of Colorado at Boulder are examples of this approach.

Beyond the massive practical exigencies of digital preservation—nothing less is at stake than the legacy and heritage of decades of human expression and innovation—there are significant overlaps with current debates in digital media studies. Preservation, with its emphasis on the underlying components of digital objects, is broadly compatible with critical and theoretical agendas being put forward under the aegis of software studies (see SOFTWARE STUDIES), platform, critical code studies, forensic computing, media archaeology, thing theory, and the so-called new materialism. What all of these approaches have in common is their acknowledgement of the deep materiality of digital objects and digital culture (see MATERIALITY). The complex interactions required to access digital objects and their interdependency on a vast array of devices and technologies constitute a major site for the exploration of not only the digital sphere but the material human world that we ineluctably inhabit. Preservation teaches us that there is no computation without representation, and that the greatest challenges to preservation are inevitably social and societal rather than technical.

■ See also ANALOG VERSUS DIGITAL, ARCHIVE, CHARACTERISTICS OF DIGITAL MEDIA, CODE, COPYRIGHT, CRITICAL EDITIONS IN THE DIGITAL AGE, DATA, GAME HISTORY, HISTORY OF COMPUTERS, MATERIALITY, MEDIA ECOLOGY, PLATFORM, SOFTWARE STUDIES

References and Further Reading

Archive Team. http://archiveteam.org/.
Bergeron, Bryan. 2002. *Dark Ages II: When the Digital Data Die.* Upper Saddle River, NJ: Prentice Hall.
Consultative Committee for Space Data Systems. 2002. *Reference Model for an Open Archival Information System.* Washington, DC: CCSDS.
The Deena Larsen Collection. 2007. College Park: Maryland Institute for Technology in the Humanities. http://mith.umd.edu/larsen/.
Depocas, Alain, Jon Ippolito, and Caitlin Jones, eds. 2003. *Permanence through Change: The Variable Media Approach.* New York: Solomon R. Guggenheim Museum and the Daniel Langlois Foundation. http://variablemedia.net/e/preserving/html/var_pub_index.html.
Dow, Elizabeth H. 2009. *Electronic Records in the Manuscript Repository.* Lanham, MD: Scarecrow Press.
Ernst, Wolfgang. 2012. *Digital Memory and the Archive.* Translated by Jussi Parikka. Minneapolis: University of Minnesota Press.

Kirschenbaum, Matthew G. 2008. *Mechanisms: New Media and the Forensic Imagination*. Cambridge, MA: MIT Press.

Kirschenbaum, Matthew G., Richard Ovenden, and Gabriela Redwine. 2010. *Digital Forensics and Born-Digital Content in Cultural Heritage Collections*. Washington, DC: Council on Library and Information Resources.

Kittler, Friedrich. 1995. "There Is No Software." *CTheory*. www.ctheory.net/articles.aspx?id=74.

Kraus, Kari, and Rachel Donahue. 2011. " 'Do You Want to Save Your Progress?' The Role of Professional and Player Communities in Preserving Virtual Worlds." *Digital Humanities Quarterly*. www.digitalhumanities.org/dhq/vol/6/2/000129/000129.html.

LOCKSS. Palo Alto, CA: Stanford University Libraries. http://lockss.stanford.edu/.

McDonough, Jerome, Robert Olendorf, Matthew Kirschenbaum, et al. 2010. *Preserving Virtual Worlds Final Report*. Champaign, IL: IDEALS. www.ideals.illinois.edu/handle/2142/17097.

Media Archaeology Lab. Boulder: University of Colorado. http://mediaarchaeologylab.com/.

Montfort, Nick, and Noah Wardrip-Fruin. 2004. *Acid Free Bits: Recommendations for Long-Lasting Electronic Literature*. UCLA: Electronic Literature Organization.

Mystery House Taken Over. 2004. http://turbulence.org/Works/mystery/.

National Digital Information Infrastructure and Preservation Program. Washington, DC: Library of Congress. www.digitalpreservation.gov/.

Smith, Abby. 1998. "Preservation in the Future Tense." *CLIR Issues* 3 (May/June).

Stille, Alexander. 2002. *The Future of the Past*. New York: Farrar, Straus and Giroux.

Thibodeau, Kenneth T. 2002. "Overview of Technological Approaches to Digital Preservation and Challenges in Coming Years." In *The State of Digital Preservation: An International Perspective*. Washington, DC: Council on Library and Information Resources.

∙∙∙

Procedural
Jonathan Lessard

The adjective *procedural* describes an object whose actual manifestation results from the strict application of a specific set of rules (or procedures) to a particular context. The main interest of procedural objects is their ability to generate varying content in response to changes in input and setting. Procedurality allows for the delivery of responses that have not been specifically authored in advance. For example, judicial systems are procedural in nature as they allow for the judgement of novel cases by the rigorous application of existing laws and procedures.

Being particularly suited to the rapid carrying out of large sets of instructions, computers have become a natural medium for procedural objects. These can be found in many aspects of digital media. In all cases, their value resides in providing for the unpredictability of interactive systems. They can even give rise to unexpected results, thus being a basis of emergence (see EMERGENCE). Procedural systems also have the advantage of being lightweight both in storage and in development for they only exist as a limited series of instructions rather than extensive pre-generated content. For example, procedurally animated virtual characters can realistically react to changes in their simulated physical environment without the need for an encyclopaedic database of prerecorded animation sequences. On the other hand, these objects usually require more processing power, which is not trivial for real-time applications. Another downside is the "generic feel" often associated with procedurally generated content, which tends to display discernible patterns in the long run.

In the context of digital literature, procedural systems have been used to create different forms of text generators. The most famous example is probably ELIZA, Weizenbaum's

1966 experiment in artificial intelligence (see ARTIFICIAL INTELLIGENCE). Janet Murray describes this chatterbot as a procedural comic character (1997, 72) (see CHATTERBOTS). Using only a limited set of rules, it creates the illusion of interacting with a particularly evasive Rogerian therapist. Despite slow progresses since, the prospect of procedural forms of narrative has kept its appeal (see INTERACTIVE NARRATIVE). In particular, it is seen as a possible answer to the problematic reconciliation of games and storytelling in computer games. By implementing a "virtual author," games could generate narrative events adapted to player action, freeing it from the limits of pre-authored content. Tavinor notes that, although promising, "it is hard to say . . . whether procedural narrative would ever be compelling or artful" (2009, 127).

The main problem of procedural literature resides in the difficulty of its authorship, which strongly differs from that of hypertexts (see HYPERTEXTUALITY) and traditional interactive fiction (see INTERACTIVE FICTION). Instead of filling a database with nodes of text providing for all possible events, authors must elaborate algorithms capable of generating meaningful original statements in response to user input (see ALGORITHM). As Bogost puts it, "To write procedurally, one authors code that enforces rules to generate some kind of representation, rather than authoring the representation itself" (2007, 4). This implies a modeling of the imagined situation as a computer-processable simulation. The complexity of even the simplest human interactions makes interesting procedural texts very difficult to design (Salen and Zimmerman 2003, 440).

■ See also COMBINATORY AND AUTOMATIC TEXT GENERATION, STORY GENERATION

References and Further Reading

Bogost, Ian. 2007. *Persuasive Games: The Expressive Power of Videogames.* Cambridge, MA: MIT Press.

Bootz, Philippe. 1996. "Un modèle fonctionnel des textes procéduraux." *Les cahiers du CIRCAV no 8,* REXCAV édition.

Murray, Janet H. 1997. *Hamlet on the Holodeck: The Future of Narrative in Cyberspace.* 1st ed. New York: Free Press.

Salen, Katie, and Eric Zimmerman. 2003. *Rules of Play: Game Design Fundamentals.* Illustrated ed. Cambridge, MA: MIT Press.

Tavinor, Grant. 2009. *The Art of Videogames.* Malden, MA: Wiley-Blackwell.

Wikidot. *Procedural Content Generation Wiki.* http://pcg.wikidot.com/.

Quest Narrative
Ragnhild Tronstad

In traditional terms, a quest narrative is the written or spoken account of a heroic journey undertaken in order to attain a specific objective. In the course of the journey, the hero will be faced with challenges, the overcoming of which becomes a source to his or her spiritual and intellectual enlightenment. Quest narratives are often inspired by popular myths, for example, the legend of the Holy Grail.

In an influential study originally published in 1949, entitled *The Hero of a Thousand Faces*, the American mythologist Joseph Campbell identified a set of structural characteristics applying to a particular kind of myth that he named the *monomyth*. The monomyth is structured as a quest narrative describing the mythical protagonist's journey from the known into the unknown, followed by his return as a transformed and enlightened being capable of bestowing his society with beneficial powers or gifts. Inspired by the French ethnographer Arnold van Gennep's work on *rites of passage* ([1909] 1960), Campbell divided the hero's journey into the three stages Departure, Initiation, and Return (Campbell [1949] 2004). Arguably, the monomyth as described by Campbell represents the archetypal quest narrative that can be identified in a vast number of myths and stories, both historical and modern.

Within the context of digital media and textuality, however, the concept of "quest narrative" takes on a slightly different meaning, relating to the phenomenon of "questing" in early text-based and contemporary graphical computer games. Computer game quests can be considered a form of interactive storytelling, combining game mechanics with elements of narrative (see INTERACTIVE FICTION, INTERACTIVE NARRATIVE). The relationship between game mechanics and narrative in computer games is complicated and has often been debated by game studies scholars. While many games provide their players with a narrative experience, the "storytelling" of games is often conducted in a radically different manner than the storytelling of noninteractive media such as literature and film. In order to identify that which distinguishes games as a storytelling medium, some game scholars have chosen to focus on the differences rather than the similarities between the media, arguing that games are not straightforward narrative, but rather performative media (see PERFORMANCE). From this theoretical perspective, a quest narrative is considered only potentially present in the quest as performed and experienced by the player, as a sequence of events that may be realized and retrospectively contemplated in the form of a story after the player character's accomplishment of the quest (Aarseth 2004; Tronstad 2001, 2003). This understanding corresponds to the traditional definition of a quest narrative as an after-the-fact story construction, separate in time and space from the quest itself.

Quests in computer games take many different forms, from shorter missions requiring that the player character fetch or deliver an object, or slay a number of low-level monsters (see NPC [NONPLAYER CHARACTER]), to long, adventurous journeys that may take days or weeks to complete, combining different types of challenges such as combat, exploration, puzzles, and riddles. It is therefore important to specify game and game genre, as well as type of quest, when discussing the characteristics of quests and quest narratives in games.

Compared with graphical computer games, text-based computer game genres such as interactive fiction (IF) and multiuser dungeons (MUDs) employ a different tool set and must rely on other techniques to construct a game world and meaningful challenges for the player to engage in (see INTERACTIVE FICTION, MUDs AND MOOs). While an interactive, textual interface may be less suited than a graphical one to represent in great detail the immediate spatial surroundings of the player character, it is a much more flexible and precise tool with which to perform complex rhetorical and literary operations. Thus, text-based computer games are able to support—and will often offer—more intricate quest narratives than graphical computer games. According to Faltin Karlsen's comparative study of quests in the text-based MUD *Discworld* and the graphical massively multiplayer online role-playing game (MMORPG) *World of Warcraft*, quests provide a distinctly more elaborate and meaningful player experience in the former than in the latter. Quests in *World of Warcraft* appear prefabricated: they resemble each other and may be solved on routine. In contrast, *Discworld* quests are unique and renowned for their nontrivial challenges. Significantly, within the MUD community of players and programmers, quests are considered "the fine art" of game design (Karlsen 2008).

MUD quests regularly combine monster slaying with exploration and puzzle solving. To explore the MUD environment is literally a matter of interacting with and examining texts. For example, the player types "<examine stone>" in order to look closer at an interesting "stone" she stumbles upon, which will trigger a text in return where the stone is described in more detail. If the stone is somehow involved in the quest plot, the text describing the stone will likely present the player with a puzzle or reveal a hint that may help the player proceed in her quest. As text is such a flexible rhetorical medium, elements of background story, puzzles, riddles, hints, and instructions can be seamlessly integrated into the description of the game world and revealed along the way as the player character explores the environment.

The text fulfils at this stage a performative function. Promising a narrative context—that the purpose and proper meaning of the player's efforts will be revealed during the course of the quest so that a sense of closure can be obtained in the end—the text shifts between partly keeping and partly deferring its promise, replacing the player's solution to a puzzle with another puzzle. This rhetorical maneuver, necessary to keep the quest in progress, continues until the quest is completed. Then, when all puzzles are solved, the performative function of the text is terminated and the quest is over. The recollection of the journey may now be narratively reconstructed and realized as a quest narrative.

Because their functionality as quest games is fundamentally tied to this performative textual rhetoric, puzzle quests and riddle-based adventures can only be performed and fully experienced as quests once by any player. Like the hero of the monomyth, the player reaches a stage of enlightenment after having completed the quest from which she can never return to her previous self—that is, to a self susceptible to be played by the quest's puzzles, still unaware of their solutions.

Quest games that do not involve puzzle solving are unaffected by such restrictions. Also, where puzzles challenge the intellectual or imaginative skills of the player, other types of challenges in quests typically address skills of the player character, such as its level of constitution, strength, agility, and intelligence.

According to Jill Walker Rettberg, in *World of Warcraft* "quests are straightforward, directions purely geographical, and the challenge lies in finding the object and killing the opponents, not in solving puzzles" (2008, 169). They are repetitive, posing "the same objectives of traveling, killing and collecting" (2008, 168), and endlessly deferring a final closure—there is always another challenge to embark on. A few of the quests in this game can be solved more than once, but most are available to the same player character one time only. However, it is not unusual that players create and alternate between several player characters with different strengths and attributes. Thus, players may well experience the same quest a number of times, from the perspective of a variety of player characters.

Many quests are designed to convey information about the fictional universe, in order to provide the players with a shared background story for identification and role-play, and to create a context for the player characters' actions. Apparently, however, few players indulge in such narrative content, but focus instead on extracting the essential information that is needed in order to complete the quest and obtain the reward(s) in the most efficient manner possible (Karlsen 2008; Walker Rettberg 2008). According to Walker Rettberg, though, during a player character's advancement through quest solving in *World of Warcraft*, "motifs and structures are repeated so steadily that they do help to shape the world" (2008, 176).

Quest narratives may also be instrumental in shaping an identity for the player character, as distinguished from that of the player (Tronstad 2008, [2004] 2009). The philosopher Paul Ricoeur has argued that our sense of a personal identity is based on subsequently configured narratives of experienced events, which together constitute the stories of our lives. In this selection of narratives, certain events will be regarded as more significant than others, and some will be forgotten altogether (Ricoeur 1991). Similarly, in the context of gameplay the subsequent construction of a memorable quest narrative does not necessarily depend on explicit narrative content during the course of a quest, but can rely on factors such as duration, causality, intensity, and the "tellability" (Ryan 1991) of the experienced events. Thus, in both games and real life, quests and events may more or less profoundly influence how we come to perceive ourselves (or our character, in the case of gameplay). A few of them we may even come to think of as *rites of passage*, marking our transition from one stage of identity to another.

■ See also GAMES AS STORIES

References and Further Reading

Aarseth, Espen. 2004. "Quest Games as Post-Narrative Discourse." In *Narrative across Media*, edited by Marie-Laure Ryan, 361–376. Lincoln: University of Nebraska Press.

Campbell, Joseph. (1949) 2004. *The Hero with a Thousand Faces*. Princeton, NJ: Princeton University Press.

Gennep, Arnold van. (1909) 1960. *The Rites of Passage*. London: Routledge.

Howard, Jeff. 2008. *Quests: Design, Theory, and History in Games and Narratives*. Wellesley, MA: A K Peters.

Karlsen, Faltin. 2008. "Quests in Context: A Comparative Analysis of *Discworld* and *World of Warcraft*." *Game Studies* 8 (1). http://gamestudies.org/0801/articles/karlsen.

Ricoeur, Paul. 1991. "Life in Quest of Narrative." In *On Paul Ricoeur: Narrative and Interpretation*, edited by David Wood, 20–33. London: Routledge.

Rouse, Richard, III. 2005. *Game Design: Theory and Practice*. Plano, TX: Wordware.

Ryan, Marie-Laure. 1991. *Possible Worlds, Artificial Intelligence, and Narrative Theory*. Bloomington: Indiana University Press.

Tosca, Susana. 2003. "The Quest Problem in Computer Games." In *Proceedings of* TIDSE 2003. Stuttgart: Fraunhofer IRB Verlag. www.itu.dk/people/tosca/quest.htm.

Tronstad, Ragnhild. 2001. "Semiotic and Nonsemiotic MUD Performance." In *COSIGN 2001: Proceedings of the 1st Conference of Computational Semiotics for Games and New Media* (Amsterdam), edited by Andy Clarke, Clive Fencott, Craig Lindley, Grethe Mitchell, and Frank Nack. www.cosignconference.org/conference/2001/papers.

———. 2003. "A Matter of Insignificance: The MUD Puzzle Quest as Seductive Discourse." In *CyberText Yearbook 2002–2003*, edited by Markku Eskelinen and Raine Koskimaa, 237–256. Saarijärvi, Finland: University of Jyväskylä, Research Centre for Contemporary Culture. http://cybertext.hum.jyu.fi/articles/119.pdf.

———. (2004) 2009. "Interpretation, Performance, Play, and Seduction: Textual Adventures in Tubmud." PhD diss. Saarbrücken, Germany: VDM.

———. 2005. "Figuring the Riddles of Adventure Games." In *Aesthetics of Play Online Proceedings*. www.aestheticsofplay.org/tronstad.php.

———. 2008. "Character Identification in *World of Warcraft*: The Relationship between Capacity and Appearance." In *Digital Culture, Play, and Identity: A World of Warcraft® Reader*, edited by Hilde G. Corneliussen and Jill Walker Rettberg, 249–263. Cambridge, MA: MIT Press.

Walker Rettberg, Jill. 2008. "Quests in *World of Warcraft*: Deferral and Repetition." In *Digital Culture, Play, and Identity: A World of Warcraft® Reader*, edited by Hilde G. Corneliussen and Jill Walker Rettberg, 167–184. Cambridge, MA: MIT Press.

R

Race and Ethnicity

Kim Knight

In 1993, the *New Yorker* published a Peter Steiner cartoon in which a dog sitting at a computer brags to a friend, "On the Internet, nobody knows you're a dog." This cartoon is often cited as an example of attitudes toward the web as a space in which markers of difference are elided. However, the affordances of the Internet operate in a context that includes a substantial history of racial ideology in the United States. In other words, race cannot be eradicated so easily. The concept of race itself is problematic. According to Michael Omi and Howard Winant, "Racial categories and the meaning of race are given concrete expression by the specific social relations and historical context in which they are embedded. Racial meanings have varied tremendously over time and between different societies" (2007, 15). Ethnicity, or the formation of group identity based on shared culture and descent, is a similarly problematic concept. It is also sociohistorical and often relies on notions of racial identity to determine inclusion (Omi and Winant 1994, 15). Though these concepts are sociohistorical, Omi and Winant are careful to insist that they are by no means illusory (2007, 19). The construction of racial meaning has material effects.

Digital media are one way in which racial meaning is constructed. They are also one of the avenues by which racial meaning can be challenged. The relationship between digital media and race/ethnicity is a complex interplay of multidirectional influences that must take into account both how race and ethnicity are given concrete expression in digital environments and how digital texts and environments are shaped by racial formations. This multidirectional relationship is exemplified in discourses about race and digital technology, digital expressions of racial meaning (including racist expressions), and global labor practices that underlie digital media and textuality.

The Steiner cartoon was just one example of early web discourses on race and technology. Popular representations and critical theorists alike suggested that the Internet held the potential for users to transcend embodied markers of racial or ethnic identity in a utopia of anonymity (see CYBORG AND POSTHUMAN). Text-based profile descriptors and the freedom to construct avatars were seen as ways of potentially refusing the notion of race. It was not long, however, before this discourse was challenged. As early as 1995, in her essay "Race in/for Cyberspace," Lisa Nakamura questioned whether such racial fluidity was possible. Although users of early community platforms such as LambdaMOO were not required to give their profiles a racial identity, race influenced identity construction in subtle ways (see MUDs AND MOOs). For instance, when racial identity went unstated, whiteness was often assumed. In addition, users would often decode other profile traits, such as hair and eye color, to align with racial identity. When users did express race in their profile construction, this was often interpreted as being a confrontational expression (Nakamura 2000, 712–713). Nakamura coined the influential term *identity tourism* to refer to users constructing online profiles pretending to be another race. She found that users often engaged in online minstrelsy in which they used reductive racial and ethnic identity traits to attach exoticism to themselves, transforming spaces of free play into "phantasmatic Imperial space" (2000, 715). In the late 1990s and early 2000s the move toward more graphical user interfaces meant the rise in creation of visual avatars (see AVATARS). Early avatar generators were often critiqued because they were generally geared toward representing normative white bodies with limited options for expressing any type of diversity. Once more options for avatar creation became available, identity tourism became possible in graphic form. According to Nakamura, one of the dangers of identity tourism is that users who pass as someone else may end up with a false sense of understanding toward the inhabited identity. If they are not treated negatively, they may assume that racism or sexism, among others, is "no big deal" (Nakamura 2011).

Far from "no big deal," one of the other commonly circulated discourses about race and technology is in relation to what is referred to as "the digital divide." In the 1990s and early 2000s, activists and thinkers concerned with social justice feared that inequities would be amplified when access to computing technologies became requisite for social mobility among underserved populations, including the poor and people of color. Others emphasized that access to computing technologies would not be enough to eliminate disparities that are perpetuated through multiple avenues in society (Everett 2008, 4). Nelson, Tu, and Hines, editors of the collection *Technicolor: Race, Technology and Everyday Life* (2001), warn against narratives that oversimplify and reduce people of color to victims of lack of access. They cite oppositional "everyday" uses of technology that empower marginalized users (2001, 3). The discourse additionally shifts with increased connectivity (Nakamura 2008, 18) and with the advent of smartphones and high-speed mobile Internet access. The emphasis becomes less about bridging the access divide and more about ensuring equitable training in digital literacies. Again, however, critics are cautioned against thinking that increased digital literacy among marginalized populations will be able to overcome structures of inequity which are embedded throughout cultures.

Another area of inequity in culture is the limited representation of people of color in mainstream or broadcast media. Digital media and textuality, particularly participatory web platforms, have provided alternative spaces for producers and performers of color (see PARTICIPATORY CULTURE). For instance, the online series *The Misadventures of Awkward Black Girl*, produced by and starring Senegalese American Issa Rae, recently won the 2012 Shorty Award for best web show (see FILM AND DIGITAL MEDIA, MOBILE GAMES, VIDEO). Rae often cites the lack of well-developed black characters on broadcast television as her inspiration for creating the series. Though race is not the focus of the show, it has received considerable media attention for Rae's role as a black producer and actor, as well as for featuring well-developed black characters. The success of digital productions like *Awkward Black Girl*, combined with the ubiquity of participatory platforms with low barriers to entry, have led to a proliferation of amateur digital content related to race and ethnicity, particularly on sites such as YouTube.

As often as digital media might be used to critique mainstream representations of race or to include traditionally marginalized people, digital platforms are also deployed to promote racism and xenophobia. Jessie Daniels's study *Cyber Racism* (2009) suggests that the affordances of digital culture produce new forms of enacting white supremacy. The structured online spaces of organized racist movements are just one way in which racism is deployed in digital contexts. Lisa Nakamura identifies five different types of online racism: visual profiling of users, voice profiling of users, racism against avatars, identity tourism (racism using avatars), and anti-immigrant racism in virtual worlds (2011). The comments on sites such as YouTube and Reddit often contain racist (and sexist and homophobic) remarks that other users dismiss as just one of the negative effects of networked social environments. In other cases, the production of racist digital media has unexpected results. In March 2011, in the wake of the Tohoku earthquake and tsunami, UCLA political science student Alexandra Wallace posted a video to YouTube entitled "Asians in the Library." In the video she evokes racial stereotypes and uses a crass imitation of someone speaking a nonsensical "Asian" language to complain about students using their cell phones in the library. Wallace experienced an immediate backlash for her so-called rant, and she removed the video within hours of having been posted. It was reposted immediately by other users and spawned a host of remixes and parodies. Many resorted to racist discourse themselves or used Wallace's sexuality as a point of criticism. However, many used the parlance of participatory media to engage in thoughtful discussion of the topics of stereotyping and racism (see PARTICIPATORY CULTURE, REMIX). We may read these responses to "Asians in the Library" as one of the forms in which "the 'unexpected occurrence' of race has the potential, by its very unexpectedness, to sabotage the ideology-machine's routines" (Nakamura 2000, 718).

Discussions of race and ethnicity which challenge the ideology machine are often carried out over blogs, web forums, social networking sites, and in digital artworks. Dara N. Byrne writes of the role of discussion forums such as *AsianAvenue*, *BlackPlanet*, and *MiGente* which provide a means of racial affirmation and contribute to the formation of collective online subjectivities. According to Byrne, the users of these sites value the "authenticity" of racial or ethnic identity, in spite of the problematic nature of defining these terms. Much of the discourse centers on establishing borders between "authentic" users and outsiders, based on community consensus for what constitutes "authentic" experience (Byrne 2008, 19). In addition, forums such as these connect diasporic populations and reinforce offline communities of race-based affinity. Blogs such as *Racialicious*, *Racebending*, and *Wide Lantern* focus on public critique of the role of race in media and popular culture, which leads to community formation and social activism (see BLOGS). Social networking sites like YouTube, Twitter, and Facebook help users circulate "gotcha" moments to bring attention to racist and xenophobic practices. One such instance was the circulation of the 2006 video of George Allen, incumbent Virginia senatorial candidate, referring to S. R. Sidarth as "macaca, or whatever his name is." The gaffe was circulated in a mode of détournement and is credited with costing Allen the election. Critiques of race-based and ethnic issues are also carried out via digital media and art. Works such as Erik Loyer's electronic literature project *Chroma* and Prema Murthy's *E.rase* examine racial identity in digital environments. Judith F. Baca's *César Chávez Digital/Mural Lab* combines art, activism, and pedagogy to produce connections between digital and offline communities. Others, such as Tamiko Thiel's *Beyond Manzanar* and Mark C. Marino's *a show of hands*, use digital platforms to investigate ethnic identity in political contexts (see ELECTRONIC LITERATURE, POLITICS AND NEW MEDIA).

In political contexts that include global capitalism, race and ethnicity must also be considered from the standpoint of the material production and disposal of the components and hardware devices that support digital media and textuality. In the edited collection *Challenging the Chip*, David A. Sonnenfeld notes that "few things characterize both the hope and desperation of social relations in the present era more than the two-headed hydra of *globalization* and *electronics*" (2006, 16; emphasis in the original). Though decisions about production and disassembly processes are often financially motivated, it is important to be aware that these jobs, with their attendant hazards, tend to be filled by people of color, immigrants, and women, regardless of where the factories are located (Smith, Sonnenfeld, and Pellow 2006, 8). The manufacture of electronics components and the recycling of hardware devices are labor-intensive processes that involve many toxic materials and solvents (Grossman 2006, n.p.). Some of this work is done in wealthy capitalist countries; however, a large portion of production/assembly/disassembly is outsourced to factories in newly industrializing nations. For instance, according to Elizabeth Grossman, loopholes in environmental regulations allow almost 80 percent of e-waste from countries such as the United States and the United Kingdom to be exported to poorer nations for recycling (2006, n.p.). In contrast, the white-collar jobs related to engineering tend to remain in a corporation's home nation. As Joseph LaDou notes, this presents a challenge in holding brand-name corporations responsible for the environmental and labor practices of their subcontractors (2006, 30) (see ETHICS IN DIGITAL MEDIA, POLITICS AND NEW MEDIA). An additional consideration is the precarious situation of software developers and coders employed as nonimmigrant workers on temporary visas in countries like the United States. Though these issues have been gaining more critical attention, the ethical implications of global labor forces still remain one of the most often overlooked ways in which race/ethnicity and digital media / textuality intersect.

This intersection is complex and multidimensional. Omi and Winant coined the term *racial formation* to refer to "the process by which social, economic and political forces determine the content and importance of racial categories, and by which they are in turn shaped by racial meanings" (2007, 16). Digital media may be only one factor in racial formation, but its influence takes many forms. We have much to learn about racial formation and challenges from examinations of discourses about race and digital technology, digital expressions of racial meaning (including racist expressions), and global labor practices that underlie digital media and textuality.

■ See also CYBERFEMINISM, GENDER AND MEDIA USE, GENDER REPRESENTATION, IDENTITY, POLITICS AND NEW MEDIA

References and Further Reading

Byrne, Dara N. 2008. "The Future of (the) 'Race': Identity, Discourse, and the Rise of Computer-Mediated Public Spheres." In *Learning Race and Ethnicity: Youth and Digital Media*, edited by Anna Everett, 15–38. Cambridge, MA: MIT Press.

Daniels, Jessie. 2009. *Cyber Racism: White Supremacy Online and the New Attack on Civil Rights.* Lanham, MD: Rowman & Littlefield.

Everett, Anna. 2008. "Introduction." In *Learning Race and Ethnicity: Youth and Digital Media*, edited by Anna Everett, 1–14. Cambridge, MA: MIT Press.

Grossman, Elizabeth. 2006. *High Tech Trash: Digital Devices, Hidden Toxics, and Human Health.* Washington, DC: Island Press.

LaDou, Joseph. 2006. "The Changing Map of Global Electronics." In *Challenging the Chip: Labor Rights and Environmental Justice in the Global Electronics Industry*, edited by Ted Smith, David A. Sonnenfeld, and David Naguib Pellow, 17–31. Philadelphia: Temple University Press.

Nakamura, Lisa. 2000. "Race in/for Cyberspace." In *The Cybercultures Reader*, edited by David Bell and Barbara M. Kennedy, 712–720. New York: Routledge.

———. 2008. "Introduction: Digital Racial Formations and Networked Images of the Body." In *Digitizing Race: Visual Cultures of the Internet*, 1–36. Minneapolis: University of Minnesota Press.

———. 2011. "Five Types of Online Racism and Why You Should Care." TedxTalks. YouTube. www.youtube.com/watch?v=DT-G0FlO07g.

Nelson, Alondra, Thuu Linh N. Tu, and Alicia Headlam Hines. 2001. "Introduction: Hidden Circuits." In *Technicolor: Race, Technology, and Everyday Life*, edited by Alondra Nelson, Thuu Linh N. Tu, and Alicia Headlam Hines, 1–12. New York: New York University Press.

Omi, Michael, and Howard Winant. 1994. *Racial Formation in the United States: From the 1960s to the 1990s.* New York: Routledge.

———. 2007. "Racial Formations." In *Race, Class, and Gender in the United States: An Integrated Study*, 7th ed., edited by Paula S. Rothenburg, 13–22. New York: St. Martin's.

Smith, Ted, David A. Sonnenfeld, and David Naguib Pellow. 2006. "The Quest for Sustainability and Justice in a High-Tech World." In *Challenging the Chip: Labor Rights and Environmental Justice in the Global Electronics Industry*, edited by Ted Smith, David A. Sonnenfeld, and David Naguib Pellow, 1–11. Philadelphia: Temple University Press.

Sonnenfeld, David. 2006. "Global Electronics." In *Challenging the Chip: Labor Rights and Environmental Justice in the Global Electronics Industry*, edited by Ted Smith, David A. Sonnenfeld, and David Naguib Pellow, 13–16. Philadelphia: Temple University Press.

Randomness

Marie-Laure Ryan

Randomness can be conceived in many ways, depending on the context in which the word is used: as lack of predictability (the result of the throw of the dice), as the failure of causality (the behavior of particles in quantum mechanics), as that which cannot be defined by an algorithm (a sequence of random numbers), and as that which we cannot control (fate), a conception particularly productive in narrative texts (see ALGORITHM). While determinists would argue that randomness does not truly exist in nature—it is just the name given to that which we cannot explain—some mystics and clairvoyants regard it as the voice of a higher power: random processes, such as drawing cards, are often used in divination.

The relation of randomness to art is ambiguous: on one hand, art means control over a medium—the opposite of randomness. Traditional poetry differs from spontaneous expression through the constraints of meter, rhyme, or alliteration, which imposes form on the signifiers. But while constraints determine which words should and should not be used, they may lead to randomness on the level of the signified, since the meaning of the text depends on what words happen to fulfill the needs of form, rather than on words carefully chosen for their ability to express preconceived ideas. In the aesthetics of classicism, authors should maintain equal control over meaning and form.

Yet the demand in art for control over the medium is counterbalanced by a demand for innovation, surprise, and estrangement from the habitual. This need rehabilitates randomness as a source of unpredictability (see GLITCH AESTHETICS). Dadaists and surrealists, who viewed randomness as a force that shakes the dust of habit and provides access to a higher, more poetic reality, adopted as their own Lautréamont's conception of beauty as "the chance meeting on a dissection table of a sewing machine and an umbrella." They devised many techniques to harness the creative energy of random encounters: *écriture automatique*, collages, cut-ups, and visual as well as verbal versions of the mad-lib party game. In this game (known in surrealist circles as "exquisite corpse," after a sentence it produced in 1918: "the exquisite corpse will drink the young wine") players provide words of a specified grammatical category to fill slots in a text they cannot see; in the visual version, they draw part of a body, fold the sheet, and pass it to another player who draws the next part. The results are often hilarious. Another technique that creates random combinations of words is combinatorics, put into practice in the algorithm used by the Oulipo author Raymond Queneau in *Cent mille milliards de poèmes* (1961) (see COMBINATORY AND AUTOMATIC TEXT GENERATION). This work consists of twelve sonnets cut into strips at every line and bound together at the spine, allowing new poems to be created by leafing through the book and combining the fragments.

As a strictly deterministic machine, the computer is fundamentally unable to generate random numbers or random events of any kind, but it can produce an *impression* of randomness by using algorithms whose output cannot be easily predicted, such as reading the last digit of its internal clock and submitting it to various operations. Since it is far more difficult to generate texts that make logical sense, such as stories (see STORY GENERATION), than to create exquisite cadaver effects, the vast majority of computer-created artistic texts rely on some kind of aleatory procedure. There are two ways to implement random word combinations. Both consist of selecting words from a database and inserting them into a target text (see DATABASE). When the database consists of lists of words of a certain grammatical category, selection can be made on the basis of a random number. In interactive systems, the user can be prompted to input words of a certain type. (There are a number of interactive mad-lib programs on the Internet.) The other way to generate incongruous word sequences, while maintaining grammaticality, is the *n*-gram technique (see N-GRAM). When the database is a text, rather than a list, a word of the proper category can be pulled out by parsing the database for a sequence of *n* words identical to the sequence of words in the target text which precede the word to be replaced; take the next word in the database: there is a high probability—a probability that increases with the size of *n*—that the found word will fit into the syntax of the target text. This folding of a text into another text has been extensively practiced by digital authors John Cayley and Noah Wardrip-Fruin (see DIGITAL POETRY).

Both of these techniques can be used to produce various degrees of randomness. If the input data of a mad-lib system are narrowly focused, as they are in Christopher Strachey's *Love Letter* (1952), arguably the first text of digital literature, the generated text may sound strange but will make some sense (see EARLY DIGITAL ART AND WRITING [PRE-1990]). Here is a sample: "DARLING CHICKPEA, MY LOVING DESIRE YEARNS FOR YOUR SYMPATHETIC LONGING. YOU ARE MY LOVING HUNGER. MY FONDNESS KEENLY YEARNS FOR YOUR ENTHUSIASM. MY BEING TREASURES YOUR ENCHANTMENT. YOU ARE MY PRECIOUS CHARM. YOURS IMPATIENTLY, M.U.C." (quoted from www.gingerbeardman .com/loveletter/). Randomness is more extensive, because the topics are not restricted, in *The Policeman's Beard Is Half Constructed* (1984), a collection of texts supposedly written by a program named Racter and promoted as "the first book ever written by a computer." Racter's poetry can reach the depth of existential anguish:

A hot and torrid bloom which
Fans with flames and begs to be
Redeemed by forces black and strong
Will now oppose my naked will
And force me into regions of despair
(1984, n.p.)

Yet as computer-generated works the poems "written" by Racter are suspicious: it is obvious that William Chamberlain, the human partner in this cyborg work (as Espen Aarseth calls any text generated partly by humans, partly by computer), not only selected the most interesting of Racter's compositions but also put his imprint on the output by writing a variety of syntactic templates. Since the algorithm is not divulged, it is difficult to disentangle the contribution of the human from the work of the computer in Racter's production, though we can guess that Racter (like Strachey's *Love Letter* program) used a fill-in-the-blanks procedure. Its hybrid nature makes it very difficult to judge *The Policeman's Beard* as an artwork: as Aarseth argues (1997, 135), we need to know its genesis in order to do so.

While the general public may assess the results of aleatory text production in terms of what they evoke to the imagination—moods, images, personal experiences—true hackers will evaluate these projects in terms of the originality of the generative algorithm. To remain ahead in the fast-paced game of experimentalism, digital artists must find ever-new ways to produce nonsense and quasi-sense, adapted to the most recent technological developments. The Google search engine has, for instance, been requisitioned by practitioners of Flarf poetry (a movement dedicated to the exploitation of "the inappropriate") to collect random words and collate them into poems (see FLARF). Another clever use of technology is Noah Wardrip-Fruin and Brion Moss's *The Impermanence Agent*, a program that searches the user's hard disk for words to be fitted into a text written by the author. Here, however, the generative algorithm is not programming virtuosity for its own sake, but an expressive device put in the service of the general theme of the work: the loss of coherence created by the invasion of the author's text by random elements reflects the gradual loss of memory of Nana, the grandmother of the narrator. Another example of a work that ties randomness to its global theme is Jason Nelson's *This Is How You Will Die*. The user is asked to pull a lever that activates a wheel and selects a fragment of text from a certain number of possibilities. Repeated four times, to fill four slots, this procedure creates a text that reveals how the user will die. While the combinatorial algorithm is not particularly original—it is formally similar to the formula of Queneau's *Cent mille milliards de poèmes*—it provides a frightening simulation of the randomness of Fate, the all-powerful mythical being who determines the way we die.

For the digital critic Roberto Simanowski (2011, 99), computer-generated texts based on aleatory procedures pose a hermeneutic problem: how can we find meaning in a text produced by a machine for which meaning does not exist? He comes up with four possibilities: (1) dismiss the possibility of meaning in the absence of an authorial intent, regardless of the aesthetic appeal of the text; (2) dissociate meaning from human authorship, so that a text can mean as long as it consists of recognizable signs; (3) see meaning in chance, as in certain techniques of divination; or (4) establish authorial intent in the text, by pretending that it is the utterance of a human being. Individual readers will decide for themselves which one of these attitudes to adopt. I would like, however, to add two more items to this list. In contrast to the other four, they are dictated by the individual features of the text, rather than by the personal predispositions of the reader: (5) ignore the exact content of the text and admire the algorithm, an attitude that amounts to focusing not on the "what" but on the "how"; or (6) interpret randomness as part of the message, as in *This Is How You Will Die*. The latter interpretation restores intentionality to the text, a move justified by the fact that even when a text is computer generated, the program is always written by a human author.

■ See also MASHUP, REMIX

References and Further Reading

Aarseth, Espen. 1997. *Cybertext: Perspectives on Ergodic Literature.* Baltimore: Johns Hopkins University Press.

Funkhouser, Christopher. 2008. "The Scope for a Reader: The Poetry of Text Generators." *Dichtung Digital.* www.dichtung-digital.org/2008/1-Funkhouser.htm.

Nelson, Jason. n.d. *This Is How You Will Die.* www.secrettechnology.com/death/deathspin.htm.

Queneau, Raymond. 1961. *Cent mille milliards de poèmes.* Paris: Gallimard.

Racter (William Chamberlain). 1984. *The Policeman's Beard Is Half Constructed.* New York: Warner Books.

Rettberg, Scott. 2008. "Dada Redux: Elements of Dadaist Practice in Contemporary Electronic Literature." *Fibreculture Journal* 11. http://eleven.fibreculturejournal.org/fcj-071-dada-redux-elements-of-dadaist-practice-in-contemporary-electronic-literature/.

Simanowski, Roberto. 2011. *Digital Art and Meaning.* Minneapolis: University of Minnesota Press.

Wardrip-Fruin, Noah. 2005. "Christopher Strachey: The First Digital Artist." *Grand Text Auto.* http://grandtextauto.org/2005/08/01/christopher-strachey-first-digital-artist/.

———. 2009. *Expressive Processing: Digital Fictions, Computer Games, and Software Studies.* Cambridge, MA: MIT Press.

Waldrip-Fruin, Noah, and Brion Moss. n.d. *The Impermanence Agent.* [No longer available.] Essay at www.impermanenceagent.com/agent/essay2/.

• •

Reading Strategies
Adalaide Morris

A reading strategy is a plan of action which provides a set of concepts and procedures by which to access and assess meanings entangled in texts. Like all strategies, it is, as Gertrude Stein would say, "a thing prepared" ([1926] 1998, 520): it precedes the encounter it anticipates and, like a battle plan, succeeds by adjusting to the contingencies it encounters.

In "Composition as Explanation," her address to Oxford and Cambridge students on the art of reading avant-garde texts, Stein compares the emergent force she calls "composition" to the improvisations of battle. An innovative text is not "a thing prepared," she argues, but "a thing made by being made" ([1926] 1998, 520). To approach it with explanations engineered to interpret texts of the past is to court the kind of catastrophe that awaited World War I generals who planned "a nineteenth century war . . . to be fought with twentieth century weapons" ([1926] 1998, 520).

N. Katherine Hayles, one of digital textuality's sharpest strategists, puts the point succinctly: "To see electronic literature only through the lens of print is," she writes, "in a significant sense, not to see it at all" (2008, 3). To attend to the specificity of digital-born, code-driven, networked, and programmable textuality, we don't have to abandon the rich traditions of print, but we may need to mothball a series of trusted terms and mobilize in their stead a newly configured array of categories and concepts.

Reading procedures for print poetry and fiction track the line left to right, the page top to bottom, the volume front to back. In the Flash programming of Brian Kim Stefans's "The Dreamlife of Letters" or the Shockwave animation of Oni Buchanan's *The Mandrake Vehicles* (2006/2011), by contrast, words shoot forward from the back of the screen and letters swerve, spin, and peel away at speeds that strain the processing capacity of a print-trained reader. In the 3D Java Applet of Daniel C. Howe and Aya Karpinska's *open.ended* (2004/2006), texts slide across the rotating surfaces of nested translucent cubes to be read singly on cube faces, sequentially across faces, or back from what appears to be a front to the cubes' sides and undersides (see FLASH/DIRECTOR). In Dan Waber and Jason Primble's *I, You, We* (2005/2006), in similar fashion, verbs arrayed across a rotating grid or lattice can be clicked and dragged along *x*-, *y*-, and *z*-axes to form phrases, front to back, sideways, or diagonally between a stable, slightly off-center, first-person singular and revolving second-person and first-person plural pronouns (see ANIMATION/KINETICISM, DIGITAL POETRY, ELECTRONIC LITERATURE).

Without revising print-driven expectations, to set out to "read" such texts is to sign on to process every word, pursue each line to its end, and move in an orderly fashion from start to finish. Like Stein's soldiers, however, interpreters who stick with this strategy march to certain defeat. For this reason, from the start, critics of digital textuality have found it simpler, more productive, and much more fun to switch into game mode and "play," "use," or "explore" these networked and programmable engines or instruments (see GAMEPLAY).

The shift from stable to dynamic textuality has consequences for all aspects of the act of interpretation. Instead of auratic reverence, for example, digital interpreters tend to practice a kind of erratic experimentation. Exploiting the protocols of the programming at hand, players click and drag, cut and paste, jump in modular fashion from part to part, and rarely override the arc of their attention. Makers of these texts, in their turn, tend to position themselves as composers or programmers rather than "authors," artisans rather than "artists," collaborators rather than solitary originals. Editorial prefaces composed for such online anthologies as the *Electronic Literature Collection*, finally, identify the programs in which the texts are written, specify optimal browser settings and screen size, provide instructions to initiate play, and supplement a brief biography of the composer with an e-mail address that allows players to direct questions to the composers themselves.

As Stein implies, then, the canniest reading strategy for things "made by being made" is to set out and see what happens. More events than objects, digital texts contain their own pedagogy: they teach the cognitive strategies they require through an array of rewards and reverses. For this reason, the most useful approaches to digital textuality are often phenomenological reports of encounters with pieces Hayles (2002b, 2006, 2008) uses as "tutor texts": her parsing, for example, of Talan Memmott's poem engine *Lexia to Perplexia*; John Cayley's text movie of transliteral morphs entitled *RiverIsland*; or Stephanie Strickland, Cynthia Lawson Jaramillo, and Paul Ryan's kinetic verbal-visual collaboration *slippingglimpse*. Foregrounding the inscription technologies that produce them, these compositions are, in Hayles's term, "technotexts" that help us imagine the implications of their computational strategies for who we are, how we live, what we know, and what we can do in the twenty-first-century ecology Alan Liu calls "the culture of information" (2004).

"Media-specific analysis," which Hayles defines as "a kind of criticism that pays attention to the material apparatus producing a literary work as physical artifact" (2002b, 29), begins with a set of pragmatic questions: What are the rules that organize the world this text generates? What moves can users make to navigate it? How do we experience its instantiations of time and space? How does it visualize information and prepare the decisions a reader must make? What ontologies build from its mesh of hardware, software, and embodied subjectivity?

One effect of digital textualities has been to spur media-specific analysis of the predecessor regimes Walter J. Ong (1982), Eric Havelock (1986), and Marshall McLuhan (1964) called orality, literacy, and secondary orality, Friedrich Kittler (1990) theorized as "discourse networks 1800/1900," and Mark Weiser, Jason Farman, and other contemporary critics are now extending to include the smartphones, GPS systems, and radio-frequency identification (RFID) tags of so-called ubiquitous or pervasive computing (see INTERFACE). Each of these approaches assumes that cognition runs through circuits or systems that link human beings with each other, with their material artifacts and tools, and, for digital textualities, with networked and programmable machines. A last but crucial strategy for reading digital textuality, then, is to develop a lexicon through which to grasp the feedback and feed-forward loops that join human beings and intelligent machines in the "dynamic heterarchy" Hayles calls "intermediation" (2008, 45).

Three concepts foundational to this project are *cybertext*, *code*, and *transcoding*. Espen J. Aarseth's term *cybertext* (1997) merges Norbert Wiener's coinage *cybernetics* (1948) with the poststructuralist term *text* to signal a broad category of dynamic computational and combinatorial writing. "Mechanical device[s] for the production and consumption of verbal signs" (Aarseth 1997, 21), cybertexts can be constructed as games, print texts, computer programs, or electronic literature, all of which function through feedback loops that run between inscription devices and their users (see CYBERNETICS).

What distinguishes digital cybertexts from the *I Ching*'s divination system or Raymond Queneau's printed combinatorial sonnets is the machine code, assembly code, and high-level languages that prepare data for display. Readings of digital textuality which do not account for coding miss a feature John Cayley (2002), Matthew Fuller (2008), Matthew Kirschenbaum (2008), and others find as foundational to digital textuality as the words that form on a screen. To function adequately, reading strategies for digital literature must include a set of critical concepts sufficient to capture the dynamic, processual interchanges between the program's code, the screenic interface, and the clicking, dragging, scrolling, and navigating options it makes available to the interpreter.

The processual aesthetic constructed through code is also, as Lev Manovich (2001), Marcus Boon (2010), McKenzie Wark (2004), and others have suggested, a cultural ontology, epistemology, and pragmatics. A final strategy for reading digital literature, then, is to attend to the phenomenon Manovich calls *transcoding*: the ongoing, open-ended loop between computer operations such as matching, sorting, copying, cutting, pasting, appropriating, sampling, searching, filtering, storing, and morphing and such emergent cultural formations as database logic, the algorithmic imagination, and the open-source ethics of the hacker. Transcoding, in this sense, is, like other strategies for reading digital literature, a way to capture what Stein would call "things made by being made," the innovative practices of an age of information.

■ See also ALGORITHM, CODE, CODE AESTHETICS, COMBINATORY AND AUTOMATIC TEXT GENERATION, CONCEPTUAL WRITING, DATABASE, MASHUP, MEDIA ECOLOGY, SAMPLING, WRITING UNDER CONSTRAINT

References and Further Reading

Aarseth, Espen J. 1997. *Cybertext: Perspectives on Ergodic Literature*. Baltimore: Johns Hopkins University Press.

Boon, Marcus. 2010. *In Praise of Copying*. Cambridge, MA: Harvard University Press.

Buchanan, Oni. 2006/2011. *The Mandrake Vehicles*. In *Electronic Literature Collection*, volume 2, edited by Laura Borràs, Talan Memmott, Rita Raley, and Brian Kim Stefans. http://collection .eliterature.org/2/works/buchanan_mandrake_vehicles.html.

Cayley, John. 2002. "The Code Is Not the Text (Unless It IS the Text)." *electronic book review*. www .electronicbookreview.com/thread/electropoetics/literal.

Farman, Jason. 2012. *Mobile Interface Theory: Embodied Space and Locative Media*. New York: Routledge.

Fuller, Matthew. 2008. *Software Studies: A Lexicon*. Cambridge, MA: MIT Press.

Havelock, Eric A. 1986. *The Muse Learns to Write: Reflections on Orality and Literacy from Antiquity to the Present*. New Haven, CT: Yale University Press.

Hayles, N. Katherine. 2002a. "Electronic Literature as Technotext: Lexia to Perplexia." In *Writing Machines*, 46–63. Cambridge, MA: MIT Press.

———. 2002b. *Writing Machines*. Cambridge, MA: MIT Press.

———. 2006. "The Time of Digital Poetry: From Object to Event." In *New Media Poetics: Contexts, Technotexts, and Theories*, edited by Adalaide Morris and Thomas Swiss, 181–209. Cambridge, MA: MIT Press.

———. 2008. *Electronic Literature: New Horizons for the Literary*. Notre Dame, IN: University of Notre Dame Press.

———. 2009. "Strickland and Lawson Jaramillo's *slippingglimpse*: Distributed Cognition at/in Work." In *Literary Art in Digital Performance: Case Studies in New Media Art and Criticism*, edited by Francisco J. Ricardo, 38–47. New York: Continuum.

Howe, Daniel C., and Aya Karpinska. 2004/2006. *open.ended*. In *Electronic Literature Collection*, volume 1, edited by N. Katherine Hayles, Nick Montfort, Scott Rettberg, and Stephanie Strickland. http://collection.eliterature.org/1/works/howe_kaprinska__open_ended.html.

Kirschenbaum, Matthew. 2008. *Mechanisms: New Media and the Forensic Imagination*. Cambridge, MA: MIT Press.

Kittler, Friedrich A. 1990. *Discourse Networks 1800/1900*. Translated by Michael Metteer, with Chris Cullens. Stanford, CA: Stanford University Press.

Liu, Alan. 2004. *The Laws of Cool: Knowledge Work and the Culture of Information*. Chicago: University of Chicago Press.

Manovich, Lev. 2001. *The Language of New Media*. Cambridge, MA: MIT Press.

McLuhan, Marshall. 1964. *Understanding Media: The Extensions of Man*. New York: McGraw-Hill.

Ong, Walter J. 1982. *Orality and Literacy: The Technologizing of the Word*. New York: Methuen.

Queneau, Raymond. 1982. *Cent mille milliards de poèmes*. Paris: Gallimard/NRE.

Stefans, Brian Kim. 2000/2006. "The Dreamlife of Letters." In *Electronic Literature Collection*, volume 1, edited by N. Katherine Hayles, Nick Montfort, Scott Rettberg, and Stephanie Strickland. http://collection.eliterature.org/1/works/stefans__the_dreamlife_of_letters.html.

Stein, Gertrude. (1926) 1998. "Composition as Explanation." In *Writings 1903–1932*, edited by Catharine R. Stimpson and Harriet Chessman, 520–529. New York: Library of America.

Waber, Dan, and Jason Primble. 2005/2006. *I, You, We*. In *Electronic Literature Collection*, volume 1, edited by N. Katherine Hayles, Nick Montfort, Scott Rettberg, and Stephanie Strickland. http://collection.eliterature.org/1/works/waber_pimble__i_you_we.html.

Wark, McKenzie. 2004. *A Hacker Manifesto*. Cambridge, MA: Harvard University Press.

Weiser, Mark. 1994. "The World Is Not a Desktop." *Interactions*, January, 7–8.
Wiener, Norbert. 1948. *Cybernetics: Or Control and Communication in the Animal and the Machine.* New York: Technology Press.

●●

Relations between Media

Philipp Schweighauser

In 1913 the German journalist and newspaper editor Wolfgang Riepl formulated what he considered "a fundamental law of the development of communication systems": "that the most simple means, forms, and methods are never fully and permanently displaced or put out of use by even the most perfect and most highly developed forms once they have become established and are found useful. But they may be compelled to search for other tasks and fields of use" (1913, 5). The example that Riepl gives in the footnote immediately following this passage is the use of the "ancient" medium of smoke signals to guide the Peruvian aviator Jorge Chávez's flight across the Simplon Pass in 1910. Riepl's account of the survival and refunctioning of older media under the pressure of new technological developments is not without its ideological impasses: his juxtaposition of "the most highly developed means, methods and forms of communication in civilized states [*Kulturstaaten*]" and "the most simple, primeval forms of various primitive peoples" (1913, 4) testifies to a primitivist evolutionism that we have learned to distrust. The empirical validity of Riepl's assertion has not gone unchallenged either: Werner Faulstich even asserts that "Riepl's Law" is "actually no law at all and simply wrong as a hypothesis" (2002, 159). Indeed, one would be hard-pressed to think of current uses of papyrus rolls, telegraphs, and floppy disks as media of communication. Smoke signals, too, have long disappeared from the world of aviation. Still, Riepl's contention helps us explain why television, CDS, and e-mail have not fully displaced the radio, vinyl records, and letters despite alarmist or celebratory announcements of their imminent demise. Riepl also helps us understand why the telephone has metamorphosed into the smartphone once it came under pressure from fully computerized forms of communication such as e-mail and online chat. More than that, half a century before Marshall McLuhan's first forages into media ecology in *The Gutenberg Galaxy: The Making of Typographic Man* (2000) and his influential assertion, in *Understanding Media: The Extensions of Man* (1964), that "the 'content' of any medium is always another medium" (1994, 8), Riepl invites us to think about the impact of new media on old media (see ME-DIA ECOLOGY, OLD MEDIA / NEW MEDIA).

Yet one should be careful not to conflate Riepl's and McLuhan's interventions in media history. McLuhan develops what he calls a "cultural ecology" (2000, 35) to study not only how old media are forced to adapt their forms and functions under the pressure of new technologies but also how the "ratio and interplay among the senses" and thus "the very constitution of rationality" (2000, 13) change when new media are introduced. It was Neil Postman who coined the term "media ecology," which largely corresponds to McLuhan's "cultural ecology": "Media ecology looks into the matter of how media of communication affect human perception, understanding, feeling, and value; and how our interaction with media facilitates or impedes our chances of survival" (Postman 1970, 61). Unlike Postman and McLuhan, Riepl focuses primarily on the technological effects of new media and has no sustained interest in their psychological and cultural impact.

Further, Riepl contends that old media take on new functions and move into new operational fields when rivaled by new media, thus focusing on what Raymond Williams calls the "residual" elements of culture, i.e., that which "has been effectively formed in the past but is still active in the cultural process, not only and often not at all as an element of the past, but as an effective element of the present" (1977, 122). By way of contrast, McLuhan argues that new media "contain" older media in the sense that they preserve and rework forms and functions of older media (see MATERIALITY). Both challenge claims that new media simply displace old media, but while Riepl's Law invites us to consider the effects of media competition on the old media themselves, McLuhan's contention that "the content of writing is speech, just as the written word is the content of print, and print is the content of the telegraph" (1994, 8) asks us to focus on how old media "live on" in new media, thus ensuring a certain "biodiversity" in media culture. In the posthumously published *Laws of Media: The New Science* (1988), McLuhan and his son Eric conceptualize these processes by way of a tetrad that captures the four fundamental social and psychological effects of the media (enhancement, obsolescence, retrieval, reversal) as a unity of simultaneous and complementary actions. Based on this model, the McLuhans formulate four laws of media as a set of four questions that are taken to apply not only to media of communication but to all technologies encompassed by McLuhan's very broad definition of media as "any extension of ourselves" (1994, 7):

1. What does the artifact enhance or intensify or make possible or accelerate? This can be asked concerning a wastebasket, a painting, a steamroller, or a zipper, as well as about a proposition in Euclid or a law of physics. It can be asked about any word or phrase in any language.
2. If some aspect of a situation is enlarged or enhanced, simultaneously the old condition or unenhanced situation is displaced thereby. What is pushed aside or obsolesced by the new "organ"?
3. What recurrence or retrieval of earlier actions and services is brought into play simultaneously by the new form? What older, previously obsolesced ground is brought back and inheres in the new form?
4. When pushed to the limits of its potential (another complementary action), the new form will tend to reverse what had been its original characteristics. What is the reversal potential of the new form? (1988, 98–99)

To ask these questions is "to draw attention to situations that are still in process, situations that are structuring new perception and shaping new environments, even while they are restructuring old ones" (1988, 116). In trying to answer them, the McLuhans hoped, media ecology would enable scholars to predict and, if necessary, correct the social and psychological effects of new media. On a more modest scale, the four laws of media also invite us to study the impact of new media on old media. The McLuhans themselves suggest this in their examples, which further emphasize the simultaneity and complementarity of the processes that make up the tetrad: "The photograph enhances pictorial realism and obsolesces portrait painting. The vacuum cleaner obsolesces the broom and the beater; the dryer pushes aside the clothes-line, and the washer the washboard and tub; the refrigerator replaces the icebox and the root cellar" (99–100). As is often the case with McLuhan, his customarily far-reaching claims need to be qualified: both portrait painting and the broom are still with us. More problematically, these examples of the complementary processes of enhancement and obsolescence are easily amenable to the kind of "epochal" media history—to use another useful term by Williams (1977)—that both McLuhan and Riepl actually reject. The case is different with "retrieval" and "reversal." Both notions serve McLuhan to counter teleological media histories that conceptualize changes in media ecologies exclusively in terms of the happy displacement of imperfect older media by more advanced new media. While reversal marks the technological, social, and physical limits of such progressivist histories, retrieval conceptualizes how old media "live on" in new media: "Money obsolesces barter, but retrieves potlatch in the form of conspicuous consumption. The digital watch displaces the old circular dial, and retrieves the sundial form, which likewise used light itself to tell the time and which also had no moving parts" (McLuhan and McLuhan 1988, 106).

Apart from McLuhan's seminal assertion that "the 'content' of any medium is always another medium," it is his reflections on retrieval that resonate most strongly in Jay David Bolter and Richard Grusin's programmatically subtitled *Remediation: Understanding New Media* (1999) (see REMEDIATION). Bolter and Grusin agree with McLuhan that media history is not a progressive series of radical ruptures. Instead, every new medium "remediates" one or several older media, i.e., it "responds to, redeploys, competes with, and reforms other media" (1999, 55) rather than displacing them. Bolter and Grusin do the important work of updating some of McLuhan's theorems for the study of digital media. Perhaps, though, their most pertinent intervention into media ecology concerns a notion that they only discuss in passing: "retrograde remediation," i.e., the process by which "a newer medium is imitated and even absorbed by an older one" (1999, 147). Thus, tablet computers remediate smartphones, motion pictures enhanced with computer-generated imagery such as Christopher Nolan's *Inception* (2010) remediate computer technology, and experimental book objects such as *McSweeney's Quarterly Concern, Issue 16* (2005)—which contains a collection of short stories, a novella, a comb, and a set of cards with text by Robert Coover which generates a different narrative whenever the cards are shuffled anew—remediate digital hypertext (see HYPERTEXTUALITY). Including processes of retrograde remediation in their discussion allows Bolter and Grusin to update not only McLuhan's studies of old media's continuing presence within new media but also Riepl's earlier reflections on the impact of new media on old media themselves. What is largely lost along the way, though, is McLuhan's focus on the psychological and cultural effects of media change—a focus that Michael Giesecke develops further in his "historical media ecology," which recognizes the necessity of multimedial, decentralized networks and synaesthetic information processing in the digital age while calling for the integration of all media and communicators, including both digital communication systems and human dialogue, in an "ecological equilibrium" (2002, 405–407).

References and Further Reading

Bolter, Jay David, and Richard Grusin. 1999. *Remediation: Understanding New Media*. Cambridge, MA: MIT Press.

Faulstich, Werner. 2002. *Einführung in die Medienwissenschaft*. Munich: Wilhelm Fink.

Giesecke, Michael. 2002. *Von den Mythen der Buchkultur zu den Visionen der Informationsgesellschaft: Trendforschungen zur kulturellen Medienökologie*. Frankfurt am Main: Suhrkamp.

McLuhan, Marshall. (1964) 1994. *Understanding Media: The Extensions of Man*. Cambridge, MA: MIT Press.

———. 2000. *The Gutenberg Galaxy: The Making of Typographic Man*. Toronto: University of Toronto Press.

McLuhan, Marshall, and Eric McLuhan. 1988. *Laws of Media: The New Science.* Toronto: University of Toronto Press.

McSweeney's Quarterly Concern, Issue 16. 2005. San Francisco: McSweeney's.

Nolan, Christopher. 2010. *Inception.* Perf. Leonardo DiCaprio, Joseph Gordon-Levitt, and Ellen Page. Warner Bros. Pictures.

Postman, Neil. 1970. "The Reformed English Curriculum." In *High School 1980: The Shape of the Future in American Secondary Education,* edited by A. C. Eurich, 160–168. New York: Pitman.

Riepl, Wolfgang. 1913. *Über das Nachrichtenwesen des Altertums: Mit besonderer Rücksicht auf die Römer.* Leipzig: Teubner.

Williams, Raymond. 1977. "Dominant, Residual, and Emergent." In *Marxism and Literature,* 121–127. Oxford: Oxford University Press.

....

Remediation
Jay David Bolter

Remediation as a term in media studies was defined by Jay David Bolter and Richard Grusin in their monograph of the same name, published in 1999. The term is meant to describe the complex relationships of rivalry and cooperation among forms and genres in a media economy (see RELATIONS BETWEEN MEDIA). Bolter and Grusin begin with the observation that new media forms do not simply spring into existence, but are instead outgrowths of technologies, techniques, and practices of older media. The medium of film, for example, grows out of a series of technologies of the moving image in the nineteenth century (such as the zoetrope, the phenokistoscope, and the zoopraxiscope). At the same time the techniques of filmic representation and the genres of film in the first decades of the twentieth century have antecedents in stage production and the novel. This relationship is universally acknowledged. However, under the influence of modernist aesthetics, media scholars and popular writers often assume that such relationships represent a beginning phase that is surpassed as the new medium or media form develops a language based on its own essential properties. Bolter and Grusin argue that these remediating relationships never end, even after the new medium has supposedly developed its own expressive forms. Newer and older media forms continue to borrow from one another as long as they remain part of a flourishing media economy. Remediation describes all the various relationships of cooperation and competition, rivalry and homage, and can involve form as well as content. Classic Hollywood film remediated nineteenth-century literature (e.g., the novels of Dickens, the Brontes, Hugo, and so on) by retelling their stories in the new visual medium. At the same time film borrowed and creatively refashioned the dramatic arc of earlier melodrama to create the standard so-called three-act film. Remediation need not be slavish borrowing; it can and often does involve creative and even radical refashioning.

Contemporary digital forms remediate a host of different forms from older media, which themselves remain important in today's media economy. The World Wide Web is a vigorous remediator. For example, news websites such as the *New York Times*'s nytimes .com remediate principally the printed version of the newspaper, while CNN's cnn.com remediates its own television networks. Web-based services (such as Hulu and Netflix) that stream television and film remediate these older media. Political blogs remediate the political pamphlet, the opinion pages of printed newspapers, and, with the addition of video, the politically oriented news channels and commentators. *Wikipedia* explicitly remediates the printed encyclopedia, whereas social networking sites such as Facebook remediate letter writing and phone calls, as well as the sharing of photographs and the playing of games among friends (see SOCIAL NETWORK SITES [SNSs]). Remediation can also function in the other direction; older media forms such as film and television can appropriate conventions and materials from digital media (see FILM AND DIGITAL MEDIA). Broadcast news shows such as CNN employ a composite screen consisting of (moving) text as well as the video image in an obvious remediation of the web page. Hollywood now often turns popular video games into films, as it has done with the *Resident Evil* or *Tomb Raider* series. The latter is a good example of what is now sometimes called cross-media or transmedia, because the original video game franchise has spawned a series of media artifacts, including comics, novels, films, and even theme park rides. The current interest in transmedia can be understood as a vindication of the premise of remediation: that media forms are intimately related and produce various strategies of cooperation and competition.

In every act of remediation, there is an implicit, if not explicit, claim of improvement. The designers or producers of the remediating form are suggesting that their product can do something better than the original. They are claiming to provide an experience that is more compelling, more authentic, or more "real" than the original. The claim of greater reality or fidelity is particularly clear when the remediation takes older material into a newer media technology. For example, Hollywood films of the 1930s often took classic novels or plays and remediated in the new medium of talking pictures. There was certainly an element of respectful remediation here, an act of homage to canonical authors and narratives of the past. At the same time, film was being offered as a superior medium for telling such narratives because it could make them vivid and visual. A contrary claim was and is still made by supporters of the older medium of print: that reading a novel is more compelling precisely because more is left to the reader's imagination. The argument about the relative power of filmic and print narrative is the classic argument of remediation: it focuses on which medium can claim the greater capacity to represent or engage with the real. A similar argument is made today between traditional Hollywood film and the newer media of video games and interactive narrative. Proponents of digital media forms emphasize the quality that these media have and that is lacking in the earlier forms of visual and verbal storytelling. Digital media are "interactive" and can therefore involve the reader (who becomes a user) as never before (see INTERACTIVITY). The reader/user participates in the story and can affect its outcome or meaning. Enthusiasts of the older forms of film or the printed novel counter that this interactivity amounts to little, because the reader/user cannot effectively participate in the story without destroying its essential, authored intentionality.

Bolter and Grusin went on to identify two general strategies of representation which artists and designers can pursue in a wide variety of media forms: immediacy and hypermediacy. The strategy of immediacy, which might be called "transparency," was favored by painters in Europe from the Renaissance until at least the nineteenth century. The development of linear perspective and other illusionist techniques enabled painters to claim that their pictures were accurate reproductions of what the eye saw when it looked on a scene in the physical world. Their techniques therefore made the painting into a transparent window onto the world, and the medium (paint on canvas) effectively disappeared for the viewer. The strategy of immediacy or transparency, which seeks to make the medium disappear for the viewer or user, remains an important aesthetic for popular media today. Hollywood cinema and so-called serious television drama gener-ally employ this strategy. The drive to create photorealistic graphics for video games and virtual reality is a contemporary example of the desire for transparency.

The counterpart of transparency is hypermediacy. If the strategy of transparency seeks to make the medium disappear, hypermediacy foregrounds the medium and the process of mediation for the viewer or user. In the twentieth century, hypermediacy was associated with avant-garde painting, photography, or film, but in recent decades hyper-mediacy has become an increasingly popular style: examples include music videos and the multimedia, multiwindowed style of many websites, including popular social net-working sites such as Facebook. The strategies of both hypermediacy and transparency can function for the remediation of other media forms. The desktop graphical user inter-face, for example, can remediate various forms of information (text, photographic im-ages and graphics, and videos) in multiple windows. The screen becomes hypermediated as the user moves back and forth among windows reading and editing all these forms. Transparency can also be a remediating strategy: for example, virtual reality has been used to allow a viewer to "walk into" a Renaissance painting.

As a media theory, remediation has been criticized as reductive and formalist. It fo-cuses on the way in which new media constitute a formal refashioning of older ones. For example, film refashions the novel by transforming prose into a visual narrative with camera work and editing. Video games refashion films by making their stories proce-dural and interactive: putting the user into the action. The criticism is that an emphasis on formal remediation ignores the socioeconomic aspects of media production and competition.

Richard Grusin (2010) has recently supplemented the notion of remediation with what he calls "premediation," calling attention to the ways in which popular media an-ticipate or prefigure future events, particularly in the political realm (war, terrorism, etc.), as in effect to lessen the trauma and potential political backlash.

■ See also ANALOG VERSUS DIGITAL, BOOK TO E-TEXT, CHARACTERISTICS OF DIGITAL MEDIA, HISTORY OF COMPUTERS, OLD MEDIA / NEW MEDIA

References and Further Reading

Bolter, Jay David, and Richard Grusin. 1999. *Remediation: Understanding New Media*. Cambridge, MA: MIT Press.

Bolter, Jay David, Blair MacIntyre, Maribeth Gandy, and Petra Schweitzer. 2006. "New Media and the Permanent Crisis of Aura." *Convergence* 12 (1): 21–39.

Grusin, Richard. 2010. *Premediation: Affect and Mediality after 9/11*. New York: Palgrave Macmillan.

Qvortrup, Lars, and Heidi Philipsen, eds. 2007. *Moving Media Studies: Remediation Revisited*. Fredriksberg, Denmark: Samfunslitteratur Press.

Remix

Aaron Angello

Remix is both a verb and a noun, a process and a product. It involves the appropriation of preexisting media (text, image, audio, video) and the recontextualization and/or reshaping of those media with the end goal of creating a new work. This new work doesn't pretend to be a unique creation of the remixer, but rather remains transparent;

the appropriated source material is generally apparent in the remix. Today, the process of remix, as well as the term *remix* itself, is particularly characterized by our current global, network culture, the free exchange of information, and "the practice of cut/copy and paste" (Navas, n.d.) and is practiced across the spectrum of cultural production, including music, literature, film, visual art, and net art. The artist, writer, or theorist, often incorporating the practice of sampling, uses existing source material(s) and combines, manipulates, and/or reshapes it (them) into a remix (see SAMPLING). Remix is closely associated with the practices of conceptual appropriation, which involves reframing existing source material without otherwise changing it, and remaking/covering.

History

Although the practice of appropriating found source material has existed for centuries, the term *remix* first began to achieve cultural significance in the world of countercultural music production (see MUSIC) in the late 1960s and early 1970s in New York City. Dance music DJs, heavily influenced by the practices of Jamaican reggae producers who would create alternate "versions" of a song on the B-side of a record (known as "dub") in which the vocals and some instrumentals were removed to highlight the "riddim tracks," began isolating percussion "breaks" from the popular records they were spinning. These "turntablists," as they were (still are) called, manipulated the breaks through scratching, beat juggling, and mixing and matching, taking the source material and making it into something of their own. The practice expanded to disco as a way of expanding tracks and highlighting the danceable rhythms, and then to hip-hop artists, who, in response to (or reaction to) disco, began isolating breaks and manipulating them. This was the original use of the term *remix*.

Concepts and procedures that are associated with remix today have been in play for centuries. One can cite the third- or fourth-century cento, a poetic form involving the assemblage of unattributed lines from other poems, as an example of early remix practice. The early twentieth century saw artists combining found objects into collage (e.g., Picasso's *Still Life with Chair Caning* [1912]) and poets and writers appropriating existing text into their own (e.g., T. S. Eliot's *The Waste Land* [1922] and Walter Benjamin's *The Arcades Project* [1927–1940]). But perhaps the early twentieth-century artist who has had the biggest impact on contemporary remix culture is Marcel Duchamp, whose appropriative works, including *Fountain* (1917) and *L.H.O.O.Q.* (1919), are often considered exemplary precursors of the practice.

Mid- to late twentieth-century artists and writers began to more fully incorporate appropriation and remix into their practices. William S. Burroughs, along with the painter Brion Gysin, famously employed the "cut-up" method, in which he took his own and others' texts, literally cut them into pieces, and reassembled them into a new text (e.g., *The Nova Trilogy*). Kathy Acker's *Blood and Guts in High School* is a mashup (see MASHUP) "of a 19th century literary character [Hester Prynne] with a much subtler caricature of her own literary presence in the late 20th century, and [she] uses this mash-up process to investigate innovative methods of manipulating both story content and traditional narrative devices" (www.remixthebook.com). The process is apparent in mid- to late twentieth-century visual arts as well. One need look no further than Andy Warhol's and Jeff Koon's appropriation of images from popular culture in their work as examples. Sherrie Levine's *Fountain (After Marcel Duchamp: A.P.)* appropriates and reinterprets Duchamp's *Fountain*, and her series *After Walker Evans*, in which she photographs Walker

Evans's photographs and displays them without manipulation, forces examination of the question of authorship in the processes of creative composition. Similarly, Cindy Sherman, in her *Film Stills* series, appropriates imagery from classic films, remaking the still with herself as protagonist.

The defining characteristic of remix today, however, is the availability of source material on the web (see SAMPLING). Marjorie Perloff, in her book *Unoriginal Genius: Poetry by Other Means in the New Century*, highlights the fact that "the language of citation . . . has found a new lease on life in our own information age" (2010, 4). Remix theorist Eduardo Navas defines remix culture as "the global activity consisting of the creative and efficient exchange of information made possible by digital technologies that is supported by the practice of cut/copy and paste" (Navas, n.d.). The ease of access to apparently limitless source material has created a culture of sampling that is unprecedented. Image, video, audio, and text are simply there for the taking, and remix has arguably become the dominant form of cultural production. From contemporary music to YouTube and *Wikipedia*, remix has become ubiquitous in our hyperconnected society.

The Four Forms of Remix

Eduardo Navas has identified four forms of remix: extended, selective, reflexive, and regenerative.

Extended remix, first appearing predominantly in DJ club culture, is the act of extending a three- to four-minute song to a much longer piece. Navas contends that this is in fact a reaction against society's desire to summarize and/or condense cultural products into easily consumable, short pieces (e.g., *Reader's Digest* and the two-minute replay of television shows). A short, consumable cultural product (a three-and-a-half-minute song, for example) is marketable within a society based on capital. The extended remix thus reexamines the idea that a song, or any other short, easily consumable cultural product, must exist within this paradigm.

Selective remix is when the remixer selectively incorporates outside source material into an existing work, or selectively removes elements of the original, while leaving the original work's aura intact. Navas cites Levine's *Fountain (After Marcel Duchamp: A.P.)* as a prime example. Levine's work is a copy of Duchamp's, but cast in brass. The "aura" of Duchamp's piece remains, but she has literally recast it as a field of new meaning, one that questions patriarchy and power within both the art world and society in general. Duchamp's urinal is clearly present in the work, as is Duchamp himself. But the fact that Levine remixes the work by recasting it in bronze alters the piece's social function. It is no longer a reframed, mass-produced object.

The reflexive remix relies heavily on the allegorical nature of the sample. Parts of other works are taken out of context and placed in juxtaposition to each other with the aim of creating an autonomous work that challenges the authority of the original. Navas says that "this strategy demands that the viewer reflect on the meaning of the work and its sources— even when knowing the original may not be possible" (Navas, n.d.). Referring to the photo collage work of Hannah Hoch, Navas says that "the authority of the image lies in the acknowledgment of each fragment individually." Each piece carries its own allegorical weight, and there is a tension in the fragments' relationship. The viewer is compelled to deal with that tension and to come to her/his own conclusion as to what it means.

The regenerative remix is entirely reliant on the web and a continuous flow of information. In a regenerative remix, the source material is constantly updated, either by a large number of users who are constantly updating information (YouTube, *Wikipedia*, Flicker) or by software that pulls information from the web and automatically includes it in the remix (generative e-poetry). The regenerative remix is particularly characterized by the fact of its plasticity; it is always in a state of change.

Copyright

The proliferation of remix culture raises questions of legality (see COPY-RIGHT) in Western society. Lawrence Lessig, the noted professor of law at Stanford and advocate for changing existing copyright laws, raises concern about "the harm to a generation from rendering criminal what comes naturally to them" (2008, 18). In his 2008 book *Remix*, he compares what he calls read/write (RW) culture to read-only (RO) culture. The RO culture is concerned with producing cultural products that are simply consumed. The RW culture, on the other hand, is characterized by "ordinary citizens" reading their culture and then "add[ing] to the culture they read by creating and re-creating the culture around them" (2008, 28). RO culture is concerned with consumption, while RW culture is concerned with creativity. Both exist, are important, and will be a part of our culture. Lessig goes on to identify two economies that are existing concurrently: the commercial economy and the sharing economy. He says, "There exists not just the commercial economy, which meters access on the simple metric of price, but by a complex set of social relations," and "these relations are insulted by the simplicity of price" (2008, 145). For Lessig, the answer to the problem of "rendering criminal" an entire generation is to establish a "hybrid economy" in which copyright laws are altered to reflect the creative and cultural benefits of remix.

Source Material Everywhere

Mark Amerika's *remixthebook* (2011a) and www.remixthebook.com (2011b) represent an important recent development in the evolution of remix theory. One of the "primary aims of the project is to create a cross-disciplinary approach to the way contemporary theory is performed and to anticipate future forms of writing that challenge traditional modes of scholarly production" (2011a, xi). Amerika is interested in expanding the very notion of "scholarly writing and publishing to include multimedia art forms composed for networked and mobile media environments" (2011b) through the process of practice-based research. The book itself, published by the University of Minnesota Press, is a collection of remixed "sampled phrases and ideas from visual artists, poets, novelists, musicians, theorists, comedians, and process philosophers" (2011a, xi). For Amerika, digital culture provides the access to unprecedented information just begging to be remixed. This is what he refers to as "source material everywhere." The role of practice-based research, or artist-generated theory, is the logical path for the future of scholarly production. To deny that source material *is* everywhere is to deny the very condition of our existence today.

■ See also CONCEPTUAL WRITING, COPYRIGHT, MASHUP, MUSIC, SAMPLING, SOUND

References and Further Reading

Amerika, Mark. 2011a. *remixthebook*. Minneapolis: University of Minnesota Press.
———. 2011b. *remixthebook*. www.remixthebook.com/.
disrupt. 2012. "Dub: King Tubby, the Black Ark, and Scientist." *Jahtari*. www.jahtari.org/magazine/reggae-history/dub.htm.

Lessig, Lawrence. 2008. *Remix: Making Art and Commerce Thrive in the Hybrid Economy*. New York: Penguin.

Miller, Paul D. 2004. *Rhythm Science*. Cambridge, MA: MIT Press.

Navas, Eduardo. n.d. *Remix Theory*. http://remixtheory.net/.

Perloff, Marjorie. 2010. *Unoriginal Genius: Poetry by Other Means in the New Century*. Chicago: University of Chicago Press.

· ·

Role-Playing Games
Olivier Caïra and Susana Pajares Tosca

Role-playing games are games in which a group of players get together to engage in a form of collective performative storytelling, based on players enacting the roles of characters in a fictional world. Interaction occurs through dialogue, while real-world actions are typically simulated by rolling dice and calculating success rates on the basis of a specific rule system.

Basing their research on a wide variety of role-playing games, Hitchens and Drachen (2008) have proposed a more open six-component definition model. For them, a role-playing game is "a game set in an imaginary world" that needs to contain a game world, participants (who adopt the roles of either characters or game masters), the possibility for players to interact with the world, and a narrative.

From War Games to Tabletop Role-Playing Games (RPGs)

The beginnings of the history of role-playing are usually tracked to the early 1970s, although the hobby was inspired by the much older pastime of war gaming, or simulating battles with tokens on a board. This type of game started in 1811 with the Prussian game *Kriegspiel* (Fine 1983, 8). War gamers were interested in both historical re-creation and the ludic possibilities of rule-based interaction.

In due time, war games spawned a more flexible form that allowed for the performance of character and storytelling (see PERFORMANCE). This new development coincided with the U.S. publication and wide distribution of J. R. R. Tolkien's *Lord of the Rings* epic, which inaugurated the high fantasy literary genre and inspired many imitations, appealing to the same demographic as war gaming. In the early 1970s, different groups of war gamers were experimenting with rules and settings, but it was Gary Gygax and David Arneson who developed the rules of what was to be the first fantasy RPG ever published, *Dungeons & Dragons*, released in 1974 by TSR Hobbies, Inc. (Fine 1983, 14). This game was based on a vague medieval setting, where players had to organize themselves into parties and explore dungeons, collect treasure, and kill monsters. Players had to roll dice to determine their six basic attributes: strength, dexterity, wisdom, constitution, intelligence, and charisma. They could also choose among seven races, each endowed with its own distinct characteristics (human, dwarf, elf, halfling, gnome, half-orc, half-elf), and four classes (fighter, magic user, cleric, and thief), which involved different abilities. Action was focused on combat, finding treasure, and collecting points. This would be the basic template upon which countless games would be designed in the following years.

It took *Dungeons & Dragons* a few years to sell well, but in the 1980s, the niche phenomenon had turned into a full-blown hobby with a solid fan base. The genre of the tabletop RPG had been born. Some notable titles of the golden era of the 1980s include *Call of Cthulhu* (1981), a game based on the universe of H. P. Lovecraft which had a strong focus on character enactment; GURPS (1984), an empty rule system that could be applied to any universe and allowed fans to develop their own fictional worlds; *Cyberpunk* (1988), which opened the door to a whole new theme in science fiction (see CYBERPUNK); and *Vampire: The Masquerade* (1991), which emphasized storytelling over treasure hunting and introduced gothic themes that appealed to a new audience. In the 1990s and later, the hobby continued to spawn new fictional worlds, where mature or socially critical themes stand side by side with humorous, light games. It has also produced experimental rule systems, some more open than the original system and others inspired by the procedural strength of the computer.

Tabletop RPGs as Ludic and Creative Experience

A tabletop RPG (also known as a pen-and-paper game) is both a product and a performance (see PERFORMANCE). The product can be a book, an electronic file, or a boxed set of rules, dice, maps, and character sheets. It displays a fictional universe and a formal system to create characters and simulate their nontrivial actions (combat, investigation, magic, racing) and their evolution from adventure to adventure (possessions, levels, physical and psychological aftereffects). Many games also contain scenarios and sample characters in their core rule book or in supplements.

As a performance, the game is organized by a game master who describes a setting and provides a plot, using natural speech: "Suddenly, as you are entering the White Boar's Inn, a young man collapses just in front of you. He seems to be holding something in his left hand." Each player describes what her character will do (for trivial actions: eating, walking, etc.) or will try to do (for nontrivial actions: lock picking, fighting, etc.). The game master determines the outcome of each action, according to the rules and to common sense, and describes the resulting situation. These loops will go on for several hours, until the plot is resolved.

Tabletop games are not only interactive but also interpretative. Players can freely simulate police interrogation, courtship, or diplomatic bargaining. The game master's description will adjust gradually to the characters' speech, rather than relying on canned responses, as in computer games. A human game master will use both rules and common sense to determine the outcome of this choice: the mate can be crippled and angry, but he can also be very excited about the evidence found in the room. In improvised fiction, the players need not consider all possible actions and lines of dialogue; they simply adjust their actions to each other's choices.

Although many adventures and campaign settings are supplied by publishers and magazines, tabletop role-playing provides an easy and cost-efficient way for game masters to create their own plots. They allow their participants to test and improve their narrative skills, often starting in their early teens. Several famous computer game designers, such as Sandy Petersen, Warren Spector, and Greg Costikyan, have first published tabletop games.

From Tabletop RPGs to Computer Games

Tabletop RPGs are generally considered to be the ancestors of many forms of computer games, from text-based MUDs and MOOs to text adventures (see INTERACTIVE FICTION, MUDS AND MOOS), single-player RPGs, and multiplayer online games such as *World of Warcraft* (see ONLINE WORLDS). They have provided inspiration for many simulation and storytelling techniques to computer games studios. Most computer RPGs use character sheets, hit points, mana pools, experience points, and levels, sometimes with explicit references to the tabletop rule books: *Neverwinter Nights* (2002) showed the result of each "dice roll" on-screen, as if a game master were using the *Dungeons & Dragons* handbook throughout the adventure. The division of time into "rounds," corresponding to discontinuous units of actions, is a way for tabletop players to slow down the action in order to simulate fights or races. It can be used as a tactical device, as in *Fallout* (1997, 1998, 2008), a series of computer games partly based on the tabletop role-playing game system *GURPS* (1986).

The relationship between tabletop and computer role-playing games is also strong in terms of ludic structures and storytelling techniques. "Dungeon crawls," adventures based on the first typical *Dungeons & Dragons* modules (exploring mazes, fighting monsters, and looting treasures), became one of the first computer game genres, from *Dungeon* (1978) and *Rogue* (1980) to *Diablo* (1996) and *Dungeons of Dredmor* (2011) (see GAME GENRES). In the 1980s came the first pen-and-paper "sandbox" campaigns, such as *Masks of Nyarlathotep* (1984) for *Call of Cthulhu* (1982): a mix of action and investigation set in an open world, based on nonlinear play and multiple subplots. This "free roam" structure became a major genre in the 3D open worlds of computer games such as *Shenmue* (1999) and *Grand Theft Auto III* (2001). Above all, pen-and-paper campaigns showed that interactive storytelling (see INTERACTIVE NARRATIVE) was not necessarily made of forking narrative threads (the structure of Choose Your Own Adventure books), but from the modular articulation of several plot elements: places, events, characters, objects, and so on.

Not all the features of tabletop role-playing can be transposed to computer gaming. As Marie-Laure Ryan explains, the epic plot, "which focuses on the struggle of the individual to survive in a hostile world . . . has long been a favorite of game designers" (2008, 6) (see PLOT TYPES AND INTERACTIVITY). A software application is better than a human game master at simulating fights and races in real time. On the other hand, Ryan's dramatic plot ("which deals with the evolution of a network of human relations") and epistemic plot ("which is propelled by the desire to solve a mystery") remain favorite structures of tabletop role-playing games, because a game master can interpret natural speech and use common sense.

An important difference between tabletop and computer games is that in the former the natural intelligence of the players and game master allows improvisation and adaptation to unforeseen situations, whereas in the latter all possible actions and outcomes must be preplanned by the designer, and all lines of dialogue must be written in advance. Whereas in tabletop role-playing games the plot is created dynamically during play time, in computer games players usually progress along predetermined plot lines, even when the plot is branching.

Research

There has been ongoing discussion about the hobby of role-playing since its beginnings in the 1970s, mostly in the form of articles in specialized magazines and fanzines. As Mason notes, the early theorizing of role-playing games was a matter of technicalities (2004, 3), such as discussing the pertinence of a particular rule or the accuracy of a game system.

The first academic study of the hobby was Gary Allan Fine's *Shared Fantasy: Role-Playing Games as Social Worlds* (1983), which looked at how participants played with different levels of identity and were able to conjure immersive worlds of fantasy. His analysis is based on an extensive ethnographic study, and its theoretical inspiration is Erwin Goffman's (1974) frame analysis. Even though the hobby has changed a lot in the meantime (for example, in the attitudes toward girl gamers or in the pool of available games), many of his conclusions are still relevant. He was the first to positively articulate the cultural potential of shared fantasy to generate social worlds (Fine 1983, 231), to identify the tensions between the fixed rules and players' creativity (1983, 234), or to speculate about the implications of these games for the everyday life of their players (1983, 240). All these topics later became central in the emergent disciplines of digital culture and computer game studies.

Paul Mason records the short-lived *Interactive Fantasy*, from 1994, as the first journal dedicated to role-playing. The four issues dealt with topics such as game system taxonomies, playing styles (puppet-play, type-play, personality-play, and mask-play), and the nature of role-playing as an art form (Mason 2004, 10).

In the Internet era of the 1990s, discussion about role-playing games moved online, where it flourished in fora and newsgroups, and continues to do so (for example, in RPG.net, the Forge, GameDev.net, and others). The debate in these communities sometimes reaches a highly theoretical level, even though it can only be described as semiacademic.

It was not until 2001 that two serious monographs dedicated to the subject appeared: Daniel Mackay's *The Fantasy Role-Playing Game: A New Performing Art* (2001), which looks at the hobby from a performance art perspective, and Robin Laws's *Robin's Laws of Good Game Mastering* (2001), written from a designer's perspective (Mason 2004, 12).

Scandinavia is a landmark in the study of role-playing games. Recent theoretical work from this part of the world includes two essay collections: *Beyond Role and Play: Tools, Toys and Theory for Harnessing the Imagination* (2004), edited by Montola and Stenros, and the Danish language publication *Rollespil i æstetisk, pædagogisk og kulturel sammenhæng* (2006), edited by Sandvik and Waade. The first of these publications is one of the many books that have sprung from the successful role-playing nordic Knutepunkt conferences, initially dedicated to LARP (live-action role-playing, a type of game that involves large numbers of participants in a real-world setting, costumes, props, several game masters, and a simple rule system to organize action). Now the conference covers role-playing in many other of its manifestations.

Also in 2006, the first peer-reviewed journal (online only) about role-playing games was born. The *International Journal of Role Playing* has now produced a few high-quality issues that link the hobby to academic areas such as computer games studies, literature, performance studies, sociology, and cultural studies.

■ See also EMERGENCE, GAMES AS STORIES, NPC (NONPLAYER CHARACTER)

References and Further Reading

Caïra, Olivier. 2007. *Jeux de rôles: les forges de la fiction*. Paris: Editions CNRS.
Fine, Gary Alan. 1983. *Role-Playing Games as Social Worlds*. Chicago: University of Chicago Press.
Goffman, Erving. 1974. *Frame Analysis*. New York: Harper Colophon Books.
Hitchens, Michael, and Anders Drachen. 2008. "The Many Faces of Role-Playing Games." *International Journal of Role Playing* 1 (1). http://journalofroleplaying.org/.
International Journal of Role Playing. http://journalofroleplaying.org/.
Laws, Robin. 2001. *Robin's Laws of Good Game Mastering*. Austin, TX: Steve Jackson Games.

Mackay, Daniel. 2001. *The Fantasy Role-Playing Game: A New Performing Art.* London: McFarland.

Mason, Paul. 2004. "In Search of the Self." In *Beyond Role and Play: Tools, Toys and Theory for Harnessing the Imagination*, ed. Markus Montola and Jaakko Stenros, 1–15. Helsinki: Ropecon ry.

Montola, Markus, and Jaakko Stenros, eds. 2004. *Beyond Role and Play: Tools, Toys and Theory for Harnessing the Imagination.* Helsinki: Ropecon ry.

Nielsen, Simon Egenfeldt, Jonas Heide Smith, and Susana Pajares Tosca. 2008. *Understanding Video Games: The Essential Introduction.* London: Routledge.

Ryan, Marie-Laure. 2008. "Interactive Narrative, Plot Types, and Interpersonal Relations." In *Interactive Storytelling: First Joint International Conference on Interactive Digital Storytelling*, ICIDS 2008, edited by Ulrike Spierling and Nicolas Szila, 6–13. Berlin: Springer.

Sandvik, Kjetil, and Anne Marit Waade. 2006. *Rollespil i æstetisk, pædagogisk og kulturel sammenhæng.* Aarhus, Denmark: Aarhus Universitetsforlag.

S

Sampling

Benjamin J. Robertson

Typically, sampling is the musical practice of inserting small bits of found material, or "samples," into otherwise original productions (to the extent that we can understand any production, artistic or otherwise, to be original). Although sampling should not be simply confused with remix, we might best understand it at the present moment, when remix has become so prominent within American if not Western culture, as a particular form within this larger category (see REMIX). Like other remix practices, sampling involves an artist's or producer's use of material not original to her. However, unlike many remix practices, which required artists to rerecord or rewrite/copy that material, sampling makes *direct* use of its sources. Whereas a musician who quotes lyrics from another act in her own voice, or one who reproduces a guitar riff on her own guitar, can be said to quote from a source, an artist who samples makes direct use of the source recording itself. Thus, Sugar Hill Gang's use of the baseline from Chic's "Freak Out" on their 1979 track "Rapper's Delight" exemplifies quotation because the baseline was rerecorded specifically for that record. By contrast, The Beastie Boys' "Rhymin' & Stealin'" samples from Led Zeppelin's "When the Levee Breaks" in that it makes use of the actual Zeppelin recording (or, at least, a copy of that recording).

Among the specific forms of remix that precede sampling are collage in the visual arts (by Braque, Picasso, and others), collage in film (by Bruce Conner and others), plagiarism and cut-up in literature (by Kathy Acker and William S. Burroughs, respectively), and the use of recorded sound in *musique concrète* (by John Cage). Despite such precedence, sampling possesses historical, technical, and cultural particularities that remain entirely its own. This entry will briefly discuss two such particularities: first, the manner in which sampling becomes possible through technological innovation and invention, and second, the manner in which sampling becomes the object of litigation in the music industry.

Sampling of found sound rose to prominence in the hip-hop communities of the 1970s and 1980s (as Public Enemy's Chuck D would later put it, rap "is a sampling sport"). Hip-hop DJs used turntables to isolate baselines and break beats from extant music (on vinyl records) for MCs to rap over. With two turntables and a crossfader, DJs found they could extend their use of small bits of sound over longer (in fact, theoretically infinite) periods of time by using two copies of the same record in tandem. Thus, the first technology of sampling was not so much an invention as an innovation, an integration of an extant technology into a new economy of production. The importance of this innovation itself cannot be underestimated as it empowered an otherwise underprivileged community to make music and demonstrated the manner in which what had once been mainly a technology of consumption (the turntable) could be transformed into a technology of production. Interestingly, the distinction between production and consumption became further confused as DJs began to buy up and hoard records with classic break beats for use in their sets.

The commercial availability of digital samplers, first in the 1970s and then more widely in the 1980s, extended the potential of this nascent practice for hip-hop DJs and others. Samplers provided sampling musicians with greater precision and flexibility in their productions. They also allowed sampling to move from the house party and the club, where it was a live and spontaneous practice, to the studio, where it would become another tool in the kit of the recording artist. By the end of the 1980s, albums such as Public Enemy's *It Takes a Nation of Millions to Hold Us Back* and the Beastie Boys' *Paul's Boutique* would take sampling to new heights. Inspired by producer Phil Spector's "wall of sound" practice, Public Enemy, for example, created music out of multiple samples, many of which blur together to form a whole that is greater, or at least other, than the sum of its parts. As Christopher Weingarten puts it in his study of *It Takes a Nation of Millions to Hold Us Back*, "Through sampling, hip-hop producers can literally borrow the song that influenced them, replay it, reuse it, rethink it, repeat it, recontextualize it. Some samples leave all the emotional weight and cultural signifiers of an existing piece of music intact—a colloidal particle that floats inside a piece of music yet maintains its inherent properties" (2010, 38).

Sampling continues today, driven in part by stand-alone and networked computers. Particularly, software such as Sony's Acid Pro and the more popular GarageBand from Apple afford professional and amateur musicians the ability to sample. Just as DJs were able to transform the turntable into a technology of production, users of such software can harness the power of their computers to make culture rather than just consume it.

However, the cultural prominence sampling achieved, driven to a large extent by the burgeoning popularity of rap music, perhaps led to it becoming a legally contested practice, one whose future viability in commercial (and even noncommercial) contexts remains unclear. Whatever philosophical questions it raises (about originality, the subjective coherence of the artist, etc.), the challenge that sampling provides for the business model of the music industry and its bottom line ultimately ended the so-called golden era of sampling in the late 1980s. Thus, by the early 1990s, copyright owners began asserting their rights to their productions and suing artists who made use of (i.e., sampled) those productions without permission (see COPYRIGHT). Although disputes over sampling have rarely gone to trial, the courts and the licensing system for sampling (or lack thereof) favor the rights of original artists over the productions of newer ones. In one notable case, *Grand Upright Music, Ltd v. Warner Bros. Records Inc.*, the court found rapper Biz Markie guilty of a sort of theft for sampling from Gilbert O'Sullivan's "Alone Again (Naturally)" and thus infringing on O'Sullivan's copyright. The judge in the case began his written decision with the biblical injunction "Thou shalt not steal" and ended it by referring what had been a civil matter for criminal prosecution. Such litigation rarely achieves this level of bombast—clearly the "theft" in this case is of a different nature than, say, grand theft auto given the fact that sampling in no way deprives O'Sullivan of a rivalrous bit of property. Nonetheless, legally, sampling has become a problematic musical practice.

Critics such as Kembrew McLeod and Peter DiCola (2011) note that sampling remains problematic in large part because, unlike the practice of "covering" music, there is no mechanical license that governs how sampling works. If a musician wishes to cover (that is, rerecord) a song by another artist, permission is automatically granted under the condition that certain predetermined fees are paid (and that the new version of the song does not constitute a transformative use of the original). However, if a musician wishes to sample, the original artist can exact any charge she wants for that right, or deny it altogether. The sampling musician is left then with a choice: to not use the sample, to use it illegally (i.e., without permission), or to record a new version of the sample (which would be governed by the mechanical license for cover songs). Of course, none of these options are desirable; the first and third lead to a possible compromise of artistic vision and the second to possible legal consequences.

Whatever its legal status, sampling appears to have gained widespread cultural acceptance. Although numerous remix practices precede it historically, only after the advent of sampling and its subsequent cultural dissemination through rap has remix generally become a popular form of expression. People routinely "sample" from popular culture in their everyday conversation (by quoting, for example, Homer Simpson), and Internet memes often rely on appropriation and repetition for their effects. None of this came about as a result of John Cage's *musique concrète* or Kathy Acker's experiments with plagiarism.

■ See also MASHUP, MUSIC, SOUND

References and Further Reading

McLeod, Kembrew. 2011. "Crashing the Spectacle: A Forgotten History of Digital Sampling, Infringement, Copyright Liberation, and the End of Recorded Music." In *Cutting across Media: Appropriation Art, Interventionist Collage, and Copyright Law*, edited by Kembrew McLeod and Rudolf Kuenzli, 164–177. Durham, NC: Duke University Press.

McLeod, Kembrew, and Peter DiCola. 2011. *Creative License: The Law and Culture of Digital Sampling*. Durham, NC: Duke University Press.

Weingarten, Christopher. 2010. *It Takes a Nation of Millions to Hold Us Back*. New York: Continuum.

Search

Yuk Hui

When computer scientist Donald Knuth started his fifth chapter on searching in the third volume of *The Art of Computing Language*, he began with the sentence, "The chapter might have been given the more pretentious title 'Storage and Retrieval of Information'; on the other hand, it might simply have been called 'Table Look-Up'" (1998, 392). In between these two terms—one that is professional and geeky and another that sounds more layman and quotidian—one can find a history of search and the evolution of search technologies from the indexations of pictograms and logograms to modern information retrieval systems characterized by automation and various algorithms such as binary search and Fibonacci search (see ALGORITHM).

Indexation precedes all searches. To search is to look for something within a larger set of items by identifying one or multiple specified features; this ranges in our daily life from choosing an apple in the grocery store to looking for a result on Google. These actions require an index that allows us to find the most relevant result. This index is often referred to as a "key" in information retrieval. Searching, sorting, and indexing are activities that can hardly be discussed separately. Conceptually speaking, indexing establishes relations between different entities, and sorting in this sense organizes these relations. To understand searching, it is necessary to understand the evolution of relations.

One can find the earliest indexing and sorting technology in the Sumerian culture toward the end of the fourth millennium BCE. The Sumerians used pictograms inscribed on clay tablets to index their stocks in order to set up an "accounting system" that recorded debts, archives for future search (Goody 1977, 75). We have to bear in mind that, strictly speaking, there is no semantic meaning in pictogram writing; what exists are *relations* created by *visual differences*. The set of visual differences present in pictograms is also the first metadata system that describes the relations between the entities, if we understand *metadata* according to its conventional definition: "data about data." Search techniques evolve according to the emergence of new relations specific to the technical natures of the writings (pictographic writing, logographic writing, analog writing, and digital writings). For example, with the introduction of morphemes and phonetics, the varieties of relations between objects and words escalate and the description of objects becomes more explicit since more and more semantic meanings can be inscribed as metadata.

We have to recognize that relations, materialized and formalized in different technical forms, are at the core of information retrieval. Searching allows us to follow these relations and thus arrive at a certain end according to specific instructions. An information system that consists of a large amount of data demands a fine order of granularity of relations, as well as algorithms that allow it to organize these relations effectively across different tables. The relational database introduced by the mathematician and information scientist Edgar F. Codd in the 1960s was the first to allow searching across multiple tables. Today we know that most information systems are built on top of relational databases, which are based on two main concepts: "(1) data independence from hardware and storage implementation and (2) automatic navigation, or a high-level, nonprocedural language for accessing data. Instead of processing one record at a time, a programmer could use the language to specify single operations that would be performed across the entire data set" (CSTB 1999, 162). The attributes of a table specify the properties and relations of the data stored in it; at the same time they also generate a "second layer" of relations among themselves through comparisons, for example, difference or sameness.

The emergence of the World Wide Web in the late 1980s posed a new challenge to search, since HTML (HyperText Markup Language) files are not databases, but more like light-weighted SGML (Standard Generalized Markup Language) annotations. Thus, we saw the emergence of search engines that archive and index contents and algorithms that display "relevant" results to users. With the development of the web and the rapid growth of user-generated data, the question of indexation and annotation became more and more crucial as the digital objects could easily get lost in the universe of data and become invisible. Early technologies such as HTML (prior to HTML5) are not expressive enough to make explicit relations among various contents. Moreover, relational databases only gave permission to authorized users, and it was difficult to query across different databases without multiple authentications. Search engines were developed to deal with this question, and different indexing methods were introduced that competed with each other in those earlier days when HTTP (Hypertext Transfer Protocol) was just one choice among other protocols. For example, among many search engines, such as Hot-Bot, Excite, Webcrawler, and Archie, we can find Veronica (Very Easy Rodent-Oriented Net-wide Index to Computer Archives, 1992), which used Gopher protocol (another TCP/IP protocol other than HTTP) for managing documents and indexation of the Internet. On the other hand, Altavista (1995) followed HTTP protocol and archived a large part of the web at the time, eventually becoming an exclusive provider of search results for Yahoo! However, the increasing amount of data produced by users and diversities of industrial standards made the status quo difficult to maintain. The web started becoming a synonym for the Internet, and within the web more and more improved protocols are being developed (HTML4.0, XML, XHTML, etc). And to solve the expanding data on the Internet, more descriptive markup languages and more sophisticated searching algorithms had to be invented.

At the beginning of the twenty-first century, we saw several significant solutions to these questions. One thing these solutions have in common is that they go beyond searching for specified features of digital objects (as one might search for a specific color red in an apple) to social searching. This new movement in search fostered three parallel movements. The first one is the development of Google's indexation technique known as PageRank. The PageRank algorithm recursively calculates an index of a web page according to the incoming links that are associated with it; the search engine then can determine where the page belongs in a search result. Google also records the online activities of its users, in the name of personalization, in order to determine the most relevant results for specific users. Google's attempt to find a compromise between "relevance of contents" through PageRank and the "relevance to users" by personalization has become an important method for producing and organizing relations.

The second of these three movements is the Semantic Web proposed by Tim Berners-Lee (2000) (see SEMANTIC WEB). The Semantic Web proposes to annotate web pages according to compulsory vocabularies, known as web ontologies, and can be understood as a semantics shared between machines and human users. This virtual "sharing" of semantics implies a certain sense of "social." The basic technical idea is to use RDF (Resource Definition Framework) tuples (ordered lists of elements) to describe web page contents in detail (by comparison with HTML). The Semantic Web aims to create a web of information which keeps all data in RDF stores, so everyone can openly search them according to semantic relations.

The third contemporary search solution is social tagging. In contrast to the Semantic Web, tagging doesn't use compulsory vocabularies, but encourages users to annotate digital objects with their own text. Searching through tagging provides an experience of serendipity based on the tags contributed by other users. It allows discoveries that are not formally related to search results. For example, by searching for a painting of shoes by Van Gogh, one can come to discover the writing of Heidegger on the origin of the work of art.

The connection between the social and the machinic has two significant implications. The first is the organization of knowledge on a global scale. All areas of knowledge—ranging from simple facts to videos on how to make bombs, academic seminars, book contents—can be searched online. Search engines are the biggest players in the contemporary organization of knowledge, since they determine which comes first and which has to disappear while relying very much on the black boxes they created in the name of algorithms, personalization, and so on. This has important political implications, in terms of privacy and information manipulation.

The second implication is the organization of cognition. Search tools provided by computational devices—including computers, mobile phones, tablets, and so on—become more and more important for our attempts to acquire knowledge, to the extent that we find it increasingly difficult to learn without them. This issue has been explored as a philosophy of externalities by such thinkers as Bernard Stiegler (tertiary retention), Andy Clark and David Chalmers (extended mind), John Haugeland (embedded mind), and Fred Dretske (externalism). Anthropologists such as André Leroi-Gourhan and Jack Goody have demonstrated the transformations of cognitive functions through writing, which create new circuits and become supports of the brain. Contemporary technologies such as search further complicate the manner in which humans think. The organization of cognition and organization of knowledge continue to converge; this is a subject that deserves exploration in the context of search.

References and Further Reading

Berners-Lee, Tim. 2000. *Weaving the Web: The Origins and Future of the World Wide Web.* Orion Business.

Brin, Sergey, and Page Larry. 1998. "The Anatomy of a Large-Scale Hypertextual Web Search Engine." *Computer Networks and* ISDN Systems 30:107–117.

Clark, Andy, and David Chalmers. 1998. "The Extended Mind." *Analysis* 58:10–23.

Codd, E. F. 1970. "A Relational Model of Data for Large Shared Data Banks." *Communications of the ACM* 13 (6): 377–387.

Computer Science and Telecommunications Board (CSTB). 1999. *Funding a Revolution: Government Support for Computing Research.* Washington, DC: National Academy Press.

Goody, Jack. 1977. *The Domestication of the Savage Mind.* Cambridge: Cambridge University Press.

Knuth, Donald Ervin. 1998. *The Art of Computer Programming.* Volume 3. Redwood City, CA: Addison Wesley Longman.

Stiegler, Bernard. 2009. *Technics and Time.* Volume 2: *Disorientation.* Stanford, CA: Stanford University Press.

Searle's Chinese Room
Inderjeet Mani

When you say "Please send the message" to your iPhone's software assistant Siri, and Siri sends it, can one infer that Siri actually understands the intended meaning of "send"? The commonsense answer is, "Of course not! No matter how much we love to anthropomorphize our gadgets, Siri is only a computer system. Any understanding is really in the minds of Siri's programmers." The philosopher John Searle (1980, 1990) makes this commonsense notion more precise, by way of a logical argument called the Chinese Room (CR). He asks us to imagine a situation where an English speaker who does not understand Chinese is locked in a room where he is provided, by Chinese speakers from outside the room, with written Chinese characters. The English speaker (let's call him X) also has available in the room basketfuls of Chinese characters, along with an English rule book that tells him what Chinese characters to substitute for the input characters, and using these he hands the corresponding output characters back to the people outside. If the inputs are questions and the outputs the answers, and the Chinese people outside judge his answers to be indistinguishable from those of a native Chinese speaker, X has satisfactorily answered questions in Chinese, without apparently understanding or learning a word of that language.

Now, let X be instead a computer processor and let the rule book be a computer program and the baskets its database. By following the instructions in the program, the system has simulated human behavior to such an extent that its own behavior is indistinguishable from that of a human, thus by definition passing the Turing test (Turing 1950) for determining whether a computer can be said to think (see TURING TEST). Yet, it is clear, Searle says, that since the man doesn't understand Chinese, neither does the computer processor. As a result, Searle argues, a computer cannot be said to possess understanding of language, or thoughts and feelings about something, or any other cognitive states.

An immediate objection to the CR is that though X doesn't know Chinese, the system as a whole does, since it can answer questions in Chinese (as in the system of Lee et al. [2007], which passes tests more stringent than the Turing test). Searle's response is that even if X memorized everything in the room and walked outside, he would still, though speaking Chinese, not understand any words of that language. Searle's idea of understanding is opposed to that of "functionalist" artificial intelligence (AI), i.e., where a cognitive state does not depend on what it is made of, but rather on its function in a containing system, specified in terms of causal relations between the mental state and the system's input, other mental states, and system output (Levin 2010) (see ARTIFICIAL INTELLIGENCE). For Searle, our cognitive states have the characteristics they do precisely because they are caused by lower-level neuronal processes. Not only do brains cause minds, but "any other system capable of causing minds would have to have causal powers (at least) equivalent to those of brains" (Searle 1990, 29). Searle also rejects a version of the CR where the program simulates the operation of the brain of a Chinese speaker at the neuronal level. He argues that such a simulation "will not produce the effects of the neurobiology of cognition," any more than one could "digest pizza by running the program that simulates such digestion" (Searle 1990, 29).

Pinker (1997) suggests that the CR is merely an exploration of the usage of the word *understand*, exposing the beliefs underlying the commonsense reluctance to use the word when the situation deviates from stereotypical conditions. Such beliefs could turn out to be no more than prejudice against thought-capable computers. A little over a century ago, people were similarly sceptical about flying machines.

References and Further Reading

Cole, David. 2009. "The Chinese Room Argument." In *The Stanford Encyclopedia of Philosophy* (Winter), edited by Edward N. Zalta. http://plato.stanford.edu/archives/win2009/entries/chinese-room/.

Lee, Cheng-Wei, Min-Yuh Day, Cheng-Lung Sung, et al. 2007. "Chinese-Chinese and English-Chinese Question Answering with ASQA at NTCIR-6 CLQA." *Proceedings of* NTCIR-6 Workshop Meeting, Tokyo, Japan. http://research.nii.ac.jp/ntcir/workshop/OnlineProceedings6/NTCIR/33.pdf.

Levin, Janet. 2010. "Functionalism." In *The Stanford Encyclopedia of Philosophy* (Summer), edited by Edward N. Zalta. http://plato.stanford.edu/archives/sum2010/entries/functionalism/.

Pinker, Steven. 1997. *How the Mind Works*. New York: Norton.

Searle, John R. 1980. "Minds, Brains, and Programs." *Behavioral and Brain Sciences* 3 (3): 417–458.

———. 1990. "Is the Brain's Mind a Computer Program?" *Scientific American*, January, 26–31.

Turing, Alan M. 1950. "Computing Machinery and Intelligence." *Mind* 59 (236): 433–460.

Self-Reflexivity in Electronic Art
Winfried Nöth

Self-reflexivity (Ryan 2007), or merely *reflexivity* (Bartlett 1992; Stam 1992), is the characteristic of a work of art that contains, suggests, or provokes—in contrast to whatever the artwork may want to say about the world beyond its own confines—reflections on its own composition; its materiality; its form, its structure; its method or purpose of creation; its artist, author, painter, or composer; or its readers, viewers, or audience and their involvement in the aesthetic process. To the degree that it is self-reflexive, an artwork makes its audience or viewers reflect on the work of art instead of on the world of things, ideas, persons, or events that it represents.

Self-reflexivity has been described as a characteristic of postmodern culture (Lawson 1985; Nöth 2011), as well as a symptom of a *crisis of representation* (Nöth and Ljungberg 2003), and it has been identified as a concomitant of media transitions, of *intermediality* and *remediation* (see REMEDIATION). In self-reflexive loops, the discourse of and about the new media and their innovative potential refers back to the precursors in media history. In particular, the subversion of Walter Benjamin's aesthetics of authenticity and the *aura* of the artwork (see Paul 2003, 28) through the unlimited iterability of electronic artworks has put the self-reflexive question of the "art after the end of art" (Santaella 2003, 315–333) on the agenda of contemporary aesthetics.

Self-reflexivity is sometimes distinguished from self-reference and metareference. According to Wolf (2007, 306), *self-reflexivity* is self-reference made noticeable or explicit; the more general phenomenon of self-reference thus includes self-reflexivity as the more specific instance of a message whose self-referentiality is brought to attention. Others define *self-reference* as the general characteristic of any message that refers more strictly to itself by directing attention to the features that it has as a message, its meaning, its logic, its truth or lack of truth, its letters, its vowels and consonants, its colors, its forms, or its sound pattern (Nöth 2007b). Dada poetry, abstract painting, and music in general are genuinely self-referential in this broader sense.

Meta-art is art about art, and *metaliterature* is literature about literature (Wolf 2009, 2011). *Metafiction* is the genre of narratives questioning the reality of what they are about by revealing their fictionality. A piece of *metamusic* is one that contains references to, or reminiscences of, other pieces of music. *Metapoetry* deals with poetry writing or reading. *Metacinema* is about filmmaking, being in a film, going to the movies, and so on. A *metapicture* is a picture about a picture: for example, one that depicts pictures, a painter who paints, a portrait being portrayed, or a painting whose being painted becomes the artwork, as in *action painting*. Metapictures are either pictures about other pictures or pictures that invite reflections on their own composition; in the latter case, they are self-referential metapictures (see Nöth 2007a).

The distinctions between self-reflexivity, self-reference, and metareference are fuzzy, and there is no general consensus about them. According to the doctrines of the nineteenth-century aesthetics of *l'art pour l'art*, whose roots are in medieval and classical aesthetics, the purpose of any work of art is to please by itself and not through whatever it may represent (see Nöth 1990, 421–428). Hence, to the degree that a work of art is self-reflexive or self-referential, it is also art about art, that is, meta-art. The distinction between self-reflexivity, self-reference, and metareference is, moreover, a matter of degree, which is another reason for the inevitable overlap between the three characteristics.

Self-reflexivity and self-reference are not restricted to works of art. They occur in many other forms of verbal and nonverbal signs, in morphology (reflexive verbs), in grammar (the rules of which always refer to grammar), and in jokes, riddles, and *paradoxes*. There are self-reflexive graphic signs in the form of *loops* and *circles*. (Actually, the etymology of the verb "to reflect" contains already the idea of circularity since in Latin *reflectere* means "to bend back.") In logic, there are vicious circles. In computer programs and game theory there are rules permitting self-application (embedding) and self-modification. In biology, autopoiesis (literally "self-creation") and self-replication are distinguishing features of life. In mythology, the idea of cosmic cycles implies a return to the origins.

Electronic art (Druckrey 1999) or *e-art* (Gagnon 2007) is a branch of cyberculture and the broader field of *aesthetic computing* (Fishwick 2006), not sharply delimited from a number of neighboring fields or subfields of artistic practice, such as *computer graphics* (Lewell 1985), *computer art, algorithmic art, information art* (Wilson 2002), *software art* (Broeckmann 2006), *digital art* (Paul 2003), *Internet art* (Barreto 2002; Greene 2004), *network* or *net.art* (Ryan 2007), *cyberart, interactive e-art* (Leopoldseder and Schöpf 2000; see INTERACTIVITY), *video e-art, digital installation art, virtual art* (Grau 2003; see DIGITAL INSTALLATION ART), *new media art* (Triebe, Reena, and Grosenick 2007), *digital poetry* (Block, Heibach, and Wenz 2004; see DIGITAL POETRY), *game art, multimedia art, robotic art, Alife (artificial life)* (Wilson 2002; see ARTIFICIAL LIFE), *genetic art* (Gerbel and Weibel 1993), as well as *electronic music, sound sculptures*, and *visual music* (see MUSIC).

The scope of the aesthetic potential of e-art can only be very selectively exemplified in the following, and its discussion must remain restricted to self-reflexivity in e-art. E-art both makes use of the traditional self-reflexive aesthetic devices and extends their potential through the enhanced possibilities offered by the Turing machine. The most fundamental computational devices contributing to the augmented creative potential characteristic of e-art are probably of *recursion, iteration, feedback*, and *looping*.

Different modes of self-reflexivity in the arts can be distinguished from the semiotic perspectives of syntactics, semantics, and pragmatics. *Syntactic* self-reflexivity evokes reflections on the formal relations between signs, irrespective of their meaning and function. The most elementary syntactic modes of self-reflexivity are repetition and symmetry (see Nöth 1998). The term *reflexive symmetry*, a synonym of *mirror symmetry*, testifies to the self-reflexive character of symmetrical forms: one-half of the image is reflected in the other. Repetition is self-reflexive insofar as each reiteration is a reflex of the reiterated form; for its aesthetics see Koch (1983).

In its traditional form, symmetry is still a device attracting creative e-artists. In Walter Giers's *Large Sliding Symmetry* of 1992, an electronic wall object, a random generator, batteries, wires, capacitors, resistors, transistors, and bulbs serve to control and create "a seemingly endless series of symmetrical patterns in a rhythmic tangle" (Peine 1997, 83).

Fractal images (Peitgen and Saupe 1988; Wilson 2002, 330–335) are a specific case of syntactic self-reference. Generated by algorithms discovered by the mathematician Benoit Mandelbrot, fractals are geometric shapes whose fragmentation into smaller forms results in reduced *copies* of the whole. The resulting fractal images evince the self-referential feature of *self-similarity*. Fractals have been explored in e-artworks since the early years of computer graphics.

Another mode of self-reflexivity can be found in e-artworks created by a random (or aleatoric) syntax (see RANDOMNESS). Aleatoric artworks, which have their roots in the concept art of the 1960s (see Nöth 1972, 41, 65), are self-referential insofar as their principle of syntactic composition is unique to each individual work, having no occurrence elsewhere. A related principle of syntactic self-reflexivity can be found in e-art created by coded errors. The net art project *Jodi.org*, for example, faces its viewers with "a screen of garbled green texts—an unintelligible jumble of punctuation marks and numerals blinking on and off on a black screen," resulting from "one of the Internet's fundamental aesthetic properties: the glitch" (quoted in Triebe, Reena, and Grosenick 2007, 50).

Coding (called *codework* by some e-artists; see Ryan 2007) has become the source of inspiration for e-artists who have discovered that the code itself may have a peculiar aesthetics of its own. One of the artists, John F. Simon Jr., declares, "I approach coding like it is a kind of creative writing" (quoted in Triebe, Reena, and Grosenick 2007, 25). Insofar as a code serves to generate the syntactic surface structure of the e-artwork and insofar as this code is equally considered an aesthetic object, such works of *code aesthetics* are syntactically self-reflexive: art generates art (see CODE AESTHETICS). Aesthetic coding breaks with the fundamental distinction between algorithmic and aesthetic computing according to which "an algorithmic rule is general and requests to be followed," whereas "an aesthetic rule is singular and only states that something could be done in this way" (Nake and Grabowski 2006, 57).

An artwork is *semantically self-reflexive* whenever it evokes reflections on meaning(s), that is, whenever it raises questions such as the following: What does it mean? What does it refer to? What does it show (represent)? How does it relate to real life? Is this a probable or an improbable scenario, character, or event? (What about its verisimilitude?) How does it relate to the contents (motifs, narratives, scenes, etc.) of other artworks? Are its contents creative? Is it coherent? Does it make sense?

Digital imaging and the computational technology of virtual reality have both a referential and a semantically self-referential potential (see VIRTUAL REALITY). They are referential insofar as they augment the potential of representation from reality to other, merely virtual worlds. At the same time, the lack of a "real" referent of virtual images makes these images self-referential since what they represent exists only through the very images that represent this reality without referents.

Internet art with its innumerable intermedial strategies of recycling text chunks borrowed from the web is a particularly good example of semantic self-reflexivity: messages are transformed in ironic, sarcastic, or otherwise distorted ways; e-mail trash becomes e-art, and ads are adbusted. In *infowars* or *netwars* (Greene 2004, 120), information becomes disinformation and culture is subverted in cybercultural attacks of culture jamming and guerilla semiotics. The self-reflexivity of such intermedial transformations lies in their metareferentiality; messages are about messages, texts reflect texts.

An artwork evinces *pragmatic self-reflexivity* whenever it deals with the aesthetic involvement of the author, the narrator, the actor, the reader, or the spectator. Happenings, living theater, and action painting were some of the historical climaxes of pragmatic self-reflexivity in the arts. Technological resources of special relevance are cameras, sensors, and other biotechnological devices that enable spectators to interact (see INTERACTIV-ITY). Interactive e-art is paradigmatic of pragmatic self-referentiality since the involvement of the spectator blurs the traditional distinction between the roles of the artists and the audience and by doing so invites reflections on the involvement of both in the aesthetic process. The question of semiotic agency (Nöth 2009) and authorship raised by an art produced by means of machines, as well as the scenario of a posthuman aesthetics (Santaella 2003), presents further topics for self-reflexive reconsiderations of the role of art in cyberculture (see CYBORG AND POSTHUMAN).

At the crossroads of art and technology, where e-artists make use of machines designed in the first place for utilitarian purposes, Vuk Cosic, the Slovenian pioneer of net art, states that his most fundamental concern is with self-reflexivity in accordance with the general aesthetic principle that art serves no other purpose than the one of being art. In a manifesto of his own aesthetics, the artist writes that his e-artworks are "carefully directed at their full uselessness from the viewpoint of everyday high tech and all its consequences" (quoted in Triebe, Reena, and Grosenick 2007, 38).

■ See also CODE AESTHETICS, DIGITAL INSTALLATION ART, DIGITAL POETRY, ELECTRONIC LITERATURE, GLITCH AESTHETICS, INTERACTIVITY, RANDOMNESS

References and Further Reading

Barreto, Ricardo, ed. 2002. *Internet Art: Festival Internacional de Linguagem Eletrônica*. São Paulo, Brazil: Paço das Artes.

Bartlett, Steven J., ed. 1992. *Reflexivity: A Source-Book*. Amsterdam: North Holland.

Block, Friedrich W., Christiane Heibach, and Karin Wenz, eds. 2004. *pOes1s: The Aesthetics of Digital Poetry*. Ostfildern-Ruit, Germany: Hatje Cantz.

Broeckmann, Andreas. 2006. "Software Art Aesthetics." www.mikro.in-berlin.de/wiki/tiki-index .php?page=Software+Art.

Druckrey, Timothy, ed. 1999. *Ars Electronica: Facing the Future*. Cambridge, MA: MIT Press.

Fishwick, Paul A., ed. 2006. *Aesthetic Computing*. Cambridge, MA: MIT Press.

Gagnon, Jean, ed. 2007. *e-art: New Technologies and Contemporary Art*. Montreal: Museum of Fine Arts.

Gerbel, Karl, and Peter Weibel, eds. 1993. *Ars Electronica 1993: Artificial Life—Genetic Art*. Wien, Austria: PSV.

Grau, Oliver. 2003. *Virtual Art*. Cambridge, MA: MIT Press.

Greene, Rachel. 2004. *Internet Art*. New York: Thames & Hudson.

Koch, Walter A. 1983. *Poetry and Science: Semiogenetical Twins*. Tübingen, Germany: Narr.

Lawson, Hilary. 1985. *Reflexivity: The Post-Modern Predicament*. London: Hutchinson.

Leopoldseder, Hannes, and Christine Schöpf. 2000. *Cyberarts 2000*. Wien, Austria: Springer.

Lewell, John. 1985. *Computer Graphics*. London: Orbis.

Nake, Frieder, and Susanne Grabowski. 2006. "The Interface as Sign and as Aesthetic Event." In *Aesthetic Computing*, edited by Paul A. Fishwick, 53–70. Cambridge, MA: MIT Press.

Nöth, Winfried. 1972. *Strukturen des Happenings*. Hildesheim, Germany: Olms.

———. 1990. *Handbook of Semiotics*. Bloomington: Indiana University Press.

———. 1998. "Symmetry in Signs and in Semiotic Systems." *Interdisciplinary Journal for Germanic Linguistics and Semiotic Analysis* 3 (1): 47–62.

———. 2007a. "Metapictures and Self-Referential Pictures." In *Self-Reference in the Media*, edited by Winfried Nöth and Nina Bishara, 61–78. Berlin: Mouton de Gruyter.

———. 2007b. "Self-Reference in the Media." In *Self-Reference in the Media*, edited by Winfried Nöth and Nina Bishara, 3–30. Berlin: Mouton de Gruyter.

———. 2009. "On the Instrumentality and Semiotic Agency of Signs, Tools, and Intelligent Machines." *Cybernetics & Human Knowing* 16 (3–4): 11–36.

———. 2011. "Self-Referential Postmodernity." *Semiotica* 183:199–218.

Nöth, Winfried, and Nina Bishara, eds. 2007. *Self-Reference in the Media*. Berlin: Mouton de Gruyter.

Nöth, Winfried, and Christina Ljungberg, eds. 2003. *The Crisis of Representation: Semiotic Foundations and Manifestations in Culture and the Media*. Berlin: Mouton de Gruyter (=*Semiotica* 143 [1–4]).

Paul, Christiane. 2003. *Digital Art*. New York: Thames & Hudson.

Peine, Sybille, comp. 1997. *ZKM: Center for Art and Media Karlsruhe*. Munich: Pestel.

Peitgen, Heinz-Otto, and Dietmar Saupe, eds. 1988. *The Science of Fractal Images*. Berlin: Springer.

Ryan, Marie-Laure. 2007. "Looking through the Computer Screen: Self-Reflexivity in Net Art." In *Self-Reference in the Media*, edited by Winfried Nöth and Nina Bishara, 269–290. Berlin: Mouton de Gruyter.

Santaella, Lucia. 2003. *Culturas e artes do pós-humano: Da cultura das mídias à cibercultura*. São Paulo, Brazil: Paulus.

Stam, Robert. 1992. *Reflexivity in Film and Literature*. New York: Columbia University Press.

Triebe, Mark, Jana Reena, and Uta Grosenick, eds. 2007. *New Media Art*. Cologne: Taschen.

Wilson, Steve. 2002. *Information Arts*. Cambridge, MA: MIT Press.

Wolf, Werner. 2007. "Metafiction and Metamusic. " In *Self-Reference in the Media*, edited by Winfried Nöth and Nina Bishara, 303–324. Berlin: Mouton de Gruyter.

———, ed. 2009. *Metareference across Media: Theory and Case Studies*. Amsterdam: Rodopi.

———, ed. 2011. *The Metareferential Turn in Contemporary Arts and Media*. Amsterdam: Rodopi.

Semantic Web

Axel-Cyrille Ngonga Ngomo

Creating a "Semantic Web" is a field of research in computer science that attempts to make the meaning of items contained in the web (web pages, multimedia, etc.) accessible to both humans and machines in an integral and consistent fashion (Berners-Lee, Hendler, and Lassila 2001; Auer, Lehmann, and Ngonga Ngomo 2011). The concepts, ideas, and technologies behind the Semantic Web grow currently at such an astounding rate that any attempt to survey them would be incomplete and would solely reflect a transitory state of research. The following thus provides a very brief overview of the concepts underlying the Semantic Web, moving from one of the key problems it addresses to the main problems it is currently faced with.

The basic idea behind the web is very simple: publish web pages, interlink and consume them. This process has been carried out by a multitude of humans over the past two decades, leading to the vast corpus of interlinked documents that we call the World Wide Web. Yet the strength of the web is also its greatest weakness. The large size of this data set makes it intrinsically difficult to query, analyze, and fathom. This very well-known problem has been addressed over the past decades by information retrieval frameworks, which allow mitigating certain aspects of the retrieval of relevant information from the web. For example, finding a movie theater called "Dream Theater" in Colorado is an easy task when using Google and similar search engines. Yet what humans do with an astounding degree of ease (i.e., consuming this knowledge and inferring upon it) is quasi-impossible for machines, as the content of websites in HyperText Markup Language (HTML) is an opaque amalgam of bits and bytes without meaning. Thus, complex information retrieval tasks such as finding the list of all movie theaters with at least two hundred seats in Colorado cannot be addressed by current search engines, although this information is available on the web.

The idea behind the Semantic Web is to make the content of the web human- and machine-processable. Just as humans read the content of a web page, represent this content according to the intrinsic scheme stored in their brain, merge it with existing knowledge, and infer supplementary facts from this newly acquired knowledge, so is the goal of the Semantic Web to allow machines to "read" the content of web pages, represent it formally, add it to their knowledge base, and infer new beliefs, facts, or even procedures to achieve certain human-set goals, such as retrieving all movie theaters with at least two hundred seats in Colorado. What sounds like an absurd vision is now becoming an integral part of the reality of the web. The language OWL (Web Ontology Language) allows the specification of ontologies for formalizing knowledge; Resource Definition Framework (RDF) allows describing resources and the relations between them; SPARQL (SPARQL Protocol and RDF Language) enables users to query large knowledge bases and to answer complex questions with a complex set of restrictions and requirements. Yet all these technologies would be useless without data upon which they can operate. Providing a large compendium of data sets from across a large number of domains in the easily processable format RDF is the idea behind the Linked Data paradigm (Heath and Bizer 2011).

The Linked Data paradigm is a compilation of methods and approaches for the publishing of structured data (mainly as RDF) that can be consumed by machines and represent the content not only of web pages but also of applications and frameworks. The main drivers behind the Linked Data paradigm seem intuitive. Firstly, just as websites are published on the web in a format that can be easily processed by humans, so should structured data be published in a format that can be processed by machines with ease. Secondly, just as humans reuse known concepts when processing new knowledge, so should identifiers for entities be reused as much as possible. Finally, the network approach to the web should be reproduced on the Web of Data, as it allows one to navigate large amounts of knowledge but also to infer supplementary knowledge. The application of this paradigm has led to the Linked Open Data (http://lod-cloud.net) cloud as we know it today. It contains more than 31 billion statements that describe millions of entities of all types (persons, locations, organizations, etc.) and the relations between them.

The Linked Data requirements might seem easy to realize, but the current solutions that try to address these challenges are still in their infancy. While publishing structured data extracted from relational data is fairly straightforward and supported by a large number of tools, dealing with unstructured data (which compose up to 80% of the current web) remains an important issue that has been solved only partly. The problem here is threefold: first, finding entity mentions in unstructured data requires frameworks that can analyze the structure of language and detect the position of named entities. While these so-called named-entity-recognition frameworks have been the subject of research in information extraction for several decades, they only achieve accuracy scores of approximately 90 percent in the best case, which means that one-tenth of their statements are wrong and they miss one-tenth of the knowledge on the web. In addition, they only find the labels of entities (Hoffart et al. 2011). Yet finding mentions of entities is not the end of the story. Discovering that "Limbe" must stand for an entity does not say which entity is actually meant in the text, as the homonym cities of Limbe in Cameroon and Limbe in Malawi share that label in text. The challenge linked with the task of discovering the entities to associate with the label discovered in unstructured data, dubbed "named entity disambiguation," is intrinsically difficult (see, e.g., FOX at http://fox.aksw .org). Tests with human experts have shown that we only achieve an accuracy of approximately 85 percent in difficult cases. Yet such scores are insufficient for machines that rely on formal inference, as the smallest inconsistencies suffice to lead to completely nonsensical knowledge bases or even an infinite processing time. Finally, named entity recognition and named entity disambiguation approaches need to be completed with relation extraction approaches, which allow discovering what is being stated about the entities mentioned in unstructured data. While this problem has received moderate attention in the Semantic Web community over the past years, successful endeavors such as the question-answering system Watson (Ferrucci et al. 2010) show that such approaches are of central importance to making machines appear as knowledgeable as humans.

Once entities and their relations have been discovered and written into a knowledge base, two main challenges remain. First, discovering links across knowledge bases is a time-consuming and complex task. Second, inferring knowledge that is both new and consistent from the large amount of available knowledge at hand remains an unsolved problem. The computation of links across knowledge bases is one of the key principles of the Linked Data web. While this principle is central for tasks such as cross-ontology question answering, large-scale inferences, and data integration, it is increasingly tedious to implement manually (Ngonga Ngomo and Auer 2011). One of the main difficulties behind the discovery of links is its intrinsic time complexity. The combination of the mere size of these knowledge bases and the quadratic a priori time complexity of link discovery leads to brute-force algorithms requiring weeks and even longer to compute links between large knowledge bases such as DBpedia (Auer et al. 2008; http://dbpedia .org) and LinkedGeoData (Auer, Lehmann, and Hellmann 2009; http://linkedgeodata .org). In addition, the manual specification of conditions for linking knowledge bases requires the specification of partly highly complex mathematical conditions. These problems are currently being addressed by link discovery frameworks such as LIMES (Ngonga Ngomo and Auer 2011) and active learning approaches such as RAVEN (Ngonga Ngomo et al. 2011). These frameworks allow interactively defining the conditions for the establishment of links between knowledge bases and computing these links efficiently. Yet checking the consistency of the generated links remains one of the many large-scale problems that cannot yet be addressed by inference frameworks. First approaches such as the Large Knowledge Collider (www.larkc.eu) aim to tackle this problem by using incomplete inferences.

As the web grows and the amount of knowledge gets more diverse in quantity and quality, the main question that remains is whether the Linked Data web will really enable humanity to regain control over this ever-growing and almost autonomous entity that the web has become. Within the current framework of the Semantic Web it is still difficult to address aspects of information essential to efficient human inference, such as trust, provenance, and partial and even voluntary inconsistency. Will machines ever be able to really help us answer the very questions we dream to have answers to?

■ See also ALGORITHM, COLLECTIVE INTELLIGENCE, NETWORKING, SEARCH

References and Further Reading

Auer, Sören, Christian Bizer, Georgi Kobilarov, Jens Lehmann, Richard Cyganiak, and Zachary Ives. 2008. "DBpedia: A Nucleus for a Web of Open Data." In *Proceedings of the 6th International Semantic Web Conference*, edited by Amit Sheth, Steffen Staab, Massimo Paolucci, Diana Maynard, Timothy Finin, and Krishnaprasad Thirunarayan, 722–735. Berlin: Springer.

Auer, Sören, Jens Lehmann, and Sebastian Hellmann. 2009. "LinkedGeoData—Adding a Spatial Dimension to the Web of Data." In *Proceedings of the 7th International Semantic Web Conference*, edited by Abraham Bernstein, David R. Karger, Tom Heath, et al., 731–746. Berlin: Springer.

Auer, Sören, Jens Lehmann, and Axel-Cyrille Ngonga Ngomo. 2011. "Introduction to Linked Data and Its Lifecycle on the Web." In *Reasoning Web: Semantic Technologies for the Web of Data*, edited by Axel Polleres, Claudia d'Amato, Marcelo Arenas, et al., 1–75. Berlin: Springer.

Berners-Lee, Tim, James Hendler, and Ora Lassila. 2001. "The Semantic Web." *Scientific American* 284 (5): 34–43.

Ferrucci, David A., Eric W. Brown, Jennifer Chu-Carroll, et al. 2010. "Building Watson: An Overview of the DeepQA Project." *AI Magazine* 31 (3): 59–79.

Heath, Tom, and Christian Bizer. 2011. *Linked Data: Evolving the Web into a Global Data Space.* 1st ed. San Rafael, CA: Morgan & Claypool.

Hoffart, Johannes, Mohamed Amir Yosef, Ilaria Bordino, et al. 2011. "Robust Disambiguation of Named Entities in Text." In *Conference on Empirical Methods in Natural Language Processing*, edited by Regina Barzilay and Mark Johnson, 782–792. Edinburgh: ACL.

Ngonga Ngomo, Axel-Cyrille, and Sören Auer. 2011. "LIMES—a Time-Efficient Approach for Large-Scale Link Discovery on the Web of Data." In *Proceedings of the International Joint Conferences on Artificial Intelligence*, edited by Toby Walsh, 2312–2317. Barcelona: IJCAI/AAAI.

Ngonga Ngomo, Axel-Cyrille, Jens Lehmann, Sören Auer, and Konrad Höffner. 2011. "RAVEN—Active Learning of Link Specifications." In *Proceedings of the Sixth International Ontology Matching Workshop at ISWC*, edited by Pavel Shvaiko, Jérôme Euzenat, Tom Heath, Christoph Quix, Ming Mao, and Isabel Cruz, 25–36. http://disi.unitn.it/~p2p/OM-2011//om2011_proceedings .pdf.

....

Simulation

Gonzalo Frasca

Historically, three groups have been the main users of simulations: the military, scientists, and children. The first two traditionally used it for understanding existing systems and predicting their future or past behaviors, as well as a tool for training. Children are also frequent users of simulations in the form of toys and games, mainly for learning and entertainment purposes.

A simulation has three main elements: a source system, a model, and a simulator. The source system is what is being simulated, such as a city, a machine, or a living organism. The model is the behavioral abstraction of the source system, "a set of instructions, rules, equations, or constraints for generating I/O [Input/Output] behavior" (Zeigler, Praehofer, and Kim 2000, 28). The third element, the simulator, is the agent that follows the model's instructions and generates output data (Zeigler, Praehofer, and Kim 2000, 28). The simulator can be a computer program—as in the case of computer simulation—but it can also be a human mind.

The invention of computers brought a major advancement to the field, allowing one to create complex, dynamic models that could be easily updated and modified, delivering rich output experiences. One of the classic examples is the flight simulator, a computer program that models the experience of flying a specific airplane. However, simulations can also be purely mechanical, such as the case of using a scaled-down wooden airplane model inside a wind tunnel for studying how it interacts with air. Toys and games can be considered to be simulations, too: when manipulated by players, a foosball table can be said to simulate a game of soccer.

The creation of simulations is an iterative process. The more a simulation is played, the more its result can be analyzed and compared with the source system. The model can then be modified and optimized to behave more closely to the system it is based on.

Additionally, not all simulations are interactive. Some only allow the modification of variables before the simulator runs it. Others, such as the flight simulator, allow the introduction of data as it is taking place, thus allowing users to steer the virtual plane.

Scientists and the military have extensively used simulation as analytical, predictive tools and also as training environments. Because of these main uses, the term has a heavy bias for "realism." In other words, simulation—and particularly computer simulation—is generally seen within these fields as a limited but somehow faithful reproduction of a nonfictitious source system. This notion, which still prevails in fields such as computer science, was challenged by the appearance of computer games. The ball's behavior in a game like *Breakout* is not consistent with our world's laws of physics. A game such as *Spore* can be described as simulating organisms; however, none of them actually exist.

It has been suggested that the semiotic relationship between representation and simulation is a matter of degree, as two extremes of a continuum (Frasca 2007). We tend to think that a painting represents a person and that a robot simulates it. There are, however, intermediary objects with simpler models, such as a statue or a doll. The statue can simulate some of the source system's behaviors, such as the ability to stand upright and deliver different textures to the touch. The doll's model is even more complex and introduces limb movement within certain limits.

After describing *Spacewar!*, the early video game created in 1962 at MIT, Brenda Laurel concludes that the computer's potential is not as a giant calculator but as a machine capable of representing "action in which the humans could participate" (1993, 1). Unlike traditional media, which can only represent actions, simulations can create actions according to different input data. Computer games have also been described as "the art of simulation," an "alternative mode of discourse, bottom up and emergent where stories are top-down and preplanned. In simulations, knowledge and experience is created by the player's actions and strategies, rather than recreated by a writer or moviemaker" (Aarseth 2004) (see GAMES AS STORIES, INTERACTIVE NARRATIVE). It is important to point out that Aarseth is referring to computer games in general and not just the genre known as "simulation games" (see GAME GENRES). In recent decades, simulations—and especially computer games—have been studied not just for their technical and pedagogical aspects but also for their aesthetics and ideology.

The interpretation of interactive simulations is heavily dependent on the user's manipulation. Obviously, an experienced player who has spent weeks on a flight simulator will become more acquainted with it than a casual player who has only spent a few hours with it. Unlike books or films, simulations will produce meaning not just when read but also when they are physically manipulated in order to modify their input variables. Aarseth describes this mode of operation as textual machines in the literal sense: machines that create meaning when manipulated (2004). This is why simulations are not just interpreted through the textual and audiovisual signs they may output but also through the manipulation of their model. The model is an abstraction of the source system. Just like the camera frames an image, models frame a system's behaviors: some of them are included, and some of them are left out. The understanding of this process is essential not only for game criticism and analysis but also for its persuasive potential (Bogost 2007; Fogg 2002; Frasca 2001, 2007).

SimCity has been not only an extremely popular simulation for entertainment but also, along with *The Sims*, a frequent object of analysis. Julian Bleecker (1995) studied the limitations of *SimCity 2000*'s model in the light of the then-recent Los Angeles riots.

Its model allowed for riots to happen, but they were never motivated by race. Rather, they were only triggered by causes such as heat or high unemployment. Race was simply not a variable included on the game's model. Ideology in a game is created not just by the signs it produces but also by the algorithms and rules within its model.

However, in spite of simulation's procedural nature, a simulation's model is only a part of what defines the user experience. In computer simulations there are multiple kinds of input and output methods (see GRAPHIC REALISM). The computer game industry has always tried to push the envelope on both. High-definition sound and graphics, as well as haptic feedback, are now the most common output methods. Traditional inputs such as the keyboard and mouse have been complemented by several other hardware accessories, such as joysticks, dancing mats, touch screens, light guns, and full-body motion sensors, just to name a few. These can radically affect the player's experience, regardless of the model's rules and instructions. For example, a dancing game such as *Dance Dance Revolution* can be controlled by a portable pad or by a dancing mat. The software may remain exactly the same in both cases, but one can be experienced while lying on a couch while the other requires the player's body to rhythmically move to the beat of a song.

In *Life on the Screen* (1995, 70–71), Sherry Turkle analyzed the players' attitudes toward simulations. She observed two main behaviors, which she called "simulation denial" and "simulation resignation." The first one described people who reject simulations because they judge the model to be oversimplified. The second described the player's resignation when she identifies the limits of the model but accepts them because they cannot be modified. Turkle also imagined a third response that could critically use simulation for consciousness raising by helping players to "challenge the model's built-in assumptions."

Just like storytelling is one of language's most relevant uses, games became one of the most popular uses for simulations. In recent years, the study of simulation has outgrown its technical and pedagogical origins, now expanding to include the humanities and social sciences.

■ See also ARTIFICIAL LIFE, EMERGENCE, GAMEPLAY, GAMES AS STORIES, GRAPHIC REALISM, IMMERSION, INTERACTIVE NARRATIVE, PROCEDURAL, VIRTUAL REALITY

References and Further Reading

Aarseth, Espen. 1997. *Cybertext: Perspectives on Ergodic Literature*. Baltimore: John Hopkins University Press.

———. 2004. "Genre Trouble." *Electronic Book Review*. www.electronicbookreview.com/thread /firstperson/vigilant.

Bleecker, Julian. 1995. "Urban Crisis: Past, Present, and Virtual." *Socialist Review* 24 (1–2): 189–221.

Bogost, Ian. 2007. *Persuasive Games: The Expressive Power of Video Games*. Cambridge, MA: MIT Press.

Breakout. 1976. Computer game. Atari.

Dance Dance Revolution (*DDR*) series. 1998–. Computer game. Konami.

Fogg, B. J. 2002. *Persuasive Technology: Using Computers to Change What We Think and Do*. San Francisco: Morgan Kaufmann.

Frasca, Gonzalo. 2001. "Videogames of the Oppressed: Videogames as a Means for Critical Thinking and Debate." Master's thesis, Georgia Institute of Technology. www.ludology.org/articles /thesis/FrascaThesisVideogames.pdf.

———. 2007. "Play the Message: Play, Game and Videogame Rhetoric." PhD diss., IT University of Copenhagen. www.powerfulrobot.com/Frasca_Play_the_Message_PhD.pdf.

Laurel, Brenda. 1993. *Computers as Theatre*. London: Addison-Wesley.

SimCity 2000. 1993. Computer game. Designed by Will Wright. Maxis / Electronic Arts.

SpaceWar! 1962. Computer game. Designed by Steve Russell et al.

Spore. 2008. Computer game. Designed by Will Wright. Electronic Arts.

Turkle, Sherry. 1995. *Life on the Screen: Identity in the Age of the Internet*. New York: Simon & Schuster.

Zeigler, Bernard P., Herbert Praehofer, and Tag Gon Kim. 2000. *Theory of Modeling and Simulation*. London: Academic Press.

Social Network Sites (SNSs)
Olga Goriunova and Chiara Bernardi

Social networking sites, platforms, and services allow users to create and maintain a dynamic representation of themselves (password-protected but publicly accessible profile of data associated with the user) and connect to other users to view and interact with their representations through the browser window. Social network sites (SNSs) offer a variety of gradients and tools to evaluate and, generally, respond to posts and connections and to manage the degree of public availability of all components of the profile (within the limits permitted by the specific platform). The technical realization of a particular SNS prescribes certain formulae for representations and evaluations (e.g., limited character length of posts on Twitter or the "Like" button on Facebook). More generally, the technical mediation of cultural processes engendered through SNSs emphasizes particular social, political, and aesthetic formulations, further explained below.

According to boyd and Ellison (2007, 214), the first SNS was started in 1997 (Sixdegrees.com), with the SNS phenomenon gaining wider traction in 2004. Whereas in 2012 the most popular SNS was Facebook, it was MySpace in 2008, and there are a variety of SNSs that differ in terms of the geography/language/identity of the communities they attract and construct (Orkut with a large Brazilian and Indian base, LinkedIn with its emphasis on the professional network, etc.); this landscape has a tendency to change quickly and abruptly in terms of the dominance of certain platforms, their focus and communities being formed, internal structures/features, and the problems they pose.

There have also been attempts to establish or at least propose noncorporate SNSs. In line with O'Reilly's (2005) prediction of the new movements for the user ownership of data, Eugene Gorny (2009) suggested a blogging service that would run on a peer-to-peer basis.

Social Change

One of the core features of an SNS, reflected in the design of its pages and in the algorithms running connections and suggestions, is the focus on the articulation and handling of a scalable but bounded network of "friends." One of the biggest ethical problems SNSs pose—and potentially a way to differentiate SNSs themselves—is privacy, having its roots in the emphasis on and the manner of friend accumulation. In most SNSs, articulation of a network of friends largely follows real-life experience: users connect to users they already know or know of (Ellison, Steinfield, and Lampe 2007). Facebook works this way, in what appears to be obedience to the site's ToS (Terms of Service), instructing the users to use real names and contacts. In order to aggregate a list of people one has encountered throughout various paths of life, it is imperative to use one's real name (thus, SNSs are called "nonymous" environments). Consequently, the aggregation and (often) public display of various kinds of data linked to a named person posit manifold threats to privacy, whether informational or institutional (Raynes-Goldie 2010; Debatin et al. 2009).

The true name / single identity issue in its relation to the revitalization of a network of acquaintances is also the means to differentiate SNSs from other forms of social organization on the Internet. Making a connection, one dimension of which is social, is the purpose of any network. If considered merely a descendent of various forms of making and maintaining connections, SNSs can be traced back to BBSs (Bulletin Board Systems) of the 1980s, the virtual communities of the early and mid-1990s, mailing lists, forums, MUDs, online chats, and other historical genres (Rheingold 1993; Turkle 1995). Each of these genres is core to the development of a particular phenomenon: for instance, the Nettime mailing list helped net art and new media theory emerge and mature in a free and exciting manner, whereas forums can be associated with the aggregation of information and advice on car-, health-, and maternity-related topics, among others. Compared to those earlier genres, most SNSs can be claimed to reinvigorate social life by extending existing connections (some still support anonymous or pseudonymous performances). Following that, if in the 1990s one of the foci of academic attention was a reinvention of the self in digital nature (Haraway 1991), an SNS is attended to in relation to, for instance, teenage bullying and abuse via Facebook or employment relying on SNS-based performance (boyd 2010). Whereas previously rape in cyberspace was a possibility (Dibbell 1993), an SNS becomes a de facto space where the drama of life is grounded.

As mentioned above, part of the research into SNSs focuses on their effects on the social life and subjectivity of teenagers (Papacharissi 2010; Ito et al. 2009; Turkle 2011; Hayles 2007; Stiegler 2010). When adult usage of SNSs is concerned with status and promotion (celebrity, music, or academic profiles), managing old acquaintances, or finding new connections, it is regarded as another social tool, albeit exposing the user to stalking, lurking, and generally depleting her privacy. A focus on children, adolescents, and young people allows for a change in tone. SNSs seem unavoidable in adolescent negotiation of self and social setting: "If you are not on MySpace, you don't exist" (Ito et al. 2009, 79); it also prescribes certain technological forms of management of friendship, emotion, love life, attention, and the process of growing up while withdrawing these from parental supervision into corporately managed and publicly available technological domains. Intimacy, romance, enquiry, social capital, and addiction through SNSs are studied ethnographically and presented with lengthy anecdotal evidence (Papacharissi 2010; Ito et al. 2009). Technologized negotiations of identity and adolescent fragility and unawareness in the face of algorithms designed nearly randomly, outside of any public scrutiny, alarm the public. In *Alone Together* (2011), Turkle argues against the enhanced sense of the social, where being worn out and isolated while maintaining a popular profile is one likely result of being connected. More than that, such critiques tune in with the overall concerns about the impact of "connectedness" on generations born with the web and SNSs. Hayles argues that "shallow" attention promoted by various online activities that require being constantly switched on changes the process of knowledge acquisition, both individual and intergenerational, and especially within traditional educational institutions (Hayles 2007).

Political Uses

From Negroponte's optimistic *Being Digital* (1996) to Turkle's pessimistic *Alone Together* (2011), the web has been regarded either as an enabler of direct democracy, participatory action, grassroots politics, and a new public sphere or as a control machine. Such debates were invigorated with Web 2.0 and SNSs (Roberts 2009). Scholars such as Zizi Papacharissi (2009), Bernhard Debatin (2008), and Philip Howard (2004) agree that the role of the Internet as enabler of direct democracy and agent for the realization of the public sphere pertains to "the past," or the beginning of the commercialization of the Internet, while Lawrence Lessig claims that Web 2.0 "re-ignited the cheerleading tendencies of the early days of the Internet" (2009).

Many academic and opinion leaders have praised the liberties offered by SNSs. Media guru Clay Shirky has repeatedly labeled events in China, Iran, Moldova, Tunisia, and Egypt as true social media revolutions without acknowledging the commercial potentials behind the formulations offered by SNSs (Langlois et al. 2009). Although political uses of SNSs have been praised or critiqued on many occasions, the significant changes that the concept of "politics" has undergone have received relatively little academic attention to date. Web 2.0, and most importantly SNSs, has undoubtedly enhanced public participation in the formulation of political thinking and political action. SNSs enable groups to be formed around issues of concern and aggregate quickly to express their viewpoints (Lind 2007). The traditional practice of gatekeeping is allegedly replaced by that of gatewatching, an activity that relies on the users' capacity to decide what they find interesting and worth sharing with their peers (Parsons 2010). Political discussion shifts from the parliament to the public. The public is usually seen as having weak political ties but strong concerns about specific issues: in such a scenario, politicians tend to "follow the flow" (Lilleker and Jackson 2009).

In the years 2010–2011, SNSs repeatedly made headline news stories when uprisings and revolutions in Tunisia, Egypt, and to some extent Yemen and Saudi Arabia were labeled "Facebook revolutions" (Shirky 2011). Several critics discuss SNSs' role in political turmoil to ascertain the intermingling of human action and a particular context and technological allowances to produce large-scale political effects, where such effects, social action, and technological artifacts are indispensable to each other (Sreberny-Muhammadi and Muhammadi 1994; Sakr 2004; Sreberny and Khiabany 2007, 2010). SNSs became a political tool, with events, groups, and profiles being supported or shut down by the platforms' owners without any public scrutiny. For instance, while Middle Eastern uprisings are widely celebrated in the Western media and Facebook makes sure to assist in setting up groups and keeping the archives (Google intervened to liberate their Egyptian executive, and Facebook reacted over the shutdown of the platform by the Egyptian government through massive campaigns), antimonarchist, antiroyalist wedding groups of Great Britain were promptly identified and closed on Facebook prior to the royal wedding in spring 2011. While SNSs clearly provide exciting new possibilities for the articulation of political concern and organization of political movements, as corporate and proprietary environments, they also become gray zones of distrust of the free and grassroots character of their products. In 2011, it was made public that the U.S. Army was developing software applications that would allow operators to manage up to forty credible SNS identities in different parts of the world, supposedly intending to stir discussion and action in certain preferential directions (Cobain 2011).

From the perspective of political communication and in relation to its uses in Western democracies, political uses of SNSs are constrained to political campaigns for winning elections, with the difference that the marketing practices for political purposes increasingly rely on social media and SNSs in particular (and Internet memes) to create interest, generate word of mouth (WOM), catch the public's attention, and instil a "call to action" (Kotler and Keller 2012). Despite the political sphere relying on the marketing practices well before Web 2.0, social media and SNSs have added a new dimension to election campaigns. More than ever, and especially with the help of SNSs, the political sphere embraces slogans; politicians become brands, and the whole election is summed up in taglines, snapshots, or, to use a traditional advertising lexicon, unique selling propositions (USPs) to engage with the public. Such strategies that seem to transpose politicians into mass products are usually related to the growing disaffection with the political class and institutions (Torcal and Montero 2006).

Political communication in the Web 2.0 era is a nascent field, very much tied to the period of elections with the proverbial "selling of a dream." The political sphere concentrates most efforts on the process of convincing the electorate to choose a specific candidate, with little research attention paid to the failure of political communication and political public relations to listen to social media users after the elections. Engagement in this case not only applies to a presence on SNSs, such as Facebook or Twitter, but refers to the capacity of the political candidate to enter into a permanent campaign through social media, monitor the moods and trends that the electorate voice through SNSs, and modify political and communicative strategy accordingly (Patrick Caddell, Memo to President Carter, 1976; see Bowman 2000). One of the most well-known examples of politics 2.0 is Barak Hussein Obama's successful presidential campaign of 2008, which centred on the USP of "Change We Can Believe In," widely diffused through SNSs. It was the most expensive electoral campaign in the United States to date, amounting to roughly $1 billion, with an expenditure on media of roughly $711 million. It gathered the support of media conglomerates, Hollywood stars, and music celebrities such as Bruce Springsteen. It lit the "dream" of a very young electorate (age 29 and below according to Pew Research) and instilled a great enthusiasm in the African American and Latin American minorities (predominantly Mexicans). However, the campaign also shows the weaknesses of political communication and political public relations in terms of the effective use of SNSs. In fact, this glamorous campaign has a less successful "follow-up," and critics have argued that the character of the president has since become stagnant, failing to proceed toward the phase of "actualisation" (Johnson 2010; Coglianese 2009).

Aesthetic Formulations

A revival of interest in the aesthetic phenomena of the "vernacular" web, stemming from net art's tinkering with the language of the network, has developed into the popular SNS-based movements of animated GIFs, formulaic web pages, and, at a different level, memes, or meme cultures (e.g., Lolcats). Social and political effects of SNSs often obscure the fact that a lot of the material created for, circulated through, and commented upon in SNSs and social media, the creative currency of SNS actors, are examples of "new media idiocy" (Goriunova 2013): jokes, pranks, funny collages, and, generally, cultural objects with obscured meaning. The circulation of memes through SNSs not only sheds light on the nature of creativity, craft, and participation but also exhibits a capacity to become a political channel in which political statements and actions are shaped by and perform as "silly" and humorous cultural production. It can be claimed that even political events are molded to fit and utilize the "Like" and "Share" button grammar: a high percentage of placards at the Bolotnaya Ploschad 2011 anti-Putin protests in Russia, for instance, were humorous, as if specifically designed to be photographed, posted, liked, reposted, linked, and liked again, to create a circular movement strong enough to further engage large-scale mass media actors, often in turn succumbing to the use of the same popular memes in their coverage.

Contemplated from this angle, SNSs and social media are not just prone to providing instant promotion to posts involving sex and crime, or the most facilely pleasant and funny, while the unsettling and disturbing is pushed out of sight (as danah boyd suggests in her "fat and sugar" theory; Pariser 2011, 14); their accumulated power and technical configuration actively shape processes and events that singularize into forms capable of becoming currency in SNSs, whose power in turn is created by those very people involved in the processes of its substantiation.

Methods to Study SNSs

SNSs, social networks, and networks share many characteristics, which is probably the basis of a certain swapping of concepts when methodology and disciplinary possessiveness are concerned. Network theory, whose language is developed by graph theory, a branch of applied mathematics, has received significant attention recently, being popularized by publications such as *Linked* by Albert-László Barabási (2003). Attention to social networks and societal interactions, on the other hand, rooted in the work of Georg Simmel (1908) at the turn of the twentieth century and revived by the sociometry of social psychologist Jakob Moreno in the 1930s and 1940s, is another set of traditions, which until recently have developed in parallel to network theory, though having borrowed mathematical models from graph theory and topology in the 1950s and 1960s (Meyer 2009; Freeman 2004). Social anthropology and work by Radcliffe-Brown and Malinowski ran in parallel to Moreno's initiatives, producing similar developments (Freeman 2004). One of the opinions is that the term *social network* was coined in 1954 by anthropologist John Barnes, who studied social ties in a Norwegian fishing village, concluding that the whole of social life could be seen as "a set of points, some of which are joined by lines" to form a "total network" of relations (Freeman 1979).

Researchers claim that SNSs transpose real-life social networks online (Lange 2008), and that "there is no hard distinction between online networks and offline ones"; hence, social network theory extends to include SNSs, often unproblematically (Hogan 2008). The concept of the network from actor-network theory (Callon and Law 1997) and the concept of the rhizome (Deleuze and Guattari 1987), which allow for actors of different nature, scale, and intensity to be part of the network, do not share a common conceptual or methodological language with social network or network theory (Hogan 2008).

There is not, therefore, such a thing as a "social media (or SNS) research method" even in quantitative analysis. To date, quantitative studies on SNSs rely on hyperlink analysis, which is primarily based on traditional statistics as applied by social network analysis (SNA). This analysis is founded on the assumption that the virtual world is made of nodes (i.e., web pages, personal profiles, blog pages) connected through hyperlinks (in-links and out-links) that form a complex and multiple network. Visualization of the network is both a tool and an intermediate finding that requires further interpretation. The density and clustering of the network are considered in order to describe the network. The principles of SNA which define "key players" are centrality and prestige. An actor is considered central when he or she has a high level of involvement in many relations, regardless of send/receive directionality or volume of activity. The three most widely used centrality measures are degree, closeness, and betweenness (Freeman 1979). Prestige takes into consideration the difference between sending and receiving links/relations. An actor is defined as prestigious when he is an object of extensive ties as a recipient. There are many more concepts and levels to study attributes of nodes, structure of their relationships, and types of community formation, as well as more advanced network measurements (Hogan 2008).

SNA uses analytical software to map social ties. The many types of software used to map the relational ties in SNSs focus on the dimension of the network or spatiality. In this view, the relevance of the nodes (which indeed can be blogs, forums, or Facebook pages) can be assessed through the number of links that each node receives (in-links) and emits (out-links). There are many limitations in the application of SNA to the study of SNSs; it is not yet possible to talk about a universally acceptable method to fully understand the relevance of and the relation between nodes (in this case the various tools offered by Web 2.0), and much of the work in the field stops at visual realizations of network maps which give hints about the size of networks and the main (central) actors within it. Software facilitates SNA quantitatively; however, this must be followed by a traditional qualitative analysis for each of the nodes on a visualized network. SNSs present a special challenge for the application of quantitative methods, as the corporations that own them do not appear to be very cooperative and would not make large data sets available. Researchers also write custom scripts to scrape data off the pages (Hogan 2008). Still, most sociological and psychological studies that focus on SNSs have to rely on user interviews, surveys, questionnaires, and sample content analysis to make conclusions about the nature of the network. Ethnographic research is also widely popular.

■ See also NETWORKING, POLITICS AND NEW MEDIA

References and Further Reading

Anstead, Nick, and Andrew Chadwick. 2009. "Parties, Election Campaigning and the Internet: Toward a Comparative Institutional Approach." In *Routledge Handbook of Internet Politics*, edited by Andrew Chadwick and P. N. Howard, 56–71. New York: Routledge.

Barabási, Albert-László. 2003. *Linked: How Everything Is Connected to Everything Else and What It Means*. London: Plume.

Barabási, Albert-László, and Réka Albert. 1999. "Emergence of Scaling in Random Networks." *Science* 286:509–512.

Bowman, Karlyn. 2000. "Polling to Campaign and to Govern." In *The Permanent Campaign and Its Future*, edited by Norman Ornstein and Thomas Mann, 54–74. Washington, DC: American Enterprise Institute for Policy Research.

boyd, danah. 2010. "Regulating the Use of Social Media Data." www.zephoria.org/thoughts /archives/2010/08/26/regulating-the-use-of-social-media-data.html.

boyd, danah, and Nicole Ellison. 2007. "Social Network Sites: Definition, History and Scholarship." *Journal of Computer-Mediated Communication* 13:210–230.

Bruns, Axel. 2008a. *Blogs, Wikipedia, Second Life and Beyond: From Production to Produsage*. New York: Peter Lang.

———. 2008b. "Gatewatching, Gatecrashing: Futures for Tactical News Media." In *Digital Media and Democracy: Tactics in Hard Times*, edited by Megan Boler, 247–270. Cambridge, MA: MIT Press.

Callon, Michael, and John Law. 1997. "After the Individual in Society: Lessons in Collectivity from Science, Technology and Society." *Canadian Journal of Sociology* 22 (2): 165–182.

Cobain, Ian, and Nick Fielding. 2011. "Revealed: US Spy Operation That Manipulates Social Media." *Guardian*, March 17. www.guardian.co.uk/technology/2011/mar/17/us-spy-operation-social-networks.

Coglianese, Cary. 2009. "The Transparency President? The Obama Administration and Open Government." *Governance* 22 (4): 529–544.

Debatin, Bernhard. 2008. "The Internet as a New Platform for Expressing Opinions and as a New Public Sphere." In *The SAGE Handbook of Public Opinion Research*, edited by Wolfgang Donsbach and Michael W. Traugott, 64–73. New York: Sage.

Debatin, Bernhard, Jennette Lovejoy, Ann-Kathrin Horn, and Brittany Hughes. 2009. "Facebook and Online Privacy: Attitudes, Behaviors, and Unintended Consequences." *Journal of Computer-Mediated Communication* 15:83–108.

Deleuze, Gilles, and Felix Guattari. 1987. *A Thousand Plateaus: Capitalism and Schizophrenia*. Minneapolis: University of Minnesota Press.

Dibbell, Julian. 1993. "A Rape in Cyberspace, or How an Evil Clown, a Haitian Trickster Spirit, Two Wizards, and a Cast of Dozens Turned a Database into a Society." *Village Voice*, December 23. www.juliandibbell.com/texts/bungle_vv.html.

Ellison, Nicole, Charles Steinfield, and Cliff Lampe. 2007. "The Benefits of Facebook 'friends': Exploring the Relationship between College Students' Use of Online Social Networks and Social Capital." *Journal of Computer-Mediated Communication* 12 (4): 1.

Freeman, Linton C. 1979. "Centrality in Social Network I. Conceptual Clarification." *Social Networks* 1:215–239.

———. 2004. *The Development of Social Network Analysis: A Study in the Sociology of Science*. Vancouver: BooSurge.

Goriunova, Olga. 2013. "New Media Idiocy." *Convergence* 19 (2): 223–235.

Gorny, Eugene. 2009. *A Creative History of the Russian Internet: Studies in Internet Creativity*. Saarbrücken, Germany: VDM.

Haraway, Donna. 1991. "A Cyborg Manifesto: Science, Technology, and Socialist-Feminism in the Late Twentieth Century." In *Simians, Cyborgs, and Women: The Reinvention of Nature*. New York: Routledge.

Hayles, Katherine N. 2007. "Hyper and Deep Attention: The Generational Divide in Cognitive Modes." In *Profession*, 187–199. http://media08.wordpress.com/2008/01/17/my-article-on-hyper-and-deep-attention/.

Hogan, Bernie. 2008. "Analysing Social Networks via the Internet." In *The Handbook of Online Research Methods*, edited by Nigel G. Fielding, Raymond M. Lee, and Grant Blank. London: Sage.

Howard, Philip, and Steve Jones. 2004. *Society Online: The Internet in Context*. Thousand Oaks, CA: Sage.

Ito, Mizuko, Sonja Baumer, Matteo Bittanti, et al. 2009. *Hanging Out, Messing Around, and Geeking Out: Kids Living and Learning with New Media*. Cambridge, MA: MIT Press.

Johnson, Leola. 2010. "Obama's Body and the Liberal Body Politic." *International Journal of Communication* 4:246–252.

Kotler, Philip, and Kevin Keller. 2012. *Marketing Management*. Englewood Cliffs, NJ: Prentice Hall.

Landowski, Eric. 1989. *La Societe Reflechie: Essais De Socio-Semiotique*. Paris: Seuil.

Lange, Patricia G. 2008. "Publicly Private and Privately Public: Social Networking on YouTube." *Journal of Computer-Mediated Communication* 13:361–380.

Langlois, Ganaele, Fenwick McKelvey, Greg Elmer, and Kenneth Werbi. 2009. "Mapping Commercial Web 2.0 Worlds: Towards a New Critical Ontogenesis." *FibreCulture* 14. http://fourteen.fibreculturejournal.org/fcj-095-mapping-commercial-web-2-0-worlds-towards-a-new-critical-ontogenesis/.

Lessig, Lawrence. 2009. "Foreword." In *The Future of the Internet: And How to Stop It*, by Jonathan Zittrain, vii–ix. London: Penguin.

Lilleker, Darren, and Nigel A. Jackson. 2009. "Building an Architecture of Participation? Political Parties and Web 2.0 in Britain." *Journal of Information Technology & Politics* 6 (3–4): 232–250.

Lind, Maria. 2007. "The Collaborative Turn." In *Taking the Matter into Common Hands: On Contemporary Art and Collaborative Practices*, edited by Johanna Billing, Maria Lind, and Lars Nilsson, 15–31 London: Black Dog.

Meyer, Katja. 2009. "On the Sociometry of Search Engines: A Historical Review of Methods." In *Deep Search: The Politics of Search beyond Google*, edited by Konrad Becker and Felix Stalder. Wien, Austria: StudienVerlag.

Mitchell, Lincoln. 2010. "The Obama Disappointment and Its Costs." *Huffington Post*, July 22.

O'Reilly, Tim. 2005. "What Is Web 2.0?" *O'Reilly Media*, September 30. http://oreilly.com/web2 /archive/what-is-web-20.html.

Papacharissi, Zizi. 2009. "The Virtual Sphere 2.0: The Internet, the Public Sphere, and Beyond." In *The Routledge Handbook of Internet Politics*, edited by Andrew Chadwich and Philip N. Howard, 230–245. New York: Routledge.

———. 2010. *A Networked Self: Identity, Community, and Culture on Social Network Sites*. New York: Routledge.

Pariser, Eli. 2011. *The Filter Bubble: What the Internet Is Hiding from You*. New York: Penguin.

Parsons, Christopher. 2010. "Moving across the Internet: Code-Bodies, Code-Corpses, and Network Architecture." *CTheory*, May. www.ctheory.net/articles.aspx?id=642.

Radio Free Europe. 2011. "Tunisia: Can We Please Stop Talking about 'Twitter Revolutions'?" www .rferl.org/content/tunisia_can_we_please_stop_talking_about_twitter_revolutions/2277052 .html?page=1&x=1#relatedInfoContainer.

Raynes-Goldie. Katie. 2010. "Aliases, Creeping and Wall Cleaning: Understanding Privacy in the Age of Facebook." *First Monday* 15 (1).

Rheingold, Howard. 1993. *The Virtual Community, Homesteading on the Electronic Frontier*. New York: Perseus Books. www.rheingold.com/vc/book/intro.html.

Roberts, Ben. 2009. "Beyond the 'Networked Public Sphere': Politics, Participation and Technics in Web 2.0." *FibreCulture* 14. http://fourteen.fibreculturejournal.org/fcj-093-beyond-the -networked-public-sphere-politics-participation-and-technics-in-web-2-0.

Sakr, Naomi. 2004. *Women and Media in the Middle East: Power through Self-Expression*. London: I. B. Tauris.

Shirky, Clay. 2011. "The Political Power of Social Media: Technology, the Public Sphere, and Political Change." *Foreign Affairs* 1 (January/February): 1–9.

Simmel, Georg. 1908. *On Individuality and Social Forms*. Chicago: University of Chicago Press.

Spyridou, Paschalia-Lia, and Andreas Veglis. 2011. "Political Parties and Web 2.0 Tools: A Shift in Power or a New Digital Bandwagon?" *International Journal of Electronic Governance* 4 (1–2): 136–155.

Sreberny, Annabelle, and Gholam Khiabany. 2007. "Becoming Intellectual: The Blogestan and Public Political Space in the Islamic Republic." *British Journal of Middle Eastern Studies* 34 (3): 267–286.

———. 2010. *Blogestan: The Internet and Politics in Iran*. London: I B Tauris.

Sreberny-Mohammadi, Annabelle, and Ali Mohammadi. 1994. *Small Media, Big Revolution: Communication, Culture and the Iranian Revolution*. Minneapolis: University of Minnesota Press.

Stiegler, Bernard. 2010. *Taking Care of Youth and the Generations*. Stanford, CA: Stanford University Press.

Torcal, Mariano, and Jose R. Montero, eds. 2006. *Political Disaffection in Contemporary Democracies: Social Capital*. New York: Routledge.

Turkle, Sherry. 1995. *Life on the Screen: Identity in the Age of the Internet*. New York: Simon & Schuster.

———. 2011. *Alone Together: Why We Expect More from Technology and Less from Each Other*. New York: Basic Books.

Watts, Duncan J. 2002. *Six Degrees: The Science of a Connected Age*. New York: W. W. Norton.

Software Studies
Matthew Fuller

The scale of the question of software and the variety of means by which it might be analyzed can be registered by thinking through the process of production of this encyclopedia in the work of coordinating and soliciting texts, work on design, editing, print, transportation, payments, and marketing, not to mention the wider ways such systems recurse in the use and mobilization of the texts herein should anyone care, or have time, to read them. Further, the construction of the entries here will occur among e-mails, dictionaries, grammar checkers, and word processors, all of which act on and guide the production of the work. Many of these factors are replacements or supplements to existing systems, but they are also novel, exhibiting kinds of speed, propensity, and agency which work in and on the circulation of ideas to the extent that even the gesture of making a book, rather than a database, takes on a certain significance (see BOOK TO E-TEXT, DATABASE). That it does not appear as a database does not mean that it is not contained, handled, recommended, and sorted by databases. The book, however, persists as a powerful media form, at the same time as its contours and capacities are articulated by powerful and mundane reconfigurations. Software studies aims to provide a context in which what is often taken for granted about such processes can be more adequately understood, not simply for the purposes of critique, but also in founding more nuanced conditions for the understanding of the significance and possibilities inherent in computational culture.

Software studies is concerned with the way in which software has become the most significant but underthought factor in contemporary culture, society, and politics. Software studies therefore consists of both integrating the disciplines and practices concerned with those broad fields in the invention and critical analysis of software and understanding the ramifications of software as it, with all its constituent logics and traits, interpolates much of culture, society, and politics. Software studies is something that proposes means to navigate, understand, and modify the terms of this recursive condition. As such, the field is one that joins research activity in cultural theory, social science, and computing, as well as being an area that is intimately formed by experimental practice through the development of software for cultural analysis and invention.

Given such variegation and spread, much of the work around software studies consists of the development of adequate points of entry to the description and analysis of computational culture. Some projects will require the study of graphical user interfaces; others study codes and programming systems, observations of behavior in cities, and archival research in the papers of labs (see ARCHIVE, CODE, INTERFACE). The clinical use and interpretation of games, word processors, image editors, content management systems, and other such systems of everyday processes are as necessary as those of more recondite and particular systems such as those articulating, planning, or making financial trades (see CHARACTERISTICS OF DIGITAL MEDIA).

Software studies, temporally speaking, has its roots, or some of them, in the moment when the cultures of the personal computer, amplified by the web, took on a materialist turn, examining or reinventing the browsers, search engines, and other forms that characterized them in the decade following the mid-1990s (Bosma et al. 1999; Manovich 2001) (see HISTORY OF COMPUTERS). (See relatedly the "Software Summer School" event at the TechNiks Festival at the Lux Gallery in London 2000.) It has other filiations of the same era to the work of science and technology studies and further roots in the free software, hacking, and software art movements (Star 1995; Fuller 2003) (see FREE AND OPEN-SOURCE SOFTWARE, HACKER). Importantly, it has sources in the more reflexive and speculative aspects of computer science, and in turn in the material aspects of digital culture in *kulturwissenschaft*, exemplified by Friedrich Kittler (2001), Wolfgang Ernst (2012), Wolfgang Hagen (2005), and in the work of scholars such as Katherine Hayles (2005) and Matthew Kirschenbaum (2007).

More recently and perhaps in scalar terms the most far removed from the minutiae of software, geography has, as a discipline, been one of those most adventurous in developing accounts of the integration of computational forms and processes into everyday life. The work of Stephen Graham (2005) examining the role social sorting systems have in shaping access to "life-chances" (favorable conditions in health, education, environment, and so on) has been complemented by that of Martin Dodge and Rob Kitchin, who, in the book *Code/Space*, set out a survey of the multitude of devices by which software is embedded into everyday life for purposes of "efficiency, productivity, safety, sustainability, and consumer choice" (2011, 224).

Software means something in itself, as an object of study, as in Adrian Mackenzie's (2011) discussion of the Viterbi algorithm, or Søren Pold's (2012) brief history of the aesthetic of buttons in graphical user interface (GUI), but also, for instance, in "On Photoshop" (2012), in which Lev Manovich assays the famous program's relation to prior forms of image manipulation, as something that relates to an outside. This may be in terms of historical influence, or, as in Mackenzie's book, something that modulates and stages forms of experience, or which creates conditions in which certain kinds of workings of the urban "hang together." At the same time, due to the tendencies of programs, such as Adobe's Creative Suite, generic forms of graphics, visualization, structuring, and handling of data and visual material tend to move across previously disparate media forms (Manovich 2007).

There is no privileged scale at which such work must take place. And while there is some truth in Vilém Flusser's claim that "the new computer codes have made us illiterate again" (2011, 55), software, and the process of digitization, is not ultimately reducible to code. In order to understand it, attention may usefully operate in the analysis of, for instance, human behaviors that are amenable to programming, or that operate as bearers or yielders of data for symbolic handling.

In this regard a number of analytical units have been offered by researchers such as Ian Bogost and Noah Wardrip-Fruin aiming to develop a sense of how processes, recognizable apart from the details of their specific implementation, become part of a new form of literacy or idiom (Bogost 2008; Wardrip-Fruin 2009). Examples would be jumping and maneuvering around platforms in games of that kind; the grammar of cut, copy, paste, and delete, to be applied to objects across applications; or the generic forms of database processes for entry, submission, and manipulation of data. These kinds of *procedural literacy*—the term is from an important essay by Michael Mateas (2005)—have been claimed to be primarily knowable through code, but might also be known with more experiential precision by those at different points in the procedure: patients waiting for an operation, those undergoing evaluation for a visa, or dancers working with movement-tracking equipment as part of their choreographic schema.

Wendy Hui Kyung Chun's *Programmed Visions* (2011) frames such questions in terms of the wider ideology and implementation of programmability. This she describes as a quality found at scales ranging from genetics to politics, one lying at the core of the implementation of the computer and generalized into an understanding of the world as being inherently codifiable and thus available to undergo certain kinds of permutation and translation. Here, the question of the underlying ontological dimensions of computing, as something historically generated in the intermixture of fields such as mathematics, logic, engineering, and management, among others—each with their specific commitments to understanding and enrolling the world, each with their particular commitments to the knowing and stabilization of certain kinds of entity and method— produces a range of exigencies in formulating methods and research programs adequate to understanding and acting in analytical and creative relation to the genesis of software. As software mutates over time into something increasingly articulated through its action in and as the social and cultural, the question of the way in which it maps and involves differing forms of relationality (as, for instance, in social media) (see SOCIAL NETWORK SITES [SNSs]) and the implicit and explicit patterns by which it does so become increasingly susceptible to new kinds of understanding. Figures of such understanding may be drawn from explicitly social and cultural fields, but such changes also establish conditions in which the social and cultural tendentially become processes themselves of computation.

As with Mackenzie's work, this question of the way in which software entails new modalities of experience also provokes enquiry in the form of software. A key component of software studies has been the development of programs as a mode of research and as a more general involvement in the culture of software. The work of researchers such as Olga Goriunova and Graham Harwood is of significance here. *Funware*, an exhibition touring the United Kingdom and the Netherlands at the end of the first decade of this century and curated by Goriunova, made, through gathering numerous artworks and historical projects, the argument that not only is software a fundamentally cultural phenomenon from its inception, but it is one that can be seen to be driven by a deep sense of fun (Goriunova 2010). This is an argument for fun not simply as frivolous and ephemeral enjoyment, which software cultures are certainly replete with (as can be ascertained from a view of any directory of apps), but also as something that is driven by noninstrumentalized, passionate engagement with the deep exploration of its condition as a mode of knowledge, communication, and being. As such, the work sets out a means by which software is something produced in the interaction between intellection, technicity, and emotion and in turn provides a constituent domain for further recensions of such interactions. Still further, such work, in software art, proposes that understanding contemporary digital society and the patterning of life with software will require the use of programs as a mode of enquiry and invention.

Harwood's work includes projects such as *Coal Fired Computers* (2010), a collaboration with ex–coal miners in the north of England which involved using a steam engine to power a computer running a database of information regarding lung diseases and mining fatalities and "visualized" this information by feeding related quanta of compressed air into a pair of preserved blackened lungs. Such work provides a "live diagram" of social relations as they are interpolated by computing; energy in the forms of heat, electricity, and kinetic muscular force; the transmogrification of forms of matter as diverse as coal and flesh; and the capacity of the computer to act as a general integrator and interpreter of such forms of relation. It is as a generalized, but disaggregate, field of action, interpretation, communication, modeling, and prediction that computing provides and entrains meaning in contemporary life. The specific forms and dynamics that it introduces, makes palpable, reinforces, oblates, and succeeds from characterize the modalities and novelty of our culture.

The research directions mentioned above form part of an array of attempts to figure out and create the adequate means of recognizing and understanding the ways in which software shapes, preempts, and responds to contemporary life in terms of ontology, idiom, and experience, among other scales. However, it is also something, as much of the work mentioned suggests, that acts on culture itself. Software studies offers an array of concerns and means of refining attention to culture which also aligns, therefore, with currents such as cultural analytics and digital methods that work with effective procedures to draw out the ways in which an understanding of software as having a fundamentally epistemic dimension may be used to analyze wider domains of culture in both "born-digital" and digitized modes (Cultural Analytics; Digital Methods Initiative).

The development of such research programs in art and in cultural analysis proposes too that the development of digital artifacts might also be driven by such concerns. This is something manifest in human computer interface research such as that of Phoebe Sengers and others in what is compellingly proposed as the third paradigm in human-computer interaction (Harrison, Sengers, and Tatar 2007). And it is manifest in the software research work aimed at "picturing the public of the network society" of Warren Sack, a sustained attempt to generate enhanced capacities of reflexivity in the network *socius*.

That software becomes both a mode and an object of such research is characteristic of the conditions of contemporary life. As software replaces text as the fulcrum of knowledge in the humanities and other disciplines, engendering new modes and problems of knowledge as it shifts and transforms their constituent media, text does not become reducible to code, implying that its tools of analysis and interpretation can be simply transposed; rather, any encounter with digital textuality will imply an expanded sense of its conjuration within computation.

References and Further Reading

Bogost, Ian. 2008. *Unit Operations: An Approach to Videogame Criticism*. Cambridge, MA: MIT Press.

Bosma, Josephine, Pauline van Mourik Broekman, Ted Byfield, et al. 1999. *README! Filtered by NETTIME: ASCII Culture and the Revenge of Knowledge*. New York: Autonomedia.

Chun, Wendy Hui Kyong. 2011. *Programmed Visions: Software and Memory*. Cambridge, MA: MIT Press.

Digital Methods Initiative, University of Amsterdam. www.digitalmethods.net/.

Dodge, Martin, and Rob Kitchin. 2011. *Code/Space: Software and Everyday Life*. Cambridge, MA: MIT Press.

Ernst, Wolfgang. 2012. *Digital Memory and the Archive*. Minneapolis: University of Minnesota Press.

Flusser, Vilém. 2011. *Does Writing Have a Future?* Translated by Nancy Ann Roth. Minneapolis: University of Minnesota Press.

Fuller, Matthew. 2003. *Behind the Blip: Essays on the Culture of Software*. New York: Autonomedia.

Goriunova, Olga, curator. 2010. *Funware* (exhibition). Arnolfini, Bristol, and Mu, Eindhoven.

Graham, Stephen. 2005. "Software-Sorted Geographies." *Progress in Human Geography* 29 (5): 562–580.

Hagen, Wolfgang. 2005. "The Style of Source Codes." In *New Media, Old Media*, edited by Wendy Hui Kyong Chun and Thomas Keenan, 157–175. New York: Routledge.

Harrison, Steve, Phoebe Sengers, and Deborah Tatar. 2007. "The Three Paradigms of HCI." *CHI 2007*. http://citeseerx.ist.psu.edu/viewdoc/summary?doi=10.1.1.96.3754.

Harwood, Graham, with Matsuko Yokokoji. 2010. *Coal Fired Computers*. AV Festival Newcastle upon Tyne. http://yoha.co.uk/cfc/.

Hayles, Katherine N. 2005. *My Mother Was a Computer: Digital Subjects and Literary Texts*. Chicago: University of Chicago Press.

Kirschenbaum, Matthew. 2007. *Mechanisms: New Media and the Forensic Imagination*. Cambridge, MA: MIT Press.

Kittler, Friedrich. 2001. "Computer Graphics: A Semi-Technical Introduction." *Grey Room* 1 (2): 30–45.

Mackenzie, Adrian. 2011. *Wirelessness: Radical Empiricism in Network Cultures*. Cambridge, MA: MIT Press.

Manovich, Lev. 2001. *The Language of New Media*. Cambridge, MA: MIT Press.

———. 2007. "Deep Remixability." *Artifact—Journal of Virtual Design* 1 (3).

———. 2012. "On Photoshop." *Computational Culture, a Journal of Software Studies* 1. www.computationalculture.net/.

Mateas, Michael. 2005. "Procedural Literacy: Educating the New Media Practitioner." *On The Horizon. Special Issue. Future of Games, Simulations and Interactive Media in Learning Contexts* 13 (1).

Pold, Søren. 2008. "Button." In *Software Studies: A Lexicon*, edited by Matthew Fuller, 31–36. Cambridge, MA: MIT Press.

Sack, Warren. http://people.ucsc.edu/~wsack/projects.html/.

Software Studies Initiative. http://lab.softwarestudies.com/.

Star, Susan Leigh, ed. 1995. *Cultures of Computing*. Sociological Review Monographs. Oxford: Blackwell.

Wardrip-Fruin, Noah. 2009. *Expressive Processing: Digital Fictions, Computer Games, and Software Studies*. Cambridge, MA: MIT Press.

Sound

Aaron Angello

Since the 1960s there has been a shift in the way people listen. In their introduction to the book *Audio Culure: Readings in Modern Music*, editors Christoph Cox and Daniel Warner say that there has been a dramatic increase in "musicians, composers, sound artists, scholars, and listeners attentive to sonic substance, the art of listening, and the creative possibilities of sound recording, playback and transmission" (2004, xiii). This is due primarily to technological advancements, from the tape recorder to the MP3 and the Internet. Academic institutions have increasingly been taking an interest in the viability of sound as a field of academic study, and galleries and museums have increasingly been accepting sound art as a legitimate art form.

Sound today, as employed in artistic practice, is heavily influenced by the sound poets of the modernist avant-garde. In the early twentieth century, futurist and Dadaist poets began experimenting with an innovative form of poetry that was meant to be heard and experienced on a level outside of the protocols of traditional meaning. Their tactical media performances replaced recognizable words with what at times came across as bombastic, absurd, or nonsensical sounds. F. T. Marinetti's "Dune, parole in libertà" (1914), Hugo Ball's "Karawane" (1916) and "Gadji beri bimba" (1916), Kurt Schwitters's "Ursonate," and Tristan Tzara's "L'amiral cherche une maison à Louer" (1916) are examples of this early work. These early sound poets explored the potentiality of sound to communicate on its own terms, outside the realm of referentiality. The advent of the tape recorder and of electronic musical instruments allowed for access to what John Cage calls, in his 1958 lecture "The Future of Music: Credo," "the entire field of sound." For the first time, composers and sound artists had access to a full range of sound that was previously limited to the sound produced by acoustic instruments. Steve Reich, for example, began experimenting with tape music in the 1960s at the San Francisco Tape Music Center, where he experimented with tape loops. In his pieces "It's Gonna Rain" (1965) and "Come Out" (1966), he played with what he called "phrasing." This process involved creating two identical loops and playing them back at slightly different speed. The loops would begin together and slowly move out of synch (classical.net). Another instance of Reich's exploration of technology and sound is the piece "Pendulum Music" (1968), in which he swung suspended microphones above amplified speakers in such a way that he could "play" the resulting feedback.

Also in the 1960s, media theorist Marshall McLuhan began to notice a shift in the human response to sound. Cox and Warner tell us that "McLuhan argued that the emergence of electronic media was causing a shift in the sensorium, deposing the visual from its millennia-old hegemony and giving way to an immersive experience exemplified by the auditory" (2004, xiii). The listener no longer necessarily associated the sound with the original source of the sound (i.e., the instrument), but with the recording, manipulation, and transmission of the sound.

John Cage's experimental compositions have had an enormous impact on the development of sound art. His compositional use of found objects, altered instruments, recording and looping, and indeterminacy have changed the landscape of sound in art. His piece "4′ 33″," a piece in which the musician sits in silence for four minutes and thirty-three seconds, allowing the audience to listen to the ambient and incidental sound in the room, has made a particularly strong impact on the history of sound art because it shifts the listener's focus from the stage and the instrument to the experience of sound generally. In "The Future of Music: Credo," Cage said, "Wherever we are, what we hear is mostly noise. When we ignore it, it disturbs us. When we listen to it, we find it fascinating. . . . We want to capture and control these sounds, to use them not as sound effects but as musical instruments" (1961, 3).

In the 1960s and 1970s, members of the Fluxus movement, a movement started by students of John Cage, continued to experiment with sound and its possibilities in art. Particular pieces of note are Yoko Ono's "Toilet Piece" (1971), Robert Watts's "Interview," (1963), and Wolf Vostell's "Elektronischer de-coll.age. Happening Raum" (1968). The Fluxus movement (from the Latin for "to flow") began with students he was teaching in a class in experimental music at the New School for Social Research. His students included Al Hansen, George Brecht, Dick Higgins, and the sound poet Jackson Mac Low. Fluxus, heavily influenced by Dada sound poetry (see above), focused intently on cultivating a DIY aesthetic in the production of sound and the use of various media.

In 1983, William Hellerman curated a show at the Sculpture Center in New York City entitled *Sound/Art*. The show included work by artists such as Carolee Schneeman, Vito Acconci, Bill and Mary Buchen, and Richard Lerman. This event marks the first time the term *sound art* was used and is generally considered the beginning of sound art as an identifiable genre in contemporary art.

Beginning in the 1990s, digital media and the Internet (see ANALOG VERSUS DIGITAL) facilitated a monumental shift in audio culture, one that continues to transform our relationship to sound to this day. The availability of inexpensive software that allows for audio recording, mixing, sampling, and manipulation has increased exponentially. Today, anyone with a computer, tablet, or smartphone (see MOBILE GAMES) can produce sound and/or music, sometimes very intuitively. The distinction between "high" and "low" art is becoming blurred to the point of making the two terms irrelevant.

Another change related to digital media is the ease with which information is exchanged. The digitization of audio and the interconnectedness of web users have allowed for unprecedented access to audio source material. This access and the increasing cultural tendency to create through the process of remix have created a vibrant audio culture that is no longer claimed by avant-garde artists and writers alone, but by everyone (see REMIX). As Bernard Schütze writes in his online essay "Samples from the Heap,"

> Mix, mix again, remix: copyleft, cut 'n' paste, digital jumble, cross-fade, dub, tweak the knob, drop the needle, spin, merge, morph, bootleg, pirate, plagiarize, enrich, sample, break down, reassemble, multiply input source, merge output, decompose, recompose, erase borders, remix again. These are among many of the possible actions involved in what can be broadly labeled "remix culture"—an umbrella term which covers a wide array of creative stances and initiatives, such as: plunderphonics, detritus.net, recombinant culture, open source, compostmodernism, mash-ups, cut-ups, bastard pop, covers, mixology, peer to peer, creative commons, "surf, sample, manipulate," and uploadphonix. (2007)

Schütze continues: "As this plethora of activities indicates, we are clearly living in a remix culture: a culture that is constantly renewing, manipulating, and modifying already mediated and mixed cultural material" (2007).

A final element of sound in the current digital environment that bears mentioning is the online digital archive (see ARCHIVE). Sites of particular note are the PennSound archive and UbuWeb. PennSound, directed by Charles Bernstein and Al Filreis, is a vast archive of sound recordings, primarily consisting of poetry readings and related lectures. UbuWeb, run by conceptual poet Kenneth Goldsmith, is an online archive of "all forms of the avant-garde" (ubu.com). It contains what appears to be the largest collection of experimental and avant-garde sound art and sound poetry on the web. Again, one of the defining characteristics of contemporary sound practice is access, and these sites, among many others, are examples of ease of access in a digital world.

■ See also ANALOG VERSUS DIGITAL, ARCHIVE, MASHUP, MUSIC, REMIX

References and Further Reading

Amerika, Mark. 2011a. *remixthebook*. Minneapolis: University of Minnesota Press.

———. 2011b. *remixthebook*. www.remixthebook.com/.

Cage, John. 1973. "The Future of Music: Credo." In *Silence: Lectures and Writings by John Cage*. Middletown, CT: Wesleyan University Press.

Cassidy, Aaron M. n.d. "Steve Reich." *Classical Net*. www.classical.net/music/comp.lst/reich.php.

Cox, Christoph, and Daniel Warner, eds. 2004. *Audio Culture: Readings in Modern Music*. New York: Continuum International Press.

PennSound. www.writing.upenn.edu/pennsound/.

Perloff, Marjorie, and Craig Dworkin. 2009. *The Sound of Poetry/The Poetry of Sound*. Chicago: University of Chicago Press.

Schütze, Bernard. 2007. "Samples from the Heap: Notes on Recycling the Detritus of a Remix Culture." *remixtheory.net*. http://remixtheory.net/?p=84.

Spinelli, Martin. 2006. "Electric Line: The Poetics of Digital Audio Editing." In *New Media Poetics: Contexts, Technologies, and Theories*, edited by Adalaide Morris and Thomas Swiss. Cambridge, MA: MIT Press.

UbuWeb. "UbuWeb: Sound." www.ubu.com/sound/.

....

Spatiality of Digital Media

Marie-Laure Ryan

In 1997, Janet Murray mentioned spatiality as one of the four major distinctive properties of digital media, along with procedural, participatory, and encyclopedic. This pronouncement, which falls in line with Fredric Jameson's (1991) claim that late twentieth-century culture is characterized by a "spatial turn," has been widely accepted by researchers. Yet the meaning of the phrase "digital media are spatial" is far from self-evident. Does "spatiality" exclude temporality? The eighteenth-century German author G. E. Lessing made a distinction between the spatial art of painting and the temporal art of poetry. This distinction rests on the medium—understood here as semiotic means of expression rather than as technology of transmission—upon which these two art forms rely: poetry (what we now call literature) is an art made of language, a mode of signification that comes to the recipient one sign at a time, each sign displacing the preceding one in the flow of perception, while painting is an art of the image, a type of sign whose various parts can be apprehended almost simultaneously because these parts coexist in space. Lessing showed that the temporality or spatiality of an art form has crucial consequences for what can be represented. Yet few (if any) media or art forms can be classified as exclusively temporal or spatial: writing gives a spatial dimension to language, film gives a temporal dimension to the image, and technologies that allow the transmission of both language (or music) and image are inherently spatiotemporal. New media incontestably belong to the spatiotemporal category; why then has their "spatiality" received more attention than their temporality (see TEMPORALITY OF DIGITAL WORKS)?

According to Murray, the specific spatiality of digital media does not lie in their ability to display images or even maps (books can do that just as well), nor in their ability to connect people across the world (the telephone, radio, and TV did that), but in "the interactive process of navigation" (1997, 82). The computer, in other words, creates spaces through which users (or their avatars) can move (see AVATARS). These spaces can be conceived in a number of different ways:

1. Computer space. As the title of N. Katherine Hayles's article "Print Is Flat, Code Is Deep" (2004) suggests, we tend to imagine the architecture and operation of computers as a communication between various layers of code leading from a deep structure of zeros and ones to the surface structure of the screen display. This supposed depth is purely metaphorical, since computers can be formally represented as a Turing machine, an automaton that operates on a one-dimensional string of zeros and ones. In a nonmetaphorical conceptualization, the visible display is simply the output resulting from the operations executed by the code on its data input. Yet authoring systems such as Flash and Director encourage the user to think in spatial terms by relying on theatrical and filmic metaphors: authors work with a two-dimensional display called the "stage," on which they place various objects connected to scripted behaviors that animate them and

create a temporal sequence called the "movie" (see AUTHORING SYSTEMS). An important feature of the stage is its layered structure: setting does not consist of a single image but of many graphic levels whose superposition creates an impression of depth. An object on a high level can hide an object on a deeper level, or levels can be made invisible when certain conditions are met, thus revealing the contents of a deeper level. Thinking in terms of layers stacked upon each other greatly facilitates the process of designing and encoding, but this architecture exists only for the designer: for the computer, there are only sequentially numbered memory cells filled with binary data, while for the users of the finished work, there is only an image (or world) on the screen with which they can interact in various ways.

2. Textual (or semiotic) space. This is the space taken by material signs out of which semiotic artifacts are made. Any message containing images or letters involves two dimensions, but when digital texts are organized as hypertext (see HYPERTEXTUALITY), they present an additional level of spatial organization: a web of data-containing nodes, connected by links. This web may or may not be accessible to the user. Through their selection of links, users are said to "navigate" the text, a conceptualization that combines nautical travel with the image of a road map. Storyspace, the name of the authoring system developed by Eastgate, reinforces the idea of the inherent spatiality of hypertext; so do other metaphors applied to hypertext, such as the labyrinth or the Borgesian image of a Garden of Forking Paths (see STORYSPACE). This spatiality is a purely cartographic phenomenon, since it resides in the two-dimensionality of the diagram through which the underlying system of nodes and links can be represented. Hypertext fiction is typically organized as a network, but digital texts can also be spatially structured as trees, radiating wheels, flowcharts, and vectors with side branches (Ryan 2006, 100–105) (see GRAPH THEORY).

While hypertext relies on the 2D space of a network, there have been some attempts to develop forms of electronic writing that unfold in a three-dimensional space. An example of 3D effect on 2D alphabetical symbols is the title of the *Star Wars* film series, which flattens out (through a half rotation around the x axis), shrinks, and disappears in outer space. In Aya Karpinska's poem "The Arrival of the Bee Box," meant to represent three-dimensionality on a 2D screen (as does perspective painting), readers can rotate virtual cubes on which words have been arranged, altering their appearance from readable to unreadable, and combining them in various ways through a process that reminds us of how the objects hanging from the branches of a mobile come together or move away from each other depending on the air flow. In *Screen*, a project developed by Noah Wardrip-Fruin for the CAVE of Brown University, words peel off from the walls on which they are inscribed and float freely as virtual images inside the CAVE, until the user bats them back onto the walls (see CAVE). In Camille Utterbeck's installation *Text Rain* (1999), similarly, words take the appearance of solid objects, and users try to catch them as they fall from the sky. Whether this is writing or pure spectacle made of alphabetic symbols depends on the meaning that can be read into the operation, and on whether this meaning depends on the lexical definition of the individual words.

3. Space of the represented world, or narrative space. It is in this type of space, which consists of either two or three dimensions (cf. *Super Mario Brothers* vs. *World of Warcraft*), that the interactive process of navigation is most fully implemented. The earliest forms of navigation and world exploration appeared in the purely textual environment of

interactive fiction (IF) (see INTERACTIVE FICTION). These games rely on a hidden map that specifies the location of various places with respect to each other; by typing commands such as "Go North" or "Go South," players move around the game world, find various useful objects, or encounter characters who help them solve a mystery. Success in the game is often a matter of being able to reconstitute the hidden map of the game world. The textual worlds of IF games are typically two-dimensional, but they can be made three-dimensional by including "go up" or "go down" commands.

The powerful graphic engines of today's video games create 3D landscapes that evolve smoothly in response to the movements of the player's avatar. The immersive quality of these games lies as much in the responsiveness of their world as in the pursuit of the game goals. In some online worlds, such as Second Life, moving through the world and exploring its content becomes an autotelic activity, rather than a means to solve problems. Video games still struggle to create emotional attachment to the characters and temporal immersion in a suspenseful plot (see IMMERSION, INTERACTIVE NARRATIVE, PLOT TYPES AND INTERACTIVITY), but they have taken the art of spatial immersion further than any other medium. In addition to allowing movement through their world, some games let the player manipulate the display, for instance, by alternating between a vertical (map) view, on which strategic moves can be planned, and a horizontal or oblique view, which counts as the world itself, while the map view is just that: a map of the territory (see WORLDS AND MAPS).

The importance of navigation and exploration in video games has led to a form of design that Henry Jenkins calls "spatial storytelling" (2004). Rather than implementing a global story line through which players progress, spatial storytelling attaches small stories to the various locations of a game world. These stories may be the legends of places, the gossip of the nonplayer characters (NPCs) who populate certain areas, or the backstory that explains the need for the quests that are given to the players (see NPC [NONPLAYER CHARACTER], QUEST NARRATIVE). In a game structured through spatial storytelling, players wander around the story world like knights errant in search of heroic deeds to perform.

Michael Nitsche (2008, 171–189) describes a number of nonnarrative spatial architectures for game worlds: there are tracks and rails, common in racing games, which limit movement to a narrow path offering no choice; labyrinths and mazes, in which the player must find the exit, while being restricted by the width of the pathway; and arenas, spaces delimited by boundaries but allowing freedom of movement within their borders. While some games are defined by one type of structure, many alternate between the three types, as they give the player a variety of tasks.

4. Real space. Digital media are notorious for building virtual worlds in which users transport themselves and live a second life by identifying with an avatar (see ONLINE WORLDS). These worlds involve a double estrangement from the real: not only do they deploy alternative spaces, but they also limit physical agency—which always takes place in real space—to hand and finger movements. Recent developments offer two ways to reconnect users of digital media to real space.

First, the dream of the pioneers of virtual reality to involve the whole body in computer-mediated experiences is becoming reality through advances in motion capture, as well as through new types of game design (see VIRTUAL REALITY). With game consoles such as Nintendo's Wii, it is not an avatar that hits a virtual tennis ball but a real body that swings a racket in physical space. Insofar as the opponent is an image on the screen, the game takes place in a hybrid space, half real and half simulated. With games such as *Guitar Hero* or *Dance Dance Revolution*, the importance of the simulated part is strongly diminished or even nonexistent: the role of the computer is not to generate a virtual world, but to function as a monitor that regulates real-world action performed with material objects, such as plastic musical instruments or a sensitive mat serving as a dance floor. While the audience and theater of *Guitar Hero* may be virtual, it is real (albeit synthesized) music that the players produce.

Second, the development of mobile technology and GPS counters the tendency of computers to lure sedentary users into virtual worlds by replacing simulated environments with real-world settings and by sending users on a treasure hunt in physical space. Three uses of digital technology covered in other entries in this guidebook tie information to specific locations: augmented reality, a general term for the superposition of digitally transmitted information and images upon real-world landmarks (see AUGMENTED REALITY); location-based narrative, designed projects that create a sense of place by linking mostly self-contained stories, such as legends, anecdotes, pieces of history, and narratives of personal experience, to specific coordinates, thereby organizing real space into the same kind of "narrative architecture" that Jenkins describes for games (see LOCATION-BASED NARRATIVE); and alternate reality gaming, collaborative projects in which players reconstitute a fictional story by chasing clues scattered in the real world as well as on the Internet (see ALTERNATE REALITY GAMING). All these phenomena are part of a growing trend to put digital technology in the service of fully corporeal outdoor activities that promote an appreciation of both urban and natural environments.

■ See also CYBERSPACE, GRAPHIC REALISM

References and Further Reading

Hayles, N. Katherine. 2004. "Print Is Flat, Code Is Deep: The Importance of Media-Specific Analysis." *Poetics Today* 25 (1): 67–90.

Jameson, Fredric. 1991. *Postmodernism; or, The Cultural Logic of Late Capitalism*. Durham, NC: Duke University Press.

Jenkins, Henry. 2004. "Game Design as Narrative Architecture." In *First Person: New Media as Story, Performance, and Game*, edited by Noah Wardrip-Fruin and Pat Harrigan, 118–130. Cambridge, MA: MIT Press.

Karpinska, Aya. "The Arrival of the Bee Box." www.poesis.net/en/projects/aya_karpinska.html.

Lessing, Gotthold Ephraim. 1984. *Laocoön: An Essay on the Limits of Painting and Poetry*. Translated and introduction by Edward Allen McCormick. Baltimore: Johns Hopkins University Press.

Murray, Janet. 1997. *Hamlet on the Holodeck: The Future of Narrative in Cyberspace*. New York: Free Press.

Nitsche, Michael. 2008. *Video Game Spaces: Image, Play and Structure in 3D Worlds*. Cambridge, MA: MIT Press.

Raley, Rita. 2006. "Writing.3D." *Iowa Review Web*. http://iowareview.uiowa.edu/TIRW/TIRW_Archive /september06/raley/editorsintro.html.

Ruston, Scott. 2010. "Storyworlds on the Move: Mobile Media and Their Implications for Narrative." *Storyworlds: A Journal of Narrative Studies* 2 (1): 101–119.

Ryan, Marie-Laure. 2003. "Cyberspace, Cybertexts, Cybermaps." *Dichtung Digital*. www.dichtung -digital.org/2004/1-Ryan.htm.

———. 2006. *Avatars of Story*. Minneapolis: University of Minnesota Press.

Schäfer, Jörgen, and Peter Gendolla. 2010. *Beyond the Screen: Transformations of Literary Structures, Interfaces and Genres*. Bielefeld, Germany: Transcript.

Utterback, Camille, and Romy Architruv. 1999. *Text Rain* (1999). Installation. www.camilleutterback
.com/textrain.html.
Wardrip-Fruin, Noah, with Josh Carroll, Robert Coover, Shawn Greenlee, Andrew McClain, and
Ben "Sascha" Shine. 2002. *Screen*. www.noahwf.com/screen/.

Story Generation

Pablo Gervás

In the field of artificial intelligence (AI) the automated generation of stories (see NARRATIVITY) has been a subject of research for over fifty years. The underlying concept of "story" in story generation research is functional and does not imply any aesthetic notion. This is important because the evaluation of generated stories does not necessarily use the criterion of a readable and appealing text. Research on storytelling systems (computational systems capable of telling a story) initially arose as part of the general trend in AI to build computational solutions that could undertake tasks that are easy for humans and difficult for machines. Some such efforts, such as computer vision and speech processing, have achieved success and given rise to commercial applications, whereas others, such as natural language understanding and story generation, still remain at the exploratory research stage.

For story generation in particular, a large part of the problem is the fact that the task is not well defined in an AI/computational perspective. If an algorithm is to be devised for a given task, it should be very clear what the inputs must be and what characteristics are expected of the output. In the generation of stories, none of these are clearly defined. When humans produce stories, it is often not transparent what inputs they are bringing to bear on the process. Moreover, saying what makes a good story remains a question open for debate. As a consequence, existing story generation systems tend to be exploratory with regard not only to the algorithms they employ but also to the set of inputs they start from, as well as the characteristics their output stories are expected to fulfill (see ALGORITHM).

There are currently a large number of storytelling systems in existence. This entry focuses on systems that generate classic sequential stories. Examples of story output are given for those systems that produce meaningful fragments small enough to be quoted (for further details, see Gervás 2009).

The first storytelling system on record is the Novel Writer system, developed by Sheldon Klein (Klein et al. 1973). Novel Writer created murder stories in a weekend party setting. This system is reputed to have generated "2100 word murder mystery stories, complete with deep structure, in less than 19 seconds." It received as input a description of the world in which the story was to take place and the characteristics of the participating characters. The story was generated based on two different algorithms: a set of rules which encodes possible changes from the current state of the world to the next, and a sequence of scenes corresponding to the type of story to be told. Though more than one story could be built by the program, differences between them were restricted to who murders whom, with what and why, and who discovers it.

Tale-Spin (Meehan 1981) is a system that generates animal stories in the style of Aesop's fables. To create a story, a character is given a goal, and then a plan is developed to solve the goal. Tale-Spin introduces character goals as triggers for action. It also introduces the possibility of having more than one problem-solving character in the story, computing separate goal lists for each of them. The system is able to model complex relations between characters such as competition, dominance, familiarity, affection, trust, deceit, and indebtedness. These relations act as preconditions to some actions and as consequences of others. A sample Tale-Spin story is given below. John Bear is given knowledge about the world and a goal to satisfy his hunger: "John Bear is somewhat hungry. John Bear wants to get some berries. John Bear wants to get near the blueberries. John Bear walks from a cave entrance to the bush by going through a pass through a valley through a meadow. John Bear takes the blueberries. John Bear eats the blueberries. The blueberries are gone. John Bear is not very hungry."

Dehn's AUTHOR (1981) was a program intended to simulate the author's mind as she makes up a story. A story is understood as "the achievement of a complex web of author goals." An author may have particular goals in mind when she sets out to write a story, but even if she does not, a number of metalevel goals drive or constrain the story-telling process (ensuring that the story is consistent, that it is plausible, that the characters are believable, that the reader's attention is retained throughout the story, etc.). These goals contribute to structuring the story and to guiding the construction process. In the final story, however, these goals are no longer visible. Dehn's assumption is that story worlds are developed by authors as a post hoc justification for events that the author has already decided will be part of the story.

Lebowitz's UNIVERSE (1985) modeled the generation of scripts for a succession of TV soap opera episodes in which a large cast of characters plays out multiple, simultaneous, overlapping stories that never end. UNIVERSE was the first storytelling system to devote special attention to the creation of characters. Complex data structures were used to represent characters, and a simple algorithm was proposed to fill these in, partly in an automatic way. But the bulk of characterization was left for the user to provide. UNIVERSE was aimed at exploring extended story generation, a continuing serial rather than a story with a beginning and an end. The system alternates between generating a new episode to continue the story and telling the most recent episode it has generated. It was initially intended as a writer's aid, with additional hopes to later develop it into an autonomous storyteller. In contrast to Dehn, who considered that the plot should drive the construction of the world, Lebowitz suggested that the world should be built first with a plot added afterward.

MINSTREL (Turner 1994) was a computer program that told stories about King Arthur and his Knights of the Round Table. The program was started based on a moral that was used as seed to build the story: for example, "Deception is a weapon difficult to aim." According to its author, MINSTREL could tell about ten stories of about one-half to one page in length, and it could also create a number of shorter story scenes. Story construction in MINSTREL operated as a two-stage process involving a planning stage (based on a combination of author goals and character goals) and a problem-solving stage that reused knowledge from previous stories.

Pérez y Pérez's MEXICA (1999) was a computer model whose purpose was to study the creative process. It was designed to generate short stories about the early inhabitants of Mexico. MEXICA switches between an engagement phase, in which new story material is progressively generated with no constraints imposed, and a reflection phase, in which the generated material is revised to ensure that generic constraints are met. MEXICA was a pioneer in that it took into account emotional links and tensions between the characters as a means for driving and evaluating ongoing stories. A MEXICA story is given below: "Jaguar knight was an inhabitant of the Great Tenochtitlan. Princess was an inhabitant of the Great Tenochtitlan. Jaguar knight was walking when Ehecatl (god of the wind) blew and an old tree collapsed, injuring badly Jaguar knight. Princess went in search of some medical plants and cured Jaguar knight. As a result, Jaguar knight was very grateful to Princess. Jaguar knight rewarded Princess with some cacauatl (cacao beans) and quetzalli (quetzal) feathers."

BRUTUS (Bringsjord and Ferrucci 1999) was a program that wrote short stories about betrayal. BRUTUS bases its storytelling ability on a logical model of betrayal. The richness of this model and the inferences that can be drawn from it enable it to produce very rich stories, though at the cost of variety. The system is also designed to take into account a large body of knowledge about literature and grammar. BRUTUS was capable of creating a story of impressive quality, with most of the features (in terms of literary tropes, dialogue, identification with the characters, etc.) one would find in a human-authored story.

FABULIST (Riedl and Young 2010) used an AI planner to generate a plot for the story. AI planners are applications that, given a description of an initial state of the world and a specific goal, identify the optimal sequence of actions to reach the goal, based on detailed descriptions of the preconditions and postconditions of all the possible actions. The use of AI planners for narrative generation is based on the assumption that a sequence of actions leading from an initial state to a goal is a good approximation of a story. Research efforts in this field have addressed issues of allowing different characters to have different goals to ensure that interesting conflicts arise. In the case of FABULIST, inputs provided included a domain model describing the initial state of the story world, possible operations that can be enacted by characters, and a desired outcome.

Story generation is an active research field that still faces a number of open questions. Progress achieved since its beginning is better measured in terms of the number of relevant questions concerning the production of narrative which have been raised by succeeding systems than in terms of the development of valuable answers for any of them. Evaluation of generated stories is improving beyond the original practice of quoting a single example of a good story produced by the system, with issues such as variety in the output and originality being considered. Nevertheless, this issue remains open, and it is very tightly linked to the purpose for which story generation systems are being built. One of the most interesting applications of story generation is to make these systems interact with human authors (and users) to produce valuable pieces with high entertainment value (see INTERACTIVE NARRATIVE).

■ See also AUTHORING SYSTEMS, COMPUTATIONAL LINGUISTICS, PLOT TYPES AND INTERACTIVITY

References and Further Reading

Bringsjord, Selmer, and David Ferrucci. 1999. *Artificial Intelligence and Literary Creativity inside the Mind of* BRUTUS, *a Storytelling Machine*. Hillsdale, NJ: Lawrence Erlbaum Associates.

Dehn, Natalie. 1981. "Story Generation after Tale-Spin." In *International Joint Conference on Artificial Intelligence*, 16–18. Los Altos, CA: William Kaufmann.

Gervás, Pablo. 2009. "Computational Approaches to Storytelling and Creativity." *AI Magazine* 30 (3): 49–62.

Klein, Sheldon, J. F. Aeschliman, D. Balsiger, et al. 1973. "Automatic Novel Writing: A Status Report." Technical Report 186. Madison, WI: University of Wisconsin, Computer Science Department.

Lebowitz, Michael. 1985. "Story-Telling as Planning and Learning." *Poetics* 14:483–502.

Meehan, James. 1981. "Tale-Spin." In *Inside Computer Understanding*, edited by Roger Schank, 197–225. Hillsdale, NJ: Lawrence Erlbaum Associates.

Pérez y Pérez, R. 1999. "MEXICA: A Computer Model of Creativity in Writing." PhD diss., University of Sussex.

Riedl, Michael, and Michael Young. 2010. "Narrative Planning: Balancing Plot and Character." *Journal of Artificial Intelligence Research* 39:217–268.

Turner, Scott. 1994. *The Creative Process: A Computer Model of Storytelling and Creativity*. Hillsdale, NJ: Lawrence Erlbaum Associates.

· ·

Storyspace
Anja Rau

Storyspace is a consumer-market hypertext authoring system that fueled the second wave of electronic literature from the mid-1980s to the late 1990s (see EARLY DIGITAL ART AND WRITING [PRE-1990]). It provided the basis for such seminal *hyperfictions* as Michael Joyce's *afternoon, a story* (created as a showcase for the original software), *Victory Garden* (Stuart Moulthrop), *Patchwork Girl* (Shelley Jackson), and *I Have Said Nothing* (J. Yellowlees Douglas), as well as nonfictional hypertexts such as Diane Greco's *Cyborg: Engineering the Body Electric* and George P. Landow's classroom collaboration *Writing at the Edge*.

Storyspace was created by Jay David Bolter, then assistant professor of classics at the University of North Carolina, Michael Joyce, then associate professor of language and literature at Jackson Community College, and John B. Smith, then professor of computer science also at the University of North Carolina. All three were active in the fields of human-computer interaction and computers and the humanities, creating fictional and nonfictional hypertexts inside and outside the classroom and, eventually, an authoring environment for their work. After negotiations with several publishers, the software was taken up by Eastgate Systems, Inc., where it is still being developed, serviced, and distributed. As of early 2012, the software will run on current Windows and Apple systems.

Storyspace is most noted for its extensive features for linking text nodes and for visualizing a text's internal and linking structure. At its center, there is a basic text editor that allows the author to create the nodes (called *writing spaces*) for her hypertext, containing both text and images. There are a number of specialized tools for linking the nodes and for controlling the linking structure, such as links that encode one-to-many relations. Most importantly, the *guard field* feature suggests a heavy usage of links that will only become active after the reader has fulfilled certain conditions, such as visiting certain nodes a certain number of times. In the final product, links may, but need not, be visible to the reader. The editor comes with several views that allow the author to compose her text sequentially or spatially.

For presentation to an audience, a Storyspace hypertext can be exported to either HyperText Markup Language (HTML), text, or a proprietary reader format. In the original version, the export option covered three different "readers" that give the audience different degrees of control over the text. The *Easy Reader* is the most basic, limiting the audience to clicking in a single text window. It draws least attention to the interface as paratext of the digital text and offers the least control to the reader. The *Page Reader*, used, for example, in *afternoon, a story*, comes with a toolbar that allows the reader to retrace her steps and to view the links pertaining to the current node. The *Storyspace Reader*, used, for example, in *I Have Said Nothing*, supplements the text window and toolbar with a map view window of the entire document, thus offering an overview of the full text and of its structure, as well as allowing the reader to access nodes without following links. All readers may contain visual representations of any level of the document structure, if the author chooses to include them manually.

■ See also AUTHORING SYSTEMS, DIGITAL FICTION, DIGITAL HUMANITIES, ELECTRONIC LITERATURE, HYPERTEXTUALITY, INTERACTIVE FICTION, INTERACTIVE NARRATIVE, INTERFACE, LINKING STRATEGIES, NONLINEAR WRITING, SPATIALITY OF DIGITAL MEDIA

References and Further Reading

Douglas, Jane Yellowlees. 1994. *I Have Said Nothing*. Watertown, MA: Eastgate Systems.
Greco, Diane. 1995. *Cyborg: Engineering the Body Electric*. Watertown, MA: Eastgate Systems.
Jackson, Shelley. 1995. *Patchwork Girl*. Watertown, MA: Eastgate Systems.
Joyce, Michael. 1987. *afternoon, a story*. Watertown, MA: Eastgate Systems.
Landow, George P. 1991. *Writing at the Edge*. Watertown, MA: Eastgate Systems.
Moulthrop, Stuart. 1992. *Victory Garden*. Watertown, MA: Eastgate Systems.

Subversion (Creative Destruction)
Davin Heckman

Our understanding of *subversion* can be traced to its Latin roots: *vertere*, which means "to turn, overthrow, or destroy," and the prefix *sub*, which means "under, beneath." Hence, subversion is literally destruction from below. This understanding carries with it two different connotations, one of which is more concrete, as a form of nonfrontal assault on a government or similar institution, by staging the attack from behind enemy lines. The second relies on the antagonistic connotations of the first, but refers to the act of turning a system upon itself from within. This treacherous understanding of subversion has been deployed by both majority groups in a pejorative sense (who routinely consider minority groups agitating for change as "subversives," especially when the horizon of change is imminent) and minority groups in a romantic sense (who routinely consider themselves "subversives," especially when the horizon of change is distant).

In the most common sense, subversion deals with questions of content or form. Subversive content consists of those discursive disruptions in which the prevailing notion is overturned by a countervailing notion presented from within. For instance, a television show might present a taboo subject in a sympathetic way, thus breaking the silence and demystifying the aura of shame associated with the taboo subject. In the case of the mashup, juxtapositions of information presented seamlessly through a single interface can disrupt the steady narrative of a particular media object, thus subverting the intended continuity of the original media objects (see MASHUP).

It is the treacherous understanding of subversion that is most commonly employed when discussing the subversive potential of digital media, as the terrain of media presupposes communication and depends to a large degree on systems of code (see CODE).

Within the context of human language, systems of representation, though flexible and indeterminate, require commonly held denotative meanings and grammatical conventions as a prerequisite for intelligibility. Thus, semiosis tends toward normativity and the relative stability of hegemony, even if the signs themselves always contain connotations in excess of their discrete value. Machine languages, on the other hand, are logical, rigidly symbolic as opposed to semiotic, and achieve expression in their application. Where humans and machines interact (at the level of programming, at the level of use, or, increasingly, at the level of subroutine), the mediation between human language and machine language is achieved through algorithms (see ALGORITHM, INTERFACE). Thus, increasingly, human experience is becoming machine-readable, and the landscape of this codification provides a large and growing target for subversion (see Cayley 2011). Ironically, however, as this target expands, its vocabulary and inertia also grow, decreasing the likelihood that subversion can achieve its desired goal of revolution.

As a consequence, contemporary subversion in postindustrial society often eschews overtly confrontational means (though these also apply in the case of distributed denial-of-service [DDOS] attacks, malicious hacking, etc.), preferring to operate by way of creative and aesthetic actions that "capture" the imagination (see Holmes 2009; Raley 2009). Consonant with the avant-garde impulse in the arts, it follows that the romantically treacherous understanding of the term would be the dominant understanding of subversion within the digital media arts. However, the spirit of the digital revolution, especially the iconoclasm associated with the "Californian Ideology" (see Barbrook and Cameron 1995), creates additional affinities between the romantically treacherous notion of subversion and the social status of the programmer. Nowhere is this subversive social role more clearly expressed than in the image of the hacker (see HACKER). And, in fact, the digital revolution has produced significant, often-unexpected changes in human thought and behavior. Furthermore, changes to the trajectory of digital media itself have been produced through the process of invention and innovation.

In the case of works that engage in formal subversion, the established codes of representation or systems of discourse are unsettled by strategic ambiguities and inconsistencies in the internal logic of the system. For instance, a prevailing style of representation might be disturbed by a counterintuitive representation that calls into question the presumed informational value of the prevailing style. In the case of media hoaxes, stylistic conventions create the impression of informational value, causing people to believe things that aren't true because they accept the form (see HOAXES). Viral videos, on the other hand, exploit emotional or intellectual desires and vulnerabilities in human users to replicate and spread the media object across a vast network, via all available means of human communication (see VIRAL AESTHETICS).

Though Marxist critical theory has historically viewed the cycles of order and chaos both as symptoms of capitalism and as the dialectical engine of human progress toward socialism, the postmodern perspective abandons the inevitability of socialism, seeing turbulence as a consistent state of affairs within late capitalism (see Jameson 1991; Harvey 1989). And, in fact, as early as the 1940s, economist Joseph Schumpeter ([1942] 1994) identified "creative destruction" within capitalist economies as a permanent state of subversion driving wave after wave of technical innovation. Michel Foucault's (1988) analysis of discourse and governmentality also concluded that the existence of norms and their transgression were the means through which power is reproduced. Thus, any discussion of subversion after postmodernism must go beyond the basic definition and take into account the larger cultural, economic, and technical norms being subverted, including our understanding of subversion itself.

From the cultural studies perspective, targets of subversion are the hegemonic structures of thought and practice which regulate, define, and normalize institutional power. Implicit in this definition is a defining power differential: subversion can only be accomplished relative to a plane of consistency. Also implicit in the definition is a strong affinity for the cybernetic (see CYBERNETICS), as the means of subversion must be present within the larger field of knowledge, and the "turning" is accomplished through a form of feedback into the system. To be considered subversive in this sense, digital media must forge a link between broader hegemonic processes and the specific qualities of the medium in question. For instance, it is possible to convey subversive political content via digital channels (blogs, e-mail, websites), and it is possible to engage in reflexive poetic practices via digital media without engaging in larger political questions (creating a new interface, writing a new program, adapting an application to an off-label use), but only when we encounter a productive friction between the technics of the digital and the broader political context of such technical systems do we have "digital media subversion." Historically, avant-garde practices in the arts have engaged in such interventions, striking strategically at internal vulnerabilities within formal and semiotic systems to disrupt the process by which such systems operate (see Renee Magritte's *La trahison des images* [1928–1929]), while unsettling epistemic assumptions.

Within the context of digital media, some areas of critical intervention have included (but are not limited to) the military/industrial foundations of computing, networked subjectivity, machine intelligence, the aura of print media, consumerism and the web, information overload, Internet hype, corporate and state censorship, and, increasingly, the specter of data mining and surveillance. In place of mere condemnation of these aspects of contemporary life, the subversive work of digital media must accomplish a response that provokes a subjectively held critical response to the phenomenon in question.

More fundamental, perhaps, is the question of subversion as it relates to the norms of digitality itself: the subversion of the "discrete" value as applied to the entirety of existence. The process of digitization, which reassembles the organic as transmissible, programmable units of abstract value, increasingly permeates all levels of social existence. From digital communication to human labor, from intelligence to food, reality is increasingly being rendered in commodity form, subject to information processing, communication, and storage. This process of creative destruction is where subversion is headed in the twenty-first century, because it is increasingly recognizable as the emergent *logos* (see www.thechurchofgoogle.org/). This emerging universal structure, then, is the definitive terrain upon which all future acts of digital subversion will be formed.

■ See also GLITCH AESTHETICS

References and Further Reading

Barbrook, Richard, and Andy Cameron. 1995. "The Californian Ideology." *Hypermedia Research Center.* www.hrc.wmin.ac.uk/theory-californianideology.html.

Cayley, John. 2011. "Writing to Be Found and Writing Readers." *Digital Humanities Quarterly* 5 (3). http://digitalhumanities.org/dhq/.

Foucault, Michel. 1988. "Technologies of the Self." In *Technologies of the Self: A Seminar with Michel Foucault*, edited by Luther H. Martin, Huck Gutman, and Patrick H. Hutton, 16–49. Amherst: University of Massachusetts Press.

Harvey, David. 1989. *The Condition of Postmodernity: An Enquiry into the Conditions of Cultural Change.* Cambridge: Blackwell.

Holmes, Brian. 2009. *Escape the Overcode: Activist Art in the Control Society.* Eindhoven, Netherlands: Van Abbemuseum. http://brianholmes.wordpress.com/2009/01/19/book-materials/.

Jameson, Fredric. 1991. *Postmodernism: The Cultural Logic of Late Capitalism.* Durham, NC: Duke University Press.

Raley, Rita. 2009. *Tactical Media.* Minneapolis: University of Minnesota Press.

Schumpeter, Joseph A. (1942) 1994. *Capitalism, Socialism and Democracy.* London: Routledge.

"Sub." *Wiktionary.* April 10, 2012. http://en.wiktionary.org/wiki/sub.

"Verto." *Wiktionary.* March 4, 2012. http://en.wiktionary.org/wiki/verto#Latin.

T

Temporality of Digital Works

John David Zuern

The computational processing and manipulation of text, images, sound, and audience feedback inevitably introduce distinctive temporal features into digital artworks. While many of these features can be viewed as extensions of earlier strategies for representing time in film (Miles 1999), in particular the use of montage (Manovich 2001, 148–155), other temporal elements of the newer media, especially those related to interactivity, cannot be easily subsumed within cinematic models (see INTERACTIVITY). In some cases, artists and writers conspicuously exploit these temporal aspects of the media to conduct creative experiments with time. Stephanie Strickland has observed that a striking number of works in digital media "explicitly address questions of time, history, and memory, often using dynamic means, Web-streaming or telepresence, in order to do it" (2001). Likewise, N. Katherine Hayles includes among the key cultural implications of the new media "the deconstruction of temporality and its reconstruction as an emergent phenomena arising from multiagent interactions" (2008, 84). Regardless of their themes, all creative endeavors in these media are shaped in some way by the specific temporal properties associated with computational systems. As Hayles suggests, the distribution of different time sequences across various agents and processes distinguishes the temporality of digital works from the temporal characteristics of works in other media.

Raine Koskimaa provides a useful four-part schema for mapping the different temporal strata of computer-based artworks (2010, 136). Koskimaa's *user time* represents the time individual users spend engaging with the work. *Discourse time* is the time the work itself takes to deliver its content to the user, for example, the length of a text or the running time of a film. *Story time* designates the temporality represented in the work itself, for example, the fictional time frame of a story like Michael Joyce's *afternoon: a story* (1990) or temporal markers within a poem like William Gibson's *Agrippa (A Book of the Dead)* (1992). *System time*, according to Koskimaa, is "the time of the cybertext system states" (2010, 136). Markku Eskelinen also uses "system time" to designate "the varying degrees of the text's permanence, in short the appearances, disappearances, and possible reappearances of its parts and phases" (2007, 181). This category can be understood to include the time it takes a computational device to process the work's code, which can vary substantially from computer to computer, and, in the case of Internet-based works, the time it takes the data composing the artwork to travel from a server to the user's display device. To different degrees and in different configurations, these four temporal domains come into play in all works that incorporate computation in meaningful ways. The interplay of user, discourse, and story time in computer-based works can be compared to temporal relationships in other media, while the complexities of system time are unique to digital artifacts.

Classical narrative theory distinguishes between discourse time, or "the time of the act of narrating," and story time, or "the time of the things narrated" (Ricoeur 1985, 5). If discourse time, understood as the audience's experience of the work's duration, is more or less fixed by the work's length or running time, user time has always been relatively elastic in the case of works in print, as individual readers parse texts at markedly different speed. Referring to Roland Barthes's notion of *tmesis*, Espen Aarseth points out that readers of print texts rarely read word for word along the precise linear path laid down on the page (1997, 47), and the amount of material readers "skip over" directly influences the duration of user time. In the case of conventional films and dramatic performances, discourse time and user time are generally much more closely aligned.

Texts in digital media tend to accentuate discrepancies between user and discourse time. A variety of structural features in digital works greatly extend the reader's capacity to affect the duration of the reading experience. Works that invite readers to participate in their unfolding, whether by making choices (as in hypertext fiction and poetry), contributing content or solving puzzles (as in interactive fiction and works employing chatterbots; see CHATTERBOTS, INTERACTIVE FICTION), or assuming the role of a character/interlocutor (as in interactive narrative and interactive drama; see INTERACTIVE DRAMA, INTERACTIVE NARRATIVE), surrender control over the duration of reading, along with control over the linear progression and logical connections of the text's statements, scenes, and events.

Many works employing animation and kineticism derive meaningful effects from the manipulation of discourse time, especially the marked acceleration or deceleration of moving texts and images (see ANIMATION/KINETICISM). Frequently cited examples of speeded-up time are the film-like, looping Flash animations of Young-hae Chang Heavy Industries, for example, *Dakota* (2001), which present their narratives in short segments at an unsettlingly fast tempo, and Stuart Moulthrop's online hypertext *Hegirascope* (1997), which is programmed to display segments of its text in thirty-second increments. Conversely, in works like John Cayley's "windsound" (2006b) and "Translation" (2006a), as well as Braxton Soderman's *mémoire involuntaire no. 1* (2010), texts transform on the screen—often moving in and out of states of legibility—at a rate much slower than an average reading time. Works that modulate pace in these ways often withhold any options for slowing down or speeding up the display, thus putting significant pressure on the viewer's attention. In some animated texts, such as Brian Kim Stefans's "The Dreamlife of Letters" (2000), accelerated animation effects are coupled with a radical decomposition of the texts into individual letters, introducing time into the dynamic morphological relationships among minimal textual units.

Manipulations of user time and discourse time frequently reinforce a work's thematic and philosophical dimensions. Some digital works, for example, Noah Wardrip-Fruin's *The Impermanence Agent* (1999) and Eugenio Tisselli's *Degenerative* (2005a) and *Regenerative* (2005b), are specifically designed to register the passage of time by tying the transformation (frequently the degradation) of their contents to user interactions. A comparable aesthetic is in play in Gibson's *Agrippa,* a digital poem famously programmed to erase itself after a single reading. In his analysis of the conspicuous deceleration in digital video projects such as Douglas Gordon's *24-Hour Psycho* (1992) and Bill Viola's *Quintet of the Astonished* (2000), Mark Hansen suggests that digitally manipulated temporalities such as these can induce affectively and physically palpable experiences of "the sensorimotor embodiment of time-consciousness" (2006, 254), thus going beyond the cerebral "time-image" Gilles Deleuze describes in his *Cinema 2* (1989).

In computer games and artworks that draw upon the conventions of games, the interrelations of user, discourse, and story time take on special characteristics that can be more precisely designated by the terms "game time," "play time," and "event time." According to Jesper Juul, "game time" is composed of "a basic duality of play time (the time the player takes to play) and event time (the time taken in the game world)" (2004, 131). Along with Anja Rau (2001, 202), Juul notes that in real-time action and shooter games, play time and event time are largely congruent, while in some adventure games and simulations, events can occur in the game world when a player is absent. The latter situation certainly holds true for online multiple-player games. In these games, as Marie-Laure Ryan notes, "if players play hooky in the real world, they will return to a changed world, like Rip van Winkle awakening from his hundred-year sleep" (2008, 259).

In hypertexts, interactive and transmedial fiction, and other works that involve the aleatory combination and generation of narrative elements, story time—the temporality represented in the work itself—is subject to fracture and distortion (see TRANSMEDIAL FICTION). In these works, the reader's choices determine the sequential ordering of events, a situation that poses a challenge to writers, who must decide whether to attempt to account for these temporal inconsistencies within the story's logic. Many game scenarios allow for unusual relationships between the time unfolding in the game world (event time) and the user's play time. Commonly cited as an example of such temporal discrepancies is the relative finality of avatar death, since it is frequently possible for users to reset the game, essentially traveling back in time to a point before their avatars were killed (Ryan 2008, 260) (see AVATARS). Moreover, as Alison Gazzard (2011) has pointed out, additional play time, in the form of "extra lives," is often a reward within the economy of the game world.

While it is the most definitive temporal aspect of digital works, system time is often the least perceptible to the user. In some cases, however, system time becomes apparent as a conspicuous element in a text. Nick Monfort's poetry generator "ppg256" (2011), for example, scrolls its output down the screen at too fast a rate for most readers to follow, and Monfort's instructions to his readers include a work-around to slow the display to a legible pace. For Lev Manovich, the cyclical, recurring time of the loop, a common strategy of programming languages and animation sequences, is fundamental to the "new temporality" of digital media (2001, 314–322). According to Hayles, fluctuations in system time from one instantiation of a work to another are definitive for the ontology of computer-based artworks, insofar as they mean that "digital texts are never self-identical" (2006, 186). Although the relevant technologies continue to improve, processing and download time remain factors in most digital artworks, and many authors still employ optimization strategies to minimize the effects of limited bandwidth and processing speed.

Finally, in regard to computer-based artworks, the passage of historical time is also an important consideration. Subject as they are to changes in their constituent technologies, including the vicissitudes of commercial hardware and software development, a great number of important digital works are threatened with obsolescence, and their preservation and the establishment of reliable archives have become pressing concerns within the academic and artistic communities emerging within the domain of the digital arts (see ARCHIVE, PRESERVATION).

■ See also DIGITAL POETRY, ELECTRONIC LITERATURE

References and Further Reading

Aarseth, Espen. 1997. *Cybertext: Perspectives on Ergodic Literature*. Baltimore: Johns Hopkins University Press.

Cayley, John. 2006a. "Translation." In *Electronic Literature Collection*, volume 1, edited by N. Katherine Hayles, Nick Montfort, Scott Rettberg, and Stephanie Strickland. http://collection.eliterature.org/1/.

———. 2006b. "windsound." In *Electronic Literature Collection*, volume 1, edited by N. Katherine Hayles, Nick Montfort, Scott Rettberg, and Stephanie Strickland. http://collection.eliterature.org/1/.

Deleuze, Gilles. 1989. *Cinema 2: The Time-Image*. Translated by Hugh Tomlinson and Robert Galeta. Minneapolis: University of Minneapolis Press.

Eskelinen, Markku. 2007. "Six Problems in Search of a Solution: The Challenge of Cybertext Theory and Ludology to Literary Theory." In *The Aesthetics of Net Literature: Writing, Reading and Playing in Programmable Media*, edited by Peter Gendolla and Jörgen Schäfer, 179–209. Bielefeld, Germany: Transcript.

Gazzard, Alison. 2011. "Unlocking the Gameworld: The Rewards of Space and Time in Videogames." *Game Studies* 11. http://gamestudies.org/1101/articles/gazzard_alison.

Gibson, William, and Dennis Ashbaugh. 1992. *Agrippa (a Book of the Dead)*. New York: Ken Begos.

Gordon, Douglas. 1992. *24-Hour Psycho*. Video.

Hansen, Mark. N. B. 2006. *New Philosophy for New Media*. Cambridge, MA: MIT Press.

Hayles, N. Katherine. 2006. "The Time of Digital Poetry: From Object to Event." In *New Media Poetics: Contexts, Technotexts, and Theories*, edited by Adalaide Morris and Thomas Swiss, 181–209. Cambridge, MA: MIT Press.

———. 2008. *Electronic Literature: New Horizons of the Literary*. Notre Dame, IN: University of Notre Dame Press.

Joyce, Michael. 1990. *afternoon: a story*. Watertown, MA: Eastgate Systems.

Juul, Jesper. 2004. "Introduction to Game Time." In *First Person: New Media as Story, Performance, and Game*, edited by Noah Wardrip-Fruin and Pat Harrigan, 131–142. Cambridge, MA: MIT Press.

Koskimaa, Raine. 2010. "Approaches to Digital Literature: Temporal Dynamics and Cyborg Authors." In *Reading Moving Letters: Digital Literature in Research and Teaching*, edited by Roberto Simanowski, Jörgen Schåfer, and Peter Gendolla, 129–143. Bielefeld, Germany: Transcript.

Manovich, Lev. 2001. *The Language of New Media*. Cambridge, MA: MIT Press.

Miles, Adrian. 1999. "Cinematic Paradigms for Hypertext." *Continuum: Journal of Media and Cultural Studies* 13 (2): 217–226.

Monfort, Nick. 2011. "ppg256." In *Electronic Literature Collection*, volume 2, edited by Laura Borrás Castanyer, Talan Memmott, Rita Raley, and Brian Kim Stefans. http://collection.eliterature.org/2/.

Moulthrop, Stuart. 1997. *Hegirascope*. Version 2. http://iat.ubalt.edu/moulthrop/hypertexts/hgs/.

Rau, Anja. 2001. "Time in Digital Fiction: Some Temporal Strategies of Adventure Games." *Kodikas/Code: Ars Semeiotica* 24 (3–4): 201–206.

Ricoeur, Paul. 1985. *Time and Narrative*. Chicago: University of Chicago Press.

Ryan, Marie-Laure. 2008. "Fictional Worlds in the Digital Age." In *A Companion to Digital Literary Studies*, edited by Susan Schreibman, Ray Siemens, and John Unsworth, 250–266. Oxford: Blackwell.

Soderman, Braxton. 2011. "mémoire involuntaire no. 1." In *Electronic Literature Collection*, volume 1, edited by N. Katherine Hayles, Nick Montfort, Scott Rettberg, and Stephanie Strickland. http://collection.eliterature.org/1/.

Stefans, Brian Kim. 2000. "The Dreamlife of Letters." In *Electronic Literature Collection*, volume 1, edited by N. Katherine Hayles, Nick Montfort, Scott Rettberg, and Stephanie Strickland. http://collection.eliterature.org/1/.

Strickland, Stephanie. 2001. "Dali Clocks: Time Dimensions of Hypermedia." *Electronic Book Review.* www.electronicbookreview.com/thread/webarts/hypertext.
Tisselli, Eugenio. 2005a. *Degenerative.* www.motorhueso.net/degenerative/.
———. 2005b. *Regenerative.* www.motorhueso.net/regenerative/regenerative.php.
Viola, Bill. 2000. *Quintet of the Astonished.* Video.
Wardrip-Fruin, Noah. 1999. *The Impermanence Agent.* www.hyperfiction.org/agent/.
Young-hae Chang Heavy Industries. 2001. *Dakota.* www.yhchang.com/DAKOTA.html.

•••

Transmedial Fiction
Christy Dena

The term *transmedial fiction* names a fictional world that exists across distinct media and art forms. A fictional world can be expanded across stories and games and is often expanded across both digital and nondigital media. This phenomenon has been observed by media, narrative, game, and art theorists alike, with varying characteristics identified.

A significant precursor to contemporary theories of transmedia is Gérard Genette's ([1982] 1997) *transtextuality*, a development of Mikhail Bakhtin's ([1930s] 1981) *dialogism*. *Transtextuality* is concerned with the study of "all that sets the text in relationship, whether obvious or concealed, with other texts" ([1982] 1997, 1). To explain these relationships, Genette introduced five top-level categories: intertextuality, paratextuality, metatextuality, architextuality, and hypertextuality. The majority of his study is concerned with hypertextuality. Genette conceived hypertextuality (not to be confused with the digital phenomenon of hypertext) as a literary text that references the fictional world of another text. Jean Racine, for instance, added a character (Antiochus) to the story of Titus and Berenice in *Bérénice* (1670). A complex example is Michel Tournier's *Vendredi*, which has a *thematic transformation* ("ideological reversal"), *transvocalization* ("the switch from first to third person"), and *spatial transfer* ("a shift from the Atlantic to the Pacific") (Genette [1982] 1997, 213).

In most cases, Genette's *hypertextual relations* are between literary texts by different authors. There are some exceptions though. Genette mentions relations between works within the same art form—such as Marcel Duchamp's *L.H.O.O.Q.* and Leonardo da Vinci's *Mona Lisa*—and terms them *hyperartistic practices*. He also observes *autotextuality*, which describes the relations between texts by the same author (such as Queneau's self-expansions). But in the end, Genette makes it clear that while *autotextuality* is a type of *transtexuality*, it has little to do with *hypertextuality*.

To further investigate the relations between works in distinct media and art form types, Aage A. Hansen-Löve (1983) introduced the notion of *intermediality*. Intermediality was needed, Werner Wolf explains, to "capture relations between literature and the visual arts," but has since developed to encompass all "heteromedial" relations (2005, 252). Indeed, *intermediality* studies relations between works of literature, paintings, performance, installations, and digital media. For instance, Peter Greenaway's *The Tulse Luper Suitcases* is a project that combines multiple feature films, art books, art installations, VJing, as well as multiple websites and digital games. An entire edition of *Image and Narrative* is dedicated to understanding Greenaway's project (Kochhar-Lindgren 2005).

To illuminate the varieties of works and relations encapsulated in *intermediality*, Wolf (2002) introduced a typology of intermediality: "intracompositional" and "extracompositional" phenomena. Intracompositional phenomena are "observed exclusively within given works" (2002, 13). It would include the study of Thomas Hardy's pictorializations in his novel *Under the Greenwood Tree* (where characters and their surroundings are described in a manner congruent with a description of a painting), or the musicalization of literature in Aldous Huxley's *Point Counter Point* (where the characteristics of the musical composition device "counterpoint" are observable in the structures of the writing). Extracompositional phenomena, on the other hand, concern relations "between works transmitted in different media" and would include studying the relations between Patrick White's novel *Voss* and Richard Meale and David Malouf's operatic version, *Singing the Nation* (2002, 20).

Another avenue of research influenced by Genette's *hypertextuality* is *transfictionality*. The term *transfictionality* captures the relations between compositions that are linked at the level of a fictional world rather than on the level of language and form ("texture"). The term was introduced by Richard Saint-Gelais (2005) as an elaboration of Lubomír Doležel's *postmodern rewrite* (Doležel 1998). Doležel was directly concerned with postmodernist rewrites of classic literary works. Specifically, he was interested in when a rewrite "confronts the canonical fictional world with contemporary aesthetic and ideological postulates" by "constructing a new, alternative fictional world" (1998, 206). To Doležel, rewrites occur when a story is preserved but relocated to a different temporal or spatial setting or both ("transposition"); when the scope of the protoworld is extended by filling of gaps, such as adding a prehistory or posthistory ("expansion"); and when the protoworld is markedly different through a redesigning of its structure and reinventing of its story ("displacement").

With *transfictionality*, Saint-Gelais extended the scope of the research area to include all fictional world expansions, not just rewrites. It covers all "practices that expand fiction beyond the boundaries of the work: sequels and continuations, return of the protagonists, biographies of characters, cycles and series," as well as literature, film, television, comics, popular culture, and experimental literature (Saint-Gelais in Ryan 2008, 386). Saint-Gelais also considers fictional world expansions by the same author or different ones, such as Conan Doyle writing Sherlock Holms, and Michael Dibdin writing *The Last Sherlock Holmes Story*.

In an effort to ensure that *transfictionality* doesn't merely duplicate *transtextuality*, Marie-Laure Ryan (2008) has investigated the research premise. Ryan argues that one of the differentiating factors in *transfictionality* hinges on the study of significant changes to the fictional world: the "term 'trans' suggests a relation between two distinct worlds and two distinct texts" (2008, 395). To identify a transfictional phenomenon, Ryan proposes a condition that the "worlds projected by the two texts must be distinct, but related to each other" (2008, 389; original emphasis removed). Texts can share the same uberfictional world, but to satisfy this condition, they need to (1) contain mutually incompatible elements or (2) have different authors.

Influenced more by drama and Internet theory, Jill Walker (2004) proposed a theory of *distributed narratives* to describe contemporary digitally oriented stories. For Walker, *distributed narratives* are "stories that aren't self-contained." Drawing on Aristotle's dramatic unities, Walker explained the characteristics of *distributed narratives* as being "disunities." A *distribution in time* occurs when the "narrative cannot be experienced in one consecutive period of time"; examples are weblogs and e-mail narratives, as well as Bevan and Wright's (2000) multiple media platform work *Online Caroline* (Walker 2004,

93). *Distribution in space* occurs when there "is no single place in which all of the narrative can be experienced," such as Nick Montfort and Scott Rettberg's sticker novel *Implementation* (2004–). *Distribution of authors* occurs when "no single author or group of authors can have complete control of the form of the narrative" (Walker 2004, 94).

These theories, while gradually expanding to include various media, have been influenced by print literary practice and theory. In media studies, Henry Jenkins (2006) initially proposed a theory of *transmedia storytelling* which distinguishes the phenomenon from previous franchises with its move away from repetition and redundancy. Jenkins's theory of *transmedia storytelling* centers on the argument that a "story unfolds across multiple media platforms with each new text making a distinctive and valuable contribution to the whole" (2006, 95). A key example is the Wachowski Brothers' *The Matrix*—a project where story lines continue across feature films, short anime films, graphic novels, and digital games (1999–2003). Such projects are unlike the current licensing system, which "typically generates works that are redundant" (2006, 105). Anything that allows "no new character background or plot development" is "redundant." A prototypical example of redundancy, according to this view, is adaptation.

To Jenkins, an important aspect of *transmedia storytelling* is *participatory culture*, for it "places new demands on consumers and depends on the active participation of knowledge communities" (2006, 22) (see PARTICIPATORY CULTURE). Jenkins warns that participation is not to be confused with interactivity, because the former is shaped by cultural and social protocols, whereas interactivity is more technology oriented. In an online update of his theory, Jenkins elaborates on the "range of different relations which fans might have to a transmedia property" (2011). These include "hunting and gathering practices" (to find elements in different media), playing through the level of a game, producing fan fiction, and engaging in cosplay (costume play of favorite characters, usually from popular culture).

Noting the differences between a media, narrative, and game studies approach to transmedial phenomena, Christy Dena (2009) introduced a theory of *transmedia practice*. She argues that focusing on the relations between stories in different media makes the phenomenon almost indistinguishable from *transtextuality*. Expansions of story lines, as opposed to the adaptations that Jenkins argues are not a trait of *transmedia storytelling*, are observable in the literary works discussed by Genette and Saint-Gelais. The continuation of a story line across media can be enacted by anyone and has been across time, and so it does not illuminate a different phenomenon. Instead, Dena argues that a more startling phenomenon is that practitioners are enacting transmedia themselves—either proactively (at the concept stage) or retroactively (after the creation of their initial monomedia project). This involves changes to how roles (writing, design, producing, directing) and work stages (development and production) operate.

In addition, since the object of most transmedial theories focuses on a certain type of transmedia project, Dena introduced a typology to highlight and encompass the variety of phenomena involved. Developing Wolf's (2002) typology of intermediality, Dena proposed *intercompositional* and *intracompositional transmedia*. To observe *intercompositional transmedia phenomena* is to study the relations between compositions in distinct media and art forms that share the same fictional world by the same "producer" or creative body. An example is the *Twin Peaks* fictional world, which is expressed through the television series (which was cocreated by David Lynch and Mark Frost), as well as the books and feature film. The alternate reality game (ARG) *I Love Bees* and the console game *Halo*

2 represent a different type of intercompositional transmedia phenomenon. As an ARG, *I Love Bees* was expressed through multiple websites, videos, live events, and, importantly, pay phones (see ALTERNATE REALITY GAMING). This makes *I Love Bees* a transmedia fiction in itself, an *intracompositional transmedia phenomenon*. But since it was commissioned as part of the greater *Halo* universe (it was actually part of a content marketing campaign), it is also *intercompositional transmedia*. Researchers can either study the ARG in itself or examine the relationship between the ARG and the digital game.

The emphasis on practices that encompass modes other than narrative was also strategic for Dena, since many transmedia projects involve digital games that rely quite heavily on the game mode for meaning making (see GAMEPLAY). The emphasis on storytelling, Dena argues, obscures the breadth and complexity of the phenomenon. Jenkins has also developed his definition to describe *transmedia storytelling* as "a process where integral elements of a fiction get dispersed systematically across multiple delivery channels for the purpose of creating a unified and coordinated entertainment experience. Ideally, each medium makes its own unique contribution to the unfolding of the story" (2011; emphasis in the original). Jenkins also now describes different transmedia "logics." Beside transmedia storytelling, there is also transmedia branding, performance, ritual, play, activism, and spectacle. *Glee* is an example of work that has at least two logics operating: storytelling and performance.

An important discussion has also been around the definition of "media" in the transmedia context. Jill Walker (2004) and game theorists Markus Montola, Jaako Stenros, and Annika Waern (2009) are careful to include "environments" as part of the meaning-making landscape. Montola explains how environments are a key part of pervasive gaming, but the role of place in *telematic arts* can already be observed in the 1960s with satellite art works (Ascott [1984] 2003). Media can also include nondigitally based objects, such as bodies (as is the case with the word tattoos on various strangers in Shelley Jackson's *Skin*).

The term *transmedial fiction* encompasses an area of research concerned with the persistence of a fictional world across time, authors, and distinct artifacts. Throughout time, people have been extending a fictional world for various reasons. The persistence of the fictional world can be official or unofficial, consistent or contradictory, by the same person or by distinct creatives, for marketing purposes or not, and with varying relations between the works. It should also be noted that many of the characteristics and practices identified in transmedial fictions can also take place in nonfiction works.

■ See also ALTERNATE REALITY GAMING, AUGMENTED REALITY, GAMEPLAY, GAMES AS STORIES, LOCATION-BASED NARRATIVE, MATERIALITY, MEDIALITY, NONLINEAR WRITING, PARTICIPATORY CULTURE

References and Further Reading

Ascott, Roy. (1984) 2003. "Art and Telematics: Towards a Network Consciousness." In *Telematic Embrace: Visionary Theories of Art, Technology, and Consciousness*, edited by Edward A. Shanken, 185–201. Berkeley: University of California Press.

Bakhtin, Mikhail. (1930s) 1981. *The Dialogic Imagination: Four Essays*, edited by Michael Holoquist, translated by Caryl Emerson and Michael Holoquist. Austin: University of Texas Press.

Bevan, Rob, and Tim Wright. 2000. *Online Caroline*. www.onlinecaroline.com.

Davidson, Drew, ed. 2010. *Cross-Media Communications: An Introduction to the Art of Creating Integrated Media Experiences*. Pittsburgh: ETC Press.

Dena, Christy. 2009. "Transmedia Practice: Theorising the Practice of Expressing a Fictional World across Distinct Media and Environments." PhD diss., University of Sydney.

Doležel, Lubomír. 1998. *Heterocosmica: Fiction and Possible Worlds*. Baltimore: Johns Hopkins University Press.

Genette, Gérard. (1982) 1997. *Palimpsests: Literature in the Second Degree*. Lincoln: University of Nebraska Press.

Hansen-Löve, Aage A. 1983. "Intermedijalnost i intertekstualnost." In *Problemi koreljacije verbalne islokovne umjetnosti—na primjeru ruske moderne*, edited by H. G. Makovic, 31–74. Zagreb, Croatia: Intertekstualnost & Intermedijalnost.

Jenkins, Henry. 2006. *Convergence Culture: Where Old and New Media Collide*. New York: New York University Press.

———. 2011. "Transmedia 202: Further Reflections." www.henryjenkins.org/2011/08/defining _transmedia_further_re.html.

Klastrup, Lizbeth, and Susana Tosca. 2004. "Transmedial Worlds: Rethinking Cyberworld Design." In *Proceedings of the International Conference on Cyberworlds 2004*, 409–416.

Kochhar-Lindgren, Gray, ed. 2005. "Opening Peter Greenaway's *Tulse Luper Suitcases*." In *Image and Narrative* 6 (2). www.imageandnarrative.be/inarchive/tulseluper/tulse_luper.htm.

Montfort, Nick, and Scott Rettberg. 2004–. *Implementation*. http://nickm.com/implementation/.

Montola, Markus, Jaako Stenros, and Annika Waern, eds. 2009. *Pervasive Games: Theory and Design*. San Francisco: Elsevier Science & Technology.

Ryan, Marie-Laure. 2008. "Transfictionality across Media." In *Theorizing Narrativity*, edited by John Pier and José Ángel García Landa, 385–418. Berlin: Walter de Gruyter.

Saint-Gelais, Richard. 2005. "Transfictionality." In *The Routledge Encyclopedia of Narrative Theory*, edited by David Herman, Manfred Jahn, and Marie-Laure Ryan, 612–613. London: Routledge.

Wagner, Richard. (1849) 2001. "Outlines of the Artwork of the Future." In *Multimedia: From Wagner to Virtual Reality*, edited by Randall Packer and Ken Jordan, 3–9. New York: Norton.

Walker, Jill. 2004. "Distributed Narrative: Telling Stories across Networks." In *Internet Research Annual 2004*, edited by Mia Consalvo and Kate O'Riordan, 91–103. Brighton, UK: Peter Lang.

Wolf, Werner. 2002. "Intermediality Revisited: Reflections on Word and Music Relations in the Context of a General Typology of Intermediality." In *Word and Music Studies 4: Essays in Honor of Steven Paul Scher on Cultural Identity and the Musical Stage*, edited by Suzanne Lodato, Suzanne Aspden, and Walter Bernhart, 13–34. Amsterdam: Rodopi.

———. 2005. "Intermediality." In *The Routledge Encyclopedia of Narrative Theory*, edited by David Herman, Manfred Jahn, and Marie-Laure Ryan, 252–253. London: Routledge.

Turing Test

Ragnhild Tronstad

In October 1950, an influential article by the British mathematician, computer scientist, and cryptanalyst Alan Turing was published in the philosophical journal *Mind*. Entitled "Computer Machinery and Intelligence," the article opens with the provocative question "Can machines think?" In order to make the question less ambiguous, and one that can be tested empirically, Turing then introduces "The Imitation Game," a precursor to what is now commonly referred to as the "Turing test" (see also www.turing .org.uk/turing/).

The imitation game involves three players: a man (A), a woman (B), and an interrogator (C) who stays in a room apart from the other two. C communicates with A and B by sending and receiving typed messages, knowing that one of them is male and one is female, but not which is either. The objective of C is to identify which player is the man and which is the woman by posing questions to each of them and evaluating their answers. B's objective is to help C in reaching the correct answer, while A's objective is to make C believe A is in fact the woman. Thus, A and B will both try to convince C that they are the woman.

Now, Turing asks, what would happen if A was replaced by a machine in the game? "Will the interrogator decide wrongly as often when the game is played like this as he does when the game is played between a man and a woman?" (Turing [1950] 2003, 50). (Note that Turing does not clearly state whether the task for the machine will be to pass as a woman or as a human. However, while the experts disagree on this question, the latter is the most common interpretation.) Instead of the initial question whether machines can think, he now suggests that we ask, "Are there imaginable digital computers which would do well in the imitation game?" Then he predicts that such a computer will be possible to program "in about fifty years' time" (Turing [1950] 2003, 55).

The Loebner Prize Competition in artificial intelligence (AI) is a contest in natural language processing that has been held annually since 1990, based on a version of Turing's imitation game (see www.loebner.net/Prizef/loebner-prize.html) (see ARTIFICIAL INTELLIGENCE). According to the organizers, the contest will run until a computer program (see CHATTERBOTS) proves able to pass an unrestricted version of the test, winning the grand prize of $100,000 and a gold medal (Epstein 1992). So far, however, no program has succeeded.

Turing's test and his idea that the ability to convincingly engage in human conversation would prove the machine to be intelligent have been discussed, as well as contested, in a variety of theoretical domains within philosophy, psychology, sociology, linguistics, and computer science (Saygin, Cicekli, and Akman 2000). John R. Searle (1980), in his thought experiment on the Chinese Room, demonstrates how it is possible, in the context of a Turing test, to display signs of understanding and intelligence without possessing either. Contrary to this view, it has been argued that while the test does prove intelligence, this test is one that concerns a *human* kind of intelligence, indistinguishable from human experience. Insofar as machines lack such experience, they can never be expected to pass the test (French 1990). In terms of the anthropocentric view of intelligence in the Turing test, some critics even argue that it has become a burden to AI research, making it the focus of the field to imitate human abilities rather than developing functional and useful AI (Ford and Hayes 1995).

References and Further Reading

Chalmers, David, and David Bourget. 2007–2009. Bibliography of papers on the Turing test. http://consc.net/mindpapers/6.1#6.1a.

Dennett, Daniel C. 1984. "Can Machines Think?" In *How We Know*, edited by M. G. Shafto. New York: Harper & Row.

Epstein, Robert. 1992. "The Quest for the Thinking Computer." *AI Magazine* 13 (2): 81–95. www.aaai.org/ojs/index.php/aimagazine/article/view/993.

Epstein, Robert, Gary Roberts, and Grace Beber, eds. 2008. *Parsing the Turing Test: Philosophical and Methodological Issues in the Quest for the Thinking Computer*. Dordrecht, Netherlands: Springer.

Ford, Kenneth, and Patrick Hayes. 1995. "Turing Test Considered Harmful." In *Proceedings of the Fourteenth International Joint Conference on Artificial Intelligence (IJCAI95-1)*, Montreal, Quebec, Canada, 972–977. www.ijcai.org/Past%20Proceedings/IJCAI-95-VOL%201/pdf/125.pdf.

French, Robert M. 1990. "Subcognition and the Limits of the Turing Test." *Mind* 99 (393): 53–65. http://leadserv.u-bourgogne.fr/rfrench/french/turing.pdf.

Hofstadter, Douglas R. 1981. "A Coffeehouse Conversation on the Turing Test." In *Metamagical Themas: Questing for the Essence of Mind and Pattern*. New York: Basic Books. www.cse.unr.edu/~sushil/class/ai/papers/coffeehouse.html.

Saygin, Ayse Pinar, Ilyas Cicekli, and Varol Akman. 2000. "Turing Test: 50 Years Later." *Minds and Machines* 10 (4): 463–518. www.cs.bilkent.edu.tr/~akman/jour-papers/mam/mam2000.pdf.

Searle, John R. 1980. "Minds, Brains, and Programs." *Behavioral and Brain Sciences* 3 (3): 417–457.

Turing, Alan. (1950) 2003. "Computing Machinery and Intelligence." In *The New Media Reader*, edited by Nick Montfort and Noah Wardrip-Fruin, 50–64. Cambridge, MA: MIT Press. Originally published in *Mind: A Quarterly Review of Psychology and Philosophy* 59 (236): 433–460.

....

Twitter, Tumblr, and Microblogging
Brian Croxall

As its name suggests, microblogging is a practice that applies a size constraint to the content of blogs (see BLOGS). While microblogging may take place on any blogging platform where an author chooses to privilege brevity, the term primarily refers to posting that takes place on specific platforms whose design either encourages or enforces brief communication.

The most notable microblogging platform—Twitter—takes the latter tack, restricting its users' posts to 140 characters or less (less than the size of this sentence). Not simply an arbitrary number, Twitter's character limit was chosen because mobile text messaging is limited to 160 characters (O'Reilly and Milstein 2009, 33). Other services that emphasize text, like Plurk, identi.ca, or Jaiku (shuttered in 2012), impose the same character limit. The 140-character limit in posts on Twitter, or "tweets," has led to the increased importance of link shorteners, tools that trim the unwieldy URLs of the Internet from hundreds of letters in length to a much more manageable string that can be as short as eleven characters.

On the other hand, a service like Tumblr does not impose length restrictions on those who use the service. Instead, the site's design pushes users toward microblogging. Many Tumblr themes use large font sizes, prompting authors to favor a short paragraph over the long-form blog post that has become the norm. Tumblr layouts often emphasize images, but the service was originally designed for users to blog a single photograph at a time (see Karp 2009). Thus, a photo-Tumblr became a photography microblog rather than a single node on a photo-sharing service. Even more important than the design of Tumblr, however, is its community of users. While it is technically possible to write long text posts in Tumblr, its users' practices have resulted in a shared aesthetic of brevity. (Prior to the ascendancy in 2006 of the term "microblogging," the 2005 neologism "tumblelog" described "a quick and dirty stream of consciousness, a bit like a remaindered links style linklog but with more than just links" [Kottke 2005].)

Given the short nature of individual posts to microblogs, many of them emphasize what the creator is doing, reading, finding, looking at, or thinking about at a particular moment, and a post's content often consists of a single image, a few sentences, or a link accompanied by some explanatory text. The ephemeral nature of the content on microblogs leads many people to question the value of what is shared with a tool like Twitter, which initially prompted users to post in answer to the question, "What are you doing?" (Stone 2009). "What," critics ask, "do I gain by knowing what you are eating for breakfast?" Cartoonist Garry Trudeau echoed these sentiments in *Doonesbury* throughout 2009 as Twitter gained increasing attention from the media and public. In March of that year, *Doonesbury*'s journalist Roland Hedley began vapidly tweeting (most often about Twitter), both in the comic strip and on the Twitter service (see Trudeau 2009; NPR 2009).

Yet the usefulness of microblogging does not lie in the single post or photo. Instead, a person's posts become useful when taken in the aggregate. If one reads quick updates over a month's time—what a person eats, listens to, and is doing—you learn a lot more about her, or at least her publicly performed identity (see IDENTITY). Writing about this phenomenon less than a year after Twitter was created, Leisa Reichelt described this awareness as "ambient intimacy": "Ambient intimacy is about being able to keep in touch with people with a level of regularity and intimacy that you wouldn't usually have access to, because time and space conspire to make it impossible. . . . There are a lot of us . . . who find great value in this ongoing noise. It helps us get to know people who would otherwise be just acquaintances" (2007). While critics of microblogging still point to what they perceive as the ephemerality of its content, it is in fact the utility of such ephemerality that continues to draw "readers."

Of course, blogs of all sizes are meant to be read. One reason for the popularization of blogging in the 2000s was the standardization of RSS (Really Simple Syndication), which enabled readers to be notified of new content without having to visit a site. RSS made it possible to follow someone's work from afar. The support for RSS found in platforms such as Tumblr and Twitter underscores the genealogical connection between microblogs and blogs. Despite this clear descent, microblogs experienced an evolutionary leap through three particular innovations. First, they allowed users to follow one another without leaving a particular site. "Following" another person on Twitter, for example, results in her short posts being wrapped into a continuously updating thread on the user's home page. While it's possible to read someone's posts in an RSS reader without "following" her on a service, it is infinitely more practical to simply use that service's follow mechanism. Since microblogs tend to display publicly whom a user follows and who follows her in return, Twitter, Tumblr, and the like are clearly social networking sites (see SOCIAL NETWORK SITES [SNSs]). The platform-centric updates (as opposed to the RSS model of blogs) helped to make microblogs "sticky." The second evolutionary tactic microblogs developed for retaining users' attention was instantaneous updates. When a user posts new content to a microblog, those who follow him get an immediate update—even on a page that appears to be delivering static content. Twitter, for example, displays a constantly incrementing counter that displays how many updates have appeared since the browser was last refreshed. Microblogging's third innovation was the ability to post or follow content from a text-only mobile device. Twitter and Plurk allow users to post updates from mobile devices using SMS short codes. It was the centrality of such mobile updates to these platforms that led, again, to the character limits they imposed on updates. More importantly, Twitter enabled users to receive updates selectively from those they followed via SMS. These updates appeared immediately following their creation, allowing Twitter users to stay continuously connected to a real-time communication network whether one was interacting with the web or SMS versions of the application. Although mobile microblogging today often depends on dedicated apps or mobile web versions of platforms, Twitter has preserved its original SMS functionality, allowing for an expanded user base. These three innovations—centrally located, instantaneous, and mobile reading and updates—helped fuel the rapid adoption of microblogs.

Integrating mobile devices with microblogs like Twitter enables users to comment publicly not only about what they were currently doing but also about newsworthy events to which they were witnesses. When US Airways flight 1549 landed in New York's Hudson River six minutes after takeoff from LaGuardia Airport, the first picture of the event was shared on Twitter (Krums 2009). Similarly, the 2008 attacks in Mumbai (Beaumont 2008) and the 2011 assassination of Osama Bin Laden were reported in real time by observers, although in the latter case the observer was unaware what was happening (Olson 2011; O'Dell 2011). But citizen journalism is not the only possibility created by a real-time, mobile communication platform like Twitter. The public nature of most microblogs means that strangers can coordinate mass social actions, such as the 2009 protests over the Iranian presidential elections or the 2011 Egyptian revolution (see Nasr 2009; Rather 2009; Hudson 2011; for a dissenting view on the importance of Twitter in Egypt, see Srinivasan 2011). Such rapid organization of large numbers of people via microblogs functions through a principle akin to "ambient intimacy" and that Clive Thompson described as a "social sixth sense": "Twitter and other constant-contact media create *social* proprioception. They give a group of people a sense of itself, making possible weird, fascinating feats of coordination" (2007; emphasis in the original). Along with enabling the 2011 England riots, then, the real-time, mobile, and public coordination of Twitter was partly responsible for the rapid organization of cleanup efforts throughout London (Wasik 2012; *BBC News* 2011). Microblogs have helped make apparent the proleptic nature of Howard Rheingold's assertion that "the 'killer apps' of tomorrow's mobile infocom industry won't be hardware devices or software programs but social practices" (2002, xii).

While the real-time updates of microblogs can help organize action in localized spaces, they also create opportunities for people to comment on events from afar. Events that draw large audiences such as U.S. presidential debates or matches at the 2010 World Cup regularly draw thousands of people simultaneously posting on microblogs about the most recent gaffe of their party's or team's rival. Occasions with much smaller audiences make similar use of microblogs for fostering a backchannel, including conference presentations and classroom discussions (see Atkinson 2010; Croxall 2010). The backchannel allows audiences, students, and others to "talk back" to the person presenting, as well as to broadcast what they are hearing and thinking with their own followers, an everting of Web 2.0 principles into the "real world." Conversations that parallel events often depend on tags or other metadata that allow participants to find other posts on the same topic. Users adopted this use of metadata for microblogs on their own, as it evolved from the tagging found elsewhere on the Internet, and the microblogging platforms have gradually incorporated this information into their information model. "Hashtags," as they are known on Twitter, allow users to follow not just immediate real-time conversations but also threads and topics that persist through time, such as conversations about electronic literature (#elit) or "alternative academic" careers (#altac) (see ELECTRONIC LITERATURE). The cultural importance of this form of metadata—and microblogs more generally—was made evident in the selection of "hashtag" as the American Dialect Society's "word of the year" for 2012 (American Dialect Society 2013).

Social practices around such backchannels—and indeed all of microblogging—are still developing (see boyd 2009), as is the understanding of other uses for such platforms. Already a site for social protest and social unrest, microblogs like Twitter and

Tumblr are also being used as a venue for publication, creative expression, short stories, collaborative narrative, and performance of all kinds (see Marino and Wittig 2013) (see COLLABORATIVE NARRATIVE, PERFORMANCE). In the future, the uses for these digital texts will certainly expand—even if their length does not.

■ See also PLATFORM, WRITING UNDER CONSTRAINT

References and Further Reading

American Dialect Society. 2013. "'Hashtag' Is the 2012 Word of the Year." *American Dialect Society*, January 4. www.americandialect.org/hashtag-2012.

Atkinson, Cliff. 2010. *The Backchannel: How Audiences Are Using Twitter and Social Media and Changing Presentations Forever*. Berkeley, CA: New Riders.

BBC News. 2011. "Twitter Users in Riots Clean-up." *BBC News*, August 9. www.bbc.co.uk/news/uk-england-london-14456857.

Beaumont, Claudine. 2008. "Mumbai Attacks: Twitter and Flickr Used to Break News." *Telegraph*, November 27. www.telegraph.co.uk/news/worldnews/asia/india/3530640/Mumbai-attacks-Twitter-and-Flickr-used-to-break-news-Bombay-India.html.

boyd, danah. 2009. "Spectacle at Web2.0 Expo . . . from My Perspective." *apophenia*, November 24. www.zephoria.org/thoughts/archives/2009/11/24/spectacle_at_we.html.

Croxall, Brian. 2010. "Reflections on Teaching with Social Media." *ProfHacker*, June 7. http://chronicle.com/blogs/profhacker/reflections-on-teaching-with-social-media/24556.

Hudson, John. 2011. "The 'Twitter Revolution' Debate: The Egyptian Test Case." *Atlantic Wire*, January 31. www.theatlanticwire.com/global/2011/01/the-twitter-revolution-debate-the-egyptian-test-case/21296/.

Karp, David. 2009. "Introducing Photosets." *Tumblr Staff Blog*, July 1. http://staff.tumblr.com/post/133573456/photosets.

Kottke, Jason. 2005. "Tumblelogs." *kottke.org*, October 19. http://kottke.org/05/10/tumblelogs.

Krums, Janis. 2009. "There's a Plane in the Hudson. I'm on the Ferry Going to Pick up the People. Crazy." *TwitPic*, January 15. http://twitpic.com/135xa.

Marino, Mark C., and Rob Wittig. 2013. "Occupying MLA." *ProfHacker*, January 14. http://chronicle.com/blogs/profhacker/occupying-mla/45357.

Nasr, Octavia. 2009. "Tear Gas and Twitter: Iranians Take Their Protests Online." *CNN.com*, June 14. http://articles.cnn.com/2009-06-14/world/iran.protests.twitter_1_facebook-president-mahmoud-ahmadinejad-supporters?_s=PM:WORLD.

NPR. 2009. "'Doonesbury' Writer Lampoons Tweeting Journalists." *NPR.org*, December 7. www.npr.org/templates/story/story.php?storyId=121155237.

O'Dell, Jolie. 2011. "One Twitter User Reports Live from Osama Bin Laden Raid." *Mashable*, May 1. http://mashable.com/2011/05/02/live-tweet-bin-laden-raid/.

Olson, Parmy. 2011. "Man Inadvertently Live Tweets Osama Bin Laden Raid." *Forbes*, May 2. www.forbes.com/sites/parmyolson/2011/05/02/man-inadvertently-live-tweets-osama-bin-laden-raid/.

O'Reilly, Tim, and Sarah Milstein. 2009. *The Twitter Book*. Sebastopol, CA: O'Reilly Media.

Rather, Dan. 2009. "Tehran, Twitter, and Tiananmen." *Daily Beast*, June 16. www.thedailybeast.com/articles/2009/06/16/tehran-twitter-and-tiananmen.html.

Reichelt, Leisa. 2007. "Ambient Intimacy." *disambiguity*, March 1. www.disambiguity.com/ambient-intimacy/.

Rheingold, Howard. 2002. *Smart Mobs: The Next Social Revolution*. Cambridge, MA: Perseus.

Srinivasan, Ramesh. 2011. "Twitter Helped to Distort Egyptian Protests." *NPR.org*, August 12. www.npr.org/2011/08/12/139570720/twitter-created-echo-chamber-during-egyptian-protests.

Stone, Biz. 2009. "What's Happening?" *Twitter Blog*, March 1. http://blog.twitter.com/2009/11/whats-happening.html.

Thompson, Clive. 2007. "Clive Thompson on How Twitter Creates a Social Sixth Sense." *WIRED*, June 26. www.wired.com/techbiz/media/magazine/15-07/st_thompson.

Trudeau, Garry. 2009. "Doonesbury Comic Strip, March 02, 2009." www.gocomics.com/doonesbury/2009/03/02.

Wasik, Bill. 2012. "#Riot: Self-Organized, Hyper-Networked Revolts—Coming to a City near You." *WIRED*, January.

V

Video

Patrick Vonderau

"Video" (from the Latin *videre*—"I see") is a *terminus technicus* introduced in the United States in the late 1930s to describe the sight channel in television, as opposed to audio, the sound channel. In the 1950s, the term became more widely used to denote the storage medium (magnetic tape), process (electronic recording and playback), and televisual displays used for the delivery of synchronized sound and image. Ever since then, *video* has developed into an umbrella term for a bewildering variety of media technologies (for instance, broadcast signals, streaming digital data, camcorders, or editing software), formats (domestic, such as V H S or Betamax, and professional, such as U-Matic), forms (feature films, video art, corporate information, amateur movies, surveillance tapes, ultrasound scans, etc.), and institutions (broadcasting networks, video stores, galleries, file-sharing communities, and the like). Although the history of video and the VCR is usually narrated as a linear trajectory, stretching from the beginnings of home video in the 1970s to an allegedly wide-reaching disruption caused by the turn from analog to digital, video remains—as opposed to film or television—an object whose histories are not yet to be told in the past: if anything, video appears to be an emergent medium enmeshed in, and constantly transformed by, heterogeneous networks of the social. Forming a node in the increasingly interlinked webs of previously separate media, video lives, as Sean Cubitt has noted, in its "potentialities which are, precisely, the relationships into which it enters" (1991, 4).

While video escapes its own theorizing, as it seems to defy any effort to pinpoint its primal source, form, or goal, and any understanding of itself as a single and unique this or that, several attempts have been made to essentialize what video as a medium is about. The two best known of these attempts focused, first, on its ways of storing information and, second, on its temporality. Following the first line of theoretical arguing, which aimed at an understanding of video as a technological means for storing representation, video appeared unique in its capacity to store video and audio information as blips of electricity, or by means of bits of information. An electronic medium, analog video primarily consists of electronic signals, stored by magnetic embedding on videotape; turning from tape to file, and from analog to digital, the bits constituting its reality come in nonlinear and discontinuous forms. From this perspective, then, video's specificity as a medium (see MEDIALITY) was tied to a double *absence*, to a loss and its anxieties: a loss of iconicity and what once constituted its material base, motion picture film. Accordingly, the aesthetics of video as a medium were identified with its moments of failure and decay—with dropouts, jittery images, or noise bars in videotapes, or the buffering of digital streamed video. But not only did video tend to be characterized by being devoid of actual or fixed pictures, as compared to motion picture film. A second line of argument defined video through a difference to television. In this view, video was something else than the extension of vision in real time, or liveness, through which television had been promoted over most of its history. Rather, video as a medium supplemented liveness by offering the opportunity to play back: the capacity to bypass broadcasting's simultaneity, and the possibility to replace television's programming flow. Understood to introduce a new, viewer-controlled regime of representation based on time-shifting, video's—or rather the VCR's—playback function thus became central in defining its mediality, since it was there that the processes of production, textuality, and reading seemed to meet. From the latter perspective then, video appeared as an "audiovisual time machine" (Zielinski 1985), essentially different in its temporality, referring to temporality both *over* time (time shifting, preservation, decay) and *in* time (as duration, or manipulated playback speed).

Given the notorious instability of contemporary media environments, it is obviously problematic to identify video with one specific mode of representation, as well as the technologies and aesthetics this mode may involve. At the same time, however, the opposite tendency to use "video" merely as an umbrella concept, and to understand it as an object that is neither an autonomous medium, free of all links with other forms of communication, nor entirely dependent on any of them, has led to a situation where video has almost become synonymous with convergence culture. Digital video can be seen as a force disrupting established production cultures and causing workflow disorder (Caldwell 2008), as a major shift in televisual programming from flow to file (Kompare 2005), as a prime instance of participatory (folk) culture (Jenkins 2006), as a defining moment in the life cycle of audiovisual commodity forms, as a symptom and propelling force of industrial exploitation, and so on. Therefore, it might be advisable to approach the phenomenon of video neither by pointing to an essential common denominator nor by leaving it entirely in the open. As an alternative, video can be explored through the multitude of specific mundane social practices it entails, practices that existed long before the latest development of its underlying technology: activities of recording, collecting, copying, repeating, deleting, or sharing. However loosely defined as a medium, video then can be studied as a "socially realized structure of communication," whereby structure is meant to include "both technological forms and their associated protocols" (Gitelman 2004). In consequence, and returning to the position of the literal "I" invoked in the Latin etymology of the term, we may explain video in light of the clutter of rules and default conditions that make up its protocols, and with an eye on the community of viewers facing those rules and conditions. Writing in 2012, the most obvious site from which to critically analyze the forms and protocols of today's video-viewing "I" would be YouTube, Google's online delivery platform, (in)famously successful in promising to "broadcast yourself."

YouTube marks the very moment in the larger history of screen practices in which the relational dimension of video—its potential to instigate connectivity between data, people, and devices—has moved to the foreground of consumption. Integrated in mobile media, web-enabled television sets, and social networking applications, YouTube videos have become a key element of the multimedia networks and machineries into which today's "viewsers" are connected. The platform's manifold video practices can be explored through metaphors that are widely used to stress, and streamline, YouTube's social, economic, and technological dimensions. YouTube is often spoken about as if it were a library, an archive, a laboratory, or a medium like television, with the respective metaphor inviting hypothetical considerations of what YouTube's possible, probable, and preferred futures might be. This clearly mirrors earlier periods in media history, with early cinema being compared to theater and vaudeville, or television to radio, cinema, and theater, in an emergent—that is, unforeseeable and uncontrolled—process of a new media phenomenon fitting into an existing culture. When changing the metaphor, one faces different horizons of use and enters a process of experiments and enterprises, each framed by a set of protocols: as archival database, screening medium, media lab, industrial workshop, and so on. When examining YouTube by way of metaphors, one is immediately confronted with a number of inherent (and not easily solvable) conflicts and problems vying for more detailed answers. How does, for instance, the practice of open access relate to traditional archival standards, legal constraints, "old" media distribution, and the entrepreneurial interests of the Google subsidary? To what extent do clip aesthetics challenge traditional notions of, for example, textuality, episodic and serial narrative, documentary forms, and also the very basic requirements of teaching and research? And finally: if YouTube is to be regarded as the world's largest archive, how do the texts and practices associated with its use work for and against cultural memory?

So even if there is no video theory, as Sean Cubitt has claimed, since video seems to prevent the very prerequisite for a theoretical approach, "that is, deciding upon an object about which you wish to know," there is still "the field of culture," a field in which a variety of intersecting activities gather around the video apparatus (1991, 5). Following video along those activities, as they become observable on platforms such as YouTube, and as they are specified on such platforms by technological forms and their associated protocols, at least allows us to explore what a video theory might look like, or rather might have looked like, from the viewpoint of a media history turning back toward a future past.

■ See also ANALOG VERSUS DIGITAL, CHARACTERISTICS OF DIGITAL MEDIA, COPYRIGHT, DATA, FILM AND DIGITAL MEDIA, MASHUP, MOBILE GAMES, OLD MEDIA / NEW MEDIA

References and Further Reading

Boddy, William. 1993. *Fifties Television: The Industry and Its Critics*. Urbana: University of Illinois Press.
———. 2004. *New Media and Popular Imagination: Launching Radio, Television, and Digital Media in the United States*. Oxford: Oxford University Press.
Caldwell, John. 2008. *Production Culture: Industrial Reflexivity and Critical Practice in Film and Television*. Durham, NC: Duke University Press.
Cubitt, Sean. 1991. *Timeshift: On Video Culture*. London: Routledge.
———. 1993. *Videography: Video Media as Art and Culture*. London: Palgrave Macmillan.
Gitelman, Lisa. 2004. "How Users Define New Media: A History of the Amusement Phonograph." In *Rethinking Media Change: The Aesthetics of Transition*, edited by David Thorburn and Henry Jenkins, 61–80. Cambridge, MA: MIT Press.
Hilderbrand, Lucas. 2009. *Bootleg Histories of Videotape and Copyright*. Durham, NC: Duke University Press.
Jenkins, Henry. 2006. *Convergence Culture: Where Old and New Media Collide*. New York: New York University Press.

Kompare, Derek. 2005. *Rerun Nation: How Repeats Invented American Television*. New York: Routledge.

Snickars, Pelle, and Patrick Vonderau, eds. 2009. *The YouTube Reader*. London: Wallflower Press.

Spigel, Lynn, and Jan Olsson, eds. 2004. *Television after* TV: Essays on a Medium in Transition. Durham, NC: Duke University Press.

Zielinski, Siegfried. 1985. *Zur Geschichte des Videorecorders*. Berlin: Spiess.

....

Viral Aesthetics
Jussi Parikka

One can approach "viral aesthetics" in differing ways, depending on which term you prioritize qualifying. One can focus on a specific notion or even genre of aesthetics that deals with virality, contagion, self-reproduction, recursion, and iterability. In addition, one can claim that there is a specific aesthetics to the viral, and that our knowledge of a biological or algorithmic entity (a virus) has a specific aesthetics to it. This would imply that our knowledge of the viral is completely embedded in aesthetic considerations—matters of representation, presentation, and visualization.

"Virality" gives us an insightful approach to the patterns of interaction and indeed aesthetics of network culture. Expressed through a range of artistic practices and works, viral aesthetics has demonstrated the need to think of the semiautonomous nature of digital aesthetics based on code and software environments. Virality can be seen as a characteristic irreducible to a single entity. It is a relation that defines its terms. Viruses are contagious agents, but more interesting is the milieu in which they function and are able to demonstrate contagious behavior. By understanding this milieu, one grasps the nature of the viral as an algorithmic procedure that is able to procreate, infect, and multiply on software platforms. This becomes clearest in the case of viral media—such as memes and other "agents" of network culture where their patterns and logic distribution, as well as spread, are more interesting than their "content." Internet memes are about the distribution of visual and other content through the logic of variation: minor tweaks and remixes are part and parcel of the memetic that itself, however, presents as if an autonomous force that is supported by network affordances. The Internet feeds on such *Lolcats* and other memetic phenomena that include a range of other gestural patterns too, as evidenced by the popularity of "gangnam style" variations since July 2012. Increasingly, one can understand the meme being one of the central modes of discourse on the Internet: repetition with the tiniest variation takes precedence over semantics or "meaning."

Viral patterns are part of a genealogy of experimental programming, which has been interested in recursion and self-referentiality, and a multiplication of variations as a strategy of evolution (Trogemann 2005, 124). As Trogemann outlines, the characteristics of selection, recombination, and mutation are themselves simulatable. Related themes include self-reproducing systems, part and parcel of computer science at least since John von Neumann's theory of self-reproducing automata (Trogemann 2005, 125). In the 1990s digital art concerned itself with genetic algorithms (e.g., the work of Karl Sims), and artificial life was similarly inspired. Evolution, adaptation, and emergence became a part of artistic methods and offered vocabularies for a new aesthetics (see ALGORITHM, ARTIFICIAL LIFE).

Alan Liu (2004) uses the term *viral aesthetics* in this sense: to refer to destructive creativity across a range of art and cultural practices in the history of network culture (see SUBVERSION [CREATIVE DESTRUCTION]). He refers to the new aesthetic practices that Critical Art Ensemble's projects have created, for instance, as well as a range of other examples. Virality as aesthetics becomes emblematic of a whole range of phenomena that characterize network culture.

Viral aesthetics is evident, for instance, in the works by Joseph Nechvatal (www .nechvatal.net/). Nechvatal's paintings introduce virality as an algorithmic distortion to digitized or digitally created abstract paintings, offering a posthuman take on the image, and forcing us to think themes of deterioration, entropy, and decay through digital software too (see CYBORG AND POSTHUMAN). Further examples of this aesthetics of deterioration include glitch artworks by Jodi (Netherlands) and Ant Scott (United Kingdom) (see GLITCH AESTHETICS). Despite not being about virality, these works have been connected to a similar field of digital art concerning noise. Besides the quite broad notion of "noise" used here, such a variety of artworks does engage with questions of nonhuman writing and processes, whether by mobilizing the power of algorithmic, semiautonomous read/write processes or other forms of glitching. Here viral aesthetics becomes an artistic methodology to investigate crashes and errors as incidental to the network culture, and hence it is perhaps connected to critical media aesthetics in a manner Rosa Menkman outlines: "On the one hand, these aesthetics show a medium in a critical state: ruined, unwanted, unrecognized, accidental and horrendous moment. This transforms the way the consumer perceives its normal operation (every accident transforms the normal) and registers the passing of a tipping point after which it is possible for the medium to be critically revealed at greater depth. On the other hand, these aesthetics critique the medium itself, as a genre, interface and expectation" (2011, 44). In music cultures, such aesthetics of failure have also been developed across glitch practices and themes of postdigital and aesthetics of failure developed by Kim Cascone (Goodman 2009, 132) (see MUSIC, SOUND).

Besides American cyberculture (for instance, the *Mondo 2000* magazine), viruses become mobilized as part of early European hacker and cyber art/activism in the early 1990s. The earliest examples of such include Italian Tommaso Tozzi's (www.tommasotozzi.it) artistic virus, which had been part of his more general hacker art approach since the 1980s. Tozzi pitched his Hacker Art as a cyberpunk-inspired ethos for democratic values and social justice, but also as an antidote to commercial cultural practices. Interestingly, Tozzi's manifesto already invoked the spirit of "anonymous practice" as well and extended the viral metaphor into an activity of social network building. For Tozzi, according to Tatiana Bazzichelli's excellent consideration of his practice, the viral becomes a way "to produce actions capable of being transmitted, communicated and contaminated in the most widespread way possible without necessarily being recognisable as artistic actions, but capable of acting in transversal sectors" (2008, 126) (see HACKER).

For sure, viruses were around anyway. While Tozzi and others, such as the VNS Matrix, used them as part of their rhetorics, we could even see some of the earliest viruses not specifically meant as art as perversions of current lulz tactics of the cyber guerrilla kind. In the late 1980s and early 1990s, MS-DOS- and Windows-based virus payloads of such programs as the Cascade dropped the screen letters to the bottom; the Melting worm captured the screen pixels in other ways, simulating what looked like melting; the Yankee Doodle virus was, as the name says, one that triggered the famous little tune.

In early 2000 important viral art projects continued the spirit of viral programs as hacker art. The situationist-styled intervention of art groups 0100101110101101.org and epidemiC introduced the Biennale virus, which spread not only in digital format but as printed and even commercial forms (see Parikka 2009). In 2002, the Frankfurt Museum of Applied Art hosted the *I Love You* exhibition focusing on viral art and practices.

In the context of digital literature, the investigation of networks and hypertext as nonlinear literary navigation space led to some interesting experiments, which showed an interest in entropy and noise. Not perhaps viral per se, but definitely part of the wider discussions concerning what Gustav Metzger already in the 1960s called self-destructive art, William Gibson's famous *Agrippa* work is important to mention. Published in the early 1990s, it was distributed on a 3.5 inch floppy disk and destroyed itself after it was read. The original idea even included the possibility of triggering the process of destruction by a virus, but that was abandoned (Edwards 1992). Such literature work emphasized the processual unfolding nature of text and/as code, both illuminating new aspects of network aesthetics (see CODE, CODE AESTHETICS, PROCEDURAL).

Besides art practices that take the viral as its method or object of investigation, we can think of aesthetics as one way to *know* about the viral, and how visualized virality offers an insight into network topologies. Vito Campanelli included a whole section on biology and science-inspired contagion approaches in his book *Web Aesthetics* (2010). Subsequently, recent popular literature on memes (contagious cultural ideas) has introduced viral aesthetics into cultural debate. Furthermore, in the sciences, the emphasis on the ways in which networks and contagion are visualized and diagrammed has its relation to our theme. The power-law and scale-free network diagrams are now popular ways of explaining networks. Such perspectives became familiar from and articulated in Albert-Laszlo Barabasi's popular science book *Linked*, which also linked the viral into the topology of scale-free. Barabasi sees computer viruses as one special case of the topology of networks in which there are a few well-connected nodes instead of many evenly connected nodes. The diagrammatics of scale-free and contagious networks are themselves, according to Barabasi's argument, emblematic of the much wider nature of epidemics, which include not only viruses and infectious diseases but also "ideas, innovations, and new products" (Barabasi 2003, 135). Viruses can also serve as means to understand the specific topologies of post–Cold War network culture (Sampson 2007).

Viruses expose networks (Parikka 2007) and help us understand the accidental nature of network society. This understanding is, however, filtered through techniques of visualization and simulation essential to production of knowledge about biological and computer viruses/networks. Indeed, the use of network technologies, mathematical epidemiology, and visualizations to track biological viruses is a good example of this; biosurveillance and virus infection maps act as outbreak control measures and are emblematic of this aesthetics of the viral communication society (Thacker 2005). Artificial life research formerly used computational simulations to understand evolutionary processes. Projects such as Tom Ray's *Tierra*, John Holland's *Echo*, Chris Adami's *Avida*, Andrew Pargellis's *Amoeba*, Tim Taylor's *Cosmos*, and Larry Yaeger's *Polyworld* contributed to what could be called the viral ecology of networks (Johnston 2009, 27–28).

A superposition of information and biological trajectories works thus to illuminate how the epistemology of concrete viruses is essentially about the aesthetics of the viral, whether biological or digital, as information visualization and the mathematization of their nature.

References and Further Reading

Barabasi, Albert-László. 2003. *Linked: How Everything Is Connected to Everything Else and What It Means for Business, Science, and Everyday Life.* London: Plume.

Bazzichelli, Tatiana. 2008. *Networking: The Net as Artwork.* Aarhus, Denmark: Digital Aesthetics Research Center. http://darc.imv.au.dk/wp-content/files/networking_bazzichelli.pdf.

Campanelli, Vito. 2010. *Web Aesthetics: How Digital Media Affect Culture and Society.* Rotterdam and the Institute of Network Cultures, Amsterdam: NAi.

Edwards, Gavin. 1992. "Cyber Lit." *Details,* June. www.textfiles.com/sf/cyberlit.txt.

Goodman, Steve. 2009. "Contagious Noise: From Digital Glitches to Audio Viruses." In *The Spam Book,* edited by Jussi Parikka and Tony Sampson, 125–140. Cresskill, NJ: Hampton Press.

Johnston, John. 2009. "Mutant and Viral: Artificial Evolution and Software Ecology." In *The Spam Book,* edited by Jussi Parikka and Tony Sampson, 23–38. Cresskill, NJ: Hampton Press.

Liu, Alan. 2004. *Laws of Cool: Knowledge Work and the Culture of Information.* Chicago: University of Chicago Press.

Menkman, Rosa. 2011. *The Glitch Momentum.* Amsterdam: Institute for Network Cultures / Network Notebooks.

Parikka, Jussi. 2007. *Digital Contagions: A Media Archaeology of Computer Viruses.* New York: Peter Lang.

———. 2009. "Archives of Software: Malicious Code and the Aesthesis of Media Accidents." In *The Spam Book,* edited by Jussi Parikka and Tony Sampson, 105–123. Cresskill, NJ: Hampton Press.

Sampson, Tony D. 2007. "The Accidental Topology of Digital Culture: How the Network Becomes Viral." *Transformations* 14, March. www.transformationsjournal.org/journal/issue_14/article_05.shtml.

Thacker, Eugene 2005. "Living Dead Networks." *Fibreculture* 4. http://four.fibreculturejournal.org/fcj-018-living-dead-networks/.

Trogemann, Georg. 2005. "Experimentelle und spekulative Informatik." In *Zukünfte des Computers,* edited by Claus Pias, 109–132. Zürich-Berlin: Diaphanes.

••

Virtual Bodies

Marco Caracciolo

The scholarly conversation surrounding virtual bodies has often problematized traditional conceptions of embodiment, and with them the apparently straightforward idea of "body." However, at first sight it is the word *virtual* that complicates the meaning of the phrase *virtual bodies* (see VIRTUALITY). In popular culture, this adjective has come to designate anything that is generated, simulated, or even mediated by computers (see SIMULATION). But the term also belongs to a philosophical tradition going back to Aristotle, whose dichotomy between the virtual—or potential—and the actual has been revived in the 1990s in the work of theorists of virtuality such as Michael Heim (1993) and Pierre Lévy (1998).

The discussion of virtual bodies in the cyberdiscourse of the same years intertwines both meanings of *virtual,* the computer generated and the potential. At the basic level, a virtual body is a computer-generated representation of a body—for instance, in a virtual reality (VR) environment (see VIRTUAL REALITY). But theorizations of virtual bodies have quickly shifted from this relatively simple definition to a complex tangle of views: far from being a self-contained representation, a virtual body is seen as a mode of being made possible by computer technology—it is a body that exists at the interface and in the interaction between a real, human body and a machine (see INTERFACE). This idea is closely bound up with sci-fi fantasies of human-machine hybrids and with posthumanist positions in the academic debate (see CYBORG AND POSTHUMAN): like prosthetic devices, computers are thought to complement and augment the human body, opening up a space where nature, culture, and technology converge and commingle. Not only is human consciousness envisioned as a machine running several programs (Dennett 1991; Hayles 1999, 6), but machines themselves are understood in biological terms—for example, in talk about "computer viruses" (Lupton 1994). The gray area between the machinic and the biological is, strictly speaking, the domain of the virtual—and it is inhabited by virtual bodies.

By blurring distinctions between machines and humans, and by casting doubt on traditional approaches to embodiment as a natural, biological "given," theorizations of virtual bodies easily lent themselves to post-structuralist and feminist agendas (Haraway 1991; see CYBERFEMINISM). Drawing on a number of post-structuralist thinkers such as Jacques Lacan and David Harvey, Katherine Hayles writes, "In the phrase 'virtual bodies,' I intend to allude to the historical separation between information and materiality and also to recall the embodied processes that resist this division" (1999, 20). This view of embodiment as a site of resistance to Cartesian-looking dichotomies between the mental and the material challenged a conception widespread in first-wave accounts of VR, according to which computer technology promised a liberation from our physical, material bodies. Having a virtual body, for the followers of VR gurus such as William Gibson and Jaron Lanier, almost borders on disembodied existence. In this vein, Heim argues that "in cyberspace minds are connected to minds, existing in perfect concord without the limitations or necessities of the physical body" (1993, 34).

By contrast, scholars such as Anne Balsamo and Hayles herself critique this disembodied conception, calling attention to the complex, and socioculturally nuanced, interrelation between our physical bodies and the computer-simulated environments with which we interact: "From a feminist perspective it is clear that the repression of the material body belies a gender bias in the supposedly disembodied (and gender-free) world of virtual reality" (Balsamo 2000, 493). For these theorists, virtual bodies provide a point of convergence between computer technologies and the sociocultural values that are inscribed in our embodied existence. By this path, the discussion surrounding virtual bodies dovetails with larger issues of human embodiment (see GENDER REPRESENTATION).

This brings us to another line of investigation that has dealt with the virtuality of our bodies from a philosophical standpoint—namely, phenomenology. Unlike the posthuman theorists discussed above, however, phenomenologists talked about virtual bodies well before the term *virtual* triggered associations with computers. In 1945, Maurice Merleau-Ponty described the body as a "virtual center of action" (2002, 121; translation modified). What he meant by this is that human embodiment does not coincide with the material boundaries of our body, since it spans the whole range of our possibilities of interaction with the world. These possibilities—which have a parallel in psychologist J. J. Gibson's (1979) notion of "affordance"—depend in key ways on our bodily makeup; and yet, they can be expanded through the acquisition of bodily skills (e.g., walking) and through the use of tools (e.g., riding a bike, grasping a fork). In sum, our embodiment is defined not only by the body that we have but also by what we *could* do with it in our coping with the world.

Seen in this light, virtuality is not a layer added to our bodies by our hybridization with computers; it is part and parcel of our embodied being. This view goes hand in hand with theorizations of embodiment in recent cognitive science, which have explicitly acknowledged a debt to Merleau-Ponty—for example, in viewing virtuality as built into human perception (Noë 2004). Theorists of extended cognition have also insisted on how tools can serve as prosthetic devices, broadening our possibilities of embodied interaction with the environment (Clark and Chalmers 1998). Philosopher John Stewart puts it very vividly: "a snow-covered mountain *becomes* an entirely different place if you have skis on your feet (and if you know how to ski!)" (2010, 28). If this is true, the virtuality of virtual (in the sense of computer-mediated) bodies is always already projected against a background of virtuality in the philosophical sense: potentialities for action shape our embodiment right from the start.

This intuition has interesting implications for accounts of users' interaction with virtual environments and more generally with computers. Scholars working in the traditions of phenomenology and "embodied" cognitive science have pointed out that computer technologies, far from widening the Cartesian divide between mind and body, interact in complex ways with our physical bodies. Despite the promises of disembodiment held out by VR gurus, our embodiment has a crucial influence on our experience of virtual worlds. This interplay usually manifests itself in the *tension* between the user's real body and its computer-simulated counterpart: "The corporeal body in the physical environment remains ever present to mind, while an electronic body image weakly echoes and competes with it" (Murray and Sixsmith 1999, 334). It is the malleability and virtuality of our embodiment that enable users to project themselves into virtual bodies significantly different from their own, giving rise to a sense of "immersion" in virtual worlds (Ryan 2001).

After the decline of the VR dream, video game scholars have leveraged the same phenomenological insights to investigate players' embodied engagements with the physical interface of computers and other game platforms. Gregerson and Grodal (2009), for instance, argue that our interaction with games involves a series of feedback loops between the interface and the audio-visual display: small movements performed by players (such as button pushes) bring about full-fledged actions in the game world (e.g., the character jumps). Innovative game systems, such as the Wii or the Xbox Kinect, make possible a high degree of similarity—or "motor congruence" (Gregersen and Grodal 2009, 68)—between the player's movements and the actions represented on the screen.

Another distinction that is clearly relevant in connection to virtual bodies is that between "body schema" and "body image." According to philosopher Shaun Gallagher (2005), the body schema includes the sensorimotor skills that we apply to our interaction with the environment in an effortless, prereflective way. The body image, by contrast, refers to more self-conscious—and socioculturally influenced—beliefs and attitudes toward our body. This distinction sheds light on some aspects of the relationship between players and avatars (see AVATARS). The embodied engagements described by Gregerson and Grodal (2009) operate at the level of the body schema, since they harness the sensorimotor skills of the player (speed, coordination, and so on). Conversely, the players' emotional bond with avatars and their visual appearance falls squarely in the realm of the body image, involving a complex interplay between the player's own body image and that of his or her avatar.

These considerations open up two avenues for investigating our engagement with computer-simulated bodies. On the one hand, phenomenology-inspired cognitive science can help us explore the correlation between the user's body schema, his or her interaction with physical interfaces, and the avatar's actions. On the other hand, the methods of ethnography (see Boellstorff 2006) seem to be particularly suited to explore the relationship between users' body image and the virtual bodies of their avatars.

■ See also COGNITIVE IMPLICATIONS OF NEW MEDIA, ROLE-PLAYING GAMES

References and Further Readings

Balsamo, Anne. 2000. "The Virtual Body in Cyberspace." In *The Cybercultures Reader*, edited by David Bell and Barbara M. Kennedy, 489–498. London: Routledge.

Boellstorff, Tom. 2006. "A Ludicrous Discipline? Ethnography and Game Studies." *Games and Culture* 1 (1): 29–35.

Clark, Andy, and David J. Chalmers. 1998. "The Extended Mind." *Analysis* 58 (1): 7–19.

Dennett, Daniel C. 1991. *Consciousness Explained*. London: Penguin.

Gallagher, Shaun. 2005. *How the Body Shapes the Mind*. New York: Basic Books.

Gibson, James J. 1979. *The Ecological Approach to Visual Perception*. Boston: Houghton Mifflin.

Gregersen, Andreas, and Torben Grodal. 2009. "Embodiment and Interface." In *The Video Game Theory Reader 2*, edited by Bernard Perron and Mark J. P. Wolf, 65–83. London: Routledge.

Haraway, Donna. 1991. "A Cyborg Manifesto: Science, Technology, and Socialist-Feminism in the Late Twentieth Century." In *Simians, Cyborgs and Women: The Reinvention of Nature*, 149–181. London: Routledge.

Hayles, N. Katherine. 1999. *How We Became Posthuman: Virtual Bodies in Cybernetics, Literature, and Informatics*. Chicago: University of Chicago Press.

Heim, Michael. 1993. *The Metaphysics of Virtual Reality*. Oxford: Oxford University Press.

Lévy, Pierre. 1998. *Becoming Virtual: Reality in the Digital Age*. Translated by Robert Bononno. New York: Plenum Trade.

Lupton, Deborah. 1994. "Panic Computing: The Viral Metaphor and Computer Technology." *Cultural Studies* 8 (3): 556–568.

Merleau-Ponty, Maurice. 2002. *Phenomenology of Perception*. Translated by Colin Smith. London: Routledge.

Murray, Craig D., and Judith Sixsmith. 1999. "The Corporeal Body in Virtual Reality." *Ethos* 27 (3): 315–343.

Noë, Alva. 2004. *Action in Perception*. Cambridge, MA: MIT Press.

Ryan, Marie-Laure. 2001. *Narrative as Virtual Reality: Immersion and Interactivity in Literature and Electronic Media*. Baltimore: Johns Hopkins University Press.

Stewart, John. 2010. "Foundational Issues in Enaction as a Paradigm for Cognitive Science: From the Origin of Life to Consciousness and Writing." In *Enaction: Toward a New Paradigm for Cognitive Science*, edited by John Stewart, Olivier Gapenne, and Ezequiel A. Di Paolo, 1–31. Cambridge, MA: MIT Press.

Virtual Economies

Edward Castronova and Travis L. Ross

A virtual economy consists of production systems by which people create virtual goods, and markets by which people trade virtual goods. A virtual good is a digital asset that has value to people. The term *digital asset* refers to an entry in a database (see DATABASE). The status of a digital asset is reported to people through a user interface that provides varying degrees of closeness to reality, yet the primary distinction between virtual goods and real goods is that virtual goods have no physical manifestation. A dollar in a bank account can in principle be withdrawn in the form of a paper dollar. However, a gold piece in a video game cannot be withdrawn in a physical form.

A virtual economy contains goods, markets, and production:

Virtual goods are a form of intangible property. Other forms of intangible property include intellectual property, reputation, and insurance. Virtual goods differ from these in that virtual goods exist only in computer databases, whereas other intangible goods, while they may be recorded in databases, exist separately from them.

Virtual markets exist only among and between real people. Exchanging a virtual good with a game character ("bot" or "merchant NPC"; see NPC [NONPLAYER CHARACTER]) just replaces one type of virtual good for another in the system's database. This is not an "exchange" in an economic sense, but rather the destruction of one virtual good and the production of another.

Virtual production occurs when a person enters commands into a database which result in the creation of a new database item and the assignment of that item to the control of a person (usually the creator). The term *control* refers to the freedom to dispose of the good as the controller desires. Disposing can include giving to or trading with other people, which means placing the good in the control of someone else.

In some systems, the virtual good is considered the legal property of the person who controls it. In others, the controller is a temporary owner (lessee, tenant, or borrower), with ownership residing in the owners of the database.

Historically, the term *virtual economy* is closely tied to the term *virtual world*, which is a persistent online space where individuals can interact (see ONLINE WORLDS). Virtual economies were first identified as such within virtual worlds in the period 1995–2001. At that time, the evidence that virtual goods had significant economic value sparked reflection and discussion about the nature of goods and their representation.

Virtual worlds were the first computer systems to establish the basic prerequisites for virtual economies on a large scale. The prerequisites for any economy to exist include the presence of goods, the ability to produce and destroy goods, and the ability to exchange goods between people. A market economy requires *gains from trade*, which means that there are at least two goods in the possession of two different people, the goods are valued by the nonowner more than they are by the owner, and the goods can be exchanged. A production economy requires *production technology*, which includes the ability to obtain inputs and transform them into new goods. Implicit in these requirements is some process for moving, storing, and recording the location and ownership of goods.

Under these requirements, any number of economies may be created. Public goods economies or "commons" economies would include items usable by all. Club goods economies would include items owned by subsets of users (such as player guilds) but not the whole. Social economies can include goods whose production and distribution depend not just on individual decisions and markets but on the decisions of a governmental authority.

In a virtual environment the rules (physical, social, or laws) of a place can be defined differently than the rules of our "real" world. In a very genuine sense, the designers of virtual economies are policy makers. Some arrangements of rules might stifle economies, while others may allow them to prosper. As an example, designers interested in creating exchange, based on the principle of gains from trade, must focus on fairly simple rules. There must be variance in the utility of items across individuals, and there must be exchange.

The attachment of economic value to virtual goods is often considered puzzling. However, the human penchant for assigning value to intangibles and things of little objective use is actually quite common and well known. Take for example the diamond market. What makes the value of a diamond "real"? Diamonds don't have a remarkable amount of utility; they are small and very hard, with a few industrial uses in cutting and grinding. They are not even the rarest substances on the Earth. Yet diamonds are accorded very high prices in markets. This has much to do with their beauty, which is an intangible property. On top of this is the social, cultural, and reputational value of diamonds (being "a girl's best friend"), which is thoroughly constructed and has nothing to do with any underlying utility or practicality. Despite being based largely on social constructs, however, the diamond's value is very real. A man who cares nothing for diamonds, yet holds several in his hand, will treat them as though they are valuable indeed. Their value becomes genuine even for him because they can be traded at a certain high price. True, the height of the price stems from thoughts that, to him, only suggest that other people are crazy. Yet this madness of others, their desire for diamonds at almost any cost, forces our skeptic to treat the diamond as a truly valuable thing simply because of the price it commands.

Drawing the line around the concept of virtual economy can be difficult. Virtual economies often mix with economies based on nonvirtual goods. Some examples of this include reward points, token economies, art, frequent flier miles, antiques, baseball cards, and intellectual property/information. It is common for players of online games to trade virtual currency for nonvirtual currency. When this mixing occurs, it is useful to deploy a concept called the *magic circle*. This notion was introduced by Dutch historian Johan Huizenga in his 1938 work *Homo Ludens*. The magic circle identified the boundary between play activity and serious activity. Historically, virtual goods emerged in play environments such as online games (see EMERGENCE). However, as their genuine economic value became apparent, they began to be traded against other goods that were not within the magic circle. A very real emergent consequence of the economic value held by virtual goods is gold farming, which is a multibillion-dollar industry. Gold farmers are individuals who work for low wages, primarily in China, and continuously harvest virtual currency for sale to Westerners. The trade of virtual for real thus blurs the distinction between what is play and what is serious.

The issues here are more than conceptual. Governmental authority extends to all goods produced and exchanged in a country, and the regimen of taxation and regulation on the economy is extensive, heavy, and critically implicated in the well-being of all the citizens. The blurring of the magic circle thus raises questions about the extent to which a virtual economy can, should, must, or must not be regulated by the state.

The History and Current State of Virtual Economies

The first virtual world was created in the late 1970s (Bartle 2004). It was named Multiuser Dungeon (MUD) and was developed at the University of Essex by Roy Trubshaw and Richard Bartle (see MUDs AND MOOs). In MUD players filled the roles of heroes in a fantasy environment. Although digital items were probably traded before that point, MUD was unique because it was persistent and this quality lent itself to making economic transactions in the game more meaningful. Persistence meant that items didn't cease to exist when the game was over and transactions could be tracked and measured.

Since MUD the scope and scale of virtual worlds and virtual economies have increased exponentially. In 1997, the Korean virtual world *Lineage* housed a persistent virtual economy with over one million users. As of this writing, *World of Warcraft* has more than ten million users on a persistent basis. These virtual worlds are all games. Non-game virtual worlds have emerged, such as Second Life and Habbo Hotel. The program *Minecraft* enables users to create and share worlds with one another. Meanwhile, non-graphical social networks such as Facebook have created large interactive economies. The Facebook meta-economy is based on the Facebook Credit, which is usable now by some five hundred million people.

It is impossible at this time to accurately measure the extent or growth of the virtual economy. A virtual economic transaction occurs whenever a computer system user cedes control over a digital asset to another person. Transactions of this sort happen in a very wide array of systems, from social networks, to marketing promotions, to games. The numbers and types of different systems are such as to defy accurate aggregation. Only a major population survey would indicate how much economic value is being created and exchanged in virtual goods economies.

Virtual Money: Inflation and Emergence

Money serves three purposes: unit of account, means of exchange, and store of value. All three functions are useful in a virtual economy, and thus it is no surprise that currency has emerged as a central part of all virtual economy design. The exchange function dominates. Currency serves as a means to solve what is known as the double coincidence of wants. If I have something that you want, but you have nothing that I want, we are suffering from this problem. In a virtual economy with a large number of items and high degree of specialization the probability that two players will both have items that can be fairly exchanged one for the other is relatively low. This creates a need for a common unit by which goods can be exchanged.

Most virtual economies are given a currency by the creators. Money is introduced to the system through "faucets," which take the form of quest rewards, currency dropped by monsters, and the sale of items to nonplayer characters (NPCs). Money is removed through "sinks," events where users return virtual currency to the system in return for a good or service.

The value of this currency as a form of money is determined by faucets, sinks, and the player economy. If it is easy for the players to create net new money, yet hard for them to create new goods, then the rate of net money inflow (faucets-minus-sinks) will exceed the rate of goods production. According to the quantity theory of money, this situation results in inflation. Inflation is the decline in purchasing power of a unit of money: more money chasing fewer goods means more units of currency are needed to purchase a unit of goods. In some virtual economies, inflation has caused the official money to lose all value, so that millions and millions of units are required to purchase even a mundane item from another player.

The storage of large numbers of units may be impractical. For example, designers may have placed limits on the size of bank accounts or wallets, and there are always hard limits on the number of digits that a computer system can display. In some virtual worlds, money was given weight, which meant that hauling large sacks of coins was a practical impossibility.

Such circumstances have led, in the past, to the emergence of new money among the users. For example, the game *Diablo II* was created with ample opportunities for players to acquire and keep gold pieces, but relatively few opportunities to spend them. Since the rate of gold acquisition exceeded the rate of goods creation, eventually gold became worthless. Due to the low value of gold, a new currency emerged in the form of "Stones of Jordan" and "Perfect Skulls." Both of these items held their value better than gold and thus were more useful as currency.

Another form of emergent money is dragon kill points, or DKP. Large monsters in games often drop one very valuable item that can be allocated to just one player, even though it may have taken fifty or two hundred to kill the monster. DKP emerged as a way for player clubs to keep track of a player's contribution to raids over time. Each time the player participates, he earns a fixed amount of DKP. The DKP is tracked by other players acting as a neutral monetary authority. When big loot drops, players may bid for it using their DKP.

These emergent properties and value of virtual economies create economic policy issues quite similar to those facing national economic policy makers. Therefore, over the course of the past decade the designers of virtual worlds have begun to employ trained economists to monitor and navigate virtual economic policy. In the future it is likely that virtual worlds will be monitored even more closely as their value increases and the magic circle dissolves.

■ See also CYBERSPACE, DATABASE, GAME HISTORY, GAMES AND EDUCATION, MUDs AND MOOs, ONLINE WORLDS

References and Further Reading

Bartle, Richard. 2004. *Designing Virtual Worlds*. Indianapolis: New Riders.
Castronova, Edward. 2005. *Synthetic Worlds: The Business and Culture of Online Games*. Chicago: University of Chicago Press.
Dibbell, Julian. 2006. *Play Money: Or, How I Quit My Day Job and Made Millions Trading Virtual Loot*. New York: Basic Books.
Huizinga, Johan. 1955. *Homo Ludens: A Study of the Play Element in Culture*. Boston: Beacon Press.
Reeves, Byron, and Leighton J. Read. 2009. *Total Engagement: Using Games and Virtual Worlds to Change the Way People Work and Businesses Compete*. Boston: Harvard Business Press.

Virtual Reality
Ken Hillis

Though the idea of a virtual reality (VR) is as old as Plato's Cave, the earliest modern use of the term occurs in French playwright and author Antonin Artaud's 1938 treatise *The Theatre and Its Double* (translated into English in 1958). In it he makes the link between alchemical practices and the theater, asserting that theater can create a virtual reality (*la réalité virtuelle*) that transforms matter from spirit or mind and in which characters, images, and objects "take on the phantasmagoric force of alchemy's visionary internal dramas" (Davis 1998, 190). Perhaps recognizing the potential of such "phantasmagoric" alchemical visions, and directly influenced by the eighteenth- and nineteenth-century panorama and the wraparound experience of Cinerama film, American cinematographer and entrepreneur Morton Heilig (1926–1997) laid the groundwork for development of VR technology. In a series of patents, he detailed the arcade-like 3D Sensorama Simulator, an "apparatus to stimulate the senses of an individual to simulate an actual experience realistically" (Patent 3,050,870; filed August 28, 1962); "a stereoscopic television apparatus for individual use" (Patent 2,955,156; filed October 4, 1960), the prototype for head-mounted displays "that a person could wear like a pair of exceptionally bulky sunglasses" (Rheingold 1992, 58); and the Experience Theater, a blueprint for what would later be known as IMAX Theater (Patent 3,469,837; filed September 30, 1969). About the future of immersive simulation technologies Heilig wrote, "The screen will not fill only 5% of your visual field as the local movie does . . . but 100%. The screen will curve past the spectator's ears on both sides and beyond his sphere of vision above and below" (1992, 283).

The influence of the desire for theatrical illusion in the development of VR and its potential for commercialization by the entertainment industry were initially overshadowed by the American defense research establishment's interest in developing computerized visualization mechanisms at the service of intelligence augmentation and problem solving. Heilig's "self-funded work had inverted the 'commonsense' temporal hierarchy often thought to exist between military-industrial inventions and later socially diverting entertainment spin-offs" (Hillis 1999, 9). In the late 1970s and early 1980s, Media Lab researchers at MIT identified the qualitative experiential difference induced when the human sensorium was surrounded by rather than facing a screen. VR theorist Brenda Laurel wrote that their work "broke new ground" in understanding "the nature of the effects that immersion could induce" (1993, 204), though Heilig's entertainment-oriented patented research had earlier mined the same wraparound terrain. It is less Heilig than Ivan Sutherland, with his connections to the defense research establishment, who is widely credited with synthesizing the trajectory of American simulation research (Krueger 1991; Biocca 1992a). In 1965, while director of the Information Processing Techniques Office (IPTO)—the computing division of the U.S. Department of Defense's Advanced Research Projects Agency (ARPA)—Sutherland proposed "The Ultimate Display," writing, "A display connected to a digital computer . . . is a looking glass into a mathematical wonderland. . . . The ultimate display would . . . be a room within which the computer can control the existence of matter. . . . Handcuffs displayed in such a room would be confining, and a bullet displayed in such a room would be fatal. With appropriate programming such a display could literally be the Wonderland in which Alice walked" (1965, 506–508). It would appear that Artaud's "phantasmagoric force of alchemy's visionary internal dramas" underpins such a theatrical virtual wonderland from the earliest moments of its narrativization.

Technologies such as VR are assemblages informed by earlier technologies and past conventions, and Sutherland—a founder of Evans and Sutherland, a leading flight simulation company—references existing flight simulation research and development: "The force required to move a joystick [within an immersive virtual environment] could be computer controlled, just as the actuation force on the controls of a Link trainer are changed to give the feel of a real airplane" (1965, 507). After moving to Harvard from the IPTO, Sutherland authored "A Head-Mounted Three Dimensional Display" (1968). It accompanied his construction of a see-through helmet at MIT's Draper Lab (Stone 1992, 95) and preceded his building in 1969 of a prototype head-mounted display (HMD). Constructed at the University of Utah and financed by ARPA, the Office of Naval Research, and Bell Labs, the HMD used a "mechanical head tracker that fastened to the ceiling" and allowed a user to look around a simulated environment simply by turning his or her head (Brooks 1991, 11). Two small cathode-ray tubes provided stereo views for each eye (Krueger 1991, 68–69), and "objects displayed [by the HMD] appear to hang in the space all around the user" (Sutherland 1968, 757). Because of the size and weight of the assembly hanging directly above the user, it was nicknamed the "Sword of Damocles" (Brooks 1991, 11).

The OED's definition of VR is "a notional image or environment generated by computer software, with which a user can interact realistically, as by using a helmet containing a screen, gloves fitted with sensors, etc." (see CYBERSPACE). The definition carries within itself an acknowledgement of the popular acceptance of the idea that VR is largely a device for the technological reproduction of the real. Yet as an information technology-cum-ecology that allows for the simulated experience of human physical presence or being in computer-generated virtual environments, VR can model imaginary worlds as well as replicate actual world settings. This idea or conceptualization of VR is often associated with the American computer scientist Jaron Lanier, who, seeking an umbrella term to describe the many simulation projects under development during the 1980s (virtual worlds, virtual cockpits, virtual workstations, virtual environments), in 1989 coined the term *virtual reality* (Krueger 1991, xiii). Lanier was a founder of VPL Research, the first firm to sell VR gloves and goggles. Earlier work on VR had assumed a single user, but VPL engineered a system—"Reality Built for Two"—to allow more than one user to share a virtual space at the same time, thereby introducing the potential for networked VR applications and environments. While Lanier is credited with popularizing the term *virtual reality* and its association with full-immersion technologies using goggles and related devices, another American computer scientist, Myron Krueger, had been working since the 1970s on developing nonimmersive simulations of three-dimensional environments. He focused his research on the creation of what he called an "artificial reality" that would situate "the body's relationship to a simulated world" (Krueger 1991, xii). One outcome was VIDEOPLACE. In Krueger's description, "two-way telecommunication between two places creates a third place consisting of the information that is available to both communicating parties simultaneously. When two-way video is used, a shared visual environment that we call VIDEOPLACE is created" (1991, 37). The promise of both Lanier's immersive VR and Krueger's nonimmersive, avatar-reliant VR (which anticipates key components of online worlds such as Second Life) is that through the use of a communication medium users will experience the presence of another person or object at a remote location as if they were actually together in the same place. This is known as "telepresence."

Krueger, who brought together his interests in the arts and computer science, and who understood, like Artaud, that when one acts one becomes someone else and therefore may come to experience reality differently, noted that a virtual environment "is a medium of experience," thereby raising the phenomenological ways by which we come to know the world and understand our place in it. The importance of experience has meant that VR remains a hybrid term with many meanings. It has come to refer not only to a suite of technologies—the HMDs, data gloves, and the virtual environments to which they allow access and permit interpersonal communication and manipulation of virtual objects therein—but also to the individual or collective human experience (and therefore the practices and techniques associated with gaining this experience) constituted through such technological forms. VR draws together the sphere of technology and its ability to represent the nonhuman parts of the natural world, with the broad and overlapping spheres of human social relations and our experience of making meaning. Michael Heim (1993) implicitly points to this synthesis of meanings in his identification of seven divergent yet overlapping concepts that guide research on and understandings of VR (see VIRTUALITY): (1) *simulation* (the creation of highly realistic images with the use of computer graphics; see SIMULATION); (2) *interaction* (the ability to interact with virtual objects such as a virtual trash can on a computer display or in virtual places such as an online classroom; see INTERACTIVITY); (3) *artificiality* (the extension of VR to cover any artificial product of human construct); (4) *immersion* (human sensory immersion in a virtual environment through the use of specific hardware, including flight simulators, HMDs, feedback gloves, joysticks, and other input devices; see IMMERSION); (5) *telepresence* (the sense of being both here and present elsewhere); (6) *full body immersion* (human sensory immersion without the use of cumbersome equipment, as in Heilig's Experience Theatre and Krueger's VIDEOPLACE); and (7) *networked communications* (VR as a communications medium in which more than one person can simultaneously share immersive virtual environments).

The idea of VR achieved its greatest popularity during the last decade of the twentieth century. Its ability to seize the technical imaginary during this period was linked to a massive amount of hype that promised a distributed VR of networked computers that would allow people to share the same virtual world and interact in real time. People were encouraged to believe that they might actually travel through "cyberspace" to exotic places without leaving their homes. Issues of cost, insufficient bandwidth, and the physical awkwardness of donning cumbersome HMDs replete with encumbering wiring all played a role in reducing public interest. While the inability of the technology to live up to industry and overheated press accounts partly explains the waning of media coverage, this in no way diminishes hype's centrality within the political economy of technology diffusion and therefore hype's necessary value to VR proponents. Neither can it account for how hype itself crucially inflects human sensory perception. At the increasingly seamless interface where popular culture meets commercially inflected desire, VR's status during this period as "the next thing" was critical in sparking consumer desire for more accessible interactive technologies that were finally commercialized less as immersive VR and more so in web formats such as multiuser virtual environments (MUVEs) like Second Life (see ONLINE WORLDS) and mobile communication technologies increasingly identified as locative media or augmented reality (AR), or a convergence of the two (see AUGMENTED REALITY). Google's 2012 announcement of Google Goggles is a case in point. Though the technology has yet to reach the door of the lab, advertisements indicate that the AR interface will be integrated into our person or at least our point of view through wearing a pair of glasses with a thumbnail-sized screen above the right eye. Aspects of VR's HMD clearly remain, but the point now is to deliver information about the real world and less to engage a wide variety of fantastical and prosaic virtual environments as a means of augmenting human intelligence.

As a technology and a research area, however, immersive VR continues to advance, particularly with respect to military, medical, and automotive diagnostic applications. For example, the University of Washington's Human Interface Technology Lab (HITLab), together with Microvision, one of its corporate spin-offs, has developed applications for burn victims' pain management, therapy for spider phobia, and management of post-traumatic stress disorder (PTSD) (HITLab, n.d.). Microvision has also developed AR products for vehicle displays, as well as wearable displays that anticipate Google Goggles and use the human retina as a screen onto which visual information is projected and perceived as geometric images floating in the "middle distance" (Hillis 2005; Microvision

2012). Retinal scanning and display achieve the kind of virtual/real hybrid of computer-generated and flesh-based vision also depicted in films such as *RoboCop* (1987) and *Iron Man* (2008). AR retains VR's formal ability to suggest to users' perceptions that its interface dispenses with a frame, but whereas fully immersive VR implies that users might become part of its display, AR presses in a different way against "the real" through its ability to demonstrate how the virtual is freeing itself from the restricted space of the display to take its place as an overlay on and merger with embodied human sight.

■ See also INTERFACE

References and Further Reading

Artaud, Antonin. (1938) 1958. *Theatre and Its Double*. Translated by Mary Caroline Richards. New York: Grove Press.

Biocca, Frank. 1992a. "Communication within Virtual Reality: Creating a Space for Research." *Journal of Communication* 42 (4): 5–22.

———. 1992b. "Virtual Reality Technology: A Tutorial." *Journal of Communication* 42 (4): 23–72.

Brooks, Fred. 1991. "Statement of Dr. Fred Brooks." In *New Developments in Computer Technology: Virtual Reality*. Hearing before the Subcommittee on Science, Technology, and Space of the Committee on Commerce, Science, and Transportation, United States Senate, S. Hrg. 102–553, May 8.

Davis, Erik. 1998. *Techgnosis: Myth, Magic and Mysticism in the Age of Information*. New York: Three Rivers Press.

Heilig, Morton. 1992. "Enter the Experiential Revolution: A VR Pioneer Looks Back to the Future." In *Cyberarts: Exploring Arts and Technology*, edited by Linda Jacobson, 292–306. San Francisco: Miller Freeman.

Heim, Michael. 1993. *The Metaphysics of Virtual Reality*. Oxford: Oxford University Press.

Hillis, Ken. 1999. *Digital Sensations: Space, Identity, and Embodiment in Virtual Reality*. Minneapolis: University of Minnesota Press.

———. 2005. "The Dream of a Virtual Life: From Plato to Microsoft." In *Dream Extensions*, 94–108. Gent, Belgium: S.M.A.K.

HITLab. n.d. "Virtual Reality Pain Reduction." www.hitl.washington.edu/projects/vrpain/.

Krueger, Myron W. 1991. *Artificial Reality II*. Reading, MA: Addison-Wesley.

Laurel, Brenda. 1993. *Computers as Theater*. Reading, MA: Addison-Wesley.

Lauria, Rita. 2001. "In Love with Our Technology: Virtual Reality: A Brief Intellectual History of the Idea of Virtuality and the Emergence of a Media Environment." *Convergence* 7 (4): 30–51.

Microvision. 2012. "Wearable Displays: Overview." www.microvision.com/displayground/tag/wearable-displays/.

Rheingold, Harold. 1992. *Virtual Reality*. New York: Simon & Schuster.

Stone, Allucquère Roseanne. 1992. "Virtual Systems." In *Incorporations*, edited by Jonathan Crary and Sanford Kwinter, 608–625. New York: Zone Books.

Sutherland, Ivan. 1965. "The Ultimate Display." In *Proceedings of the International Federation of Information Processing Societies*, 506–508. New York: IFIPS Congress.

———. 1968. "A Head-Mounted Three Dimensional Display." In *AFIPS Conference Proceedings* 33.1, 757–764. Washington, DC: Thompson.

Virtuality
Michael Heim

The paradox of virtuality runs through twists and turns in the history of language. The "virtual" for first-century Romans indicated manly strength and straightforward power (Latin *vir*), what Italian courtiers would in the Renaissance dub *virtu*.

Medieval thinkers downshifted the meaning of the Roman word as scholastics such as Thomas Aquinas (ca. 1250) distinguished a power existing in something "inherently" or *virtualiter* as opposed to essentially (*essentialiter*) or actually (*actualiter*). Here the virtuality of a thing is no longer its power to be present straightforwardly with strength. The strong but now less visibly intrinsic power fades even more in the fourteenth-century English term, which was borrowed from the French *virtuel*, by which "virtual" came to mean something that is implicit but not formally recognized, something that is indeed present but not openly admitted—something there virtually but not really or actually there. This weaker, nearly invisible virtuality would blossom into a new semantic flower as the need for a computer-based aesthetics arose in the 1980s. Computers began to simulate digitized objects as recognizably vivid phenomena. The newly digitized phenomena were visible with many of the characteristics of primary realities and needed a new descriptive term. The virtual object was now a functional object—even reproduced as a three-dimensional object—but now generated in a digital environment. The historical linguistic paradox—strong presence dimmed to near invisibility followed by subtle presence—parallels the broader general paradox of contemporary virtuality.

The paradox: virtuality succeeds by disappearing. At its diaphanous best, virtuality vanishes into sheer transparency. Once software flows smoothly throughout the contours of human gestures, needs, and desires, there is a feeling of unmediated activity. One deals with the things themselves, not with software or virtuality as such. As virtual reality (VR) advocates claimed in the 1980s and 1990s, the computer will eventually disappear, and so will virtuality itself. With cultural adaptation, the realities themselves exist in the virtual, and as wrinkles smooth out, old habits and entire economies assume a new configuration. The high profile of stand-alone virtuality fades into an early stage of epochal realignment.

Virtuality is at first highly visible. Prior to routine digitization, a Platonic yearning wants to carve out a separate uncontaminated space, an independent realm of pure computer control. Thus idealized, VR enjoys hermetic properties and stimulates speculative imagination. For Ivan Sutherland (1968) virtuality was a set of floating light cubes perceived through boom-style monitors. For Myron Krueger (1991) virtuality was a "smart environment" where bodily movements evoke real-time computer responses perceived by simultaneous users who physically share the same artificial setting. For Jaron Lanier (whose data glove was patented in 1989) VR was a data glove and goggles that manipulate a cornucopia of three-dimensional objects that can outrun the symbols of spoken language. Decades later, mobile microcomputing would replace the holy grail of "full-blown" VR with mundane smartphones, digital office tools, and a wide variety of electronic toys for the home. Virtuality recedes as it becomes ubiquitous, a subconscious component of everyday life. What was once a transcendent research goal merges with everyday activities as they float suspended in the cloud of nested computer networks. The semantic need fades for a specialized vocabulary to isolate "virtual worlds," "avatars," and "telepresence." The semantic remnants of the terms now scatter across every field of routine activity.

Two major phases of virtuality mark its evolution:

1. VR as portal to a private world of simulation where physical senses are immersed in sensory data passed through prosthetic devices where users temporarily "forget" their primary sensory world (1980–2000).

2. VR as a convenient communication tool where human contact transcends the constrictions imposed by limited sensory data transmitted by electronic networks (2000–present).

Straddling both phases is the computer gaming industry, where compelling action reduces the need for full-scale visualization and where commercial design continually pushes the envelope for richer graphics and cinematic production values. Of the two phases, the second phase dominates as human contact and commerce expand exponentially on computers. This second trend overcomes sensory constrictions by supporting shared connectivity under the changing conditions of mobility and convenience.

To some, virtuality is an alternate universe; to others, it is simply an additional layer in the given conditions of human interaction. Immersive VR elevates the holy grail of realism to metaphysical heights. The pursuit of realism can push beyond the aesthetic trompe l'oeil to project a new mission for humanity: uploading mind, body, and cultural world to an artificial plane free from the restrictions imposed by nature. The final fantasy of transhumanism is to release carbon-based mind-bodies from temporal and spatial forms, enabling escape from planet Earth in the search for other solar habitations. This transhumanist or utopian teleology faces serious problems of data conversion.

For continental theorists of the 1980s and 1990s, virtuality became a metonymic trope for mapping a whole gamut of postmodern phenomena. Abandoning metaphysics for Saussurean linguistics, many semioticians, such as Jean Baudrillard, collapsed the virtuality/reality distinction into a social system of binary oppositions that inscribe social hierarchies and that function as conventions in communication. A finely constructed system of cultural signs then replaces any ontological anchors, and the theorist then analyzes, parses, and/or deconstructs the significance of the symbols. Thus, Baudrillard (1987) views virtuality as an all-encompassing drive toward ungrounded simulations (simulacra), which in extreme form yield hyperreal social fabrications that mask or deny reality, even though actualities are already suspended by Saussurean semiotics. Virtuality becomes the technological proliferation of simulacra that lack ontological referents. For dystopian Baudrillard, the postmodern population is a passive victim of technomedia that have twisted the Enlightenment's goals to master and control experience. The seductive obsession with digital phantoms leads to an apocalyptic "end of reality" in which communal sensation (Gibson's "collective hallucination"; see CYBERPUNK) usurps individual experience and theory itself emerges as sensationalist commentary (Baudrillard's "The Gulf War never happened"). Individual power to control or adapt virtual technology fades for Baudrillard as corporate media admits personal agency only to consumers, and consumer activities are limited to choices made for packaged commodities. Baudrillard's references to "Late Capitalism" may imply leftovers of the grand Marxist narrative of economic determinism, but this emancipatory story is not argued in his works.

Opposite Baudrillard on the spectrum of optimism/pessimism is the French theorist Pierre Lévy. Lévy's (1999) notion of collective intelligence acknowledges virtuality as having a distinct relationship to actual items in the world. The virtual, while standing in a relationship to the actual, forms its own independent culture or "cyberculture" (Lévy 2001). Lévy sees cyberculture as developing nonnatural or supernatural properties. As a collective memory is built in cyberspace networks, individual human choices are assembled and sorted through enormously complex algorithms (see CYBERSPACE). The process is so vast in scope and accuracy that human intelligence—as human-computer artifact—improves over time. Collective intelligence, not unlike Teilhard de Chardin's "noosphere," is a new global entity whose development marks a shift in history. The virtual is more than simply a new artifact that reflects the actual world; it also belongs to cyberculture, and cyberculture opens new possibilities for actually existing things. Thus, Lévy recognizes a complex dialectic between the virtual and the actual. The potential for things uploaded to cyberculture does not create a detached and obsessive hallucination, as in Baudrillard, but instead offers a positively helpful interplay between humans and the items of the actual world. Cyberculture transforms things into media artifacts, but the artifacts stand in relationship to actual things themselves. So Lévy celebrates an expanding human awareness achieved by connectivity on the global scale and by the digitization of things available to human experience. This two-pronged process of cyberculture transforms both things and human awareness. In this way, Lévy avoids the narcissistic focus of transhumanism while also acknowledging a power increase that digitization brings to research, development, and most facets of everyday life. Lévy's work continues to have relevance to the twenty-first century, although his unbridled enthusiasm for collective improvement may not match the felt experience of people in the actual workplace.

The contemporary workplace, where most people spend much of their time, shows a reluctance to adopt full-blown VR. An instinctive resistance to VR may signal a healthy psychological need to counterbalance technology trends. Office workers today who work, paradoxically, from home tend to develop mixed versions of telepresence rather than using integrated virtual worlds. They tend to use

- mobile access to shared data on the web;
- avatars composed of selected photo fragments;
- instant messaging and shared desktops;
- webcasts for company meetings rather than in-world events; and
- telephone voice conferences with shared desktops.

A loose and inventive approach to using the computer grid may indicate a collective movement away from the single-minded pursuit of virtuality. The single mind can envision deeply immersive systems, but the mind is inevitably engaged in a socially constructed world that lifts the visions of "reality for one" into the broader network of social communication (see ONLINE WORDS, SOCIAL NETWORK SITES [SNSs]).

The paradox of virtuality prompts a look at past speculative trends, how they change, and how the present trend now unfolds toward possible futures. The terms that once beamed a numinous radiance are now stamped into the everyday coins of commerce: "avatars" can suggest a wide range of composited aesthetic elements; "virtual worlds" and "virtual reality" are spread tenuously and used loosely. Social adoption brings new uses for old things. The new normal comes from things once held strange and wonderful. "The Street," as cyberpunk Gibson puts it, "finds its own uses for things—uses the manufacturers never imagined" (quoted in Benedikt 1991, 29).

Idealized virtuality can sketch abstract artifacts that change under conditions of actual usage. Twentieth-century philosophy, led by Heidegger and Wittgenstein, criticized the modern tendency to disengage models or paradigms from their at-hand applications. The disengaged and external vantage point is an abstraction that lacks the give-and-take of applied experience. Both Heidegger's *Lichtung* and Wittgenstein's *Lebensform* point to the need for a repeated re-grounding of ideals in the grit of human activity where things are "defined" more by existential practice than by the imaginings of a disengaged speculative mind. The normalization of technology, its "street use," suggests that, rather than construct theories about virtuality, it is more fruitful to attend to the many very particular practices that currently infiltrate everyday activities. Contemporary life is replete with virtuality in different shapes and forms, and there is little need to construct a special model to understand virtuality. The "Street" continues to surprise, delight, and refute any and all ideas of what VR is or can be. The term *virtual* belongs to the heyday of a creative digitization that will soon look and sound quaint. The normalization of technology is the other side of Wittgenstein's motto to the *Philosophical Investigations*: "Progress always seems larger than it really is." A careful look at past speculation can help adjust the illusions that appear in the rearview mirror as the drive to progress steers ever forward.

518
Virtuality

■ See also AUGMENTED REALITY, CROWDSOURCING, HISTORY OF COMPUTERS, IMMERSION, INTERACTIVITY

References and Further Reading

Barfield, Woodrow, and Thomas A. Furness, eds. 1995. *Virtual Environments and Advanced Interface Design*. New York: Oxford University Press.

Baudrillard, Jean. 1995. *Simulacra and Simulation*. Translated by Sheila Faria Glaser. Ann Arbor: University of Michigan Press.

Benedikt, Michael L., ed. 1991. *Cyberspace: First Steps*. Cambridge, MA: MIT Press.

Bracken, Cheryl Campanella, and Paul D. Skalsi, eds. 2010. *Immersed in Media: Telepresence in Everyday Life*. New York: Taylor & Francis.

Burdea, Grigore, and Philippe Coiffet, eds. 2003. *Virtual Reality Technology*. 2nd ed. New Jersey: John Wiley & Sons.

Cahill, Kevin. 2006. "The Concept of Progress in Wittgenstein's Thought." *Review of Metaphysics* 60:71–100.

Coyne, Richard. 2001. *Technoromanticism: Digital Narrative, Holism, and the Romance of the Real*. Cambridge, MA: MIT Press.

Ellis, Stephen R., Mary K. Kaiser, and Arthur C. Grunwald, eds. 1991. *Pictorial Communication in Virtual and Real Environments*. New York: Taylor & Francis.

Gibson, William. 1989. "Rocket Radio." *Rolling Stone*, June 15.

Hayles, Katherine. 1999. *How We Became Posthuman: Virtual Bodies in Cybernetics, Literature, and Informatics*. Chicago: University of Chicago Press.

Heim, Michael. (1987) 1999. *Electric Language: A Philosophy Study of Word Processing*. New Haven, CT: Yale University Press.

———. 1993. *The Metaphysics of Virtual Reality*. New York: Oxford University Press.

———. 1998. *Virtual Realism*. New York: Oxford University Press.

Jakobsson, Mikael. 2003. "A Virtual Realist Primer to Virtual World Design." In *Searching Voices: Towards a Canon for Interaction Design*, edited by Pelle Ehn and Jonas Löwgren, 73–87. Malmö, Sweden: Malmö University Press.

Krueger, Myron. 1991. *Artificial Reality II*. Reading, MA: Addison-Wesley.

Lévy, Pierre. 1999. *Collective Intelligence: Mankind's Emerging World in Cyberspace*. Translated by Robert Bononno. New York: Basic Books.

———, ed. 2001. *Cyberculture*. 1st ed. Minneapolis: University of Minnesota Press.

Lunenfeld, Peter, ed. 2000. *The Digital Dialectic: New Essays on New Media*. Cambridge, MA: MIT Press.

Ommeln, Miriam. 2005. *Die Technologie der Virtuellen Realitaet*. Frankfurt am Main: Peter Lang.

Papacharissi, Zizi A., ed. 2011. *A Networked Self: Identity, Community and Culture on Social Network Sites*. New York: Taylor & Francis.

Pearce, Celia, and Artemesia. 2009. *Communities of Play: Emergent Cultures in Multiplayer Games and Virtual Worlds*. Cambridge, MA: MIT Press.

Rheingold, Howard. 1991. *Virtual Reality*. New York: Summit Books.

Rossi, Diego. 2010. *L'estasi dell'uomo sperimentale*. Rome: Aracne.

Schroeder, Ralph, and Ann-Sofie Axelsson, eds. 2010. *Avatars at Work and Play: Collaboration and Interaction in Shared Virtual Environments*. Dordrecht, Netherlands: Springer.

Stanney, Kay M., ed. 2002. *The Handbook of Virtual Environments: Design, Implementation, and Applications*. Mahwah, NJ: Lawrence Erlbaum Associates.

Sutherland, Ivan. 1968. "A Head-Mounted Three Dimensional Display." In *Proceedings of Fall Joint Computer Conference*, 757–764. http://portal.acm.org/citation.cfm?id=1476686.

Taylor, Charles. 1995. "Lichtung or Lebensform: Parallels between Heidegger and Wittgenstein." In *Philosophical Arguments*, 61–78. Cambridge, MA: Harvard University Press.

Zudilova-Seinstra, Elena, Tony Adriaansen, and Robert van Liere, eds. 2009. *Trends in Interactive Visualization: State-of-the-Art*. London: Springer.

Walkthrough

Frederik De Grove and Jan Van Looy

In its most basic form, a walkthrough is a text describing step by step how to complete (part of) a digital game. In practice, walkthroughs often comprise additional information such as maps of the game space, lists of items and their characteristics, cheat codes, tips on how to build characters, and strategies to use. Hence, there can be considerable overlap with other types of paratext to the game such as game guides, strategy guides, and frequently asked questions (FAQs) (Crawford 2012).

Walkthroughs are sometimes commercially provided, but in most cases they are created by players. This requires a significant amount of time, effort, and mastery of the game and is often a collaborative project by several authors based on requests by the broader community (Karaganis 2007; Newman, 2005, 2008). Providing a walkthrough generally rewards the author(s) with a certain status within the game community. Thus, the practices of producing, adapting, and making use of walkthroughs are firmly rooted within fan culture and the broader game community (see GAMES AND EDUCATION, PARTICIPATORY CULTURE).

Whereas in the past walkthroughs consisted mostly of written text, the popularity of video-sharing platforms has given rise to a multitude of walkthroughs in audiovisual formats. Due to the nature of the medium, audiovisual walkthroughs tend to focus on showing how players can complete (parts of) the game. Written text, on the other hand, is generally deemed more suited to providing additional information such as maps and lists of items and their corresponding features.

■ See also CHEATS, WORLDS AND MAPS

References and Further Reading

Crawford, Garry. 2012. *Video Gamers*. London: Routledge.
Karaganis, Joe. 2007. *Structures of Participation in Digital Culture*. New York: Social Science Research Council.
Newman, James. 2005. "Playing (with) Videogames." *Convergence: The International Journal of Research into New Media Technologies* 11 (1): 48.
———. 2008. *Playing with Videogames*. London: Routledge.

Web Comics

Karin Kukkonen

Web comics are comics (primarily) published on and distributed through the Internet. Some, but by far not all, of these comics make use of the affordances of digitalization. Web comics are usually individual and nonprofessional efforts, and even though larger infrastructures exist, no web comics industry comparable to the print comics industry has emerged.

Reportedly, the first web comic was Erik Milikin's *Witches and Stiches*, which began its run in 1985. In the 1990s, the number of web comics rose steadily, with the arrival of now-established web comics such as *PhD* (1997–), *Penny Arcade* (1998–), and *PvP* (1998–). The 2000s saw an explosion of web comics, as collectives were established and more and more creators put their work online. Most established web comics update on a regular basis, often one to three times a week. In some cases, this leads to run numbers of over one thousand installments (the run of *Sluggy Freelance*, for example, is currently four thousand). However, web comics can also change their URLS rapidly, end their run abruptly, or be taken off the web entirely. Because of the less professionalized environment of web comics, the majority of them only exist as long as the author has interest in them.

In *Reinventing Comics* (2000), McCloud outlines three revolutions connected to web comics: digital production, digital delivery, and digital comics. Not only web comics but also increasingly print comics are produced digitally. However, digital delivery (or distribution) is the point at which web comics differ most clearly from printed comics. Even if they do not often make use of digital affordances, web comics are "pure information" in the sense that they are distributed in digital form through the Internet.

Distribution and Infrastructures

Distribution through the Internet means that creators with their own web page can reach a large audience without having to work for a comics publisher and having to rely on their distribution networks with comics shops and booksellers. These creator web pages feature the latest installment of the web comic, an archive of previous installments, information on the creator, a forum for communication with and between readers, and sometimes a web store (Allen 2001; Partridge 2005; Zanfei 2008). Successful web comics, such as *Penny Arcade* or *Ctrl+Alt+Del*, have a wide readership and monthly viewings in the millions (according to their self-report), and they can rely on income from advertising and merchandise. Other successful creators publish print anthologies of their web comics (like *Sinfest* or *PvP*), or their web comic is syndicated into newspapers (like *PhD—Piled Higher and Deeper* in the *Times Higher Education*). In turn, many popular newspaper comics are published in online syndication as well as in the print medium.

Apart from creator web pages, a number of web comic collectives have emerged, which host web comics (such as *Drunk Duck*, *Webcomics Nation*, *Comic Genesis*, and *ComicFury*). These comics collectives publish individual work on their pages, but they also present crossover narratives (combining characters and storylines from their different comics) and sometimes list comics according to popularity. DC Comics, an established print comics publisher, began its own web comic collective, Zuda Comics, in 2007, with editorially driven web comics and structured talent submissions, but it subsequently closed down in 2010. There are a number of general services and web pages dedicated to web comics, such as wikis for web comics and web comics–related topics (such as *Comix-Pedia*). Web comics listings with synopses of content and links (e.g., *Belfry WebComics Listing, The Webcomic List*), blogs (e.g., *WebSnark*), and podcasts (e.g., *The Webcomic Beacon, Webcomics Weekly*) provide readers and amateur creators of web comics with orientation in this frequently changing field. Between 2001 and 2008, Web Cartoonists' Choice Awards were given out. In the past decade, organizations that generally honor print comics, such as the Eisner Awards, have introduced categories for web comics or digital comics. However, no wide-ranging institutionalization of web comics has taken place as of yet.

522
Web Comics

Properties of Digital Comics

Like printed comics, web comics combine images and words in panel sequences in order to tell a story. The images depict the situation, setting, and characters involved in an exchange. Written words are included in captions (i.e., text boxes) when the speech is not located, temporally and/or spatially, in the image. They are included in speech bubbles or thought bubbles when the speech is attributed to a character in the image. Panel sequences can either represent different parts of the same scene, sometimes located in the fictional mind of a character, or associate different scenes by combining them. Web comics usually take the form of either a comic strip (a row of panels) or a comics page.

The row of panels in the comic strip is the most convenient for display on a computer screen, and therefore highly popular for web comics, but there are also a significant number of page-based web comics. The web comics in the comic strip format usually tell short, humorous narratives building up to a punch line and stand in the tradition of the newspaper comic strip. Often, they have a consistent set of characters which is revisited in the different installments (like in *Sinfest*), or they feature the persona of the writer(s) (like in *Penny Arcade*). Web comics that use the traditional page format tend to tell longer stories in their installments. The genres vary from adventure (like *Dr McNinja*) to horror and science fiction (like *Gone with the Blastwave*). Web comics tend to reflect on communities of heavy computer users and their cultural expressions, such as computer games, science fiction, anime, and role-playing (Fenty, Houp, and Taylor 2004). As the character Strongbad puts it in a parody about web comics, "They're all about video games, gamernerds, webgeeks, dorknerds, gamewads, nerdgames, webwebs, and elves" (on *TV Tropes*). Examples of this trend, which contributes to a strong intermediality in web comics, are *Order of the Stick, Ctrl+Alt+Delete*, and *Penny Arcade*. However, by no means do all web comics service only the target audience of heavy computer users.

As Scott McCloud puts it in *Reinventing Comics*, "digital comics are comics that exist as pure information" (2000, 203). It seems, however, that in general web comics did not capitalize on the affordances that the malleability of the digital medium brings. Only very few comics (e.g., *Argon Zark!*) experiment with animations in the panel images, Easter egg effects that unfold as readers move the mouse over the image, or speech bubbles that appear one by one on the screen (see EASTER EGGS).

Web comics mostly employ drawing techniques similar to printed comics, from simple black outlines in the drawings to detailed colored renderings. Some web comics use photography (such as *Irregular Webcomic!*, which features photographs of LEGO figurines) or reproduce nineteenth-century prints in their images (such as *New Adventures of Queen Victoria* and *Edison Hate Future*). Some other web comics reproduce the same image in each of their panels, changing only the dialogue (e.g., *Dinosaur Comics*). Some web comics are drawn digitally (e.g., *T.H.E. Fox, Order of the Stick*), or they are created using a pastiche of computer game characters (e.g., *8bit Theatre*). Each of these techniques, however, is well within the affordances of printed comics, as the photo novel genre and printed comics based on digitally rendered images (e.g., Gaiman and McKean's *Mr. Punch*) document.

Scott McCloud, a comics author himself, presents a number of examples of the uses of digital effects in web comics on his web page: in "The Right Number," readers click into the middle of a panel to move to the next panel in a combination of hyperlink and zoom animation. Animations rotating the panels or moving the eyes of the characters are added for narrative effect. In "Carl," readers initially see the first and the last panel of the narrative. By clicking, they can add extra panels in between. These additional panels give new information, bring new characters and events, and force readers to continually recast their inferences about the chain of events making up the plot, as well as the motivations of characters. In "Mimi's Last Coffee," readers see the entire sequence of panels in miniature strings of images. In order to read the comic, readers need to zoom in by clicking on an individual panel. As the plot forks, so do the strings of panel sequences, and readers need to decide which direction to keep scrolling into.

McCloud calls comics like "Mimi's Last Coffee," which feature a panel sequence extending beyond the screen, "infinite canvas" comics. Infinite canvas comics have no cut-off points in the panel sequence like traditional newspaper comics or comic books, a feature that most web comics carried across the media boundary. For infinite canvas comics, the monitor functions not as a page but as a window (McCloud 2000, 222) on the "temporal map" of the narrative (2000, 215). McCloud moves away from the seriality of traditional comics narratives and suggests supplanting this feature with a rendition of continuous spatial imagination similar to William Gibson's cyberspace (2000, 231). Some of the comics on McCloud's web page, as well as comics by other creators, such as *Wormworld Saga* and *When I Am King*, explore the narrative possibilities of infinite canvas comics, but the majority of web comics remain serialized, contained panel sequences connected by hyperlinks.

At the end of the 1990s, web comics seemed to promise a new revolution in the field of comics, after movements for creators' rights, diversification, and reevaluations for printed comics had stopped in their tracks (see McCloud 2000). From today's point of view, web comics have offered a new platform for independent and alternative comics (see also Fenty, Houp, and Taylor 2004). The expectation of a radical innovation of the way comics tell their stories has not been borne out, however, and most web comics either concern themselves with issues close to web user communities (such as gamers) or place themselves firmly in the tradition of the newspaper strip. With the fluidity of the digital medium, however, this landscape might change rapidly.

■ See also DIGITAL AND NET ART, ELECTRONIC LITERATURE, GLITCH AESTHETICS, INTERACTIVITY, INTERFACE, MEDIALITY, NONLINEAR WRITING, WORD-IMAGE

References and Further Reading

Allen, Jeremy. 2001. "A Virtual Revolution: Australian Comic Creators and the Web." *International Journal of Comic Art* 3 (1): 22–37.

Fenty, Sean, Trena Houp, and Laurie Taylor. 2004. "Webcomics: The Influence and Continuation of the Comix Revolution." *ImageText: Interdisciplinary Comics Studies* 1 (2). www.english.ufl.edu /imagetext/archives/v1_2/group/.

McCloud, Scott. 2000. *Reinventing Comics: How Imagination and Technology Are Revolutionizing an Art Form.* New York: Perennial.

Partridge, Myra. 2005. "Webtoonists: Making a Living Online." *International Journal of Comic Art* 7 (1): 504–512.

"Webcomics." 2011. *TV Tropes,* June 5. http://tvtropes.org/pmwiki/pmwiki.php/Main/Webcomics.

Zanfei, Anna. 2008. "Defining Webcomics and Graphic Novels." *International Journal of Comics Art* 10 (1): 55–61.

Selected Web Comics

Argon Zark! 2007. Created by Charley Parker. www.zark.com/.

Gone with the Blastwave. 2011. Created by Kimmo Lemetti. www.blastwave-comic.com/index.php.

Irregular Webcomic! 2011. Created by David Morgan-Mar. www.irregularwebcomic.net/.

McCloud, Scott. 2009. "Webcomics." *Scottmccloud.com.* http://scottmccloud.com/1-webcomics /index.html.

Penny Arcade. 2011. Written by Jerry Holkins, illustrated by Mike Krahulik. www.penny-arcade .com/.

Sinfest. 2011. Created by Tatsuya Ishida. www.sinfest.net/.

....

Wiki Writing

Seth Perlow

Wiki writing enables users of a website to collaboratively add, edit, or delete content from the site through a browser-based interface. A typical wiki site consists of multiple distinct pages hyperlinked to one another and structured as independent articles, each covering a particular topic. Most wikis open with a welcome page offering news and announcements, an article search field, and excerpts from featured articles. Each article initially displays as a noneditable web page that may include text, hyperlinks, pictures and graphics, video, and other multimedia objects. Users can then choose to edit an article; to view the article's "talk" page, where users discuss possible changes or additions; and in some cases to view the article's history, which records the date and time of each edit and the username or IP address of the user who made it. Since the invention of wiki writing in the mid-1990s, numerous wikis have facilitated knowledge sharing and information management in many different contexts. The most notable such site is *Wikipedia,* a publicly editable online encyclopedia founded in 2001.

Wiki means "fast" in Hawaiian. Inspired by the interlinked structure of Apple's HyperCard program, Ward Cunningham developed and named the wiki protocol in 1994, and he launched the first wiki site, WikiWikiWeb, in March 1995. Cunningham wrote the original wiki software using the Perl programming language, but there are now dozens of wiki software packages, both proprietary and open-source, that utilize a variety of languages and file systems. Most wikis employ a syntax called "wiki markup" for editing, a simpler alternative to HyperText Markup Language (HTML), but many editing interfaces can display editable content as it will appear after changes are saved.

The authorship of most wikis is functionally anonymous. Because of a wiki's collaborative structure, a given text may have been edited by many different users, and because the default view omits editing history to improve readability, casual users do not consider authorship. This functional anonymity has sparked debate about the reliability of *Wikipedia* and other wikis as sources of information and tools for academic research (see COLLECTIVE INTELLIGENCE). A study in *Nature* compared scientific articles in *Wikipedia* with their equivalents in the *Encyclopedia Britannica*, concluding that the two were comparably reliable (Giles 2005). Subsequent studies have produced similar results but have illuminated the differences between wikis and conventional references. Wiki writing relies on a large population of users to produce articles on a breadth of topics, but research suggests that wiki articles provide less depth of information, fail to balance attention to all aspects of a topic, and may omit important facts. A public wiki is open to vandalism, and in some cases individuals or corporations have removed negative facts about themselves. Conventional reference sources rely on the expertise of their authors and editors to provide more reliable and balanced articles, but the large number of users on some wikis enables swift and effective error correction, often within minutes of an error's appearance. Despite its advantages, scholars have proved reluctant to accept wiki writing as a reliable means of sharing information.

■ See also AUTHORING SYSTEMS, COLLECTIVE INTELLIGENCE, FREE AND OPEN-SOURCE SOFTWARE, LINKING STRATEGIES, OLD MEDIA / NEW MEDIA, PARTICIPATORY CULTURE

References and Further Reading

Cunningham, Ward, and Bo Leuf. 2001. *The Wiki Way: Quick Collaboration on the Web*. Boston: Addison-Wesley.

Giles, Jim. 2005. "Internet Encyclopedias Go Head to Head." *Nature* 438:900–901.

Lih, Andrew. 2009. *The Wikipedia Revolution: How a Bunch of Nobodies Created the World's Greatest Encyclopedia*. New York: Hyperion.

Reagle, Joseph Michael, Jr. 2010. *Good Faith Collaboration: The Culture of Wikipedia*. Cambridge, MA: MIT Press.

Shirky, Clay. 2008. *Here Comes Everybody: The Power of Organizing without Organizations*. New York: Penguin.

Windows

Jay David Bolter

The window is one of the principle metaphors in the "graphical user interface" (GUI), which remains the primary visual interface for desktop and laptop computers. Elements of the GUI are sometimes summarized in the acronym WIMP (windows, icons, menus, and pointing device). The window is typically a resizable, framed rectangle on the computer screen containing various forms of information: text, graphics, video, or combinations of these three. In the 1960s Douglas Engelbart's NLS (On-Line System) had pioneered the presentation of multiple data areas on the screen. In the 1970s a team at Xerox PARC including Alan Kay developed a coherent interface in which overlapping windows, with title bars and scrolling, constituted a key feature. Steve Jobs and his collaborators at Apple Computer made the Xerox GUI interface, including windows, into a successful part of the personal computer in the 1980s by applying modernist design principles to the drab but functional Xerox design. After Microsoft adopted and adapted the Apple design for its eponymous Windows interface in the late 1980s, it became clear that nearly all users of desktop and laptop systems would be examining and manipulating data in windows on their screens. This is still true today, although the advent of smartphones and tablets is now providing successful and widely used alternate interfaces for the first time in two decades.

The window has long served as an important metaphor in the history of Western representation. The Renaissance artist Leon Battista Alberti claimed that the goal of his painting was to turn the frame into a window onto a represented world. As André Bazin argued in the 1940s in the "Ontology of the Photographic Image," Renaissance painting committed the "original sin" in adopting the goal of illusionistic representation. Despite important changes in style, the goal of illusionistic representation remained dominant in Western painting until the impressionists (see IMMERSION). From the mid-nineteenth century on, artists challenged and often rejected this notion of "realism" in the elite art of painting, but the notion remained powerful, especially in popular culture with the growth of photography and film as media forms. The photograph came to define our culture's notion of the realistic or objective representation. As Bazin argued, film possesses the same ontology: a film, after all, is composed of a large number of photographs displayed in succession. In the 1960s and 1970s, the assumption of photorealism was taken up by the technical pioneers who developed the methods of computer graphics. The windowed interface became the frame through which computer graphics and other data could be clearly presented. The goal of the interface design became and remains the transparent presentation of data to the user. The goal of the window is to allow the user to see and manipulate the data seamlessly. Whether they realized it or not, the inventors of the GUI were the heirs to Alberti's metaphor.

■ See also GRAPHIC REALISM, INTERFACE

References and Further Reading

Bazin, André. (1967) 1980. "The Ontology of the Photographic Image." In *Classic Essays in Photography*, edited by Alan Trachtenberg, 237–244. New Haven, CT: Leete's Islands Books.

Bolter, Jay David, and Diane Gromala. 2003. *Windows and Mirrors: Interaction Design, Digital Art, and the Myth of Transparency*. Cambridge, MA: MIT Press.

Engelbart, Douglas, and William English. 2003. "A Research Center for Augmenting Human Intellect." In *The New Media Reader*, edited by Nick Montfort and Noah Wardrip-Fruin, 233–246. Cambridge, MA: MIT Press.

Kay, Alan, and Adele Goldberg. 1977. "Personal Dynamic Media." *Computer* 10 (3): 31–41. March 1977.

Manovich, Lev. 2001. *The Language of New Media*. Cambridge, MA: MIT Press.

Word-Image

Maria Engberg

What literary critic W. J. T. Mitchell calls "an extraordinarily ancient problem" (2003), the relationships between word and image continue to be relevant today in digital textuality. Word-and-image studies are concerned with the study of encounters and tensions, collaborations and hostilities between verbal and visual languages. Historically a field of study in the visual arts and literature, the interest in word-and-image relations has spread into newer academic fields such as visual culture and media studies. Today, there are journals, professional organizations, and scholarly networks devoted to a wide range of word-and-image issues and concerns, which at times include their relevance for digital textuality. Journals such as *Word & Image* and *Image & Narrative*, as well as organizations such as the *International Association of Word and Image Studies*, are devoted to verbal-visual studies.

Comparisons between the visual and the verbal arts and the dynamics between word and image in art and literature have long been a source of theoretical debate. There is by now a large body of critical work. Historically, two main schools of thought can be discerned. The first centers around the idea that word and image are to be understood as essentially equal. *Ut pictoria poesis*, as is painting so is poetry, was Horace's formulation in *Ars Poetica*, in which he argues for the same treatment of writing as was given painting. That is, their aesthetic foundations are viewed as similar and painting and poetry should be considered as sister arts. In the classic sense, the aesthetic principles they share are based in mimesis, the imitation of ideas or natural things. The other school of thought, evolving as a critique of the sister arts, emanates from Gotthold Ephraim Lessing's argument in *Laocoon; or, The Limits of Poetry and Painting* ([1766] 1836). In *Laocoon*, Lessing argues that poetry (word) and painting (image) should be viewed as "two just and friendly neighbors," each with their particular character. He argues that poetry arranges words as extended in time, and the image is arranged in parallel, that is, spatially. Therefore, the relationship of word and image is also thought of as a concern of temporality and spatiality in literature and the arts.

There are different fields of study in the arts and literature concerned with the dynamic of word and image: concepts like ekphrasis, iconology, and pictorial narrativity are invested in exploring the relationships and negotiations between verbal and visual text. Ekphrasis is largely understood as the literary evocation of spatial art, therefore "an umbrella term that subsumes various forms of rendering the visual object into words" (Yacobi 1995, 600). As Tamar Yacobi and others have noted, the one work's representation of the world then becomes the other's re-presentation, albeit not an unproblematic one.

Related to the notion of word-and-image relations is the question of literacy and the cultural valence of a medium at a particular time. The increasing ubiquity of multimedia texts in traditional and digital media has prompted renewed debates about the changing nature of literacy since the advent of digital technology. Digital literacy, or sometimes multimedia or visual literacy, includes the ability to read and interpret media (not just words). It can be said that words and images make up the core of what is digital textuality. It has been argued that our culture has taken a turn toward pictorial dominance. The concept of the pictorial turn was introduced by W. J. T. Mitchell in an article in *Artforum* in 1992 and reached a broader audience through its reprint in *Picture Theory*, published two years later. Since then, it has gained wide currency as a catchphrase taken to mean that societies are today picture dominated. Visual culture theorist Nicholas Mirzoeff, for instance, writes in the introduction to the *Visual Culture Reader* that "Western philosophy and science now use a pictorial, rather than textual, model of the world, marking a significant challenge to the notion of the world as a written text" (1998, 5). Many observe that the rise of the image is linked to the fall of the word and that images are "fast replacing words as our primary language" (Stephens 1998, 11). Others, such as Roland Barthes, argue that writing and speech still are of importance: "It appears that the linguistic message is indeed present in every image: as title, caption, accompanying press article, film dialogue, comic strip balloon. Which shows that it is not very accurate to talk of a civilization of the image—we are still, and more than ever, a civilization of writing, writing and speech continuing to be the full terms of the informational structure" (1977, 3).

Discussions about the relationship between word and image in digital media appear often in the context of changes in how our culture defines literacy. Speaking of a shift in this definition, Jay David Bolter suggests that in a digital environment increasingly dominated by visual modes of representation, "the verbal text has to struggle to hold on to its cultural legitimacy" (1996). Along with literary critics such as Murray Krieger (1992), Bolter reminds us that in ancient rhetoric ekphrasis set out to demonstrate the superiority of the rhetorical art over painting or sculpture. In contemporary culture, however, the dominance of the word over the image is shifting toward a culture that favors multimodality. Therefore, many studies are concerned with the nature of the digital image alone, such as William J. Mitchell's *The Reconfigured Eye: Visual Truth in the Post-Photographic Era* (1994b).

Another dimension of digital word-and-image relations can be found in concepts such as multimedia, a word that partly fell out of fashion in critical discourse after the 1990s but still has a commercial presence. Multimedia refers to any combination of two or more media in a digital text: word-and-image relations then form part of those possible combinations. The "late age of print" (Bolter 1991) is characterized by what Terry Harpold has called "conflations of letter and graphic" (2009, 83) in all forms of media: windows and menus of software, advertisements, myriads of web pages, television screens that resemble web pages (Bolter and Grusin 1999), and printed literary works that increasingly include visual material since they are created with ease with desktop publishing software (Hayles 2008). Rather than a battle between word and image, some theorists view the reconfigured relationship of word and image in digital media as one in which they operate dialogically in dynamic interplay (Hocks and Kendrick 2005). In addition, as Johanna Drucker (1998, 2008) reminds us, writing has binary qualities: written words exist materially as images and function as elements of language. The advent of desktop publishing has prompted an increase of digital texts that can easily incorporate visual dimensions through the use of color, fonts, and layout. Web design, too, has verbal-visual constructions at its core.

Word-and-image combinations can thus be said to be found in most contemporary digital text genres. The use of several modes of expression is the rule rather than the exception. Apart from the overwhelmingly wide range of aesthetic forms present on websites, particular genres of digital textuality are also characterized by word-and-image relationships (see DIGITAL POETRY, EARLY DIGITAL ART AND WRITING [PRE-1990], ELECTRONIC LITERATURE, INTERACTIVE NARRATIVE). Digital poetry, digital fiction, hypertext fiction (second-generation hypertext is defined by its inclusion of images)—there are arguably more digital forms, established and emerging ones, that include images or graphic elements alongside words than there are purely textual ones (see NONLINEAR WRITING). There are also expressive arts, with an increasing digital presence, that are inherently made up of word-and-image combinations, such as comics and graphic novels. Web comics are growing, ranging from merely digitized panels to new experiments in graphic narratives in digital forms (see WEB COMICS). In visual culture in general, commercial digital texts, advertisements, visualizations, and, more generally,

websites tend to include word...
each other may fall under est*abli*_{*l*}*ed* ... *ges as a d*fault, although their relationship to
Most of the digital texts in the to-date...*entions of* representation.
tion share that they combine word and image, along... *ith other media, to create their ar-* ... *onic Literature Collec-*
tifice. Terms such as *word-and-image*, or *verbal-vis*...
keywords of the volume. Digital literary works such as Rob... however, not included in the
Brian Kim Stefans's "The Dreamlife of Letters" (2000), and Kate F ... ndall's "Faith" (2002),
Joseph's *Inanimate Alice* (2005), to name a few from the first volume, combin... er and Chris
well as the visuality of the word itself with images and animation. Digital texts that fall
under the rubric of visual and concrete poetry also have a particular interest in the visual
dimensions of words. There are by now a host of digital poems that continue the aesthetic program of visual poetry into digital form. In scholarship about digital, or electronic, literature, Loss Pequeño Glazier (2001), Chris Funkhouser (2007), and N. Katherine Hayles (2008), among others, have explored verbal-visual dynamics. However, they
have most often done so with little or no reference to specialty fields such as word-and-
image studies and ekphrastic studies. On the other hand, literary scholars working in
those fields by and large have not included digital works to any significant degree in their
studies. Thus, academic studies on word-and-image relations in contemporary digital
culture can be said to coexist beside each other in various disciplines rather than in extended dialogue.

■ See also DIGITAL AND NET ART, DIGITAL POETRY, EARLY DIGITAL ART AND
WRITING (PRE-1990), ELECTRONIC LITERATURE, GLITCH AESTHETICS,
INTERACTIVE NARRATIVE, OLD MEDIA / NEW MEDIA

References and Further Reading

Bolter, Jay David. 1991. *Writing Space: The Computer, Hypertext, and the History of Writing*. Hillsdale, NJ: Lawrence Erlbaum Associates.

———. 1996. "Ekphrasis, Virtual Reality and the Future of Writing." In *The Future of the
Book*, edited by Geoffrey Nurnberg, 253–272. Berkeley: University of California Press.

Bolter, Jay David, and Richard Grusin. 1999. *Remediation: Understanding New Media*. Cambridge,
MA: MIT Press.

Drucker, Johanna. 1998. *Figuring the Word: Essays on Books, Writing, and Visual Poetics*. New York:
Granary Books.

———. 2008. "Graphic Devices: Narration and Navigation." *Narrative* 16 (2): 121–139.

Funkhouser, Chris. 2007. *Prehistoric Digital Poetry: An Archaeology of Forms, 1959–1995*. Tuscaloosa:
University of Alabama Press.

Glazier, Loss Pequeño. 2001. *Digital Poetics: Hypertext, Visual-Kinetic Text and Writing in Programmable
Media*. Tuscaloosa: University of Alabama Press.

Harpold, Terry. 2009. *Ex-foliations: Reading Machines and the Upgrade Path*. Minneapolis: University
of Minnesota Press.

Hayles, Katherine N. 2008. *Electronic Literature: New Horizons for the Literary*. Notre Dame, IN:
University of Notre Dame.

Hocks, Mary E., and Michelle R Kendrick. 2005. *Eloquent Images: Word and Image in the Age of New
Media*. Cambridge, MA: MIT Press.

Kendall, Robert. 2002. "Faith." http://collection.eliterature.org/1/works/kendall__faith.html.

Krieger, Murray. 1992. *Ekphrasis: The Illusion of the Natural Sign*. Baltimore: Johns Hopkins University Press.

Lessing, Gotthold Ephraim. (1766) 1836. *Laocoon; or, The Limits of Poetry and Painting*. Translated
by William Ross. London: Ridgeway.

Routledge.

Mirzoeff, Nicholas, ed. 1998. ⸻. ⸻ ⸻ ⸻ ⸻ ⸻ University of Chicago Press.

Mitchell, W. J. T. 1986. *Iconology: I*⸻

⸻. 1992. "The P⸻⸻⸻ ⸻⸻⸻ *resentation.* Chicago: University of

⸻. 1994a. *Picture Theory: Essays* ⸻

Chicago Press. ⸻ *ritical Terms for Art History,* edited by Robert S. Nelson and

⸻. 2003. "Word and Image." University of Chicago Press.

Richard Shiff, 51–59. *The Reconfigured Eye: Visual Truth in the Post-Photographic Era.* Cam-

Mitchell, William ⸻. MIT Press.

bri⸻

⸻llinger, Kate, and Chris Joseph. 2005. *Inanimate Alice.* http://www.inanimatealice.com.

Stefans, Brian Kim. 2000. "The Dreamlife of Letters." http://collection.eliterature.org/1/works/stefans__the_dreamlife_of_letters.html.

Stephens, Mitchell. 1998. *The Rise of the Image, the Fall of the Word.* Oxford: Oxford University Press.

Walsh, Richard. 2006. "The Narrative Imagination across Media." *MFS Modern Fiction Studies* 52 (4): 855–868.

Yacobi, Tamar. 1995. "Pictorial Models and Narrative Ekphrasis." *Poetics Today* 16 (4): 599–649.

....

Worlds and Maps

Bjarke Liboriussen

When mapmaking relates to fictional worlds, rather than to the real world, it is best thought of as a constructive rather than as a descriptive practice. It is a practice that does not necessarily involve storytelling. Robert Louis Stevenson constructed his Treasure Island on a map, in cooperation with his father and stepson, and it was only later on that Stevenson decided to use the island as the setting for a tale of pirates and hidden treasure (Padrón 2007, 265). J. R. R. Tolkien began the construction of the arguably most popular fantastical world, Middle-earth, in 1917. In the early 1930s, Tolkien started writing the story that became *The Hobbit* (1937), expanding the world of the story as necessity dictated. It was only after the story was completed that Tolkien decided that *The Hobbit* had in fact taken place in Middle-earth (Sibley 1995, 15). Tolkien made many other decisions regarding events and characters of *The Hobbit* retrospectively, but he did draw a map of the protagonist's journey early on. The map guided Tolkien in his storytelling, and he was to make similar use of cartography during the twelve years it took him to write *The Lord of the Rings* (published 1954–55). Maps were made and changed during storytelling, and Tolkien went as far as to say, "It is impossible to make a map of a story after it has been written" (Tolkien quoted in Sibley 1995, 16). To Tolkien, maps were dynamic tools in the construction of both world and story, not descriptive summaries produced after the fact.

Other examples of mapmaking involved in the construction of nondigital, fictional worlds can be found in the realm of pen-and-paper role-playing games. Sociologist Gary Allan Fine (1983, chap. 4) has, for instance, made a detailed case study of M. A. R. Barker's construction of the world of Tekumel. Additionally, David Cohen and Stephen MacKeith (1991) have published case studies of imaginary worlds created and maintained by children, with references to mapmaking.

Mapmaking is not only a tool in world creation; it can also be a useful aide for the "nontrivial" effort required for traversing the fictional worlds of "ergodic literature," Espen Aarseth's term for cybertexts such as Choose Your Own Adventure–style books, tabletop role-playing games (see ROLE-PLAYING GAMES), text-based adventure games (see INTERACTIVE FICTION), as well as some MUDs and MOOs (see MUDS AND MOOS; see Aarseth [1997], though Aarseth makes no reference to mapmaking). Without direct, visual access to the fictional world, mapmaking might be useful or even necessary in order to find one's way through worlds often purposefully laid out as labyrinths. A host of fan-made cybertext mappings can be found online, many of which are in fact flow-charts of the stories whose construction the cybertext allows for, rather than maps describing the spatial layout of a fictional world.

When digital worlds became three-dimensional in the 1990s, maps assumed an even greater role in their construction. As Bartle writes, "Authors of epic Fantasy novels often start with a map. Similarly, designers of virtual worlds often choose a map as the first concrete realization of their dreams" (2004, 269). For the user, however, the function of maps—and indeed the very meaning of the word *map*—changed profoundly with the advent of three-dimensional, digital worlds. Not only did the user now have direct, visual access to the world, but it also became the norm to rely on an abundance of maps. A small map (which is sometimes called a "mini-map" and might be semitransparent) is typically found in the corner of the screen and allows for peripheral attention to location in the digital world while steering one's avatar through the world (see AVATARS); I will use examples where an avatar is available as a focus for the user's agency, but similar points can be made for worlds experienced in what some film scholars would call optical point of view, that is, worlds in which the avatar is only implied. A larger map can often be called up instantly on the screen with the touch of a button. Thus, the user might choose, for some time, to navigate the maps rather than the world itself, focusing attention on the little, moveable map symbol representing his or her location, rather than on the avatar.

Here it is important to note that the maps of contemporary, three-dimensional, digital worlds are in fact not maps in any traditional sense. The maps are not potentially flawed representations of the world—made after exploring and measuring the world—but two-dimensional *renderings* of the world carrying exactly the same ontological weight as the "world proper," that is, the "world" understood as that three-dimensional space to which the avatar belongs. From an ontological perspective, *I am* just as much the little, moveable map symbol as *I am* my avatar. The avatar does not precede the map symbol in the manner of a thing preceding its representation, nor does three-dimensional space precede two-dimensional map, hence their equal, ontological weight. From an experiential perspective, however, no confusing of world and map is possible. What is important in the perspective of user experience is not where I am *per se* but where *I act*—one identifies with a contextualized point of action, perception, and emotion rather than with a point of pure being—and the highest potential for action lies in the avatar's relation to its environment, not its symbol on the map. Thus, the map is experienced as a representation in the sense of something secondary to the world, but the perceived secondariness stems from a relatively limited sense of agency, not from the description being ontologically secondary to a primary world.

Users of contemporary, three-dimensional, digital worlds engage in various kinds of mapmaking activities, some of which are unique to such worlds, for example, the making of "maps" in the sense of *levels*. This practice is particularly popular for first-person shooter games such as *DOOM*, *Quake*, and *Half-Life*. Strictly speaking, and bearing the above discussion of ontology in mind, the practice of making a *DOOM* "map" is *cartogenetic* rather than *cartographic*: creation of the world and drawing of the map are two sides of the same coin (additionally, the map-creating user can decide features such as lighting and surface textures, but basic spatial layout, the "mapping" proper, comes first in the design process).

A more traditional—that is, descriptive—kind of cartography is the automated grass-roots cartography widespread among users of online game worlds such as *World of Warcraft* (see ONLINE WORLDS). Players typically spend a large amount of time obtaining resources, for example, by mining ore, collecting herbs, or killing and subsequently skinning animals. Some time after harvesting, resources reappear in fixed patterns. It is obviously useful for players to be aware of those patterns if they want to collect resources effectively. To explicate the resource patterns of the game world, players band together in an informal way by installing a so-called *add-on* to their game, a small program that uploads information about their resource gathering to a central database. The collectively gathered information then forms the basis for automatically generated maps of resource patterns which can be found online and aid the player toward efficiency. Here cartography is descriptive and secondary to the already-existing world, yet it utilizes unique, digital possibilities in a communal manner characteristic of Internet-based media consumption (see, e.g., Dovey and Kennedy 2006; Jenkins 2006).

The practice of explicating the resource structures of *World of Warcraft* through cartography, and perhaps also the practice of creating flowcharts of Choose Your Own Adventure–style books mentioned in passing above, could be interpreted as activities aimed at mastery and control. Mary Fuller and Henry Jenkins (1994) have explored the link between mapping and mastery with attention to the so-called New World travel writing produced by colonists and Nintendo games, respectively. Fuller associates mastery with a type of mapping aimed at overview, whereas Jenkins, drawing on Michel de Certeau, associates mastery with mapping aimed at the production of routes. Hence, a conceptual disagreement underlies Fuller and Jenkins's "dialogue," adding nuance to the text and making it an excellent starting point for critical reflection on the relationship between worlds and maps (see Harley [1988] for a strong analysis of the connections between maps, knowledge, and power, with numerous references to relevant literature).

■ See also ONLINE WORLDS, SPATIALITY OF DIGITAL MEDIA

References and Further Reading

Aarseth, Espen J. 1997. *Cybertext: Perspectives on Ergodic Literature.* Baltimore: John Hopkins University Press.

Bartle, Richard A. 2004. *Designing Virtual Worlds.* Berkeley: New Riders.

Cohen, David, and Stephen A. MacKeith. 1991. *The Development of Imagination: The Private Worlds of Childhood.* London: Routledge.

Dovey, Jon, and Helen W. Kennedy. 2006. *Game Cultures: Computer Games as New Media.* Maidenhead, UK: Open University Press.

Fine, Gary Alan. 1983. *Shared Fantasy: Role-Playing Games as Social Worlds.* Chicago: University of Chicago Press.

Fuller, Mary, and Henry Jenkins. 1994. "Nintendo® and New World Travel Writing: A Dialogue." In *Cybersociety: Computer-Mediated Communication and Community*, edited by Steven G. Jones, 57–72. Thousand Oaks, CA: Sage.

Harley, J. B. 1988. "Maps, Knowledge, and Power." In *The Iconography of Landscape: Essays on the Symbolic Representation, Design and Use of Past Environments*, edited by Denis Cosgrove and Stephen Daniels, 277–311. Cambridge: Cambridge University Press.

Jenkins, Henry. 2006. *Convergence Culture: Where Old and New Media Collide*. New York: New York University Press.

Padrón, Richard. 2007. "Mapping Imaginary Worlds." In *Maps: Finding Our Place in the World*, edited by James R. Akerman and Rovert W. Karrow Jr., 255–287. Chicago: University of Chicago Press.

Sibley, Brian. 1995. "There and Back Again: About the Map of the Hobbit." In *There and Back Again: The Map of the Hobbit*, 5–23. London: HarperCollins.

. . . .

Writing under Constraint
Anastasia Salter

Writing under constraint is a concept that precedes digital media but has also been adapted to probe at and reveal the process of construction behind electronic literature (see ELECTRONIC LITERATURE). Jan Baetens defines constrained writing as "the use of any type of formal technique or program whose application is able to produce a sense of its making text by itself, if need be without any previous 'idea' from the writer" (1997, 1). This definition distinguishes intentional writing under constraint from simply following the traditional rules governing communication or working within a medium. Poetry inherently embraces styles that could be called writing under constraint: a sonnet or haiku, for instance, certainly has inherent structural limitations that must be obeyed (see DIGITAL POETRY). Constraint-based writing can be purposeful, such as the work of Dr. Seuss with its limited vocabulary to raise the quality of beginner reader experiences, the result of which includes classics such as *The Cat in the Hat* (1957). However, writing under constraint is less about the formal structures imposed by outside forces and rules and more about an author's deliberate decision to embrace constraints as a path to creation.

In digital media, writing under constraint can begin by playing with the possibilities within an inherently limited form. Some forms of writing under constraint are clearly tied to the technical limitations of a device or network. For instance, both Twitter and cell phone communications are limited to 140- or 160-character bursts, with pauses forced by the medium (see TWITTER, TUMBLR, AND MICROBLOGGING). However, while all participants in these networks work under the same constraints, only some use the limitations as a basis for creative literature. Writers of cell phone novels embrace the tempo and adapted language of abbreviations and "leet" associated with the medium to tell stories that take place over time, while Twitter users can either create characters or tell stories composed for a single tweet, rather akin to haiku (see E-MAIL NOVEL). Those who use Twitter's constraints as the starting point for a creative work often add additional constraints to the process or incorporate the medium into other experiments in electronic literature.

The concept of writing under constraint was first popularized by the Oulipians, members of the Oulipo group founded by Raymond Queneau in 1960. While the work of the Oulipians preceded digital media, it did introduce often structurally demanding ways of generating texts and working with limited frameworks. Some of the constraints Oulipo experimented with lend themselves even more appropriately to digital forms. Raymond Queneau's *One Hundred Trillion Poems* consists of ten sonnets, sliced and bound in a book, so that the random formation of strips always creates a new sonnet—each sonnet was written with the intention of keeping the syntax consistent across the whole to allow for the combination to hold. The interdependency of the sonnets constrains their forms just as the slicing of the pages releases them into previously uncharted combinations. Likewise, William Gillespie's "11,1112,006,825,5558,016 Sonnets" uses a digital generator combined with Gillespie's own writing to form an automated collection. In each case, part of the appeal is that it is impossible to create such a sheer quantity of poetry through traditional means, and similarly there is more to experience within either work than can readily be known. While each individual sonnet appears to have depth of meaning, thanks to the adherence to the formal constraints of their connections, it is not itself formed as an intentional piece in the traditional understanding of authorial control. Thus, the question of who "created" the sonnet blurs, as the reader has the power to arrange while the author creates the content and the system itself determines what is possible.

Writing under these types of seemingly arbitrary constraints, from forgoing the use of the letter "e" to only using monosyllables, adds a playful element that is part of constraint-based writing's appeal. Harry Matthews (1996) offers a parallel between constraints and gameplay, as constraints, like rules in a game, narrow the realm of what is possible to draw sharp focus on a particular objective or structure. Games cannot function without the rules that tie the magic circle of the desired experience into a formal structure. In the case of Gillespie's and Queneau's poems, the composition process, by its very strict rules, allows for possibilities that could not otherwise be achieved: the constraint is not merely a restriction but the system that allows for meaning in the potential chaos of the reordered and sundered sonnets.

Writing under constraint is only one example of the process of production for electronic literature or "technotexts"—N. Katherine Hayles's term for texts that are inherently connected with the technology of their production and whose forms and language are understood best within that context (2002, 25–26). Hayles's categorization of the technotext links the "physical" form, or the materiality, of a text to the texts' contents and production. Her argument is a reminder that just as stories composed for the oral tradition are dramatically different from the composition of prose for the printed page, so too does digital media have its own material constraints (see MATERIALITY). Because of this free digital materiality, electronic literature resembles poetry in its constraints, but not necessarily in its outcomes: while the structures of the poetic forms suit the written page, the electronic space can at first seem to lack those same demands. Storage space has gradually risen to the point of seeming limitless, and the screen acts as a portal rather than a finite viewpoint for approaching a text. In this context, constraints can draw attention to the real limitations of the structures behind the screen, which might otherwise be transparent to the reader.

Nick Montfort and William Gillespie's "2002: A Palindrome Story" (2002) is one example of a technotext whose production was heavily tied to digital tools and thus illuminated those structures. The work embraces the constraint of a palindrome in all aspects of its creation: it is exactly 2002 words long, was published to the web on February 20, 2002, and, of course, it reads the same backward and forward. A digital version of the text also allows for exploring the mirrored tale, viewing the two directions simultaneously. Nick Montfort notes that the program is not the coauthor—it does not contribute anything new—but the palindrome constraint itself guides the text: "With restrictive rather than generative procedures this point is less clear, but it is worth noting: if there was a non-human co-author of 2002, it was almost certainly the palindrome constraint itself, which led us to certain discoveries about the names and natures of characters and how the story should progress. By bounding the set of possible texts, only those which read the same forwards and backwards being permitted, the palindrome determined a far smaller set of possible 2002-word stories than in the general case; from this set of stories Gillespie and I chose one" (2003). This fits the model of obsessive production that Alan Sondheim describes as part of the meaning of writing under constraint observed in palindromic literature: the tightness of authorial control allows for meaning to emerge through the "interaction between the constraint and the content" and thus emphasizes the mechanical coauthor (2004). In this project the program "Deep Speed" was the digital embodiment of the palindromic constraint, used as an automated tool to both verify and manage the writing of the text, and thus another voice of authorship within the work.

Other forms of writing under constraint rely more on the nature of programming, such as the genre of "codework"—formal code within the text, or in strongly constrained examples, code that must compile and run. In these, the laws of code themselves provide the constraints, and those rules are more demanding than that of grammar, and the workings of the medium provide part of the message: Rita Raley described codework as "making exterior the interior workings" (2005), but in practice this work is rarely in the binary language of the machine but instead exists many layers above. More common is pseudocode, which places the human reader first, as in the pseudocode "mezangelle language" of Mary-Anne Breeze, better known as Mez. In the *Electronic Literature Collection*, volume 2, the work _cross.ova.ing][4rm.blog.2.log][_ is described as "a 'netwurk repository' that's been in operation since 2003. these 'wurks' r inscribed using the infamous polysemic language system termed _mezangelle_ . . . 2 _mezangelle_ means 2 take words>wordstrings>sentences + alter them in such a way as 2 /x/tend + /n/hance meaning beyond the predicted +/or /x/pected" (Mez 2010). The invented language draws upon both the language of the Internet and the structures of code, but the final outcome only gestures at the machine's interpretive forms (see CODE, CODE AESTHETICS, ELECTRONIC LITERATURE ORGANIZATION).

The intention echoes the outcomes of constrained writing: take elements and alter them to enhance meaning beyond the predicted or expected. Constrained writing uses seemingly procedural and algorithmic methods to reveal the unexpected and, in doing so, to interrogate the relationship between the work and the means of digital production.

■ See also ALGORITHM, DIGITAL POETRY

References and Further Reading

Baetens, Jan. 1997. "Free Writing, Constrained Writing: The Ideology of Form." *Poetics Today* 18 (1). www.jstor.org/pss/1773230.

Gillespie, William. 1999. "11,112,006,825,558,016 Sonnets." Spineless Books. http://spinelessbooks .com/electronicliterature/archive/index.html.

Hayles, N. Katherine. 2002. *Writing Machines*. Cambridge, MA: MIT Press.

Mathews, Harry. 1996. "Translation and the Oulipo: The Case of the Persevering Maltese." *Electronic Book Review*. www.altx.com/ebr/ebr5/mathews.htm.

Mez. 2010. _cross.ova.ing][4rm.blog.2.log][_ . In *Electronic Literature Collection*, volume 2. http:// collection.eliterature.org/2/works/mez_crossovaing.html.

Montfort, Nick. 2003. "The Coding and Execution of the Author." In *The Cybertext Yearbook*, edited by Markku Eskelinen and Raine Kosimaa, 201–217. Jyväskylä, Finland: Research Centre for

Contemporary Culture. http://nickm.com/writing/essays/coding_and_execution_of_the_author
.html.

Montfort, Nick, and William Gillespie. 2002. "2002: A Palindrome Story." Spineless Books. www
.spinelessbooks.com/2002/palindrome/index.html.

Morris, Adalaide. 2007. "How to Think (with) Tinkertoys: Electronic Literature Collection, Volume
1." *Electronic Book Review*. www.electronicbookreview.com/thread/electropoetics/distributed.

Raley, Rita. 2005. "Interferences: [Net.Writing] and the Practice of Codework." *Electronic Book Review*. www.electronicbookreview.com/thread/electropoetics/net.writing.

Sondheim, Alan. 2004. "Verse in Reverse." *Electronic Book Review*. www.electronicbookreview.com
/thread/wuc/stuttered.

Susana, Stéphane. 2000. "A Roundup of Constrained Writing on the Web." *Electronic Book Review*.
www.altx.com/ebr/ebr10/10sus.htm.

CONTRIBUTORS

Angello, Aaron: Remix; Sound

Baron, Naomi S.: Language Use in Online and Mobile Communication

Bernardi, Chiara: Social Network Sites (SNSs)

Berry, David M.: Code Aesthetics

Bogost, Ian: Platform

Bolter, Jay David: Augmented Reality; Remediation; Windows

Bootz, Philippe: Animated Poetry; Combinatory and Automatic Text Generation

Brough, Melissa: Participatory Culture

Buckley, Jake: Analog versus Digital

Caïra, Olivier: Role-Playing Games

Caracciolo, Marco: Virtual Bodies

Castronova, Edward: Virtual Economies

Cayley, John: Cave; N-gram

Ciccoricco, David: Games as Art/Literature; Games as Stories

Clivaz, Claire: Critical Editions in the Digital Age

Coleman, E. Gabriella: Hacker

Croxall, Brian: Twitter, Tumblr, and Microblogging

Davenport, Glorianna: Interactive Cinema

De Grove, Frederik: Walkthrough

Dena, Christy: Transmedial Fiction

Doran, Steven Edward: Identity

Drucker, Johanna: E-books

Duda, John: Collective Intelligence

Eder, Jens: Film and Digital Media

Elson, David: Artificial Intelligence

Emerson, Lori: Glitch Aesthetics

Engberg, Maria: Digital Fiction; Word-Image

Ensslin, Astrid: Hypertextuality; Nonlinear Writing

Ess, Charles: Ethics in Digital Media

Evens, Aden: Music

Flores, Leonardo: Digital Poetry

Frasca, Gonzalo: Simulation

Fuller, Matthew: Data; Software Studies

Funkhouser, Christopher: Combinatory and Automatic Text Generation; Early Digital Art and Writing (Pre-1990)

Gaudenzi, Sandra: Interactive Documentary

Geoghegan, Bernard: Cybernetics

Gervás, Pablo: Story Generation

Goddard, Michael: Media Ecology

Gold, Matthew K.: Digital Humanities

Golumbia, David: Characteristics of Digital Media; Critical Theory

Goriunova, Olga: Social Network Sites (SNSs)

Hamidović, David: Critical Editions in the Digital Age

Hands, Joss: Politics and New Media

Harris, Katherine: Archive

Heckman, Davin: Subversion (Creative Destruction)

Heim, Michael: Virtuality

Hellekson, Karen: Fan Fiction

Hillis, Ken: Virtual Reality

Hjorth, Larissa: Cell Phone Novel

Hui, Yuk: Search

Jensen, Jens: Interactive Television

Juul, Jesper: Gameplay

Kac, Eduardo: Biopoetry; Holopoetry

Kirschenbaum, Matthew: Preservation

Klastrup, Lisbeth: Online Worlds